Pastor's COMPLETE HANDBOOK of MODEL SERMONS

LOWELL D. STREIKER

PRENTICE HALL
Englewood Cliffs, New Jersey 07632

Prentice-Hall International, Inc., *London*
Prentice-Hall of Australia, Pty. Ltd., *Sydney*
Prentice-Hall of Canada, Inc., *Toronto*
Prentice-Hall Hispanoamericana, S.A., *Mexico*
Prentice-Hall of India Private Ltd., *New Delhi*
Prentice-Hall of Japan, Inc. *Tokyo*
Prentice-Hall of Southeast Asia Pte., Ltd., *Singapore*
Editora Prentice-Hall do Brasil Ltda., *Rio de Janeiro*

10 9 8 7 6 5 4 3 2 1

Library of Congress Cataloging-in-Publication Data

Streiker, Lowell D.
Pastor's complete handbook of model sermons / Lowell D. Streiker.
p. cm.
Includes bibliographical references and indexes.
ISBN 0-13-653379-5
1. Sermons—Outlines, syllabi, etc. I. Title
BV4223.S87 1992
251'.02—dc20 92-7927
CIP

ISBN 0-13-653379-5

PRENTICE HALL
Professional Publishing
Englewood Cliffs, NJ 07632
Simon & Schuster, A Paramount Communications Company

PRINTED IN THE UNITED STATES OF AMERICA

ACKNOWLEDGMENTS

In bringing these materials together, I have been assisted by numerous pastors and church administrators from several traditions. I am particularly grateful to the many contributors whose selections have been added to my own to round out this book. In addition, I gratefully acknowledge the help of the following:

Dorothy Stoft, who proofread and made many helpful stylistic suggestions.

Special thanks belongs to

The staff of Foster City Public Library for many courtesies.

Betty Johnson, my mother-in-law, who keyed in many sermons and the indexes.

The editors/staff of Saratoga Press, Prentice Hall, Seven Worlds Publishing, NavPress Software, Paraclete Software, Parsons Technology, Abingdon Press, and *Preaching Today* for their generous assistance.

My wife, Connie Streiker, and my friend Gil Gray, for many helpful suggestions. Special thanks to my editor, Tom Power; Production Editor, Jacqueline Roulette; Copy Editor, Sally Ann Bailey; my agent, Bert Holtje; and Mike Hodgins, who enriched my knowledge of illustrations.

The manuscript was prepared using *WordStar* 6.0, *Right Writer*, and a Hewlett-Packard LaserJet Series II with a Pacific Page Postscript cartridge. Bible study software from NavPress and Paraclete Software was of particular value as was the computer diskette version of *Parables, Etc.* and *Pastor's Story File* (when teamed with *Gofer*, my favorite quick-search, quick-insert utility).

Thanks also to the congregation of Island United Church, Foster City, California, where I first preached several of these sermons, and to my present congregation, Ladera Community Church, Portola Valley, California, for whom most of these messages were prepared and preached.

As a preacher-writer-communicator, I consider myself a lucky and blessed man. Week after week, I get to do what I love doing. Thank you, Lord, and thank you, Ladera!

HOW THIS BOOK WILL HELP YOU

"A funny (or not so funny) thing happened to me on the way to the pulpit this week. I simply did not have time to prepare my sermon." That is how many ministers feel, week after week. The administrative needs of their congregations are so pressing that they scarcely have time to think about their sermons. Emergencies crop up that leave them without the quiet periods necessary for thoughtful homiletic effort.

The typical parish minister is called upon to serve in many capacities—as preacher, teacher, administrator, counselor, social worker, visitor of the sick, membership recruiter, congregational representative to civic groups, delegate to denominational and ecumenical gatherings, and so on. Regardless of how busy his or her week may be, the congregation assumes that the minister will have something to say on Sunday morning and that the way the message is presented will be powerful and skillful. As any experienced minister can tell you, given the stresses and strains of most weeks, that is expecting a lot.

In the words of Leander E. Keck, dean and Winkley Professor of Biblical Theology at Yale Divinity School, the pastor

> . . . who still devotes a major block of his time preparing sermons—particularly scholarly or biblical ones—has been on the endangered species list for a long time. . . . *sundry matters have displaced Sunday matters*. The proliferation of tasks has squeezed virtually to the vanishing point blocks of time free from interruption, time essential for sermon preparation and especially for long-range reading and reflection.[1]

Pastor's Complete Handbook of Model Sermons provides parish ministers, priests, and others who preach regularly with hints, tips, and samples to speed the work of sermon preparation. It offers models that can be woven into the preacher's own sermon. For those who preach only

[1] Leander E. Keck, *The Bible in the Pulpit* (Nashville, TN: Abingdon Press, 1978), p. 15 (emphasis added).

now and then or have been called on to preach for the very first time, *Pastor's Complete Handbook of Model Sermons* is a source of homilies that can be readily adapted to the preacher's specific situation. For those who preach occasionally or regularly, this book is intended as grist for the homiletic mill. Referring to his book should not replace a minister's sermon preparation, but enhance it. In these pages, the preacher will find new ideas and novel forms of expression.

The Indexes

The sermons in this book are arranged by topic in twelve chapters (e.g., "Faith and Hope," "Discipleship," "Building the Christian Community," "Transformation and Change"). Headings preceding each sermon contain the following information: the suggested date for presentation (e.g., "Easter, Year A," "Pentecost Sunday, Year B," "Any Sunday"), a one- or two-sentence summary of the theme of the sermon, a brief list of the major subjects covered, and the sermon title.

The sermon collection is indexed by subject, by date (church year calendar and secular holidays), and by Scripture text. To be more specific,

Topical Index

Each sermon is indexed by two or more major topics. Use this index if you are preparing to preach on "faith," "forgiveness," "service," "stewardship," and so on. More than 120 topics are included.

Index of Dates, Holidays, and Special Occasions

The Index of Dates, Holidays, and Special Occasions arranges all the sermons according to the New Common Lectionary, a widely used series of Bible lessons designed to be read as part of weekly worship services. The Lectionary readings for each Sunday and special holy days consist of a Psalm as well as a reading from each of the following: the Old Testament, the Epistles, and the Gospels. Over a three-year period (referred to, respectively, as Year A, Year B, and Year C), the Lectionary presents all the major themes of the Bible.

Each Christian Year begins in Advent, the four-week period before Christmas, and continues until late November of the following year. Year A begins with the First Sunday in Advent in 1992 and three years later in 1995. Year B begins with the First Sunday in Advent in 1993 and 1996. Year C begins in 1991, 1994, and 1997.

Turn to Index of Dates, Holidays, and Special Occasions to find material for Christmas, Good Friday, Easter and the various Sundays of Advent, After Epiphany, Lent, Easter, After Pentecost, and so on. Several selections are offered for "Common Time," the more than twenty Sundays between Pentecost and Advent.

This index is also a guide to materials for holidays and other special observances such as Presidents' Day, Mother's Day, Father's Day, Independence Day, and Thanksgiving.

Scripture Text Index

Each sermon is indexed according to the major Scripture reading or readings on which it is based. The headings also provide collateral readings from the Revised Common Lectionary.[2] The major text or texts upon which the sermon is based are indicated in bold type.

Copyright © 1992, Consultation on Common Texts.

Since the Revised Common Lectionary for each Sunday provides four Scripture selections (Old Testament, Psalm, Epistle, and Gospel), I have been able to provide only a representative sample. After all, fifty-two Sundays times three years times four weekly lectionary readings would require several hundred sermons!

The Revised Common Lectionary is used (with minor variations) by several Protestant denomiations and the Roman Catholic Church. In some cases, I have made alterations or have chosen to follow the previous version, the New Common Lectionary (abbreviated "NCL" in the text.)

Authorship, Word Count, and Timing

This collection of sermons was written by myself and seventeen contributors. The name of the author appears at the end of each sermon. The names, addresses, and brief descriptions of the contributors are listed at the back of the book.

The length of each sermon is indicated in words and minutes. Timing, of course, depends on the rate at which the material is read and the number of digressions, interpolations, and so on. I recommend an oral presentation speed of one hundred words a minute.

How to Use the Sermons in This Book

The sermons in this book may be used in a number of ways. Here are a few suggestions:

1. Consider a given sermon as a resource for the preparation of your own original sermon. Read the prepared sermon in this book several times. Then put it aside for a day (or at least a few hours). If you have time, consult other materials, such as those mentioned in Resources for Preaching (pp. 420-424).

   Then adapt the general structure and approach of the selected sermon and prepare your own version, either as a detailed outline or a complete manuscript. Or use two or more sermons on related topics as the basis for constructing your own sermon. Adapt material from more than one sermon, using the topical or Scripture text index.

   If your preparation time is severely limited, read the selected sermon several times, and lay it aside for at least an hour. Outline the sermon, expressing its major points in your own words.
2. Use a given sermon as though it were your own first draft. Type the complete text or input it on your computer. Now, wherever possible, express the thoughts of the sermon in your own words. Add illustrations based on your own experience, or replace first-person material by the writer of the selected sermon with your own stories or stories drawn from the lives of your friends, relatives, or fellow church members.
3. Use the sermon as a *script*. "Take my sermon—please!" There will be occasions in which it will be proper and appropriate for you to read a sermon from this book aloud. Many who turn to this book are not regular preachers, but find themselves filling in for a minister who is called away because of an unforeseen emergency or are last-minute backups due to special circumstances. This book was prepared with such situations in mind. We would be honored if our sermons were to be heard through others.

   If you plan to recite a sermon virtually word for word as it appears in this book, I recommend that you read it to yourself several times and that you type it out or write it longhand. Mark appropriate pauses and underline words that you think should be emphasized.

If there is absolutely no time for preparation, have your church secretary or your local copy shop make an enlarged photocopied version of the sermon for you. When I preach, the manuscript of the sermon manuscript I carry into the pulpit is usually printed in at least 16-point type (via my laser printer) or enlarged at least 20 percent so that it may be easily scanned at arm's length. When enlarged 35 percent on a photocopier, an 8½" × 11" original typescript with 1" margins on all sides will neatly fit an 8½" × 14" page. (Since 8½" × 7" pages are easier to handle in the pulpit, I cut each page in half.)

4. Practice, practice, practice! Whichever approach you take, set aside time for a trial run. Preach the sermon to your spouse or a friend and encourage constructive criticism. (Try not to be defensive. Your friendly critic is just trying to represent to you how your material and approach will be perceived by the average man or woman in the pew.)

   Try preaching the sermon before a mirror. Or preach it in an empty auditorium or church. Or record it on audiotape or videotape and give it careful attention—with or without a friendly critic.

5. If you are reasonably confident of your ability to speak extemporaneously, read the selected sermon to yourself a few times, outline its major points and illustrations on a few 3" × 5" cards, and launch out on your own, referring to your cards as needed.

6. If you just cannot get comfortable with a sermon, don't use it. There are plenty of others in this collection. And many of these sermons can be adapted for occasions other than those suggested. For example, the talk for a sports awards banquet can be used as a Sunday sermon on virtually any date.

7. A special caution about the first-person material. Several of the writers (including myself) routinely use illustrations based on their own experience. If you cannot replace such confessional material with stories based on your own experience, then attribute the first-person accounts to their respective writers, for instance, "Deborah Streeter, who is both a mother and a minister, recalls the first time she felt her the movement of her then unborn son," or "Lowell Streiker, a pastor, father, and grandfather, remembers when his own father taught him to ride a bicycle," or "Harold Rucker, a clergyman in California, describes his childhood experience of caring for his brother while both of his parents worked."

In addition to suggesting what to preach, this book also provides suggestions on how to preach. Throughout the text of this book, I have added ruled boxes filled with "tips and pointers."

A last word of advice—as you prepare and preach, never lose sight of the ultimate nature of the issues you are inviting your hearers to consider. And never forget that the word of God to your audience is found not in your eloquence but in their hearing and that God's word to you may be found there also.

CONTENTS

❦ CHAPTER ONE

FAITH AND HOPE

According to the sermons of this chapter, faith is more than belief. Faith is a matter of perspective, springing from the awareness of what we most treasure. To the eyes of faith, all of life is a miracle. Faith is the recognition that God has ordained a purpose for the existence of every human being—a purpose individual and unique to each of us.

Faith produces self-esteem and courage. It empowers us to create, to change, and to hope. But faith is not magic. It has no power of its own and is not an end in itself. Only God can guarantee that our hopes are not in vain.

For Christians, Jesus is the image of God. Through him we know a God of compassion, who experiences our deepest sorrows as well as our greatest joys. For the Christian preacher, the themes of triumph and tragedy are inseparable. Hence, the Sunday commemorating Jesus' final entrance into Jerusalem is at once Palm Sunday and Passion Sunday.

Through faith, we receive the gift of God's grace. But faith without works is dead. Faith yields acts of faithfulness and love as surely as the sun produces heat and light. Christians are not merely called to believe; they are chosen to go forth in service. To those Jesus sends, he gives the peace of the Holy Spirit. In the midst of the insanity of modern existence, the God of the ages offers us an oasis of rest and renewal. All that we need to fill our hearts is at hand and available. It is up to us to reach out for it!

❦ *Sermon 1*

❦ *Date:* Sixteenth Sunday After Pentecost, Year B

Texts: (NCL)
Proverbs 2:1-8
James 1:17-27
Mark 7:24-37

Theme: Faith is a matter of gaining perspective and telling your story.
Subject: Treasure

❦ *Title:* Click!

TIP | This sermon may be used as part of a memorial service.

*My child, if you . . . call out for insight and cry aloud for understanding, and if you look for it as for silver and search for it as for hidden treasure, then you will understand the fear of the LORD and find the knowledge of God. For the LORD gives wisdom, and from His mouth come knowledge and understanding. (Proverbs 2:1–6, selected)**

Every good and perfect gift is from above, coming down from the Father of the heavenly lights, who does not change like shifting shadows. (James 1:17)

Jesus commanded them not to tell anyone. But the more he did so, the more they kept talking about it. People were overwhelmed with amazement. "He has done everything well," they said. "He even makes the deaf hear and the mute speak." (Mark 7:36–37)

Jesus taught: ". . . where your treasure is, there your heart will be also" (Matthew 6:21). Treasures of the heart—all three of our Scripture readings for this morning tell us of God's gifts and how to receive them.

In the Book of Proverbs, the wise parent instructs his child to search for understanding as though it were more valuable than a winning lottery ticket.

James, a leader of the early church, speaks of a wisdom that transforms us from within—a wisdom that is not the accumulation of information or degrees but a wisdom that is characterized by self-control, especially by control of one's tongue; a wisdom that reveals itself in acts of generosity and mercy.

And, finally, our Gospel passage teaches us about a healing that cannot be silenced.

> Despite the fact that the healer himself asked that the story be hushed up, the one who experienced the miracle proclaimed the experience wherever he went—and he did so loudly. The more dramatic the deliverance, the more irrepressible the testimony. Arguments from Scripture and proofs from logic may have their place, but nothing is quite as effective as the personal story of one who . . . was blind and now can see, was deaf and now can hear, was addicted and now can stay sober, was lost and now can find the way.[1]

---

*Biblical reference, e.g., "Proverbs 2:1-6, selected" should not be read aloud. They are included for identification.

[1] *Prayers for Worship*, New Berlin, Wisconsin Liturgical Publications, Inc., September 8, 1991.

Gaining Perspective and Telling One's Story

It is all a matter of gaining perspective and telling one's story from a newfound point of view. There's a word that covers personal perspective and one's story—a very abused word. The word is "faith."

The faith that really counts is not mental assent to doctrine. It is not accepting what we do not know and cannot know because someone says it is so. Proverbs, James, and Jesus have no patience with people who think they are better than others because of their orthodox beliefs. The faith that saves us, that makes us whole and alive, is the meaning we see and the story we tell.

When everything clicks into place, that is faith. When we look at everyday life and see the bright, shiny pennies, that is faith. When we find love and comfort and are comforted, make commitments, share the good days and the not so good days with someone else, that is faith. When we go through the photo albums and remember with gratitude, that is faith.

What does God have to do with this? Everything. We have been spoiled by those stories we learned in Sunday School. We expect a God who intervenes, who gives us whatever we want whenever we want it. We expect a God who is in control, who never lets us get sick or suffer or hurt or die. And when it doesn't come out that way, we get mad.

"Where was God when I needed him?" we demand. And then we look back on the last decade or the last twenty years or the last fifty and as we tell our story, we see. There is a pattern there. At first glance, I see what has gone before. At second glance, I see it as something, as my life, my history, my story. I look once again, it is a story about me and many, many others. I take a final look and the big picture emerges. My story is part of a larger tale—a story that embraces past, present, and future; a story encompassing the living and the dead; a story encompassing men, women, and children of every nation and society; a story encompassing humankind, nature, and being itself. My story has merged into God's. Something has gone "click"!

"The Little Tin Box"

Perhaps a story can make the point. This one is called "The Little Tin Box" and is adapted from Edward Hays's book, *Twelve and One-Half Keys.*[2]

> The long gravel driveway that led up from the highway was filled with cars and pickup trucks. The two-story, white farmhouse and large barn were surrounded by tractors and other farm machinery, together with furniture and a variety of household articles. The farm had been in their family now for two generations, and, like so many other Midwestern farms, it had been sold recently to some European businessmen. Today, Tom and Mary would sell their furniture and all of their farm machinery. After trying different solutions, even a part-time job in town, Tom was giving up at attempting to make a living from farming.
>
> The farm auction had attracted neighbors and strangers alike.... After the furniture and antiques came the machinery....

Most of the items had been sold when the auctioneer held up a small tin box. "How much do I hear?" he asked.

Before a single bid could be placed, Tom shouted, "Sorry, friends, the tin box is not

---

[2] Edward Hays, *Twelve and One-Half Keys*, (Leavenworth, KS: Forest of Peace Books, Inc. 1981), pp. 139ff. For a list of publications, write Forest of Peace Books, 251 Muncie Road, Levenworth, KS 66048

for sale . . . everything else is, but not that!"

Tom took the box and walked away. In a few minutes, the auction was over.

The day also began to quickly disappear. . . . The pickup trucks slowly rolled down the gravel driveway, the life possessions of Tom and Mary stacked on them or being towed behind. . . . Tom settled with the auctioneer, who echoed the sympathies of their neighbors about having to sell. He placed his fee into a worn-out brown billfold and drove down the drive . . . the last car.

. . .

Tom and Mary had planned on leaving the farm that night. Their suitcases and a pile of cardboard boxes stood ready by the door.

They sat in silence, eating ham sandwiches and drinking coffee.

The tin box had a place of honor in the center of the kitchen table. Mary was the first to speak: "They almost sold your little tin box."

"Yeah, that was close, wasn't it?" said Tom, as he slowly opened the lid of the box. To the average eye the box appeared to be empty, but in reality it was filled almost to the top. The old battered tin box was filled with memories. Mary opened a suitcase and removed a small tin box [of her own]. Slowly, one after another, they took out memories from their tin boxes and passed them to each other. One memory would awaken another one or be the leader of an entire parade of memories: "Remember the first night we stayed together after we were married . . . or when Dick came home from the Army . . . or that Christmas day in the 50s when we and the kids were snowbound?" Their little tin boxes held memories that went back to their early childhoods. . . .

These small tin boxes were what made Tom and Mary the richest people in the county. Early in life they had learned a great secret from Tom's grandfather. "The purpose of any possession," the old man had said, "is to make memories! The only purpose of money—only purpose—is to make memories. Things and possessions only rust and age, but memories, Tommy, memories are like fine wine . . . they grow in value with time." Now that the farm sale and auction had completely dispossessed them of their belongings, they knew the wisdom of what grandfather had said to them. . . .

Tom returned the last memory to his tin box. He had to rearrange some memories for it to fit. He closed the lid and looked at his watch. They had visited over their memories so long it seemed too late now and too much trouble to drive into town to their new apartment. Instead, they decided to spend just one more night at the farm. Mary unpacked the sheets from one of the cardboard boxes by the door and made the bed.

Thank goodness, they had not included the old bed in the sale. It had belonged to Tom's parents and was solid walnut. They had given it to one of their sons. Tomorrow he and his wife would pick it up.

Tom placed his little tin box on the windowsill as he climbed into the ancient great bed. Their last night on the farm was one of the most beautiful of their lives. Mary was asleep as Tom arose and stood by the open window. The fields, the barn, the windmill, and, off in the distance, the cottonwoods along the creek were all silent but beautiful, bathed in the light of the giant moon.

Tom smiled as he opened, once again, his little tin box and gently placed inside it the memory of this beautiful night. He attempted to close the lid, but it wouldn't close, the box was so full. Gently he rearranged the memories so they would all fit. Then he closed the lid. As he did, it made a strange click that he had never heard before. Tom placed the old tin box on the windowsill and slowly laid back on the bed. He closed his eyes and was asleep almost at once. The next morning, when she awoke, Mary found him sleeping peacefully in the gentle arms of death.

Three nights later, Mary and her children entered the funeral home. Their friends and neighbors were there—the same friends and neighbors who had been at the auction. "Poor Tom," they murmured, "losing the farm was just too much for him." But Mary knew better. She stood by the casket, looking down at her husband.

Tom looked peaceful, his weatherworn face relaxed, his hands folded across his chest. His fingers still had tiny grease-darkened lines from all the years of hard work. Intertwined among his fingers was a black rosary.

Mary opened her pocketbook. She removed the rosary from Tom's hands. From her handbag she took the little tin box and placed it in Tom's hands. The parish priest stepped forward and in his authoritarian but hushed voice said to her, "Mary, Mary, you can't do that!" He reached for the tin box.

"Leave it there, Father . . . *that's* Tom's rosary. Hardly a day would pass that he wouldn't take some memory out of that box and be filled with gratitude. He was a holy man, and he understood what poverty and prayer were all about. No, Father, the box remains because it's the only thing he's taking with him to heaven."

. . .

When the wake was over, and family and friends had all departed, Mary returned to her apartment. Her black dress hung on the back of the bedroom door as she sat on the bed and smiled, thinking how much Tom would have approved of what she had done that night. Then she carefully took out her own little tin box and opened it. She placed the memory of the wake—the many, many kind words about Tom, even the expression on Father [Ed's] face—all of it, into her little tin box. The lid fit perfectly on the very top of the full box. As she closed the lid, it made a strange little click. Mary smiled and lay back on the pillow. She was asleep, peacefully, almost at once.

And Jesus said: "Do not store up for yourselves treasures on earth, where moth and rust destroy, and where thieves break in and steal. But store up for yourselves treasures in heaven, where moth and rust do not destroy, and where thieves do not break in and steal. For where your treasure is, there your heart will be also" (Matthew 6:19–21).

CLICK!

Amen.

—LDS

[1876 words]
[19 minutes]

❦ *Sermon 2*

❦ *Date:* Sunday Between August 7 and August 13 inclusive Pentecost, Year A

Texts:
Genesis 37:1-4, 12-28
Psalm 105:1-16, 16-22, 45b
Romans 10:5-15
Matthew 14:22–33

Theme: To the eyes of faith, all of life is a miracle.
Subject: Faith and miracles

❦ *Title:* When the Small Black Cat in the Big, Dark Room Is Really an Elephant

Miracles make me uncomfortable. I guess I have been forever influenced by Jack Webb's Sergeant Friday. You know—"The facts, ma'am. Just the facts." I live in a world of observation, confirmation, and predictability. I live in a universe governed by natural law. I expect the sun to rise in the east every morning. If I drop a lead weight, I expect it to hit the floor. If I put my hand into a flame, I expect my fingers to be burned. I do not expect God to suspend the laws of the physical universe on my account. No matter how righteous I may be, I expect to get as wet as any sinner when it rains.

Miracles make me uncomfortable. Miracles are events that cannot be explained according to the known laws of science. People who believe in them think that natural law can be suspended at any time. They are fond of the exceptions that prove the rule—the one-in-a-million, inexplicable healing at Lourdes, for example. I am more impressed by the other 999,999 cases. Isn't the God of the miraculous just plain arbitrary and capricious?

Three of our four lectionary readings for this Sunday speak of miracles. Our Old Testament passage is the Exodus account of the escape from Egypt—the parting of the Red Sea, the destruction of the pursuing Egyptian army, the divine presence in the pillar of cloud—here is the central miracle around which the entire theology of the Old Testament revolves.

The psalm for today is a reflection on this same miracle. Writing centuries after the exodus, the psalmist looks forward to God's forthcoming rescue of his people—from foreign enemies, from military setbacks. He confesses that he and his contemporaries have repeated the sin of their ancestors when they were in Egypt. The generation of the exodus had not remembered the abundance of God's steadfast love, and, in consequence, they had rebelled against him. They doubted that he would keep his promises to save them from the enemies that pursued them.

The descendants of those escaped slaves had likewise forgotten God's steadfast love. Even though they had grown into a mighty nation, they had forgotten the God who never forgot, who never welshed on his promises.

Who is this God who liberated the Hebrew slaves from their oppressors, who never forgot his people even when they "forgot to remember" him? As depicted in our Old Testament passages for today, he is no still small voice, no subtle inner sense guiding human conscience, no gradual evolution of self-discovery. In the exodus event, God does not whisper to us, he overwhelms us with his power.

Likewise, the Jesus of today's Gospel account does not appeal to his disciples with clever stories or try to lure them into the new way of life he offers by his moral example and teachings. No, he stuns them into paralysis by displaying the same power over the elements that had created a nation out of fleeing slaves at the time of Moses.

Looking for the Cat That May Not Be There

All too often, we live our spiritual lives as though we were feeling around in a large, dark room for a small black cat that may not be there anyway. In our readings for today, God is no elusive, hard-to-find, possibly nonexistent being. His presence and power are so overwhelming that neither the fleeing children of Israel nor the disciples in that fishing boat could doubt them for an instant.

That does not mean that they could not misinterpret God's presence and power, make them into something else, pigeonhole them, domesticate them, explain them away, or—worst of all—simply file them away as unique and fascinating events and forget them. "That Moses sure can concoct some splendid special effects," the escaped slaves agreed, "but can he get us out of the wilderness? Can he feed us and find water for us?" And one by one, the survivors of Egyptian enslavement died and left their bones in the desert of Sinai, although the promised land was only a few miles away. No matter what the God of the covenant did for them, they soon rationalized it, diminished it, explained it away—or forgot it.

Are we like the children of the exodus? Do we soon forget what God has done our behalf?

Are we like Peter? Eager to step out on faith but in the end overcome by our own pettiness and fear.

Have we seen the power of God? To the eyes of faith, all of life is a miracle. Two of us live through almost identical days. One of us sees that day as just a day like all other days. The other sees that day as a gift of God's grace, evidence of God's presence, a sign of his steadfast love. That's what a miracle is—not a special effect, not an apparent violation of physical law that we cannot rationally explain.

Did God part the Red Sea so the children of Israel could pass over? Did he drown Pharaoh's army? One fact we cannot dispute. The children of Israel escaped from their oppressors. However they managed this, it was to the eyes of faith a gift of God's grace. It was evidence of God's presence, a manifestation of God's steadfast love.

Did Jesus really walk on the water or did the sleepy disciples misperceive his arrival? Let us not be sidetracked. The message—"Take heart, it is I; have no fear"—is more important than the means by which Jesus traveled. It is obvious that Matthew believed that the disciples reexperienced the exodus event. Whatever may have happened, they had the same choice as those who followed Moses. They could forget the whole thing or remember it as a gift of God's grace. They could let the exodus event fade away, or they could embrace it as evidence of God's presence and steadfast love.

This Jesus was something else! They could not doubt that for each of them God's power was right here and now—inescapable, unavoidable. They could not explain him. They could not interpret him. They could not understand him. And, above all, they could not forget him.

The Miracles of Grace

I still have trouble with miracles. There are no voices from burning bushes, parting of the seas, or raising of the dead in my daily life. And I am suspicious of the motives of modern miracle workers and the credulity of those who follow them. However, when I pause to reflect on the course of my life, I am struck at how little of significance that has happened in my life has been because of my planning or doing and how much I owe to surprises. Things happen. Things that I never would have expected. And I am changed forever in consequence. Sometimes I am enhanced, sometimes chastened. Sometimes I am blessed, and sometimes I am a blessing. Sometimes I lose my way—stumble, stagger, even fall—but I am always lifted up by a tender hand. I am always reminded that I am loved and called to love others.

And whatever happens, I am overwhelmed by a sense that each day is a gift of God's grace, evidence of God's presence, a manifestation of God's steadfast love.

God is no small black cat that may or may not be in the darkness of our lives and the murkiness of our world. To the eyes of faith, he is as unavoidable and present as the miracle of the exodus was to fugitive Hebrews. His power and grace are as close to us today as the company of Jesus was to the awestruck disciple in that tiny boat two thousand years ago.

Miracles still bother me, but I never forget them. As Lily Tomlin's character, the infant Edith Ann, would say to Sergeant Friday: "And that's the truth!"

Amen.

—LDS

[1300 words]
[13 minutes]

Sermon 3

Date: Sunday Between June 19 and 25 inclusive (if after Trinity Sunday)
Year A

Texts:
Genesis 21:8-21
Psalm 86:1-10, 16-7
Romans 6:1b-11
Matthew 10:24–39

Theme: We are caught in a prison of low-self-esteem, trying desperately to be something we are not, until we hear the gospel message of confidence.
Subject: Self-esteem, faith

Title: On Feeling Unimportant

She was only a small girl in a town in Texas, but the whole nation held its breath as her life trembled in the balance. She had slipped into a narrow well near her home and had become wedged in it, twenty feet below ground. Her cries brought help, and soon the word spread. As construction crews worked feverishly to dig down and rescue her, the whole nation heard of her plight, and radios and television carried continuous coverage as the effort went on. Just a small girl, previously unknown to anyone outside her family and friends, but hundreds of millions of people watched to see whether she would make it or not.

He was a businessman in Indianapolis. A crazed man had entered his office, wired a gun to his head, and demanded certain concessions. The crisis went on for more than 24 hours, and again, the world watched. Just an ordinary businessman, but everyone knew his name now, he was very special, and prayers and hopes for his rescue abounded.

They were very ordinary people in both cases, people like you and me. But suddenly both were center stage as their lives hung in balance. Now isn't it remarkable to think that such would be the case if it were you or I in such a desperate situation. No matter how unimportant we feel, if it were one of us, again the eyes of the world would be focused here, and millions would watch to see whether our story would end in despair or in joy.

There is good biblical precedent for this. "Two sparrows are sold for a penny," said Jesus. "But one of them falls to the ground without the father's knowledge. Even the very hairs on your head are numbered" (Matthew 10:29). The shepherd who had a hundred sheep brought all but one safely into the fold at night. But one was missing, one was in danger. No matter that 99 percent were in safely—where was the lost one? The shepherd went out, and all of heaven's energies were turned to finding the one lost sheep.

It is remarkable, in view of these circumstances, that one of the diseases of the spirit that most frequently gets us down is a feeling that we are unimportant, that we don't count for much, a feeling of inferiority. Someone put it this way: "Stick your hand into a bucket full of water, and then pull it out and see how big a hole is left. That'll tell you how important you are," and that feeling of personal inferiority occurs in the most unexpected places.

When God called Moses to service, this trembling man asked, "Who am I that I should go to Pharaoh and bring out the sons of Israel?" (Exodus 3:11). Gideon was one of the heroes of the Old Testament, but he responded to God's call by saying, "My clan is the weakest in the tribe, and I am the least in my clan" (Judges 6:15). Jeremiah, the prophet, said, "Oh, Lord, I do not know how to speak, for I am only a youth" (Jeremiah 1:6). I heard a popular woman politician tell of her anxiety on entering politics. "Inadequacy and insecurity," she said, "are old friends of mine."

Small wonder, then, that this disease of the spirit should be found among us ordinary people. Despite the fact that our lives are unique, that many people care about us, we suffer from a lack of self-esteem.

The Desire to Be Somebody

I. Look what we try to do about this. We reach for a feeling of importance, and the less self-esteem we have, the more frantic our reach. We search for things that will make us feel like we amount to something. Other people's approval becomes one of the ways we reach for self-esteem. If enough other people think well of me, then surely I can think well of myself!

Thus, we spend our lives playing to audiences. Each one of us selects an audience to play before. What do they like? What will impress them? What can I do to make them believe that I am somebody? We try to get our feelings of self-worth from outside ourselves. If we do not have it already inside us, we get it stamped on us from outside by what other people think. All this rings true to psychologist Alfred Adler's claim that the strongest human drive is the desire for recognition, the desire to be somebody.

A recent article from the sports pages illustrates this in a poignant way. The article tells of the shooting death of the young boxer Tyrone Everett. He was the number one contender for the lightweight boxing championship, having fought his way up from the streets of Philadelphia. "The 25-year-old boxer," says the article, "was a flashy dresser who loved the ladies and money. Everett made enough money to buy a bar, two apartment houses, and a Cadillac. 'Money is the only reason I'm fighting,' he said. 'Man, you gotta be out of your mind to say you like to fight. Who wants to get in the ring and get beat up?'"

"But he also talked of his dream of some day wearing the championship belt. 'I see myself coming into the ring,' he said. 'I have the championship belt around my waist—and the lights go down, and the spotlight hits me, and I hear all the girls in the audience screaming, 'Whooee, look at Tyrone Everett!'"

Most of us have some kind of dream like that, little dreams that "give us a temporary lift over the low opinion we have of ourselves." And so we select some audience that is important to us, our professional colleagues, our bridge club, the neighbors, the country club, our brothers-in-law, the Sunday School class. We select some such audience and we play out our lives before them, reaching for a feeling of self-worth stamped on from outside, hoping that if enough other people say, "He is somebody," we'll begin to believe it ourselves!

Reaching After Self-Importance

II. This reach for self-esteem is usually so awkwardly done that much harm comes from it, both to ourselves and others. Someone has put it into blank verse in this fashion:

> Half of the harm that is done in this world
> Is due to people who want to feel important.
> They don't mean to do harm, but the harm does not interest them,
> Or they do not see it, or they justify it,
> Because they are absorbed in the endless struggle
> To think well of themselves.

We play little games of self-importance, reaching again for the stamp of approval or recognition from others, and we look foolish in the process. But worse than this, we do harm to ourselves. Keith Miller tells of the young couple who got married, and everything they reached for came to them. They wanted all the marks of success, and quickly and in order, they got them. His work was a success, her involvement in the community was spectacular, their children were attractive and admired, they achieved membership in the right clubs. But every new success, every new step up the ladder, brought more fighting and arguing.

"What's wrong with us?" they wondered. "It must be this house. It just won't do." The husband was in a rapid financial climb, and in the next few years they built four new houses, each larger than the one before. "Finally," the wife said later, "we built a beautiful 15-room house in the nicest part of the city. And after the builder left we sat down in the living room of that magnificent house and had the worst fight of our marriage. Right then we realized the problem wasn't the house!"[1]

The author goes on to observe that many of us never get in a position to discover this, so we keep striving for material things, hoping against hope that they will give us security or esteem. "But when people realize that the reaching of a material goal or status is not the solution, a real identity crisis can arise. And this type of crisis has reached almost epidemic proportions in America because so many people are achieving their material goals at an early age."[2] Analysts, looking back on the 1980's are calling it the "me" decade.

A feeling of self-worth, then, is not stamped on from outside by a climb up the ladder, as by an accumulation of honors or possessions, and we do harm to ourselves when we forget this.

The Source of Self-Esteem

III. The most liberating moment any of us faces is when we feel our own self-worth, when we realize that as children of God, our worth does not depend on what someone else thinks of us. Our worth comes because God has created us as unique human beings, his children, custom-made and special. We don't have to perform before an audience any more! What difference does it really make what someone else thinks about us? Our stamp of self-worth comes from within us, and God put it there.

What this involves is simply the confidence that God loves us, that we are his children. I am somebody, not because I drive a certain kind of car, or live in a certain house, or have earned a certain degree, or belong to a certain club; I am somebody because God brought me into being.

---

[1] Miller, Keith, *The Becomers* (Waco, TX: Word Books, 1973), p. 152.

[2] Ibid.

The genius of Jesus was that he helped people see this. Matthew was a traitor to his people, a tax collector with little to offer. But Jesus came by and said, "Matthew, I want you!" and Matthew followed. Peter and Andrew were fishermen, a dime a dozen in that day, uneducated and uncouth, but Jesus cast his net over them and took the gifts they had to offer. Mary and Martha were two sisters living together, with hospitality as their only gift, but they gave it, and Jesus welcomed it warmly.

And for many others, each with some limited gift to give, Jesus blessed the gift, and the giver's life was enriched because of it. Our world is filled with people who feel little self-worth, people trying to give gifts they don't have, people trying to be what they are not. Jesus enters our hearts, breaks into that low-esteem, and says, "Little children, the very hairs on your head are numbered, you are so precious in your father's sight. He has made you little less than gods, and has crowned you with glory and honor."

Listen, how many of us need to hear that message. Caught in a prison of low self-esteem, trying desperately to be something we are not, our lives are crippled because of it. The Gospel's message is not inferiority, but confidence. "Beloved, you are God's children now, and it does not yet appear what you shall become!"

Charlotte Elliott, born in 1789, found that life did not go exactly as she had planned. Her older brother had become a minister in England, and Charlotte had hopes of finding some kind of meaningful work to do as well. But her health failed her, and in her late twenties she had to move in with her brother's family, a complete invalid.

She resented her helplessness, her utter uselessness, until a friend reminded her that she should put herself in God's hands and come to Christ, "just as you are." Charlotte Elliott took that word to heart. Although she regretted the fact that she could not help her brother with his work, something clicked inside her, a thought, a message. She sat down and wrote a poem for her brother to set to music, and that poem which expressed her feelings became one of the church's great hymns. It is a hymn for all those of us who come wondering at our own self-worth, and it moves us from inferiority to confidence. The words crippled and useless Charlotte Elliott wrote were these:

Just as I am, without one plea,
But that thy blood was shed for me,
And that thou bidst me come to thee,
O lamb of God, I come, I come.

Just as I am, though tossed about,
With many a conflict, many a doubt.
fightings and fears, within, without,
O lamb of God, I come, I come.

Just as I am, Thou wilt receive,
Wilt welcome, pardon, cleanse, relieve,
Because thy promise I believe,
O lamb of God, I come, I come.

Amen.

—Eugene Brice

[2100 words]
[21 minutes]

Sermon 4

Date: Second Sunday After Epiphany, Year A

Texts:
Isaiah 49:1–7
Psalm 40:1–11
1 Corinthians 1:1–9
John 1:29-42

Theme: God has ordained a purpose for my existence, different from the purpose of any other human being.
Subject: Self-image, identity

Title: God Named My Name

> *The Lord called me from the womb, from the body of my mother he named my name. (Isaiah 49:1 RSV)*

God named my name. What did the prophet mean? He was saying something like this: God knows me inside and out even before birth. God has ordained a purpose for my existence, different from the purpose of any other human being. Machine parts are interchangeable, people are not.

As Diane L. Harvey, pastor of the Rochester (New York) Congregational Church, explains:

> To be named is to be given an identity. Parents spend hours trying to find just the right names for their children to mark them as special and unique. Our names tell us who we are. For God to name our name is to hear our Heavenly Parent reaching out to us in love, marking us as God's own, and calling us to take our part in the endless community of the faithful.[1]

God Knows Who I Am

God and only God knows who I really am. For God has named my name. Among many peoples, name and reality are one and the same. To know a person's name is to have power over him. To know the name of a deity is to be able to conjure him or her up at will and make the god do our bidding. The Hebrews so zealously guarded the name of Yahweh or Jehovah that no one knows how his name was pronounced.

---

[1] Rear cover text, United Church of Christ Sunday Bulletin Service, Second Sunday After Epiphany, Year A (January 14, 1990).

The Importance of Names

My name discloses and yet conceals who I really am. When we hear a person's name, we think we know something about him or her and we react accordingly. What do you expect when you are introduced to a woman named Prudence or a man named Shirley? What do you anticipate when you meet a Mark or a Keith or a Kim or a Cindy? How will we feel at the end of this century when we meet grandparents named Bambi or Rock?

Naming a child identifies, predicts, and influences what that child will become. A distinctive name suggests distinctive achievements. Failure to live up to that name is viewed as a profound tragedy. To be saddled with the name of a famous parent or forebear can be particularly disastrous, or it can open doors of opportunity for the rest of one's life.

Nicknames are a powerful form of naming that can influence personal development. I think of some of our acquaintances from the South, people in their advanced years, with names like "Little Miss Bess" or "Bitsy." My wife knew a man whose nickname of "Chubby" followed him into adult life. The only nicknames I have ever had were "Lolly" and "Doc." Would I be a different person today if my parents had named me "Mike" or my friends had called me "Bubba"?

Changing One's Name

Changing one's names is often an attempt to change one's identity. When I was a child some of my favorite movie stars were

Frederick Austerlitz (Fred Astaire)
Betty Persky (Lauren Bacall)
Bernie Schwartz (Tony Curtis)
Doris Kapelhoff (Doris Day)

They got rid of foreign-sounding, ethnic names in order to makes themselves acceptable to a Middle American audience.

Other favorites of mine were:

Dianne Belmont (Lucille Ball)
Lucy Johnson (Ava Gardner)

By changing their names, they left behind no-nonsense, straightforward mundaneness and attained glamor and appeal. Still others such as Archibald Leach (Cary Grant), Leonard Slye (Roy Rogers), and Marion Morrison (John Wayne) rid themselves of "sissy names" so that each of them could be just "one of the boys."

As I grew older, I became fond of the comedy of Allen Stewart Konigsberg (Woody Allen) and the short stories of William Sidney Porter (O. Henry). Doesn't "Houdini" have more mystery than Erich Weiss? Doesn't "Babe" Ruth sound more approachable than "George Herman" Ruth? Aren't you glad that the San Francisco 49ers are led by a guy named Joe rather than by a "Boomer" or a "Bubby"? Do you think Gerald Ford would have been elected to any public office if he had retained his original name, Leslie L. King, Jr.?

Last names also have a significance and a lasting influence. There is something comfortable, trustworthy about a common name. By the way, the most common last names in United States, in order, are:

Smith
Johnson
Williams

Jones
Brown
Miller
Davis
Anderson
Wilson
Thompson

Unusual last names suggest unusual potential—potential for good or for evil, and such names create lifelong stress for the bearer. Having a common name is a good way to hide from scrutiny and expectation.

When I see the names of writers Irving Wallace and David Wallechinsky joined together, I realize how far we have come from the generation that wanted to be like everyone else and thus Americanized their family names to a generation in desperate search for roots, continuity, and a sense of heritage. I hope someday to introduce you to my friend, Sacheen Littlefeather, the American Indian activist, who was born Maria Cruz.

Name Calling and Discrimination

Calling a person by a name is a way of reducing him or her from being real to being a category to be filed away or dismissed. One day, I toured the wards at a state mental hospital and was given access to many treatment records. In case after case, I discovered that certain patients were "clinically depressed," "manic depressive," "schizophrenic," or all three! And that was all. If the case records were very, very old, the patient might have been diagnosed as "catatonic" at one time. The "manic depressives" were treated with appropriate medication such as lithium carbonate, the "clinically depressed" with antidepressants, and the "schizophrenics" with antipsychotic agents. Nobody was allowed to be "catatonic" anymore. It was out of vogue.

It seemed to me as a layperson that no one at the state hospital had the foggiest idea of what was wrong with the chronic patients or any concept of who any of the patients really were. The reality of these human beings had been swallowed up in the categories of "clinically depressed," "manic depressive," and "schizophrenic." The staff readily fell into the temptation to name each patient's condition and then respond not to the patient but to his or her designation.

Living Up to Who We Are

God has named our name. The challenge is to bring our name in touch with the reality of who we are. Each of us directly names who we are. We are the sources from which most people learn our names. Listen carefully, for I am saying something deeper than you are the one who says to others, "Hello, my name is _______." You and you alone attach to that name its significance and value. Consider the name of the man whose birthday we honor tomorrow, Martin Luther King, Jr. What a burden was placed on him by his parents—to be named not only for his father but for the instigator of the Protestant Reformation. What a name to be lived up to!

The point is that Martin Luther King, Jr., did just that. His life—his deeds and his words—filled in what his name only outlined. What his name means to us today is a result of how he assumed and lived that name. He could have betrayed his name. He could have rejected his calling. His name could have been as empty as the names chosen by advertisers to give the illusion of substance while concealing in gaudy colored, bulky packaging only empty promises and junk.

God named my name—before I was born. And that is not the name on my birth certificate or the name by which I am known at work or the pet name by which my spouse addresses me or the nickname known only by my buddies. God has given me the outline of who I am and what I can become. And he works with me to fill in the details, to establish my character. (I often wonder if when I am gone those who have known me will recall: "What character!" or "What a character!" I hope it is a combination of both!)

Do you remember what the voice from the burning bush said to Moses when Moses demanded to know his name? The voice replied: "I AM WHO I AM" (Exodus 3:14). As Flip Wilson's alter ego, Josephine, has been saying for many years: "What you see is what you get!" Each of us asks, "What is your name, Lord?" And God responds: "I do what I say I will do. I keep my promises. My name is, 'The One Who Can Be Counted On.'"

God has given each of us the same name: "The One Who Can Be Counted On." Will we respond when he calls us by name? Will the content of our separate and distinct names, our diverse personal identities, be filled in? Or will the masks behind which we hide fall away to reveal nothing at all?

When our children and grandchildren and great-grandchildren find our names in their family tree, will our names be full with significance? Will we be remembered as those who could be counted on?

Can we say with the prophet, "God named my name"? Can we bring to reality what he confessed: God knows me inside and out even before birth; God has ordained a purpose for my existence, different from the purpose of any other human being; I am who I am; you can count on it.

Amen.

—LDS
[1600 words]
[16 minutes]

❦ *Sermon 5*

❦ *Date:* Sunday between August 7 and 13 inclusive, Year C

Texts:
Hebrews 11:1–3, 8–16
Luke 12:32–40

Theme: Where your treasure is, there is your heart.
Subject: Treasures

❦ *Titles:* Treasures

The Small Cedar Chest

When I was a little girl, I owned a small cedar chest, handed down to me by my Auntie Anne. It must have been at least a hundred years old, this chest, just the right size for a little girl, and when you opened the hinged lid and took a deep breath, you could still catch a whiff of the cedar, delicate as angel wings.

When this chest was given to me, it contained two remarkable things: a handstitched cloth doll dating from the turn of the century and a faded black skullcap that had belonged to some male member of the distant Jewish branch of my family. Pity that I never knew the names of the original owners of the doll, the skullcap, or the chest, or even how I am related to them. But I don't know, and the people who might have known are all dead now. Someday, no doubt, I will hand them down to my own daughter and make up some fantastic story about them, so at least she will have the good sense not to give them away.

The doll and the skullcap collected dust on the closet floor, but the little cedar chest became a place for keeping treasures. Safely hidden under the bed, it held the odds and ends that were the inexplicable artifacts of my childhood. There was my complete collection of Walt Disney plastic figurines (including two of Pluto). There was also a small bagful of salt that I had collected at the Great Salt Lake in Utah on one of our family car trips and a little blue clown on a ball bearing that rolled across the floor—I'd gotten that from a gum machine for a nickel in 1962. There was a cheap little stuffed bear that I had won at the Williamson County fair one year for selecting out of the water the winning combination of floating ducks. Aside from that, there was the usual collection of bright stones, beads, doll dishes, a piece of stale pineapple candy from Hawaii, and a seashell or two.

I think that every child has a box like this, at one time or another. Often it is a cigar box, but it might as easily be a drawer or a purse or a paper bag. Who can explain the junk that is precious to children? It is simply the stuff of which wonder is made, no different from the icons and sacred texts and hosts of our holy places.

If you had asked me when I was a child, "Where is your treasure?" I would have pulled the little cedar chest out from under the bed and lovingly shown you each precious item, perhaps even allowed you to touch and hold them. But if you were to ask me now, "Where is your treasure?" I would have to think a moment or two. There is no cedar chest anymore, you see, no repository of sacred objects to pull out from a hiding place. Oh, I have a box of letters and ticket stubs, concert programs and newspaper clippings, but it's hardly the same thing. The contents of that box do not describe me quite like the little cedar chest did.

My Treasures and My Heart

So if you asked me now, "Where is your treasure?" I would have to dig a little deeper and a little more painfully, until I found the dark place where memory lives . . . the place where my heart beats and my soul breathes. And even then, it would not be a simple answer. It would be more like a swirling constellation of things: Callie Lou, my golden retriever, would be there; and the dozens of roses given to me by my husband, Curt; a few lines of William Faulkner; an aria from a Bach cantata; a family photograph posed in front of the fireplace mantle; a song about a shoemaker that my grandmother used to sing; the smell of fresh mint in iced tea on hot Sunday afternoons; and the kiss I received on my first prom night.

I know that there would also be some pain there, because there has been so much pain, and so much learned from pain—the pain of loss, of betrayal, of irrevocable decisions. But there would be blessings as well—the blessing of my niece Libby when she lifts her face to kiss mine, the blessing of a friend's hand on my shoulder, the blessing of a day's hard work and a night's refreshing sleep.

Jesus said, "Provide yourselves with purses that do not grow old, with a treasure in the heavens that does not fail, where no thief approaches and no moth destroys. For where your treasure is, there will your heart be also" (Luke 12:33b–34).

If you ask me, "Where is your treasure?" I will point to that place where memory lives. Because that is where I go when I need to remember how to love, how to risk, how to trust, how to mend, how to forgive. If God lives in that place, and I believe God does, then my treasure is also with God. That is where my treasure is, because that is the stuff of which I am made. Like the contents of the cedar chest hidden under a little girl's bed, that is what describes me.

But unlike the little cedar chest, which someday might be broken or stolen or eaten up by termites, this treasure is in a place where no thief may approach and no moth may destroy; it may grow old, but it cannot fail. Jesus was right: where my treasure is, there will my heart be also. I have a treasure, in this place where my heart is. I have it. I will always have it. There are no words for the gratitude.

Amen.

—Elizabeth Chandler Felts
[970 words]
[10 minutes]

Sermon 6

Date: Second Sunday of Advent, Year A

Texts:
Isaiah 11:1–10
Psalm 1-7, 18-19
Romans 15:4–13
Matthew 3:1–12

or Sunday Between July 17 and July 23 inclusive, Year B
Texts:
Jeremiah 23:1–6
Ephesians 2:11–22
Mark 6:30–34, 53-56

Theme: God always keeps his promises.
Subject: Hope

Title: The God of Hope

Tip

> For the sake of variety, change the structure of your sermons from time to time. If you usually present your material with a well-articulated outline ("Point 1. . . . Point 2. . . . Point 3. . . .), preach a sermon without an obvious outline. If you usually explain or expound your text and then make practical suggestions, try reversing the order as in this sermon.
> Remember: Familiarity breeds wandering minds.

Stress Kills

Stress kills. We have seen it, felt it. Reducing stress can save our lives. We have known that most of our lives. We also know that stress can drain the meaning and value from our personal existence, our family lives, and our careers. But even more fundamental is the recognition that hope or expectancy is an essential component in well-being. Without hope, fear and worry throw the body as well as the mind into a constant state of disequilibrium or "disease." In simplest terms, fear, the obsessive concern for what can go wrong, disempowers and disrupts; hope, the preoccupation with what can go right, empowers, harmonizes, and restores.

Hope is more than wishful thinking, just as faith is more than belief. Faith and hope are twin expressions of the fundamental commitments that give meaning to our lives, that enable us to find ourselves meaningfully related to the universe and the universe meaningfully related to us. Faith and hope are basic tendencies of the spiritually grounded consciousness to create significance and purpose.

Hope is more than a sigh of resignation when nothing more can be done. Hope is a major force of life, a vital impulse that protects us against illness and stimulates the proper functioning of all physical systems, including the heart, circulation, respiration, digestion, muscles, skin, nervous system, brain, and the senses. In addition, faith and hope are major contributors to mental well-being.

Hope Revives

Hope enlivens. It makes life worthwhile. It pulls us from the dead past and the disappointing present toward a future bright with promise. The most exciting parts of our lives are those in which we have the most to look forward to. Many of us look back with fondness to the days when we struggled, scrimped, and saved—all for the sake of our hopes. Getting what we want is always dull and boring compared to the agony and ecstasy of discovering what we want, overcoming obstacles as we pursue it, defeating foes that stand in our way, and making allies who join us in the quest for our goals. Measure success not in attainment but in enthusiasm—the very roots of the word reminding us that the enthusiast is one who is possessed by God (*en theos*).

To lose hope is to surrender to death and to become an agent of death. We are surrounded by grim reminders of disappointed hopes or the utter lack of hope. The sometimes invisible mass murderers in our midst—substance abuse, depression, anxiety—and the all too obvious killers—family violence, rage, crime, suicide—are all the fruits of hopelessness. A man with no expectations, no vision of a hopeful future, is a dangerous man—dangerous to himself and others. A woman who is trapped in the anguish of blasted dreams or of no dreams at all is a hazardous woman—hazardous to herself, her loved ones, and her friends. Families trapped by circumstances and aimlessness in quiet lives of lonely desperation are ticking time bombs looking for a place to explode.

Hope itself can kill. It can distract us from the pain and pleasure of the moment when our attention is most sorely needed in the here and now. Hope can be irresponsible, an excuse for not planning ahead or preparing for the future. Hope can be irrational, the blind pursuit of a delusion. To exist by false hopes is to postpone living, to act as though this life were a practice session for the real thing. Of one thing I am sure—this life is no dress rehearsal.

The Guarantor of Hope

What determines if our hopes vitalize or our hopes kill? The answer lies in distinction between the guarantee and the guarantor of our hopes. In this life, I submit, there are no guarantees but there is an absolutely reliable guarantor. In the words of a gospel song, "I know not what the future holds but I know who holds the future."

"Hope" is a key word in Paul's letter to the Romans. Paul uses it at least 14 times. For Paul, "hope" is the expectancy that God will keep his promises. God promised Abraham a son. Abraham believed God. Paul observes: "Against all hope, Abraham in hope believed and so became the father of many nations" (Romans 4:18). God kept his word.

Through the prophets of the Hebrew Scriptures, God promised to send his son as the anointed one as the redeemer of the Jewish people and as a light to the Gentiles (Romans 15:8–12). God kept his word.

The willful disobedience, selfishness, and stupidity of the human race, says Paul, has subjected the entire creation "to frustration," has placed it in "bondage to decay" (Romans 8:20–21). Hear his profoundly moving words:

> *the pains of childbirth right up to the present time. Not only so, but we ourselves, who have the firstfruits of the Spirit, groan inwardly as we wait eagerly for our adoption as sons, the redemption of our bodies. For in this hope we were saved. But hope that is seen is no hope at all. Who hopes for what he already has? But if we hope for what we do not yet have, we wait for it patiently. (Romans 8:22–25)*

How can Paul "wait . . . patiently" for an end to death and decay? Doesn't he know that the whales need to be saved? that the rain forests are disappearing? that humankind, drowning in its own garbage, is finding it increasingly difficult to be either human or kind?

Paul had no guarantees but he had a guarantor. Hear his exuberant utterance of faith:

> *Who shall separate us from the love of Christ? Shall trouble or hardship or persecution or famine or nakedness or danger or sword? . . . No, in all these things we are more than conquerors through him who loved us. For I am convinced that neither death nor life, neither angels nor demons, neither the present nor the future, nor any powers, neither height nor depth, nor anything else in all creation, will be able to separate us from the love of God that is in Christ Jesus our Lord. (Romans 8:35–39)*

Sharing What Cannot Be Proved

You still need to be convinced. You want me to prove that there is a God and that he cares for you, that he will accept you if you only accept his acceptance. You want me to demonstrate that the kingdom of God is coming, that death does not speak the final word, that the planet will be rescued from its derelict caretakers.

I can't convince you. But I can tell you what I expect. I can articulate my hope and share it with you. I will live as though there is a a loving, caring, and saving God, and I expect that, having so chosen, life will be different than if I were to live as though there were not a loving, caring, and saving God. I will commit myself to this community of those who have covenanted to live according to the teaching of Jesus, and I expect that, having so chosen, life will be different than if I had made no such covenant. In other words, I will live by faith, in hope, and for the sake of love.

So you are still not convinced. Like Thomas you want to see before you believe. But you can't see. As Paul says,

> *For in this hope we were saved. But hope that is seen is no hope at all. Who hopes for what he already has? But if we hope for what we do not yet have, we wait for it patiently. (Romans 8:24–25)*

"Faith," says the author of the letter to the Hebrews, "is the substance of things hoped for, the evidence of things not seen" (11:1). And the alternative to hope is not merely perpetually unsatisfied intellectual curiosity but despair. To quote Paul's letter to the Ephesians, *from citizenship in Israel and foreigners to the covenants of the promise, without hope and without God in the world. But now in Christ Jesus you who once were far away have been brought near . . . (Ephesians 2:12–3)*

Being described as being "without hope and without God in the world" sounds a lot colder and more painful than describing oneself as being an "open-minded seeker." Paul says, in effect, *at some point you have to make a commitment to life; if you keep your mind open too long your brains may roll out.*

Hope as the Power of God

So far, I haven't told you anything about the context in which these words of Paul appear. I haven't forgotten. I've saved that for last. The early church at Rome was divided into two factions: the so-called "strong" and the so-called "weak" Christians. The Christians that Paul termed "weak" were vegetarians; the strong Christians were not. (Was that church in Rome or Marin County?) Paul considered himself one of the "strong" Christians, but he feared that arguments about food would destroy the work of God. So, he counseled, let's put up with the vegetarians and not make an issue of what we eat. Don't live to please yourself, but live to please your neighbor, says Paul (15:1), so that you may live in harmony.

Now living in accord can be a rough job—human beings being what they are—but it is never an impossible job. Commitment to pleasing one's brother or sister in the local church requires the patience, steadfastness, and personal integrity that only God can give. Live to serve, and you will find patience, steadfastness, and personal integrity ever present. Live to serve, and your life will never lack the dimension of hope. For hope is the power of God, holding your life together and sustaining the universe.

Don't take my word for it. Take the word of the God of hope, the God who always keeps his promises.

Amen.

—LDS
[1600 words]
[16 minutes]

❦ *Sermon 7*

❦ *Date:* Palm/Passion Sunday, Year B

Texts:
Isaiah 50:4–9a
Psalm 118:1-2, 19–29
Philippians 2:5–11
Mark 11:1–11 and Mark 15:1–39

Theme: What kind of king is Jesus anyway? Respecting this day as both Palm Sunday and Passion Sunday provides the answer.
Subject: Palm/Passion Sunday

❦ *Title:* Hail to the Conquering Loser!

Note

> The basic sermon is about eighteen minutes long. The optional opening and closing poems about two minutes. Reading the Scripture passage as part of the sermons adds an additional seven minutes. The biblical text is indicated by italics.

Tip

> Have the organist begin by playing joyously, "Lift Up Your Heads" and then diminish into a minor-key and segue into "Were You There When They Crucified My Lord?"

Hark, how the children shrill and high
"Hosanna" cry;
Their joys provoke the distant sky,
Where thrones and seraphim reply;
And their own angels shine and sing
In a bright ring;
Such young, sweet mirth
Makes heaven and earth
Join in a joyful symphony.[1]

The Triumph of Palm Sunday

Today is Palm Sunday. Today we remember our Lord's triumphant entry into Jerusalem. Today we join the crowd and cry out "Hosanna!"—"Save us, Lord; save us now!" Like the throng, we are fervent with anticipation. We want Jesus to come to our rescue, to free us from all that troubles us. We want him to be our king, our hero.

But he rides into Jerusalem and into our lives on a pathetic-looking donkey. He mocks our notion of what a king should be.

He does not come to rule and reward us for our virtue, but to die for our sins. We know the story well. Within a few short days, he will be gone. So we pay heed to every detail of his final week, this Holy Week. We do not jump from the sham glory of Palm Sunday to the splendor of Easter Sunday. We know that today is not only Palm Sunday but Passion Sunday. We know that the road to Jerusalem leads to Gethsemane and Golgotha. And we cherish every moment of this week.

Writing of his deceased father, southern humorist Lewis Grizzard says:

> Some of [my] memories are nearly forty years old, but they are indelible and they are a comfort.
>
> To love someone unconditionally—as I loved Daddy—is to remember isolated and long-past moments together, to remember nuances that made such an object of love unique and impossible to replace.
>
> That is why I remember, and cherish, the memories of the man's hair, his smell, his likes and dislikes, his speech, and his idiosyncrasies.

---

[1] Vaughan, Henry, *Works*, second edition (Oxford: Clarendon Press, 1914).

> We had such a little time together. War took him away.
>
> Then he came back for a short time before he was gone again. He never would return on a full-time basis.
>
> Maybe that is why each of the nuances, each of the jokes and stories, each of the memories is so priceless to me. I have some pictures of my father. I have that packet of war records. I have the flag that was across his casket. I have his Bronze Star and his Purple Hearts in a frame and they hang on my wall.
>
> But what I don't have anymore is him. There will be no new memories made. That is why I cling to those I have with such tenacity.[2]

Not in Control

Very early in the morning, the chief priests, with the elders, the teachers of the law and the whole Sanhedrin, reached a decision. They bound Jesus, led him away and handed him over to Pilate.

There is an amazing restraint to Mark's passion narrative. He does not pile up "gory details to milk melancholy from the story" or "to create sympathetic sadness or to draw tears." He respects us. He knows that "feeling bad about [the passion] is hardly faith" and that manipulated emotions are scarcely repentance.[3]

But what is more remarkable about Mark's narrative is that it is a story of what happened to Jesus rather than of what Jesus did. After all, that's what "passion" means—being passive, being on the receiving end of life.

Reginald Fuller notes that

> there are striking differences between the passion story and the rest of the Gospel. The earlier chapters had portrayed Jesus as one who acted with power and taught with authority. Now all that vanished. Jesus is stripped of that power, and his authoritarian speech is silenced.[4]

Earlier in Mark's Gospel, Jesus is depicted as an irresistible force, as someone in charge. He is in constant movement—healing, teaching, traveling, mingling with the crowds, touching and being touched by humanity. He is always in control. But during the final week of his life, he is "conspired against, . . . denied, betrayed, captured, tried, sentenced, mocked, crucified, buried."[5] In the words of Fred B. Craddock, "If the incarnation means anything, it means Jesus identified with the experience of not being in control."[6]

---

[2] Grizzard, Lewis, *My Daddy Was a Pistol and I'm a Son of a Gun* (New York: Dell, 1986), pp. 113–114.

[3] Craddock, Fred B., *Preaching the New Common Lectionary: Lent, Holy Week, Easter, Year B* (Nashville, TN: Abingdon Press, 1984), p. 87.

[4] Fuller, Reginald, *Proclamation 3, Holy Week, Series B* (Philadelphia: Fortress Press, 1984), pp. 14–15.

[5] Craddock, ibid.

[6] Ibid.

> *"Are you the king of the Jews?" asked Pilate.*
> *"Yes, it is as you say," Jesus replied.*

We want Jesus to be in control. We want him to protect us against frustrations and humiliations and financial setbacks and upsets and arguments with our spouses and disagreements with our children. When we have a rotten day, we want to say to him, "Jesus, just what kind of king are you anyway?" But now and then it dawns on us that Jesus isn't the kind of king we insist upon at all. Rambo wouldn't have put up with Holy Week. He would have come down off the cross with a howitzer under his arm and a nuclear missile in his hands and blown the scum away. But Jesus wasn't that kind of hero—and he still isn't.

The King Who Kneels

Jesus is a king who stoops to wash feet, to kneel before people like you and me and wash away the dust of life from our daily existence. As Lucy Rose observes, he is not "a king with super power, interested only in making everything right, but a king who recognizes the pain and frustration, the fragmentation and chaos of life." Maybe there are days in which nothing comes together and every effort is wasted. Maybe folks we love get cancer and

> bombs explode and innocent folks are killed and who knows why—and Jesus comes riding up on a donkey with a towel and a basin, ready to wash away the filth and the tears and to pass the towel on to us. Maybe that's how Jesus is the king.[7]

The Case Is Fixed

The chief priests accused him of many things. So again Pilate asked him, "Aren't you going to answer? See how many things they are accusing you of."

But Jesus still made no reply, and Pilate was amazed.

Now it was the custom at the Feast to release a prisoner whom the people requested. A man called Barabbas was in prison with the insurrectionists who had committed murder in the uprising. The crowd came up and asked Pilate to do for them what he usually did.

"Do you want me to release to you the king of the Jews?" asked Pilate, knowing it was out of envy that the chief priests had handed Jesus over to him. But the chief priests stirred up the crowd to have Pilate release Barabbas instead.

"What shall I do, then, with the one you call the king of the Jews?" Pilate asked them.

"Crucify him! " they shouted.

"Why? What crime has he committed? " asked Pilate.

But they shouted all the louder, "Crucify him!"

Wanting to satisfy the crowd, Pilate released Barabbas to them. He had Jesus flogged, and handed him over to be crucified.

The soldiers led Jesus away into the palace (that is, the Praetorium) and called together the whole company of soldiers. They put a purple robe on him, then twisted together a crown of thorns and set it on him. And they began to call out to him, "Hail, king of the Jews!" Again and again they struck him on the head with a staff and spit on him. Falling on their knees, they paid homage

---

[7] Rose, Lucy, "Hail, King Jesus," *Abingdon Preacher's Annual 1991* (Nashville, TN: Abingdon Press, 1991) pp. 88–89.

to him. And when they had mocked him, they took off the purple robe and put his own clothes on him. Then they led him out to crucify him.

So the judge caves in to pressure. The mayor and the D.A. want this conviction. They need it for their reelection campaigns. The cops take the suspect away and have a good time at his expense. The forces charged with maintaining law and order become forces of disorder. The protectors of human rights become the enemies of human dignity. The men in uniform whom we so desperately want to regard as our allies turn on our one true friend and turn on us. They beat our hero because of his race, because he is powerless, because they are frustrated and feel like taking it out on someone, because he is in their hands, because they can get away with it.

In Jesus the Christ, God surrenders himself to our state and fate. He identifies with those who are not in charge. He suffers with the powerless.

The Ecology of God

A certain man from Cyrene, Simon, the father of Alexander and Rufus, was passing by on his way in from the country, and they forced him to carry the cross. They brought Jesus to the place called Golgotha (which means The Place of the Skull). Then they offered him wine mixed with myrrh, but he did not take it. And they crucified him. Dividing up his clothes, they cast lots to see what each would get.

A black man from the crowd is forced to carry the cross. Why him? Probably just because he is black. Black men and women, yellow men and women, red men and women, poor men and women, homeless men and women, sick men and women, elderly men and women—they all carry the cross.

But this Simon from Libya was not a faceless, undocumented peon. We know his name and his place of birth and even the names of his children, Alexander and Rufus. For in the midst of the helplessness and passivity of Jesus, God is at work, calling, wooing, building his new community. And there from the start is the family of Simon of Cyrene. In the ecology of God, nothing is wasted.

Hope of the Helpless

It was the third hour when they crucified him. The written notice of the charge against him read: THE KING OF THE JEWS. They crucified two robbers with him, one on his right and one on his left. Those who passed by hurled insults at him, shaking their heads and saying, "So! You who are going to destroy the temple and build it in three days, come down from the cross and save yourself!"

In the same way the chief priests and the teachers of the law mocked him among themselves. "He saved others," they said, "but he can't save himself! Let this Christ, this King of Israel, come down now from the cross, that we may see and believe." Those crucified with him also heaped insults on him.

"Hosanna," which originally meant "save us," has the same root in Hebrew as the word Jesus. Remember the declaration of the angel to Mary, "He shall be named Jesus for he shall save his people from their sins."[8] And now at the cross, his name and the revelry of a few days past are used to taunt him. How many who hailed him as king on Palm Sunday revile him in his helplessness? How many of us call him king on Sunday and daily turn from those as helpless as he?

---

[8] Matthew 1:21. Jesus is the Greek form of Yeshua or Joshua, which means "the LORD saves."

At the sixth hour darkness came over the whole land until the ninth hour. And at the ninth hour Jesus cried out in a loud voice, "Eloi, Eloi, lama sabachthani?"—which means, "My God, my God, why have you forsaken me?"

When some of those standing near heard this, they said, "Listen, he's calling Elijah."

One man ran, filled a sponge with wine vinegar, put it on a stick, and offered it to Jesus to drink. "Now leave him alone. Let's see if Elijah comes to take him down," he said.

There is a cloud over the cross like a fog blotting out an airport. Nothing can get in. Nothing can get out. Nothing can get through. Jesus is alone. So alone. As Reginald Fuller reminds us,

> Mark emphasizes the loneliness of Jesus in his passion. The disciples fall asleep while Jesus wrestles alone in prayer in the Garden of Gethsemane. They desert him at the moment of his arrest. Peter . . . [denies] him three times. The High Priest manipulates the Sanhedrin to pronounce Jesus guilty and deserving of death. Some of the bystanders spit upon him, blindfold him, and mockingly challenge him to play the prophet, the police strike him. . . . Even two crucified with him join in the mockery—no penitent thief in Mark. . . .Finally, [he is] forsaken in the end by even God himself. He dies bereft and in utter loneliness.[9]

An old African-American spiritual laments, "Nobody knows the troubles I've seen. Nobody knows but Jesus." Nobody in the midst of sorrow or pain can say to God, "You don't understand." God understands.

With a loud cry, Jesus breathed his last.

The curtain of the temple was torn in two from top to bottom. And when the centurion, who stood there in front of Jesus, heard his cry and saw how he died, he said, "Surely this man was the Son of God!"

Lifting of the Fog

Watching someone you love die is a terrible thing. As Stephen Weissman remarks,

> At first you deny that it is happening. . . .
>
> Then, when the inevitable becomes undeniable, and you can see your friend is dying, then you are angry. You fume and curse and strike out. . . .
>
> Rather than face that, you hide.[10]

Until Good Friday, we managed to hide from God and he managed to hide from us. Weissman adds:

> Every time contact had been made—at Moriah, with Abraham; at Sinai, with Moses; at Solomon's Temple, by the waters of Babylon, and in the Torah and in sacrifice—every time, contact had been faint, jammed by interference.[11]

---

[9] Fuller, *Proclamation 3,* p. 15.

[10] Weissman, Stephen, *Word & Witness,* March 24, 1991, p. 4.

[11] Ibid.

We human beings had not been idle. For centuries, we had been trying to make contact, too. But our efforts had been less than satisfactory.

> For every Moriah, an Ishmael; for every Sinai, a gold calf; for every temple, a megalomaniac King; for every prophet, a torturer of prophets; for every holy book, an indifferent reader; for every law court, a venal judge and a mob yelling "crucify him."[12]

We tried but we just couldn't hear or be heard. Until Good Friday. For at the foot of the cross, God and humanity get through to each other at last.

God gets through to Simon the Libyan. The unnamed centurion at the foot of the cross gets the message. The fog begins to lift. A few rays of light begin to spread and spread until they reach to the ends of the earth. God gets through to us and we to him.

Jesus has come as our king—and we hail him with glad hosannas. Jesus has come to die for us and we stand ready to receive and embrace the pains and sorrows of life. Jesus has come to reign—not on an earthly throne, but in our hearts and lives. And we abdicate. We give up the illusion of being in control.

After Lewis Grizzard had scrounged together every detail of his father's life he or his family could recall and every item to which his father's friends could bear witness, he observed:

> But what I don't have anymore is him. There will be no new memories made. That is why I cling to those I have with such tenacity.[13]

But the story of Jesus does not end this week—it only begins. It always begins anew. For if we will walk with him through the suffering of this week, he will break through to us and we to him. And nothing can stop that.

> Lord, come away;
> Why dost Thou stay?
> Thy road is ready and Thy paths made straight
> With longing expectation wait
> The consecration of Thy beauteous feet.
> Ride on triumphantly: behold! we lay
> Our lusts and proud wills in Thy way.
> Hosannah! welcome to our hearts: Lord, here
> Thou hast a temple too, and full as dear
> as that of Sion; and as full of sin—
> Nothing but thieves and robbers dwell therein;
> Enter, and chase them forth, and cleanse the floor,
> Crucify them, that they may never more
> Profane that holy place
> Where Thou hast chose to set Thy face.
> and then if our still tongues shall be
> Mute in the praises of Thy deity,
> The stones out of the temple wall

---

[12] Ibid.

[13] Grizzard, *My Daddy Was a Pistol*, pp. 113–114.

Shall cry aloud and call
Hosannah! and Thy glorious footsteps greet.[14]

Amen.

—LDS

[2700 words with Scripture text; 2000 words without text]
[27 minutes with Scripture text; 20 minutes without]

❦ *Sermon 8*

❦ *Date:* Palm/Passion Sunday, any year

Texts:
Year A
Isaiah 50:4-9a
Philippians 2:5–11
Matthew 21:1–11
Year B
Isaiah 50:4-9a
Hebrews 12:1–6
Mark 11:1–11
Year C
Isaiah 59:14–20
1 Timothy 1:12–17
Luke 19:28–40 or Luke 24:14-23:56 or 23:1-49

Theme: Without the suffering and death of Jesus, Easter has no meaning. It is what is between Palm Sunday and Easter that counts: the hard words: "No pain, no gain. No cross, no crown."
Subject: Palm Sunday, suffering

❦ *Title:* The King's Parade

[Organ: "I Love a Parade"]

The Parade We Love

"I love a parade!" exclaims the Gershwin song. We all love a parade. How can we help but love the one observed today?

Worship services on Palm Sunday and Easter boast the highest attendance of any Sundays of the church year. And why not? As religious observances go, these two Sundays are uppers! They exalt and excite our spirits! Palm Sunday with its circus-like frivolity, the waving of ceremonial palms, the shouts of the excited crowds is as joyous as any holiday of any kind.

And next Sunday is Easter egg hunts, new Easter clothes, Easter baskets, Easter bunnies, Easter bonnets, Easter vacation, and the Easter ham dinner at Gramma's.

---

[14] Jeremy Taylor in *Masterpieces of Religious Verse*, edited by James Morrison (New York: Harper & Brothers, 1948).

There are two kinds of Holy Week observers (both, I would hasten to add, loved of God), those who bask in the joy of Palm Sunday and Easter; and those who wrestle with the reality of all eight days of Holy Week.

Those who attend church on the two Sundays of Holy Week can completely avoid the unpleasantness of the intervening six days. They can have the best of times—the triumphal procession today and the resurrection next Sunday—without subjecting themselves to the worst of times. They can avoid the pain and still claim the gain. They can wear the crown without bearing the cross. At least they think so.

As commentator David Tiede observes, "A society that prefers to deny the reality of sin and death [will] love Palm Sunday and Easter." But the message of the Gospel is simple, unavoidable, and direct: "No pain, no gain. No cross, no crown."

Today is Palm Sunday, but it is also known by many Christians as the Sunday of the Passion. This parade will end with the death of the Son of David. The crowds who today cry "Hosanna" will in a few days shout "crucify him!"

Who Is This Man?

Who is this man who enters Jerusalem scant days before the Feast of Passover? And why should we care?

Who is this man? He is Jesus the clown. Look at him on his unsure saddle of cloaks thrown on a donkey's back. Is he riding that one tiny beast of burden or should we take Matthew literally and believe that he was riding both donkey and foal?

Jesus the clown. He mocks what we take most seriously—our solemnity, our dignity, our accomplishments, our standing in the community. He asks us to laugh at ourselves, to stop taking our petty concerns so seriously. He offers us not only light but lightness as well.

Who is this man? He is Jesus the scandal. Who would want to associate with this rowdy, this friend of extortionists (they were called "tax collectors"), women of questionable reputation, social outcasts, the poor, the homeless, carriers of deadly diseases? He is so unpredictable, so dangerous. I did not say he was unpredictable and dangerous—he *is*. Why should we want to have anything to do with him? But he does not seem to give us a choice. He stands at the door of our life and knocks. He lurks like a panther about to pounce in the back of our minds, in the corners of our consciousness, in the recesses of our hearts, in the depths of our consciences.

Who is this man? He is Jesus the earthquake. Matthew says, "When Jesus entered Jerusalem, the whole city was stirred." What a weak translation! Was the whole Bay Area "stirred" when the World Series was interrupted by the shake of '89? Were our lives merely "stirred"?

Jesus is an earthquake. He shakes us to the very foundations of our being. He comforts us when we are afflicted and afflicts us when we are comfortable. And he produces people who are just like him—indispensable, exciting, and uncontrollable. Remember the Chinese curse: "I pray that you may be born in an exciting time"? Let Jesus the earthquake get close to you and look out. Let any of his disciples within earshot of your life and stand back.

Who is this man? He is Jesus the king. He is on Palm Sunday what he always is—dignity within riot. We distort his message. We try to make him like us and unlike everyone else. But he never loses hold on who he is. He does not allow the cheers of his suddenly won friends to distract him any more than he permits the jeers of his opponents to set his priorities.

Who is this man? He is Jesus the offering. His coming to Jerusalem, swollen by pilgrims to a population of a million and a half, was not to rule but to die. He came to die—not as a victim, not as a martyr, but as a willing sacrifice. His death was not an unfortunate accident. It was, if we are to believe him, God's plan. From the beginning of his ministry, he had set his face like a flint.

His life had been in danger practically from the day of his birth. He knew it, and yet he came to Jerusalem to die.

Who is this man? He is Jesus the king—not a king who rules with force and terror, but a king who can lay aside his garments, clothe himself in a towel, and wash the feet of his disciples. He is not a king who demands obedience but a friend who wins it. He is a king who surrenders everything for his subjects even his life, a king who empties himself, humbles himself in order to serve. He does not bring us new, esoteric doctrines or teach us yogic postures or improve our diet or teach us how to be successful or how to walk on hot coals. Instead he models God. He images God. He sets an example and leaves it to us to do what God has done, to exalt him, to give him the name in our lives that is above all names, to confess that he is Lord to the glory of God the Father.

Who is this man? "Jesus Christ is Lord" shout the writers of the New Testament. This absurd donkey rider is Lord? "Jesus is Lord?" we muse. Nearly two millennia have passed and still the questions remain as fresh as they were when he led his feeble parade: "Is he a man like any other man? Is he God in the flesh? a teacher? a prophet? an example?"

Beginning of the End or End of the Beginning?

Palm Sunday, the Sunday of Passion, is the beginning of the end. But more decisively it is the end of the beginning. Within a few days, this one solitary life will seem to be terminated in ignominy and defeat. But it does not end. Why not? Why does he still hold on to our yearnings and imagination two thousand years after the events of these eight days? What trick has been worked by this clown-king, this Passover sacrifice, this claimant to the throne of our hearts?

The answer is not to be found on the Sundays of triumph. For without the suffering and death of Jesus they have no meaning. It is what is between Palm Sunday and Easter that counts: the hard words—No pain, no gain. No cross, no crown. There is no free lunch. Life is unfair. If you can't endure the darkness, you will never recognize the light.

But once we willingly enter the cloud of pain and confusion, once we are willing to pay the cost, to take up our cross and follow him, the stone rolls away, the sun rises, the light breaks through, and God is God.

Let us rejoice then that our king has come! Let us join the parade and welcome him. Let us go with him to the Upper Room and Gethsemane. Let us stand at the foot of his cross. And let us know in our lives the power of his resurrection.

Amen.

—LDS

[1322 words]
[13 minutes]

❦ *Sermon 9*

❦ *Date:* Easter Sunday, Year A, B, or C

Texts:
Year A
Acts 10:34–43 or Jeremiah 31:1–6
Psalm 118:1-2, 14–24
Colossians 3:1–4 or Acts 10:34–43
John 20:1–18 or **Matthew 28:1–10**

Year B
Acts 10:34–43 or Isaiah 25:6–9
Psalm 118:1-2, 14–24
1 Corinthians 15:1–11 or Acts 10:34–43
John 20:1–18 or **Mark 16:1–8**
Year C
Acts 10:34–43 or Isaiah 65:17–25
Psalm 118:1-2, 14–24
1 Corinthians 15:19–26 or Acts 10:34–43
John 20:1–18 or **Luke 24:1–12**

Theme: We honor Mary Magdalene for her unfailing love and attempt to repair her reputation. To those who love him as she did, in spite of inconveniences, anxieties, doubts, and dangers, Jesus is alive.
Subject: Love, faith, faithfulness

Title: First, First, and Always: The Truth About Mary Magdalene

[Solo: "I Don't Know How to Love Him" from Andrew Lloyd Webber's rock opera, Jesus Christ Superstar.]

Mary was there—first, last and always. For nearly two thousand years, Mary Magdalene has been revered by the Christian Church as the first person to see the risen Jesus. But who was she? Was she a reformed woman of easy virtue or a maligned, pious disciple?

In numerous works of fiction, Mary Magdalene has become a notorious repentant sinner. In Nikos Kazantzakis's novel, The Last Temptation of Christ, she is the love of Jesus' youth, embittered because he has forsaken her for God. It is to her that Jesus comes for forgiveness before he can begin his solitary quest for his mission.

In Andrew Lloyd Webber's rock opera, Jesus Christ Superstar, Mary Magdalene has all the best songs. It is Mary who sings "I Don't Know How to Love Him." Again, she is a woman with a past, who has given up her sinful ways to care for Jesus during his wandering ministry.

Does such speculation find any support in the Gospel accounts? Let us look then at what the Gospels have to stay about this intriguing woman.

Mary Magdalene in the Gospel According to Mark

In Mark, the earliest of the Gospels, Mary Magdalene is one of a group of women who watched the crucifixion of Jesus "from a distance" (15:39). We note that Mary Magdalene's is the first name mentioned—as is the case in similar lists throughout the Gospels. It is clear that she was somebody in the early church.

Mark tells us that "in Galilee these women had followed him and cared for his needs" and adds, "Many other women who had come up with him to Jerusalem were also there" (v. 40).

When the body of Jesus was buried by Joseph of Arimathea in a tomb cut into the rock and was sealed with a large stone, it was Mary who "saw where he was laid" (v. 46).

When the Sabbath was over, it was Mary who came with spices and linen to anoint their teacher's body. Mark tells us that she discovered that the stone had been rolled away and that they encountered a mysterious young man in white who told them: "Don't be alarmed. You are looking for Jesus the Nazarene, who was crucified. He has risen! He is not here. See the place where they laid him. But go, tell his disciples and Peter, 'He is going ahead of you into Galilee. There you will see him, just as he told you.'"

But, says Mark, she was too frightened and bewildered to tell anyone, and so she said nothing.

The picture of Mary Magdalene we gain from Mark is straightforward. Her reputation is unsullied. This Mary was a Galilean. Her name tells us that she was from the village of Magdala on the western shore of the Sea of Galilee near Tiberias. She had followed Jesus from the beginning of his public ministry and cared for his needs. She was there at the end of his life. She was a devout Jew, who would not violate the Sabbath to care for his body.

Mary Magdalene in the Gospel According to Matthew

Matthew (27:54 and following) adds little to our knowledge. He also puts Mary near the scene of the crucifixion, concurring with Mark's description of her as one of the women who had followed Jesus from Galilee to care for his needs.

According to Matthew, Mary Magdalene was more than a furtive discoverer of the tomb of Jesus. He adds that she seated herself opposite the tomb when it was sealed—a brave thing to do at the grave of a felon executed for sedition and blasphemy.

In Matthew's account, Mary was there at dawn when a violent earthquake signaled that an angel of the Lord has rolled back the stone. While the guards were paralyzed with fear, the angel spoke to her:

> *"Do not be afraid, for I know that you are looking for Jesus, who was crucified. He is not here; he has risen, just as he said. . . . go quickly and tell his disciples: 'He has risen from the dead and is going ahead of you into Galilee. There you will see him.'"*

According to Matthew's report, Mary was not the least bit intimidated. She rushed to tell the others what she had witnessed, only to be stopped by none other than Jesus himself, who addresses her almost nonchalantly, "Kairete," which means, "Good day. I am glad to see you." He instructs her not to be afraid and sends her to tell "his brothers" that they should go to Galilee where he will meet them later.

The picture that emerges from Matthew's depiction of Mary Magdalene may be summarized in two words: constancy and bravery.

Mary Magdalene in the Gospel According to Luke

It is Luke who adds to our knowledge and prepares the way for the confusion that has forever hounded the memory of Mary Magdalene. In chapter 7 of his Gospel, Luke tells us of a sinful woman who interrupted Jesus' dinner at the home of Simon the Pharisee, washing his feet with her tears, kissing them, anointing them with ointment, and wiping them with her hair.

The Pharisee was shocked that Jesus would welcome the attentions of such a woman. Jesus seized the occasion to teach Simon a lesson about love and forgiveness. He concluded: "I tell you, her many sins have been forgiven—for she loved much. But he who has been forgiven little loves little."

Immediately after telling the story, Luke comments:

> *After this, Jesus traveled about from one town and village to another, proclaiming the good news of the kingdom of God. The Twelve were with him, and also some women who had been cured of evil spirits and diseases: Mary (called Magdalene) from whom seven*

demons had come out; Joanna the wife of Cuza, the manager of Herod's household; Susanna; and many others. These women were helping to support them out of their own means. (8:1)

Later centuries would confuse Mary Magdalene, who was cured by Jesus of maladies not specified in the biblical record, with the unnamed sinful woman of the previous chapter. It was an easy leap from this mistake to lumping in the account found in some manuscripts of the Gospel of John of the woman taken in adultery and pardoned by Jesus with the exhortation: "Go now and sin no more."

The early church was careful to distinguish Mary Magdalene from the mystical Mary of Bethany and from the penitent woman whose sins Jesus forgave. It was Pope Gregory I in about the year 600 who forever endangered Mary Magdalene's reputation by insisting that the three women were one and the same person and by adopting the veneration of "St. Mary Magdalene, the repentant prostitute to whom the risen Christ first appeared."

Luke repeats the story of angelic visitors at the empty tomb but tells us that it was the angels and not Jesus who upbraid the women for seeking the living among the dead and sends them to proclaim the resurrection to the apostles. Luke informs us that several women were present, but once again it is Mary Magdalene who heads it.

Luke has added one significant detail to our image of Mary Magdalene. She had been healed by Jesus of several afflictions—perhaps psychological as well as physical maladies. Mary Magdalene was not only constant and brave; she was grateful. And from her gratitude came a life of service.

Mary Magdalene in the Gospel According to John

The Gospel of John again places our Mary near the cross. But in the community to which John belonged, she had dropped in the listings. Three women including Mary the mother of Jesus are mentioned ahead of Mary Magdalene. Yet John validates Mary's claim to having been the first to whom the risen Jesus appeared. He even provides the missing details in an account replete with personal touches that he could have learned only from Mary herself.

Mary, relates John, mistook Jesus for the cemetery gardener. She did not recognize him until he called her by name. She tried to embrace him, to restore their relationship to what it had been during his ministry. But he rebuffed her and established with her the relationship that he would have with all his disciples throughout the centuries. Henceforth, he would be more than their teacher or rabbi; he would be their Lord, and his Spirit would comfort and guide them.

Mary Magdalene in Tradition and Myth

According to Eastern Orthodox tradition, Mary accompanied the Apostle John to Ephesus, where she died and was buried. Later legends maintain that she was John's wife.

Mary was important to the Gnostics. These early Christian heretics believed that matter is evil and redemption is attained by an enlightened elite who possess a special divine revelation. They regarded Mary as a medium of a secret wisdom. Medieval Catholics believed that she had been the first to preach the Gospel in Provence.

Well into the present century, Mary Magdalene continues to appear in our imaginings, dreams, and visions. In 1912, C. Austin Miles, received a strange challenge from Adam Geibel, the music publisher and hymnist. Geibel asked Miles to write a hymn that would be "sympathetic in tone, breathing tenderness in every line; one that would bring hope to the hopeless, rest for the weary, and downy pillows to dying beds."

One day as Miles sat in the dark room where he kept his photographic equipment, he opened his Bible and his eye fell upon the twentieth chapter of John—his favorite chapter. As he thought about Mary Magdalene's meeting with Jesus, he felt as though he had faded into that scene, as though he had traveled back through time to the first Easter morning. Miles recalled:

> I seemed to be standing at the entrance of a garden, looking down a gently winding path, shaded in olive branches. A woman in white, with head bowed, hand clasping her throat, as if to choke back her sobs, walked slowly into the shadows. It was Mary. As she came to the tomb, upon which she placed her hand, she bent over to look in, and hurried away.[1]

He saw John appear, "looking into the tomb"; then came Peter, "who entered the tomb, followed slowly by John." He watched as they departed, then as Mary reappeared. He reported:

> leaning her head upon her arm at the tomb, she wept. Turning herself, she saw Jesus. . . . She knelt before him, with arms outstretched and looking into his face cried "Rabboni [my teacher]!"[2]

Suddenly the scene faded away. As though he had just wakened from a dream, Miles found himself again in the dark room. A strange tingling sensation ran through his body. In a matter of moments the words of a poem based on his experience formed in his mind. In hours, a melody flooded his consciousness. It was the hymn that Adam Geibel had asked him for, the only hymn for which C. Austin Miles is known, one of the most popular and moving gospel songs ever written. It is a hymn about Jesus and Mary Magdalene. It is a song about you and me as we come to the risen Jesus, as we hear him call us by name and meet him "in the garden." "In the Garden" is, of course, the name of Miles's song. In a moment, we shall join our hearts and voices as we sing it together.

Who was Mary Magdalene? She was the one who was always there when Jesus needed her, who paid the price for being there. I honor her for her spirit of gratitude that overflowed into a life of service. I honor her this Easter morning not as a reformed sinner but as the constant companion whose devotion never wavered—not even in the face of death. I honor her and all like her, who nurture, encourage, and enhance the daily existence of their fellow human beings.

To those who love him as she did, in spite of inconveniences, anxieties, doubts, and dangers, Jesus is alive. In the lives of those who receive his healing touch and dedicate their lives to healing others, Jesus lives.

Alleluia!

Amen.

[Concluding song: "In the Garden"]

—LDS

[2000 words]
[20 minutes]

---

[1] Osbeck, Kenneth W., *101 Hymn Stories* (Grand Rapids, MI: Kregel Publications, 1982), p. 124.

[2] Ibid.

❦ *Sermon 10*

❦ *Date:* Second Sunday of Easter, Year B

Texts:
Acts 4:32–35
Psalm 133
1 John 1:1–2:2
John 20:19–31

Theme: Jesus offers his peace to those whom he sends.
Subject: Peace, faith, doubt, Holy Spirit

❦ *Title:* Peace for a Doubting Thomas

[Choir or Congregation: "Come, Thou Long-Expected Jesus"]

Tip

> The following sermon integrates music, Scripture reading, and message into a single presentation. If possible, the Scripture text should be read by someone other than the preacher.

[Choir: "Come, Thou Long-Expected Jesus," verse 1]

> Come, thou long-expected Jesus, Born to set thy people free;
> From our fears and sins release us; let us find our rest in thee.
> Israel's strength and consolation, hope of all the earth thou art;
> Dear desire of every nation, joy of every longing heart.
>
> —Charles Wesley

The Peace of His Injured Humanity

On the evening of that first day of the week, when the disciples were together, with the doors locked for fear of the Jews, Jesus came and stood among them and said, "Peace be with you!" After he said this, he showed them his hands and side. The disciples were overjoyed when they saw the Lord.

A group of senior citizens at a retirement home was having a great time discussing their various aches, pains, and ills. One had arthritis; another indigestion (or was it an ulcer?); a third complained about insomnia. And on and on it went. Finally an 85-year-old man said: "Think of it this way, my friends. It just proves that old age isn't for sissies!"[1]

And being a Christian isn't for sissies either!

Frightened and confused, the followers of Jesus huddled together behind locked doors. They hadn't been sleeping well. The horrors of Jesus' betrayal, arrest, torture, and execution were too immediate and real for them. The incredible reports of an empty tomb and of Mary Magdalene's vision or hallucination added to their inner turmoil. "Could it be true?" they wondered. "Could it

---

[1] Adapted from *Parables, Etc.*, April 1991, p. 1.

possibly be true? Could Jesus be alive? Or is it all a trick to bring us out into the open so the authorities can arrest us and murder us as well."

"Shalom," said Jesus. Shalom—the most common greeting in Palestine then and now.

Three times during his brief visit to his fearful disciples, Jesus says "Shalom." He wouldn't have repeated it if they had gotten the message the first time. He wouldn't have offered peace to his friends if they already had it. Peace is a slippery commodity. No matter how tenaciously one clings to it, it always slips away. Yet it is infinitely renewable—if one knows how to find it.

What is God's Shalom? What is the "peace of God" of which we often speak and for which we frequently pray? Shalom means hello and goodbye and so much more. In the Old Testament, shalom is wholeness or well-being. To have peace is to have security and prosperity. To have peace is to live in a land committed to justice. Peace exists between people or between people and God. The idea of peace as individual harmony with God or inner spiritual tranquility is alien to the Old Testament.

In the New Testament, peace is the absence of strife or conflict. Peace is associated not with prosperity and security but with righteousness, grace, mercy, joy, love, and life itself. Without such spiritual endowments there is no peace. Without peace, no spiritual endowments.

Peace is God's gift to humanity. Through the sacrifice of his son, he has broken down the wall of separation between heaven and earth. In Jesus the Christ, God is with us and for us. We are a forgiven, restored people and, in consequence, a forgiving and restoring people.

God's gift of peace is the very heart of the Easter message. The world is a place of trial and tribulation, of suffering and dying. On planet Earth it is always Good Friday. Yet in the midst of death, we are renewed. In the crushing coils of mortality, we are daily born anew. The God of hope and the hope of God fill us with peace. At the heart of the blackness is a light so bright and penetrating that it cannot be hidden. In us and between us, it is always Easter Sunday. Alleluia!

"Shalom," he said, the first time, and showed them his hands and side. Here was the resurrected, glorified Christ, but his body still bore the wounds of Good Friday. His body will always bear those wounds.

God knows. God understands. God stands with us.
The body of his son is scarred.
And by those scars we are healed. We are made whole. We receive courage and joy.

[Choir: "So Send I You," stanzas 1 and 2]

So send I you—to labor unrewarded,
To serve unpaid, unloved, unsought, unknown,
To bear rebuke, to suffer scorn and scoffing—
So send I you, to toil for Me alone.

So send I you—to bind the bruised and broken,
O'er wandering souls to work, to weep, to wake,
To bear the burdens of a world aweary—
So send I you, to suffer for My sake.

"As the Father hath sent Me, So send I you."

John W. Peterson

The Peace of the Spirit

Again Jesus said, "Peace be with you! As the Father has sent me, I am sending you." And with that he breathed on them and said, "Receive the Holy Spirit. If you forgive anyone his sins, they are forgiven; if you do not forgive them, they are not forgiven."

"Shalom," he said the second time and told them both to "go" and to "receive."

This shalom means "Pack now! Get ready to go! I am sending you."

This shalom also means "Pack right! Go well equipped!" He gave them the Spirit.

And this shalom means "Pack light! Get rid of the excess baggage!" Having the Spirit is simple. Being spiritual is being forgiven by God and returning the favor by forgiving others.

Is that too simple? Would you prefer supernatural endowments like speaking in tongues or the power to work miracles or the strength of Samson or the ability to raise the dead? John lets Jesus cut to the chase. Being spiritual is saying "thank you" to God, accepting your acceptance. Being spiritual means reaching out to others in the power of that acceptance. Being spiritual means being welcoming and accepting to others.

He breathed on them. They each took a deep breath of their own. Join them now. Take a deep breath. As they exhaled, they imagined that all the fear, uncertainty, guilt, and tension of the past days flowed down and out of them like water into the ground. They inhaled and felt new strength, vigor, and vitality flow into their bodies. They exhaled again, letting go of all their anger and hostility—toward one another, toward the cruelty of life and fate, toward those who did not meet their expectations. They let go of disappointment and frustrations, let them pour out down their limbs, into the floor, into oblivion. They drew another breath, and as they did they felt God's forgiveness, God's peace uniting them with him, with one another. They felt safe and secure in God's embrace and reached out to enfold one another in a circle of reunion.

[Choir: "Breathe on Me,"]

Holy Spirit, breathe on me, Until my heart is clean;
Let sunshine fill its inmost part, With not a cloud between.

REFRAIN: Breathe on me, breathe on me,
Holy Spirit, breathe on me,
Take Thou my heart, cleanse every part,
Holy Spirit, breathe on me.

Holy Spirit, breathe on me, My stubborn will subdue;
Teach me in words of living flame What Christ would have me do.

Holy Spirit, breathe on me, Fill me with power divine;
Kindle a flame of love and zeal Within this heart of mine.

Holy Spirit, breathe on me, Till I am all Thine own,
Until my will is lost in Thine, To live for Thee alone.

The Peace of Not Getting What You Want but Getting What You Need

Now Thomas (called Didymus),one of the Twelve, was not with the disciples when Jesus came. So the other disciples told him, "We have seen the Lord!"

But he said to them, "Unless I see the nail marks in his hands and put my finger where the nails were, and put my hand into his side, I will not believe it."

A week later his disciples were in the house again, and Thomas was with them. Though the doors were locked, Jesus came and stood among them and said, "Peace be with you!" Then he said to Thomas, "Put your finger here; see my hands. Reach out your hand and put it into my side. Stop doubting and believe."

Thomas said to him, "My Lord and my God!"

Then Jesus told him, "Because you have seen me, you have believed; blessed are those who have not seen and yet have believed."

Jesus did many other miraculous signs in the presence of his disciples, which are not recorded in this book. But these are written that you may believe that Jesus is the Christ, the Son of God, and that by believing you may have life in his name.

"Shalom," he said a third time and told them and us to stop doubting and to trust.

The New Testament story of Thomas, as brief as it is, is a story of courage, loyalty, and limitation. When Jesus told his disciples of his determination to go to Jerusalem, they protested that such a move could cost him his life (John 11:8). It was Thomas who declared, "Let us also go, that we may die with him" (11:16). When Jesus predicted that he would go ahead of them to his Father's house and there prepare places for them, it was Thomas who objected, "Lord, we don't know where you are going, so how can we know the way?" (14:1, 5) And now in this locked room, Thomas speaks again, speaks the words that will forever brand him as "Doubting Thomas": "Unless I see . . . I will not believe."

What an injustice history has done this brave, honest man. John tells us that his nickname was "the Twin." If he is anyone's twin, he is yours and mine. Call him Frightened Thomas. Call him Confused Thomas. Call him Practical Thomas. Call him Seeking Thomas. We should have no difficulty identifying with his fear, his confusion, his struggle.

He needed neither more nor less than any of us. He did not need theological argumentation or airtight evidence. He needed the presence of the living Christ.

I recently read a report of a dialogue between a man whose life had been transformed by his faith and a skeptical friend:

"So you have been converted to Christ?"

"Yes."

"Then you must know a great deal about Christ? Tell me, what country was he born in?"

"I don't know."

"What was his age when he died?"

"I don't know."

"How many sermons did he preach?"

"I don't know."

"You certainly know very little for a man who claims to be converted to Christ!"

"You are right. I am ashamed at how little I know about him. But this much I do know: Three years ago I was a drunkard. I was in debt. My family was falling to pieces. My wife and children would dread my return home every evening. But now I have given up drink; we are out of debt; ours is now a happy home. All this Christ has done for me. This much I know of him."[2]

The point of the story of Thomas's doubt is simple: believing is seeing. That is not so strange. It is a teacher's belief in a student that transforms a mediocre pupil into a scholar, a "discipline problem" into a self-respecting individual. It is that student's belief in his or her own specialness that works the magic of transformation—that continues to work the magic for years and years to come. Because Mr. Johnson (or Miss Jones) believed in me, I found that I could believe in myself. The hard-hearted, hardnosed, bottom-line-watching world says, "Seeing is believing." But the heart knows better. It knows "Believing is seeing."

Thomas wanted what you and I want. He wanted love that was there for him—love irresistibly and undeniably his. The risen Christ never reproved Thomas for his doubts. Doubts are usually just excuses anyway. Some doubts are rationalizations for not making commitments or for not honoring commitments. Other doubts arise from our unwillingness to let go of the unsatisfactory religion of our childhood. We think that we have successfully rebelled and left the authoritarian repressions of Mom and Dad's faith behind. But we have no more successfully divorced

---

[2] De Mello, Anthony, "The Song of the Bird," included in *Parables, Etc.*, April 1991, p. 3.

ourselves from yesterday's dogmas and doctrines than we have from Mom and Dad themselves. Yesterday's religion clatters and chatters in our consciousness until we courageously face it.

"I will not believe unless . . . ," declared Thomas. Jesus paid no attention to Thomas's mental reservations. He ignored Thomas's need to work out Thomas's own infantile faith. Jesus offered Thomas what Thomas really needed—himself. *It is the courage to risk intimacy that silences doubt. It is the giving and accepting of love that settle the demand for certainty.*

In the words of Jewish novelist Isaac Bashevis Singer: "Doubt is part of all religion. All the religious thinkers were doubters." Casanova recognized, "Doubt begins only at the last frontiers of what is possible." Einstein felt that while certainty is of value, "the important thing is not to stop questioning." Wilson Mizner observed, "I respect faith, but doubt is what gives you an education." And Francis Bacon echoed, "If a man will begin with certainties, he will end in doubts; but if he will be content to begin with doubts, he will end in certainties." And, finally, the most profound word about the triumph of courage over doubt was spoken by Thomas Carlyle: "If you are ever in doubt as to whether or not you should kiss a pretty girl, always give her the benefit of the doubt."

Doubting Thomas began with doubts and ended in certainties. If life had been a pretty girl, he would not only have kissed her, he would have proposed marriage.

Thomas had insisted that God meet his expectations. He learned that God is at large. God is free and full of surprises. God is on the loose. Alleluia!

Amen.

[Choir or Congregation: "Come, Thou Long-Expected Jesus, verse 2"]

Born thy people to deliver, born a child, and yet a king,
Born to reign in us forever, now thy gracious kingdom bring.
By thine own eternal Spirit rule in all our hearts alone;
By thine all-sufficient merit, raise us to Thy glorious throne.
—Charles Wesley

—LDS

[23 minutes with music]

❦ *Sermon 11*

❦ *Date:* Fourth Sunday of Easter, Year B

Texts:
Acts 4:5–12
Psalm 23
1 John 3:16–24
John 10:11–18

Theme: In a world of VCRs, fax machines, and silicon chips, it still makes sense to say that the Lord is our shepherd.
Subject: Peace, security

❦ *Title:* Shepherd of the Silicon Chips?

"The Lord is my shepherd." Those words bothered me when I was a child. A shepherd? The only shepherds I ever saw were German shepherds—and I avoided them whenever I could.

I could understand someone addressing God as father or grandfather or Santa Claus for that matter. "The Lord is my president" would have seemed OK. Or perhaps God was a Hollywood movie star. Movie stars seemed to live in some far off heaven, to be all-knowing and all-powerful, to have everything they wanted, and could, from time to time, reward their worshipers with gifts.

But God is a shepherd? I asked my friends at the men's prayer breakfast how they thought David would conceptualize God if he were alive today.

Perhaps today we should think of God as a TV set, one opined. God looks at us while we look at him, makes us to lie down on stuffed sofas, and provides what we want during commercials.

Another said that God is a multinational conglomerate. (Exxon giveth and Exxon taketh away, blessed be the name of Exxon!)

Perhaps, said one, David would speak of God as a football coach. Then the psalm would go something like this:

> The Lord is my head coach, I shall not want,
> He bringeth me to green artificial turf with perfectly drawn yard lines,
> He leadeth me beside the Gatorade and Coke machines,
> He restoreth my starting position,
> He leadeth me through the play book for the sake of repeat Super Bowl rings.
> Yea though I walk through the cheap shots of middle line backers and nose guards, I will fear neither injuries nor quick flags, for Coach is with me.
> He prepareth a massage table and pain killers for me in the presence of nosy newspaper reporters. He rubbeth my muscles with liniment; my locker with bonus money overfloweth. Surely no-cut guarantees and commercial endorsements will follow me all of my playing days, and I will dwell in the broadcasting booth with John Madden for a very long time.

In a world of VCRs, fax machines, and silicon chips, does it still make sense to say that the Lord is our shepherd? Does Psalm 23, David's beautiful shepherd song, have any relevance for us. Let's take a look.

1. A psalm of David. The LORD is my shepherd, I shall not be in want.

The words "sheep" and "shepherd" appear hundreds of times in the Bible. While the vast majority of uses are literal, sheep and shepherds are used metaphorically, particularly in the New Testament to describe the relationship of God and humankind. "Shepherd" was one of Jesus' favorite descriptions of himself.

The original Hebrew tribes were nomadic shepherds. Abraham, Isaac, Jacob, and their sons were shepherds. Moses spent time as a shepherd. King David and Micah the prophet had been shepherds.

Sheep provided the necessities of life: milk, meat, and wool. Ram horns were used as containers for oil or as musical instruments. From the skins of sheep came not college degrees but clothing and the inner covering of the tabernacle.

Wool was a precious good and an important item of trade. In 2 Kings 3:4, we read that Mesha, king of the Moabites, paid to the king of Israel an annual tribute of the wool of a hundred thousand rams.

If there had been tabloid newspapers in their day, the stories would have provided details of sheep-breeding, sheep-rustling, and the private antics of sheepherders whose flocks numbered more than a million.

If you spend too much time with too many sheep, strange things are bound to happen to you. You will stop associating with human beings except for fellow shepherds. This is because you will have less and less in common with ordinary folk and also because ordinary folk will always want to stay upwind of you.

You will become highly protective to the point of paranoia. And you will become as fond of sheep as of your own children. You may actually prefer the sheep. Finally, you will come to think of everything in images drawn from the relationship of sheep to shepherds.

"The Lord is my shepherd," said David. This is a comforting image but not a flattering one. It means that David thought of himself as a sheep. And as he well knew, sheep are convivial, dim-witted, heedless of danger, and totally dependent.

David was king over all Israel. He had everything he could possible want or need, including limitless access to money, power, and sex. The tabloids would have loved him. Yet he knew his own heart. He knew that if he followed his own inclinations, he would stray from the path of virtue every time. He knew that he was easily influenced by the opinions of others. He knew that his perceptions and thoughts were easily distorted by his self-interest. He also knew that he was totally dependent on God.

There was no social security then, no Medicare, no United Way, no IRAs, no life insurance, and probably very little real estate appreciation. To live was to be dependent and to know that one was dependent.

And the only real difference between us and them is that they knew. And when we realize that life is a gift, that the more we receive from life, the more life continues to give, rather pronounced changes in our attitude and behavior ensue. We become generous. We give gladly and sacrificially to others. And life laughs at us and keeps giving—endlessly, boundlessly, if we but open our eyes to see, our hands to receive and to give, and our hearts to be grateful.

2. He makes me lie down in green pastures, he leads me beside quiet waters.

If you had been a shepherd during biblical times, you would have been constantly in search of greener pastures and adequate shelter for your flock. And you would have spent much of your life looking for water—not just any source of water. If you led your stupid flock to a stream with a fast current, they would wade right in and be swept away.

How well David remembered those rare occasions in which the pasture was lush and the water clean and still. How he longed for the times when his own heart would be at peace with God and humankind.

In the midst of even the busiest, most stress-filled, most exasperating lives, there is an oasis. No matter how fast the current of our existence flows, there is time for stillness. There is no day so choked with cares and responsibilities that there is not room for God, for joy, for love, for being human. For all of us, the oasis is there. But for too many of us, the intention is lacking. You can have season tickets to the 49ers, the As, the Giants, the opera, the theater, and the symphony. But if you fail to get yourself there, you have wasted your money. And likewise God has given us everything we need to prosper as intellectual, aesthetic, and spiritual beings, but getting there requires our cooperation.

3. He restores my soul. He guides me in paths of righteousness for his name's sake.

And, of course, sheep were a major sacrificial animal. Shepherds like David knew about death. Their sheep died for them again and again. They died to provide mutton flesh and hides. They died in the tabernacle and later in the temple in the place of their owners. They died to settle the account.

How deeply ingrained in Christianity is the image of the sacrificial sheep. When John the Baptist saw Jesus approach, he cried out: "Behold the lamb of God who takes away the sin of the world." But this lamb is no helpless victim, no innocent incapable of finding his own way or fending for himself. He is at one and the same time sheep and shepherd. He leads the flock yet he is a member of the flock. He lays down his life so that we might have life and have it abundantly.

Christianity is not some prosperity cult that promises health, wealth, and success through the recitation of magic formulas or belief in arcane doctrines. Being a Christian is entering a world full of suffering, contradiction, and pain with one's eyes wide open. God does not guarantee instant eternal bliss. He promises us that we will never be alone or forsaken whether our lives are as placid as a calm sea or as rough as a squall.

4. Even though I walk through the valley of the shadow of death, I will fear no evil, for you are with me; your rod and your staff, they comfort me.

The shepherd was responsible for the protection of his flock. His was the job of defending them against predators and thieves. His shepherd's crook was a weapon with which he defended the flock. It was also a rod of correction which could be turned against a recalcitrant sheep.

God, the Good Shepherd, does not coerce us. He gives us the freedom to wander wherever we choose to wander. But he is not an infinitely permissive father. No matter how lost we become or how far from our own true nature we stray, there is within us an inborn compass, pointing and pulling us back toward home. And God sets limits to our freedom, limits which we transgress at our peril. Reality can be a harsh taskmaster. Sometimes the shepherd's crook gently taps us on the shoulder and sometimes it grabs us by the throat.

5. You prepare a table before me in the presence of my enemies. You anoint my head with oil; my cup overflows.

In this verse, images of human hospitality seem to run together with metaphors drawn from the shepherd's way of life. Among ancient near-eastern shepherds, "to prepare the table" was an expression meaning to groom the pasture for the sheep. This involved removing harmful weeds, killing snakes, and removing scorpions. Moreover, the shepherd was the only veterinarian his flocks knew. Many an hour was spent applying oils externally as salves and internally as medication.

And a particularly winsome and personable lamb could become a family pet, practically a member of the family. Such a favored lamb would share the shepherd's food, drink from his cup, and even sleep in his arms (see 2 Samuel 12:1–10).

We try so hard to do what is right, to do what will make us acceptable in our own eyes and in the eyes of our employers (or employees), our parents, our spouse, our children, our neighbors, and so on. And God just nuzzles up with us, wears us like a comfortable old pair of slippers, and loves us for absolutely no reason whatsoever.

6. Surely goodness and love will follow me all the days of my life, and I will dwell in the house of the LORD forever.

When David dreamed of his youthful days and nights with his father's flocks, he remembered with affection his constant companions and guardians, his sheep dogs. They were his eyes and ears.

They gathered the flock, nipped at the heels of stragglers, warned at the approach of strangers, kept wolves and lions at bay.

He didn't have to call their names or whistle for them. They were always there, always following him. What were the names of those wonderful dogs? I'd like to hazard a guess. They were named "Goodness" and "Mercy."

I am not a perfect human being and yet God unconditionally loves me and showers me with his gifts. I do not have everything I want, but I have everything I need. I sin and I fall short of what God expects of me and of what I truly can be again and again. But God never forsakes me. Through his love and through the fellowship of my fellow Christians, I am forgiven and restored. Day by day, I am born from above and given a fresh start.

In the midst of a hectic life filled with demands and responsibilities, there is an oasis for me within me and between me and others in the church.

And when I look back, I discover that all the things I thought I had accomplished were gifts of grace. And scampering after me like two faithful dogs are goodness and mercy.

This is one deal I can't resist. I plan to enjoy it for a long, long time.

Maybe I don't know a shepherd from a shoemaker or a sheep from a shirttail, but I know an oasis when I find one. May God give this dumb sheep—and all of us poor little lambs—the sense to stay with him forever.

Amen.

—LDS

[2100 words]
[21 minutes]

❦ *Sermon 12*

❦ *Date:* Pentecost Sunday or any Sunday

Text:
Acts 2:1–21

Theme: The power of Pentecost is readily available.
Subject: Pentecostal power

❦ *Title:* "Turn the Spigot!"

Pentecost is the shortest season of the Christian Year. It lasts all of one Sunday. That's just enough time to change the altar cloth from the white of Eastertide to red, symbolizing the fire of the Spirit's presence.

Pentecost Sunday recalls the birthday of the Christian Church—the giving of the Holy Spirit to the first disciples of Jesus. A week later, we begin a six-month season known only as "after Pentecost." It is as though the makers of the Christian calendar ran out of imagination and relied on reruns until Advent, the first Sunday in December.

What the Church needs is a Season of Pentecost, lasting several weeks. So until further notice, that is what we shall observe at this church.

A Spirit-filled church is a Christ-centered church and a biblically literate church. God gives us everything we need to live productive Christian lives and to prosper as a community. Here are a few thoughts on the presence of the Spirit (all inspired by the current California drought). A Lutheran newsletter reports,

> After the end of World War One the famous desert fighter, Lawrence of Arabia, brought several Arab leaders to Paris to represent their interests at the Versailles Peace Conference. Those sons of the desert were filled with astonishment at the sights of Paris, but nothing intrigued them quite as much as the running water in their hotel rooms. In the desert water was such a luxury and here in their rooms it seemed to be free and never ending, at the turning of a tap. When it was time to leave Paris, Lawrence found those Arabs removing the faucets, believing that those magic instruments would give them water at will in their native Arabia. Only with great difficulty did he finally convince them that the faucets were no good if detached from the water supply.[1]

"No good if detached!" How true that is in our relationship with God. Only when we remain "fully hooked up" does the power and peace of the Spirit flow through us.

Often we are ignorant of the riches we possess. Talking to a friend in the petroleum industry put me in mind of the following story:

> In West Texas there is a famous oil field known as the Yates pool. During the depression this field was a sheep ranch, owned by a man named Yates.
>
> Mr. Yates was not able to make enough money on his ranching operation to pay the principal and interest on the mortgage, so he was in danger of losing his ranch. With little money for clothes or food, his family, like many others, had to live on a government subsidy. Day after day, as he grazed his sheep over those rolling west Texas hills, he was no doubt greatly troubled about how he would be able to pay his bills.
>
> Then a seismographic crew from an oil company came into the area and told Mr. Yates that there might be oil on his land. They asked permission to drill a wildcat well and he signed a lease.
>
> At 1,115 feet they struck a huge oil reserve, giving 80,000 barrels a day. In fact, 30 years after the discovery, a government test of one of the wells showed that it still could flow 125,000 barrels of oil a day. And Mr. Yates owned it all! The day he purchased the land he received the oil and mineral rights. Yet, he was living on relief. A multimillionaire living in poverty! What was the problem? He did not know the oil was there. He owned it, but he not possess it.[2]

Back to the water shortage: When I was sixteen, my parents moved into their "dream house" in the Chicago suburb of Westchester, a few miles from my mother's childhood home of Maywood. The new subdivision had one serious problem. The outmoded water system could not provide the needs of the new housing. Strict water rationing was imposed. That hot summer our new lawn turned brown and perished as did the yards of our neighbors. Swimming pools were closed. Every glass of water was a luxury.

One day a civil engineer from Chicago was looking over the water works. He was astonished to hear of the water shortage. Apparently he knew what the local had forgotten. The local district did not draw its water from its ancient wells, but directly from Lake Michigan. He turned a handle and the phantom drought ended. A virtually limitless supply of water had been available all the time!

---

[1] *Parables, Etc.*, February 1989.

[2] *Parables, Etc.*, January 1984, 3.11.

Everything we need to quench our spiritual thirst and make our church grow is within our reach. It is up to us to take possession of what we already own. Turn the spigot!

Amen.

—LDS

[789 words]
[8 minutes]

❦ *Sermon 13*

❦ *Date:* Fifth Sunday After Epiphany, Year C

Text:
Isaiah 6:1–8

Theme: The basic reason why we have such a hard time loving God is because God is holy and we are not holy, and that causes problems.
Subject: Holiness of God

❦ *Title:* Loving a Holy God

The philosopher Pascal confessed, "The heart has its reasons of which reason knows not." Pascal had a problem, didn't he, between knowing God and loving God. But that problem gets intensified when we hear God say not only are we supposed to love him but we're supposed to love him with all of our hearts and with all of our minds, all our souls, and all of our strength.

Nobody in this room has loved God with all of their heart in the last five minutes—you know that. I know I haven't loved God with all of my heart for five minutes in my whole life. Sometimes I ask, "Why do we have such a hard time loving God?" I suppose there are lots of reasons and we could get very complex about it. But if we could jump quickly to the bottom line, I find in the Book that the basic reason why we have such a hard time loving God is because God is holy and we are not holy, and that causes problems.

Isaiah in the Temple

I think, frankly, the most poignant example of the problem that we find anywhere in Scripture is found in the Old Testament, and I want to take you through it quickly. In that very famous passage, we find where the prophet Isaiah is given his call to the ministry. Find it in the beginning of the sixth chapter of the Book of Isaiah where Isaiah says this: "In the year that King Uzziah died, I was the Lord seated on a throne, high and exalted, and the train of this robe filled the temple. Above him were the seraphim, each with six wings: With two wings they covered their faces, with two they covered their feet, and with two they were flying. And they were calling to one another: 'Holy, holy, holy is the Lord Almighty; the whole earth is full of his glory.'"

We don't have time to go into a lengthy exposition of this text, but I want to focus our attention, if we can, on a couple of highlights that take place here in this man's life. Isaiah is one of the most respected and most righteous men in all of the nation. He emerges not only as a prophet but as a statesman who is a consultant to at least three kings.

He comes into the temple because the king has died and it's a crisis for his people. And when he comes into the temple, he has a vision of the majesty and of the exalted, awesome excellence of God seated upon the throne. As he sees this vision in the church, he sees these weird creatures—birds or something—with six wings, flying all over the place in the temple.

And we know when we look at nature, there's a certain efficiency built into creatures God has made. Fish have fins and gills because they live in the water, and they don't need wings because they don't fly up in the air. But birds have wings; they fly in the air. They don't have gills because they don't need gills to fly up in the air. They have bills not gills because they function as birds.

But did you ever see a bird with six wings?" Well, these aren't birds, right? They're creatures that God has made to serve him in his immediate presence. And so he equips them that they might adapt to their environment. Two wings to do what? To cover their face, because, my dear friends, the glory and the brilliance and the dazzling light that come from the face of God is so intense, even the angels can't stand to look at it directly. And two wings to cover their feet, to cover their creatureliness.

But I'm not so much interested here in the anatomy of the seraphim as I am in their message, in their song. To adore God—to worship him—is one of the most fantastic experiences that any creature can ever have.

The Value of Repetition

I love music. And I like to hear both church music, and country-western music. I like all kinds of music. When I get a choir up there in the back singing Handel's "Messiah," that just sends chills up and down my spine.

But can you imagine an anthem written in heaven itself, what it would sound like to hear the angels sing? What in the world would they say? Well, Isaiah tells us about the anthem he hears when he sees God. The angels are singing, "Holy, holy, holy, is the Lord Almighty; the whole earth is full of his glory."

I know we have a hymn like that in our traditional church music, and we've heard this a jillion times. But there's something going on here in this text that maybe you missed. We have an example here of something that occurs rarely in the Bible.

The Jewish people had ways of speaking and ways of emphasizing things that were different from our ways. For example, if I want to say that something is important or if I want to emphasize a point I'm writing, I may underline it, or I may set it in italics, or boldface it, or put five exclamation points or quotation marks around it, or put it in parentheses. There are all these different ways that I have to communicate emphasis.

The Jews did all those things, but they also had their own special way of calling attention to something that was very important. They did it by repetition. They would say it over again.

Do you remember Paul when he admonishes the Galatians and tells them, "Hey, don't let anybody ever tell you any other gospel except the gospel that you received. And even if an angel from heaven comes and tells you another gospel, kick him in the seat of his ethereal pants and get him out of there." And then he says, "I say it again; don't let anybody ever tell you another gospel." It's as if he's saying, "If you didn't catch it the first time around, I'm going to make sure you get the point by repeating it."

Jesus does it frequently. When he's teaching his disciples, you know what he says? When he gets to that important point that he doesn't want them ever to forget, he says, "verily, verily" or "truly, truly," depending whether Jesus spoke in King James or in RSV, right? Really what he said in Aramaic was, "Amen, amen," which is a strange thing. In Israel, when did the people say Amen? Not at the beginning of the sermon. It was at the end of the sermon, or after the point was made, that all the people said, "Amen," which means, "Hey, that's true."

Jesus turns that around and starts his sermon by saying, "Amen, amen, I say unto you." That's like the captain on a ship getting on the horn and saying, "This is the captain speaking; now here this." Repetition.

A humorous illustration of it was given to me—that's really a lie; I stole it from John Guest, a friend of mine, an Episcopalian evangelist back in Pittsburgh, and he stole it, too—where back in the book of Genesis we have one of these situations where the people of God are being pursued by the bad guys, the wicked kings. And the wicked kings have the advantages of the Iron Age; they have chariots. They're bearing down on the people of God, and the Bible tells us that at the last second, just when they're going to get run over, these chariots get caught in the slime pits.

Well, at least that's what one translation says. Another translation said they get caught in the tar pits. Another one says they get caught in the bitumen. Another one said they get caught in the asphalt pits, and still another English translation simply says they got caught in the great pits.

The problem the translator has there is that the Jew simply uses the Hebrew word for pit twice, and the English translator said, "I can't translate this literally, because no American will understand it. If I do this it would say: "The chariots got caught in the pit pit."

Now what in the world is a pit pit? There are pits and there are pits, and a pit pit is the pittiest kind of pit the Jew could think of. You get in a pit pit and you're never going to get out! So that was the way the Jew did it. He made his point of emphasis by repetition.

But less than five times in all of the Bible do we ever find anything repeated to the superlative degree. And, my dear friends, only once in all of Scripture is an attribute of God elevated to the third level.

The song of the angels is not imply that God is holy. And it isn't even that they're so jealous for us to understand them that they say God is holy, holy, but that God is holy, holy, holy! The Bible never says that God is love, love, love, or mercy, mercy, mercy, or justice, justice, justice, or wrath, wrath, wrath, or sovereign, sovereign, sovereign, or anything, anything, anything,—except that God is holy, holy, holy.

"Woe is me . . ."

And when Isaiah said that, what happened? He's on his face. And listen to what he says: "Woe is me, for I am undone."

Now there's something else here that we could easily miss that we just can't miss. Sometimes we try so hard to bring the Bible up to date that we lose something in our translation. Who in the world today talks in terms of "Woe is me"? My Jewish friends in New York still say it in Yiddish when they say, "Oi vey." Now that's Yiddish for "Woe is me."

But who talks about woe? That's like saying "alas and alack" or "forsooth." Nobody talks like that where I live anymore. So why keep it in the text?

Well, again, the translators are doing us a favor. There's a reason for it, because in the Old Testament when God called a person to be a prophet, God took God's words and put them into the mouth of the prophet. When the prophet spoke, he prefaced his remarks by saying, "This saith the Lord," he would deliver this announcement that came from God.

The form the prophet used was called the oracle. Remember the Oracle of Delphi? He was like Jimmy the Greek in the ancient world. He would give his predictions, and he would do it in the form of an oracle. But there were two kinds of oracles; there were good oracles and there were bad oracles. There was good news and there was bad news; oracles of weal—of prosperity—and oracles of woe or calamity.

Jesus uses the form of the oracles in the most famous sermon that was ever preached. The good oracle was prefaced by the word blessed. That is, you are blessed of God if you are poor in spirit or if you know how to mourn or if you know how to be hungry and thirsty for righteousness or if you are a peacemaker. Jesus pronounced a divine benediction on people who lived out certain virtues.

But Jesus also used the oracles of doom from time to time, particularly with one group. Remember who that was? "Woe unto you, scribes and Pharisees, hypocrites! You go over land and sea to make one convert, and after you've made him, you make him twice the child of hell that you are yourselves."

And Amos—remember he did the same thing to the cities and the nations around Israel and then lowered the boom on Israel, because it's an awful thing to hear God's malediction.

You go to the end of the Bible in the book of Revelation, and all that stuff is taking place. The trumpets are blowing and the bowls of wrath are being poured out, and again, these bizarre creatures are flying through the air. And when things really get grim in the last days, you have this eagle or something flying around the sky. What's he singing? "Woe, woe, woe." Whoa! That's all the woe I want to hear. When you start hearing a bird flying over crying, "woe" you better look out, because there's trouble right here in River City.

So we see that formula used prophetically in the Bible. But look what happens here.

Here is a man who pronounces the woe—the curse of God—upon himself. "Woe is me, I'm undone. I'm coming apart. I came in here having it together. I felt like a whole person. I thought I had integrity until I had one glimpse of the living God. And now I experience disintegration." Why? "Because I'm a man of unclean lips. I have a dirty mouth. And I cannot stand it."

Now my friends, when Isaiah saw the holiness of God, it was the most excruciating experience in his life. And it's not isolated. If we look throughout Scripture, Scripture everywhere, uniformly, consistently shows us the same pattern.

Job is ticked, and he screams at God and he demands an answer. And when God finally shows up, what does Job do? "I abhor myself. I repent in dust and ashes. I'll speak no more."

Habakkuk gets up in his watch tower and says, "Okay, God, I don't like what I'm seeing down here. There's injustice all over the place, and you're responsible for it. You better get your act together and you better explain yourself to me." And God shows up, and Habakkuk says, "My lip quivered."

I have a four-year-old granddaughter and a six-month-old grandson, and I forgot what that quivering lip meant until I watched those kids. When they get in trouble, that lip starts to go, and you know what's coming next.

Habakkuk says, "My lips quivered, my belly trembled, and rottenness came into my bones." Do you like to feel like that? I sure don't.

The Holiness of Christ

The most perfect incarnation of holiness was in the person of Christ. And do you know how his best friends struggled in getting along with him? They're out fishing one night, a violent storm comes up on the Sea of Galilee, and Jesus is taking a nap in the back of the boat.

Do you like people like that? I know people like that. I was on an airplane once in the most violent thunderstorm and lightning storm that God ever visited on this planet. And being a Calvinist, I was terrified, because I thought God's eternal plan was about to come to pass in my life—and it wasn't so good! And I have white knuckles, hanging on—literally. On this airplane flight, the flight attendants were screaming in panic. And the guy next to me was sound asleep! I hated him. I wanted to grab him by the throat and say, "Stupid, don't you know what's going on out here?"

So I can relate to those guys in the boat when this storm has 10-foot-tall waves and the boat's ready to go under, and Jesus is in "tranquil repose" in the back of the boat. The Bible tells us they were afraid—you bet your neck they were afraid! And so Peter or somebody runs back there, and he's irritated: "Master, do something or we're going to perish!"

You know the story. Jesus doesn't say anything to these guys. He turns around and looks at the sea, and starts talking to it, yelling at it: "Peace! be still!" Wham! the sea's like glass—not a ripple, not a zephyr in the air.

Now the thing that drives me crazy when I read that is what the Bible says next: "And they became very much afraid." They ask a heavy question here; this was the first Christological inquiry in antiquity, and it hasn't been answered adequately yet. "What a manner of man is this?" What kind of man is this? What category can I place him into? I need to have categories for you; I need to know whether you're fundamentalist or liberal, a Methodist, a Baptist, a dispensationalist, an Armenian, a Catholic, a Jew, a black, a Puerto Rican, or what you are, because I suffer from xenophobia like everybody else in the human race, a fear of forms, of people who are different from what I am.

Well, where do you put this guy? The fundamental meaning of holiness means otherness, something different, really different, transcending. And suddenly these guys knew that they were in the presence of something that transcended the very powers of nature and was more terrifying than nature itself.

One more sea story and I'll quit. Same guys. Same boat. Same lake. Not the same story. They're out fishing all night and they come back. Peter's mad because they had a lousy night, and Jesus says, "Well, how did it go, fellas?"

And they say, "We couldn't find any fish."

And Jesus says, "Well, Peter, why don't you put the net over on that side of the boat?"

You know the biblical profile of Peter. Let me have a little bit of license here to read between the lines. I mean this was in the original, but it was expurgated because Peter started to swear—he was really mad: "What do you mean, 'Put it on the other side of the boat'? Where do you think it's been all night? Look, Jesus, you're an incredible theologian, the best rabbi and miracle worker we've ever seen, but give us some credit, for crying out loud! We fish this place every night, and we know what we're doing."

Instead he says to the guys, "Humor him. Throw the net over on that side of the boat." So they threw the net over on the other side of the boat, and you know the story: every fish in the Sea of Galilee jumped in the net. And so they try to drag the net into the boat and the boat starts to sink. The other boat comes along, and that boat starts to sink.

And then Peter rushes over to Jesus and he pulls out a contract: "Equal partners: 'Simon Barjonas . . .' no, 'Jesus Barjoseph (top billing)—Simon Barjonas, Inc.' Fifty percent of the profits, and all you have to do is come down here one day a month for five minutes." Right? That's what I would have done.

That's not what Peter did. Instead, Peter said, "Depart from me, for I'm a sinful man." He said, "Jesus, please leave. I can't take it. You're holy; I'm not. Leave."

"Then flew one of the seraphim to Isaiah with a live coal in his hand, which he had taken with tongs from the altar." And Isaiah says, "With that he touched my mouth."

I think authentic repentance is one of the most painful experiences a human being can ever go through. Look what God did to Isaiah; he took a live coal. Imagine this—try to think about it—you're having a barbecue in the back yard, and somebody goes over and takes one of those white-hot coals and comes over and puts it on your mouth. I mean if he put it on my arm, that would be bad enough, but put it on my mouth! And my mouth is immediately blistered. I'm screaming with pain.

But why does God do that? Because God's sadistic? Because he wants to torture him? No. He cauterized him. Isaiah had a dirty mouth. And God comes down and cleans it, and he says, "Behold, your sin is taken away; your iniquity is forgiven."

Love and Forgiveness

How do you love a holy God? You get forgiven by him.

When we experience forgiveness from a God who is in the business of just, you know —"Hey, boys will be boys and girls will be girls. We're all the children of God and God is love, love, love. Never mind that he's holy, holy, holy," that kind of forgiveness is what Bonhoeffer called "cheap grace." It doesn't mean anything to anybody.

When a holy God says to you, "You're forgiven," how can you not love him?

Isaiah's down there, blisters all over his mouth, and God says, "Who will go for me? Who will I send?"

And Isaiah's mumbling through all these blisters, he's saying, "Here am I." Not "Here I am," as if he's trying to tell God where to find him. But he's saying, "Here am I. Send me!" This was a guy who five minutes earlier was putting curses on his own head and was disintegrated.

See, that's what we fear from a holy God, that if we meet him, he's going to destroy us. Instead he's going to heal us. He wants to put us back together so that we want to go wherever he sends us.

Amen.

—R.C. Sproul

[3498 words]
[35 minutes]

❦ CHAPTER TWO

SPIRITUALITY AND BEARING WITNESS

Spirituality is letting God be God. Spirituality is putting first things first, refusing to allow the petty and mundane to crowd out the real and vital.

A spiritual life hears the Word behind all words. It is open and directed towards God. It is a response to a God who call and demands.

Being born from above is taking one's place with the people of God as one who is open to God's Spirit within the context of a faithful community. God's voice is best heard in moments of silent reflection. The Spirit's presence keeps us from being torn apart by our irreconcilable inner demons. It is our best resource in the struggle against loneliness.

Spiritual development is not only a personal journey; it is the evolution of a "team spirit." So join the best team you can. Get the best coach. And work! Develop a lust for a life fully lived in God's presence.

Primary spiritual activities are worship and witness. We are made to worship God. Church is not a filling station; it is a place to serve. Church is a place to foster our dreams of community, peace, and justice. And it is where we do something about these dreams!

In sum, seek God's just rule and leave the rest to him. Recognize that your life is a miracle and share the sense of awe and wonder. The proclamation of God's powerful Word of mercy and reconciliation belongs not only to ministers but to the whole people of God. We are all called to the task of bearing witness.

Sermon 14

Date: Easter Sunday, Any Year

Texts:
Year A
Acts 10:34–43 or Jeremiah 31:1–6
Psalm 118:1-2, 14–24
Colossians 3:1–4 or Acts 10:34–43
John 20:1–18 or Matthew 28:1–10
Year B
Acts 10:34–43 or Isaiah 25:6–9
Psalm 118:1-2, 14–24
1 Corinthians 15:1–11 or Acts 10:34–43
John 20:1–18 or Mark 16:1–8
Year C
Acts 10:34–43 or Isaiah 65:17–25
Psalm 118:1-2,14–24
1 Corinthians 15:19–26 or Acts 10:34–43
John 20:1–18 or Luke 24:1–12

Theme: The resurrected Jesus greets Mary Magdalene and makes a claim upon her life—as he does upon ours.
Subject: Grace, unexpected miracles

Title: Mary's Miracle

Prayer: Our Great and Gracious God: we wait with eager ears to hear your truth through the drama of the Easter story. Let us hear, let us be moved, let us respond. Amen.

Something happened that day. Something so breathtaking, so unbelievable, that the sighs of those who witnessed it echo and shudder through twenty long centuries. Even we can hear it.

On this holiest of holy days, we listen in wonder to a story. A story that does not make complete sense to us, but a story of such beauty and power that even the most cynical and rational among us, still our breathing to hear. And even the most believing among us, find our breath taken away.

Early on the first day of the week, while it was still dark, Mary Magdalene came to the tomb and saw that the stone had been removed from the tomb.

Why did she come? Why was she here? She came to attend to the unfinished business of grief. Mary, remember, was one of Jesus' closest friends, probably a wealthy patron of his ministry. Only she could have afforded to buy the perfumed oils and ointments that were used in biblical times to anoint the bodies of the dead. Mary came, her hands heavy with spices and oils, her heart heavy with sorrow.

She came to the tomb while it was still dark. It was still dark. Was she restless? Couldn't sleep? Was she afraid to be seen performing loving rituals for one who had been executed for blasphemy and high treason?

She found the doorway gaping open. Something was wrong—terribly wrong. The expensive flasks of oil slipped from her limp hands and shattered on the rocks. Without a word, she turned and ran to get Simon Peter and the unnamed disciple whom Jesus loved. She wrenched them out of sleep, crying, "They have taken the Lord out of the tomb, and we do not know where they have laid him!"

They reached the tomb, breathless, and Simon Peter crawled inside. John tells us that "he saw the linen wrappings lying there, and the cloth that had been on Jesus' head, not lying with the linen wrappings, but rolled up in a place by itself." Why has John recorded such careful detail about these burial wrappings? Did the shocking contract of rumpled white cloth against empty gray stone sear forever in Peter's memory this image—to be told, and told, and told again, like a ghost story?

Or was John trying to tell us something about how Jesus left? That his departure was not sudden or dramatic but rather, unhurried? Leisurely? Plenty of time to roll up the linen wrappings and tidy up the place?

Peter scrutinized the scene, but didn't get the point. The other disciple took one look and understood everything. John tells us that he believed. No wonder this disciple was so beloved by Jesus. No wonder Peter so often disappointed Jesus.

Peter and the disciple made their way back home. To bed? To tell the others? We're not told. But Mary stayed behind. The disciples' footsteps grew more distant and the stillness gathered around her. Quietly, slowly, she fell to pieces. What has happened? What has happened?

She walked over to the tomb and bent down to look inside. At first, she saw nothing—darkness against darkness. But as her eyes began to adjust, she could just make out two white shapes. Blinking her eyes, she finally saw them—two angels sitting where the body of Jesus had been lying.

The angels spoke. "Woman, why are you weeping?"

All the exhaustion, the rage, and the ache closed down over Mary, and the words flowed out like a lonely, mournful wail—"They have taken my Lord away, and I don't know where they have laid him!"

And for one breathless, excruciating heartbeat of a moment, they stood there together in silence.

"It's no use, no use," she thought. "He's gone."

"It's no use," he thought. "She'll never know it's me."

"Mary," he said.

He called her by name. Just as he had done a thousand times before, he called her by name. And something happened inside her. In the time it takes to say one word, she suddenly saw things in a new and startling way. All that she had ever heard about life and death and the ways of God's love just fell into place with the shuddering sound of her own name. "Mary," he said. And the word hung in the air between them, shimmering in the twilight of dawn. And she knew in her heart.

There are times in our lives when we stand, like Mary, suspended somewhere between tears and laughter, somewhere between death and life. Times when a person comes into our life like a gift, and speaks our name, and calls us into hearing, into understanding, into living. Times when we hear, in the calling of that name, a claim on our life. And we know beyond all knowing that we have been in the presence of Christ resurrected.

Mary walked home that morning, just as the sun was breaking over the Judean hills. Most of Jerusalem was still asleep. Only the sounds of animals stirring, the crackle of breakfast fires, the echo of her quickening footsteps.

When she saw the house, she started running. She threw herself against the door, and pounded with both fists, and called out, "Wake up! Wake up!"

They came to the door at once, and flung it open, and squinted out with sleepy eyes. There was Mary, laughing like a madwoman, tears streaming down her cheeks.

"It's a miracle," she gasped. "My name is Mary! Mary! He called me Mary!"

Something happened that day. Something so breathtaking, so unbelievable, that the sighs of those who witnessed it echo and shudder through twenty long centuries. Even we can hear it.

Christ is risen. Christ is risen indeed. Alleluia.

Amen.

—Elizabeth Chandler Felts

[987 words]
[10 minutes]

Sermon 15

Date: Second Sunday of Easter, Year A, B or C

Texts:
John 20:19–31

Theme: Spirituality is reminding ourselves that the Christ is with us, twenty-four hours a day.
Subject: Spirituality

Title: What is Spirituality?

Jesus breathed on them and said, receive the Holy Spirit. (John 20:22)

In this post-Eastertime we all have a sense of waiting. What is going to happen next? How is this Easter story going to play itself out in the life of Bethel church? In each of our lives, there is a sense of wonder, What is going to happen in your life as you are caught up in this new life the risen Christ has declared for all of us?

My text this morning is found in the twenty-second verse of John chapter 20. The two Marys who had talked with the risen Christ had reported this unbelievable information about Jesus to the disciples. To the shock of the disciples Jesus appeared to them behind locked doors. The risen Christ first gave a blessing: "Peace be with you." Then he breathed on them and said, "Receive the Holy Spirit." That act of Jesus triggers the beginning of our spirituality.

Why a sermon on spirituality? Is not all preaching about spirituality? Yes and no. Preaching should proclaim God's will, proclaim what is right, what we should be doing and what we should not be doing. But a lot of preaching gets bogged down in the petty details of trying to help people move from eating spiritual baby food to maybe a hamburger of faith. There is far too much psychology and emotion and too many ineffective stories in today's preaching.

And worst of all is the prosperity preaching from many of our TV preachers who tell you that God will make you prosper if you send dollars, big dollars, to their ministry. In the last few years we have learned how big donations really are spent.

Not too long ago, Malcolm Warford, the president of our seminary in Bangor, Maine, said, "We are living at the end of an era. We have lived off our heritage. We have diluted our heritage as much as we can. The well has gone dry. It is time for us to say what we stand for."

Let's begin this morning by examining the spiritual content of the biblical passages you heard earlier. Of the first four commandments, the first one deals with the nature and reality of God. It stresses that God is one and no other gods are to be tolerated. The second commandment stresses the spiritual nature of God in that no images can be made of God—no idols. The third commandment declares God's name to be holy and to be honored as such. I feel pain every time I hear swear words which are tossed off with the flip of the tongue. To me it is like a needle being stuck into my body!

The Sanctity of the Sabbath

In the fourth commandment, one whole day in the week is to be devoted focusing on God's holiness. We frequently refer to these commandments as law, but what is the law about? This law declares the spirituality of God. One God. No image. Name is special, a reminder twenty-four hours long.

We don't grab the spirituality of God with the speed that we use to get our Big Mac and fries! It takes time and intention. That's why Mr. Warford said our well is dry. We have not been intentional about opening ourselves to God. But a whole day? Let's think about that.

In three of the Gospels we find Jesus dealing with this problem. On a Sabbath, some Pharisees caught his disciples rubbing out some grains of wheat and eating them. Shelling out grains of wheat is classified as work and is therefore forbidden.

How did Jesus handle this? With some sarcasm, he asked if they had never read what David and his companions did. They had gone into the temple and eaten the Bread of Presence which was only lawful for priests to eat. And the temple did not fall down!

Jesus declared that God had made the Sabbath for humans, not the other way around. God knew that it was difficult for human beings to comprehend all that God was, so the Sabbath was created as the opportunity for human beings to comprehend the spiritual nature and power of God.

What have we done with that Sabbath opportunity? What do Christians and Jews do with that opportunity? Do we use the opportunity to worship? Do we use the opportunity to pray? to study God's word? to rest? to relax and refresh our bodies and our souls? The Holy Spirit has a tough time getting into a body that is doing six things at one time!

When you go shopping on Sunday, you are forcing others to work. The days of the blue laws are gone. The city or state has no business in telling merchants they can only be open certain days or telling us when we must worship or where we must pray, such as in school. If we believe that we are the children of God, then our own convictions should force us to ask what is necessary for us to have a healthy spiritual life. How much shopping is really necessary on Sunday for us?

When God Is God

This is what spirituality is all about. Spirituality is acknowledging that God is God. Spirituality is being open to God. I am not talking about being mentally or intellectually open to God. Our spirit, our soul needs to be open to God and that cannot be the case if we are concentrating on a TV show or arguing with the family or fighting traffic to get to one more party.

Spirituality is letting God be so big in your life that the mean and petty are crowded out, there is no room to feel you have to get even with someone or be first or make more money so you can buy another car.

Let Christ be big in your life.

As you heard the Second Psalm read this morning you probably wondered what this coronation of a king with all the bluster of rebellion, has to do with this first Sunday after Easter. If you do a little hunting around in this Psalm you will begin to find some clues in the phrases, "his anointed, Zion, my holy hill, serve the Lord with fear, with trembling kiss his feet."

The ancient Hebrews thought of their kings as channels of blessing. These kings represented the preference of God to the people. It is no surprise that the people were expected to kiss their feet. These were holy acts. Sometimes it is hard for us to comprehend how people two to four thousand years ago experienced the spiritual nature of God.

Spiritual renewal is simply reminding ourselves of this reality, the Christ is with us, twenty-four hours a day while we are living—and with us in death.

Times for Remembering

Nothing is too common to be exalted. In the course of a day there are at least twelve times when we need to remind ourselves God is with us. We need to sense God's presence in

The alarm clock that rouses us from sleep—THANK GOD FOR THE GIFT OF TIME.

The cup of coffee or the hurried breakfast—THANK GOD FOR THE GIFT OF FOOD.

The crowded subway, bus, train, or highway where everyone does the unexpected—THANK GOD FOR THE GIFT OF MOVEMENT.

Arriving at work, same old station but with an urgent note "Do this first"—THANK GOD FOR THE GIFT OF WORK WHICH CREATES.

In the course of the workday, someone yells, "I've had fourteen complaints about such and such; "Don't do that again."—THANK GOD FOR CHALLENGES.

Once in a while someone says "Just had word from Joe that he really liked what you did with that project."—THANK GOD FOR THE GIFT OF SATISFACTION.

At a break or lunchtime, gossip, jokes, sports, or TV reviews—THANK GOD FOR THE GIFT OF FRIENDS.

At the end of the day, in spite of ups and downs—THANK GOD FOR THE GIFT OF ACCOMPLISHMENT.

Going home—THANK GOD FOR THE GIFT OF FAMILY.

Fun in the evening—THANK GOD FOR THE GIFT OF LEISURE.

When your head hits the pillow—THANK GOD FOR THE GIFT OF SLEEP.

In your dreams—THANK GOD FOR THE GIFT OF LIFE.

Concern for spirituality is showing up all across the United Church of Christ and many other denominations too. This concern for spirituality is not a denial of the prophetic witness that our church has borne for many years. But the truth of the matter is that some of us have been so busy with the protests and demonstrations that we have lost touch with the spiritual power God provides. Too many of us have just assumed that we know what needs to be done and that God is blessing what we do when in fact we have forgotten that God exists!

Spirituality: The Threefold Disciple

I commend a threefold spiritual discipline to you.

1. Be aware that God exists in your life.
2. Do specific things because you are thinking of God—for example, worship, prayer.

3. Meditate. At least once a day, for five minutes, turn off the radio, turn off the TV, turn off the stereo, shut the door. Turn your mind, your thought processes loose with God. Acknowledge that God is in that room, in your body. Ask God what you should do. Listen for God's answer.

Spirituality takes time and intention. Spirituality is acknowledging that God is God. Spirituality is being open to God. Spirituality is letting God be so big in your life that the mean and petty are crowded out.

Let Christ be big in your life.

Amen.

—Eugene Schneider

[1600 words]
[16 minutes]

❦ *Sermon 16*

❦ *Date:* Second Sunday in Lent, Year A
or First Sunday After Pentecost, Year B (Trinity Sunday)

Texts: Year A	Year B
Genesis 12:1–4a	Isaiah 6:1-8
Psalm 121	Psalm 29
Romans 4:1–5, 13–17	Romans 8:12-17
John 3:1–17	**John 3:1-17**

Theme: Reconception is Nicodemus' misconception—and Nicodemus has a whole lot of company.
Subject: Spiritual rebirth, conversion, being born again

❦ *Title:* Under Cover of Darkness

> This sermon contains a short passage from Thornton Wilder's classic play, *Our Town.* The selection may be read by the preacher or enacted by members of the congregation.

We are conceived in the dark. For many months, we gestate in the darkness of our mother's womb. During all our days, the light and the darkness provide the basic rhythm and structure for our existence. When the light of our lives fails, we return to the darkness. That we not remain in the dark all of our lives is the major concern of the author of the Fourth Gospel.

As I reread and studied our Gospel text for today from the third chapter of John, two possible sermon titles came to mind: "Lord, You Mix Me Up!" and "How Not to Be Born Again." John's report of the nighttime conversation between Jesus and Nicodemus takes advantage of deliberate confusions and ambiguities. I am sure that Nicodemus left his evening meeting with Jesus as confused as he came—just as I am convinced that most references I have heard in my life to the oft-quoted words of this chapter are products of systematic misunderstanding of what Jesus was saying.

John the beloved disciple is deliberately ambiguous. He loves symbolism, puns, double meanings, and irony. John was a theologian and a preacher more than a reporter. He never remains behind the camera as do Matthew, Mark, and Luke. He is a character in his own production. He is never far from the center of the action. He rests on Jesus' bosom at the Last Supper. He stands with Mary at the foot of the cross. He and Peter were the first to hear Mary Magdalene's report of the empty tomb. He was one of the seven disciples to whom Jesus appeared by the Sea of Tiberius.

John's interest is the significance more than the facts. When he tells a story, it is difficult to tell when the tale ends and his sermon on the story begins. Thus, commentators and translators are hard pressed to know where the conversation between Jesus and Nicodemus ends and where John's interpretation begins. Could Jesus have said: "God so loved the world that he gave his only begotten son," and so on?

Born From Above

There is so much interesting and challenging material in these verses, but since time is limited, I would like to focus on the words that are usually translated "You must be born again" (gennethénai anothen). The original Greek is ambiguous. The words can mean either "You must be born again" or "You must be born from above." Or to be even more literal, they say, "You must be generated again" or "You must be generated from above."

Jesus tells Nicodemus: "No one can see the kingdom of God unless he is born ánothen." It is clear from the context and from John's consistent use of the word ánothen throughout the Gospel that he means "from above"—that unless God acts to open our eyes to spiritual reality, we will remain blind to his presence in our lives and world. According to the Synoptic Gospels (Matthew, Mark, and Luke), the kingdom of God, God's just rule over the affairs of humankind, was a central emphasis of the teachings of Jesus—as it had been in the preaching of John the Baptist. Yet in the Fourth Gospel, the kingdom of God is mentioned only here in John 3.

John is saying something important to his readers, to the first-century Christian church, and to us. The kingdom of God is not a new sociopolitical order like the Roman empire or the kingdom of Alexander the Great. As Jesus will later say to Pilate, "My kingship is not of this world"(18: 36 RSV). John is taking us beyond this world and pointing toward a new dimension or order of existence. And yet this new dimension is here at the center of our daily lives.

If that sounds confusing, you are getting the point. The demand that Nicodemus be "born again" or "born from above" is intentionally confusing. Nicodemus misunderstood Jesus and so have most translators of this text. In this case as in so many others, careless translation has led to sloppy theology. So-called born-again Christians, assuming that the born-again experience is a "by the numbers," routinized stimulation of a momentary emotional excitement have appropriated these words for themselves.

"Are You Born Again?"

When such Christians ask me if I am born again, I want to tell them that, of course, I am. After all, I have been regenerated from above more times than I can remember. And God keeps planting his seed in my life, and with or without my cooperation, it keeps growing. Day by day, I am born from above every time I open my heart to the grace of God in my life and respond with thanks and joy.

Being born from above is not the experience of crisis conversion, the sense of relief and release that follows confessing one's sins and asking Jesus into one's heart. Being born from above is taking one's place with the people of God as one who is open and responsive to God's Spirit. Being born from above is being committed to walking in the light even as God gives us light within the context of a faithful community.

Jesus did not say, "Unless a person is born of the right emotional agitation" or "of the right beliefs" or "of the right lifestyle." He said, "Unless a man is born of water and the Spirit, he cannot enter the kingdom of God." John does not quote Jesus as saying to Nicodemus, "You must be regenerated" or "You must be reborn." He says, "You must be born from above." Reconception is Nicodemus' misconception—and Nicodemus has a whole lot of company.

Opening Our Eyes to the Presence of God

Abraham, about whom today's Old Testament and Epistle readings speak, was called to leave his home and go where God commanded. Likewise Nicodemus was called to leave his prejudices, his presuppositions, and his position in society. He was called to join those who have been born of water and of spirit. Both men were summoned to strike out in ways they could scarcely have imagined.

When I drive home the same way day after day, I scarcely see the passing scenery. When I take a new way home, I am aware of my surroundings—as though they had just been created for my benefit. To be born from below is to drive on through life without stopping to live. To be born from below is to be a spectator to one's own life rather than a participant in it. To be born from above is truly to live. To be born from above is have one's eyes open to the presence and grace of God in our lives as individuals and in our midst as a church.

The call to Abraham was heard and obeyed. We are not told what Abraham said. But we know what he did. He lived life fully. He saw the presence and grace of God at work in his life. He was awestruck and appreciative. He was open to the possibilities of his life. He was alert and aware. Through him all the nations of the world have truly been blessed. From the faithfulness of Abraham springs the great monotheistic faiths of humankind—Judaism, Christianity, and Islam.

Nicodemus' response to his calling was to discuss it, object to it, think it over, meditate upon it, and seriously consider it. As John describes him, Nicodemus was a victim of "the paralysis of analysis." Nicodemus came in the dark and left the same way. His life remained two-dimensional. He was too busy attending to his responsibilities to have time to open himself to the spontaneity, to the excitement, to the danger of really living.

To be fair, Jesus' late-night conversation with Nicodemus was not entirely in vain. Nicodemus would later defend Jesus before the Sanhedrin (7:50), insisting on a fair trial, and, when his words were ignored and Jesus was juridically lynched, he would have the courage to come openly by day with Joseph of Arimathea to help prepare Jesus' body for burial (19:39). The disciples loved by Jesus fled like roaches exposed to the light, but this man who had so much to lose—his status and standing as one of the highest officials of his people—risked it all to give the strange teacher from Galilee a decent burial.

Nicodemus never understood Jesus. He never came out and publicly acknowledged him to be the Messiah. He never joined the church of his day. Yet he had the courage to live—to risk his life for the sake of the wonder worker he never comprehended.

Choosing Life

The choice between living one's life and merely existing finds eloquent expression in Thornton Wilder's ageless play, Our Town. The concluding act is set in a New England cemetery. The townspeople who have died sit facing the audience in a dozen ordinary chairs in three openly spaced rows. The chairs represent their graves. Emily Gibbs, a young woman, enters their ranks. She has just died in childbirth and misses her family. She greets her new companions but tells them her greatest wish is to return to her family. They strongly advise against it. Simon Stimson, the bitterest of the dead, reminds her of the ignorance and blindness of the living. He tells her that being alive is

> To move about in a cloud of ignorance; to go up and down trampling on the feelings of those . . . about you. To spend and waste time as though you had a million years. To be always at the mercy of one self-centered passion, or another.

Emily tries to go back as a witness to one of the happiest days in her life, her twelfth birthday party, but she discovers that the living don't appreciate life. They take too much for granted. Finally she cries out:

> I can't. I can't go on. It goes so fast. We don't have time to look at one another.
>
> I didn't realize. So all that was going on and we never noticed. Take me back—up the hill—to my grave. But first: Wait! One more look.
>
> Good-by, Good-by, world. Good-by, Grover's Corners. . . Mama and Papa. Good-by to clocks ticking. . . and Mama's sunflowers. And food and coffee. And new-ironed dresses and hot baths. . . and sleeping and waking up. Oh, earth, you're too wonderful for anybody to realize you."

And then she turns toward the stage manager, who rules over this play like God, and asks:

> Do any human beings ever realize life while they live it?—every, every minute?

And he replies:

> No. (Pause.) The saints and poets, maybe—they do some.

Dying in Order to Live

All God's gifts are undervalued—sunsets, music, food, nature, friendships. Must we die before we can see life for the gift it really is?

In a way, we must. We must die to our self-centered, me-first, self-justifying existence. We must die to "I'm too busy to live now, I'll start living as soon as the I get my promotion, or get the children through college, or retire, or. . . ." We must stop pursuing the cheap counterfeit versions of life. God so loved the world that he gave his one and only son that we might have real life, the life of the ages. When John speaks of eternal life, he is not talking about life after death. He was not looking forward to reclining on a cloud while playing a harp. He is talking about life that is lived in the light—not under cover of darkness. "Eternal life" is the "life of the Eternal." It is God's life, offered to us, lived through us, realized in our midst.

Do any human beings ever realize how precious life is while they live it—every, every minute? No. There is too much darkness in us, too many bad habits, too much sadness and pain, too many excuses, too much anger. We spend so much time under cover of darkness that it is a wonder that we see anything at all. It is a miracle that the light can break through at all. But now and then it does. God speaks and we hear. God calls and we respond. God changes the itinerary and we are alert and aware, all the way home. We are born from above.

Amen.

—LDS

[2100 words]
[21 minutes]

Sermon 17

Date: Sixth Sunday After Epiphany, Year A

Texts:
Deuteronomy 30:15–20
Psalm 119:1–8
1 Corinthians 3:1–9
Matthew 5:17–37

Theme: What is spirituality? Realizing that God is present in Jesus the Christ, that God demands perfection, and that although striving cannot overcome imperfection, surrender and service can.
Subject: Spirituality

Title: Only God Gives the Growth—Who Is Really Spiritual?

But I, brothers, could not address you as spiritual men but as men of the flesh—as mere infants in Christ. . . . I planted the seed, Apollos watered it, but God made it grow. So neither he who plants nor he who waters is anything, but only God, who makes things grow. (1 Corinthians 3:1, 6–7)

Who is really spiritual? One hears a great deal of talk these days about spirituality. A few years ago, the Fifteenth General Synod of the United Church of Christ adopted spiritual renewal as one of the priorities of the denomination. Nearly half of all UCC congregations followed suit, officially adopting spiritual renewal as a priority or an area of special concern. During the past five years, I have heard more talk in the United Church of Christ about expressions of spirituality than in the previous three decades.

Spiritual Pains in the Neck

All right, spirituality has suddenly become a subject of interest. But the question remains, who is really spiritual? The Apostle Paul had much to say about this subject. His first letter to the Corinthians is an essay on the difference between true and false spirituality. The Corinthians thought that they were spiritual. They were convinced of it. More than that—they were proud of it. They were so spiritual it hurt! They flocked to the most popular religious teachers. They had ecstatic religious experiences: they spoke in tongues, worked miracles, healed the sick, and uttered prophecies. Their community was filled with talented church administrators, preachers, and missionaries.

If they were alive today, I am sure that we would find them conversant with the current religious best-sellers, flavoring their speech with the most fashionable religious clichés, and attending the trendiest workshops and retreats. We would expect them to be at church school and worship services every Sunday morning, Sunday evening, Wednesday night, and whenever else church activities might be scheduled. During the week, they could be counted on to study the Bible, say grace at meals, and pursue personal devotional lives by praying and meditating regularly. In their homes, we would no doubt find Christian periodicals, Christian music, Christian books, and Christian art. A perusal of their check stubs would reveal their giving to be systematic and substantial.

And if the Apostle Paul were to visit them today, he would find them a colossal pain in the neck. They would think of themselves as spiritual downhill racers of championship caliber. Paul would see them as fit only for God's bunny slope.

The trouble with the Corinthians was that they thought of themselves as extraordinary and special. Paul found them ordinary and boring. As spiritual as they thought they were, they were such an opinionated lot that they couldn't even get along with one another. They claimed that they were truly spiritual—the Greek word is *pneumatikos*, but Paul regarded them as still carnal, of the flesh (*sarkikos*). To put this in a more contemporary mode, they thought they were filled with the Spirit, but Paul was convinced that they were "airheads." I love this distinction, the pneumatics versus the meatheads! Those who put God and others first versus those who were enmeshed in pride and selfishness. Those with a capacity to love and be Christlike versus the arrogant and self-satisfied, who thought they were spiritual.

Who Then Is Spiritual?

Who is spiritual? As a Christian, finding the answer to this question is important—if not vital—for me. As a longtime counselor of individuals suffering from spiritual indigestion, from being too religious for their own good or any one else's, determining what the word "spiritual" means has become a virtual obsession.

The following often pass for spirituality: dreams, daydreams, and mysteries; gurus, mind games, hugs, self-examination, and talking about one's feelings; feminism, ecology, and the unconscious; above all, anything exotic, preferably if it is from a remote place or a distant time.

Among some of my Christian friends, a spiritual person is one who quotes the Bible a lot, says "Praise the Lord," and works "God" into conversation whenever possible. A spiritual person is one with an overly tender conscience, someone who can't do anything without feeling guilty. A spiritual person is one who speaks in tongues (to the outsider, kind of inarticulate babytalk), or has been healed of an illness or an addiction. A spiritual person is one who eschews materialism and lives simply and meagerly. And, above all, a spiritual person is one who is better than other Christians.

Among other Christians of my acquaintance, spiritual persons are those who interpret the Bible in Jungian categories, who "let their child out" by putting on clown makeup, who keep journals of their inner journey, who control their posture and their breathing, who visualize, or who avoid meat. To yet another group of Christians with whom I spend time, to be spiritual is to avoid conspicuous consumption and to demand social justice in the world.

Among my non-Christian friends, a spiritual person is one who has psychic experiences, uses ESP, engages in astral projection, or channels beings from a higher plane or another world. A spiritual person is one who can predict the future, see auras, read Tarot cards, heal ailments with crystals, transform reality by thinking positively, or quote from Kahlil Gibran, the Bhagavad Gita, or the Kama Sutra. A spiritual person is one who overcomes dependence (on alcohol, drugs, food, romance) through a twelve-step program, and so on, and so on.

Tools of Spirituality

Now in the past few paragraphs I have mentioned a large number of allegedly spiritual pursuits. And I am neither condemning them nor giving them my unconditional endorsement. They are just tools. Don't get me wrong, tools are absolutely essential, but they are still tools. And the problem is that we tend to collect the tools of spirituality, play with them, display them, catalog them, be entertained by them, acquire a modicum of skill in using them, and bamboozle ourselves into thinking that the tools of spirituality make us spiritual, and that because we are spiritual we are better than everybody else.

Conversely, many of us in the liberal and permissive United Church of Christ family have conned ourselves into thinking that because we are not spiritual—because we are too rational to be taken in by the fanatics, fakers, and phonies—we are better than other human beings.

The illusion of spirituality, the trap into which seekers fall, is believing that because we experience something real, learn something real, feel something real, we are Real (with a capital R). The *Tao Te Ching* says it so well: "The one who knows does not say; the one who says does not know." The truly spiritual person is the one who does not know that he or she is spiritual, does not say that he or she is spiritual, but just is. A rose does not know it is beautiful any more than a Van Gogh painting does, it just is. Anyone who claims to be spiritually superior to another human being is deluded.

The tools we choose are important. Knowledge of one's faith—its scriptures, its heroes, its history—is extremely significant. Spiritual guides—lovers of our souls, mirrors and lures, partners—are also indispensable. In many ways, spirituality is a social activity like speech. It requires the support and challenge of others, especially of those who know its nuances, syntax, grammar, and style.

The Initiative Is God's

Spirituality emerges spontaneously in every human soul. But left unnourished by soulmates, psalms, songs, worship, scriptures, and confessions, it withers and dies. True spirituality must constantly express itself. It cannot avoid expressing itself—not only in worship and praise of the giver of the eternal Spirit but in acts of loving service. If God is present in me, he is present in all human beings. I cannot truly worship him unless I acknowledge that every person is a temple of his Spirit. If I am spiritual, every one is spiritual.

Spirituality is also what a person does in the depths of his or her solitude. It is pursuit of the inner light, the Christ within, the God who is heard in silence, the love of one's true self that is the basis of one's love for others.

We turn spirituality into easy answers—into techniques or tricks or tips. We divide up into teams—the holy, the holier, and the holiest—and we quibble as to who is which. And in the midst of all of our spiritual seeking, we forget that in true spirituality the initiative is God's, not ours. That is my whole sermon in a single sentence: in the midst of all of our spiritual seeking, we forget that in true spirituality the initiative is God's, not ours. Many of the activities I have mentioned are useful self-help. They bolster the ego, the imagination, the feelings, the intellect. But are they spiritual? They serve the needs of the human spirit, which is not antagonistic to true spirituality. But unless they arise within and among us because the divine spirit is brooding over the face of the deep, they are something less than spiritual. Moreover, unless they attach themselves to the Word and Sacraments of our churches, they run the risk of fading away when the next trend emerges.

Eighteen Words Too Many?

When I was a child, relatively untainted by the religious notions of my elders, I was aware of three powerful images that dominated my being. There was the sense of an ever-present friend. Sometimes this friend was an imaginary playmate; sometimes it was Jesus. There was the awareness of a monitor or judge, an ever-present inner "Watchbird." There was the consciousness of comfort, resting on the bosom of the universe, an experience recaptured in nature, in dreams or daydreams, in the presence of comforting persons, such as my maternal grandmother. Spirituality would for the rest of my life be formed and shaped by these three images.

What is the true nature of spirituality? For me, it is whatever nurtures my sense of being ultimately befriended, being subject to unconditional imperatives, and being finally at peace. If we are very, very careful when we use the word "love," I would say that accepting love, responding as love demands, breaking down the barriers to love is another way of saying the same thing.

What I have found and what has found me is a Christian spirituality. It depends on God, Jesus, the Church, and the Bible. Yet, as befits the spirituality of a UCC Christian, it is never final, never dogmatic, and certainly not a required spirituality for anyone else. For me, the key to spiritual life may be summarized in three assertions:

> God is present in Jesus the Christ.
>
> God demands perfection.
>
> Striving cannot overcome imperfection; surrender and service can.

It has taken me eighteen words and a lifetime to say that—and I probably have used eighteen words too many.

Amen.

—LDS

[1900 words]
[19 minutes]

Sermon 18

Date: Fourth Sunday After Epiphany, Year B

Texts:
Deuteronomy 18:15–20
Psalm 111
1 Corinthians 8:1–13
Mark 1:21–28

Theme: Authority comes from silence.
Subject: Silence

Title: Shh!

Note

> This sermon and the one following may be used as a series on "Spiritual Authority and the Overcoming of Evil."

[Piano: "The Sound of Silence" by Paul Simon]

Hello darkness, my old friend,
I have come to talk with you again,
because a vision softly creeping,

left its seeds while I was sleeping,
and the vision that was planted in my brain
still remains within the sound of silence.
—Paul Simon, "The Sound of Silence"

"They went to Capernaum." Why Capernaum? The baptism of Jesus and his forty days of solitude took place in the wilderness of Jordan. That's about a hundred miles away from Capernaum and about a hundred miles away from Nazareth in Galilee where Jesus had resided as a child and a young man.

Jesus goes to the coastal city of Capernaum on the shore of the Sea of Galilee, and he calls a group of men to be his followers. According to Mark he begins his public ministry here on the seashore. Why not in Nazareth? why not in wilderness with the followers of John the Baptist? why not in Jerusalem?

The Fascination of the Sea

Jesus had a feeling of attraction, a fascination for the sea. The sea is profoundly symbolic in Judaism in the Old Testament. The sea represents all the creative energy and chaos of everything that is. The sea represents a world not yet formed and waiting to be formed. In Genesis 1 we read of the Spirit of God brooding over the surface of the deep. We know this story comes from an earlier creation story, a Sumerian account, in which a good god struggles with an evil god, who tries to pull creation back into chaos and turn it into debris.

In our own lives there are impulses and urges and needs that are constantly warring with one another. Order and chaos contend for control of our inner selves. And I feel the struggle, as I am sure you do, every time I go to the sea. For at the sea I find myself in the presence of something which is profoundly moving and stirring, yet at the same time which is full of chaos capable of overwhelming me.

Years ago I went to visit Hannah Tillich, the widow of Paul Tillich, one of the greatest theologians of the twentieth century. The Tillichs lived way out on the end of Long Island, and Long Island is a long, long island. Mrs. Tillich told me about a time in which a hurricane-force storm struck the area. The roads were awash. Trees were being toppled and power lines were coming down. Her husband was missing and she was terrified. They found him out on a little spit of land sticking out into the Atlantic Ocean right in the middle of the storm savoring it like a small child who had found a fascinating toy.

The Quiet Center

Relishing the force, the power, the utter chaos, and in the midst of it finding a calm in the very core of his personality—that's what Jesus was like. We read that after he went to see John the Baptist, he heard a voice from heaven that said, "You are my beloved Son in whom I am well pleased." Jesus went to the wilderness and for forty days he lived in silence. That silence is probably the most neglected and ignored feature of his ministry. Again and again, we find him retreating from the maelstrom, finding himself, centering himself, and then returning.

Like most Protestants I have tended to think of him as going off in a retreat and praying—talking to God. But now I am not so sure that there was anything more there than what is most needed—silence. Silence that anchors, silence that speaks to the core of our being, silence that then equips us to return to a life that is too busy and is too filled, too overwhelmed by circumstances.

A man was possessed by an evil spirit and he cried out. Now this is one of the most peculiar things to us about the New Testament, and yet it is characteristic of the New Testament. If we were to take all of the things that Jesus did during his earthly career and make a statistical analysis of them, the thing that he is recorded in the gospels as having done the most was healing. The thing that we would find number two on our list would be casting out evil spirits. Jesus was an exorcist! And if we continue down the list, the third most common thing was that Jesus was a teacher.

Jesus cast out evil spirits. This activity is so strange to us. In our scientific and rational universe, who casts out evil spirits? As a counselor, I have dealt with many people who believed they were possessed by evil spirits. And if you and I were this morning visiting with a Pentecostal church, a church that emphasized gifts of the spirit such as healing and speaking in tongues, in such a tradition it would not be unusual at all to speak about evil spirits, about forces, demonic forces which are an explanation for what's wrong. Such churches emphasize a surrender to "unconscious forces" to the sources of chaos and creativity within us.

The Authority of Silence

I don't know what evil spirits are. I will admit that. But I know this—that there are forces you and I contend within ourselves and in our world that make for chaos. There are forces that do what evil spirits do in the Gospel accounts, they undo the creation. They unmake everything that we do. And spirituality is a constant contending with the forces that would undo the creation. Be quiet, Jesus says to these forces.

In the Synoptic tradition—the Gospels according to Matthew, Mark, and Luke—we have the doctrine of the messianic secret: when Jesus is revealed as the Christ, as the Son of God, as the Savior, he says to the one who identifies him, "Shh." In the Synoptic Gospels there is a clear reason for that: until the church has passed through the experience of the crucifixion of Jesus, the apparent triumph of chaos over meaning, and until the church has passed through the resurrection in which God reverses and redeems this apparent defeat, until Jesus has passed through death and resurrection, until the church has passed through his death and resurrection, until we in our own lives have passed through suffering and death of self and entered into a life of discipleship and newness and creativity, the life of Jesus is without significance and meaning and our life is without significance and meaning. Be quiet. The centered life is the powerful life. Listening is greater than speaking. Silence the inner chattering. And they heard Jesus and they said, here is a new teaching and with authority.

There was a young second lieutenant at Fort Dix who walked up to a beverage machine and discovered Cokes were 75 cents. He looked through his pockets but he didn't have any change. He called over a PFC who was walking by and he asked, "Private, by any chance, would you have change for a dollar?" The PFC replied, "I'm sure if I dig around in my pockets I could find change." And the second lieutenant said: "That's no way to speak to an officer. Let's do it again. Do you have change for a dollar?" The PFC snapped to attention, saluted smartly, and said, "No, sir."

The more the second lieutenant asserted himself, the less influence he had. The less the PFC said, the more powerful he became. There was authority to this private. There is authority to you. That authority comes from the silence. If you would find the power that overcomes chaos, heed the instruction of Jesus: "Shh!"

"The jackass brays mightily but the forest does not tremble. The tiger's paw barely presses the fallen leaf and all rush for shelter."

Amen.

—LDS

[1304 words]
[13 minutes]

❦ *Sermon 19*

❦ *Date:* Sunday Between June 5 and June 11 inclusive (if after Trinity, Sunday) Pentecost, Year B

Texts:
1 Samuel 8:4-11, 16-20
Psalm 138
2 Corinthians 4:13–5:1
Mark 3:20–35

Theme: By joining Jesus we can avoid being torn apart by our irreconcilable "demons."
Subject: Wholeness, evil

❦ *Title:* "Hold Your Horses!"

Jesus the Exorcist

It was around them everywhere like smoke in a chimney. All around them. They could see it; they could feel it; they could taste it.

Evil. The people of Jesus' time lived in a world of evil. The writers of the New Testament spoke of evil as an ever-present aspect of our personalities, our experiences, and the world in which we live. They spoke of evil hearts, evil thoughts, evil consciences, and evil surmising. They spoke of evil reports, evil days, evil work, evil deeds, evil people, evil spirits. Evil woke up beside them every morning, and walked beside them every day. It was inescapable, like our own shadow.

The people for whom Mark wrote this Gospel believed they lived in a world where evil had the upper hand. They felt powerless. They believed they were hostages to fate. Until one day, when God established a beachhead within evil's domain. Until one day, when God sent a raiding party into that world. That raiding party was Jesus. Wherever Jesus was in that world, his authority held sway over evil and chaos. Jesus got a foot in the door and opened it just wide enough for the church to slip inside. And we, the Body of Christ, God's beachhead, have been waging the battle against evil ever since.

If we made a statistical analysis of all of the acts that Jesus performed, we would discover that what he did the most was healing. We would find that his second most common activity was casting out evil spirits. Jesus was an exorcist. In fact, the Gospels report that he cast out evil spirits more often than he taught.

Jesus cast out evil spirits. This is so strange to us. In our scientific and rational Western universe, we deal with demonic spirits only from the safe distance of our theater seats. We regard them as the product of the overactive imaginations of movie screenplay writers, Holy Rollers, and small children at bedtime. But Jesus believed in evil spirits. He was an exorcist.

Jesus came home to Capernaum one day. And some of the Jewish religious authorities—scribes in town from Jerusalem for the day—began to gossip about him. "He has Beelzebul," they claimed, "and by the ruler of the demons, he casts out demons." The scribes accused Jesus of being in league with Satan. He was calling demons out of possessed people as a child would call a friend out to play after supper.

Jesus demanded: "How can Satan cast out Satan? If a kingdom is divided against itself, that kingdom cannot stand. And if Satan has risen up against himself and is divided, he cannot stand, but his end has come."

Forces of Chaos

I don't know what evil spirits are. I will admit that. But I do know this: there are forces that you and I contend with in our selves and our world that make for chaos. There are forces in our lives that do what the evil spirits did in the Gospel accounts. They unmake everything that we do. And consciously or unconsciously we contend with those forces every day of our lives.

Sometimes, evil is easy to identify: prejudice and discrimination. Or pride, greed, and envy. Or drug abuse, theft, and violence. Sometimes, it is not so easy to identify, because they are familiar parts of our everyday lives. We take them for granted and think that we are immune to them.

In our lives, there are impulses and urges and needs that are constantly warring with one another. It is as if each of us were harnessed to four powerful horses. When things are well with us, the horses pull together, in the same direction. But now and then—more often than we care to admit—they pull in different directions. They pull so powerfully that we feel torn apart.

The Four Horses

What are these four horses? Let us call them body, mind, soul, and spirit. Or let us call them family loyalty, personal fulfillment, community obligation, and financial success.

We may not call them demons, but we feel their pull and tug, feel ourselves being torn apart by them. We may not call them demons, but they do to us what demons did to the lives of the possessed people to whom Jesus ministered. They turn the order and structure of our serene lives into utter confusion. They undo God's creation—in our personal lives, in our families, in our communities, and in our world. And most tragically of all, they destroy the oneness of God's family, the Christian Church, setting us against one another. In those times, we feel like that house of which Jesus spoke—that house that is divided against itself, that house that cannot stand.

Body, mind, soul, and spirit. Family loyalty, personal fulfillment, community obligation, and financial success. All tugging away inside us, like four uncontrollable horses.

The pull and tug have always been part of our lives, and they always will. We can try to escape through narcotics, through relationships. We can try to escape through a constant search for possessions, experiences, adventures, power. We can try to escape the pull and tug by handing responsibility for our lives over to a cause, a program, a guru, even a church. We can try to escape by surrendering our souls to despair, deadness, and depression. We can, and at times, we do.

The Unpardonable Sin and a Better Way

But Jesus came to give us a better way. To tell us that our separate lives are part of a larger life, to tell us that the heart of God beats within each of us, even in the midst of our pain and confusion. Jesus came to tell us that all of life is a gift. He came to reawaken in us our lost sense of awe and wonder and mystery. He came to tell us that none of us can find a better way on our own, but together, we can; through him, we can.

Jesus came to warn us against making the greatest mistake of all: to think for one minute that we can get up in the morning and make it through another day by anything other than the grace of God; to assume that we are self-made persons who have no one to thank for what we are and what we have; to attribute the mighty acts of God to our own efforts or to random chance. That is what it means to blaspheme against the Holy Spirit. It is as simple as that. And it is unforgivable.

And when the scribes accused Jesus of casting out demons through the power of Satan, they were blaspheming against the Holy Spirit too. Because it was not by the power of Satan that Jesus cast out demons. It was by the power of God. To witness God's power at work—and see only human power or even Satan's power—that is blasphemy. And it is unforgivable.

Why is blasphemy against the Holy Spirit unforgivable? When we live without God in our lives, we live estranged from the power than can pull together the scattered fragments of our lives, that can reconcile us with one another and with ourselves, that can restore us to wholeness. When we live as though God is not at work in our lives, we lose touch with the very thing that makes us human. We forget who we are, and who we belong to. We cannot see the image of God in ourselves, or in others. We cannot see the texture and pattern of God's life within us. And the call of God—that claim that God makes upon our lives, that claim that gives us vision and direction—falls upon our own deaf ears. That is when the horses tear us apart.

Jesus came to show us how to handle those four horses. In the midst of conflict and tension, he knew who he was. Day by day, moment by moment, he heard the call of God and responded to it. He responded by serving, by loving, by forgiving. He responded with all that he was, with integrity, humor, and compassion. He held nothing back.

The horses did not tear him apart. They traveled side by side with him as he walked his road. And when we join him on that road, when we acknowledge the presence of God in our lives and respond with everything we have to God's call, the forces that have been tearing us apart line up and lead us on life's journey. For I am convinced that when we join Jesus, there is healing for divided families, divided loyalties, and divided lives.

It is around us everywhere—like smoke in a chimney. All around us is the presence, the power, the grace of God.

Amen.

—Elizabeth Chandler Felts and LDS

[1985 words]
[20 minutes]

❦ *Sermon 20*

❦ *Date:* Sunday Between June 19 and June 25 inclusive (if after Trinity Sunday) Pentecost, Year C

Texts:
1 Kings 19:1–4, 8-15a
Psalm 42 and 43
Galatians 3:23–29
Luke 8:26-39

Theme: The best resource for loneliness is the presence in our lives of the still small voice of God.
Subject: Loneliness

❦ *Title:* On Feeling Lonely

A Happy Sermon on Loneliness?

"I saw in the church paper that your sermon topic is loneliness," he said.

"That's right," I said, "Loneliness is a problem we all face."

"Make it a happy sermon!"

A happy sermon on loneliness? That is a challenge beyond a doubt, for loneliness, by itself, is not a happy subject. We are all familiar with it, and probably some of us could offer some dictionary definitions to describe it for us. But specific illustrations are always better than definitions, and here are a few to open the door on the subject.

What Is Loneliness?

What is loneliness? He was eighty-nine and by reason of hard work and a born-into-him vigor, he had outlived all of his friends and most of his family. His past life had been outgoing, and he had poured his interests, his enthusiasm into his church and his community to the betterment of both. But now, he was in a nursing home in a large city. The attendants gave him minimal, but adequate, care. They had heard all his stories, they knew them by heart, and they were too busy to hear them again. His church sent occasional visitors, but they didn't stay long. His only nephew lived in Des Moines, and there was no other family. He sat dispiritedly and described his predicament. He could take the physical ailments, but the uninterrupted silence of his life was too much. His greatest problem was loneliness.

What is loneliness? She was thirty-two, a young mother. Three children, ages two, five, and eight. Her husband was rising in his company, and she was proud of that, but it required frequent trips out of the city, and the family's care rested on her shoulders. She tried to get out some, but the second car was often not running, the baby had earaches all winter, and her life had dissolved into tubs of laundry water and Ivory Soap. "I'm tired of talking to people three feet tall," she said in despair. "I want to be with some people and be alive again." Her basic problem in the midst of an unbelievably hectic schedule was loneliness.

What is loneliness? He was a twenty-six-year-old graduate student, and Keith Miller tells about him. "We were standing in front of a computer in the room next to the regional computer bank at the University of Texas. For a group of graduate students in psychology, we were strangely quiet. The young lady leading us through the center said, "Here's a simple model. You can talk to it—through that typewriter. Ask it anything you want to." The twenty-six-year-old student sat down and typed out, "Howdy—hello!" and in less time than it takes to say this, the machine began to type back, "Well, hello, there. Welcome to the University of Texas!" When it stopped, the young man sat there a few seconds, then turned to us and said rather wistfully. "That's the warmest thing that's been said to me around here in three years." What was his problem? It was loneliness.

It's a problem then not limited to single people living alone—it is found among all of us at one time or another. Thomas Wolfe put it like this: "The whole conviction of my life now rests on the belief that loneliness, far from being a rare and curious phenomenon, is the central and inevitable fact of human experience."

The Cure for Loneliness

Then preach a happy sermon on loneliness! Is there a way to do it? There's only one way I know, and that is to hold up for our attention a man who faced critical loneliness, and lived through it. Or more than lived through it—he overcame it and emerged on the other side of loneliness a stronger man because of it.

His name was Elijah. He lived about eight hundred years before Christ, and we are surprised to find him lonely. Elijah had just lived through one of the most magnificent days of his life. A prophet of God, Elijah had fought against the priests of the pagan god Baal. In a great contest on Mount Carmel, Elijah had singlehandedly taken on 450 priests of Baal, and their sponsoring Queen Jezebel. He emerged completely victorious. It was an overwhelming victory, and strangely, now, we find Elijah, the morning after, lonely and despairing.

But most of us know that we are most vulnerable to loneliness on all the "days after," when the party has ended, the family gone home, the tree taken down and put away. It is the feeling we get on December 26 when we pull a bit of tinsel out from beneath the sofa and are unexpectedly touched by loneliness. The Duke of Wellington once said it with insight: "Nothing, except a battle lost, is half so melancholy as a battle won." Elijah's battle was won, and now his words identify his new enemy: "It is enough, now, Oh, Lord, take away my life—for I, even I alone am left, and they seek my life, to take it away." (1 Kings 19:4, 10)

Like our friend in the nursing home and our young housewife and our graduate student, Elijah was lonely, and there's not much happy about that! But let's follow him through this experience, and watch God lead him through this valley of loneliness. We are going to see God use different strategies to deal with Elijah's loneliness, and all of them are available to us.

People and Loneliness

I. First, the most obvious. "Elijah," God said, "What are you doing here?" Elijah was hiding in a cave on a mountain back in the wilderness. "No wonder you feel that you are left all alone—you are all alone!" God was saying. The fact is that there are settings that produce loneliness, and Elijah had found one. In effect, God was scolding Elijah for complaining of loneliness, on the one hand, while confining himself in isolation in the mountain cave.

Back in the horse and buggy days, farmers delighted in telling the story of the fellow who came driving his wagon down the road. He shouted out to a man sitting on a front porch, "How much longer does this hill last?" The front porch observer shouted out to him, "You aren't on no hill, mister. Your hind wheels are off."

When hind wheels are off, all the world looks uphill, and when hidden away from people, all the world looks lonely, and God saw this quickly. "Here's what I want you to do, Elijah. Go back to Damascus and anoint Hazael king over Syria, and anoint Jehu to be king over Israel, and see if you can get Elisha to follow in your steps as prophet."

People are the most obvious antidote to loneliness, so God took Elijah out of his self-imposed isolation and put him back in circulation again.

This is, no doubt, the best argument for an open, creative marriage. Having someone with whom we can share our deepest feelings helps dispel the loneliness into which we were born. Socrates told an interesting story that pictured this graphically. In the beginning, he said man was a round creature with four legs, four arms, and two faces, looking different ways. He was very strong and very happy and exceeding wise. This worried the gods. So as a measure of safety, Zeus split him right down the middle, to weaken them. Since then, man is only half a creature, and each half goes about with a passionate longing to find the other half and become whole again. This longing for reunion with the lost half of oneself is what we call love.

Obviously, this describes marriage at its best. There's no doubt that there can be loneliness within marriage. And there are other ways than marriage to find companionship. Our work, our hobbies, our volunteer work—all involve people, and God sent Elijah to people to alleviate his loneliness.

But this cannot be the whole answer to our loneliness, nor could it be for Elijah. People have a way of moving on—the crowds dwindle away, people we have grown dependent on are taken from us. In the cycle of life we know, we move from the loneliness of birth, to family, to school and friends, to a spouse, to some people we grow ourselves, our children —and life is at its fullest. But the cycle continues and they begin to go from us.

People of my generation get regular reminders of this just walking down the hall at home and passing bedrooms that were once as noisy as they were cluttered, filled with all the debris of adolescence. But now they are unnaturally quiet and neat, and the house has a hollow sound about it. People help us here. They are aspirin that reduce the fever of loneliness, but they don't eliminate the infection.

Inner Resources and Loneliness

II. So God pointed Elijah to another direction as well. Make sure your inner resources are strong, he said. He reminded Elijah of the basics. Rest up. Eat enough. Then get up. Inasmuch as loneliness is an inner condition, the solution to it must in part be inward.

The Saturday Review recently carried a want ad that made this offer: "Lonely? Like to receive a personalized card on your birthday, or at Christmas, or other holiday? Send $10 and the five occasions you choose to Anne, Box 38, North Star, Michigan, 48049."

Ingenious, isn't it? But deep down we know when the greeting cards are from ourselves, and the telephone calls are recorded messages, and all our mail is marked "Occupant." There has to be some resource, some strength inside us when loneliness comes, and too often there isn't. Too often, when the party is over and the children are gone and the visitors are departed, we reach down into the cistern of our soul, and find it empty. It was in order to put something there that God moved Elijah out of his wilderness cave and up to the mountain top and there showed him the final and best resource against loneliness.

God and Loneliness

III. Listen, as the scripture tells it again. "And behold, the Lord passed by, and a great and strong wind tore the mountains . . ., but the Lord was not in the wind, and after the wind an earthquake, but the Lord was not in the earthquake, and after the earthquake a fire, but the Lord was not in the fire, and after the fire, a still small voice." (1 Kings 19:11–12)

The best resource for loneliness is the presence in our lives of that still small voice of God, one which we can feel and lean on. An old nineteenth-century hymn had a verse that says: "Something within me holds the reins, something within that banishes pain, something within me I cannot explain. All that I know—there is something within." And that is a happy message!

This is the special gift of Christian faith, and quite frankly, one which many of us never do use, the awareness of the constant presence of God. It is distressing how many persons grow up and participate in our churches, yet never feel that presence, or feel it only late in life. "I never did really know Jesus Christ until this special moment," someone says. What do they mean? They mean that they knew the vocabulary of faith, its ritual, its history, its theology, and its duties, and they had done these well. But faith's greatest gift had eluded them, the feeling that through the hardest day and the darkest night they were not alone; that someone was with them.

These are faith's highest promises, "I will not leave you comfortless." Jesus said, "I will come to you." And Jesus' followers felt this. Paul said, "I am convinced that there is nothing in death or life, in the world as it is or the world as it shall become, nothing in all creation that can separate us from the love of God in Jesus Christ our Lord."

This is the Christian's extra gift, and the best resource for loneliness, the knowledge that we are never alone in our lives as his children. And this was the message that sent Elijah back down the mountain and into the fight again. Never alone, Elijah! Never alone, whatever wind and the fire and the earthquake might do, or through it all, in the nursing home at age eighty-nine, or a home in piles of laundry and dishes, or at school with its tensions, never alone, for that still small voice is always there, saying, "Lo, I am with you always, to the close of the age," and if you can feel that, it is, indeed, a happy message about loneliness.

Amen.

—Eugene Brice

[2100 words]
[21 minutes]

Sermon 21

Occasion: Sports Awards Banquet or Any Sunday

Texts:
1 Corinthians 9:24–27
Hebrews 12:1–2
Philippians 3:12–14

Theme: Compete to win both physically and spiritually
Subject: Spiritual development

Title: A Thorn in My Path, third in a series [or Winners in the Race of Life]

Note: This sermon may be used as part of a 3-part series, "Three Thorny Sermons." See sermons 102 and 59. Each sermon may be used independently.

Cathy and her boyfriend Irving, who is a golfing fanatic, are on vacation. They are on the golf course.

Cathy: Here's your ball, Irving! It was over in the weeds!

Irving: AACK! You moved the ball! You're not allowed to move the ball, Cathy!

Cathy: Who cares? We're the only ones out here!

Irving: It's against the rules! You can't break the rules!!

Cathy: You **hate** rules!

Irving: But this is a **SPORT!** It's no fun without rules! It's pointless unless everyone plays by the exact same rules!

As Irving walks away, Cathy follows after, writing in her notebook, "To do after vacation. Get relationships declared a 'sport' and print up rule book for all the men."[1]

---

[1] "Cathy," July 10, 1991.

Sports and Life

Sports are a metaphor for life. They represent life not as it is but as it ought to be. Sports are much like religion in that way.

Religious writer Eugene Peterson is a baseball fan. When he is feeling confused about life, he likes to drive to Memorial Stadium in Baltimore and watch the Orioles play baseball. He reports:

> For a couple of hours I am in a world that is defined by exactly measured lines and precise, geometric patterns. Every motion on the playing field is graceful and poised. Sloppy behavior is not tolerated. Complex physical feats are carried out with immense skill. Errors are instantly detected and their consequences immediately experienced. Rule infractions are punished directly. Unruly conduct is banished. The person who refused to play by the rules is ejected. Outstanding performance is recognized and applauded on the spot. While the game is being played, people of widely divergent temperaments, moral values, religious commitments, and cultural backgrounds agree on a goal and the means for pursuing it. When the game is over, everyone knows who won and who lost. It is a world from which all uncertainty is banished, a world in which everything is clear and obvious. Afterward the entire experience is summarized in the starkly unambiguous vocabulary of numbers, exact to the third decimal point.[2]

Then he goes back to the real world. He comments:

> The world to which I return when the game is over contains all the elements that were visible in the stadium—elegance and sloppiness, grace and unruliness, victory and defeat, diversity and unity, reward and punishment, boundary and risk, indolence and excellence—but with a significant difference: instead of being sharply distinguished they are hopelessly muddled. What is going on at any particular time is almost never exactly clear. None of the lines are precise. The boundaries are not clear. Goals are not agreed upon. Means are in constant dispute. . . . At the end of the day—or the week, or the year—there is no agreement on who has won and who has lost.[3]

Not all sports enthusiasts can tell the difference between sports and reality. Sports have their fans (derived from the word "fanatic"), their true believers, and their addicts. In our area, there are a lot of football addicts.

> I was seated next to one—a lady—at a football game not too long ago. There was an empty seat beside her. "It was my husband's, but he died," she explained. "Oh, I'm sorry," I said. Then as an afterthought I asked, "Isn't there someone else in the family who could use the ticket?" "No," she replied, "They are all at the funeral."[4]

Paul the Sports Fan

Paul was a sports fan. That's right. The Apostle Paul, whose letters or epistles constitute half the books in the New Testament, was an avid sports fan. He was fascinated with the Olympics—and

---

[2] *Run With the Horses* (Downers Grove, IL: Inter-Varsity, 1983), pp. 193–194.

[3] Ibid.

[4] Ibid.

especially with the running events. Images drawn from foot racing turn up again and again in his writings.

For example, in his first letter to the Corinthians, he asks: "Do you not know that in a race all the runners run, but only one gets the prize?" And then he advises his readers, "Run in such a way as to get the prize." (9:24)

Paul's point is straightforward: If you are going to compete in the race of life, run to win. And how does one do that? The answer is not on the playing field but in the training room. In Paul's words,

> *Everyone who competes in the games goes into strict training. They do it to get a crown that will not last; but we do it to get a crown that will last forever. Therefore I do not run like a man running aimlessly; I do not fight like a man beating the air. No, I beat my body and make it my slave so that after I have preached to others, I myself will not be disqualified for the prize. (9:25–27)*

The final victory demands more than determination. It depends on the self-control of the athlete. It requires discipline. Your old coach was telling you the truth after all. Michigan State football coach Duffy Daugherty tells of Dave Kaiser's winning field goal against UCLA.

> The game was in Los Angeles and the field goal gave [us] a 17–14 victory. As Dave Kaiser came back to the bench to meet the roaring enthusiasm of his teammates, I said, "Nice going, Dave, but I noticed you didn't watch the ball after you kicked it. How come?"
>
> Kaiser replied, "You're right coach, I didn't watch the ball. I was watching the referee to see how he would call it. You see, I forgot my contact lenses. They are back at the hotel. I couldn't even see the goal posts!"
>
> I was shocked and at first very angry that Kaiser had not told me about his contact lenses. But after I thought it over I changed my mind entirely. Why shouldn't Kaiser kick without his contact lenses? He was a disciplined kicker and had practiced for long hours. He knew well the angle and the distance to the goal even though he could not see it. The whole process of kicking the ball was programmed into his body and mind by the ongoing discipline of daily practice. In that moment, when the ball went through the goal posts, discipline paid off.[5]

So if you jump into a taxicab and ask the driver, "How do I get to the World Series?" or "How do I get to the Super Bowl?" don't be too surprised if he replies, "Practice! Practice!"

For Paul, physical training is a metaphor, an illustration of a spiritual truth. A total human being is more than just a well-developed physique with an educated mind. A well-rounded person has his or her body and mind under control. And the source of this self-control is a sense of purpose and direction, a spiritual calling, a vocation. Until an athlete has found God's direction for his or her life, the athlete will run a dark, rocky, and thorn-strewn path.

For just as important as those long, grueling hours spent sharpening up your competitive skills is running a straight and intentional course. If you get confused and turned around while fielding the kickoff, you just might return it the wrong way. If you hit a home run but trot to third base, second, and first before going home, your effort will count for nothing. You can be the fleetest

---

[5] *Pastor's Digest*, adapted.

athlete in the world, but if you don't stay on course, it's not likely you'll find your way into the record books—except as a bad example.

If your life isn't together, if you don't know to whom you belong and to whom you are accountable in life, you won't make it past the starting blocks. Until your life is for something, it is dead weight. You are trying to sprint with a bowling ball tied to each track shoe.

Keeping Your Eye on the Goal

A similar image appears in the letter to the Hebrews:

> *since we are surrounded by such a great cloud of witnesses, let us throw off everything that hinders and the sin that so easily entangles, and let us run with perseverance the race marked out for us. Let us fix our eyes on Jesus, the author and perfecter of our faith, who for the joy set before him endured the cross, scorning its shame, and sat down at the right hand of the throne of God. (12:1–2)*

We are on the track waiting for the starter's signal. Everyone who has ever cared for us is sitting in the stands, cheering for us. But we can't start the race until we get rid of the monkeys on our back, until we get rid of our selfishness and arrogance. At the finish line waits the all-time world record holder and judge. If we just keep our eyes on him, we will be all right. If we just run the race as he did, we cannot lose.

Paul makes the same point in his letter to the Philippians:

> *Not that I have already . . . been made perfect, but I press on. . . Forgetting what is behind and straining toward what is ahead, I press on toward the goal to win the prize for which God has called me heavenward in Christ Jesus. (3:12–14)*

You can't run a race looking over your shoulder. And you can't live your life fully if you are bogged down with unfinished business—regrets, grievances, hurt feelings. Get your eyes on the goal. Paul had learned to put first things first, to do what Jesus had required of his followers, before everything else to seek God's dominion and his justice and to let everything else fall into place.

It's like the imaginary conversation between Liz and Gil Gray:

Liz: "Gil, you promised you would be home at 4:00. It's now 8:00."

Gil: "Honey, please listen to me. Poor ol' Roger is in the hospital. He was knocked unconscious by a stray shot on the eighth green."

Liz: "Oh, that's awful."

Gil: "It surely was. For the rest of the game it was hit the ball, drag Roger, hit the ball, drag Roger.

If we are to get anywhere in the event known as life, we have to stop dragging Roger! [Note: Liz, Gil, and Roger are actual members of my congregation. Gil and Roger are avid golfers. Use the names of members of your church who will enjoy the attention.]

Don't Run in Vain

In his letter to the Galatians, Paul tells us that when he first received his life's mission to preach the Gospel among the Gentiles he went in secret to the leaders of the Jerusalem church because he was afraid, in his words, "that I was running or had run my race in vain". (Gal. 2:2)

His point is: Don't run for nothing. If you are going to pour your life into any enthusiasm, get the best advice you can get. If you feel called to be an athlete, get the best mentor you can find. If you are going to live your life in response to God's will for your life, find a church in which you can invest your time and talents. Support a church with a pastor you can respect. Look for a spiritual coach as perceptive as Alabama's Paul (Bear) Bryant, who explained his technique as follows:

> I'm just a plow hand from Arkansas, but I have learned how to hold a team together. How to lift some men up, how to calm down others, until finally they've got one heartbeat together, a team. There's just three things I'd ever say:
> If anything goes bad, I did it.
> If anything goes semigood, then we did it.
> If anything goes real good, then you did it.
> That's all it takes to get people to win football games for you.

The Apostle Paul warns the Galatians:

> *You were running a good race. Who cut in on you and kept you from obeying the truth? (Galatians 5:7)*

In other words, don't let spiritually immature believers distract you. Find a community of like-minded "spiritual athletes" with whom you can train for what really counts. With their help and encouragement, run your race—the race to which God is calling you—not the other guy's.

Running to Win

Finally, in his second letter to Timothy, Paul says:

> *I have finished the race, I have kept the faith. Now there is in store for me the crown of righteousness, which the Lord, the righteous Judge, will award to me on that day. . . . (4:7–8)*

Paul had a profound sense of the one who had called him, the God to whom he had committed his life. Paul knew God not as an abstraction or a vague idea. He knew him as his trainer, teammate, and judge. Paul was sure that his life would carry him across the finish line as a winner. He could almost feel the gold medal on his chest, could see the laurel wreaths being placed on his head, could hear the cheers of those whose opinion really counted.

To put it all together, if you are going to compete in the race of life, run to win. And that means developing your total being—physically, mentally, and spiritually. Know where you are going. Don't run in vain. Join the best team you can find with the best coach. Avoid distractions and run your race until you cross God's finish line.

Amen.

—LDS

[2169 words]
[21 minutes]

Sermon 22

Date: Any Sunday

Text:
Revelations 2:1–7

Theme: We are made to worship God.
Subject: Worship

Title: Made to Worship God

Are the details of life bogging you down? Are you feeling that much of what you do isn't really that important? Maybe sometimes you ask yourself, "What can I do that's truly significant?" Well, the Lord has made you to worship him. It's a great and high calling, and it's yours.

Staying in Tune

A shepherd in Idaho once wrote to Ted Malone, whose morning radio show he liked to listen to. He had a funny request. He wrote, "Would you please play the note 'A' on your broadcast? I'm a sheepherder 'way out here on a ranch, far away from a piano. My violin is all out of tune. If you'd be willing to strike an 'A,' I could get this thing back in tune."

You and I sometimes get out of tune, in a way we get caught up in many things. Good things. But not central. We need to have an "A" note struck so we can get back in harmony again.

Your basic business is to worship God. That's the note "A," my friend! He must be the basis of everything. Your humble bowing in acknowledgment of the Lord and worship of Him must be the most basic, most important function of your life.

God has made you with resources of energy, feelings, skills, intelligence, and emotions. If you don't spend them on God, you'll spend them on yourself. It really is "either, or." You'll either honor or worship the Lord, laying all you are and have before Him, or you'll do your thing and become self-centered and self-destructive—and that would be a tragedy. You were made for better. Learn to worship the Lord. Love Him wholeheartedly! Fulfill your highest and most noble purpose—worship the Lord.

The Apostle John spent the last years of his life as a prisoner in exile on the island of Patmos. It wasn't exactly what he had planned for his life. But in that situation God gave John visions of God's glory and the Lord's future triumph. He saw Angels and men worshiping the Lord, and he, too, fell down to worship Him.

Your life may not have turned out as you had hoped. You may be feeling as isolated or as unfulfilled right now as John on that island! But whatever your circumstances, like John, you, too, can get caught up in the awe of His presence and worship God. He's available. He's there. And you can choose to be unhappy and frustrated, or you can choose to worship and enjoy Him.

Rick Floyd is a Wycliffe missionary to the Quechua (Ket′ chu-a) Indians in Peru. He's working on translating the Bible into their language. A few months ago he had to have sudden surgery and was stuck in bed for weeks. Then, just as he was starting to recover, he came down with hepatitis. More weeks flat on his back, unable to work. And during those long weeks, Rick wrote home that he'd discovered through his hard time that the purpose of his life isn't work, it's worship! It's acknowledging and loving God! He could do those things even on his sickbed, and it's any person's primary function. Right now, where you are, worship God.

You were made to worship God. That's your purpose. It's the basic business of your life. Serving God, knowing the Bible, witnessing—those things are all important, but loving and worshiping the Lord has got to be first and most of all.

Do you remember the awe and thrill you felt when you were a brand-new Christian? God Himself was interested in you! The one who made the universe! You felt almost childlike.

A little child looks up to his father. He thinks he's just about perfect, and he knows everything. But as the kid grows up he loses his awe! "Familiarity breeds contempt," they say. Now, human fathers aren't perfect, but our Heavenly Father is, and yet we seem to lose our awe of Him. Jesus tells us to be like children.

The old Wesley hymn describes being "lost in wonder love and praise." Does that describe you? When you think about the Lord, is it with reverence and awe? That's the basis of worship. If God has become ordinary and dull to you, your worship won't really be worship!

Have you lost your first love? Revelation 2:5 says, "Repent, and do the things you did at first." God is too great for you to settle for a correct but dull relationship to Him. Repent, and tell the Lord He's wonderful. Learn again to love Him wholeheartedly and with reverence.

Why Worship Is Not Easy

Worshiping the Lord is right, but it's not easy. Self-centeredness is our natural bent, and it's the enemy of worship. Preoccupation with self is a terrible disease! It grows in us; it wants to take over. Even when we think we're worshiping the Lord we can get lured again into occupation with self. Do you find yourself talking about what God does for you, or what worship was like for you? That's too much you. Ask God to heal you of self-absorption. You need to get away from you and look at Him. Pray for hunger for Christ Himself, not just hunger for worship but hunger for God.

Then seek Him. Spend time in the Bible searching out God's character, His perfection, His beauty. Get to know Him. Well—and in freshness day by day.

The Lord of Glory is too big to be described in ordinary terms. He's "WOW" and "incredible" beyond your wildest imaginings. At the very least, you have to shut your mouth and bow in humility and worship.

Not knowing Him well enough is dangerous. Not understanding Him can make you irreverent, even cocky. You think of Him as "the Man upstairs," someone to help you with your plans, to pull out of your pocket when you need Him. Oh no! Don't ever, ever diminish the Lord God! He is full of authority and wisdom and perception. Worship Him!

Worship and Service

We call Sunday morning—sometimes Saturday morning—a worship service. That's the right name for it because that's what it's supposed to be—God's people coming from a week of seeking to exalt the Lord individually, to exalt Him as a body together—to lift Him up in a unified hallelujah.

But if you're not worshiping the Lord Monday through Saturday, you won't know what to do Sunday. Too many Christians see Sunday morning as a gas station. "Fill 'er up, Jesus!" But Christ isn't there to service them. He doesn't give rubdowns. He's not for water between boxing rounds. Church isn't a pit stop. It's not for you at all; it's for God!

When you come to worship, seek to meet His needs. Ask Him, "What do you want, Lord? How can I please you?" Lay aside your own interests; be concerned for God's interest. "He must increase; you must decrease." Minister to the Lord. Never mind what others around you are doing; you worship God.

Come to church early. Friends can wait till afterward. You get to God. Submit and respond to the Lord in the music, the prayers, the preaching—be saying, "Lord, this is all for you. You're God. You're great. I'm your servant, here to love and listen and obey." That's worship.

That's what life is all about. If you go through your life with that attitude, your life will be vital and fresh, and joyful and useful. Give yourself to worship the Lord.

Amen.

—Ray Ortlund[1]

[1255 words]
[12 minutes]

Sermon 23

Date: Epiphany Sunday, Any Year

Texts:
Isaiah 60:1–6
Psalm 72:1-7, 10–14
Ephesians 3:1–12
Matthew 2:1–12

Theme: The story of the Magi is really a tale of two kings: King Herod and King Jesus. Which king do we seek?
Subject: Worship

Title: A Tale of Two Kings

They came in search of a king. We don't know their names, or how many of them there were, or exactly where they came from.

They did not come to the manger. Jesus and his family were long since gone. Mary and Joseph had a house now. Also long gone were the celestial chorus, the shepherds, the crowds, and the gawkers. Yes, it was like the aftermath of any Christmas. The excitement dies down, the relatives go home, and life goes on.

They came in search of a king. Later tradition would call them the Three Kings, would give them names like Balthazar, Gaspar, and Melchior. Over the centuries, pious imagination would even provide distinctive personalities, life histories, and places of burial. Ten centuries after the story of the visitors was first told, relics of the Three Kings would reach Cologne.

But Matthew never said that there were three visitors or that they were kings or that they had arrived at the manger as they do in present-day Nativity pageants. His story is not about three kings at all. It is about two—King Herod and King Jesus.

---

[1] *Haven of Rest,* broadcast, November 14, 1990, used with permission.

King Herod the Great

The first king was known as "Herod the Great." He restored much of the splendor of former times. He conquered Idumea, Samaria, Galilee, and Jerusalem. He allied himself with the Romans, building the Mediterranean port of Caesarea, an elegant colonnaded city, "Roman in law, Greek in culture." He rebuilt Samaria and renamed it "Sebaste" in honor of Augustus Caesar, whose Greek name was Sebastos.

Throughout his realms, he constructed stadiums, theaters, amphitheaters, and temples to the gods of the Hellenistic world. For his Jewish subjects, he rebuilt the Temple at Jerusalem, the world center of their faith and practice. But no matter what he did for them, they despised him because he was not one of them. He was an Edomite, a descendent of Esau, the brother of Jacob and, thus, the product of a race against whom the Hebrews had warred for centuries.

Herod ruled with an iron hand. His fear of real or imagined threats led him to murder Mariamne, the most beloved of his ten wives as well as Mariamne's brother, her grandfather, and some of his own children.

Through brilliance, boldness, diplomacy, and ruthlessness, he held on to power for more than forty years. His reign was almost at an end when the party of Babylonian astrologers came to town. These stargazers were an incredibly naive bunch to ask Herod the address of the one born "king of the Jews." Herod was a dying man who knew his days were numbered. But as far as Herod was concerned, the Jews had all the kings they needed.

Who Rules Today?

And so do we. No single despot rules us. We have kings and queens galore. We have King I-Want-What-I-Want-When-I-Want-It and Queen My-Career-Comes-First, King I-Just-Want-to-Be-Like-Everybody-Else and Queen If-You-Promise-to-Like-Me-I-Will-Do-Whatever-You-Want. There is King Easy-Answers and Queen Who-Says-Money-Can't-Buy-Happiness? We are governed by false expectations, prejudices, advertising, the media, unexamined assumptions, carelessness, and a host of other petty monarchs.

They came in search of a king. Herod knew a threat when he heard one. And he knew how to deal with it. The petty monarchs of today are just as easily threatened and every bit as murderous. They kill ability, creativity, compassion. Above all, they kill compassion. And once compassion is gone, they then do exactly what Herod did. They kill our children. Literally and figuratively, they kill our children.

Looking for a King

They came in search of a king. There was only room for one king then and only room for one now. There are the Herods of today, who would give us places of entertainment and power over the helpless and even houses of worship in exchange for our lives. And there is the child king of Bethlehem. We find him today as the Magi found him then—in the midst of dependence, poverty, vulnerability, and powerlessness. In the midst of *his* dependence, poverty, vulnerability, and powerlessness. In the midst of the dependence, poverty, vulnerability, and powerlessness *of others*. In the midst of *our own* dependence, poverty, vulnerability, and powerlessness.

We have seen his star. Seen it in our quiet moments, in our yearnings for something real, in our dreams of a better world, in our awareness that we are called to a higher purpose, in our hunger for community, in our thirst for peace, in our commitment to justice.

They came in search of a king. And we come with them. For we have seen his star and come to worship him.

Amen.

—LDS

[800 words]
[8 minutes]

❦ *Sermon 24*

❦ *Occasion:* Address to a Youth Group

Texts:
Ecclesiastes 12:1
Matthew 19:20–24

Theme: Advice to the young: remember your Creator now.
Subject: Youth

❦ *Title:* First Things First

"Remember also your Creator in the days of your youth, before the evil days come, and the years draw nigh, when you will say, 'I have no pleasure in them' . . . " (Ecclesiastes 12:1).

These words from the ancient book of wisdom known to readers of the Bible as Ecclesiastes were written by one who seemingly had soured on life, who had seen it all, had it all, and found that nothing truly satisfied him. However, he had not become a sour, squeezed out, lifeless recluse. Rather he had gained perspective. He had learned, at long last, to put first things first, and to put his life in order.

And he came to realize that the time to set things in proper perspective is not when one has sown his or her wild oats, not when one has earned respect and position in the community, not when one has a beautiful home, a loving spouse and perfect children, not when one is too old to worry about anything but eternity. The time to put first things first is at the beginning of one's life.

How to Find Eternal Life

In the Gospel according to Matthew (19:20–24), we read of a young person who came to Jesus and asked "What good deed must I do to have eternal life?"

"Keep the Commandments," Jesus replied.

"This I have done, but something seems to be missing. There is this empty space in my life and I don't know what to fill it with. Can you help me? Can you tell me what I need?" the youth asked.

Jesus told him: "If you would be perfect, go, sell what you possess and give it to the poor, and you will have treasure in heaven; and come, follow me." In other words, said Jesus, "Don't let the things you own own you." But the young man could not deal with this advice. As Matthew tells us: when he heard this, "he went away sorrowful; for he had great possessions."

Then Jesus instructed his disciples, " it is easier for a camel to go through the eye of a needle than for a rich man to enter the kingdom of God."

It is easy for you to dodge the significance of what Jesus was teaching. After all, most of you are from modest, middle-class families. You may have an automobile, a stereo, a color TV, and a closet full of clothes, but you scarcely think of yourselves as rich. And yet compared to most of the planet's population, you are well housed, well fed, and well dressed and are surrounded with luxuries. And you expect even more—if you work hard enough, go to the right school, find the right job, marry the right person, or are just plain lucky.

Of course, you are nobody's dummies. You know that nothing is guaranteed. You have looked around at the lives of your parents, their friends and business associates. You read the newspapers and watch the TV news and the "movies of the week." You know the score. You know that life is not always easy, not always fair—that bad things happen to even the best of people.

You also know that people can get lost in the pursuit of what they want and forget who they are and what really counts. You already have seen the lives of some of our friends and acquaintances get terribly screwed up by drugs. Perhaps some of you may have lost friends to automobile accidents or suicide.

The plain fact is that people get lost—whether they are sixteen or thirty or sixty. They lose their way. They forget who they are and to whom they belong and to whom they are responsible. They make getting things more important than loving and caring for one another. They pay no attention to what it costs to ignore the needs of others, of their own families, of their community or of their world. They gain dollars and toys and honors and lose their own souls in the process.

Putting First Things First

Remember your Creator *now*, says the author of Ecclesiastes. Put first things first. Open your eyes to the presence of God in your life. Welcome the friendship of the living Christ who is always with you. Get close to those who support what you value and are looking for what really counts in life. Decide today what your priorities are, what is important, what makes your life special and worth living. Don't just passively let things happen, enter into partnership with God to make them happen.

I am not saying that your teenage years are not for fun, that you have to be a "gloomy Gus" or a "serious Sarah" every minute of every day. Jesus knew how to have a good time with his friends. The self-righteous types of his day never could understand that. He wanted to be wherever life is lived, to share it, to enhance it, to take away the pain and deepen the joy. But he never forgot who he was, to whom he belonged or where his life was going. He kept his eye on his goal, on his calling, on his sense of purpose. And he expects the same of each of us.

"Give up the things that own you," said Jesus to the rich young man, "and concentrate instead on the satisfactions that last forever." Or to paraphrase what he said at another time, to another audience, "Don't be so uptight about what to wear or what to eat. Your heavenly Father knows what you need. Seek first God's rule and God's justice and everything else will fall into place." (Matthew 6:31-33)

Amen.

—LDS

[940 words]
[9 minutes]

Sermon 25

Date: Sunday Between July 31 and August 6 inclusive Pentecost, Year C

Texts:
Colossians 3:1–11
Luke 12:13–21

or Sunday Between October 16 and October 22 inclusive Pentecost, Year A

Texts:
1 Thessalonians 1:1–10
Matthew 22:15–22

Theme: Greed is good and healthy. The trick is learning to be greedy for the right things.
Subject: Greed

Title: The Gospel of Greed

TIP

> The often-quoted words from the movie *Wall Street* provided a point of departure and helped the listeners to remember what the preacher had to say.
> Also this quotation was used because the congregation is made up of "fast-track," work-ethic oriented individuals.
> Give thought to the characteristics, needs, and situations of your hearers. Choose illustrations from the common language of cultural expressions and clichés.

"Greed is good"—or at least it seems so. In 1968, only 39 out of every 100 college freshmen deemed affluence an essential goal. Money was considered secondary to developing "a meaningful philosophy of life." Today, only two decades later, more than three-quarters of first-year college students think that getting rich is what life is all about. Commenting on a survey by the American Council of Education of more than 200,000 students, *U.S. News & World Report* observes: "the idea of college as a place to gain wisdom seems distinctly passé. Most students now say that a key reason they entered college was to make more money, and a quarter name business as their chosen field."[1]

Almost one hundred years ago, American philosopher Charles Sanders Peirce, one of the most brilliant minds ever produced in this country, declared:

> The gospel of Christ says that progress comes from every individual merging his individuality in sympathy with his neighbors. On the other side, the conviction of the

[1] *U.S. News & World Report,* January 25, 1988, p. 10.

> nineteenth century is that progress takes place in virtue of every individual's striving for himself with all his might and trampling his neighbor underfoot whenever he gets a chance to do so. This may accurately be called the Gospel of Greed.[2]

Peirce's words seem as appropriate today as they did then.

Nearly two thousand years ago, the Apostle Paul instructed the church at Colossae:

> *Put to death . . . whatever belongs to your earthly nature: sexual immorality, impurity, lust, evil desires and greed, which is idolatry. Because of these, the wrath of God is coming. (Colossians 3:5–6)*

And Jesus taught:

> *Watch out! Be on your guard against all kinds of greed; a man's life does not consist in the abundance of his possessions. (Luke 12:15)*

"Greed Is Good"

What would happen if we took Paul and Jesus seriously? Would the wheels of commerce grind to a halt? Would we return to lives of simplicity—lives devoid of such modern conveniences as the automobile, the telephone, television, and the microwave oven? In our own day, we are counseled by the fictional exemplar of the Gospel of Greed, Gordon Gekko, as follows:

> The point is, ladies and gentlemen, greed is good. Greed works. Greed in all its forms, greed for life, money, love, knowledge, has marked the upward surge of mankind.

Gekko's real-life counterpart, financier Ivan Boesky, had the following advice for a 1985 graduation of business students at the University of California.

> Greed is all right, by the way. I want you to know that. I think greed is healthy. You can be greedy and still feel good about yourself.[3]

I have often heard it said that the Bible teaches that money is the root of all evil. As we all know, that is a misquotation. The King James text of 1 Timothy 6:10 actually says: "the love of money is the root of all evil." I like the New International Version's rendering: "the love of money is a root of all kinds of evil."

And what I would add is that the drive for money, the lust to acquire, is also the root of all kinds of good.

One of the most difficult aspects of counseling individuals suffering from depression is to get them to lust after anything at all. Ask a depressed person what he or she wants, and the answer is likely to be, "I don't know." It is as though he or she has made a decision to be undecided. I have a far greater problem getting my clients to indulge their evil impulses than to get my greedy clients to redirect their lust for money and things.

---

[2] Cited by Konstantin Kolenda, "The Gospel of Greed," *The Humanist*, September/October 1985, p. 41.

[3] Cited by Loudon Wainright, "Moola, Moola," *Life*, February 1988, p. 17.

When Greed Is Idolatry

Jesus and Paul make a theological issue of greed. Greed is arrogant presumption, says Jesus. The greedy man of his parable thought that he had all his bases covered. He had deluded himself into thinking that the means are the end. Jesus reminds us that no matter what we want, no matter what we get in life, there is no security in things. None of us really knows what he or she needs or what will happen whether or not we get it. As Christians, "We know not what the future holds but we know who holds the future."

According to Paul and to Jesus, greed is idolatry, greed is failure to put first things first. If they were alive today, they would surely condemn our preoccupation with status, with the tokens and symbols of prosperity, with what William James derided as "our national disease . . ., the worship of the bitch-goddess SUCCESS."[4]

What they are both saying is simple—let God be God; don't count on any finite, limited, ephemeral thing to provide you with satisfaction or fulfillment.

Greed is idolatry. "Idolatry" seems a strong word. Let's consider its background for a moment. Prior to the exile, the Hebrews had worshiped a jealous god, one who would brook no competition. The gods of the heathen were very real to the children of Israel and to their pagan neighbors. They seemed powerful and seductive. During and after the exile, the emphasis shifted. The gods of the Gentiles are derided as inanimate things of stone and wood with no power to save those who turned to them.

I find both teachings instructive. What we worship becomes real. If we are preoccupied with getting and having, then getting and having control us. We end up being gotten and had, and we forget what is really central to our lives. But ultimately we find ourselves on a treadmill. The more we have, the more we think we need. The more we get, the less we feel ourselves fulfilled. No, I am not saying that rich people are miserable people. What I am saying is that those whose lives have no center, who belong to no one but themselves, who want what they want simply because they want it, are poor indeed.

Paul was particularly radical on the subject. He thought that the world was coming to an end within his lifetime and that anything that distracted Christians from the proclamation of the Good News should be shunned. And to the extent to which one devalues the present age, concern for material things is idolatry. But if we regard the world as inevitably being guided by God toward its eventual redemption, and we think of our lives as individuals and as a community as God's beachhead in the retaking of the world, then wealth becomes a weapon in the struggle.

Money is simply congealed energy, a means of exchanging one form of energy for another. Money is power, and like all expressions of power, it is neither good nor evil. When viewed as an end in itself, as something to be sought for its own sake, it is seductive and destructive—just like the gods of Israel's pagan neighbors. But it is also a power for good.

Good and Evil Impulses

Nothing is good or evil in itself but good or evil only with respect to the purpose and intention of one's life. Rabbinic theology speaks of conflicting human *yetzerim* or impulses: *ha-yetzer-ha-ra* (the evil impulse) and *ha-yetzer-ha-tov* (the good impulse). Were it not for the acquisitive, erotic *yetzer-ha-ra,* human beings would never build homes, marry, beget children, or engage in business. Thus, even the so-called "evil impulse" may become the instrument of good. However, when the

---

[4] *The Philosophy of William James,* selected by Horace M. Kallen (New York: Modern Library, 1953), p. 305.

yetzer-ha-ra remains without direction or purpose, it becomes the source of all the griefs that flesh is heir to—war, inhumanity, injustice, exploitation, and cruelty.

It is our task as human beings not to extirpate our inclination toward evil but to direct it to the actualization of good. Evil is yielding to impulse, good is giving it direction. Openness to others, directing greed and all other impulses as aspects of one's vocation, calling, or direction in life is ultimately good, while giving in to the impulse of the moment, being controlled rather than taking control, is evil.

Good is that which a human being does with the wholeness of one's being, evil that which concerns only a part or segment of one's total experience. Goodness is not achieved by the overcoming or suppression of some possibilities by others. Virtue is not the denial of given impulses, talents, and proclivities. Virtue is the actualization of whatever enables a person to attain his or her distinct selfhood.

It is probably impossible to define human fulfillment, but, says social psychologist Kenneth Keniston, "some of its results can be defined." "A whole man or woman," he declares, "has the capacity for zest, exuberance, and passion." The deepest drives of such persons are the sources of their strength but not the dictators of their action. "We recognize whole men and women," Keniston concludes, "because their wholeness is manifest in their lives: what they do is 'of a piece.'"[5] In other words, they are greedy for life, but their lives are for something.

Gordon Gekko and Ivan Boesky are right—as far as they go. Greed is good. Greed is healthy. You can be greedy and still feel good about yourself. The trick is learning to be greedy for the right things. Lust after life, after love, after relatedness, after wholeness, after the opportunity to make a difference in the lives of others. Be greedy for vitality, intimacy, and creativity. Lust after knowledge, after personal growth, after the means of being generous and caring to others. Acquire for yourself all the memories you can of hours spent with those who need you and whom you need. Store up your memories of loving and being loved like wheat in a granary. I think that is what Jesus had in mind when he told his audience the story about the rich fool who forgot to put first things first. You can choose not to make his mistake. You can choose to become rich in the eyes of God. With jest and passion, you can each day lustily embrace the opportunities for love and service, the chance to find self-fulfillment, the freedom to live in the Spirit.

Amen.

—LDS

[1700 words]
[17 minutes]

❦ *Sermon 26*

❦ *Date:* Third Sunday of Easter, Year B

Texts:
Acts 3:12–19
Psalm 4
1 John 3:1–7
Luke 24:35–48

---

[5] Keniston, Kenneth, *The Uncommitted* (New York: Harcourt, Brace & World, 1965), pp. 441–442.

Theme: Witnessing grows from the recognition that one's life is a miracle. Witnessing is sharing the sense of awe and wonder.
Subject: Witnessing

❦ *Title:* God's Eye-Witness News Team

We are all witnesses—whether we volunteer for the job or not. There are various styles of witnessing:

1. The witness of religious truth—telling others what God wants them to know
2. The witness of social conscience—telling others what God wants them to do
3. The witness of integrity—being what God wants you (singular and plural) to be, which includes what you know and do

The Witness of Integrity

As an example of the witness of integrity, I think of two friends and exemplars from my late teens, Miss T. and Charles. Miss T. was my supervisor at Moody Press in Chicago. She encouraged me to return to college and even offered to lend me the money for tuition. Charles, an Old Testament scholar, arranged a scholarship for me at Temple University in Philadelphia.

They were both dedicated Christians. They didn't just believe, they believed in me! And that made all the difference. They didn't just teach, they modeled!

Phil Donahue, in his autobiography, tells of the time he was starting out as a young television reporter. He was sent to cover a mine disaster. It was late at night. Snow was on the ground. It was freezing cold. The rescue team was down in the mine shaft. The worried relatives and friends were gathered at the opening of the mine, waiting anxiously for some word of hope.

Someone began to sing, "What a Friend We Have in Jesus." Other people joined in singing, "all our sins and grief to bear." Still more voices joined in, "What a privilege to carry everything to God in prayer."

Then it was quiet. A minister stepped out of the crowd and said, "Let us pray . . .". It was a brief but very moving prayer. Donahue said it was such a moving scene that he got goose bumps. The only problem was that it was so cold that the television camera froze up, couldn't use it. Donahue held the camera against his body, and got it functioning. He went to the minister, asked him to repeat the prayer.

The minister said, "No."

Donahue said, "I'm a TV reporter. I represent 260 stations. Millions of people will be able to see you and to hear your beautiful prayer."

The minister said, "No."

Donahue said, "Perhaps you don't understand. I'm not representing some local TV station. I'm with CBS. The whole nation will be able to see this."

The old country preacher said, "No," and walked away.

Donahue was dumbfounded and furious. He couldn't understand it. But about a year later he said it hit him. He realized that he had witnessed something called "integrity." He wrote: "The man wouldn't showbiz for Jesus. He wouldn't sell his soul for TV, not even for national TV, not even . . . praise God . . . for CBS."

That was the witness of integrity.

Letting God Show Through

As Gandhi taught, "The rose does not propagate its perfume. It just is." The story is told of an Easterner who walked into a Western saloon and was amazed to see a dog sitting at a table playing poker with three men. He asked, "Can that dog really play cards?" One of the men answered, "Yeah, but he ain't much of a player. Whenever he gets a good hand he wags his tail."[1]

Don't hide your feelings. Witnessing grows from the recognition that one's life is a miracle. Share the awe. Don't be afraid to wag your tail!

One Sunday on their way home from church, a little girl turned to her mother and said, "Mommy, the preacher's sermon this morning confused me." The mother said, "Oh, why is that?"

The little girl replied, "Well, he said that God is bigger than we are. Is that true?"

The mother replied, "Yes, that's true, honey."

"And he also said that God lives in us? Is that true, Mommy?"

Again the mother replied, "Yes."

"Well," said the little girl, "If God is bigger than us and he lives in us, wouldn't He show through?"[2]

Scientists have learned that the nucleus of most snowflakes is a tiny piece of snow from another snowflake. It takes snow to make snow. Likewise, it takes faith to make faith. You have to have it to share it. It takes love to make love. It takes responsible responsiveness to build a community of the faithful. Jesus calls us to fellowship. We respond by becoming God's Eye-Witness News Team.

The power of God's Spirit is here and now—in our midst and in our lives. And we are his witnesses.

Amen.

—LDS

[740 words]
[7 minutes]

❦ *Sermon 27*

❦ *Date:* Sunday Between June 19 and 25 inclusive (if after Trinity Sunday), Year A

Text:
Matthew 10:24-39

Theme: The proclamation of God's Word belongs to the whole people of God, who are sent into the world.
Subject: Proclamation

❦ *Title:* Words We Tremble to Say Aloud

The Gospel lesson you have just heard is the one assigned for next Sunday by the Common Lectionary. It's not one I would have chosen because it's too cryptic, too ominous. The whole tenth chapter of Matthew sounds the same way. Jesus is giving the disciples instructions for their

---

[1] *Parables, Etc.*, October 1984, 4.8.

[2] *Parables, Etc.*, September 1986.

first missionary journey without him. Before he sends them out, he tells them the truth: They'll be persecuted wherever they go. They'll be flogged and arrested and chased from town to town. They may even be put to death. But he tells them they are not to fear those who kill the body. Better they should fear the death of their souls, which cannot happen as long as they claim and proclaim the God who has claimed them.

For the church in Matthew's day, it was a comforting word. They were living the kind of life Jesus described. They were being flogged, arrested, and chased from town to town. Hearing the accuracy of Christ's predictions was their assurance that he knew them well. He not only knew what would happen to them, but because he had gone before them, he also knew how it would turn out in the end. "Have no fear." That is what they heard him say to them. "Have no fear. Fear not. Do not fear."

Where Is Persecution Today?

Jesus says the same thing to us today, but it sounds so foreign, so antique. There are places in the world where people are persecuted for proclaiming their faith in Christ. For most of us, religious persecution is something happening somewhere to someone, but not in our communities.

My most recent persecutor was a young man in my congregation who insisted we vote on whether to use the service of Morning Prayer or Holy Communion on Sunday mornings. I also have had some trouble with a Bible salesman. Beyond those two, my missionary is relatively free from persecution. No one stands up and storms out of the church during my sermons or writes me threatening letters on Monday mornings. Most people shake my hand at the door and say, "Thanks, I liked what you said." Sometimes I want to tell them they weren't supposed to like it. They were supposed to be moved, heartbroken, challenged, changed. But I don't say any of that; I say, "Good, I'm glad you liked it. I'll see you next week."

Even the church doesn't come in for much persecution these days, at least not where I live. In the South, going to church is what well-connected people do. They go to church to find mates. They go to church to socialize their children, to make business contacts, to see and be seen. Many of them even go to church to worship God. They read their Bibles, pray, and staff the night shelter. They take meals to shut-ins. They spend a lot of time in and around the church.

What they hear at church makes sense to them. It's a word they don't hear many other places in their lives, and they are grateful to hear it said aloud. They would like to speak it themselves, but most of them don't know how. When they think about trying it out at work or at home, they get self-conscious. What would people think? What would people say?

The Moat Around the Church

It's almost as if there's a moat around the church, separating it from the world. Everyone's welcome to come inside, sing the old songs, and hear the old stories. Everyone is welcome to seek the presence of the living God. In the church, ordinary rules are suspended for a time. People are free to say what they believe and use language that would sound strange if it were spoken anywhere else. Here they confess their sins, praise God, and ask for the guidance of the Holy Spirit.

When the service ends, the drawbridge goes up, and there's another week to wait until it comes back down again. Everyone knows that the words we use on Sunday morning are not appropriate on Monday. Words that sounded just right in the bosom of the community sound strange, stark, and a little assertive when spoken on the street. We utter them, and we feel exposed.

We started something we don't know how to finish. The words want a response, and almost no one is responding.

On the way here yesterday, I passed an ordinary-looking man. He leaned against the wall right where people get on the train to go to the airport concourses. He wore an old green suit and a brown hat. He looked sad to me—sad and tired. Maybe I thought that because of the wooden cane leaning on the wall beside him. Maybe it was the sign around his neck that read, "'Everyone who calls on the name of the Lord will be saved.' Romans 10–13"

He didn't look the kind of a man who would wear a sign. He looked like someone's grandfather who should be sitting on a bench outside a filling station, whittling a stick or patting an old dog. The big sign covered the top half of his body. I wondered if he had started out with a smaller sign and worked his way up in the hopes that a bigger sign would get him better results. He still wasn't having much luck. Hundreds of people walked past him as if he weren't even there. It didn't seem to bother him much. Maybe he was used to it. I smiled at him when I got on the train, and he smiled back at me—as shyly and sweetly as a boy—like we shared a secret no one else know.

"When I tell you in the dark, speak in the daylight; what is whispered in your ear, proclaim from the roofs."

The Danger of Being Ignored

Persecution is not the problem where most of us live. The odds are much greater that we will be ignored. People walk past without acknowledging we exist. Every now and then one of us gets invited to pray at a baccalaureate, a basketball game, or a Rotary Club. In most cases we're happy to oblige. We stand there awkwardly in our dark suits and good shoes asking God's blessing on the team, the school, the business community. If you have done that thing very often, you know it goes downhill from there. When your prayer is over, no one knows what to do with you. The people assigned to sit with you strain to find suitable conversation, usually landing on their fond memories of the church they attended as a child.

A little persecution might liven things up. That's what I think when I'm being small talked to death, when I'm spending my days shifting piles of religious trivia from one place on my desk to another, or when I watch the church loitering outside the corridors of power in this society. A little persecution might do us some good.

The church we know and love today is no less marginal than Matthew's church. It's just marginal for a different reason. If the early church was attacked by the empire for being a threat, then I fear that we are shunned for being a bore, being trite, being predictable, holding our tongues, and staying in our places.

Even when we've got a good thing going—God is in our midst and we know it—we're guilty of staying on our own side of the moat keeping the good news to ourselves. We don't know how to share it without sounding offensive, so we end up whispering in thc dark what has been given to us to utter in the light.

After a particularly comfortable Sunday morning service, I begin to worry that the persecution of a church is the measure of its faithfulness. Is a preacher who sends no one storming out of the room no preacher at all?

Jesus did not send his twelve out to draw fire. He didn't send them out with instructions to rile people up and aggravate the authorities whenever they could. He knew that would happen. He knew his servants would rate no better treatment than their master; that worried him. He went through great pain to encourage them, to feed their faith, to stoke their courage. But he did not send them out to be persecuted. He sent them out to proclaim God's Word—a different matter altogether.

The Power of God's Word

From the beginning of time, the speaking of God's Word has been an incredible act of power. "God said, 'Let there be light,' and there was light." Moses delivered the law to Israel, and Torah became the covenant of their life together. John the Baptist cried in the wilderness saying, "Prepare the way of the Lord," and the way was prepared. His very words paved the desert where Jesus would walk.

Sometimes the power of the Word is not so evident. Jeremiah was a laughingstock, Hosea a cuckold, and Ezekiel an exile—which may be God's way of telling us that no one can judge the efficacy of God's Word by the results. God is in charge of the results. It's enough for us to proclaim the Word and to believe that in doing so we change the world whether the world knows it or not—whether we know it or not—simply by standing and speaking the words that have been given to us, words of love and challenge, words of judgment and grace, words of truth and such terrible clarity that sometimes we tremble to say them out loud.

You don't need a grand pulpit; any old housetop will do. Even the sun room will do at the nursing home, where you stand by the piano surrounded by wheelchairs full of old people. Some of those old people are dozing, some whimpering, and less than half of them are aware you are there. Say "Resurrection!" in their presence. Say "Life everlasting!" Say "Remember!" Just let those words loose in the room; just utter them in the light, and trust them to do their work.

Speak to a support group for people with AIDS. Worship with them, laying hands on their heads and praying for their healing. Say "Mercy!" to them. Say "Comfort!" Say "Beloved children of God!" Just let those words loose in the room; just utter them and trust in their power to make people whole.

Let something you care about lead you to the steps of city hall, where you stand staring into television cameras, wondering what in the world you have gotten yourself into. Say "Justice," "Peace," "The righteousness of God!" Never mind what other people say. Never mind that they walk past you without reading your sign or put you in the back of the paddy wagon and take you away. God is in charge of the results. Wherever you are and whatever happens to you, just speak the word that has been given to you to say, whatever it may be.

Never forget that the very act of speaking sets God's Word into motion. Your own willingness to utter it out loud is the best proof that it's an active Word as true and lively now as it was when it separated light from darkness and filled the earth with living things. Dare to create a new world with God's Words. Give the people who listen to you new images of a world full of new people.

Be careful of the power you have been given. Treat it as carefully as a stick of dynamite, and use it with as much respect. Learn all that you can about the Word you proclaim. Study it. Argue with it. Fear it. Love it. Live it. Then let it go; set it fee.

Utter the Word in the light, and proclaim it upon the housetops, understanding that when you do, you show other people how, people who need and want to know how. Every time you step into the pulpit you show them how it is done. Week after week, you are their best bet at learning how to speak the language of faith, so they can speak it themselves.

Where did we ever get the idea that preaching the Word of God is our job alone? The proclamation of God's Word belongs to the whole people of God, who are sent into the world. Some places we will never go—hospitals, schools, offices, factories, prisons, banks, shelters, and courtrooms. We're sent to speak the Word of God and say, "God is near. You are valuable. Lift up your hearts. Your sins are forgiven. Peace be with you. Have no fear."

People want to know how to say those things. Here's the plan: God showed Jesus how; Jesus shows us how; we show the whole people of God how; they show the world how. We are all sent. Every one of us is sent. If we were not sent, our words might be perfectly fine words, but they would not be God's Word. We dare to speak only because we believe we are sent across the moat, into the world, onto the housetops, and into the light to proclaim God's Word, with God's help, in God's name.

Amen.[1]

—Barbara Taylor

[2200 words]
[22 minutes]

❦ CHAPTER THREE
DISCIPLESHIP

Discipleship arises from a sense of our debt and duty to God. Discipleship is living with the realization that God's just rule is *here* and *now* and *yet to come*. God's reign is *here* in our midst and in our lives. It is *now* in the unconditional demand on us to love one another. It is *yet to come* as God day by day transforms the world and transfigures us in the image of his Son.

Jesus is our example of selfless service to others. He lives in us, through us, and despite us. The Christian life is a spiral leading from faith to love, from love to service, from service to heaven.

The Gospel of Jesus Christ demands our total commitment. Our lives are of value to those in need or they are as worthless as bounced checks. The choice is ours.

Being a Christian means taking up one's cross in the power of Christ's resurrection. In the words of the Apostle Paul, "living is Christ and dying is gain." By the grace of God, we will succeed unless we pronounce our own failure. No matter how powerless we may seem in our own eyes, through faith God gives us the strength to do, to be, and to make a difference.

Sermon 28

Date: Maundy Thursday, Any Year

Texts:
Exodus 12:1–14
Psalm 116:1-2, 12-19
1 Corinthians 11:23–26
John 13:1–17, 31b-35

or Fifth Sunday of Lent, Year B

Texts:
Jeremiah 31:31–34
Psalm 51:1–12
Hebrews 5:5–10
John 12:20–33

Theme: The word testament sums up our debt and our duty to God—our part in the New Covenant.
Subject: Communion, Eucharist, the Lord's Supper

Title: The Reading of His Will

Covenants and Contracts

"This cup is the new covenant in my blood . . .". We have heard these words hundreds perhaps thousands of times—whenever we have received the sacrament of the Lord's Supper. But what do these words mean? What is the "covenant" of which they speak?

As the character Mrs. Antrobus says to her husband in Thornton Wilder's play, *The Skin of Our Teeth*, "I didn't marry you because you were perfect. . . . I married you because you gave me a promise." She takes off her ring and examines it. "That promise made up for your faults and the promise I gave you made up for mine. Two imperfect people got married and it was the promise that made the marriage."

A covenant is a promise. A covenant is an agreement sworn before God in the presence of the congregation of the faithful. A covenant is a human response to a sense of God's invitation or calling. It is freely entered into by its earthly parties with a conviction that God has hallowed and sanctified this binding together of individuals. A covenant recognizes that God is more committed than the human parties could ever be to the fulfillment of the agreement.

Within the church, marriage is a covenant. In marriage, two persons acknowledge that God has given them to one another and that through his abiding presence their lives together may attain levels of satisfaction and communion that they would never achieve alone. It is God who initiates this covenant. The bride and groom accept it as God's gift to them. Finally, and often overlooked, it is the congregation who add their "yes" or "amen" to the proceedings and, in so doing, commit themselves to support and sustain "what God has joined together."

Contrast this understanding of marriage as a covenant with the notion that marriage is a contract. A contract is also a promise. A contract is joined into by two or more persons. It is based on a consideration, such as money or something of monetary worth. No matter how specific its terms, it is based on the goodwill and integrity of the parties. Its terms are subject to later reinterpretation by courts of law. As my father taught me, "Where there's a will, there's a lawyer to contest it."

If marriage is a contract, it depends only on the two parties involved. The congregation (if any) is reduced to the status of witnesses. As such, they have no responsibility before, during, or after the marriage. Likewise, God is reduced to the role of provider of the hall if the wedding is in a church, the supplier of the master of ceremonies if the wedding is performed by a minister, and the source of some archaic words and sentiments if anything like a traditional wedding ceremony is used. Where marriage is a contract, the church becomes the place for marrying and burying and little else.

Covenants are foundational to life. They are the binding promises without which life would be formless and chaotic. It is our solemn commitments made before God and our fellow human beings that form the guideposts of our lives. Many of us have made promises like those demanded by the following questions:

"Do you promise to love, honor, and cherish?"

"Do you swear to tell the truth, the whole truth, and nothing but the truth, so help you God?"

"Do you swear to protect and defend this country against all enemies, foreign or domestic?"

"Do you accept and own with us this covenant of our church?"

"Do you now engage upon your part to perform those things needful that the goodwill and love of the heavenly father be not hidden from your child?"

Such covenants change lives forever.

God and the Human Race

Throughout the Bible, the word "covenant" is used to describe solemn promises made by individuals. But far more essential and common in Scripture is the use of "covenant" to describe relationships entered into between God and the human race.

The book that we call the Old Testament or Old Covenant contains several: the covenants between God and Adam, God and Noah, God and Abraham, God and David, as well as the central covenant from which the Old Testament draws its name: the covenant between God and Israel. In every case God promises spiritual blessings, protection, and prosperity, and, in return, God demands faithfulness.

The covenant between God and the nation Israel required of the entire people that they accept and obey the laws of God, receive and cherish God's revelation of himself, and reveal God to the other peoples of the world. And God committed himself to establishing his people as a nation in the promised land, causing them to prosper, providing for them, protecting them, and revealing himself to them.

Despite the faithfulness of God, this covenant failed. God promised a New Covenant, one not dependent on laws, reward, and punishments. In the words of the Prophet Jeremiah: "The time is coming," declares the Lord, "when I will make a new covenant with the house of Israel and with the house of Judah" (Jeremiah 31:31).

Jesus had the words of Jeremiah in mind when at his last supper he claimed to establish the promised New Covenant through his death. The Greek word for covenant or testament used by Jesus is worth noting. It is *diatheke.* The usual Greek word for a covenant between two people is *suntheke.* For example, a marriage covenant or a business agreement would be spoken of as a *suntheke. Diatheke* normally means a will rather than a covenant.

Agreements and Testaments

To simplify matters a bit, let us use the English words "agreement" and "testament" in place of *suntheke* and *diatheke.* The reason for the choice of testament instead of agreement is apparent. An agreement is a contract made between parties on equal terms, which either party can alter. But the testament of which Jesus spoke is something radically different. God and man do not meet on equal terms. God, of his own choice and by his grace, offers us this relationship. We can accept it or reject it. But we cannot alter or annul this covenant. Thus, the New Covenant is like a last will and testament that offers a bequest that may be accepted or refused, but the terms of which cannot be altered.

The Apostles were aware of another reason for the use of a word that means "last will and testament." The validity and operation of a testament depends on the death of its author. Hence, Jesus says, "This is the new testament in my blood." The visiting Greeks of John 12 wanted to see Jesus. Perhaps they had heard of his miracles and hoped to receive a demonstration. Maybe they had learned of his teaching and wanted to argue philosophy with him. What they got was the paradox of the New Covenant: death produces life, suffering leads to joy.

Now Jesus was not a masochist nor has he called us to suffer for the sake of suffering. We are not called to suffer injustice. We are called to risk and endure the suffering that eliminates the suffering that can be ended. But, of equal importance, we are called to risk and endure the suffering that comes from standing with those whose suffering cannot be ended. We are called to put an end to injustice and, if we cannot, to bear the pain of those crushed by injustice.[1]

The true Christian life is living within the paradox of faith:

> We see unseen things; we conquer by yielding; we find rest under a yoke; we reign by serving; we are made great by becoming little; we are exalted by being humble; we become wise by being fools for Christ's sake; we are made free by becoming his slaves; we possess all things by having nothing; we wax strong by being weak; we triumph by defeat; we find victory by glorying in our infirmities; and we live by dying.[2]

Hear the Gospel paradox: We live by dying. The death of one produces the life of many. The word testament sums up our debt and our duty to God—our part in the New Covenant.

We are in debt because our relationship to God is entirely due to him and not to anything we have ever done.

We have a duty because in accepting this covenant we have to accept God's conditions of love and faith and obedience, and we cannot alter them. To accept God's New Covenant with us is to embrace the paradox—to seek life in death, joy in sorrow, purpose in chaos. To accept God's New Covenant is to suffer so that the suffering of others may cease or to stand in solidarity with those whose suffering cannot be ended.

---

[1] Charles Rice, *Word and Witness,* March 17, 1991, p. 3.

[2] *InfoSearch, Sermon Illustrations,* (computer software) (Colorado Springs, CO: NavPress Software, 1990), adapted.

Every act of Christian worship—every sacrament, every ceremony—is, in effect, a reading of Christ's will. We come as recipients of covenant blessings through the death of our benefactor. We come as faithful executors, ready and willing by God's grace to carry out God's conditions. We come because we are invited. We come as heirs. We come to share fully in the joy and sorrow of life courageously lived. And we come with grateful hearts.

Amen.

—LDS

[1538 words]
[15 minutes]

Sermon 29

Date: Sunday Between October 2 and October 8 inclusive Pentecost, Year A

Texts:
Numbers 27:12–23
Exodus 20:1-4, 7-9, 12-20
Psalm 19
Philippians 4b-21
Matthew 21:33–46

Theme: The Kingdom of God is here and now and yet to come.
Subject: God's rule

Title: Here and Now and Yet to Come

The kingdom is here . . . and now . . . and yet to come.

In the words of the Apostle Paul, "this one thing I do: forgetting what lies behind and straining forward to what lies ahead, I press on toward the goal for the prize of the heavenly call of God in Christ Jesus". (3:13–14 NRSV)

Is our salvation a gift of God's grace? Or is it a prize for running the race of life with all of our might? It is clear from Paul's many letters that salvation is not earned or achieved by anything we do or attained, by anything we have earned by anything we can be. God has accepted us and requires of us only that we accept his acceptance.

Sometimes we act as though we are not so sure. We strive to please God, to make everyone happy. In consequence, our lives reflect a sense of frustration and drudgery. At times, our lives seem an unrewarding struggle. The race that we run is replete with blisters, bone spurs, shin splints, and muscle pulls!

And sometimes we act as though we are a bunch of privileged characters who, in George Peck's phrase, "can sit back and be carried to heaven in indolent comfort."[1] We don't take part in the race as much as we sit in the bleachers and watch it being run by others—sometimes cheering them on and sometimes criticizing their performance.

For Paul, the chief proponent of salvation by grace through faith, salvation, which is received as a gift, manifests itself in a life of striving and discipline. Either one's life marks one as a citizen

---

[1] *Proclamation 3, Series A, Pentecost 3* (Philadelphia: Fortress Press, 1987), p. 15.

in God's kingdom or it does not. As Peck comments, "to be given the vineyard is to be required to deliver the harvest."[2]

The New Testament proclaims the "good news" that God is with us, that his kingdom is *here* and *now* and *yet to come*. The kingdom is *here*, in the person and work of Jesus of Nazareth. Through his chosen one, we learn, God has invaded our existence, transformed (and complicated) our lives, taken us as partners, surrendered himself to our state and fate, given us the opportunity to transcend suffering, tragedy, and death. He has called and chosen us as recruits to His kingdom, deepened our capacity to feel all human emotions, forced us to contend with enhanced ups and cruel downs. God gives us life more abundant, ecstatic, and fruitful even as we come to know life's enemies—pain, disappointment, and failure—more intensely than ever.

The kingdom of God is *here* because the King is here in our midst. The kingdom is now because the presence of God in our lives as Christians is unavoidable. God has broken into our daily existence, changed our nature, and empowered us. We are neither better nor worse than other human beings. In a sense, our lives are more difficult, more complex. Whether we want it or not, there is a sensitivity, a responsiveness in our lives.

The kingdom of God is *coming*. It is always beyond our grasp. It lures us like some beautiful butterfly that we would snare for our collection, and then it eludes us. As God's partners, we are able to actualize it for brief moments here and there. "Not that I have already reached the goal; but I press on to make it my own, because Christ Jesus has made me his own," says Paul. (Philippians 3:12 NRSV).

We are used as instruments of peace. We find love that we do not deserve or understand. We serve others and are served by others. We are lured on and on by a love that will not let us go.

But the age in which we live dooms us to frustration, suffering, loneliness, and death. So why bother? Why care? Why love? Surely we will be misunderstood, humiliated, and rejected—no matter how pure our motives may be. Our own failings and limitations will ultimately negate everything we accomplish. This world's cacophony of greed, lust, and selfishness will drown out our quiet songs of faith, hope, and charity. And, finally, each of us will die and be forgotten. The unfeeling world machine will grind on remorselessly—war after war, death after death, calamity after calamity.

Until the new age. Until the promise made by God in the Messiah's death and resurrection is kept. "Our citizenship," says Paul, "is in heaven, and it is from there that we are expecting a Savior, the Lord Jesus Christ." (3:20 NRSV) Someday, the Christian faith boldly affirms, we will study war no more. Someday, peace will prevail not only in the affairs of nations but in the petty differences that set people against one another. There will be no more angry words, no feeling that what you have should have been mine, no shortage of caring, no lack of love, no divorce, no selfishness, no theft, no victims. Someday nature will not be at odds with humankind or humankind with nature. Someday there will be no disease, no famine, no earthquakes, no tidal waves, no hurricanes. And, finally, individuals will no longer be at war with themselves. Loneliness, frustration, fear, stress, meaninglessness, and confusion will be forgotten like so many discarded fashions.

Says Paul, Jesus "will transform the body of our humiliation that it may be conformed to the body of his glory, by the power that also enables him to make all things subject to himself" (3:21). How do we know that all this will be so? That we will beat our swords into plowshares? That what we lost in the fall of Adam will be restored through the Christ, the founder of a new race? That God will be all in all? We don't know. We, as Christians, have taken Jesus at his word. From the world's point of view, we are fools, simpletons, and children. We wait for God's inevitable triumph, tasting it, longing for it, spying it through the murk of everyday struggle, and affirming it in our prayers: ". . . your kingdom come, your will be done. . . ."

---

[2] Ibid.

And now and then, that kingdom is very real and present for us. Jesus began his ministry by restoring the ostracized and forsaken to human fellowship. When out of gratitude, those whom he returned to health and sanity tried to join his traveling company, he ordered them to remain in the hometowns to which they rightfully belonged. Jesus healed hundreds, perhaps thousands. But those whom he called to give up their families, friends, and vocations for the sake of "full-time Christian service" were limited to a handful. It is easy to use being a Christian as an excuse to avoid the really hard job of being a human being, belonging to a family, living in a community. But the kingdom which Jesus proclaims requires very few of us to do anything else.

Of course, how we are human, how we are part of our families, how we respond to the needs of our neighbors makes all the difference in the world. Just because we run the race of life with our eyes on the prize, just because we are citizens of a commonwealth that transcends human experience, we are not excused from living here and now. To live, however, only for the here and now, only for material possessions, only for one's career, only for one's family, only for one's nation, only for one's pleasures is ultimately to live for impermanent things.

For Paul it is a matter of putting first things first. The Christian life for him is holding fast with all of one's might—heart, mind, soul, and spirit—to the God whose grip is stronger than Krazy Glue. In Philippians 2, Paul expresses this in a wonderful paradox: "work out your own salvation with fear and trembling; for it is God who is at work in you, enabling you both to will and to work for his good pleasure." (v. 12 NRSV)

The kingdom of God is here and now and yet to be. It is here in our midst and in our lives. It is now in the unconditional demand on us to love one another. It is yet to be as God transforms his world, as he transfigures us in the image of his Son.

Amen.

—LDS

[1380 words]
[14 minutes]

❦ *Sermon 30*

❦ *Date:* Last Sunday After Pentecost, Year C

Texts: (NCL)
2 Samuel 5:1–5
Psalm 95
Colossians 1:11–20
John 12:9–19

Theme: Will we go after Jesus and follow his example of selfless service to others?
Subject: Discipleship

❦ *Title:* ". . . the world has gone after him"

Tip

> Notice how the previous day's newspaper provides the central illustration. Headlines can provide a bridge between the biblical world and the congregation's. You can replace the citations with up-to-date items from your own daily newspaper.

When Walls Come Down

"You see that you can do nothing; look, the world has gone after him." (John 12:19)

These unnamed Pharisees were wrong. The world has not gone after Jesus. The world goes on. Some of us go after him and some of us do not. And those who go after him may be divided into two groups: those who deliberately follow and those who follow unwittingly.

Throughout the world, the walls of oppression seem to be tumbling down. The Prince of Peace is luring men and women to lives of freedom and justice, whether they honor him or not. Who would have thought that in our time the unchallenged champion of world peace, military deescalation, the enfranchisement of those oppressed by totalitarian systems would be the highest ranking official of the Soviet Union? Who would have dreamed that the one-party rule in Poland would be overthrown without as much as the smashing of a single window?

In yesterday's newspaper, I read

> a remarkable civility . . . characterizes Czechoslovakians.
> Amid all the turmoil and excitement of the country's political reawakening of recent days, those pressing for change have maintained an unusual sense of consideration for their fellow citizens.
>
> It is a polite revolution.
>
> It is a movement whose foot soldiers in the streets—mainly students—throw flowers, not rocks, and light candles to show their protest. Even in the jostling crush of the massive demonstrations in central Wenceslas Square, anyone stepping on another's toes immediately, profusely apologizes.
>
> At Wednesday's rally, for example, one fifth of a million people quickly and quietly parted when a speaker asked that an ambulance be let through.
>
> When a toddler in her mother's arms screamed she had dropped a toy, the crowd quickly shuffled backward, creating a small space around the pair, eventually revealing a little plastic car.[1]

On the other side of the ledger, the headlines reveal "36 die as violence continues in Indian elections." Follow-up stories remind us that only a few days ago peacemakers were brutally murdered in Lebanon and El Salvador.

When Walls Refuse to Crumble

Some walls are crumbling. Other walls are firmly in place, separating neighbor from neighbor, rich from poor, white from black, from Asian, from Hispanics. There are still those who refuse to go after Jesus, who would murder, oppress, stifle, and spit in the face of humanity as they spit in his face. There are those who will continue to exploit the dispossessed, turn misery into profit, sell poison to their neighbors and their neighbors' children. But are they as secure in their heedlessness as they were a few years ago? They must be petrified with fear as they see the new wonder workers in their midst, those who will lay it all on the line—their lives, their positions, their fortunes, their sacred honor—for the sake of a vision of a world that works for everyone.

---

[1] Marshall, Tyler, "Civil Unrest Truly Civil in Prague," *Los Angeles Times*, in *San Jose Mercury News*, November 25, 1989, A-1, A-5.

Who will go after the Galilean and throw out the money traders? Who will say "enough" to the multinational corporations who despoil the rain forests and pollute the seas and the air? Who will say that humankind cannot live by bread alone and we certainly cannot live by junk food and junk media and junk politics and junk bonds? Who will offer to our children a vision of a hopeful life—a life that requires no drug-induced euphoria, religious obscurantism, or phony political nostrums.

Will we go after Jesus and follow his example of selfless service to others? The one among you who would be greatest, he taught, must be servant of all (Mark 9:35). Servant of all—not the wisest of all, or the one who amasses the most toys, or the cleverest deal maker, or even the most spiritually adept. The greatest among you is the one who serves the most.

Tip

> When the preacher admits his or her own doubts and confusions, it binds him to the listener and the listener to him instead of setting them apart.

Who Is This Jesus?

I don't always know what to think about Jesus. The confessions of two thousand years of church history challenge me and make me want to know more about this one solitary life. "He is the image of the invisible God," says the author of the letter to the Colossians. "The Father and I are one. . . . He who has seen me has seen the Father," he is quoted as saying by the writer of the Fourth Gospel. In Philippians 2, Paul quotes a hymn of the early church, which says of Jesus

> *Who, being in very nature God, did not consider equality with God something to be grasped, but made himself nothing, taking the very nature of a servant, being made in human likeness. And being found in appearance as a man, he humbled himself and became obedient to death—even death on a cross! Therefore God exalted him to the highest place and gave him the name that is above every name, that at the name of Jesus every knee should bow, in heaven and on earth and under the earth, and every tongue confess that Jesus Christ is Lord, to the glory of God the Father. (Philippians 2:6–11)*

The message of these early Christians is as direct as it is wholehearted: if you want to know what God is all about just look at the life and ministry of Jesus. Jesus is the pattern. He is what the human race was designed to be, what you and I were designed to be. We are created in God's image. He is God's image.

The King Who Serves

Ours is a service economy. The trouble is each and every one of us assumes the role of servees. We live to be served by others. We expect to be served, insist on being served, complain if we are not served cheerfully, immediately, upon demand. But Jesus inaugurated a servants' society, a community of servers. Jesus lived to serve and to give himself for others. Shortly before his arrest, he washed his disciples feet. What he said to them is the heart of his teaching: "I have given you an example, that you also should do as I have done to you" (John: 14:15). Whatever God is, Jesus is. In Jesus, God has surrendered himself to our state and fate. In a life given totally to and for others, Jesus shows us, concretely and unavoidably, what God intended when he created us in his image.

I don't always know how to conceptualize this, how to package it neatly, how to say it in ways that will satisfy my mind as well as my heart. But one thing is for sure. Jesus the Christ is my companion, my guide, my goal, my standard, and my standard bearer. He lures me into fellowship, into caring and giving of myself, into forgetting my petty and self-centered ways. He lives in me and through me and despite me. He is with me in the midst of those to whom I join myself. He is always just ahead of me, inviting me to catch up, as I do what I cannot help doing, as I go after him. As you and I together go after him.

Amen.

—LDS

[1200 words]
[12 minutes]

Sermon 31

Date: Third Sunday After Epiphany, Year A

Texts:
Isaiah 9:1–4
Psalm 27:1–6
1 Corinthians 1:10–18
Matthew 4:12–23

or Third Sunday After Epiphany, Year B

Texts:
Jonah 3:1–5, 10
1 Corinthians 7:29–31
Mark 1:14–20

or Fifth Sunday in Lent, Year B

Texts:
Jeremiah 31:31–34
Hebrews 5:7–10
John 12:20–33

Theme: Following Jesus is like climbing a spiral staircase.
Subject: Discipleship

Title: "Come follow me"—the Spiral Staircase

[Suggested special music before sermon: "We Are Climbing Jacob's Ladder" and "Follow Me Where I Go."]

And Jesus said: "Come follow me, and I will make you fishers of men" (Matthew 4:19). "Follow me," he says today.

Misguided Followers

Barabbas thought he was following Jesus. Do you remember the 1962 film *Barabbas,* in which Anthony Quinn played the thief Jesus replaced on the cross? The crude, violent Barabbas claws his way from the living hell of the mines to success as a gladiator. Haunted by his memories of the crucifixion and fascinated by the persecuted sect of Christians, who worship the very man who died in his place, Barabbas falls prey to their belief that God is about to judge the world by fire. When sections of Rome are set on fire by agents of the emperor, a crazed Barabbas runs through the streets setting fires, shouting "Lord, I won't fail you this time!" He is arrested, his misguided effort to help usher in God's kingdom providing the authorities with the pretext to blame the Christians for the conflagration. The not-so-innocent Barabbas and the totally guiltless Christians are crucified for arson. In the end, Barabbas looks heavenward and demands of God: "Why can't you make yourself clear?"

When I was counseling, I had a client whose husband tried to follow Jesus. Like Jesus he healed the sick and cast out demons. His fame as a counselor and healer spread far and wide, and he attracted a sizable following. Then he told one of his followers, a diabetic, to accept by faith a miracle of healing and to throw away his insulin. While the group surrounded the young man, prayed, and cast out demons, the diabetic went into shock, turned blue, and died. Even then the group, which included the young man's parents and closest friends, continued to pray, believing that their faith could raise the young man from the dead. They failed.

The Gentle Giant

I knew an opera singer once, when I was in my teens. His name was Bill Carle. He had known the ups and downs of a career in the entertainment world. He had been the soloist at President Roosevelt's funeral. He had appeared weekly in a highly successful radio series. (He played Daddy Snooks, the father of Fannie Brice's "Baby Snooks.") He had a beautiful, moving bass singing voice. But his spirit was restless and unsatisfied. He gave up his show business career for a new calling. He became a follower of Jesus.

When I met him, he was touring the country, singing and speaking to teenagers at Youth for Christ rallies and church-sponsored meetings. He had become a born-again Christian and had found a sense of peace and purpose. He was a soft, caring giant of a man, who let his light shine brightly. And everywhere he went, he taught his audiences a new gospel song that had been translated from its original Swedish into German, then into Russian and finally into English. It was called "How Great Thou Art!" and has since become the most popular hymn of the twentieth century. I have forgotten almost all of the hundreds of sermons and testimonies I heard during my teenage years in evangelical Christianity, but I have never forgotten the warm, tender man who taught me, "How Great Thou Art!"

Francis and Martin

Francis of Assisi, for whom San Francisco is named, heard Jesus say, "Come follow me." He gave up wealth and position to found an order of mendicant priests. He healed the sick, attempted to reform the Christian church, tried to bring peace to the warring nations of his time, and taught his followers to respect all living things and the source of their being. The words of his "Canticle to the Sun" are inscribed on the wall to my right. Be sure to read them before you leave today.

Martin Luther King, Jr., responded to the call of Jesus. He had every excuse to hate those who oppressed his people. He could have led a violent uprising to redress the grievances and indignities of a century of Jim Crow, terrorism, and repression. He could have taught an eye for an eye, a lynching for a lynching, a fire bomb for a fire bomb, a racial slur for a racial slur. But he was a follower not of brutality nor of expediency. He was a follower of the Christ.

It is not easy to follow Jesus, we tell ourselves. It is too hard to discern his will, to distinguish between our personal agenda and his. We do not want to be like the misdirected Barabbas or the fanatic faith healer. We are a little embarrassed by the Bill Carles as well. And which of us would claim to be another St. Francis or Martin Luther King, Jr.?

And just when we think we can get comfortable and excuse ourselves from his call, Jesus pops up in our consciousness and takes hold of our imaginations. We resist him, of course, maintaining that we aren't even sure if we believe in him or what we have been taught about him.

Following Jesus: The Spiral Staircase

What I have learned after nearly four decades of seeking and finding and being found is that what I believe is of relatively little importance. What counts is what I cannot not believe. I cannot prove that God exists or that he cares for me, but I cannot live as though he does not exist, as though he does not care. I cannot prove that the path I have chosen is God's choice for my life, but I cannot live any other way.

I do not know why other sincere men and women follow ways other than mine, have beliefs other than mine, do things in the name of God that are repugnant to me. I also cannot explain how I am able to overcome so much of the rhetoric and maintain a sense of oneness with those with whom I disagree and who disagree with me.

I know that one can follow Jesus and make mistakes, that one can follow Jesus and make a fool of oneself.

Following Jesus is like climbing a spiral staircase. Sometimes it seems as though we are just circling around, getting nowhere. But then we notice that the circle is getting bigger and bigger and that our perspective is getting higher and higher. More and more experience is being absorbed and integrated. Our perspective is becoming less and less self-centered and other directed and more and more God ordained. We are being guided by an unseen hand that, even in the midst of suffering and setbacks, enriches and enhances our lives. In the words of the song, "We are climbing Jacob's ladder."

I have always loved this spiritual. Somehow it says it all:

We are climbing Jacob's ladder . . .
Every round goes higher, higher . . .
Brother, do you love my Jesus . . .
If you love him, why not serve him . . .

What fascinates me is the progression. First, there is the image of climbing Jacob's ladder, a reference to Genesis 28. As you may recall, Jacob, fleeing from his brother Esau, whom he had defrauded out of his birthright, slept in the wilderness and had a strange dream. In his dream, he saw a ladder or staircase between heaven and earth, on which the angels of God ascended and descended. Jacob's ladder, the connection between heaven and earth, I would say, is the Christ nature of each human being, the often-sullied but never eradicated image of God in each of us.

Some versions of the spiritual, holding to the ladder image, say "Every rung goes higher, higher." Others read, "Every round goes higher, higher"—a beautiful ambiguity, the ladder blending into the spiral.

And how does one ascend the ladder to God? How does one climb the stairway to heaven? By loving Jesus and serving him, by loving the brothers and sisters of the Christ and serving them. And as we follow the Christ, as we ascend, develop, and grow as spiritual beings, heaven descends toward our world, the Word becomes flesh and dwells among us, full of grace and truth. God incarnates himself not only in the life and work of his Son but in our lives and our work.

And Jesus said: "Come follow me, and I will make you fishers of men" (Matthew 4:19). They left their nets and followed him. There are times to leave our nets, to put aside the worries and the rat race, the car pools and the swimming lessons, the buying and the selling. There is a time for this world and a time for the world beyond. There is a time for getting and having and a time for giving it all up. There is a time to stream forth from the source of our being and a time to return to the one from whom all blessings flow. Sunday mornings are such a time, but they should not be the only time.

And there are times to return to our nets. Jesus says to fishermen today, "Come follow me and I will make you fishers of men—not as apostles, missionaries, or preachers, but as fishermen." He says to each of us, "Do not give up your talents and career, but consecrate them to me. Come follow me in the marketplace, at school, at home, at play. Do not give up who you are for the sake of the Gospel, but be who you are to the fullest of your ability."

Heaven and earth, the sacred and the profane, the holy and the mundane are separated by less than a hair's breadth. They impinge upon and intermingle with one another like different colored strands in a tapestry. Heaven and earth have come together in the life of the Christ. They combine and coalesce in ever fascinating kaleidoscopic patterns in the life of each one of us—as we climb Jacob's ladder, as we follow the Christ.

And Jesus said: "Come follow me, and I will make you fishers of men" (Matthew 4:19). "Follow me," he says today.

Amen.

—LDS

[1650 words]
[16 minutes]

Sermon 32

Date: Sunday Between September 4 and September 10 inclusive, Year B

Texts:
James 2:1–5, 8–10, 14–17

Theme: Faith without works is dead.
Subject: Good works

Title: The Check That Bounced

Unbelievable Promises and Bounced Checks

My cousin Charlotte was a few months younger than me. We were once best friends. Somewhere in our teens we lost one another. The last time I saw her was at our grandmother's funeral. I gave Charlotte a hug and told her I loved her. "Don't *tell me* you love me," she said, "*Show me!*" She needed more than promises. I didn't know it at the time but she was terminally ill—just barely in her thirties and dying. "Don't *tell me* you love me. *Show me!*"

According to George Will, the "three least credible sentences in the English language" are the following: "The check is in the mail." "Of course I'll respect you in the morning." "I'm from the government and I'm here to help you."[1]

---

[1] Will, George F., "The Squeeze," *The Pursuit of Happiness and Other Sobering Thoughts* (New York: Harper & Row, 1978).

Our focus this morning is on the first of these promises: "The check is in the mail."

We can think of each individual life as though it were a handful of checks. The spiritual life of each of us is fashioned out of thousands of interwoven commitments and the way in which each of us honors them. In our lives, the check is always in the mail. Sometimes it is a good check. Sometimes it is not.

We are a fellowship of people who have committed ourselves to live by the teachings of Jesus. To the extent we do, our commitments are valid. The check is valid. When we fail, our commitments are checks that bounce. But, one way or the other, the check is always in the mail.

For several years, I counseled families distressed by the conversion of a loved one to a fanatic cult. I became very aware of one central truth: cults, sects, and extremist groups are the Christian church's bounced checks. When young adults could not find a sense of belonging, a community that needed them and provided them with guidance, they turned to cults. When they were lacking in moral direction and personal discipline, they turned to demanding, authoritarian leaders. Their search was motivated by a desire for a genuine spiritual community, a yearning for a genuine religious life. God was beckoning to them, but when they tried to hear the voice of the divine in traditional religion, they found that voice muffled and drowned out.

They had a taste for real religion but no way of living it or expressing it. Hence, they were vulnerable to the appeal of spiritual counterfeits. For these seekers, the church was a bounced check.

Throughout my life, I have known many ethically sensitive, morally honorable individuals who were ready and willing to devote their lives to a cause greater than themselves. Some of the issues that inspired them were saving the environment, women's rights, world peace, and economic justice. Unfortunately, they could see no connection between their moral intuitions, their sense of the way things ought to be, and the actions of the local churches in their respective communities.

For these sincere but unchurched persons, religion was not a way of transforming the world, of overcoming prejudice and hostility. Instead religion was just another limited expression of everything that is wrong with the world—including prejudice and hostility. The church was a check that bounced.

Such seekers have a perception that God stands in solidarity with the powerless and the wronged. When they look to the church for leadership, what they see is that, at worst, the church stands in solidarity with the powerful and the exploitative; at best, they find the church sitting idly by, examining its own inner working, while the world goes to hell in a handbasket.

Doing Something Practical

Sometimes the local church is like the little boy who was talking to the girl next door: "I wonder what my mother would like for Mother's Day."

The girl answers: "Well, you could promise to keep your room clean and orderly—you could go to bed as soon as she tells you—you could go to her as soon as she calls you—you could brush your teeth after eating—you could quit fighting with your brothers and sisters, especially at the dinner table."

The boy looked at her and said, "No, I mean something practical."[2]

What Mother Earth would like is our living according to her rules and respecting the fragile nature of our environment, cleaning up our messes, returning to nature more than we take. What a world filled with conflict and suffering needs is a model community that devotes its energies to doing, week by week, the small tasks to which it is called and for which it exists—worshiping

---

[2] *Pastor's Story File*, May 1987. p. 186

God, praying, telling its story, providing guidance to the young, feeding the hungry, clothing the naked.

If we worship God on Sunday and exist Monday through Saturday as though God makes no difference in our lives, we are practical atheists. But if we worship, pray, tell our story, guide the young, feed the hungry, clothe the hungry, Sunday through Sunday, then we are truly God's people. We have given God, God's children, and God's creation something practical.

Being responsive and responsible is a slippery slope. It is all too easy to do an occasional good work because it makes us feel good. However, no good deed is a true act of charity unless attention is focused on the needs of the recipient rather than on the feelings of the doer. Consider the fifteen-year-old boy who came bounding into the house at the end of a school day and found his mother still in bed. She had been sick for several days and he was truly concerned. "Mom, are you feeling any better?" he asked.

When his mother said that, as a matter of fact, she didn't feel too well, the boy replied, "Well, don't worry a bit about dinner. I'll be happy to carry you down to the stove."[3]

The Moral Test of Our Faith

Hubert Humphrey once said something that so impressed Tip O'Neill that O'Neill hung these words on the wall of his office: "The moral test of government is how it treats those who are in the dawn of life—the children; those who are in the twilight of life—the aged; and those who are in the shadows of life—the sick, the needy and the handicapped."

Truly, the moral test of our lives, the test determining whether the check is valid or the check bounces, is how we treat those in the dawn of life, those in the twilight of life, and those in the shadows of life. And if we think that government will do the job for us, we have another thing coming. There was a man who injured his thumb on the job. His foreman told him to go to the clinic.

> He stepped inside and saw an empty room with only a desk and two chairs. Toward the back of the room there were two doors—one marked "Illness" and the other marked "Injury." The man thought to himself, "I am not sick, I have just hurt my thumb." He walked through the door marked "Injury." He found himself in a second room. It was empty except for a desk and two chairs. Toward the back door were two doors—one marked "Internal" the other marked "External." The man thought to himself, "It's my thumb that is hurt, not something inside." He walked through the door marked "External." He found himself in still another room. It was empty except for a desk and two chairs. Toward the back of the room there were two doors, one marked "Therapy" and one marked "Treatment." He thought to himself, "I don't need counseling or therapy. What I need is to have this thumb treated." He walked through the door marked "Treatment." He found himself in still a fourth room. It was empty except for a desk and two chairs. Toward the back of the room there were two doors—one was marked "Major" and the other marked "Minor." He thought to himself, "This isn't a major illness, it's just my thumb that is hurt." He walked through the door marked "Minor." He found himself outside the clinic on the street. He walked back to the building and went to work.
>
> The foreman saw him and said, "Were they able to help you?" The man said, "I'm

---

[3] Adapted from Malvina Leiner, *Parables, Etc.*, May 1985, 5.3.

not sure—but I will tell you one thing, that is the best organized outfit I have ever seen!"[4]

Organization is important, but organization without compassion, without personal involvement, is barren. As my friend King Duncan has noted:

An effective church needs to be well organized. But the best organized church in the world might as well be torn down if it is not truly helping people.

Responding to the needs of others is not always an easy job. It requires compassion, responsiveness, and a dollop of common sense. Without informed, sound judgment, our good works are like those of a certain little girl, the sister of the fifteen-year-old I mentioned a few minutes ago whose mother had been sick in bed for several days. Her six-year-old daughter decided to make her mom some hot tea to make her feel better. The child brought the tea

into the room and she waited as her mother drank it, so that she could be properly congratulated for her good deed. Her mother drank the tea, and then asked the little girl how she went about making it.

"Just like you do, mommy," replied the girl. "First I took the tea leaves and boiled them, then I strained them," she went on.

"What did you use to strain them?" her mother asked.

"Oh," replied the girl, "I couldn't find the strainer, so I used the fly swatter." Sensing that she had said something wrong, the daughter tried to put her mind at ease and said, "Oh, not the new fly swatter—I used the old one."[5]

Sometimes there are limits on what any of us as individuals or as a group can do.

A certain man made an application for a position and was being interviewed by the personnel manager. He was told that the company had group insurance for their employees but that each employee paid for his own coverage. The cost would be deducted from the first paycheck of each month. The man looked very disappointed. Noting his disappointment, the interviewer asked him if that presented a problem.

"At my last place of employment, the company paid for everything," he said. "They paid for our life insurance, dental insurance, health insurance, three weeks paid vacation, a Christmas bonus, and unlimited sick leave."

"I can't imagine why you would leave such a generous employer," the personnel man said.

After a moment of silence the man said sheepishly, "They went bankrupt."[6]

There are risks in doing what we are called to do—in being decent and caring human beings in a heartless and uncaring world. It is like the hen and the pig who were making a journey together.

After a time they became hungry. They began looking for a restaurant. Finally they came to one that had a sign out front: "Ham and Eggs are our specialty." The hen wanted to go in, but the pig refused. When the hen became upset, the pig is said to

---

[4] As told by King Duncan in *King's Treasury of Humor*, computer diskette (Knoxville, TN: Seven Worlds Publishing, 1991).

[5] Ibid.

[6] Ibid.

have replied: "It's easy enough for you to say, my dear, all they expect from you is a contribution—from me they will expect total commitment."[7]

The Gospel of Jesus Christ expects more than our contributions. It demands our total commitment. The Gospel of Jesus Christ demands not only our cash but our common sense. The Gospel of Jesus Christ demands not only that we feed the hungry and clothe the naked but that we work to change the rules of the game so that our society works not just for the privileged but for all its citizens.

Our lives are either of value to those in need or they are of no value. The checks we write with our lives are either good checks or rubber checks. Either we make a difference or we are invalid. Either we pay off or we are checks that bounce. And the check is in the mail.

Amen.

—LDS

[2030 words]
[20 minutes]

❦ *Sermon 33*

❦ *Date:* Sunday Between August 21 and August 27 inclusive, Year A

Texts:
Exodus 1:8-2:10
Psalm 124
Romans 12:1-8
Matthew 16:13–20

Theme: Being a Christian means taking up the cross in the power of the resurrection. No cross, no crown. No pain, no gain.
Subject: Grace, faith

❦ *Title:* "Dear Matt, Your Gospel Gets Thumbs Up!"

A letter from Simon Peter, apostle of Jesus Christ, to Matthew the Evangelist

Dear Matt: It was with great pleasure that I just received your recently published Gospel. The imperial mails being what they are—it took eighteen months for my copy to catch up with me here in Rome. I'm afraid that by the time this reaches you it may be too late for my comments to be of much use.

Since we are quite busy here at the capital, I'll have to restrict my comments to just one part of your account—an incident that was quite central to my life—the conversation between the Lord and us disciples at Caesarea Philippi.

As you quite correctly recount, it had been quite a week. We were up to our tunic tops in sick people. There were not enough hours in a day to get them organized so we could take them to the Lord in small groups, let alone one at a time. The Lord had just received news of the execution of his cousin John. He didn't say a word. He just had us take him away in our boat for a few days, during which he said nothing. I didn't pick up on it at the time, but I guess he was thinking of where his career was going.

---

[7] Ibid.

We had picked an isolated spot. Somehow the mob of sick and dying and crazy and crippled found out where we were. And you know what happened then—how with just five loaves and two fish, the Lord fed five thousand. Also I remember that he sent us on ahead in the boat while he dismissed the crowd—although how he ever got away from them remains a mystery to me.

Now your account of his walking on the water and my sinking in the water—well, I remember it a little differently. When I recognized the Lord, I said to my brother James, "I wish I had the faith to walk right out and meet him." And whenever I have faced controversies among fellow Christians or persecutions by the authorities, I have always remembered that strange morning and the way Jesus commanded the elements just as Moses had done when our people crossed over the Red Sea. And when I told the story to my fellow Christians, it would calm them and together we would confess, "Jesus is truly the Son of God."

But I honestly don't remember trying to walk on the water or getting chewed out for being of little faith. Of course, if I had been, it would not have been the first or last time. The Lord was always calling us his "little of faith." It was a kind of pet name.

The healings and the miracles continued, as you described them. And there was another mass feeding—four thousand this time. And those curious, veiled remarks about rejection and conflict with our people—you got those right.

Finally, we came to Caesarea Philippi—here we were surrounded by Gentiles and their temples in this center of Pagan worship named for Tiberius Caesar himself. I don't have to tell you that the place gave me the spooks. Out of nowhere, Jesus asks, "Who do men say that the Son of Man is?" Well, we knew all the stock answers: "John the Baptist, Elijah, Jeremiah, one of the other prophets." And then he asks, "Who do you say that I am?"

I didn't stop to think. I just said what was in my heart. And I wasn't just saying it for myself. When I thought it over later, my sense was that I was speaking for all the disciples. "You are the Messiah, the Son of the living God." "Messiah, the anointed one, the Christ, the one chosen by God"—that seemed natural enough. As for "Son of God," I don't know if any of us had actually said that before, even though we thought it. How else could we speak of the close relationship between the Lord and our Father in heaven — a relationship so close that what our Father did, the Lord did. "Son" seemed to cover the territory.

When the Lord blessed me, I felt unworthy. I hadn't confessed my faith because I was smarter than the other disciple or more sensitive or more perceptive. Any of them could have said what I did. And when the Lord changed my name to Peter the Rockman and said that on this rock he would build his church, I didn't know what to say. Now maybe you ought to add a comment or two so your readers don't get this wrong.

First, the Lord had never used the word "church" before. We had thought that as God's anointed one he would usher in God's kingdom, a restored Jewish theocracy of some sort. But the notion of a church and all that a church would entail, it simply had not crossed our minds—could not have crossed our minds at the time.

Now isn't it funny how that word, "cross," came cropping up just then? I had no idea what lay ahead—of the death of the Lord, of my own shameful behavior, of the resurrection, of the Lord's appearances to me, of the giving of the Spirit, of the mission to the Gentiles, of the dropping of the requirement that new converts should first become observant Jews before becoming baptized Christians. We were so ignorant then and I most of all.

Jesus called me the Rockman. What a rock I was! Simon the unstable would have been more appropriate. Simple Simon. Simon with rocks in his head. Simon the stumbling block. Simon who was all talk and no action. Simon who would run away when the going got tough. Some foundation for a church, huh?

Look, Matt, I want you to get this right. It was on my faith—not on me—that the Lord has built his church. And not on just my faith. On the faith of all the disciples who came through those awful days in Jerusalem together. And our faith isn't something that we have done or made for ourselves. What the Lord said to me goes for all of us. Faith is our Father's gift.

I mentioned those awful days in Jerusalem a few lines ago. Things haven't changed much, have they, Matt? The rulers of our people and the rulers of the empire have sure killed off a lot of us old timers. I didn't think anyone would want to harm my brother James or the Lord's brother James. But they are both gone. And our buddy Paul is in prison. Things don't look good for him. I'm sure you know that he and the Rockman haven't always seen eye to eye—but he is a brother beloved and a first-rate preacher of the Gospel. If the Lord can put up with me, I can't complain too much about the tent maker. If only he could say things more clearly. His letter to the church here in Rome gives me a headache—yet it is so impressive.

I guess the Lord uses each of us—talents, education, lack of education, shortcomings, and all—in his own way. I don't think I'd get much of argument from you. I still remember when we first met. There you were living in your fine tollhouse, extorting excise taxes from the caravans and travelers. So I started out catching fish and ended up catching men and women while you started out keeping track of camels and merchandise and ended up collecting accounts of the sayings and doings of the Lord. Who would have guessed?

You know what keeps coming back to me? It happened just as you described it. After my confession and the Lord's benediction, Jesus looked at us as sternly as I ever saw him look and ordered us not to tell anyone that he was the Messiah. Without everything that was yet to happen, it just would not have meant anything to those who flocked to him or those who spied on him for the authorities or the authorities themselves. It scarcely meant anything to us—so little did we then understand.

I don't know how many I've received into the church during the past thirty years. I'm not as good at counting as you are. And some of these converts realize that to be a Christian is to start just where I did at Caesarea Philippi, to start with the simplest faith and to pass through all the contradictions and sufferings of the cross. And some think that being a Christian is luxuriating in the power of the resurrection. And a few, very few, seem to know that being a Christian is both.

May God bless you.

Your Good Friend and Brother in Christ, Pete.

Amen.

—LDS

[1500 words]
[15 minutes]

❦ *Sermon 34*

❦ *Date:* Sunday Between September 18 and September 24 inclusive Pentecost, Year A

Texts:
Exodus 16:2-15
Psalm 105:1-6, 37-45
Philippians 1:21–27
Matthew 20:1–16

Theme: "For to me living is Christ, and dying is gain." This sentence from Paul's letter to the Philippians not only provides a summation of the man who wrote it but expresses the challenge and opportunity of the Christian life.

Subject: Gratitude, Christian life

Title: The Power of Thanksliving

"For to me living is Christ, and dying is gain."

This sentence from Paul's letter to the Philippians not only provides a summation of the man who wrote it, but expresses the greatest challenge and opportunity of the Christian life. For these few words articulate a faith worth living for and a cause worth dying for.

Paul's Life and Mission

"For to me living is Christ, and dying is gain." Paul's life had a mission, a direction, a purpose. It was not free of conflict and hardship. Becoming a Christian had not transported Paul into some magic fantasy land. He still had to work for a living. He had trouble making ends meet. He depended on the charity of friends. His motives were questioned. He was repeatedly arrested as a troublemaker—riots had a way of breaking out wherever he preached.

In the end, he would die a martyr to his faith. Paul's life and death expressed what two thousand years of Christian history proclaim: the central symbol of our faith is the cross—not the happy face of a smile button.

Paul's mission was not carried out in isolation. He may have looked like a vagrant and a vagabond. But he was not alone like some solitary artist whose worth would be discovered only after his death. No, Paul had friends—friends who valued him, appreciated him, and stood by him in his adversity.

When Paul wrote these words, he was in prison—again! Whether he was in Rome awaiting the verdict that would end his life or in some provincial jail charged with disturbing the peace, we cannot tell. And he felt a strange, mixed sense of exaltation and resignation. He was a man who had everything to gain and nothing to lose.

His sole purpose for living was to preach the Gospel of Jesus the Christ. If he were freed, he would return to his mission, and the Gospel would be proclaimed. If he remained in jail, his imprisonment would call attention to the faith that had led him there. Mahatma Gandhi, Martin Luther King, Jr., Nelson Mandela, and countless other prisoners of conscience down through the ages would understand his point of view. If worst came to worst—as we would judge the situation—and he was executed, his death would unleash a wave of outrage, sympathy, and interest that would speak more eloquently than any of his sermons or letters could ever do.

The Resilience of Paul

You could beat Paul down, but you could never crush him. You could kill him, but you could not silence him. His friends, his spiritual sons and daughters would arise in his place by the hundreds, the thousands, and ultimately the millions.

"For, to me, living is Christ, and dying is gain." Living and dying—Paul knew how to do both. He knew how to die to self and live for others. He knew how to dedicate each moment of life to the service of the church and its message. He knew how to trust in a God who would never forsake him even as he walked through the valley of the shadow of death.

Paul knew the secret of abundant life. As he wrote to the Galatians, "I am crucified with Christ. Nevertheless I live. Yet not I, but Christ lives in me. And the life that I now live in the flesh I live by the faith of the Son of God, who loved me and gave himself for me" (Galatians 2:20).

The center of Paul's existence was gratitude. His life was an unbroken act of thanksgiving to God. There is a simple poem that says

> Were thanks with every gift expressed,
> Each day would be Thanksgiving;
> Were gratitude its very best,
> Each life would be thanksliving.
> —Chauncey R. Piety

The Conversion of Paul and the Face of Christ

We remember that pre-Christian Paul, Saul of Tarsus, don't we? We remember Saul the fanatic defender of orthodox Judaism who stood by while Stephen was stoned to death. We remember Saul, who considered the new messianic sect of Jesus of Nazareth a cancer of the Jewish body politic a tumor that should be excised with all haste lest it destroy the nation.

Years after his conversion, after being struck down on the road to Damascus by the blinding presence of the very Jesus whose name he had sought to erase from human recollection—years after he had humbly placed his fate in the hands of a ragtag band of fugitives, Paul would write, "If any person is in Christ, he is a new creation. Old Things have passed away, and, look, everything is brand new." (2 Corinthians 5:17)

"If any person is in Christ. . . ." For Paul, Jesus of Nazareth was not a moralist or a storyteller or a wonder worker or a failed revolutionary. Paul was not trying to build a museum to house the memorabilia of a fallen hero. He was not raising funds for a library where pious legends and personal reminiscences could be preserved for posterity. No, Paul was a man "in Christ." The living Christ filled his heart and mind and dreams and imagination and yearnings as though he were a tangible presence never more than an arm's reach away. Sometimes it was as though the ego of Paul had been replaced by the personality of Jesus the Christ—as though it was Jesus who walked, talked, preached, healed, wrote, cajoled, advised, and meditated in and through the persona of Paul.

At times, Paul must have felt as though he were the mask of Jesus. Until he was hungry or thirsty or felt unappreciated by his converts or unfairly criticized by other Christian leaders or threatened by smooth-talking purveyors of heretical doctrines. Then he knew that his job was being Paul not Jesus, that God had called him not to give up being Paul but to the be the best, most authentic, most self-actualizing, most fulfilled Paul he could be.

Paul and the Philippians

Paul was a minister of Jesus Christ. All Christians are, but many are not aware of it. His life was not lived in a vacuum. He was not some desert holy man, some recluse in a hermitage. He was a minister of Jesus Christ. Nobody can be a minister without those to whom he or she ministers. Nor can anyone be a minister without those who minister to that minister. Ministry for all Christians is a two-way street. No one gives without receiving, and no one receives without giving.

Paul knew that, and, fortunately for him, so did the Philippians. He was their spiritual "daddy." He had brought the gospel to them, not as a packaged product. He had given them himself—his faith, knowledge, concern, loving, caring, correcting. He had given them more than a handbook of orthodox doctrines and a list of ethical dos and don'ts. He had cleaned up their messes and been there for them despite their suspicions, fears, misguided enthusiasms, and partisan bickering.

And they had never forgotten. He was in trouble. They would not let him down. He was alone. They sent Epaphroditus. He was hungry. They sent food. He was sick. They sent medicine. His old bones were chilled. They sent warm clothing. He didn't have enough money to buy parchment and ink so that he could write them. They took up a collection and sent that along. Why? Because they were grateful. Because no matter where he was, he was with them and always would be.

They worried about old Paul because they loved him. And old Paul, did he complain to them that none of his other spiritual children ever came to visit him? No, he worried right back. He remembered the terrible squabbles they could get into. He recalled the temptation to give up the difficult business of being Christians and lapse back into their pagan ways. He was concerned about the ease with which some of them had liked being converts so much that they had gone shopping for newer, farther out spiritual paths.

But what could Paul do about it? Here he was in an imperial prison with only sickly Epaphroditus and his stalwart friend Timothy for company. What could he do for his beloved Philippians? What could he give them in return for their generosity?

There were only three things he could give and he gave all three. He sent Epaphroditus back to them. He sent his dearest spiritual child, Timothy, to them—Timothy, his only trusted and faithful friend. And he sent a letter full of joy, encouragement, and counsel.

As always, he did exactly what Jesus would have done. Not because he remembered a maxim or teaching that said "It is more blessed to give than to receive," but because Jesus the Christ was alive and well and living in Paul. "For to me living is Christ, and dying is gain."

Resisting the Preacher's Temptation!

As a minister, I am tempted to do what preachers always do, tell you about this wonderful man of faith and encourage you to follow his example. But if I did, I would be misleading you. Rather I say, be who you are in Christ. In the way that is fitting and proper for you, discover how Christ lives in you. Be grateful for who you are and who you can be in the lives of others.

You have friends here in this church. Be who God has called you to be and we will not let life beat you down. We will not let disappointments crush you. We will not let misunderstandings silence you. Sow abundantly with us that we may reap abundantly together, that with exuberance we may add our voices to Paul's and declare, "For to me living is Christ, and dying is gain."

Amen.

—LDS

[1600 words]
[16 minutes]

Sermon 35

Date: Any Sunday

Theme: As long as there is the grace of God, you do not fail until you pronounce your own failure.
Subject: Determination

Title: "If at first you don't succeed . . . ."

"If at first you don't succeed"—you know the rest—"try, try again." Now that's a maxim that we all grew up with. From time to time we are all conscious of failure. Some may recall tragic and terrible failure, when you failed yourself—your best self—or you failed as a father, or as a husband, or as a son, or as a daughter, or as a mother, or as a wife. Maybe you failed some of your friends. Some, too—and there are many failures of this sort—have to come face to face with the fact that they have failed Christ. They have failed as Christians.

If any of you fall into any of those categories, have I got a story for you! It's straight out of the Word of God, beginning at Mark, chapter 14, verse 52, where it declares: "And [John Mark] fled from them naked."

It's midnight in Jerusalem, and everybody's asleep. All is asleep, except, of course, guilt and hate and sorrow and sickness. The Lord's Supper—the Last Supper—has ended, and the traitor has gone out. Jesus and his disciples have already made their way up to Gethsemane, where Jesus took the chosen three along with him farther on and had them sit and watch and pray. Time passes. The three chosen ones fall asleep. There's commotion; soldiers, Pharisees, and Judas Iscariot, the traitor, return to take Jesus away.

But there is one hiding himself in the bushes, way back there in the shadows of the trees of the garden. It is John Mark. John Mark watches as Jesus is taken captive and is led off toward the city. Now a couple of soldiers apparently spot John Mark hiding back there in the bushes—maybe he has a white robe on because he was hastily dressed—and one of them seizes him. John Mark twists and turns in a moment of panic and flees, leaving his cloak and his robe in the arms of the soldier. John Mark runs away naked.

There's the deep failure. And there's the story for us, because if you look at that, you've got a deserter. You have a quitter; you have a coward. If John Mark had merely had the courage to be taken prisoner, he might have been able to stand by Jesus Christ our Lord in our Lord's hour of trial. Just by his very presence, he might have been able to be an encouragement and a help to our Lord. But that night in his first trial and confronted with his first grand opportunity, Mark failed. He fled naked, stripped not only of his garments, but also of his self-respect and his honor.

But there's a word of hope for him, isn't there? It goes like this: "If at first you don't succeed, try, try again." And there's a word of warning here for us. The warning is this: Don't write off any of your Christian believers too soon. Don't write them off, because this is not the end of the story for John Mark.

I can think of the man who bought a home, and in the back yard of the home was a tree. It was wintertime—nothing special about this tree; just an ordinary tree. Spring came, and lovely pink buds appeared on the tree. The man thought to himself, Marvelous! I have a blossoming flower tree in my back yard and I shall watch it all summer long. A heavy wind came, and the pink blossoms blew off—scattering all over. The man thought, What a terrible tree! But that's not the end of the story of the tree.

And it wasn't the end of the story of Mark, because we go to a second passage of Scripture: Acts 13:13. It declares in the Word of God that "John Mark, departing from them, returned to Jerusalem." Fifteen years have passed since that time of disrespect and dishonor in the Garden of Gethsemane. Now it's springtime at the harbor of Seleucia, and in the harbor is a small boat. On the small boat stand three men, three men whom nobody really notices. Yet these three men are setting off on one of the most memorable journeys of all history, the beginning of Christian missions in service to Jesus Christ. They journey; they preach. They come to Cyprus and preach Jesus Christ.

Then they take a ship to Perga in Pamphylia on the southern shore of Asia Minor. There, just as they were about to depart into that high country, the interior, where there are thieves and brigands and robbers, Mark turns back. Mark quits again! He turns back and leaves them, and from the attitude Paul took later in expressing himself on this, we know there was no good reason why

Mark should turn back. It was dangerous country—rough, interior country—toward which they were headed now. They were getting into the dangerous territory of robbers and thieves, and Mark turns back.

Even today that territory looks bleak and wild to the eye of the traveler. Apparently Mark had an ebb in his zeal for Jesus Christ the Lord. His courage had failed him at that point. And in the time of danger, when the elderly Barnabas and the frail Paul could have used him as a minister and helper in going through the mountain passes, that's when John Mark decided to return to Jerusalem.

This is a story for any of us who have tried and failed, because John Mark had failed. He failed in his first trial in the garden; he failed in his second trial. He had a great opportunity to stand by Barnabas, to stand by Paul, as they went through Asia Minor preaching the gospel on that memorable journey, but he backed out. So much so, that when Paul was going to go on the next great journey, he wouldn't even take John Mark with him. He said, "No way!" Paul had branded John Mark a deserter and quitter.

Mark was a man who had put his hand to the plow and turned backward and went backward. That's the last we see of Mark for some time—the man had failed, the person who had not made it. Men will forgive almost anything, but they are reluctant to forgive cowardice. And that's apparently what Mark became marked with: not fit to go into the dangerous journeys anymore.

But, John Mark, there is a word of hope for you. "If at first you don't succeed, try, try again." And there's also a word of warning here for us: Don't write off Christian people. Be open to what God can do with them. Try trusting in God concerning their difficulties before you dismiss them or relegate them to a category of "not worthy of your trust and your love," because this is not the whole story of Mark—oh no, not by a long shot—just as it wasn't the whole story of that tree in the back yard.

The spring winds came and blew the blossoms away. Summer passed, and one day the owner of that home looked out in the back yard and noticed large growths on that tree, about the size of a large nut. They were green. He said, "My goodness! What is this?" He went out, took one off the tree, took a bite out of it, and said, "Blecch! What a horrible and bitter flavor!" He threw it away and said to himself, When winter comes I shall cut down that tree. But it's not the end of the story of the tree. It wasn't the end of the story of Mark.

Ten more years passed. Where is Mark now? Is he the one who was utterly discouraged by his failures? Is he the one who was embittered by the uncompromising and rather staunch and rigid view of Paul not wanting to have anything more to do with him on a journey in the name of Jesus Christ?

The answer is found in the greeting at the end of Peter's first letter, where Peter says, "The church which is at Babylon greets you and salutes you, and so does my son, Mark." That tells you what happened to Mark, the failure, the quitter, the coward. Mark had failed by himself. Mark had failed dismally with Paul. But given one more chance, he not only made a comeback and succeeded as a companion of Peter, there's something very touching that happens.

Peter himself knew failure, knew what it meant to deny Jesus Christ the Lord and go out and weep the bitter tears of remorse. Peter sympathizes and embraces and supports Mark in his trial. Just as Jesus said to Peter, "Go and feed my sheep," and Peter made a grand actualization of that command, so Mark is given the opportunity. Jesus Christ in his mercy and kindness touches Mark and changes his life. No wonder, then, that Peter took a particular interest in Mark.

This really is a sermon for us, all right, but what about Paul? What about Paul, who wanted nothing more to do with him? It's the sunset of Paul's life now. He's in the cold, damp Mamertine prison. He writes a letter to Timothy, probably through the hands of Luke, and he says, "Timothy, come before winter. And bring my cloak and the parchments with you, Timothy." Just as Jesus

Christ had his chosen three, now in the hour of his death, in the sunset, the shadows of his life, Paul wants three with him also.

He has Luke and he will have Timothy. Who is the third man Paul wants with him? Is it Epaphroditus? Is it Titus? Is it any of that glorious company of friends of Paul when he's alone and he says "Demas has forsaken me because he has loved the world?" Paul wants a third man. And who is this third man? Who is this friend to be? Well it's none of Paul's other friends. It's in the message that Paul wrote. This was the man whom he desired to have at his side in the last great hour when he's about to face the mouth of the lion (2 Timothy 4:11): "Take Mark"—Mark! "and bring him with you, for he is profitable to me in the ministry." In that last great hour when Paul is about to face the mouth of the lion, he wants Mark—Mark who had fled naked when he ought to have stood by Jesus Christ, stripped not only of his garment but of his self respect; Mark who had left Jesus in the hands of his enemies; Mark who had left Paul and Barnabas to climb alone the rugged mountains, to ford the swollen streams by themselves, and to face the mobs of Antioch, Lystra, and Iconium. He wants Mark, who went back to Jerusalem. Mark he wants—the quitter and the coward—"for he is profitable to me in the ministry."

So Mark passes from the New Testament records. He had failed in two trials, two examinations, but now he passes magna cum laude. This is a story for us, because it tells us that it takes more than one defeat to make a failure. Babe Ruth struck out 1330 times. It tells us that great people like Mark are ordinary people like us with extraordinary amounts of determination.

There was a young captain in the regular army in the Oregon territory in 1854, and he had fallen into some bad habits. He missed his wife; he missed his baby back in Missouri. He was the quartermaster, the paymaster. On the day when he was to distribute the pay, he was intoxicated. His superior officer, rather a marinet, a very strict man, said, "All right. You have two options. One is to resign your commission and the other is to go before a court-martial." This individual resigned his commission. The young captain, after having resigned his commission, went to New York and fell penniless on the shores there.

Time pass—ten years—and in 1864 an army officer steps into the Willard Hotel in Washington. He is holding a small boy by the hand. Rather indifferently, the clerk spins the register around to him and says, "Please sign." He signs and whirls the register back to the clerk. The clerk is astonished, for on the register is written the name Ulysses S. Grant and son. Ten years before, dismissed from the army for intoxication; and now a lieutenant general and supreme commander of the Armies of the Union.

Some people, when they face the indictment of their weaknesses and failures and are rebuked as severely as Paul rebuked John Mark, often will refuse to yield. They become ensconced in a bitterness and resentment that will take them farther off into dishonor. But with Mark, it was the reverse. Instead of being angry with Paul, instead of defiantly abandoning the purposes and ways of God, he sees the fault with himself and not with God or God's people. Mark resolves in his heart that he will show Paul he can make a man out of himself yet.

"If at first you don't succeed, try, try again."

Mark recovered. He recovered because he had determination. Great people like Mark are ordinary people like us with extraordinary amounts of determination. Mark had that, but he didn't do it alone. He needed the help of his friends just as we need the help of our friends. Peter was there. And that can make all the difference in the world. It really can sometimes when you have someone draw alongside you and stand by you with support and sympathy during your failure. Peter was the one who did that for Mark.

Long ago an ambassador to Germany, Andrew White, who was the president of Cornell University and later taught at the University of Michigan, had a student who was impudent—a smart aleck, always mouthing off to him in the classroom. But White endeavored to support him, to stand by him, to encourage him. And he won the student's friendship. That student, however, was later expelled from college because he was connected, indirectly, with a tragic happening in which another student was killed. That student came to President White and said, "I thank you for what you've tried to do for me, and I tell you this: I will make a man out of myself yet." He had the support. He had the help.

Later on in the Civil War, which was just breaking out, he enlisted. Then came Gettysburg, and there was a brigadier general at Gettysburg, a brigadier general who had just been awarded his office due to gallantry and bravery and fidelity. A command was given this brigadier general to attack the Confederate Army. It was an impossible command; it was a hopeless command; and it was a mistaken command. Yet this brigadier general led a gallant charge into impossible odds and fell with nobility and bravery in the Confederate lines. That officer's name was General E. J. Farnsworth, the same student who had been expelled from the university yet encouraged and supported by Dr. White. Farnsworth had made good his promise that he would make a man out of himself yet.

No matter what the mistakes, no matter what the failures or blunders, there is the possibility of noble and honorable success if the will and the purpose are there and with just a little help from our friends. And you have a friend who sticks closer than a brother—Jesus Christ the Lord.

What is marvelous about this account of Mark and his failures and his regaining of the virtue of nobility in his life is not the account of his determination. That is not really the greatness. Nor is it his resolve. Nor is it the sympathy and kindness given him by Peter. That is not it, either. Nor is it the forgiveness of Paul. But what is of supreme importance here is the love and grace of God given in Jesus Christ the Lord. Oh, the depth of the riches of the love of God for you!

As long as there is the grace of God, you do not fail until you pronounce your own failure. As long as there is the grace of God in Jesus Christ, there is still time for another battle. And as long as there is the grace of God in Jesus Christ, remember this story of Mark and take heart and take hope. Lift up your hearts, because the deserter, the quitter, the coward, one of the worst failures on the pages of biblical history is left in the light of the golden text of Paul which reads: "Take Mark and bring him with you, for he is profitable to me in the ministry." That is the end of the story of Mark, but we will have the story of the tree to wind up.

It is to say this: as long as there is the grace of God in Jesus Christ the Lord, as long as this grace of God is operative in yielded Christian lives, then don't write off your Christian brother or your Christian sister. Don't do that.

That man wanted to cut down the tree in his back yard, but that tree took little notice of him. That tree did notice the graciousness and abundant provision of God the father. And that tree continued determinedly to draw water from the ground and to gain sympathy and warmth from the sun. In the late fall, that tree produced crisp, red, delicious apples. Yes, it really did.

Some of us see Christians with their early pink blossoms of happiness and think they should be that way forever. Or we see nut-sized green apples of bitterness in their lives and we're sure they'll never bear the fruit of joy. Could it be that we forget some of the best fruit is still to come?

Some of the best fruit is still to come in our lives and in the life of our church, especially if the time has that perspective in Jesus Christ the risen Lord that says, "If at first you don't succeed, try, try again."

Amen.

—R. Geoffrey Brown

[3051 words]
[30 minutes]

❦ *Sermon 36*

❦ *Date:* Sunday Between July 3 and July 9 inclusive, Year B

Texts:
Mark 6:7–13

Theme: We are commissioned to do the Gospel, traveling light.
Subject: Removing hindrances

❦ *Title:* Traveling Light

Prayer: God who leads us beside still waters: In the Scriptures, you pour yourself out upon us. Let us turn thirsty hearts to you, and drink deeply. Amen.

When my father and stepmother came to visit me from St. Louis recently, they brought an awful lot of luggage. They brought two heavy, full-sized suitcases, a weekend bag, a garment bag, a makeup case, and a large camera bag. My stepmother admitted she packed ten pairs of shoes. All this for a ten-day stay.

When we loaded the car to take them to the Oregon coast for a few days, my husband and I added our own luggage to the pile. We brought two full-sized suitcases, two duffel bags, another bag for maps and books, two sets of golf clubs, and our tennis racquets. He and I brought eight different pairs of athletic shoes. At the last minute, we decided not to bring along our bicycles, simply because we had no room for our cycling shoes.

No doubt about it, my family would be confounded by Jesus' instructions to his disciples when he sent them out to be missionaries. They were to travel, two by two. Their carry-on luggage was limited to one pair of sandals and a walking stick. They were not to take any money or extra provisions—no traveler's checks, no granola bars—but were to depend on the hospitality of those who received them. They were not to shop around for the most comfortable lodgings, but they were to stay where they were first invited. And if they entered a village where people were hostile and would not receive them, they were simply to shake the dust from their feet, before leaving quietly.

This was no sight-seeing trip; no summer vacation. The disciples were not invited to bring along the wife and kids for a little getaway on the company's expense account. Jesus sent them out to continue the work that he had begun: to preach and to cast out demons. This was to be their commission, their assignment, their vocation. And they were launched on this career path with practically nothing to go on but their wits and their guts.

The commissioning of the twelve disciples marked a turning point in the ministry of Jesus. Before that, Jesus had been doing it all by himself—all the teaching, all the exorcisms, all the healing. He had not always had a good press; his opponents sometimes accused him of running a magic show and performing miracles by sleight of hand. Most recently, he had been ridiculed and rejected in his own home base, Capernaum. The townspeople were upset over his healing of the daughter of Jairus and the woman with the uncontrollable flow of blood. After all, this was Jesus, who was—or used to be—one of their own. A simple carpenter. Who does he think he is, performing tricks and telling us what to do?

Jesus responded to this rejection—not by giving up his ministry, but rather by extending it. Extending it and sharing it. He invited the Twelve to share his work and his power. He sent them out to preach and gave them authority to cast out evil spirits. And when they started exorcising and healing, it proved that Jesus was not some charlatan or magician who deceived his audiences through trickery and illusion. Look! Even his followers—the common people, the fisherfolk, and tax collectors—even they had the same Spirit that was in him.

And he advised them, when they left on their missionary trips, that if they were rejected, as he had been in Capernaum, they were not to dwell on their failure or waste time and energy in hurling judgment upon those who rejected them. No. They were simply to shake the dust from their feet—dust that was there in the first place because no one had extended the basic Jewish courtesy of offering a vessel of water to wash up. The disciples were to dust off their feet, and walk away.

The evangelist Mark committed this story to writing because he wanted it to be a teaching for his church. Now, remember, Mark was writing nearly forty years after the death of Jesus. He wanted to remind his church that, just as the Twelve were commissioned, so too were they commissioned. Commissioned to do just what the Twelve had done, and what Jesus had done—to preach the gospel of repentance and cast out demons. And to do it all, traveling light.

We who hear this passage today and claim the scripture as authority in our lives, also need to remember that we, too, are commissioned. Commissioned to do just what the Twelve did, and what Jesus did. And to do it all, traveling light.

There are many ways in which our ability to carry out this commission is compromised by the extra baggage we carry. We load up our lives with luxuries and possessions, which we have to insure against theft and loss. We load up our bank accounts with cash, which we have to invest wisely for the highest possible yield. We load up our professional lives with power lunches and savvy maneuvering and groveling, because it is important to have leverage and credentials.

We load up our days with busywork so that we fall exhausted into bed every night. We load up our calendar with endless social obligations, because we want to be popular, we are afraid of being lonely. We load up our hearts with meddling in people's lives and problems when they are none of our business.

In the end, we are weighted down with excess baggage. We are overcrowded, overindebted, overcommitted, overstressed. And we are no closer than we ever were to doing what Jesus commissioned us to do: to share the message of repentance, and justice, and mercy; to exorcise the demons that dehumanize our daily lives.

How we yearn to simplify. How many times we have wanted to reassess our priorities and disentangle our lives. But our motives are personal ones, selfish ones. We want to travel light, so we can handle our problems and enjoy life.

When have our motives ever been spiritual ones? When have we ever wanted to simplify our lives so that we could be more effective witnesses to the Gospel? When have we paused to consider that our complex and burdened lives might be a hindrance—a real obstruction—to Christian living? When have we stopped to realize that our homeless brothers and sisters—who, ironically, have the simplest of all possible lives—are far better equipped than we to hear and understand what Jesus taught and lived for? And to go out and do what he asked.

Jesus calls us to examine our motives, our priorities. Jesus calls us to peel away the layers of possessions and busyness and credentials that protect us. They protect us, but they also burden us, numb us, build walls around us. We hide behind those walls. And after a while, we become dependent upon them to hold us up. We begin to believe that, without them, we are worthless, we are empty, we are nothing.

Think about it. If we no longer depend upon our money, or our possessions, or our job status, or our social position, or our family connections, to support us and give us meaning, what is left? What is left?

Now there is a question for the Twelve who went out with only a pair of sandals and a walking stick. There is a question for the homeless who beg for change on the streets. There is a question for us. What is left?

What is left is faith: a faith that is like a walking stick, that gives us support and strength; a faith that is like a pair of sandals, that protects us and eases our journey; a faith that is like a commission, that gives us direction, and tells us how to live; a faith that is like an empty hand, that asks and receives and knows the pain, and the grace, of survival.

That is what we have left, when we're traveling light. Nothing more. But nothing less.

Amen.

—Elizabeth Chandler Felts

[1376 words]
[14 minutes]

Sermon 37

Date: Fourth Sunday of Advent, Year C

Texts:
Micah 5:2–5a
Psalm 80:1–7
Hebrews 10:5–10
Luke 1:39–55

Theme: Individuals, God's "little ones," can make a difference.
Subject: Power and powerlessness

Title: Promises Kept Through the Lowly

In a world of complex problems, massive dislocations, and international implications, it is hard to believe that we, as individuals, "little ones," can make a difference in the world. What the scripture says this morning, however, is that little people, blessed by the power of God, can make a difference. Both texts are a celebration of the newness wrought by God through the obedience of the "little ones." In both texts, the Bible has noticed that large concentrations of power and authority have caused deep human trouble.

The Micah text is addressed to Jerusalem, which is, at this point in history, a center of power, wealth, and influence. Assyria is on the ascendancy, but Jerusalem believes it can fend off the influences of this international power by compromise and political manipulation. Micah prophesies that the city cannot save itself; surrounded by its enemy it is doomed to failure.

The village of Bethlehem is contrasted with massive Jerusalem. The city, Jerusalem, the embodiment of arrogance and power, has always looked down with pity on poor Bethlehem, an agricultural village—its name means "House of Bread." On the other hand, every listening Israelite would remember that Bethlehem was the home of David. But, over the long period of history, Jerusalem preempted Bethlehem for royal claims.

The proof of a prophet is always hindsight. At first, Micah was ridiculed because Judah, the southern kingdom of which Jerusalem was the capital, survived the siege of Sennacherib, though in a weakened, vassal state. Judah had survived the political machinations of the age. Micah was wrong. He lost what my son calls a "See bet." That's when you can stand and say in someone else's face, "See—I told you so."

Micah, however, is proved right in the long run. Judah finally falls to Babylon in 587 B.C., and the new passage we read this morning, promising a new king, free of Jerusalem, who will restore the fortunes of Israel, comes 130 years after Micah's original prediction. It is this new king who will cope with Israel's enemies, who will be the faithful shepherd of Israel, who will be the source of well-being and security which is the biblical conception of peace.

It is easy to see why the early church made use of this poetry (Matthew 2:6). The contrast between Jerusalem and Bethlehem is now transposed to be a contrast between mighty Herod and modest Jesus. Herod embodies all the might, arrogance, and political legitimacy of the ruthless, urban elite. Jesus, by contrast, carries the hopes and possibilities of village life which has no imperial ambitions. The wave of Israel's future is not with Jerusalem and all its Herods, but with the new king who is no party to such arrogant ambition.

Do you hear how much this sounds like American politics: the urban elite, Eastern intellectual effete snobs, as opposed to the silent majority of rural, Middle America? The struggle between entrenched bureaucracy, and the voice of the people is an old, old story.

Our Gospel lesson speaks from the voice of the small town, and the silent, but righteous, majority. It concerns the faith of Mary. She is indeed a nobody from whom no one expected anything. But she is to be the mother of "my Lord" (v. 43).

It is interesting to note how this information is revealed. Many of you have watched Bill Moyer's conversation with Joseph Campbell (America's best-known expert on religious myths) on PBS. Campbell commented that sexual initiation rights for males are often violent, while female initiation rights into adult sexuality are more often marked by times of separation and contemplation on the meaning of creating and nurturing new life.

Notice that after the annunciation Mary goes to the hill country to visit her cousin Elizabeth. It is Elizabeth, who after hearing the experience of the visitation of the angel, feels her child leap in the womb, and she exclaims with a loud cry, "Blessed are you among women, and blessed is the fruit of your womb." Then Mary experiences her own private ecstasy. And she says: "My soul magnifies the Lord. . .".

In a land called "holy," in a time we call sacred there are two women: One, Elizabeth, was unable to bear a child until late in her life, and the other is Mary, who was too young by modern standards to be either betrothed or pregnant. These women had no wealth, no social position, or special training. They came from a small Roman colony, their men had no special standing.

The Message of the Humble

Yet from the lowly such as these, comes good news. They embody the humble way God comes to us. They tell us Jesus is coming with no imperial ambitions, but dreams of a new set of social relations free of exploitation and fear. The wave of Israel's future is not with Jerusalem and all its Herods, but with the new king who is no party to such arrogant ambition. It is this unencumbered king who has the power to save.

Now, Mary has been portrayed, especially by Protestant theologians, as an example of a meek and submissive female nature, accepting her lot in life. This takes away from Mary her power of faith, because even in powerlessness there is a choice. In the highly acclaimed play *Fences*, by August Wilson, there appears the story of a strong and powerful black man and his wife. It is the story of "no room in the inn."

Rose: "I married your Daddy and settled down to cooking his supper and keeping clean sheets on the bed. When your daddy walked through the house he was so big he filled it up. That was my first mistake. Not to make him leave room for me. But at that time I wanted that. I wanted a house I could sing in. And that's what your daddy gave me. I didn't know to keep up his strength I had to give up little pieces of mine. I did that. I took on his life as mine and mixed up the pieces so that you could hardly tell which was which anymore. It was my choice. It was my life and I didn't have to live it like that. But that's what life offered me in the way of being a woman and I took it. I grabbed hold of it with both hands."

The Radical Mary

That is the choice of many women, but notice what a different model Mary presents. She doesn't grab, she receives in wonder, and she is not asked to give up herself, she is asked to give her son. The power of Mary's faith is not that she believes in what little she can get, but in how much God will fulfill the promises made. She believes God is faithful to God's word and that God has power to keep the promises.

The promise is that a son will be born, but, in the larger sense, the son would rescue God's people and transform this oppressed community into a people of joy and wellbeing. This is the meaning of peace in the Hebrew *"Shalom."*

So Mary sings (vss. 46–55). She sings the best loved hymn of the church which is also the most radical and subversive of all our songs. Did you know that the military junta of Argentina banned the public speaking of the Magnificat? This ban was not rescinded until the reestablishment of democracy in this decade.

Mary sings of a radical inversion of values in which martyrs rather than tyrants rule. Some theologians have even said that history is a footnote to the Magnificat: her son shall bring mercy on those who fear him, show strength with his arm, scatter the proud, put down the mighty, send the rich away, and exalt the low among many other works. Soren Kierkegaard puts this historical footnote in a nutshell: "The tyrant dies and his rule is over; the martyr dies and his rule begins."

This radical inversion is articulated in verses 51–53. Life is going to be transformed in astonishing ways. The proud will be brought low. The now established powers (all the Herods and all the Jerusalems) will be dethroned. In their place will come those of low degree and low estate. Not only will the hungry be filled but the rich will be sent away hungry. Now the ones who have fed off the suffering of the poor will be banished.

This is extraordinary good news—if you are among the waiting, the watching hungry. It is raw bad news for the affluent. In receiving this poem it matters if we are among the "hungry" or the "rich." In this country we think of the "hungry" as the minority, the eccentric few—and we ignore them, cast them aside. We do not listen to them seriously, because we are in power.

What the Advent Gospel is trying to tell us, and what has been played out again and again in our history, is that there is a restlessness among the villagers of Bethlehem who resent the rapaciousness of Jerusalem. From the mouth of Mary, in her meditation, comes a prophetic word as strong as Isaiah or Micah; there will be a reckoning, a reordering. It will be wrought by the power of God—through the little ones.

Dangerous and Transforming News

These two poems from Micah and Mary are an invitation for us to look again at the map of our economic world. We notice the regions of affluence, the concentrations of wealth, and the wide spaces of neediness. We notice the region which we inhabit. Is it one of plenty or want? We need to ask "What promises of God are on the move in our world, promises for well-being and food?"

"Where is God's peace being proclaimed?" Advent is a time to ponder the change that needs to happen—and then to imagine how we might participate in that change.

The change to come will be wrought by the presence of God. Both Micah and Mary sing of undefeated promises. Those promises will be wrought by the "little ones" who have been neglected. Think! Who are the people crying for justice? Those in power call for a measured approach, "constructive engagement," but real change occurs by those who have been given a fresh power in the hope that their hunger will be filled.

These are dangerous and transformative issues. Caesars have proclaimed themselves to be gods and they have fallen from their thrones. Empires as long-lived as Rome and as short-lived as

Nazi Germany have proclaimed themselves masters of the world and they have disappeared from the face of the earth. Napoleons and Hitlers by many names have set out to subdue all nations under their feet, and they all lie in their graves marked with shame. For "he has scattered the proud in the imagination of their hearts, he has put down the mighty from their thrones."

A simple, surprised young girl from Nazareth in Galilee remains, standing humbly among the ruins of fallen giants because she believed in her heart: "[God] has exalted those of low estate." Advent is a story that shocks us into the resolve not to disregard the urgency of the text or its reality among us.

Amen.

—W. Matthew Broadbent

[1875 words]
[19 minutes]

❦ CHAPTER FOUR

PERSONAL GROWTH/ CHRISTIAN LIVING

Jesus says to those who follow him, "You are the light of the world." What an amazing thought! He invites each of us, in the words of poet Gerard Manley Hopkins, to "let Him easter in us, be a dayspring to the dimness in us." Walking with Jesus is neither painless nor easy. It requires responding with the fullness of our being to those in need and being there for the hurting, the unloved, and the unlovable.

Sometimes we experience Jesus as comforting us in our afflictions. At other times, he afflicts us in our comfort. Sometimes, we know him as flexible and forgiving; at other times, as uncompromising and insistent.

For Christians, personal growth is impossible unless we accept God's forgiveness and extend it to others. The local Christian Church is a community of those who are forgiven and forgiving—or it is nothing. A heart full of grudges is a heart devoid of God.

We cannot respect others until we learn to respect ourselves. We are designed by God to serve and to lead. God made each of us as a being with authority who grows in leadership by giving and serving.

As human beings, we are doing the best we can—but that's no excuse! We must set aside the American myths of success and learn to see things from God's perspective.

Jesus gives us the gift to be simple and thus to be free. He rescues us from the delusion that it is all right not to honor our commitments.

We are constantly tested—tempted by distorted priorities, tempted to ignore reality, tempted by our own impatience. By overcoming trials and tragedies, we respond to God's call to our true vocation.

Sermon 38

Date: Fifth Sunday After Epiphany, Year A

Texts:
Isaiah 58:1–9a
Psalm 12:1–10
1 Corinthians 2:1–12
Matthew 5:13–20

Theme: The light of God in each of us can be exposed or hidden, well focused or out of focus.
Subject: Christian life, church

Title: "You are the light of the world!"

"You are the light of the world."—Jesus said that [pause] *to us*! What an amazing thought! It sounds wrong, doesn't it? "Not me, Lord," we want to say. "'The light of the world'? Me, a light to anyone? Why, when it comes to life and its problems, I have trouble keeping myself from bumping into the furniture of the universe. And my spouse—when it comes to moral or spiritual choices he [or she] can scarcely see the tunnel, let alone the light at its end. As for our kids, 'light of the world,' you're joking, right? Why if they encountered a dead horse in the middle of their bedroom floor some night, they would just step over it."

Jesus said, "You are the light of the world." First, note the context. These familiar words are found in a section of the Gospel according to Matthew known as the Sermon on the Mount. Following the overall theme that Jesus is the new lawgiver, the second Moses, the one who fulfills the message of the Law and the prophets, Matthew weaves together many recollections or oral traditions to form a single, coherent presentation. There are five such collections of material in Matthew's Gospel, a not accidental parallel to the Five Books of Moses, known as the Law or Torah. The resulting "sermon" may be called "the rule book of the kingdom of heaven" or "the charter of the just society." It sets forth in clear, ringing phrases not only the guidelines that citizens of the kingdom are expected to follow but the attitudes without which obedience becomes mere hypocrisy.

The Sermon on the Mount

To whom is the Sermon directed? In his description of the audience, Matthew employs an interesting ambiguity. He tells us of huge crowds attracted by reports of our Lord's teaching and healing. "Seeing the crowds," says Matthew, Jesus "went up on the mountain, and when he sat down his disciples came to him," the suggestion being that the Sermon on the Mount is directed not to the multitudes but to the handful that can be termed "disciples." Yet when the Sermon concludes (7:28), Matthew comments: "the crowds were astonished at his teaching, for he taught them as one who had authority, and not as their scribes."

The Sermon, as Matthew has structured it, incorporates spiritual and psychological wisdom from which any human being can benefit. However, it is directed primarily to those who are willing to pay the cost of discipleship, to those who are more concerned with God's reign and God's justice than with anything else. The two striking metaphors, "salt of the earth" and "light of the world," immediately follow the Beatitudes. In particular they come after that jolting change from third person to second person pronouns: "Blessed are those who are persecuted for righteousness sake" becomes "blessed are you when men revile you." When Matthew arranged his materials, he was thinking of the situation of the Christians of his day, Jewish and Gentile converts, who found themselves objects of derision and discrimination because they had chosen to respond to God's call to follow the Christ.

Jesus said, "You are the light of the world." There is no question in my mind that this saying about the capacity of Christians for revealing and concealing God's light is an authentic saying of Jesus'. It is found a total of four times in Matthew, Mark, and Luke. In Mark 4, Jesus says to his listeners:

> *"Do you bring in a lamp to put it under a bowl or a bed? Instead, don't you put it on its stand? For whatever is hidden is meant to be disclosed, and whatever is concealed is meant to be brought out into the open. If anyone has ears to hear, let him hear." (vss. 21-23)*

Mark is telling us something about the way that Jesus taught—in parables rather than directly. The message of Jesus is transmitted to humankind like a radio broadcast sent into the atmosphere. If you don't happen to be tuned in, you will miss the message. There is no moral imperative in Mark's version of the saying. We are not asked to do anything but keep our ears open—if we have ears.

Notice the subtle but real difference in the way in which Luke uses the same material:

> *"No one lights a lamp and hides it in a jar or puts it under a bed. Instead, he puts it on a stand, so that those who come in can see the light. For there is nothing hidden that will not be disclosed, and nothing concealed that will not be known or brought out into the open. Therefore consider carefully how you listen. Whoever has will be given more; whoever does not have, even what he thinks he has will be taken from him." (Luke 8:16-18)*

We have the same imagery but a slightly different point. Like Mark, Luke is explaining why Jesus taught in parables. But he places the responsibility for getting the message squarely on our shoulders. Pay attention to what God is telling you, for if you fail to do so, not only will you miss out on what God has to say but you will lose what you thought you already knew. In simplest terms, use it or lose it. The Gospel is a self-recharging flashlight with no shelf life. The more you use it, the brighter it glows. Fail to use it, and it cannot be rekindled.

The remaining use of the saying on light is found in Luke 11 (verses 33–36). After excoriating his generation for demanding a sign, Jesus says:

> *No one lights a lamp and puts it in a place where it will be hidden, or under a bowl. Instead he puts it on its stand, so that those who come in may see the light. Your eye is the lamp of your body. When your eyes are good, your whole body also is full of light. But when they are bad, your body also is full of darkness. See to it, then, that the light within you is not darkness. Therefore, if your whole body is full of light, and no part of it dark, it will be completely lighted, as when the light of a lamp shines on you.*

As Fred B. Craddock comments: "The . . . sayings on light are placed here to say that to the person of integrity and openness to light, Jesus' message is clear enough and able to give the light of God to one's life."[1] Again, we have the language of moral imperative. If something is wrong or deficient with your spiritual perspective, do something about it. In contemporary idiom, if you can't see clearly, get your eyes examined by an optometrist and get new glasses. If your spirit is dim, tune

---

[1] *Harper's Bible Commentary* (San Francisco: Harper & Row Publishers, 1988), p. 1030.

up your integrity and your openness to the light. This use of the material is echoed in the sixth Beatitude: "Blessed are the pure in heart, for they shall see God." (Matthew 5:8)

Each Christian Is the Light of the World

Matthew goes one step beyond the other Gospel accounts. He prefaces the material on revealing and concealing light with the stark declaration: "You are the light of the world."You are not urged to be the light of the world. You are the light of the world. Matthew is not exhorting Christians; he is reminding them what they essentially are. We are, to be sure, God's reflected light. In the Prologue to the Gospel of John, Jesus is described as the true light that illumines every one. In the eighth chapter of John, Jesus says: "I am the light of the world. Whoever follows me will never walk in darkness, but will have the light of life" (v. 12). In chapter 9, he says, "While I am in the world, I am the light of the world" (v. 5). But now and until the end of the age, we are the light of the world.

That light in each of us can be exposed or hidden, well focused or out of focus, diffused into glorious rainbow patterns or reflected into empty space. In other words, Christians can be lamp stands, beacons, lenses, and prisms, or we can be black-out curtains, burned out headlights, and reading lamps of inadequate wattage. We can walk in the light, sharing the light with others, or we can stumble about in our own inner darkness.

Jesus said, "You are the light of the world." The "you" of this sentence is plural. It refers to the church. Now the church to which Matthew belonged must have been a rough bunch. If it were otherwise, he would not have to have constantly reminded them of their imperfections—the point of the parable of the wheat and the tares, the teachings on dealing with anger and the need for forgiveness, and constant warnings such as Matthew 7: 21: "Not every one who says to me, 'Lord, Lord,' shall enter the kingdom of heaven, but he who does the will of my Father who is in heaven," the one who "does what my father in heaven wants."

If the church that Matthew attended had been perfect he would never have used the straightforward, startling image of the coming king who will not divide the sheep from the goats on the basis of the purity of their doctrine or the record of their attainments but on whether or not they responded to those in need: "The King will reply,'I tell you the truth, whatever you did for one of the least of these brothers of mine, you did for me.'" . . . . 'I tell you the truth, whatever you did not do for one of the least of these, you did not do for me.'" (Matthew 25:40 and 45)

The Church as the Light of the World

Just as I said a few moments ago about individuals, I now say about this church. Now and until the end of the age, this church is the light of the world. That light can be exposed or hidden, well focused or out of focus, diffused into glorious rainbow patterns or reflected into empty space. In other words, this church can be a lamp stand, a beacon, a lens, or a prism or it can be a black-out curtain, a burned out headlight, a reading lamp of inadequate wattage.

I believe that here at this church the torch of the Gospel will continue to burn bright. The light of God will shine in our midst and in our community. The searchlight of God's justice will scatter the darkness. The bright rays of God's hope will drive out despair and aimlessness. We are coming out of the hollow and onto the hilltop, out of a season in which we banked the furnace and kept the embers glowing into an era in which we shall become a bonfire.

Jesus says: "You are the light of the world." He does not say, "I urge you to be the light of the world" or "Will you think about being the light of the world and get back to me on it?" or "If you have nothing better to do, will you be the light of the world?" Jesus says: "You are the light of the world."

Amen.

—LDS

[2000 words]
[20 minutes]

❦ *Sermon 39*

❦ *Date:* Third Sunday of Easter, Year A

Texts:
Acts 2:14a, 36–41
Psalm 116:1-4, 12–19
1 Peter 1:17–23
Luke 24:13–35

or Easter, Year C

Texts:
Exodus 15:1–11
1 Corinthians 15:20–26
Luke 24:13–35

Theme: Jesus invites us to be "eastered."
Subject: Christian life

❦ *Title:* Burning Hearts in an Icebox World

The Road to Emmaus

It was a hot and dusty road. A lonesome road. A seemingly endless road. On the first Easter, they walked the road to Emmaus. They started out with confusion and bewilderment. They arrived with hope and fervor. When they set out, they had problems—they were bits and pieces of the problem. When they arrived, they were part of the solution. At the beginning of the road, they had nothing to look forward to but more road. At the end, they had everything!

We don't know exactly where Emmaus was. Most ancient manuscripts of the Gospel of Luke place Emmaus 7 miles from Jerusalem, but others prefer 20 miles. A town named Emmaus did exist at the latter distance. Twenty miles—a good day's walk—plenty of time to mull over and discuss the events of the previous week.

There are four important characters in the drama of the road to Emmaus—an unnamed disciple (I think it was Luke, the author of the account), Cleopas (about whom we know nothing), the unrecognized Jesus, and Simon Peter (who remains offstage during the entire scene). So our little play is set on the way to an unknown place, and its cast comprises two nonentities, a mystery figure, and an absent coward. We don't know where we're going, we don't know who is going with us, and we don't know what awaits us when we get there. It all sounds familiar. It is just like our own lives.

Luke reports that the unnamed disciple and Cleopas were having a heated conversation. Then Jesus joined them and asked what was on their minds. We discover that, like most of us, they were sharing with one another their misunderstandings and misconceptions. They thought of Jesus as a prophet, a wonder worker, and as a political liberator. He had seemed so powerful in word and deed, but he had disappointed their expectations by proving so utterly powerless that the ruling elite had been able to kill him.

And now there were confused and contradictory reports that his tomb was empty, that angels had told some of Jesus' women followers that he was alive. What was going on?Had his body been stolen? Were the women seeing things? Could Jesus' death have just been a bad dream? If he were alive, where was he and why hadn't he started to set up God's kingdom?

We live as they did in the midst of confused and contradictory reports. We want to do what is best for our families, our society, our world, and ourselves. But it is all so foggy, nebulous, and ambiguous. We aren't even sure how we should feel about the threats, challenges, and opportunities that surround us, let alone what we should do about them. And no matter what we do, we make mistakes. We flee from one set of problems to the next—from one unsatisfactory relationship to another, from one therapist to another, from one job to another. We do exactly what these two disciples did: we head for the suburbs! But the tranquility we find there is leavened with pain, suffering, and uncertainty. There is so little time and so much to do, so few good friends. There is so little money for the special schools, the activities, the hundred-fifty-dollar sneakers, the orthodontia our children need. There is such an abundance of what we don't need—loneliness, fear of the future, heartbreak.

They Knew Him in the Breaking of the Bread

And then this stranger told them the truth about suffering, death, and glory. No pain, no gain. No cross, no crown. He broke bread and gave it to them. In the process, he shared his brokenness with them and they shared theirs with him. And they recognized him.

For us today, Jesus is known in the breaking of the bread. He is known as we remember the breaking of his body and the outpouring of his blood in the Lord's Supper.The disciples wanted easy answers to their problems. Jesus offered them a church service, complete with an exposition of the Scriptures, a prayer of thanksgiving, and a sharing of the bread and wine to remind them of his death—as these elements have reminded Christians for two thousand years of his death.

Our church is not a memorial to a dead hero. It is a place where he lives and is known through word and sacrament, through the open Bible and the broken bread.

He gave thanks and they recognized him. Whenever we are grateful to God for his gifts—for the material things that sustain us or for the spiritual gifts that give our lives nobility and meaning, Jesus emerges. Whenever we assemble in his name to honor his teachings and his example, he is here.

Jesus is known as his body is broken, again and again, in the sufferings of the wretched of the earth—our brothers and sisters with whom we are one. Whenever we respond, sharing our lives and substance, caring enough to live as examples, concerned enough to speak from the heart, committed to making a difference in the lives of others, Jesus is known.

Jesus is known in our own brokenness—in our hurt and suffering. Being a Christian is not being given a free pass through life's afflictions. Being a Christian is knowing God in the midst of contradiction and sorrow.

The poet Gerard Manley Hopkins has written of Jesus:

Let Him easter in us,
be a dayspring to the dimness in us.

In the words of one commentator:

> The living Christ easters our sorrows, our tears (especially on the days that have limped so badly that we are glad to spank them and put them to bed and be done with them), our loneliness, our hopes, our humanity.[1]

In the calendar of the liturgical year, there is not one Easter Sunday but seven—today is the third. The calendar seems to preach that Easter no more happened *once* than it happened once upon a time. As surely as lengthening days, warming temperatures, and the emergence of flowers herald the coming of spring, so, day by day, does the power of God within, the healing of distressed minds, the budding of loving relationships, the reconciliation of adversaries, the growth of caring communities, the reemergence of conscience in an all-too-amoral world. All these are signs that Jesus lives and that we are being eastered.

He Has Appeared to Simon

He has appeared to Simon the unstable—not to Peter the Rockman. We note that according to Luke's account in chapter 2 of Acts, it was not "Simon" but "Peter" who spoke to the crowd in Jerusalem on the Day of Pentecost. In the six weeks between the crucifixion of Jesus and Pentecost, what had happened to this man? What had transformed him from coward to hero? from discredited, ineffectual buffoon to a determined and forceful leader?

He had lost the fear that had made him Simon who denied Jesus. He had lost the fear of death. He had encountered one who had triumphed over the grave. As Peter preached about Jesus a few weeks later, "it was impossible for death to keep its hold on him" (Acts 2:24). Peter had been eastered. The living Jesus had become the dayspring, the dawn, to the darkness in him. The light of the world had flickered, but it had not gone out. The darkness in Simon's heart could not overcome it. The darkness in our hearts can never extinguish it.

The Lord has appeared to Simon! Simon did not conjure him up through some correctly performed religious rite. Simon did not earn the privilege of beholding him. Simon's sorrow, contrition, and repentance had not won him the right to see Jesus. The Lord has appeared to Simon! The initiative—as always—is God's.

Simon the braggart who had sworn never to forsake Jesus, Simon the show-off who waved a sword in the face of those who came to arrest his Lord, Simon who could not get away from danger fast enough, Simon who had thrice denied his master—this Simon was crucified and dead with Christ. Yet as Peter the rock he was alive, his faith and faithfulness so firm that the gates of hell could not prevail against them.

Years later, Peter would write in his first letter:

> it was not with perishable things such as silver or gold that you were redeemed from the empty way of life handed down to you from your forefathers, but with the precious blood of Christ. (1 Peter 1:18)
>
> Now that you have purified yourselves by obeying the truth so that you have sincere love for your brothers, love one another deeply, from the heart. (1 Peter 1:22)

Jesus had turned on Peter's heartlight! Jesus had turned Peter's whimpering and whining into dancing! Peter had been eastered!

---

[1] Garrison, R. Benjamin, *Word & Witness*, April 29, 1990, p. 3.

A Sunday Like Other Sundays

For the disciples on the road to Emmaus, it proved to be a Sunday like the Sundays that have come and gone for two thousand years. It was a Sunday like this Sunday—here and throughout the world. There is the word and the sacrament. There is a yearning for God's message to our hearts and lives. There is a passion within us. As the prophet Jeremiah exclaimed: "if I say, 'I will not mention him or speak any more in his name,' his word is in my heart like a fire, a fire shut up in my bones. I am weary of holding it in; indeed, I cannot." (Jeremiah 20:9)

But it is not only a Sunday. Jesus is known by his disciples not in a miracle such as the feeding of the multitudes but in the simplest of all human acts—talking and eating. We tend to look for Jesus in the unique, the wondrous, the inexplicable. We set aside Sunday to seek him. And sometimes we forget that he is beside us Monday through Saturday. He is present as we earn our daily bread, as we share it, as we are nourished and nurtured by it.

The test of our faith as Christians is not whether we can recognize him for an hour on Sunday but what we do with the other 167 hours of the week. An hour of worship is painless and easy. Walking with Jesus—responding with the fullness of one's being to those in need; discerning what is right and wrong in a world perpetually out-of-order; being there for the hurting, the unloved, and the unlovable—is neither painless nor easy.

So why bother? Why not just be laid-back Californians and go with the flow?

Because we are eastered again and again. Jesus dawns in our lives and dispels the dimness in us. He appears to us not because we want him to or ask him to—certainly not because we merit his appearing.

In the words of Methodist pastor R. Benjamin Garrison:

> Jesus comes knocking at the door—of the bereaved and lonely, of the hopeless and helpless. But he does not force the lock.
> He walks with us![2]

Jesus comes knocking at the door of our homes, of our places of work and recreation, and of our hearts. When I was a child, the most exciting words I could hear were those of a pal: "Can Lowell come out and play?" And the most important request that any of us will ever hear is God's summons to come out and live. He invites us to be eastered. In the midst of an icebox world, he invites us to let our hearts burn with our love for him and for one another.

Amen.

—LDS

[1950 words]
[20 minutes]

❦ *Sermon 40*

❦ *Date:* Second Sunday of Advent, Year B

Texts:
Isaiah 40:1–11
Psalm 85:1-2, 8–13

---

[2] Ibid.

2 Peter 3:8–15a
Mark 1:1–8

Theme: There is a time to comfort, a time to be comforted, a time to afflict, and a time to be afflicted.
Subject: Comfort

Title: The Desert on the Road to Bethlehem

John the Disturber

Advent belongs to John the Baptist, not to Jesus. As much as we want to jump the gun and begin celebrating Christmas, Advent is the season to prepare our hearts and lives for the coming of Christ. As much as we want to resist the call to quiet self-examination, "Advent pilgrims on the way to the manger must pass through the desert where John is preaching."[1]

It is actually possible to sentimentalize Jesus, to tame him, to turn him into a buddy as comfortable as an old pair of slippers, and to ignore him. But John the Baptist is another story. Trying to snuggle up with John is like trying to relax during the last two minutes of a Super Bowl when your team is behind by six points. John is simply not comfortable.

Many years ago, I was manuscript editor at a religious publishing house in Chicago. One of the projects for which I was responsible was a book about preaching to which several prominent ministers contributed. Each minister wrote an essay on how to prepare a sermon and submitted a sample of his own work. Although I read the material many times as it passed from the original typescripts to a single, unified manuscript to galley proofs to page proofs and finally into the final bound version, the contents of the book is a blur in my memory—except for one sentence. It is a sentiment I have quoted a thousand times. One of the ministers explained the preacher's job as follows: "Our task is to comfort the afflicted and to afflict the comfortable."

Priestly Versus Prophetic Religion

There are two kinds of religious experience: priestly and prophetic. Priestly religion underwrites the status quo. It views God as the guarantor and guardian of society. It reduces religion to rules, mores, and ceremonies. It offers comfort and security. Do what is required by the norms of society, your family's expectations, and the rituals of the religious establishment and you will be OK—in this world and the next.

Prophetic religion, on the other hand, sees things not as they are but as they ought to be. Prophetic religion demands change, repentance, a return to basics. It takes chances, gives up security, and detests compromises. Prophetic religion makes unconditional demands and expects total commitment. The message of the prophets is not "I'm OK, you're OK." The message of the prophets is "I'm not OK, neither are you, neither is our society, and something ought to be done about it—now!"

Priestly religion comforts the afflicted. Prophetic religion afflicts the comfortable.

---

[1] Craddock, Fred B., *Preaching the New Common Lectionary. Year B, Advent, Christmas, Epiphany* (Nashville, TN: Abingdon Press, 1987), p. 31.

After forty years of studying the religions of humankind while traveling on my own personal faith journey, I am sure there is a time to comfort, a time to be comforted, a time to afflict, and a time to be afflicted.

We live in a time requiring all of these. There are millions in need of the most basic comforts of life: food, shelter, meaningful work, stable families, dependable friends, and caring life partners. It is a time for you and me to comfort the comfortless.

It is a time of confusion and peril. Many parts of the world are in danger of sinking into chaos. The Soviet Union and many Eastern bloc nations are teetering on the edge of an abyss. The United States is running the risk of war the way toddlers attending a day care center run the risk of catching cold. The economy of this country and many others seems to be hanging by a thread.

It is a time for you and me to seek comfort where it truly may be found—not in our possessions or drugs or distractions, not in frenzied busyness or endless self-examination, not even in religion. It is time to renew our connection with the God who, in the words of our Old Testament reading for today, "tends his flock like a shepherd: . . . gathers the lambs in his arms and carries them close to his heart." (Isaiah 40:1–11)

It is a time to afflict the comfortable, to realize that the world cannot persist with one tiny minority of its population stripping the rest of their natural resources and returning to the world mountains of garbage and rivers of toxic waste. It is time to set aside the myth that each of us can live as he or she desires with no consideration of the consequences. It is time to realize that we do not live in a "no harm, no foul" world. It is a time to understand that we live in a world governed by a single moral premise:

"The only thing necessary for the triumph of evil is for good men [and good women!] to do nothing."[2]

It is a time to afflict and to be afflicted.

Time for a Change

And it is a time to change. As Fred Craddock summarizes the message of John the Baptist:

> Repent of the arrogant assumption that you alone are favored, that you are exempt from the moral demands put on others, that being better than your worst neighbors is your salvation, as though God grades on the curve. Repent. . . .[3]

There are times in my life when I would have said to John the Baptist, "I don't come here to be insulted. I come to be consoled. I don't want to feel like a bad person, like a failure. I want to feel accepted. I come here for peace of mind. I come for comfort."

When Comfort Is Not Enough

But what is comfort?

Is comfort having enough to pay all the bills? Is it being able to afford luxuries—electronic playthings, sports cars, jewelry, furs, works of art, travel abroad?

---

[2] Attributed to Edmund Burke, *Bartlett's Familiar Quotations*, edited by Emily Morison Beck (Boston: Little, Brown and Company, 1980), p. 374.

[3] Craddock, ibid.

A woman I knew when I was a child in Chicago drove her husband and family remorselessly for years to save enough money to buy a house in the suburbs. If she could just get out of the crowded tenement and have a place of her own, she would be happy, she thought. She scrimped and saved and denied herself and her loved ones every pleasure until, finally, she had just enough for the down payment for her dream house.

But when she and her family moved to their suburban paradise, she was not happy at all. In many ways, she was more miserable than she had ever been in her life. Having what she wanted did not solve her problems.

Years ago I had a friend who was a brilliant, compassionate, and generous man. He was a sensitive and caring psychotherapist. Truly, he was a comfort. He was also heir to a sizable estate. One day, he received a check for several million dollars. For weeks, he wandered the streets of Philadelphia's Center City, trying to decide what he really wanted, what would make him happy. He stood outside the most exclusive jewelry store in the city, thinking to himself: "I can buy anything I want in this store. As a matter of fact, if I wanted to, I could buy the store!"

He came to the conclusion that there were only four things he really wanted: a Mercedes, a house in the country, a painting by Tintoretto, and a silver flute. He bought all four and became a hermit. The brilliance, compassion, and generosity disappeared behind his mansion walls. When he became comfortable, he was no longer comforting.

"A Little Roll With Butter"

The story is told of a simple man, a very good man, who died and went to heaven. His life having been blameless and exemplary in every respect, he was welcomed by God and offered anything he desired—pleasure, knowledge, riches, power—anything. His only request: "Every morning for breakfast, couldn't I just have a little roll with butter?"

What any of us really needs in order to be comforted is very simple. What any of us needs to give to others to comfort them is just as simple.

Once I was in Boston for a conference. I had arrived early and went to the hotel restaurant for lunch. It was terribly crowded and I was seated at a table with three strangers. I immediately recognized them as three of America's most successful authors, men for whom I had great admiration and envy. The first writer asked the others what it was they "really wanted in life." The first writer said, "I know what I want. I want to be rich—not just a millionaire. I want to be as rich as Aristotle Onassis. I want to own a Greek island." The next writer said: "I want to be powerful—as powerful as the president of the United States." The third writer did not like the way the conversation was going, became visibly agitated, and left.

I sat there like a fly on the wall, silently observing. The first writer tried to draw me into the conversation. He said: "Tell us, young man, what is it you really want?"

"I want to be known," I replied.

"Sure," said one of the writers, "just like us. You want to be famous, to see your picture on the cover of Time magazine, to be interviewed on the Today Show. That's what we all want."

"No. That's not what I mean," I protested. "I don't want to be famous. I want to be known. I want someone to care so much about me that they will want to know who I am, what I am, and that person or those persons will not stop until they know."

The first writer interrupted me, trying to help clarify what I was saying. "You're not talking about being known. You're talking about being loved. In other words, you want to be loved for who you really are."

"I guess so," I answered.

The two famous writers looked at me for a few seconds, at one another, and then back at me. Then one of them spoke: "What we want is easy compared to what you want."

And as they continued to speak, I stopped a waitress, who asked me what it was that I wanted, and I almost said, "Every morning for breakfast, couldn't I just have a little roll with butter?" "What is it that I want?" I want to be known. I want to be loved for who I am. I want to be comforted.

There is a time to comfort, a time to be comforted, a time to afflict, and a time to be afflicted. Advent belongs to John the Baptist, who was called to comfort the afflicted and to afflict the comfortable. Before we can get to the manger, we must pass through the desert where John is preaching.

Amen.

—LDS

[1700 words]
[18 minutes]

❦ *Sermon 41*

❦ *Date:* Sunday Between July 24 and Jyly 30 inclusive Pentecost, Year C

Texts:
Colossians 2:6–15
Luke 11:1–13
[Special reading: **John 8:2–10.** Use in place of or in addition to the passage from Luke.]

Theme: Jesus was flexible in approach yet uncompromising in principle.
Subject: New beginnings
[This sermon and the one following should be presented as a series on successive Sundays.]

❦ *Title:* Pictures of Jesus: The Flexibility of Jesus

"We've gotcha!" That's what the Scribes and Pharisees must have thought when they asked Jesus the question. The scene was the courtyard of the temple in Jerusalem, and these fellows had come with a miserable woman and a bag of stones. "Teacher," they said, "This woman has been caught in the act of adultery. The law says for us to stone her to death. What do you say?" (John 8:2–10) And they stood, waiting his answer.

No wonder they thought, "We've gotcha!" How could Jesus safely answer their question? If he said, "Yes, go ahead and kill her," what would happen to his reputation for gentleness and forgiving love? But if he said, "No, don't kill her," he would be going against what the law required. (Leviticus 20:10) Indeed, they had him. Neither answer would do. "We've gotcha!"

But they didn't. What happened next has become one of the most familiar of our pictures of Jesus. "Do we stone her, as the law requires, or do we let her go?" Pausing for a moment, Jesus said, "Let him who is without sin among you be the one to throw the first stone." Another pause, and now the "gotcha" was reversed. He had them. "But when they heard it, they went away, one by one, beginning with the eldest." Jesus said to the woman, "Where are they? Has no one condemned you?" She said, "No one, Lord." And Jesus said to her. "Neither do I condemn you. Go, and do not sin again." The flexibility of Jesus!

Now the question: Do you like this picture of Jesus? "Of course," many would say, "What's wrong with it? It's great." And yet, check your own New Testament to see whether this story is even included. The earliest manuscripts of the New Testament almost all omitted it. It is included in only one of them. Two others left blank spaces where it would go, but left it out. Later New Testament manuscripts included it, but they weren't sure where to put this story. It is put in different places in the Gospel of John, and one even locates it in Luke's Gospel.

Present-day editors who print Bibles for you and me to read aren't quite sure where to put it either. In the RSV it is a footnote to John 8. The New English Bible puts it as an addendum at the end of John. Now what's the problem here? What was it about this story that troubled the earliest compilers of the New Testament?

The answer is that many early Christians were embarrassed by this picture of a flexible Jesus. St. Augustine explained that this story about Jesus was dangerous. It seemed to imply that Jesus didn't care about adultery. Therefore, many of these early Christians took down this picture from the pages of the New Testament. It was purged, left out.

What about you? Would you hang this picture of a flexible, forgiving Jesus on the wall of your faith? Think about it for a moment. There is the scene again—the arrogant crowd, the miserable woman, and Jesus. Listen to the interchange. "Let him who is without sin among you throw the first stone at her." Watch them melt away.

As we look at this story from different angles and let the light move across it, it becomes richer, deeper. Maybe as we think on that scene, we can hear Jesus asking four basic questions that are worth considering today.

Love and Flexible Rules

I. "Listen, you are the leaders of your church, your faith," he was saying to the Scribes and Pharisees. "You are the cream of the crop. Don't you really think that this woman is more important than the rules about adultery?"

People can fall in love with rules occasionally, so that the rules become more important than the folk they serve. The Pharisees were champion rule makers. They had devised rules about almost every conceivable situation, and they often forgot that the rules were there to bring people closer to God, to enable them to live rich, full lives. Jesus believed in rules, too. He believed in rules about the proper use of the Sabbath day, but he was flexible with those rules when human need appeared to conflict with them.

And the more we love people, the more likely we are to use flexibility in applying the rules. I recall about eleven years ago, not long after arriving here, one Sunday morning, during the sermon, there was a loud clatter back there behind the chancel, the thump, thump, thump of adolescent feet running up and down the back stairs. At our staff meeting the next morning, I urged, "find out whose those kids were, contact their parents, and let's get this under control." One of the staff members pointed out that the father of one of the kids was the minister of education and the father of the other was the senior minister. We decided to drop the issue and work on it privately.

Jesus always operated on the premise that every racer up and down the stairs, every adulterer, every cross-bound thief, was his own child, his own brother or sister, and their lives were more important than any rule devised. "Don't you really think this woman is more important than the rule?"

The Narrow Gap Between Saints and Sinners

II. Then, more directly to the point, Jesus seemed to say, "OK, assuming the rule is this important, is there anyone here who thinks he is pure enough to judge this woman?" He frequently spoke of the perils of quick judgment. "Don't judge," he said simply. "It's too easy to see the speck in your brother's eye and not notice the log in your own." (Matthew 7:1-5) The Pharisees had become a group of professional speck seekers. This is always the peril of having too many rules, even at home. Someone has to be the enforcer, the judge. "And who of you," Jesus was asking, "who of you is without sin, so that he can throw the first stone."

Even the saintliest among us have too many memories to declare ourselves qualified here. What a narrow line there is between sainthood and sinfulness, and what chance keeps us on one side or another. I read somewhere that Adolf Hitler's greatest ambition as a youngster was to study at the Art Institute in Vienna. In his late teens, he applied for entrance. And he was turned down! Flat rejected! What would have happened, do you suppose, had the committee approved his application?

What small hinges history turns on! What narrow lines there are between happy endings and tragedy, between saints and sinner. I would wager that there are none here who could not, in the privacy of their own minds, describe in detail a stupid, awful mistake they made in the past, and they got by with it! No real damage was done. The normal consequence was escaped. No one saw. We were luckier than we deserved. Jesus knew this about us, and was not hesitant to say, in effect, "All right, sure, go ahead and kill this woman. But let the one among you who is without sin throw the first stone!"

The Hazard of the Second Stones

III. And more than this, in this picture frozen there before us in this story, I can hear Jesus asking, "Is there anyone here who knows enough about this woman to judge her? Who are her parents. Is she married? Does she have any children? Has something gone wrong in her life? And where is the man involved in all this? Does anyone here know all this?"

"Why should we know all this" the accusing faces might reply. "Didn't you hear? She was taken in adultery—" (and here the lips purse, the eyes harden)"in the very act!" Jesus does not say it, but he might have responded, "Whose word are you taking? Surely this whole committee didn't catch her in the very act! Someone has reported this to you, haven't they? And you believed them. But you, yourself, do you know enough first hand, do you really know enough to kill this woman?"

Do we ever know enough to slander, to condemn? A West Texas town has a story about a woman given to gossip. She circulated the tale that a leading citizen of the town was a drunk. She hadn't actually seen him drunk, mind you, but she knew because the man's horse was tied in front of the town saloon all night. The very next night, the man left his horse tied all night right in front of the woman's house.

The utter audacity of gossip! Some people go equipped with their bags of stones, waiting for a target. Maybe they don't throw the first stone, but gossip is always a matter of throwing second stones, and third and fourth. And first stones, for that matter, seldom do the killing. The killing is done by the throwers of the second stones, the happy carriers of the story. "In the act, did you hear? In the very act!" And the story goes wider and wider, the hearers more distant, and stones are lobbed in from a long way off. And say it again, like missiles aimed at continents we can't even see, those distant stones, they do the killing.

"Is there anyone here who knows enough about this woman to judge her?"

The Power of New Beginnings

IV. And then I hear one other unspoken question, Jesus is asking these sharp eyed men. "Is there anyone here who doesn't think a person can change? Can't she change? And isn't this what you want, really?"

It's one of the characteristics of Jesus most appealing to me, the part of the picture I like best, his enormous faith in our ability to change, to start over. He believed the lost sheep could be found, the Prodigal son could come to himself and return home. He believed Zacchaeus could come down out of his tree, that a woman caught in adultery could begin again clean and fresh.

"Before you kill her, ask yourself, Don't you believe she can change?" Be sure to note that Jesus didn't say, "Oh for goodness sakes, why are you picking on her? Taken in adultery? What difference does it make. We're all adults here. It doesn't matter." It mattered then and it does today, too, and all the timid, muted ethics that come out of the religious world don't alter that. We are good at inventing new jargon and say that in our enlightened day we are freed up from old inhibitions, we have alternate life-styles, we control our own bodies, we do our own things, and those indiscretions, those shoddy shortcuts in ethics that enable us to do whatever we please, they don't matter. But down in the hidden crevices of the heart, we know it does matter, it matters a great deal.

But you can change. You can change. You can put all this behind you and start over. "Neither do I condemn you. Go, and do not sin again."

In the late nineteenth century, a controversy erupted among educators about a brand-new invention. For decades, students had used lead pencils in doing their exercises, but in 1880, a technological breakthrough came. For the first time, manufacturers started sticking rubber erasers on the ends of pencils. It had never been done before. Many educators opposed the use of this new fangled pencil on the ground that it encouraged students to make mistakes. "Let them avoid errors in the first place, and they won't need an eraser." Put most simply, Jesus insisted on an eraser on the pencil of life. Old errors can be erased, and new beginnings made.

That's our picture of Jesus, then. There is the story. Do you want it included in your New Testament, or left out? More important, do you want it in your own life? Look at it again. The hostile crowd, a miserable woman, and Jesus.

Is anyone here aimless enough to condemn her?
Does anyone here know enough to condemn her?
Does anyone here believe she can change?

And they melt away, and as they do, into the circle of forgiveness and new beginning comes a child of God, brought back by the forgiving flexibility of Jesus.

Amen.

—Eugene Brice

[2040 words]
[20 minutes]

❦ *Sermon 42*

❦ *Date:* Sunday Between July 31 and August 6 inclusive Pentecost, Year C

Texts:
Colossians 3:1–11
Luke 12:13–21

Theme: Jesus was flexible yet uncompromising.
Subject: Setting limits
[This sermon and the one preceding should be presented as a series on successive Sundays.]

❦ *Title:* Pictures of Jesus: The Inflexibility of Jesus

"Say," the fellow said, "I liked that picture of Jesus we looked at last Sunday. His acceptance of the woman caught in adultery, his flexible, nonjudgmental attitude, that was terrific. Let's hear some more stories like that this week."

OK, great! Here are a few other stories Jesus told. I will summarize them briefly, and as I do, see if you can detect something that does not ring quite true.

1. Once there was a king who gave a marriage feast for his son. One of the guests apparently took his invitation lightly, for he arrived in very casual dress. The king said, "Friend, how did you get in here without a wedding garment? Go home, change clothes, and get back here in time for dinner, and do not do this again." (Matthew 22:11)
2. There's another story. In the last judgment, the Lord will gather a group of people and say to them, "I was hungry and you never fed me, thirsty and you gave me no drink, sick and you never visited me." "Lord," they will say, "when did this happen?" And he will say, "Inasmuch as you never did it to me, return to your home, pay attention to human needs, and do not sin again." (Matthew 25:31)
3. Or a third story. Once there was a wedding and ten maidens came with their lamps to take part. It got dark, and only five of the ten had brought extra oil for their lamps. The five foolish maidens ran out of oil, and while they ran to get more, the wedding party arrived. When the five maidens got back, they knocked on the door, saying, "Let us in!" The bridegroom opened his door and said, "Anyone can forget extra oil. Come on in, and do not forget again." (Matthew 25:1) See how flexible and forgiving these stories of Jesus are?
4. Try one other story, our Scripture for today. A rich man was very successful, but he built bigger and bigger barns to hold his property. But one night, an angel came to him and said, "You fool, whose will all these things be if you die? Tomorrow, you do some hard thinking about your priorities, and do not sin again." (Luke 12:16)

Now, you wanted more stories about gentle, nonjudgmental Jesus, so there they are. But way in the back a hand goes up and someone says, "Wait a minute! What translation are you using? None of those stories end like that in my New Testament." And he is right, dead right. As sweet as those imaginary endings are, Jesus didn't end those stories that way. Here is the way he really ended them:

1. The improperly dressed wedding guest? Jesus had the king say to his servants, "Why did he not prepare for the feast? Bind this man, and cast him into outer darkness where men weep and gnash their teeth." (Matthew 22:13)
2. The fellows on the day of judgment who never fed the hungry or given the thirsty to drink? Jesus ended that story by saying, "Truly I say to you, as you did it not to the least of these, you did it not unto me. And they will go away into eternal punishment." (Matthew 25:46)
3. And what about the maidens at the wedding who arrived without enough oil for their lamps and came pounding late on the door? Jesus ended that story by having the bridegroom come out and say to them, "Truly I say to you, I do not know you." (Matthew 25:12) And the door was shut!
4. And finally the man who built the bigger barns? Did the angel send him back for another try? No, not the way Jesus told it. The angel said, "You fool, this night your soul is required of you, and the things you have prepared, whose will they be?" (Luke 12:20)

Wait a minute, we say. What has happened to the easy flexibility of Jesus? We like stories with happy endings, stories with lots of second chances. But these four stories we have told here, and a dozen other stories Jesus told, don't end that way. What we see here is another side of Jesus, an inflexibility that stands out sharply in his teachings. The late Senator Everett Dirksen used to say, "I am a man of firm and unbending principle, and my first firm and unending principle is to be flexible at all times!"

Flexible at all times! That's what we would prefer to find in Jesus, but it can't be found there. Perhaps it is more accurate to say that Jesus recognized an inflexibility in this world of ours, and in his stories he made sure we would see it, too. God's love lasts forever, Jesus knew, but our opportunities to claim it run out. God's mercy never ends, but our time to accept it does, and with amazing frequency, Jesus makes that point.

"Listen to me," Jesus pleaded in his stories. "Opportunities run out! Time runs out." And this flexible Jesus told stories about the inflexibility of life, stories of tardy maidens locked out of the wedding feast, and rich men dying in the middle of the night. Can we hear that urgency echoing down to our own day? Because we believe so strongly that God's love is limitless, do we think our opportunities and our time are, too?

Opportunities Run Out

I. Listen, Jesus says to us, opportunities run out! That story he told of the poorly prepared maidens wanting to get in to the wedding after it had started is about an inflexible as a story can get. So they forgot to bring extra oil! A thousand excuses could be given, a thousand reasons why they hadn't prepared. And they wanted in so badly, and they were good people, surely, and—All the "ands" in the world could not change the fact that the door that was once open was now shut, the wedding was well underway, and the opportunity gone.

Doors of opportunity get closed. Surely we ought to know that. As parents, opportunities to enter creatively into a child's life have a way of moving quickly away, and while we are out looking for oil, the doors get closed. "The film of childhood," someone has said, "can never be run through for a second showing." As husbands, as wives, we find life full of the sound of opening and closing doors, and what poor timing we often have in using them.

Francis Faber once said, "Each hour comes with a little piece of God's will fastened on its back." It crawls through life, in and out of our reach so quickly, and is gone. And it never comes back again, not this opportunity.

Yesterday, when I had my sermon all finished, a letter arrived at the church. Let me share it with you. "Dear Dr. Brice," it said. "My husband, two teenagers, and I had the privilege of worshiping in your church last Sunday. We were attending the Big Eight basketball tournament. I wanted you to know that we were very blessed by all parts of your service. The execution of the service is tight but not cold, the female associate has a lovely speaking voice and wonderful presence, the sermon was meaningful, the organist was solid and tasteful, and the music of the University of Nebraska Choir was exceptional and touched me deeply. Of course, it goes without saying that the sanctuary is stunning. Your church was recommended to us by the people where we were staying. Thanks for the privilege of sharing with you in the Lord. Our morning would have been perfect had even one person spoken to us. Yours sincerely, Barbara (From Oklahoma City)."

Talk about being lured up the mountain, only to be pushed off! Now I can say a lot of things in response to that letter: How did you get by our greeters at the door? Our church has the reputation for being among the most open and friendly in town; maybe the people sitting next to you were visitors, too! But what I really wanted to do was go pounding on her door and say, "Let us in! Here's the oil! Here's the greeting, the friendly word." But, you see, this opportunity with this child of God was gone forever, this door closed! Maybe we almost greeted her, but we did not.

I discovered not long ago where the word "mediocre" comes from. From the Greek. It means, literally, "half way up a mountain." Drawn by the good we recognize in Christianity, we begin the journey, but half way up, the way becomes hard, and the opportunity is gone in mediocrity, half way up the mountain.

Jesus saw all among him the inflexibility of missed opportunity, and his stories reflect it.

Time Runs Out

II. But he also saw the inflexibility of time, how it moves on so quickly, and before we know it, it is gone. A little girl became fascinated by her mother's egg timer, the kind that looks like a miniature hourglass filled with sand. Her mother explained to her that it took exactly three minutes for the timer to empty, and then she would turn it over so that it would do the same thing over again. That afternoon the little girl brought her playmate to her mother's kitchen and was showing her the egg timer. "See?" she said, "you run it like this, and then you just turn it upside down and get your three minutes back."

Would that it worked that way! Oh to have those three minutes back, those three years, those three decades back again! But it doesn't work like that. It's the tyranny of time Jesus recognized, and he knew it could be our worst enemy. We run out of time—all of us do, no exceptions. Time is a commodity we cannot borrow or steal. The richest among us cannot buy it, the poorest among us cannot hoard it or beg it, or create it. We simply watch it go by and try to use it as best we can.

Among my earliest memories of church is one set in a farm community of East Texas, watching those ruddy-faced farmers and their families coming for worship, and so frequently singing the hymn that must surely have been No. 1 on whatever hymn Hit Parade there was in those days. Do you remember it?

> Work for the night is coming, work thro' the sunny noon,
> Fill brightest hours with labor, rest comes sure and soon.
> Give every flying minute something to keep in store,
> Work for the night is coming when man works no more.
>
> Work til the last beam fadeth, fadeth to shine no more,
> Work for the night is coming when man's work is o'er.

That hymn comes from a statement Jesus himself made in John 9:4. "We must work the works of him who sent me, while it is day. Night comes, when no one can work anymore." We sang it there in that little rural church, and 90 percent of those who sang it are now gone, for night came for them. In the mountains of Puerto Rico, I heard the same song, only in Spanish, "Trabaje porque la noche viene," and it was as true for them as for any of us. "Night comes, when we work no more."

It is the one absolutely inflexible, absolutely universal fact we all face. I've not heard the song sung there, but I've look around and recognized its truth while worshiping at Riverside Church in New York, and St. Paul's in London, and Notre-Dame in Paris, and the temple in Karnak (Egypt) and the Church of the Holy Sepulchre in Jerusalem—all of us, all of us, caught in the swift movement of time. Night comes, Jesus says, time runs out, doors are closed, opportunities are gone. He said it over and over again.

Along with the flexible, forgiving love of Jesus comes his urgent teaching about this inflexible truth of life—sooner or later, we run out of both time and opportunity, so any good you want to do with your life, any love you want to express to another, any service you want to render to God, friends, do it now. Do it now!

There is an ancient Zoroastrian story about Satan choosing three apprentice devils to send to earth to do their worst. In a sort of contest, Satan asked each what he proposed to do, how he would operate, to see which would be more effective in leading people astray. The first one said, "I will tell people there is no God." Satan did not think that would be too effective, because people knew in their hearts there was a God.

The second one said, "I will tell people there is no hell." Again, Satan ruled that out because people had experienced enough of hell in their own hearts to know it must exist. At last Satan chose the winner, because the third agent said simply, "When I arrive on earth, I will tell people there is no hurry."

Amen.

—Eugene Brice

[2170 words]
[22 minutes]

❦ *Sermon 43*

❦ *Date:* Sunday Between September 11 and September 17 inclusive Pentecost, Year A

Texts:
Exodus 14:19-31
Psalm 114
Romans 14:1–12
Matthew 18:21–35

or The Fourth Sunday in Lent, Year C

Texts:
Joshua 5:9–12
Psalm 34:1–8
2 Corinthians 5:16–21
Luke 15:1–3, 11–31

Theme: Forgiveness is the doorstep to the presence of God. If you're forgiven and you know it, pass it on!
Subject: Forgiveness

❦ *Title:* The Threshold to the House of God

Being forgiven by God and not extending that forgiveness to others is putting one's soul on a starvation diet. Trying to keep God's forgiveness to oneself is like owning the patent to the greatest invention in the history of the human race and locking the plans in a safety deposit box without even building a prototype.

The local Christian church is a community of those who are forgiven and forgiving—or it is nothing. That seems abundantly clear from the most cursory reading of the New Testament. Yet attempting to forgive often seems like Captain Ahab's pursuit of the great white whale. It tasks us.

"Just how far must I go to forgive my brother?" asks Peter (Matthew 18:21). "How about if I forgive him seven times? That sounds fair, doesn't it?" After all, "Rabbinic law at the time held forgiving three times fulfilled one's religious obligations, and Peter had doubled that and added one more for good measure."[1]

Good-hearted, impetuous Peter must have been quite proud of himself. But, as usual, Jesus quickly deflated him. "Not seven times, but seventy-seven."

"Seventy-seven times!" Peter must have thought to himself. "Seventy-seven times! Lord, you might as well have said seventy million." Seventy-seven times! Maybe when Peter heard "seventy-seven" he thought of that strange story about Lamech recorded in Genesis 4. Lamech, who was the father of Noah and probably the progenitor of Rambo, bragged about killing a young man who had in some way harmed him. He is quoted as saying: "If Cain is avenged seven times, then Lamech seventy-seven times" (vss. 23–24). Lamech had exacted the most awful, terrible, and complete revenge of which a human being is capable. He had killed his tormentor. Was Jesus now insisting that when a brother or sister offends or wounds me that I must be every bit as complete and unconditional in my forgiveness as Lamech had been in exacting his retribution?

The Man Who Owed a Fortune

As Peter mulled it over ("Seventy-seven times! Seventy-seven times!"), Jesus interrupted him with a remarkable story about a man (we'll call him Ernest) who owed a ruler a staggering sum of money, an amount that it would take a working man 150,000 years to earn! Big bucks!

Now the ruler was so moved by the man's piteous pleas for mercy that he canceled the debt. And do you know what that man did when he left the ruler's presence. He was so transformed by the ruler's generosity that he got an honest job and amassed a fortune and donated it to charity? Wrong. He ran into a friend (let's call him Vern) who owed him a few hundred dollars, and when Vern could not pay him the money, he grabbed him by the throat and said, "Pay up or go to jail."

You can imagine what the ruler thought when he heard about that! He was the head guy, the Man, and he had kept a duplicate copy of Ernest's bill. Ernie was in big trouble again.

Picture two friends, Bob and Ray, standing in line at the 7-11, waiting to buy lottery tickets. It turns out that Bob has forgotten his wallet, so he borrows two dollars from Ray and buys two lottery tickets. Ray buys two himself. And Ray wins twenty million dollars.

A week later, new millionaire Ray runs into his old friend Bob in the parking lot outside of Pizza Hut. "Give me my two dollars, you thief!" Ray screams. "I can't," says Bob. "I just spent

[1] Felker, Bruce, *Word & Witness*, September 16, 1990, p. 4.

all of my money on this cheese pizza. Here, you can have it." But Ray only becomes more enraged. He hails a passing squad car and tries to have Bob arrested.

If you were Judge Wapner how would you rule in this case? You would probably want to fine Ray twenty million dollars and the cost of Doug Llewelyn's hair mousse.

What God's Free Gift Really Costs

What our Lord's parable makes clear is that the giveness of God's grace provides a base for the human response. Because much has been given, we have much to share. Because much has been given, much is required of us.

Before we can forgive, there must be an appreciation of what has been given for us. God forgives our sins and ignores our failings. He accepts us despite our constant confusion and never-ending perversity. He invites us to the fellowship of his church, and re-creates us in Christ Jesus.

For us, on our behalf, in our place, God has given his Son. Given for us. Remember that verse that you learned in Sunday School? "God so loved the world that he gave his only begotten Son . . ." (John 3:16).

Jesus calls for unlimited forgiveness, a forgiveness that passes all understanding. And the only way that the church can do this is by "passing on" its appreciation of all that God has given for us. I know, it sounds like the lyrics to a camp song: "If you're forgiven and you know it, pass it on!"

Pigpen Forgiveness

We all remember the Parable of the Prodigal Son, one of the greatest stories ever told. The point of the parable is the love of God is unconditional, but without repentance and conversion, we remain in life's hog wallow. Years ago I heard an alternative version of the Parable of the Prodigal Son told by A.W. Tozer. I call it the Parable of the First Church of the Pigpens. It went something like this:

> The prodigal son went to the big city and spent all his substance on riotous living. He ended up working as a swineherd. One day, as he was sitting in the mud, chewing on a corn husk, a man wandered by, distributing pamphlets. He gave one to the prodigal son. The pamphlet read, "You can go home. Your father loves you."
>
> The prodigal was exceeding glad and called together all the other swineherds. He gave each of them a copy of the pamphlet and when they read it, they were also exceeding glad. "We can go home. Our father loves us," they exclaimed.
>
> Soon they established the First Church of the Pigpens. On Sunday mornings they got together and read aloud the words of the pamphlet: "You can go home. Your father loves you." Now no one else in their community would have anything to do with them. After all, they were swineherds and they smelled different from other folk!
>
> As the good people of the town passed, careful to remain upwind of the First Church of the Pigpens, the swineherd shook their fists at the townspeople and shouted, "So persecuted you the prophets who were before us." Then the swineherd read once more the words of the pamphlet: "You can go home. Your father loves you." But they never went home!

God has forgiven us. If we do not forgive others, what difference does it make—to us or to them? God has accepted us. If we cannot approach one another honestly, openly, and with humility, so what? God stands at the threshold of our lives and we stand in the shadow of his presence. If we gossip about one another, question one another's motives, choose sides and gang up on one another, who cares? We keep telling one another: "You can go home. Your father loves you." But we never go home!

Forgiving the Sin, Saving the Sinner

But, preacher, you may protest, if I have to forgive others does this mean that I have to ignore their behavior? Should I abandon all my ethical expectations?

Should we condone evil when we see it? Should we mouth "I forgive you" and avert our eyes? Clearly, that is not what Jesus did. He loved his enemies and devoted his life to saving them from their evil ways by word, deed, and example. Yet even in his darkest hour, as he hung on the cross, his prayer was "Father forgive them. . ." (Luke 23:24). How he loved us sinners! How he hated our sins.

Forgive the sin; rescue the sinner—that's the formula. I know that sounds like hairsplitting. But it really is not so far-fetched. We do it all the time. We overlook our own failures and go on with life as though nothing had happened. We don't fall out of love with ourselves! As C.S. Lewis has written,

> For a long time I used to think this a silly . . . distinction: how could you hate what a man did and not hate the man? But years later it occurred to me that there was one man to whom I had been doing this all my life—namely myself. However much I might dislike my own cowardice or conceit or greed, I went on loving myself. There had never been the slightest difficulty about it. In fact, the very reason why I hated the things was that I love the man. Just because I loved myself, I was sorry to find that I was the sort of man who did those things.[2]

The Gospel proclaims not only the unconditional forgiveness of our sins but the absolute demand that we live as though God's acceptance of us makes a difference in our conduct toward others. We are expected to love as God loves. We are called to accept and affirm others without reducing by one iota the hatred we feel for selfishness and insensitivity. We ought to hate cruelty and treachery, but as Lewis insists, Christianity wants us

> to hate them in the same way in which we hate things in ourselves: being sorry that the man should have done such things, and hoping, if it is anyway possible, that somehow, sometime, somewhere, he can be cured and made human again.[3]

But What Will I Do . . .?

"But what's in it for me, preacher?" you may ask. "You have no idea how lovely spite can be, how much fun there is in entertaining old grudges, displaying old wounds like combat medals. You expect me to give that up? What will I do for fun?" It's like the two elderly men, Sam and Max,

---

[2] Lewis, C.S., *Mere Christianity* (New York: Macmillan, 1943), pp. 104–106.

[3] Ibid.

who ran into one another in Miami Beach. They were both from the same neighborhood in New York, but they had not seen one another in twenty years. "Sam," said the first man, "how is your wife, Ida?"

"Ida died four years ago," the second man replied.

Max pounded his forehead in disbelief and exclaimed, "Ida died four years ago! What do you do for aggravation?"

Some of us hold on to our grudges as though they were blue-chip securities in a bull market. But unforgiven grudges pay no dividends. They simply tie up our spiritual capital and keep us from making more productive uses of our inner resources.

The Doorstep to God's Presence

Forgiveness of others is the ultimate expression of love, of one's own sense of security, of the presence of God within one's own life. The one who is forgiven knows the presence of God. In the midst of futility and despair, we are suddenly seized by the certainty that we are forgiven. The fire of love is rekindled. That is the greatest experience of which a human being is capable.

> In the words of Paul Tillich: "We can *live* only because our guilt is forgiven and thus *eternally* forgotten. And we can love only because we forgive and are forgiven."[4]

The one who is forgiven knows the presence of God. The one who knows the presence of God knows life not as a random succession of things that happen and of which he or she is a victim. Rather, the one who knows the presence of God experiences life as a calling, a vocation, a partnership. The fire of love begins to burn again, and out of the fullness of our hearts, we forgive.

But, I would warn you, be careful. This forgiving is dangerous business. The experience of forgiving is the threshold to God and his forgiving love. Experiencing that love will make you even more forgiving, which will bring you, again and again, to God. And the demands of God on your life are every bit as unconditional as his love and forgiveness.

A heart full of grudges is a heart devoid of God. When God is absent, the vacuum fills itself with cynicism, sarcasm, and despair. A heart full of grudges is a heart full of hurt.

God has forgiven you! God accepts you! Be glad. When I learned to fence many years ago, my instructor told me to hold my foil as though it were a live bird. "Hold it too tight and you smother it. Too loose and it flies away." Try to keep God's forgiveness to yourself and it rots within you. Spread it around and it enhances your life, now and forever.

Amen.

—LDS

[2100 words]
[21 minutes]

---

[4] *The Eternal Now* (New York: Charles Scribner's Sons, 1963), p. 32.

❦ *Sermon 44*

❦ *Date:* Sunday Between July 3 and July 9 inclusive Pentecost, Year B

Texts:
2 Samuel 5:1-5, 9-10
Psalm 48
2 Corinthians 12:1-10
Mark 6:1–13

Theme: We are without honor until we learn to respect ourselves.
Subject: Honor

❦ *Title:* Prophets Without Honor

Honor as Cash Value

"Prophets are not without honor, except in their hometown, and among their own kin, and in their own house." (Mark 6:4 NRSV) The basic meaning of the Greek word translated *honor* is price or worth in dollars and cents. "Honorarium" is one of its meanings. We might say, "cash value."

The practical relatives and neighbors of Jesus found him of little monetary worth. Healings, exorcisms, and parables brought little on the open market.

All too often, we, too, confuse honor with honorarium, worth with cash value.

There is the story about an upper-crust banquet attended by George Bernard Shaw. Shaw playfully asked his hostess if she would sleep with him for a hundred thousand pounds.

"Of course," she replied.

Then he asked her if she would sleep with him for ten pounds.

"What do you think I am?" the offended aristocrat snarled.

Said Shaw: "That we have already determined. What we are haggling over is the price!"

The trouble with most of us is we fail to determine what we are (and what we have to offer) before we set the price. In consequence, we end up disappointed with the wages life pays us.

Honor as What One Treasures

The second meaning of the word translated *honor* is that which one finds valuable, that which one treasures.

The trouble is that we seldom communicate to others what we really find valuable, what we really want. So we are frustrated when we don't get what we want.

That reminds me of a story

> about a man and wife who were celebrating their Golden Wedding Anniversary—fifty years of married life. Having spent most of the day with relatives and friends at a big party given in their honor, they were back home again. They decided, before retiring, to have a little snack of tea with bread and butter. They went into the kitchen where the husband opened up a new loaf of bread and handed the end piece (the heel) to his wife.

> Whereupon she exploded! She said, "For fifty years you have been dumping the heel of the bread on me. I will not take it anymore; this lack of concern for me and what I like." On and on she went in the bitterest of terms, for offering her the heel of the bread. The husband was absolutely astonished at her tirade. When she had finished he said to her quietly, "But it's my favorite piece."[1]

When others fail to value you for who you are it may be because you're not letting anyone know.

Honor as Esteem

The third meaning of the word translated *honor* is esteem. We confuse acclaim with esteem, fame with appreciation. Fame is fickle and fleeting and often a poor measure of value.

I think of my mother's Aunt Clara, a quiet manicurist, who didn't seem to fit into my mother's family of successful overachievers—architects, musicians, college professors, engineers. Maybe that's why she divorced my mother's uncle and retired to Florida. Then, in her eighties, Aunt Clara uttered one immortal line and became more famous and acclaimed than any member of my mother's illustrious family. The line? "Where's the beef?" Surely, you remember the little old lady in the Wendy's commercial. That was Clara Peller, my mother's aunt.

We are all sensitive to criticism. Yet sometimes the grudging respect of our family members and friends is a spur to greater accomplishment. I have heard that

> Fritz Kreisler, the great violinist, had one big problem all his life: he hated to practice. His wife, who was deeply concerned about his career, kept after him all the time: "Have you practiced today? How much have you practiced? Be sure to practice!" And he was constantly coming up with all sorts of excuses and rationalizations not to practice.
>
> Toward the end of his life, a great banquet was held in Kreisler's honor. One speaker after another—great conductors and musicians—rose to speak of him in glowing terms. One even said, "He is the world's greatest living musician." Beaming, Fritz Kreisler turned to his wife and said, "Did you ever hear such praise?"
>
> Without cracking a smile, Mrs. Kreisler said, "Yes, but think what they could have said if you had practiced!"[2]

A constructive critic is the best friend any of us will ever have. And a hostile or destructive critic is the worst!

Hostile critics thwarted Jesus. The power of God flows through us and between us. The power of God flows when we are in agreement, when we respect differences, when we appreciate others even if they are not like us. But when we discount one another, gossip about one another, disrespect one another, that power cannot be transmitted.

---

[1] *Parables, Etc.*, January 1984, 3.11.

[2] *Sunday Sermons*, Ventnor, NJ: Voicing Publications, Vol. 12, No. 4 (July/August 1982).

Honor as Dignity

The fourth meaning of the word translated honor is dignity. We confuse position with dignity, career with meaning.

Let me tell you about one of the most unhappy men I ever met. The year was 1972 and I was in Jacksonville, Florida, pursuing my duties as associate director of a statewide presidential primary campaign. As I lounged in the sun reading my Sunday newspaper, I glanced across the lawn and spotted a familiar face and a body covered with so many scars it looked zippered. I went over, asked the man if I could join him, and struck up a conversation. After about a minute I asked if he were George Blanda. He was pleased I recognized him.

We started talking about the wonderful season he had enjoyed—all those last-minute heroics and the adulation of the media as well as the admiration of all us out-of-shape middle-aged Monday morning quarterbacks.

Suddenly Blanda became disgusted. "Where was the media coverage when I was in my twenties and thirties? When I was really good? All those years in Chicago and Houston?"

Honor and glory had come to George Blanda in the declining years of his athletic career. It would have been more than enough for most of us. But not for a fierce competitor like Blanda.

Like many of us, Blanda had confused who he was, his worth in the eyes of God, with what he did. And he made what others said of him more important than what he thought of himself. To be fair to Blanda, maybe when we spoke he was having a bad day. Maybe there were other days when he basked not only in the Florida sun but in the sense of satisfaction for a job well done. He certainly earned it. In the words of a recent television commercial, "Lamonica would play with the flu. Blanda would play if he were dead!"

The best respect is self-respect. And that comes not from acclaim, applause, or monetary reward. Self-respect comes from making commitments and honoring them, from giving one's word and keeping it.

One observer recalls:

> In the 1920's [George] Mallory led an expedition to try to conquer Mount Everest. The first expedition failed, as did the second. Then, with a team of the best quality and ability, Mallory made a third assault. But in spite of careful planning and extensive safety precautions, disaster struck: an avalanche hit, and Mallory and most of his party were killed.[3]

That happened in 1924. When the avalanche swept them away, Mallory and a companion were only eight hundred feet from the summit.

The story continues:

> When the few who did survive returned to England, they held a . . . banquet saluting the great people of Mallory's final expedition. As the leader of the survivors stood to acknowledge the applause, he looked around the hall at the framed pictures of Mallory and his comrades who had died. Then he turned his back to the crowds to face the huge picture of Mount Everest, which stood looming like a silent, unconquerable giant behind the banquet table. With tears streaming down his face, he addressed the mountain on behalf of Mallory and his dead friends. "I speak to you, Mount Everest, in the name of all brave men living and those yet unborn," he began. "Mount Everest,

[3] *Parables, Etc.*, April 1990.

you defeated us once, you defeated us twice; you defeated us three times. But Mount Everest, we shall someday defeat you, because you can't get any bigger and we can!"

Each of us has his or her personal Mount Everest. Each of us daily faces disappointment and risks disaster—if we are human beings, if we are alive. And occasionally the avalanches crash down on us and we are lucky to survive. But then some force gathers the broken pieces of our existence and glues them back together. We become stronger and bigger than we ever were before. That force is the grace of God, and by the grace of God, we defeat our Mount Everest. And then, no matter what any one else says to us or about us, we know the meaning of self-respect.

In a "Peanuts" cartoon, Linus and Lucy are talking. Linus: "I've been thinking. Charlie Brown has really been a dedicated baseball manager. He's devoted his whole life to the team. We should give him a testimonial dinner."

Lucy: "Is he that deserving? How about a testimonial snack?"

So my advice to each of you this morning is give yourself a testimonial snack. Honor yourself. For prophets, it seems to me, are without honor until they learn to respect themselves.

Amen.

—LDS

[1545 words]
[15 minutes]

Sermon 45

Date: Any Sunday

Texts:
Genesis 1:26–31
Psalm 8:1–9
Luke 19:11–27

Theme: We were designed to rule with God.
Subject: Service, leadership

Title: Designed to Be a Human

One day Charlie Brown is seated at Lucy's Psychiatric Help booth—5 cents per session. He is pouring out his heart, saying, "I want people to say, 'Here comes Good ol' Charlie Brown . . . Now everything will be all right!' I want to be a special person . . . I want to be needed . . . It's kind of hard to explain."

He turns plaintively to Lucy and says, "Do you understand? I mean, do you know what I'm talking about?"

She says, "Sure, I understand perfectly." He looks at her longingly and asks, "Well?" In the last frame she says "Forget it! Five cents, please!"

My concern, this morning, is to elevate your concept of who you are as a human being, as a man or woman—that you might walk out of here lifted in your awareness of who you are—what you are designed to be by God—in being a woman, a man, a human being.

I want to explore some of the basics of our essential humanity. What are God's original intentions in our design? Designed for what, to be what? What does it mean when the Bible says we were designed in the image of God?

My premise is that if we know what we were actually designed for then we might have a better chance to live better lives, more realistically functioning lives. For I believe we live in a world of confused design where things that are designed for one thing are being used for something else.

When I was a kid I got in trouble with my mom a number of times trying to use one of the family's good silverware table knives as a screwdriver. As she explained with enthusiasm, that wasn't what it was designed for.

We have seen in our culture lamps that are made out of wine bottles, or fog horns, or carburetors. Hotels that are made out of ships, like the *Queen Mary,* sitting intractably dockside. The *Spruce Goose* has been caged and made into a tourist attraction, and I understand now they are talking about moving it to Las Vegas and may be turning it into an Orange Julius stand or a cocktail lounge, or a casino, or a wedding chapel, or whatever.

We live in a world of confused design. In Irvine, California, a silo has been turned into a motel. It is weird, having concrete hexagonal (maybe even octagonal?) walls in a motel room. Lots of things in our world are not being used in the manner for which they were first designed.

We have a large rusty milk can from a dairy farm by our front door. I hate to disillusion you, but there is no milk in it. Nor will their probably ever be.

When we were walking about North Lake early yesterday morning I noticed an old fashioned barrel that had been cut in half. It was hung by its side, and it was full of flowering plants. It had become a planter, not what it was designed to be.

Designed for Dominion

What were we designed for? I would like to suggest just one thing:

In Psalm 8.6 we read that God gave man domination. We find this spelled out in Genesis 1:26-28 where we read man was given dominion over the fish, the birds, and every living creature.

So also we read in Luke 19:11-18, in Jesus' parable of the pounds. A nobleman gave each of his ten servants money to invest—they were each given ten pounds and told to trade with this money until he returned. When he returned, he rewarded the faithful stewards according to their wisdom and success in investing—and the reward was dominion. Those who made ten pounds were given dominion over ten cities, those who only made five pounds were given dominion over five cities. To be a faithful steward in God's kingdom is to be rewarded with increased dominion.

In 1 Corinthians, Paul laments over lawsuits between Christian brothers. He says, "Do you know that the saints will judge the world and if the world is to be judged by you are you not competent to try trivial cases? Do you not know that we are to judge angels? How much more matters pertaining to this life?" So also in 2 Timothy 2:12 we read, "If we endure we shall also reign with him."

Revelation 3:21

"He who conquers I will grant him to *sit with me on my throne* as I myself conquered and sat down with my father on his throne." Revelation 20:4, 6 speaks of "Thrones . . . those to whom judgment has been committed . . . they shall reign with him a thousand years." The apocalyptic vision for the redeemed woman or man of God is a vision of *reigning with Christ.*

Paul writes to Titus in Titus 2:15, "Declare these things, exhort, and reprove with all authority. Let no one disregard you!" Does this mean we are designed to be dictators? I don't really think so. When we leave the apocalyptic descriptions of this topic and get into the plain teachings of Jesus we find a marvelous paradox about ruling authority for God's people.

Mark 10:42-45

"And Jesus called them to him and said to them, 'You know that those who are supposed to rule over the Gentiles lord it over them, and their great men exercise authority over them. But it shall not be so among you; but whoever would be great among you must be your servant, and whoever would be first among you must be slave of all. For the Son of man also came not to be served but to serve, and to give his life as a ransom for many.'" We reign, not by violence and coercion, but through serving.

Consider the example of Moses in his early career in Exodus 2:11, when he interjected himself into a fight between an Egyptian and a Hebrew and murdered the Egyptian. When he came back the next day and found two Hebrews fighting he added his two bits worth and they questioned his authority, saying "Who made you a prince and a judge over us? Do you mean to kill me as you killed the Egyptian?" In a sense, as Moses made this first clumsy and ill-advised attempt at leadership he was using the methodology of the world—leadership through violence. But that wasn't the kind of leadership authority he needed and he had to flee into the desert. And he began his long sojourn at DCLD (Desert College of Leadership Development), first of all, by serving the watering and protection needs of the seven daughters of Reuel (or Jethro), the priest of Midian. It was only after some forty years of serving in the desert that Moses was ready to rule God's people.

Designed to Have Authority

As God's creation and child, God designed you to embody authority, to be able to rule, to make decisions, to have potency, to have influence over the world, animals, and nature.

God designed you to have clout, his clout, the right kind of clout. One of the great crises is the problem of people without clout, without authority in the church. Many such people tend to follow demagogues who exemplify false and attractive authority. They are swept away by every wind of doctrine that the world dishes out.

One day Charlie Brown is talking to Lucy, at her psychiatrist's booth. He says, "Lucy, you're the kind of person with all the answers, aren't you?"

Lucy says, "Yes, that's true!"

They stare at each other for a moment.

Then Charlie Brown turns to walk away and says, "You have no idea how overwhelming that is to someone without even any questions."

You see, Charlie Brown has no clout, and he suffers from the fact that he is surrounded with people who seem to carry a great deal of clout.

How do you define clout? I like the word *hegemony*, having to do with the preponderant influence or authority over an area of life. God designed us to have increasing hegemony. Are you fulfilling your design to have domination? How big? What is the nature, the quality of your dominion, what are the particular areas of your reign? The areas you have gained influence over—by serving?

Who do you really have significant influence over in life? the dog? the cat? the canary? your family? some friends? Who do you make a real authoritative difference with? How do you influence them?

You were designed to have dominion! Christ revealed that such rule is to be acquired through the servant role. Simply put, we are to gain clout by serving others in the name and power and love of Jesus Christ.

It is for you to choose how you view life, whether you will attack it with vigor and enthusiasm and leadership, rejoicing in the fact that God has called you to triumph through service to become a ruler in life. Will you rust and atrophy? Or will you shine with use?

God designed you to be a marvel, a special creation, a being with authority who grows in leadership by giving and serving. Therefore, give and serve that you may be fulfilled and God may be served.

Amen.

—James S. Hewett

[1534 words]
[15 minutes]

❦ *Sermon 46*

❦ *Date:* New Year, Any Year
or First Sunday After Pentecost (Trinity Sunday), Year C

Texts:
Year A or B
Psalm 8

Year C
Proverbs 8:1-4, 22–31
Psalm 8
Romans 5:1–5
John 16:12–15

Theme: The human race is doing the best it can, but that's no excuse!
Subject: Humanity defined, humility

❦ *Title:* When Being Human is No Excuse: A Conversation Between David and Job

Tip

> The best speaking is dramatic speaking, the ebb and flow of contrasting viewpoints. With the following sermon, I wanted to raise questions and issues rather than resolve them. When I presented the following sermon, I read the David lines from the pulpit and a member of the church read the Job lines from the lectern.

I take you on a journey of imagination. Come with me to the halls of eternity and listen to a conversation between two men who have become friends over the passage of centuries. In eternity both men have come to identify themselves as writers or literary figures. In life, one of them had been king of Israel—among other things. His name is David. The other had been the central figure in the greatest drama of the Old Testament. We know him as Job. However, in eternity David is much more content to be known as the author of psalms, as a poet, and Job as a thinker who has meditated for millennia on the frailty of human nature, seeing millions come and go, and recalling their observations on life. Their conversation:

> ***David:*** . . . what is man that thou art mindful of him,
> and the son of man that thou dost care for him?
> Yet thou has made him little less than God,
> and dost crown him with glory and honor.[1]

Or as my good buddy Will Shakespeare put it:

> What a piece of work is man! how noble in reason! how infinite in faculties! in form and moving how express and admirable, in action how like an angel! in apprehension how like a god! the beauty of the world! the paragon of animals![2]

> ***Job:*** My friend Abraham is quoted as saying to God: "Behold, I have taken upon myself to speak to the LORD, I who am but dust and ashes."[3] And even I lamented: "God has cast me into the mire, and I have become like dust and ashes."[4]
>
> Sometimes I agree with W.S. Gilbert: "Man is Nature's sole mistake!" and with a roach named Archy who communicated with the human race by jumping on the keys of a manual typewriter. Said Archy:

> I suppose the human race
> is doing the best it can
> but hells bells that's
> only an explanation
> its not an excuse[5]

And you know what Mark Twain had to say:

> The noblest work of God? Man. Who found it out? Man.

> ***David:*** And yet this has been the century of humankind's greatest technical achievements. Can a century that has given us the following be all bad: powered flight, jet flight, rocket flight, electricity, the phonograph, the motion picture, radio, television, the computer, long-distance telephone, antibiotics, the Salk vaccine, the extirpation of small pox, organ transplants, nylon, polyester, plastic, Teflon, Velcro, the Xerox machine, and the Pill?

> ***Job:*** Don't forget that this has been the century in which humankind has despoiled the planet, damaged the environment, perforated the ozone layer, polluted the seas, and, in general, poisoned everything we touched.

---

[1] Psalm 8:4-5.

[2] *Hamlet,* Act II, Scene 2, lines 300–304.

[3] Genesis 18:27.

[4] Job 30:19.

[5] Don Marquis, "Archy says," *Archy Does His Part,* 1935; cited in *The International Thesaurus of Quotations,* compiled by Rhoda Thomas Tripp (New York: Perennial Library, Harper & Row, Publishers, 1970), p. 558, number 34.

David: We also invented the atomic bomb, used it twice, and never, never used it again—not for 45 years. Maybe we are learning.

This has been the century in which many voices other than John Lennon's have been proclaiming: "All we are saying is give peace a chance." Think of Mahatma Gandhi, Pope John XXIII, Martin Luther King, Jr., Bishop Desmond Tutu, Mikhail Gorbachev, and Mother Teresa.

Job: Now just a moment, David, haven't you noticed the millions who have moved into the neighborhood during the present century because of humankind's terrible blood lust, its willingness to kill for the sake of anything or for nothing? Have you forgotten Auschwitz and the gulags, the killing fields of Cambodia, or the hundreds who have died of starvation, of neglect, of treatable or preventable diseases, and of abuse?

David: OK. So man is not an angel. I admitted that in the beginning. I was certainly no angel. But I had potential—and that made the difference. Man is not a preprogrammed machine. He is not an animal with built-in, irresistible instincts. Man requires his fellows, to love him, mirror him, criticize him, judge him, confirm him.

Human beings are wonderful—or at least they can be.

Job: I remember what you once said, in one of those prayers that mortals call the Psalms: "I praise you because I am fearfully and wonderfully made; your works are wonderful, I know that full well." I have to admit you said it so well, so succinctly. Have you heard how that new fellow down the street, Buckminster Fuller, says the same thing?

Voice: Man is a self-balancing, 28-jointed adapter-base biped with the following:
. . . Millions of warning signal, railroad, and conveyor systems
. . . Crushers and cranes (of which the arms are magnificent 23-jointed affairs with self-surfacing and lubricating systems)
. . . A universally distributed telephone system needing no service for 70 years if well managed
. . . An electrochemical reduction-plant, integral with segregated stowages of special energy extracts in storage batteries, for subsequent actuation of thousands of hydraulic and pneumatic pumps, with motors attached
. . . 62,000 miles of capillaries
. . . And the whole, extraordinarily complex mechanism is guided with exquisite precision from a turret in which are located telescopic and microscopic self-registering and recording range finders, a spectroscope, etc., and the turret control being closely allied with an air conditioning intake-and-exhaust, with a main fuel intake.
Within a few cubic inches which house the turret mechanism, there is room also for
Two sound-wave and sound-direction-finder recording diaphragms
An expertly devised analytical laboratory large enough not only to contain minute records of every last and continual event of up to 70 years of experience, or more, but to extend, by computation and abstract fabrication, this experience with relative accuracy into all corners of the observed universe
A forecasting and tactical plotting department for the reduction of future possibilities and probabilities to generally successful specific choice
"A man," indeed! Dismissed with the appellation "Mr. Jones!"

Job: That's what annoys me so much about human beings—they make so much of themselves. They have such little sense of proportion and such arrogance. They are fascinating, gifted creatures to be sure, but they use so little of what they have for productive purposes.

Why, in some so-called advanced nations, every other person is a lawyer, who spends all of his time afflicting humankind with legislation and litigation. Surely you remember that nuisance suit in Illinois about 150 years ago.

Voice: . . . a rich man in Springfield, Illinois, . . . insisted that a certain poor man owed him $2.50. When the claim was denied, the rich man decided to sue him. He contacted a young lawyer . . . , who at first hesitated to take the case. On second thought he agreed—if he'd be paid a fee of $10 cash in advance.

Job: What a waste of time and talent.

David: That's true, but you've neglected to tell how that lawyer, young Mr. Abraham Lincoln, disposed of the matter.

Voice: The client readily produced the money, whereupon Lincoln went to the poor man and offered him $5 if he would immediately settle the alleged debt. Thus Lincoln received $5 for himself, the poor man got $2.50, and the claim was satisfied. The rich man foolishly paid three times the original debt, just to gain his rights.

David: And young Mr. Lincoln had a good laugh at his client's expense. That's why I love Abe so much. No matter how exasperated or frustrated he was by his fellow human beings, he never lost his sense of balance, to say nothing of his sense of humor. Balance and humor—even the worst humans have them. That adds some highlights to your gloomy picture, doesn't it?

Job: But do individuals ever learn? Do they change? Can they?

David: The individual is an abstraction, a figment of the imagination. Each of us belongs to others, who help us become what we can become. Through them and despite them—but never without them—we are truly human. God is our partner in every meeting of human being with human being. God is present, as his son Jesus said, whenever two or three are gathered in God's name. That's why I wrote hymns of praise and worship. That's why I wanted to build a temple in Jerusalem for God and all who worship him.

Job: But you failed—and although your son Solomon built the Temple, within a few generations, it was in ruins.

David: Yes, but it wasn't in vain. The dream remains. Men and women of every age, race, and condition still strive after the City of God—still attain in their special moments the blessedness of unity. The dream leaves them better than it finds them, at one with one another and with God. I have to believe that. I cannot not believe that.

Job: They call that the placebo effect, David. Because you believe, you feel better. But does it really count? Really make a difference?

David: "Really?" The jury is still out, Job.

Job: So how should men and women live in the meantime—in these very mean times?

David: They should wear a garment with two pockets. In one pocket there should be a piece of paper that says, "The world was made for me." This is to remind them that they are just a little lower than God. That their potential for weal and woe is infinite. In the other pocket they should carry a piece of paper that says, "I am dust and ashes." The trick is knowing when to read paper number one and paper number two.

Amen.

—LDS

[1557 words]
[16 minutes]

❦ *Sermon 47*

❦ *Date:* Second Sunday in Lent, Year B

Texts:
Genesis 17:1–7, 15–16
Psalm 22:23-31
Romans 4:13–25
Mark 8:31–38

Theme: During the season of Lent, we turn from looking at things from the human perspective to seeing them from God's.
Subject: Lent

❦ *Title:* Everything to Lose, Everything to Gain

The Way of the World

Jesus said to Peter, "You do not have in mind the things of God, but the things of men."

When I hear these words, I think of the myths we Americans so readily believe, the myths promulgated by television:

The fittest survive.

Happiness consists of limitless material acquisition.

Consumption is inherently good.

Property, wealth, and power are more important than people.[1]

William Fore maintains that "the whole weight of Christian history, thought and teaching stands diametrically opposed to the media world and its values." In other words, "You do not have in mind the things of God, but the things of men."

A study of employees at two Silicon Valley companies reveals that "baby boomers are a selfish, independent group with contradictory needs for independence and approval."[2] They are

---

[1] William F. Fore, "Mass Media's Mythic World: At Odds with Christian Values," *Christian Century*, January 19, 1977, pp. 34–35.

[2] "Workers Climb the Corporate Ladder on Others' Backs," *San Francisco Examiner*, February 23, 1991, p. A-1.

obsessed with getting ahead at the expense of others. They show little loyalty to their employers or to their fellow employees. Women surveyed proved no more humane than their male colleagues.

The fittest survive.

Happiness consists of limitless material acquisition.

Consumption is inherently good.

Property, wealth, and power are more important than people.

I read in the *Peninsula Times-Tribune* that the Woolworth store in the Stanford Shopping Center will be closing soon.[3] The store, a genuine piece of Americana, is an original tenant of the center and has been there for thirty-five years.

What is the cause of this closing? Hard times? Lack of profitability? Not at all. As columnist Tim Goode notes: "The fact is, the store was unceremoniously bounced out of the . . . Center. So long, and thanks for 35 years of rent." Goode explains: "Woolworth was considered an uncouth crasher at a formal party." It seems, to quote the Center's director of operations, Woolworth "doesn't fit the Stanford image."

And just what is that image? Says Goode:

> The guess is the "Stanford image" the shopping center directors want to perpetrate is one of the mall as a place where upper-class people see other upper-class people spending money on lavish gifts and fancy goods like upper-class people should.

In other words,

The fittest survive.

Happiness consists of limitless material acquisition.

Consumption is inherently good.

Property, wealth, and power are more important than people.

The elitism of the shopping center is so much like America's besetting sin of racism. The Seventeenth General Synod of the United Church of Christ declared:

> Racism is a sin and an evil that stands as an affront to the Christian faith. Racism is an expression of idolatry, replacing faith in God, who created all peoples equal in the image of God, with the belief in the superiority of one race over another. When this idolatry is expressed by those who possess economic and political power, it leads to a cruel and extensive repression of selected peoples and negation of their identity and value as given by God.

Inherent in racism are the same assumptions:

The fittest survive.

Happiness consists of limitless material acquisition.

Consumption is inherently good.

Property, wealth, and power are more important than people.

---

[3] Tim Goode, "Goodbye to Yesterday: The Closing of Woolworth Means More than the End of an Era," *The Peninsula Times-Tribune* (Palo Alto, California), February 9, 1991, p. B5.

Questioning Our Assumptions

Lent is a time to question these assumptions. Lent is a time to reflect on the words of Jesus: "If anyone would come after me, he must deny himself and take up his cross and follow me. For whoever wants to save his life will lose it, but whoever loses his life for me and for the Gospel will save it. What good is it for a man to gain the whole world, yet forfeit his soul? Or what can a man give in exchange for his soul?"

Lent is a time of engagement with God, of repentance and prayer, a time of reflection on what it means to be a Christian, and a time to look forward to joy. "Lent looks toward God's act in the resurrection. Sober awareness of sin is appropriate, to be sure, but so is profound joy."[4]

What am I giving up for Lent? Whatever stands between me and my determination to use this season as a time of spiritual renewal. I'm giving up an unexamined life. I'm giving up the preoccupation with self that prevents me from sharing in the joy of others. I'm giving up my defensiveness, my always having to be right. I'm giving up my refusal to live. In simplest terms, I'm giving up my excuses.

As one businessman observed: "We are all manufacturers in a way—making good, making trouble, or making excuses."

Tired of hearing the same, hackneyed excuses for why people don't attend church services, the Reverend Sydney Laing of Dublin, Ireland, penned for his parish paper "Ten Reasons Why I Never Wash":

1. I was made to wash as a child.
2. People who wash are hypocrites . . . they think they are cleaner than other people.
3. There are so many different kinds of soap—I could never decide which one was right.
4. I used to wash, but it got boring so I stopped.
5. I still wash on special occasions, like Christmas and Easter.
6. None of my friends wash.
7. I'm still young—when I'm older and have gotten a bit dirtier I might start washing.
8. I really don't have time.
9. The bathroom's never warm enough.
10. People who make soap are only after your money.[5]

In *Parables, Etc.*, I read about a girls' college dorm where some of the students

> had the problem of what to do when they wanted to turn down a date from someone they didn't want to go out with. To solve the problem one of them wrote a list of ten handy excuses and tacked them up next to the phone in the hall. It worked pretty good except for the time one girl got flustered and said to the earnest caller, "I'd love to go out with you, Tom, but I can't—because of Number Seven."[6]

---

[4] Gene M. Tucker *et al., Preaching the New Common Lectionary, Year B. Lent, Holy Week, Easter* (Nashville, TN: Abingdon Press, 1984), p. 12.

[5] *Parables, Etc.*, December 1989.

[6] Ibid., September 1982, 2.7.

Giving Up Our Excuses

We offer our lame excuses for not following Jesus, for not caring, for not making a difference, for saving our self-centered lives, for not taking up the cross of discipleship. But we know they are only excuses. God doesn't want our excuses. He wants us.

Bob Benson writes of sending a son off to college:

Nearly a year ago Peg and I
had a very hard week. . . .

SUNDAY NIGHT
we were home and [our son Mike] was
700 miles away in Chapman 309

Now we have been through this before
Bob Jr. had gone away to college
and we had gathered ourselves together
until we had gotten over it. . . .

So we thought we knew
how to handle separation pretty well
but we came away too lonely and blue.

Oh, our hearts were filled with pride
at a fine young man
and our minds were filled with memories
from tricycles to commencements
but deep down inside somewhere
we just ached with loneliness and pain.

Somebody said you still have three at home—
three fine kids and there is
still plenty of noise—
plenty of ball games to go to—
plenty of responsibilities—
plenty of laughter—
plenty of everything . . .
EXCEPT MIKE.
And in parental math
five minus one
just doesn't equal plenty.

And I was thinking about God
He sure has plenty of children—
plenty of artists,
plenty of singers,
and carpenters,
and candlestick makers,
and preachers,
plenty of everybody . . .
EXCEPT YOU
and all of them together
can never take your place.

And there will always be
an empty spot in His heart—
and a vacant chair at His table
when you're not home.

And if once in a while
it seems He's crowding you a bit—
try to forgive Him.
It may be one of those nights
when He misses you so much
He can hardly stand it.[7]

Give up the excuses. It is time to look at things from God's perspective. It is time to begin the adventure of losing your life in order to find it.[8] It is time to come home.

Amen.

—LDS

[1310 words]
[13 minutes]

❦ *Sermon 48*

❦ *Date:* Thanksgiving Day, Year B

Texts:
Joel 2:21–27
Psalm 126
1 Timothy 2:1–7
Matthew 6:25–33

Theme: Simplify!
Subject: Simplicity

❦ *Title:* The Simplicity of Jesus

Tip

Have a soloist or ensemble sing "The Gift to Be Simple" before and after the sermon.

The man came struggling down the trail high up in the Sangre de Cristo Mountains in Colorado. The backpack he was carrying must have weighed 75 pounds, so he was more than willing to stop for a moment and chat. "This is my second day out," he said, "and the mistake I made was in bringing too much. I've got gourmet food in here and a portable CD player and several books and binoculars and enough camera equipment to start a store. I'm debating right now whether to dump some of it and go on. I've got so much clutter with me that the trip isn't much fun."

---

[7] *Parables, Etc.*, September 1982, 2.7.

[8] Ted Loder, *Guerillas of Grace: Prayers for the Battle* (San Diego, CA: LuraMedia, 1984), p. 117.

We left him there trying to muster the courage to simplify his life by getting rid of some of his unnecessary baggage. Often when I am reading the marvelous teachings of Jesus, I think of that burdened-down backpacker and the clutter he was carrying. Like a scarlet thread running through Jesus' teachings is this advice: Simplify! Don't clutter your life with unnecessary burdens. Even when it's classy clutter, it's still clutter!

The early American group of Christians called Shakers must have recognized that and accepted it. They came up with a life-style that carried simplicity to an extreme, but they also came up with what must be among the most beautiful American hymns—"The Gift to Be Simple." Aaron Copland took the tune of it as the theme of his symphony Appalachian Spring. Remember the words? "Oh the gift to be simple is the gift to be free, the gift to come down where we ought to be. And when we find ourselves in the place just right, twill be in the valley of love and delight."

Jesus' teachings echo through that claim: The gift to be simple is the gift to be free. That burdened-down backpacker in the Sangre de Cristos would have understood the claim, and so should we—if you want to be free, then simplify! Simplify! Look how this theme recurs in the teachings of Jesus.

Speaking Simply

I. Start with something as basic as language itself, the way we talk. It is interesting how often Jesus referred to the need for simple, direct language.

"In praying," he said, "do not heap up empty phrases as the Gentiles do, for they think they will be heard for their many words." (Matthew 6:7) "Let your yes be yes and your no be no." (Matthew 5:37)

If too frequently our prayers seem in retrospect to have been heaps of empty phrases, a lot of words but not much meaning, then simplify. Who are we trying to impress in our prayers? Even in prayer, the clutter may be classy, but it is still clutter. Look at the picture of Jesus we have in the New Testament—what simplicity of language is there!

When Jesus taught he spoke of flowers in the field, of sparrows falling from a tree. He told of lost coins and sheep that strayed, of a boy who ran away, of a woman kneading bread, of an injured traveler, of specks in your eyes and houses built on sand. Simplicity! Simplicity!

Strange, then, that we often feel that to honor him, to explain him, we have to resort to virtually unintelligible jargon. There is something inside us that fears simplicity, that wars against it. Haven't you noticed what we do with language, the jargon we develop? For example, what does this phrase mean: The chronological gifted? Chronologically gifted? That's a new, up-to-date way to say "older people." Instead of saying "handicapped," some groups are saying "the differently abled." And champion of all, do you know what some medical groups mean when they use the phrase, "negative patient care outcome"? That means dying—negative patient care outcome.

Why don't they say that? This is what Jesus argued for—whatever you mean, say it, say it simply. *The Reader's Digest* tells of young Matthew, age 4, eating an apple in the back seat of the car. "Daddy," said Matthew, "why is my apple turning brown?" The father explained, "Because after you ate the skin off, the meat of the apple came in contact with the air which caused it to oxidize, thus changing its molecular structure and turning it into a different color." There was a long silence, and then Matthew asked softly, "Daddy, are you talking to me?"[1]

Matthew's question is the right one. To whom are we talking? What do we want to say? Whether in the language of prayer, or in simple conversation, it follows through, if you don't feel you have to carry with you the need to appear sophisticated, to appear philosophical or theological

[1] *Reader's Digest,* December 1988, p. 208.

or clever, if you can truly find the courage to be simple, then you can be free. No more worry about what someone will think about your comment here, your question there. The gift to be simple in speech is the gift to be free.

Thinking Simply

II. But Jesus went on from there. Don't clutter your mind with unnecessary worry. "Therefore, I tell you, do not be anxious about your life, what you shall eat or what you shall drink, not about your body, what you shall put on. Is not life more than food, and the body more than clothing? (Matthew 6:25)

Now the fact is that few of us here are greatly worried about having enough to eat today. We have food and clothing and a home. So we load up our backpack with lesser concerns that weigh just as much. As quickly as one concern is dealt with, we find another to carry along. If Jesus could tell his friends to simplify their lives by not worrying about having enough food to eat, what would he say to those of us who collect such an astounding array of less important things to worry us? Who says we have to be concerned with all this?

George Buttrick told of meeting a friend one day, and the friend seemed uncharacteristically happy. What had happened? "George," said the friend, "I have just resigned as General Manager of the Universe, and it's amazing how fast my resignation was accepted." Isn't it Jesus again? Why do you carry all these unnecessary concerns with you?

A minister friend came by some time ago to talk over an issue he was greatly concerned with. His brow was furrowed, his face worried. The situation was causing him great distress. But as he described it in full, it became clear that there really was nothing he could do about it. It was someone else's problem, and there was actually no way he could change their situation. He went away having unloaded a part of his backpack having resigned as General Manager of the Universe.

We have to be careful here not to overstate this, for there are many painful issues of our society people of conscience must be involved in, but Jesus' main point was this: In the journey of life, you don't have to carry everybody's baggage. The gift to be simple, to concentrate on your own life and what you can do, is the gift to be free.

Don't let your speech be cluttered up, Jesus said. And don't let unnecessary worry clutter your mind.

Living Simply

III. And don't let possessions clutter your life and so burden you down that you lose your freedom entirely. Jesus said it over and again—don't let your possessions become your master. "Do not lay up for yourselves treasures on earth," he said. (Matthew 6:19) "A person's life does not consist in the abundance of his possessions." (Luke 12:15)

Ed Cohn tells of a California woman who received word that one of those canyon fires was racing toward her house, that she had only an hour or so to collect a few things and leave. What would she take? She wrote: "All of a sudden, articles began to have a spirit, a soul, a life of their own. Here was a book owned by my father, a pitcher from which my mother poured milk. I walked through rooms where I had spent my childhood. Here we laughed and cried. Here I had argued, celebrated, worried." And then came this intriguing statement. She said, "We define who we are by what we take and what we leave behind."

How did Jesus say it? "A person's life does not consist of the abundance of his possessions." The fact is that life can get so bound up by possessions that we can never again be really free. The more we have, the more we have to lose; and the more we have to lose, the less free we become. Many a person has discovered to his or her great surprise and disappointment that life can get so crusted over with present possessions and expectations of more, with appetites satisfied that it becomes increasingly hard to have a truly joyous moment again. But even in possessions, the gift to be simple is the gift to be free.

I read an account written by a woman born near the turn of the century. It was a firsthand account of the challenge of raising a family on a farm—of all the testing and hard times that went with it. One chapter told of a terrible winter when they were almost broken. It centered on their 18-month-old daughter who came down with a cold, then flu, then pneumonia, then diphtheria.

Living 18 miles from town, they resorted to home remedies and the neighbors rallied to help nurse the baby. Her condition went downhill rapidly and they grew more desperate. The worst night, the woman wrote, was when snow fell, making any more travel to town extremely difficult. That night the baby lay virtually lifeless, and the father wrote in his journal, "Heavy snow. How can we bury our baby in this? The blackest day of my life thus far."

The next day the doctor did come out from town, making the last 8 miles of the trip on horseback over terrible roads. He said that the infection seemed to be lessened, but that she was very near death. If they could just get some nourishment of some kind down her, with a bit of strength and a lot of luck, she might make it. Maybe, he said, an egg would help.

An egg! Simple suggestion, but it was the dead of winter and the hens were not laying and there was no way to get to town. Someone went to the recently installed rural party line and rang the neighbors. The word went out quickly. Did anyone have an egg? The baby's life depended on it. And one distant neighbor did! One egg was found, and the neighbor rode over with it. And into the house he came as they rejoiced. The baby was given an eggnog of sorts, and whether that was really what did it, no one would ever know, but the crisis was over, and the baby was soon well again.

The woman who wrote that account of life on an East Texas farm was my mother, the baby my twin sister. And I have thought of this occasionally when opening the refrigerator door I have seen the eggs stacked neatly there in every season of the year. So often I have compared my life, all that I have, with theirs in those far more difficult days when, in comparison to us, they had so little.

And yet I occasionally wonder if in my entire life I have ever felt the depth of joy they felt when that one egg was brought carefully into the house on that snowy December day of 1932. "A person's life," Jesus said, "does not consist of the abundance of his possessions."

Sometimes I picture him sitting there beside the trail, that overloaded backpacker in Colorado, trying to decide what to take with him and what to leave behind. And I know that each one of us is doing exactly the same, right now. How cluttered up is our speech? How many unnecessary worries are we carrying along with us? How many possessions? The picture Jesus painted was well said by the Shakers —

> The gift to be simple is the gift to be free.
> The gift to come down where we ought to be,
> And when we find ourselves in the place just right,
> Twill be in the valley of love and delight.

Amen.

—Eugene Brice

[2068 words]
[21 minutes]

Sermon 49

Date: Sunday Between May 29 and June 4 inclusive (if after Trinity Sunday) Pentecost, Year A

Texts: (NCL)
Genesis 12:1–9
Psalm 33:12–22
Romans 3:21–28
Matthew 7:21–29

Theme: Sin is deluding ourselves into believing that it is all right not to honor our commitments.
Subject: Sin

Title: The Wages of Sin; the Gift of God

Tip

> Don't be afraid to pour new meaning into overused or abused texts. Reclaim them for yourself as though you had discovered a valuable antique in a dusty attic or had bought a thoroughbred that was pulling a junk cart.

My port of entry into the Christian Church—and, hopefully, into the Kingdom of God—was evangelical revivalism. I was converted to Christianity at a Youth for Christ evangelistic rally at Orchestra Hall in Chicago when I was fifteen. The Bible as I first learned it could be reduced to a few major proof texts—one of which I have just read. The Gospel that I heard preached at various evangelistic meetings and revivals was based on Romans 3:23, Romans 6:23 ("For the wages of sin is death; but the gift of God is eternal life through Jesus Christ our Lord"), and, of course, John 3:16 ("For God so loved the world, that he gave his only begotten son, that whosoever believeth in Him should not perish, but have eternal life").

More times than I can recall or recount, I heard this string of sentences, cited with no sense of the context in which these words appear in Paul's letter to the Romans and the Gospel of John, used as a basis for inducing in the hearer an emotional catharsis. It was not a difficult task to convince an individual that he was a sinner, that he had fallen short of what he expected of himself—let alone of what a just God required. Youth evangelists were particularly adept at turning the teenagers' unavoidable, awkward first encounters with sexual impulses into manifestations of human depravity. And the solution to the anxiety which the revivalist himself had elicited was a brief prayer of repentance, followed by an intense inner sense of relief and release.

I am not saying that such staged and induced conversions are or are not of God. That is between each individual convert and his Maker. And I am not saying that the words of Paul and John should be ignored. I wish that every Christian were familiar with their message—for that matter all the contents of the New Testament. George Bernard Shaw declared that youth is a wonderful thing, which, unfortunately, is wasted on the young. The teachings of Jesus as recorded in the Gospels and those of the Apostles as preserved in the other books of the New Testament are a wonderful thing—what a pity they are wasted on us Christians, most of whom ignore them, a few of whom twist them according to strange, inhumane ways of reasoning, picking and choosing, majoring only in minors.

I have my own theory about the Bible—that it was meant to be read to us as much as to be read by us. And I would strongly recommend that each of you buy a copy of the New Testament on cassette tape recordings and play it for yourself, chapter after chapter, book after book. Recordings of several versions of the New Testament are available from Christian bookstores.

Sin: A Fresh Look

Our focus this morning is sin. As a counselor of individuals and families, I am constantly overwhelmed by the depth and persistence of human perversity. Each of us seems to want diametrical opposites all the time. None of us will allow himself or herself to be content. The ability of individuals to grasp defeat from the jaws of victory, to turn happiness into misery, to act contrary to his or her own self-interest never ceases to amaze me. It is simple to explain drug addiction, shyness, depression, lack of assertion, suicidal behavior, or cult involvement as manifestations of low self-esteem. But that presupposes that there is a readily available alternative. The problem is that most "normal, well-adjusted" people do not seem to like themselves any more than those known to be at risk. Not only is there an epidemic of inferiority complexes but the fact is most these complexes are totally justified. For when it comes to any standard that we would set for ourselves, we fall short.

This morning, I want to emphasize two senses of the word "sin": sin as failure to keep one's word, and sin as refusal to accept responsibility for one's words and acts. Sin is living as though the other guy is supposed to honor his commitments but excusing ourselves for not keeping ours. God made a contract with Adam and Eve. They broke it. God made a covenant with the nation Israel. They turned to other gods and neglected the demands of justice to which they had pledged themselves. Jesus Christ offered the new covenant sealed with his blood, a community of Spirit-endowed brothers and sisters whose life would manifest the lordship of God. We have all committed ourselves to live by our Lord's example of self-sacrifice and service. We have given our word repeatedly in the worship and sacraments of this church and by voluntarily accepting membership in this community. But do we keep our word?

Refusing to Keep Our Word

Sin is deluding ourselves into believing that it is all right not to honor our commitments. Sin is each of us accepting his or her own feeble excuses—"everybody else does it; it really doesn't make any difference; I'm only one person; rules are made to be broken; there are always exceptions, the other guy will understand that I was too busy," and so on. Sin is not only an individual failing, it is a national menace. Why has America lost its leadership in the industrial world? Because we offer and accept of one another excuses instead of excellence. Why do Americans feel so little confidence in our national leaders? They have lied to us too often.

We often speak about the twentieth century as an age of anxiety. Anxiety is a direct result of never knowing whom to believe, whose word is bond, whose product is dependable, which politician will keep his campaign promises, what advertising campaign is the dissemination of accurate information, and what advertising is psychological manipulation. Anxiety is the natural result of fearing that my spouse will be faithless, my employees dishonest, my environment poisoned, the money in my pockets debased by inflation, the wheels will fall off of my new car, the washer repairman will not show up on Wednesday morning even though I have stayed home from work in order to let him in, the can opener that I just bought will not open cans, the physician will misdiagnose my condition and recommend unneeded surgery. Anxiety is not being able to take my brothers and sisters in Christ at their word when they offer me their caring, support, and love.

We are so overwhelmed when our friends or employees or employers or business associates or spouses or professionals or manufacturers of goods or tradesmen who provide services do keep their word, actually perform as we expect them to perform, really deliver what we have paid them for, that we feel like nominating them for the Nobel Peace Prize! I recently phoned the distributor of a software program that I had bought to thank him because his program worked. That it worked was a surprise to me—and my phone call a bigger surprise to him.

We have become so conditioned to accepting less than we pay for, to scaling down our expectations, to maintaining modest hopes. We are part of an unspoken conspiracy to tolerate incompetence, dishonesty, and inferiority. Why? So that as individuals each of us will accept his or her own incompetence, dishonesty, and inferiority?

Dodging Responsibility

Sin is refusing to honor one's word. To put it a somewhat different way, sin is dodging responsibility. "Why did you disobey my instructions?" God asked Adam in the Garden of Eden. Adam's response, a classic of shifting the blame, was: "The woman you gave me—she told me to."

I learned a long time ago that I would never know for sure whether what I believed was true or false. So I would have to decide for myself how I was going to live. Was I going to live as though there were a just and loving God? As though I were accountable for my actions? As though I could make a difference in my own life and in the lives of others? Or was I going to live a life of excuses? (There are plenty of excuses available. If you need some, perhaps you would like to borrow some of the following: I can't help being the way I am; I had an unhappy childhood; I married too young; I have been unlucky, gotten bad breaks; I was born under the wrong sign of the Zodiac; I have allergies; I am hypoglycemic; my parents were alcoholics; I was abused as a child; my husband or wife didn't love me enough. . . .)

I wonder if any society at any time in history has entertained more excuses, more ways to dodge responsibility. Look at the role of psychiatric witnesses in murder trials. Without going into details about some of the more celebrated cases, let me point out that the acceptance of the notion that individuals are machines that are programmed by circumstances and triggered by stress into committing horrendous acts for which these machines are not responsible is the inevitable culmination of the accepting of excuses. As a counselor, I long ago abandoned as my goal the "understanding" of my clients—that is, the assigning of external causes which enabled them to blame their present distress on someone or something else. I am in the business of facilitating change in the lives of those who want to change and of motivating the desire for change in the lives of those who are not yet ready.

Jesus had a special contempt for those he called hypocrites—those who professed a standard of conduct, condemned others who feel short of the mark, but excused themselves from the wholehearted observance of the rules of the game. He made clear that attending religious services, giving money to charity, even preaching and working miracles in his name could not substitute for doing what the Father wants. And what does God want? The words are simple: justice, mercy, humility, love, service. Every moment of every day is a demand, an invitation, an opportunity. We may respond with the wholeness of our being, accept responsibility, commit ourselves or we can drift from one immediate satisfaction to the next, forever justifying the unjustifiable, excusing the inexcusable.

Sin's Fatal Power

The wages of sin is death. Paul tells us that in the sixth chapter of Romans. Death is being cut off from the love of others as the result of our selfishness. Death is ending up with no character at all because the excuses that we offer become more real to our family and friends than the deeds which express who we are. Death is a society without direction in which everyone is for himself or herself. Death is life without a sense that what I do counts, that I stand for something, that my acts, deeds, and work are of value. Death is always having to be right and ending up right and alone forever.

But the gift of God is life—abundant life, life of the ages, life energized by the presence of God himself, life shared and replenished in a community of brothers and sisters. The faith that saves us from death is not a momentary rush of excitement at an evangelistic rally—although it certainly may start or be nurtured there. Faith is faithfulness, commitment, realizing that life is precious and significant. Faith is living as though it is natural that I will keep my word, that I will do the job for which I am being paid, that I will stop running off at the mouth with self-pitying lamentations and that I will open my ears and my heart to those to whom I have pledged myself—including my brothers and sisters in Christ.

And the pay off for keeping one's word, for accepting responsibility, for responding with love and concern? The payoff is that by living as though there is a just and loving God, we experience a just and loving God. By living as though our individual lives have significance and meaning, they have significance and meaning. By acting and speaking as though our church is a community of those who bear one another's burdens, our church becomes a community of those who bear one another's burdens.

When Moses asked the name of God, the voice from the burning bush responded: "I AM THAT I AM." In God, promise and fulfillment are one. God keeps his word. He is his word.

Amen.

—LDS

[2000 words]
[20 minutes]

❦ *Sermon 50*

❦ *Date:* First Three Weeks in Lent, Year A or C

Texts:
Matthew 4:1–11 or
Luke 4:1–13

Theme: We are tested as was the Christ.
Subjects: Temptation, priorities, reality, delusion, evil, impatience

❦ *Titles:*
Being Tested With the Christ (a series)
The First Temptation: Distorted Priorities
The Second Temptation: Ignoring Reality
The Third Temptation: Impatience

> The following is a series of three sermons intended for use during Lent. These sermons are based on the account of the temptation of Jesus, found in both Matthew's and Luke's Gospels. When the pericope for the First Sunday in Lent uses the account from Matthew (Year A), adopt the order that follows. When Luke is used (Year C), reverse the second and third sermons in accordance with Luke's order, and employ the concluding paragraphs of the third sermon below at the end of the second sermon below.

The Calling of the Christ

Until he was thirty, Jesus lived an ordinary, unremarkable existence as a carpenter, the son of a carpenter, in a provincial backwater. His neighbors apparently knew nothing of the signs and wonders which had attended his birth. They had not been told of the angel's startling conversations with Mary and Joseph, of the manager at Bethlehem, of the shepherds and the heavenly chorus, or of the stargazers who came in search of the newborn king of the Jews. Since the death of the tyrant Herod, the family of Mary and Joseph had lived quietly among the residents of Nazareth. If the Nazarenes were aware of Jesus at all, they knew him for the furniture, tools, and farm implements that he made and repaired. If they honored him at all, it was for the houses and barns that he constructed and embellished.

And then one day he was gone. His neighbors probably thought that he had become bored with small town existence and was headed for the big city, Jerusalem. A few of them might have imagined the truth, that he had gone to see his strange cousin, John the Baptizer. The Nazarenes had heard of John, a notorious "religious fanatic," who haunted the wilderness, preaching to crowds from Jerusalem who sought him out that men should turn away from their unrighteous deeds before the anointed one, the Messiah or Christ, appeared on the scene astride a white horse, sword in hand, to mete out the judgment of God.

Suddenly, perhaps while receiving John's rite of cleansing, Jesus realized that he was the Christ. For forty days and nights, he hid in the lonely, empty solitude of the desert and struggled to sort out who he was, to whom he belonged, to whom he was responsible, and to what ministry he had been called. Ignoring thirst and hunger, the scorching heat of the day, the bone-chilling cold of the night, the wind storms and apparitions, he attended only to those terrible conflicting inner voices which contended for possession of his soul. He agonized over what lay ahead as intensely and fervently as his forefather Jacob had wrestled with the angel of God.

During those forty days in the wilderness, Jesus must have thought much about the forty-year odyssey of his ancestors in the desert of Sinai. He recalled how God had sent Moses the deliverer, how he brought the fugitive slaves out of Egypt through the miracle of the Red Sea, how He gave them the Law and bound them to Him as His people and Himself to them as their God. Jesus remembered the frailty of those freed slaves—their anxieties, their impatience, their lack of faith, and their constant rebellion against their calling and destiny as the chosen people of God.

Hearing the Word of God

And when his own emotions—excitement, loneliness, and confusion—engulfed him, and the desert-born hallucinations became more real than the weariness of his emaciated and dehydrated body, Jesus anchored his being and sanity in the Word of God. He must have recited to himself every syllable of Scripture he could remember. His mind fastened on the book we know as Deuteronomy, the final sermon of Moses to the wilderness nation. Perhaps Jesus started with the Shema, the words most precious to a devout Jew: *"Shema Yisrael, Adonai Elohainu, Adonai Echod"* ("Hear, O Israel, the Lord our God is one Lord") (Deuteronomy 6:4). And then he would have recited the words which follow the Shema: "And you shall love the Lord your God with all your heart, and with all your soul, and with all your might." And a few verses later: "You shall not put the Lord your God to the test . . . " (6:16) A few minutes later, his memory would bring him to the words: "And he humbled you and let you hunger and fed you with manna. . .; that he might make you know that man does not live by bread alone, but that man lives by everything that proceeds out of the mouth of the Lord" (8:3-4). As Jesus stared out into the desert, it would have been so appropriate to think of Moses and the children of Israel and to recall the final words of Moses contained in the fifth scroll of the Law.

And as the words of the Law, Writings, and Prophets ran through his mind, he realized, with an assurance that could never be shaken who he was, to whom he belonged, and to what he had been called. Then the tempter came!

And the tempter said to him, "If you are the Son of God, command these stones to become loaves of bread." Jesus knew that he was the Son of God. He did not need to prove it to himself. He was also hungry. But he realized that his powers like those of Moses before him were not cheap tricks to satisfy his physical needs or his ego. Yielding to just such a temptation had cost Moses entrance into the promised land.

Jesus was being tempted to put himself and his needs first and his calling second. He dismissed this temptation with a reference to the heavenly manna which had fed the Israelites in the desert. What he was saying to the tempter was, "I will put God first, responding with the fullness of my being to who I am, to whom I am responsible, to my calling. That is all that I can do."

This awareness would echo throughout his ministry. When those who followed him were more concerned with food, shelter, and clothing than about the kingdom of God, the teaching of Jesus was clear: Don't worry about such things. Seek first God's kingdom and righteousness and let God take care of the rest. (Matthew 6:33; Luke 12:31)

Partnership with God

Man's first concern should be the God who calls him to partnership in the ongoing redemptive struggle. "Man shall not live by bread alone, but by every word that proceeds from the mouth of God." And where may we today hear the word that proceeds from the mouth of God to our ears?

The word of God to us is to be found in the Bible. For the spiritual message of the prophets, chroniclers, psalmists, sages, evangelists, and apostles will speak to our hearts if we immerse ourselves in it so that it may wash over our consciousness, infuse our dreams and aspirations, inform and ennoble our character.

As Protestants, we boast that we are the people of the open Bible. Yet for many of us it remains a closed and dusty tome. It should be read, studied, meditated upon, recited aloud, discussed, and cherished. It should not be worshiped, twisted, distorted, or set above the God to whom it points. But it surely should never be ignored.

On a more personal level, each of us should listen as God speaks to us as we fully and without reservation respond to one another as brothers and sisters in Christ. For in our age, God does not demand our attention with unavoidable signs and wonders but whispers to us with a still, small voice that says: "as you did it to one of the least of these my brethren, you did it to me." (Matthew 25:40)

And he speaks to you and me as individuals—calling each of us to be what he or she alone can be, to use talents and abilities to serve others, to use genius and artistic creativity "to tame the savage beast and make noble the way of man," to meet without whimpering or complaining the challenges, threats, and opportunities of ordinary existence. For to each of us is given a unique direction, a calling, a vocation, a life that may be lived with the fullness and totality of our being.

Remember as Jesus did: You "shall not live by bread alone, but by every word that proceeds from the mouth of God."

Amen.

—LDS

[1300 words]
[13 minutes]

❦ *Sermon 51*

The Second Temptation: Ignoring Reality

The Stubbornness of Evil

Sometimes evil is as stubborn as ring around the collar, as persistent as the IRS. The devil transported Jesus to Jerusalem and placed him on the pinnacle of the Temple, and taunted him: "If you are the Son of God, throw yourself down; for it is written, 'He will give his angels charge of you,' and 'On their hands will bear you up, lest you strike your foot against a stone.'"

To paraphrase the devil, "If God loves you, you can't get hurt." And by implication, "If you can get hurt, God doesn't love you." It makes sense, doesn't it? And Satan can even quote scriptural justification, the ninety-first Psalm. What is interesting is the way that Satan sets the truth of "first things first" on its head. "Seek righteousness first and God will take care of the rest," is twisted into "if you believe in God, you no longer have to take any responsibility for your own life."

Once again, Jesus focuses his attention on the wandering Israelites. No matter what God did for them, they grumbled and complained—just as we do! Instead of receiving the gifts of God with thankfulness and gratitude, they wanted more and more. They were spoiled children demanding "If you really love me, you will give me what I want." They had lost touch with reality.

Jesus did not succumb to that temptation. He knew how the world was—even for the Son of God. Later, he would teach his disciple to pray: "Lead us not into temptation but deliver us from evil." The Greek text of these words is ambiguous. The words can be translated: "deliver us from evil" or "deliver us from the evil one." I have often wondered which Jesus had in mind. Were we to ask the Father to deliver us from our own evil inclinations or from the devil?

The writers of the New Testament spoke of evil as a ubiquitous and persistent aspect of our personalities, our experiences, and the world in which we live. They refer to evil hearts, evil thoughts, evil consciences, evil surmising, evil reports, evil days, evil work, evil workers, evil deeds, evil men, and evil spirits. They remind us that we live in "the present evil world," that this age is corrupt, out of balance, and insane. The world in which Jesus found himself—and which you and I know—is characterized by suffering, confusion, illness, death, and despair. God is not the ruler of the world, this present age. If he were, there would be no suffering, no disease, no death. Evil is king. Sin reigns in us and in our world. It spreads like some hideous disease which invades a healthy body and cannot be destroyed without killing its host.

Sin is not a minor irritation—an occasional outburst of bad manners or a brief time of turmoil which disrupts the habitual peace. War is the natural state of the human race. Discord, calamity, death are the way things are.

Tip

> Go one step beyond citing well-known words. Write your own version of them to illustrate your message.

At War Until the End

Do you remember those words which interrupted our family gathering one Sunday forty-five years ago? Or the words of our president the following day?

> Yesterday, December 7, 1941—a date which will live in infamy—the United States of America was suddenly and deliberately attacked by naval and air forces of the Empire of Japan . . . . With confidence in our armed forces—with the unbounded determination of our people—we will gain the inevitable triumph—so help us God.

In the days that followed we set aside pettiness and bickering and united as never before to assure the defeat of our common enemies. Along the way, we endured separation, hardship, and shortages, as well as the postponement of career and family plans. And some of our neighbors and loved ones sacrificed a great deal more. For we were convinced, as President Roosevelt confidently predicted on December 9 in his "fireside chat," "We are going to win the war, and we are going to win the peace that follows."

> We interrupt this regularly scheduled program to bring you a special message from God. At every moment of every day since the birth of his son, special forces under the command of goodness have invaded the human race and begun the final conquest of evil by good. Though God's beachheads are small in our age, our nation, our community, our homes, and our individual lives, God has assured us of his ultimate victory. And he calls upon each of us to sacrifice profit, pleasure, and convenience, and to join him in this final struggle.

"You shall not tempt the Lord your God," Jesus insisted. Tempting the Lord is living as if there is no struggle, as if there is no piper to pay, as if we do not reap what we sow, as if it makes no difference what any one of us does, as if there really is a free lunch. "You shall not tempt the Lord your God" means "Don't leave it to God to do what you are responsible for doing. Don't be careless and claim that you are just trusting God. Don't neglect your spouse, children, parents, or community and say that God will take care of them. Don't shirk the hard work of building your own character or of providing an example of character building for your children. Don't excuse your failure to keep your word and to honor your commitments by saying "It's not my fault. That's just the way things are. It must be the way God intended them."

"You shall not tempt the Lord your God" means accept responsibility for your own life. Keep your word. Stop making excuses, and stop accepting them.

The rules of the game called life are very straightforward: Life is hard. Life is unfair. There are no survivors. We all depend on one another. No one else can live my life for me. To live as if any of these rules does not exist is like trying to fool providence. "Again it is written, 'You shall not tempt the Lord your God.'"

Amen.

—LDS

[1000 words]
[10 minutes]

❦ *Sermon 52*

The Third Temptation: Impatience

The Final Offer

The devil displayed for Jesus "all the kingdoms of the world and the glory of them," and the tempter said to Jesus, "All these I will give you, if you will fall down and worship me."

Obviously, the devil considers the kingdoms of the world his to give. God, it would appear, has given him a temporary sublease. Fundamentally, they belong to God, and someday, according to the divine plan, they will revert to his Son. As John proclaims in the eleventh chapter of Revelation (and as we echo whenever we sing Handel's *Messiah*): "And the seventh angel sounded; and there were great voices in heaven, saying, The kingdoms of this world have become the kingdoms of our Lord, and of his Christ; and he shall reign for ever and ever" (11:15). So if they are going to be his anyway, why shouldn't the Son of God claim them now?

The forty days of meditation on the lessons of Deuteronomy reminded him of the forty years in which the children of Israel had tried the patience of God. Jesus realized that even the most faithful continually tempt God through impatience, lack of faith, forcing God's hand, having to do things our way.

Throughout his career, his audience "tempted" him. The word "temptation" is used in the Gospels to describe an incredible number of encounters between Jesus and the smart alecs of his time. They tried to belittle him, to make him look foolish, and to make themselves look wise. They tried to bait him into losing his temper or saying something that would get him in trouble with the authorities. They tried to get him to make some grand gesture, such as leading an armed insurrection or calling down fire from heaven against the Romans. But all of the temptations added up to one and the same thing. Jesus was tempted to twist God's arm, to make things happen now, to do things his way rather than God's, to avoid the long, costly road that led to Calvary. And he was tempted to override our wills, to make us be obedient and righteous whether we wanted to be or not, to bring in the kingdom of God without having to put up with our confusion, uncertainty, failures, and ineptitudes.

Instead of forcing God's hand, Jesus surrendered himself to the state and fate of humankind. He experienced every temptation. (Hebrews 2:18) He served us when we should have been serving him. He was obedient unto death even the death of the cross. (Philippians 2:8)

Wrestling with Evil

"You shall worship the Lord your God, and him only shall you serve." These words remind us that the fear of the Lord is the beginning of wisdom; that for our individual lives to have meaning, each of us must discover for himself or herself a sense of perspective, a feeling of belonging, an awareness that the universe is tilted to reward justice, good conscience, unselfishness.

Is it true? I don't know. I can't prove it. But I can choose to live it. I can choose to let God be God. I can remind myself daily not to set preliminary concerns before the ultimate; not to let anything less than God be God. I can demand of myself that what I consider important, vital, and central in my life really is important, vital, and central. I can resist the temptation to have to be liked, loved, and appreciated. I can resist the temptation to always have to be right.

We struggle with evil because we have no choice. We wrestle with our own evil inclinations and with the evil one, Satan, the tempter. We are tempted to cut corners, take shortcuts, do it now, do it our way. But God's way may be summarized in one word: "serve." "You shall worship the Lord your God, and him only shall you serve." How may I serve you, O king of kings? Again, the still small voice replies: ". . . as you did it to one of the least of these my brethren, you did it to me." And as Jesus, the disguised king, prepares to lay down his life, he gives a final example, he washes the feet of his disciples. (John 13:3–18) He might as well have counseled a friend who was anxious, depressed, confused, or angry. The message would have been the same. Whenever any one of us helps a friend to respond to the challenges, threats, or opportunities of his or her life, we serve the king. "If he you know these things," Jesus adds, "blessed are you if you do them." (John 13:18).

Note | The following concluding material may be moved to the end of the previous sermon when the Gospel pericope is from Luke.

Despite temptation, Jesus remained focused on who he was, to whom he was responsible, and to what he had been called. The forty days in the desert provided a foundation for his ministry. And despite the rejection by the masses, the instability of his followers, and the hostility of the spiritual and civil leaders of his day, he never forgot who he was.

I can hear the struggles of the forty days echoed in the Lord's Prayer, which he taught his disciples shortly after his trials in the wilderness. His memory of the hunger he felt produces the prayer, "Give us this day our daily bread." The temptation to take things into his own hand and do things his way instead of his Father's inspires the teaching: "Forgive us our sins as we have forgiven those who have sinned against us. Do not put us to the test." The conflict he experienced between the demands of false gods—wrong priorities, delusions, and impatience—and the will of the true God are heard throughout the prayer, especially in the petition, "Deliver us from evil," from the evil of our own hearts and minds and from the evil over which we have no control.

In my mind's eye, I see him in the midst of crisis and turmoil returning again and again to the forty days in the wilderness. I hear him whispering to himself the scriptural lessons that gave him the backbone to resist both temptation and the evil one, the scriptural lessons which are every bit as fresh, meaningful, and significant to us today as we courageously serve and love:

> Man shall not live by bread alone, but by every word that proceeds from the mouth of God.
>
> You shall not tempt the Lord your God.
>
> You shall worship the Lord your God, and him only shall you serve.

Amen.

—LDS

[1100 words]
[11 minutes]

Sermon 53

Date: Sunday Between October 30 and November 5 inclusive Pentecost, Year A

Texts: (NCL)
Ruth 4:7–17
Psalm 127
1 Thessalonians 2:9–13
Matthew 23:1–12

Theme: Setbacks in life may reveal God's call to our true vocation.
Subject: Triumph over tragedy

Title: Women of the World: Temptresses, Wives, Mothers, and the Purposes of God
[Third in a series: "More than Is Required"—The Book of Ruth and Women of Today. Each sermon may be used independently. See also sermons 103 and 104.]

Naomi's Complaint

Naomi complained to God and about God. She was the prosecutor, the star witness, and the jury all rolled into one. God is unfair, she lamented. I have never done anything to him, yet he has deprived me of husband, sons, grandchildren, security, and protection.

And all the while Naomi whimpered and whined, God stood right next to her.

Our charming tale is as much the Book of Naomi as it is the Book of Ruth.

Naomi complains that God is unfair. When she and her daughter-in-law return to Bethlehem, she tells her old friends, "Don't call me Naomi," which means "the sweet one," "the pleasant one." "Call me Mara, which means the bitter one, because the Almighty has made my life very bitter."

And all the while, the means of her triumph over adversity stands at her side.

Naomi's Trap

Naomi cannot trust God to run his universe any more. She knows what should be done and she sets out to do it. She may be a complainer, but she is also a woman of valor.

When her wealthy distant cousin Boaz shows an interest in her Moabite daughter-in-law, offering Ruth his protection and allowing her to glean with his servant girls, Naomi advises Ruth to take that offer. The wheels are turning.

When the time of harvest is over and the season for threshing begins, Naomi stops being reactive and starts giving fate a gentle shove. She knows that Boaz and his workers will be sleeping at the threshing floor in order to protect their grain. Ruth has taken good care of Naomi. Now it is time for her to take care of Ruth.

So Naomi says: "Bathe yourself and anoint your body with oil. Put on your fanciest, frilliest frock. Splash on that good perfume you used to wear when you were married to my son. Here, take my best jewelry. And, for goodness sake, comb your hair and put on some makeup."

Meanwhile Boaz had found himself a comfortable spot behind a pile of barley. He had enjoyed a good meal, a couple of skins of cabernet, had sung a few songs with the guys. He was in good spirits and he soon drifted off to sleep and was dreaming about dancing girls.

In the middle of the night, something woke him. It seemed to be one of those dancing girls he had been dreaming about! "Who are you?" he asked.

"It's Ruth," she whispered.

"Ruth! What are you doing here?"

"Do you remember that blessing you pronounced when we met in your field? "May the Lord, the God of Israel, take you under his wing." She lifted the skirt of the robe in which he slept and cuddled next to him. The Hebrews called that portion of the garment a wing. She was under Boaz's wing and God's. And she said no more.

Boaz was overwhelmed. He was flattered. He was excited. And he was very confused. Boaz was not a young man. He knew that marrying Ruth would mean added responsibilities and complications. If he married her, he would have to support her and Naomi. And there was the matter of that parcel of land that Naomi owned. During the long years, Naomi had been away, squatters had taken it over. And Naomi's brother-in-law Tob had prior claim. It made Boaz's head swim, but the warmth and fragrance of Ruth soon distracted him.

Boaz's Response

The next morning, within hours, Boaz took care of everything. He convinced Tob that he already had enough on his plate with his own wife and children. Why marry Ruth? Yes, she was young and good looking. Yes, she was a hard worker. But she was apparently barren. Tob could not expect strong sons to help him farm the new field and earn back the purchase price. And in the bargain did Tob want to adopt Naomi—bitter, cynical, Naomi? And did Tob have the muscle to push the nesters off of Naomi's land? It was more than Tob could handle. He bowed out.

So Boaz and Ruth were married. Naomi was not so bitter any more. Perhaps God had not deserted her after all. Now if only Boaz and Ruth could have a son so that Ruth and Naomi could be provided for. After all, Boaz was an old man, almost Naomi's age. If he died, Naomi and Ruth would be right back where they started. And neither Boaz nor Ruth had ever had a child. Was it too much to ask?

Nine months later, Naomi's prayers were answered. The women of the village were ecstatic. They sang to Naomi:

> Praise be to the Lord, who this day has not left you without a kinsman-redeemer. May he become famous throughout Israel! He will renew your life and sustain you in your old age. For your daughter-in-law, who loves you and is better to you than seven sons, has given him birth.

And Naomi took the child from Ruth, lifted him as high in air as she could reach, twirled around before her friends and relatives, and in her heart she thought a single word: "Mine!" Naomi was never bitter again.

We curse our fate and act as though life were through with us. And sometimes we convince ourselves. But God is at our elbow. Tragedy does not speak the last word. It merely writes "the end" to one chapter of our lives and opens the next. Not getting what we want or getting what we don't want does not shut us down, cancel or annul us. It enables us to hear the voice of God calling us to be.

There will never be enough of what you want. There will always be an abundance of what you don't. So when you feel yourself slipping into bitterness, put on your best apparel and your most courageous frame of mind, and expect God to be right there at your side, whispering in your ear, calling you to your true vocation.

Amen.

—LDS

[1000 words]
[10 minutes]

❦ *CHAPTER FIVE*

CELEBRATION, JOY, AND GRATITUDE

As Christians we celebrate God's presence in our lives, our communities, and our world. Enthusiasm is a sure sign that God is in us. Joy is the most undeniable evidence of God's presence.

God's gifts are most appreciated by those who have most recently received them. Yet, whether we know it or not, the Gospel is proclaimed in, through, and despite each of us. We are all the Gospel's converts and its missionaries. We are the only Bibles that many of our neighbors will ever read!

Being appreciated is wonderful. When we realize who we are in Christ, we are freed to appreciate others and, in the end, appreciate ourselves. So show appreciation—now, while you have the chance. It makes a difference and it pays off.

When we celebrate God's transforming love, we know God's peace. We gain a perspective where worry just does not fit. We spontaneously, joyfully pray. We become aware that God gives us more than we could ever deserve or imagine.

God lives and God gives—ceaselessly, abundantly, with no strings attached. And when we consciously receive God's blessings with thanksgiving, our hearts expand to give, to share, to reach out to others.

❦ *Sermon 54*

❦ *Date:* Thanksgiving Day, Year A

Texts:
Deuteronomy 8:7–18
Psalm 65
2 Corinthians 9:6–15
Luke 17:11–19

or Twenty-first Sunday After Pentecost, Year C

Micah 1:2; 2:1–10
Psalm 26
2 Timothy 2:8–15
Luke 17:11–19

Theme: Christians without a sense of gratitude and mission are outcasts indeed.
Subject: Thankfulness

❦ *Title:* When the Story Makes No Sense

Here is a story that makes no sense. It is a passage that raises more questions than it answers. The story seems sandwiched in. It doesn't fit the itinerary. Luke has Jesus and the disciples backtrack to the border of Samaria and Galilee on their way to Jerusalem. That is like saying that John Smith was on his way from New York to Salt Lake City, and, as he got to the Utah border, something happened to him near Chicago.

The moral aspects of the story are equally puzzling. Why did Jesus praise the one leper and disparage the other nine, who had done exactly what he had told them to do and what the Law of Moses required? Was this grateful outcast more healed than the obedient nine?

What was Luke trying to tell us? As my years as a counselor have taught me, when the story makes no sense, embrace the ambiguity. Enjoy it. Then listen again with great care and read between the lines. There are four facets of this text to which I would call our attention: (1) the relationship of Jesus and the Samaritans, (2) what it meant to be a Samaritan and a Leper, (3) why Luke told this story, and (4) the lesson of the story to us.

The Relationship of Jesus and the Samaritans

Who were the Samaritans? Samaria was the central province of Palestine, sitting between Jesus' home province of Galilee to the north and the province of Judea to the south, where Jerusalem and the temple were located. The Samaritans considered themselves God's true chosen people and viewed the Judeans and all who observed the ways of the temple at Jerusalem as heretics and usurpers.

No doubt the Samaritans of Jesus' day were descendants of Israelites and others who had lived in the land over the previous seven hundred years. When the remnant of the southern kingdom of Judah had returned from the Babylonian exile around 500 b.c., the tension between the two related peoples had been fierce. The Israelites of the north had been banned from assisting in the reconstruction of the temple and had done what they could to harass and interfere with the builders. (Ezra 4)

Shut out by the Judeans or Jews of the South, the Samaritans clung to their own traditions, accepting only the five books of Moses as canonical. When the Judeans rebuilt the temple on Mount Zion, the Samaritans built one of their own on Mount Gerazim, about 35 miles away. The Jews regarded the Samaritans as aliens and troublemakers and barred them from the sacred precincts of the temple at Jerusalem. The Samaritans, for their part, were embittered by the war that the Maccabean kings of Judea had fought against them, which had destroyed both of their principal cities, Samaria and Schechem, leaving much of their land open for resettlement.

The relationship between Jesus and the Samaritans was hostile. Jesus was a Jew, and the Samaritans were his people's enemy. Yet, in this instance and in the most celebrated of his parables, the Parable of the Good Samaritan (Luke 10:29–37), Jesus used their despised status to make the point that God plays no favorites, that his mercy extends to all, and that the one who responds to others with compassion is the true model of the divine grace.

What It Meant to Be a Samaritan and a Leper

In the Old Testament, leprosy was an annoying but easily cured skin condition—nothing like the disfiguring affliction known today as Hansen's disease. The sufferer washed himself and his possessions, and the disease went away. Why the Hebrews so feared the condition, regarding it as a divine punishment and a grave ritual pollution, is far from clear.

As to the nature of leprosy in the New Testament, we are at a loss. (It probably was the dreaded illness now known as Hansen's disease.) Whether it was the Old Testament skin condition or a worse malady, no one can say. Lepers of the first century were outcasts who lived in their own communities on the outskirts of established villages and cities upon which the lepers depended for alms. Jesus healed lepers and commissioned his disciples to do the same. Yet he prohibited his disciples from preaching among the Samaritans. To be both a leper and a Samaritan was to be doubly cursed.

The nine miraculously cleansed Jewish lepers did exactly what the Law of Moses and Jesus commanded. But what did Jesus expect the healed Samaritan to do? The double outcast of our story did not go with the other nine lepers to the temple. He could not. He was unwelcome there—as unwelcome as Jesus had been in the village of the Samaritans.

To be a Samaritan and a leper was to be twice cursed. But to hear the Gospel in the midst of one's suffering and rejection and gratefully to receive God's gift of unconditional acceptance is to be made truly whole. The point is that God does not promise freedom from pain and misunderstanding but that he will be with us if we but open our eyes to his presence.

Why Luke Told This Story

Why was it so important to Luke to tell this story? For the same reason he had honored this despised ethnic group in the Parable of the Good Samaritan—another story recorded only by Luke. The answer is found in the history of the early church, also recorded by Luke in the fifth book of the New Testament, the Acts of the Apostles.

In Acts 1 we read that Jesus' last words to his disciple before his ascension were: "you shall receive power when the Holy Spirit has come upon you; and you shall be my witnesses in Jerusalem and in all Judea and Samaria and to the end of the earth" (v. 8). There is no evidence that the first Christians ever attempted to evangelize their hated northern neighbors until circumstances intervened. When Stephen, the church's first martyr, was executed, the Jerusalem church went underground, and its leaders scattered. The apostle Philip, whose suspiciously Greek name suggests that he would be at home among Samaria's Hellenistic populace, went to Samaria to preach. Philip's mission, says Luke, carried him "to many villages of Samaria." Apparently Philip and the other apostles were extremely successful. With the conversion at this time of their greatest opponent, Saul of Tarsus, we read, "the church throughout all Judea and Galilee and Samaria had peace and was built up." (Acts 9:31)

The success of Philip's mission ensured the emergence of the Christian faith as more than a new sectarian movement within Judaism, more than a breakaway cult, more than an obscure clique based on an odd interpretation of the Hebrew scriptures. In Samaria, among the despised and the foreigners, the church began to obey the final command of Jesus, and Christianity became a faith for all who would respond to its message.

And that is why Luke loved and revered the Samaritans. Because the Gospel had been preached to them, it had been proclaimed to Gentiles like himself.

The Lesson of the Double Outcast

Who are the grateful foreigners today?

The ethnic minorities and poor within our community?

The homeless?

The poor in spirit?

Or are we the double outcasts?

Do we, like the Samaritans, think that we are better than our neighbors because we are faithful, normal, and accepted?

Perhaps our faithfulness, normality, and acceptability are mere figments of our imagination. To this day, the Samaritans of Palestine exist as a separate, distinguishable minority in modern Israel—but their number has declined to a few hundred. Could that happen to us?

Like the lepers of the Gospel account, we are in danger of becoming ghettoized, of restricting ourselves to preaching only to the converted, of addressing the needs only of our own kind—ordinary, normal, upper-middle-class, educated, OK people. But what will become of us if the supply of ordinary, normal, upper-middle-class, educated, OK people declines? Or if they become too busy to need us or if they find their needs better met elsewhere?

How do we reverse the trend? How do we break out of our confines? Today's text suggests a few possibilities.

First, we need to learn to be grateful—grateful to our tradition, to our Church, to our God. We need to appreciate who we are as members of this particular church in this special place at this unprecedented time in history. We need to begin and to end each day with a prayer of thanksgiving for what has been entrusted to us. As Meister Eckhart said many centuries ago, "If the only prayer you say in your whole life is 'thank you,' that is enough."

God gives ceaselessly, abundantly, with no strings attached. And when we consciously receive with thankful hearts, our hearts expand to give and to receive even more. The power of God is present in our lives whether or not we acknowledge it. But without thanks, it is like an uncashed check.

Second, we need to express our thanks, to stop keeping it a secret. Of course, we appreciate what we have. The problem is we take it for granted and that we keep it to ourselves.

The failure of mainstream churches like ours has not been that we were too concerned with the issues of the day, but that we have failed to communicate why we cared in the first place. Our weakness has been not in our social conscience but in our failure to educate. We have done the right thing without letting anyone—our fellow church members, our neighbors, or our children—know who we were, what we believed, to whom we held ourselves accountable. We were not always so sure ourselves, and it showed.

If we want to be more than benched, sideline players, we must deliberately give voice to our gratitude. We have to own up to who we are, to what we believe. And that means changing our attitude about the church, seeing it not only as a warm and congenial group of friends but as a lifelong learning center. As Malcolm Warford, the president of the UCC seminary in Bangor, Maine, warns, "We are living at the end of an era. We have lived off our heritage. We have diluted our heritage as much as we can. The well has gone dry. It is time for us to say what we stand for." If we do not *learn* who we are and what we believe, and *teach* who we are and what we believe, and *live* who we are and what we believe, and *offer* to others who we are and what we believe, ours will truly be a story that makes no sense.

Third, we must find our Samaria, our special opportunity to proclaim the Good News. And that requires answering these questions: What are the needs of this community? What can we do to respond to those needs? The answers will not come in the form of new programs or priorities but in an opening of our arms to accept our neighbors, to respond to their needs with love, compassion, and imagination.

Why was the story of the grateful Samaritan leper important to Luke? It enabled him to say that he was grateful, to declare that he had not taken God's bounty for granted, and to remind us that Christians without a sense of gratitude and mission are outcasts indeed.

Amen.

—LDS

[1940 words]
[20 minutes]

Sermon 55

Date: Thanksgiving Day or Thanksgiving Sunday
(the Sunday Before Thanksgiving)

Text:
Philippians 4:4–9

Theme: "An attitude of gratitude is a beatitude, which is no platitude!"
Subject: Thankfulness

Title: An Attitude of Gratitude

Tip 1

> In obvious appreciation to Robert Schuller, I here used an outrageous pun as both the title of the sermon and as the main point. It caught the congregation's attention and was much discussed. It also provided a good laugh and reminded some of my congregants that the preacher is not a "Gloomy Gus."

Tip 2

> The historical background of major American holidays and special occasions is poorly understood. Congregations sit up and take notice when the preacher adds to their scant store of data.

Today is Thanksgiving Day, our annual national holiday celebrating the harvest and other blessings of the past year. This morning I would direct our attention to the meaning of this special day of gratitude and to the lessons it provides—for the significance of this day reveals to us the secret of the victorious Christian life.

The Pilgrim Thanksgiving

As we all know, Thanksgiving originated in the autumn of 1621 when Massachusetts Bay colony governor William Bradford invited neighboring Indians to join the Pilgrims for a three-day festival of feasting and diversion. In our mind's eye, we see the magazine cover depictions, the grade school plays, the commercial displays—the Pilgrim fathers with their funny hats and shiny shoe buckles hunting wild turkey with their absurd blunderbusses while Pilgrim mothers in bonnets and plain dresses baked pies and played with Pilgrimettes. We forget what a near thing that first Thanksgiving was.

After arriving in the New World, the Pilgrims spent their first winter aboard ship. Forty-seven of the 102 immigrants succumbed to disease, probably the same plague that had killed 95,000 of New England's 100,000 coastal Indians.

In the spring, the *Mayflower* returned to England, leaving the hardy survivors atop Cole's Hill, where they buried their dead and planted seed to conceal their tragedy. It was not a good idea to let the possibly hostile indigenous people know just how badly depleted their numbers were.

In March, a tall Indian named Samoset appeared, shouting a peace cry in English: "Much welcome, Englishmen! Much welcome, Englishmen!" The small band of settlers and the decimated natives desperately needed each other. Samoset introduced the Pilgrims to his friend Massasoit, the local chief. Among Massasoit's braves was Squanto, once a slave in Spain and later a resident in the home of an English gentlemen from whom he had learned English. In this strange way, providence had provided the newcomers with an interpreter, guide, and teacher.

The thirty-five religious nonconformists and the sixty-seven assorted adventurers, soldiers, and tradesmen had come seeking freedom and opportunity. Hundreds of millions would follow them in pursuit of the same vision. But in 1621 the tenacious handful of pioneers and their Indian friends had little time to think of lofty goals and aspirations. We today are grateful to them for having founded a nation. They were content that they had survived.

Lincoln's Proclamation

Over the ensuing decades, the custom of thanking God for his bounty during the harvest season spread and was widely observed, particularly in New England. Not until a descendent of early New Englanders, Abraham Lincoln, was in the White House did the fall festival receive official status. In 1863, at the height of the Civil War, President Lincoln officially proclaimed Thanksgiving as a national holiday. At a time when Americans were dying by the hundreds of thousands to preserve the nation that the Pilgrims had founded, Lincoln must have felt a need to set first things first, to remind the nation of the just God who is the Author of liberty and the source of all its blessings.

Perhaps Lincoln, a devout but unchurched spirit, had learned of the importance of thankfulness from the Apostle Paul. Perhaps Lincoln had read the words of today's text from Paul's letter to the Philippians. Lincoln's mother, Nancy Hanks, is described by her contemporaries as a person who was pious to the point of fanaticism. And in the Indiana hovel of Abraham Lincoln's childhood there was only one family-owned book—the Bible.

The Thankful Apostle

Thanksgiving is not an incidental theme in Paul's letter to the Christians of Philippi. It is central to the epistle as it was to Paul's ministry. The letter opens with gratitude: "I thank my God in all my remembrance of you, always in every prayer of mine . . ., thankful for your partnership" (1:3–6). It closes with an expression of appreciation to the Philippians for their generosity to him. Of all the churches he had founded, only the Philippians contributed to his financial support. While Paul languished in chains in a Roman prison, they had sent Epaphroditus, one of their number, to care for him.

Paul was grateful, but he was also concerned. From Epaphroditus he had learned that there was trouble among the Philippians. That was nothing new. As much as Paul loved them, he knew that the Philippians could be a tempestuous lot. Paul's visit to the city of Philippi had been joyous, painful, and exciting—rather like surviving a 7.1 earthquake in northern California.

In about A.D. 50, Paul, Silas, and Timothy had founded the church in Philippi. Their stay in that city (recorded in Acts 16) was like a vacation planned by a mad travel agent. Paul had met Lydia, the seller of purple, at a Jewish prayer meeting outside the city. She was his first convert and his hostess. So far, so good. A chance encounter with a possessed slave girl, probably a snake-handling oracle, led to a dispute with her masters. Before it was over, Paul and Silas had been beaten and imprisoned, an earthquake had flung the prison gates open, and the terrified jailer and his family has been converted. When the authorities discovered that Paul was a Roman citizen, they apologized and sent the party of missionaries on their way.

The church at Philippi felt bound to their founder as grateful children do to their parents. They frequently sent gifts to support Paul's mission, and through the exchange of letters Paul and the Philippians kept in touch.

But there was one problem—or should I say two problems?—with the church at Philippi. The names were *Euodia* (Eu-o-DEE-a) and *Syntyche* (Sin-TOO-kay)—one old preacher of my youth referred to them as "Odious" and "Soon-touchy."

Odious and Soon-touchy were dedicated Christians. They were founding members of the first church in Europe. They were pillars of their community. They were probably generous donors to the special fund that supported Paul. The trouble with these two was that they could not get along with one another and their constant quibbling and backbiting had badly divided the church.

Paul felt he could straighten things out if he could get Odious and Soon-touchy to forget their petty squabbles and focus on all that God had given them. He urged them to be Christ-minded, to get out of their "I-need-I-want-I've got to have" mode of thinking and to consider others. To make his point he reminded them of the words of an early Christian hymn. In Philippians 2, Paul says

> *Each of you should look not only to your own interests, but also to the interests of others. Your attitude should be the same as that of Christ Jesus: Who, being in very nature God, did not consider equality with God something to be grasped, but made himself nothing, taking the very nature of a servant, being made in human likeness. And being found in appearance as a man, he humbled himself and became obedient to death—even death on a*

cross! Therefore God exalted him to the highest place and gave him the name that is above every name, that at the name of Jesus every knee should bow, in heaven and on earth and under the earth, and every tongue confess that Jesus Christ is Lord, to the glory of God the Father. (vss. 2:5-11)

As important as the example of the servant-Christ might be, Paul went further. He told them the secret that is the very heart of the Christian life: playful, prayerful thanks. He taught the Philippians the power of gratitude, the magic of knowing the difference between what seems important and what really matters. To paraphrase his words,

Rejoicing is imperative. In 1989, President Bush quoted a Polish patriot who said it well. When asked how she could sit at the same table as those who had oppressed her, she replied: "Our joy at what is happening now is more powerful than our bitter memories." What a lesson for all of us this morning: knocking off our "poor me" games and realizing how blessed we are makes all the difference in the world. Each of us can choose to wallow in self-pity and self-righteousness, or we can allow ourselves to be thankful and generous. The individual who is right all the time buys himself or herself a one-way ticket to loneliness and frustration. Appreciation attracts appreciation. The appreciative person is the appreciated person. The point is so important that Paul repeats it: "Again I say, Rejoice!"

The Power of Thanksgiving

Prayer makes a difference, especially prayers of thanksgiving. As Meister Eckhart taught centuries ago, "If the only prayer you say in your whole life is 'thank you,' that is enough."

Thanks changes things. The spirits of all human beings shrivel when appreciation is denied them and blossom when gratitude is expressed. Do not allow a day to pass without expressing your thanks. Not only will it benefit the recipient but it will enlarge and enhance your life as well. Do you remember Shakespeare's lovely words in The Merchant of Venice? "The quality of mercy is not strained; It droppeth as the gentle rain from heaven Upon the place beneath. It is twice blessed—It blesseth him that gives and him that takes." That's exactly what Paul was getting at. And Paul did more than advise the Philippians to be thankful. He provided them with a model. He was what he taught.

The *prayerful, thankful heart is the peaceful heart.* Success cannot buy peace of mind. Spiritual exercises and devotions cannot guarantee happiness. Counseling, drugs, a great social life, a perfect mate, wonderful children, a whirl of socially significant activities cannot do for any of us what a grateful heart can achieve. Forgive the Robert Schuller–like affectation, but "An attitude of gratitude is a beatitude, which is no platitude!"

Finally, Paul tells the Philippians that *some things are worth thinking about and some things aren't.* If he were alive today, he would be saying some television programs are worth watching, some aren't; some books are worth reading, some aren't; some music is worth hearing, some isn't; some political leaders are worth heeding, some aren't; all friendships are worth keeping, petty bickering is not. At times I fear that the verdict of later generations on our times will be a single headline: "They were drunk on junk and bunk!"

Paul's message is simple: if you want your life to be excellent, to have real value, to really matter, set your mind and your heart on what is excellent, what has real value, what really matters (1:10). He echoes the familiar teaching of Jesus: "Seek first God's kingdom and his righteousness, and everything you need will be yours as well" (Matthew 6:33, paraphrased).

And so this morning we remember the example of the Pilgrims who were thankful and who were neither too proud to accept their neighbors' help nor too selfish to share with them the bounty of the earth.

We remember Abraham Lincoln who renewed the Pilgrim's dream of freedom, who called his people to a renewal of its purpose, "that this nation, under God, shall have a new birth of freedom—and that government of the people, by the people, for the people shall not perish from the earth."

We remember the Apostle Paul who knew how to express his appreciation to others and who never forgot what really matters. Together with them, we look to the God who created and sustains us, and to his children, the loving ones who comfort and encourage us, and we say "thank you."

Amen.

—LDS

[1900 words]
[19 minutes]

Sermon 56

Date: Thanksgiving Day or Thanksgiving Sunday
(the Sunday Before Thanksgiving)

Text:
2 Corinthians 6:1–10

Theme: God lives! Give thanks!
Subject: Thankfulness

Title: God Lives! Give Thanks!

Christ, Our Anchor, Holds Firm

Turn back the pages of history with me to the land of Jesus when Tiberius was the emperor of Rome. See that band of men, their faces aglow, their bodies pulsing with life. They are more than men of purpose. They are men possessed with a passion, and from each of their lips comes the same jubilant cry: "Good news! Good news!" Follow them as they are stoned and beaten; listen as the echo comes from the cave: "We are pressed on every side, yet not straightened; perplexed, yet not unto despair; pursued, yet not forsaken; smitten down, yet not destroyed." Listen as the judge asks Andrew if he has a final request before his execution. "Yes, I am not worthy to be crucified as was my Lord. Crucify my body in the form of an X." And from that cross, even as he died, came the testimony of the good news: "In Christ we have an anchor for the soul."

Turn the pages of history with me. Observe these men called Christians. No obstacle is too great. Death itself cannot stop them, for they are men possessed with a hope and a joy of thanksgiving. We stand in admiration before such men; we marvel at their courage. See them there, their robes tattered, their faces tired, their bodies bruised—a mighty company of God's heroes, from every land, from every age, and from their lips comes a mighty chorus: "Thanks be to God for his unspeakable gift."

How could these men give thanks when their bodies were racked with pain? How could Paul write, with a pen dipped in blood from a prison cell, "In everything, give thanks"? How could these men face the dungeon and death with such an unconquerable spirit? It was because they had within their hearts the deep conviction that they were not alone, that God was with them. They knew God! God was not an imaginative fulfillment of their wishful thinking. God was not an expedient theory to give meaning to their logic. God was not an opiate to shield them from reality. God was not a tradition adapted from their fathers. God was a real, moving, compelling experience within their souls. They knew God! God was with them. The eternal Creator of this universe, the alpha and omega, was in them and with them. Why should they fear the dungeon? Why should they fear the lion? Why should they become despondent and discouraged? Why should they sink to the hell of despondency? God was alive in their hearts. So even from the dungeon came their jubilant song of thanksgiving, "God lives! God is with us!"

This is the triumphant affirmation that has stirred the hearts of men of all ages, changing them from weak, complaining men to stalwart soldiers of the faith.

One day Moses, tending the flock of his father-in-law Jethro, heard the call of God: "Come, therefore, and I will send thee unto Pharaoh that thou mayest bring my people, the people of Israel, out of Egypt." But Moses looked within himself and, because of his inadequacies, cried, "Who am I that I should go unto Pharaoh?" But God said, "I will be with thee," and Moses became a new man. And Pharaoh trembled.

One day Jeremiah heard the call of God coming to him, saying, "Go and speak in my name." But Jeremiah looking within himself and, because of his weakness and inadequacies, cried, "Lord God, behold, I cannot speak for I am a child." But the Lord God said to Jeremiah, "Say not I am a child, for thou shalt go to all that I shall send thee and whatsoever I shall command thee thou shalt speak. Be not afraid of their faces, for I am with thee." And kings trembled at the sound of his voice.

Listen to the words of Governor Bradford, one of the early governors of the Plymouth Colony, as he describes America through the Pilgrims' eyes:

> The whole country, full of woods and thickets, represented a wild and savage hue. If they looked behind them, there was the mighty ocean which they had passed, and was now as a main bar and gulf to separate them from all the civil parts of the world. What could now sustain them but the spirit of God and his grace? May not and ought not the children of these fathers rightly say, "Our fathers came over this great ocean, and were ready to perish in this wilderness; but they cried unto the Lord, and he heard their voices, and looked on their adversity. Let them therefore praise the Lord, because he is good and his mercies endure forever."

Look with me into the notorious Dachau concentration camp on Christmas Eve 1944. I know that place. I see its long, low, green houses, now, for I was with that first wave of troops that went across that low, green field to Dachau. I shall never forget those skeletonlike men who came to greet us. There stands Martin Niemoeller, on that Christmas Eve 1944, delivering a sermon to his fellow Christian prisoners. When Christmas must be celebrated in prison, it is a dismal affair. But then, as he recalls the name of Jesus, Immanuel, God with us, his voice carries a new strength: "We are not alone amid the horrors of these years, cut off though we are from the outside world. We are in the hands of God—the God of Jesus Christ, who is with us in this dismal and lonely place, to uphold and comfort us and keep hope alive in our hearts." God with us!

God Is with Us

Ah, Christians, do you know what that means this morning? To be sure, we want to give thanks for the abundance of these material things, large and small, that God has showered upon each one of us. We have much to be thankful for, who live amid the plenty while others starve and freeze. But these things become insignificant as we become conscious anew on this Thanksgiving Day of this great gift of God. God lives! God is with us! Let every heart rejoice! Let every heart give thanks! God lives with us! Let that man suffering there on his bed of pain give thanks! God is with him. Let that mother whose son is in a far-off land give thanks: God is with him. Let that family who stands by the open grave give thanks: God is with them. Let those who are hungry, and tired, and discouraged, and cold, and sorrowful, even unto death give thanks this morning: God is with us.

> . . . Is by our beds of pain;
> We touch him in life's throng and press,
> And we are whole again.

> The Lord is my shepherd; I shall not want.
> He maketh me to lie down in green pastures;
> He leadeth me beside the still waters.
> He restoreth my soul;
> He leadeth me in the paths of righteousness for his name's sake.
> Yea, through I walk through the valley of the shadow of death,
> I will fear no evil; for thou art with me. . . .

The Triumph of the Cross

A second affirmation that filled the hearts of these early Christians with thanksgiving and gave them the courage and will to push always onward, always higher upward toward the goal, was the triumph of the cross. This way of the cross was God's way of love, and it had proved victorious.

All the forces of evil and sin were pooled on that day of long ago to win a final victory over goodness and righteousness, and so they nailed upon a cross him who personified theses virtues.

> They nailed him on a cross and thought that they had won,
> That love was lost and goodness died and truth forever done.

But they forgot that this was God's world, God spoke! Christ arose! And the battle for truth was won!

Do you capture the significance of this truth this morning? It means that truth cannot be forever nailed to a scaffold. It means that love cannot be buried in a grave. It means that the goodness in your friend cannot be covered in a wooden box. It means that "Though the cause of evil prosper, yet 'tis God alone stands." This was the faith that enabled those early Christians, and indeed Christians of all ages, to carry on because, regardless of discouragements, reverses, and temporary defeats, they knew that in the end theirs would be the victory, for they labored on the side of God.

This is the kind of triumphant faith that we need in a world such as ours today. When rival forces battle for our allegiance, when nothing seems stable and secure, when confusion and hysteria awaken anew fears within us, and the wars and rumors of wars frighten us without; we need the sense of stability and courage to stand for the truth and for the best. We cannot stand unless we have the encouragement of this triumphant faith, that God's is the victory.

During the war, St. Philip's Church in London was twice bombed and left in ruin. Many thought that it was devastated, that it could never be put to any use again. But there were those of an unconquerable spirit that were determined that something should be built from those fragments, and so they set forth to built a new structure that was to be used for community worship. A drama was given as part of the program of the dedication of the new building. The prologue of the drama sounded these words.

There lives a beauty that men cannot kill, yea that shall kill all ugliness at last. Yes, God lives! Let him who works for good, who longs for truth and hopes for the right, give thanks.

> Our struggles will not end in defeat.
> Our sacrifices will not be lost.
> God lives! God's is the victory!

Triumph Over Death

Finally, the affirmation that filled the hearts of these early Christians with such a joy of thanksgiving was the good news that death was swallowed up in victory, that death was not the end but the beginning, that as God lived, so men could live eternally. Though the gates of hell themselves would rise up against them, they would not be cast down; for they had no fear of him who could destroy the body but could not harm the soul. When the storms of this life covered the skies with darkness, they too like John could capture a vision of the new Jerusalem and could say with him:

And I John saw the Holy City, the new Jerusalem, coming down from God out of heaven, prepared as a bride adorned for her husband. And I heard a great voice out of heaven saying, "Behold, the tabernacle of God is with men, and he will dwell with them, and they shall be his people, and God himself shall be with them, and be their God. And God shall wipe away all tears from their eyes, and there shall be no more death, neither sorrow, nor crying, neither shall there be any more pain: for the former things are passed away."

Yet, when a man has that vision he can stand. When a man has that vision, he can live. Life is no longer a tale told by an idiot, full of sound and fury, signifying nothing. But every moment in every day lived now has meaning because these moments and these days make the man who can live eternally. We shall not grow and mature here only to be cut down to decay as an animal of the field, but we shall live on to grow and grow again in God's eternal kingdom. Our work for which we have labored shall not be ended at harvest time, but we shall go on to labor in the heavenly vineyard and reap the harvest.

Victor Hugo caught this vision when he wrote:

> For half a century I have been writing my thoughts in prose and in verse. But I feel I have not said the thousandth part of what is in me. When I go down to the grave I can say, like many others, I have finished my day's work. But I cannot say, I have finished my life. My day's work will begin again the next morning. The tomb is not a blind alley, it is a thoroughfare. It closes on the twilight, it opens on the dawn.

This is a faith to live by as well as to die by; for if we can really believe an affirmation like this, it will make a difference in how we live now. It will make a difference in how we use our time. It will make a difference in how we treat our neighbor. It will make a difference as to what things we put first. It will make a difference as to what things we work for and how hard we work. It will make us rethink our philosophy of life. It will make us ask ourselves the question: Am I just an animal to live for the senses of the moment, or am I a soul destined for eternity? Though Paul lacked many of the material blessings of life, though he suffered persecution and affliction for the cause of Christ, he believed that God was with him. And believing that the way of the Cross would triumph, believing that his soul would live eternally, he could say, "I have nothing and yet I possess all things." God lives! Give thanks!

Amen.

—Chaplain Donald E. Lewis[1]

[2264 words]
[23 minutes]

---

[1] From *Best Sermons, 1955 Edition* (New York: McGraw-Hill, 1955), pp. 335–341.

Sermon 57

Date: Any Sunday

Texts:
Matthew 16:21–28
Acts 2:42–47

or Fourth Sunday of Easter, Year A

Texts:
Acts 2:42–47
Psalm 23
1 Peter 2:19–25
John 10:1–10

Theme: Enthusiastic Christians are God-filled Christians.
Subject: Enthusiasm

Title: Enthusiasm

Joe shook his head. "Did you see what the preacher's topic is this Sunday?" he said. "I can't believe it. It's 'Enthusiasm.'" Joe and Bill were having coffee, and they were talking about their church. Bill said, "Well, he's having this series of sermons on specific words that he thinks are important words like 'cherish' and 'resilience' and 'boundaries' and 'responsibility.'" "Yeah, I know that," Joe replied, "and those words are O.K. But enthusiasm? What is this—some kind of motivational seminar or church? And the fact is that we're born either enthusiastic or not, just like we're born blue-eyed or not, and there's nothing we can do about it."

Joe took another sip of coffee. "And anyway, what does enthusiasm have to do with the gospel of Jesus Christ? "Beats me," said Bill, "But, say, Joe who do you think is going to win the Series?"

Leaving Joe and Bill to their coffee and conversation, we return here to the scene of the crime, where, sure enough, the word for today is enthusiasm. What do we say about it?

The Sign of God's Presence

First, we must respond to Joe's criticism. "What does enthusiasm have to do with the gospel of Jesus Christ?" Joe, we would say, don't you agree that few things are more damaging to Christianity than glum, lifeless Christians?

And don't you realize that enthusiasm is a religious word? Coming straight from the Greeks, it is made up of two parts, the preposition "in" and the work "theos," which means "God." "Entheos" becomes "enthuse," which means, literally, "God inside" or "God filled." An enthusiastic person is a "God-filled" person. One of the most frequently repeated assertions of the New Testament is that believing people are filled with the presence of God. They are, quite literally, "enthused," God filled.

Jesus said to his followers, "Abide in me, and I in you." (John 15:4) He said, "I am in my father, and my father is in me, and I am in you." (John 14:20) Jesus said, "Lo, I am with you always." (Matthew 28:20) What does being God filled, enthused, have to do with the gospel? Everything! Forget Simon and Andrew and Paul and all their cousins, and recognize it. Jesus was saying to all who would be his followers, to you and me, "I am in you." We are God filled.

And how do genuinely God-filled people act? They act with enthusiasm, with joy. On the last evening of his life, Jesus said to his followers, "All these things I have spoken to you that my joy may be in you and that your joy may be complete." (John 15:11) Enthusiasm is faith that has been set fire.

Listen, Joe, we have to say, enthusiasm is not just one of a long list of personality traits. It is a religious word, a sure sign that God is inside, and it has everything to do with the gospel of Jesus Christ.

Recognizing Reality

A second point: To be enthusiastic does not mean to deny reality. This is why some people are suspicious of enthusiasm. How can anyone who is aware of the weight of world problems today, drugs and war and broken families and struggling churches and scandals, how can anyone come chirping onto this scene with any optimistic enthusiasm. Don't they know what's going on?

And there is something to that, all right. Unbridled, unthinking good cheer does get on the nerves. Sometime ago, I went out and played tennis with a Lutheran pastor, a Jewish rabbi, and a Congregational minister. This sounds like the beginning of one of those jokes: "There was once these Protestant ministers who played tennis with a rabbi and a priest." Believe me, it was no joke. The doubles match was pretty good except for one thing. In an excess of gallantry, everybody kept complimenting everyone else. "Great shot! Good hit! Good try! Great serve! No matter how utterly inept a shot was, somebody would find a compliment. "Good footwork there! Nice warm-up suit." After an hour or so of this, I was yearning for my regular Tuesday morning group where compliments are paid when deserved, but where we recognize and honor bad shots for what they are, and share a good number of friendly insults after each.

There are a lot of bad shots in this life, and genuine enthusiasm is not blind to them. It does, however, focus on the good ones. And that is basically what Paul was saying in our text for today. "You've had some sour quarrels in your church there at Philippi," he pointed out, "and there's lots to be anxious about. But brethren," he said, "Whatever is true, whatever is honorable, whatever is pure, whatever is lovely, whatever is gracious, if there is any excellence, if there is anything worthy of praise, think about these things...and the God of Peace will be with you" (Philippians 4:8–9).

And those problems that exist? Don't deny them, but turn them into promises. Make your complaint into your job description, and see what a God filled life can do with it.

The Power of Enthusiasm

And a third observation. Enthusiasm has a remarkable effect on other people. The Proverb says, "A cheerful heart is good medicine, but a downcast spirit dries up the bones" (Proverbs 17:22). And it is true. Surely you have seen it proven over and again. I have. I attend a considerable number of community meetings where there are speakers on a variety of subjects—politics, education, the Kansas City Chiefs, drugs, and so on. It is fun to watch the speakers' techniques and strategies and observe how we listeners respond.

It usually takes only about thirty seconds to know whether the message will be heard or not. And it isn't the speaker's credentials or topic that makes the difference. It is his or her spirit, or enthusiasm. Some make the audience want to listen. That speaker is clearly glad to be here, has something he or she wants to say, is sold on the subject. Some make the listeners check how close they are to the door to see if early exit is possible.

The speaker largely determines the response. This, no doubt, explains the instructions an eighteenth-century New England preacher gave the ushers at his church in the event someone went to sleep during the sermon. Here is the instruction: "In the event that someone goes to sleep during the sermon, the usher is to go immediately and wake up the preacher." If the spirit is there, the enthusiasm, people will listen.

And this surely explains the success of the early church. Listen as Acts describes it. "And day by day, attending the temple together and breaking bread in their homes, they partook of food with glad and generous hearts, praising God and having favor with all people." (Acts 2:46) You catch the spirit showing in that verse? No wonder the next verse says, "And the Lord added to their number day by day those who were being saved." (Acts 2:47) And what was Joe's question? "What does enthusiasm have to do with the gospel of Jesus Christ?"

Whether we like it or not, we Christians are walking advertisements of our faith. Does Christ abide in us? Often it takes only thirty seconds or so of listening to a person's witness about life itself to know. We don't have a choice in this. A few months ago a landscape expert came by the church parsonage to talk about putting some new shrubs and flowers out in the yard. "What I want to do," he told me, "is have my partner come by and visit with you a little to get a reading on your personality so that we will know what kind of a statement you want to make with your front yard."

That ended the project, because (1) I didn't dare run the risk of seeing how they would translate my personality into shrubs and flowers and (2) all I really wanted was green grass and no weeds, which may say enough about personality right there.

But if even our front yard makes a statement about who and what we are, what about our spirit, our enthusiasm? Whether we like it or not, we are walking advertisements of our faith, so that our enthusiasm has a remarkable effect on others.

The Value of Enthusiasm

And, finally, enthusiasm has a remarkable effect on the self. It energizes us and makes us able to do our jobs better. Someone put it pretty bluntly about the challenges a lot of us face in our work: "If you aren't fired with enthusiasm, you are likely to be fired—with enthusiasm."

"But wait a minute," someone says, "what about Joe's other criticism of the subject today? He said that we are born either enthusiastic or not, just as we are born blue-eyed or not. Isn't that true? Some of us are not the exuberant, enthusiastic type. What if we, in all honesty, just don't feel enthusiastic?"

But listen! You don't have to feel enthusiastic in order to act enthusiastic, just as you don't have to feel loving in order to act loving. Why should feeling have more power than will? William James devised and defined what he called the "as if" principle. If you want to be brave and courageous, act as if you are brave and courageous. As Shakespeare said, "assume a virtue if you have it or not."

What do you think of this "as if" approach? It has often been observed that it is easier to act your way into a new way of thinking than to think your way into a new way of acting. This is the "as if" principle all over again. And it can have a remarkable effect on the way you look at life.

If you don't believe it, talk to one of Kansas City's heroes, Charlie Plumb. Many of us have heard him speak about his experience in a North Vietnamese prison camp. Shot down, captured, tortured, mistreated, caged, Charlie Plumb found himself bitterly blaming the president, the builder of his plane, the Congress, anyone—until a fellow POW got hold of him and told him about what he called prison thinking. Self-pity and blaming others were the first symptoms, and it was inevitably fatal to prisoners. To survive this ordeal, he had to break out of prison in his own mind.

Did he do it? Six years later, 2,103 days later, he stumbled out of that prison and came home. He survived because he came to see that an inner enthusiasm, a spiritfilled life, could never be prevented by prison bars, "Keeping a positive, optimistic spirit," he said, "was the only way to survive."[1]

The word for today is enthusiasm, and what have we said? First, enthusiasm is a religious word meaning literally, God filled. Second, to be enthusiastic does not mean we are blind to the problems of this world—we simply put them in perspective. Third, enthusiasm has a remarkably positive effect on people and groups about us. And, finally, enthusiasm has a creative, positive effect on ourselves.

A father and child once stood looking at Holman Hunt's picture, titled *Christ Standing at the Door Knocking*. They gazed for a few moments at the picture of Jesus standing motionless before that closed door, his hand raised as if knocking repeatedly. The father said to the child, "I wonder why they don't let him in?" And after a moment's thought, the child replied, "I know why. I'll bet they're down in the basement, and they can't hear him knocking."

Listen, too often that's where we are, down in the dark basement of faith, so that we miss out on the joy he promised. If you want your own faith to be stronger and more effective, if you want the causes you believe in to prosper, there's a way to do it. It's not always easy, of course, but it is possible. The word for today is Enthusiasm.

Amen.

—Eugene Brice

[2000 words]
[20 minutes]

❦ *Sermon 58*

❦ *Date:* Eleventh Sunday After Pentecost, Year A

Texts: (NCL)
Exodus 16:2–15
Psalm 78:1–3, 10–20
Romans 11:13–16, 29–32
Matthew 15:21–28

or Christmas Day, Year C

Texts:
Isaiah 52:7–10
Hebrews 1:1-4
John 1:1–14

---

[1] *Kansas City Star*, September 4, 1986.

or Second Sunday of Easter, Year B

Texts:
Acts 4:32–35
1 John 5:1–6
Matthew 28:11–20

Theme: Christians are all missionaries and converts.
Subject: Appreciation, missionaries

❦ *Title:* The Mystery of the Unconverted Missionary

The Unappreciated Gift

The cobbler's children have no shoes. The orthodontist's wife has crooked teeth. The tailor's mother wears rags. And sometimes missionaries neglect not only the souls of their children but their own as well.

If you give your child a hundred Christmas presents, that child will probably appreciate none of them. All too often, we Christians are that way with the blessings of God.

God's gifts, I have noticed, are best appreciated by those who have most recently received them and least esteemed by those who have had them the longest.

Many would insist that the history of Christianity is no longer in the hands of Western European or North American Christians. We are not where the action is! The future of the Christian church depends now on Latin America, Africa, Asia, and, Eastern Europe. So it is said.

And that is entirely consistent with the way humankind has always responded to the revelation of God. God offered his gifts to the descendants of Abraham, Isaac, and Jacob. And, again and again, they ignored them.

He sent his son, Jesus the Christ. In the words of the Fourth Gospel, Jesus came to his own and his own did not receive him. And so the torch was passed from Jew to Gentile. The old covenant of rules, laws, and ritual observances was replaced by a new way.

Jesus came to his own, and his own did not receive him. However, the message does not end here. He came to his own, and his own did not receive him, but to all who received him he gave the right to become children of God (John 1:11–12).

Jesus the Christ has given us the right to be children of God. Do we exercise that right? God has heaped on us the priceless treasures of grace, but don't we act more like spiritual paupers? Have we been exposed to the Gospel for so long that we have gotten used to it? Have we become a little bored with it? Have we grown immune to it?

Have you ever lost something valuable among the junk mail and bills that collect on your kitchen table or desk? More often than I care to admit, just after I have weathered a financial storm, I have found an uncashed check hidden amid my personal papers—a check that had been there for days. Isn't that exactly how we treat the authority given to us to be God's children?

The ancient Israelites were no better or worse than we are. Like us, they forgot God when things were going well and turned to him when things were not. Along the way they tried to hedge their bets by worshiping a few local deities to ensure fertile fields, flocks, and families. Good old Yahweh might be all right when it came to international affairs or military matters, but when it was imperative that the crops were adequate or that the lambs were healthy or that your wife bore strong sons, what could it hurt to get on friendly terms with the gods who had looked after such things in the neighborhood long before the Israelites appeared on the scene?

It was simply a matter of thinking globally but acting locally. We do that in our own way, don't we? Worshiping God on Sunday but living Monday through Saturday as though he were irrelevant? And along the way we bow our knees to gods named "getting ahead," "doing what's expected," "I'm only human," and "a man (or a woman) has gotta do what a man (or a woman) has gotta do." The ancient Israelites would have understood us all too well!

The Sin of Forgetfulness

Now the lapses of the Israelites in the strict fidelity demanded by Yahweh were small potatoes compared to their basic forgetfulness. Yahweh was the God of the oppressed. He had shown compassion to them when the Egyptians oppressed them. When they did not show the same sympathy to one another or to strangers in their midst, it kindled his rage. More than idolatry, it was injustice that doomed them. The disparity between a handful of the wealthy and the ever-increasing multitude of the poor weakened them. Selling justice to the highest bidder and denying it to the poor—that was something the prophets could not stomach and the God of the prophets could not ignore.

God Tries Again

So God tried again—with a new covenant and a new people. "This is the new covenant in my blood which is shed for many for the remission of sins." As the centuries passed, the Good News spread to every corner of the earth. From the faith of a few semiliterate peasants would spring the church numbering hundreds of millions.

The course of this people of God would have even more twists and turns than the history of ancient Israel. The persecuted minority of the first few centuries after the founding of the church would become the church triumphant of the Middle Ages. And when everyone is a Christian by imperial decree, nobody has to work very hard at being a Christian. Reformers would arise to call the church back to its own true nature, as the prophets had arisen in the kingdoms of Israel and Judah. Millions would perish in wars between followers of the Protestant reformation and Catholic loyalists. The vehemence and violence between Christians would only abate when their attention turned from matter of dogma to concerns for economic advantage, nationalism, geographic expansion, the enslavement of non-Christian peoples, and, now and then, the murder of Jews. It is not a pretty picture.

Along the way, western Christians of various denominational loyalties would offer the gospel, this divine treasure carried in all too human vessels, to Asia, Africa, South America, and so on. No matter how spiritual the aims of the missionaries, the sword was often the traveling companion of the cross. "Before the gospel came to my country," the leader of one indigenous people after another would exclaim, "we had lands but no Bibles. Now we have Bibles but no lands!"

As it had been when the prophets condemned those who found self-justification in the rote observance of the state religion while neglecting the needs of their countrymen, as it had been when Jesus of Nazareth preached that the last shall be first and the first shall be last, that the greatest among you is the one who serves the rest, so it was during all these years. The flame of the gospel flickered but never failed.

Despite Christian bickering, dissension, hypocrisy, and insensitivity, the gospel continued to be preached, the sacraments to be observed, humankind somehow kept in touch with its humanity, and God remained in his heaven.

Converts and Missionaries

Millions who have received the gospel through missionaries and evangelists can testify as follows:

> I came into the Christian church as a convert from another religion. For me, it was all fresh and new and exciting. What I was not prepared for was that it was not all fresh and new and exciting for all Christians. Or that I would encounter prejudice based on my origins. There is so much confusion among Christians. They do not know the difference between the gospel and the middle-class mores and social prejudices of the countries of their birth.

When I was seventeen, there was a missionary emphasis week at the Christian college I attended. A missionary from the then Belgian Congo spoke as follows:

> Before the gospel came to the Congo, the men of the village where I was sent wore skirts. Now that the gospel has come to village, they wear trousers.
>
> Before the gospel came to the Congo, the people of the village lived in mud huts. Now that the gospel has come to the village, they live in brick houses.
>
> Before the gospel came to the Congo, each man of the village ate dinner apart from his wife and children. Now that the gospel has come to the village, each man eats with his wife and children.

This missionary did not know the difference between wearing trousers and bearing the cross! He did not know the difference between being a Rotarian or a Junior Leaguer and being a Christian! He apparently thought that Norman Rockwell had been portraying Jesus and the Apostles on all those covers of Saturday Evening Post!

We are all missionaries—each and every one of us. We all preach the Gospel of Jesus Christ by our affirmations and our doubts, in our lucid moments and in our most confused. We all mix up unexamined social prejudices and self-interest with the Good News. Even when we don't believe and say we don't believe, we still proclaim the gospel. Whether or not we agree with Jesus, he sets the agenda for most of us as long as we live.

God's Prudent Ecology

God is ecologically prudent. In his universe nothing is wasted. The gospel is proclaimed in, through, and despite each of us.

And just as we are all missionaries, so also are we all converts. We are both the evangelists and the evangelized. We are the Good News even as we continually receive the Good News. We are the only Bibles that many of our neighbors, our co-workers, and our family members will ever read. Scary isn't it?

We all bring who we were to who we are. We spend our lives working out the difference between what our parents believed and what we believe. Even when we rebel against them, they speak the last word. Right or wrong, pietistic Christians, agnostics, or atheists, we can never quite get them out of our hearts and minds or stop reacting to them.

Further, no matter how miraculous and instantaneous conversion to the Christian way may seem, it is always a process and never a product. It is like a great painting to which layer upon layer is added, day by day, year after year. The Christian life is no Polaroid snapshot.

I have often said that discerning the presence of God is not as difficult as we make it. That is the essence of the Good News. Now for the corresponding "bad news": we will never overcome our prejudices or selfish ways. No matter how hard we try to comprehend God, we will misunderstand him and distort what he has to say to us as individuals and as a people. Yet God will cherish us and call us to be his people nonetheless.

Avoiding God is not easy. I would say it is virtually impossible. And it is not always easy to live as what we are—the carriers of the Good News and those most in need of the Good News. That's what we are. We are God's missionaries and his converts, the evangelists and the evangelized of the gospel of Jesus Christ.

We are the Good News even as we continually receive the Good News. God is ecologically prudent. In his universe nothing is wasted. The cobbler's offspring may go barefoot, but God's children are never neglected.

Amen.

—LDS

[1800 words]
[18 minutes]

Sermon 59

Date: Sunday Between July 3 and July 9 inclusive Pentecost, Year B

Texts:
2 Samuel 5:1-5, 9-10
Psalm 48
2 Corinthians 12:1–10
Mark 6:1–13

Theme: Lack of appreciation is a thorn in the flesh.
Subject: Appreciation, gratitude

Title: A Thorn in My Flesh

[First in a series. To be followed with "A Thorn in My Paw" (102) and "A Thorn in My Path" (21). Each sermon may also be used separately.]

Being appreciated is wonderful. Not being appreciated is the pits. It's as simple as that.

The desire for recognition and appreciation is as powerful as any craving we experience. If we were automobiles, our bumper stickers would read, "Appreciate Me Now and Avoid the Rush." If we were teeshirts, our chests would read, "I May Not Be Totally Perfect, But Parts of Me Are Excellent."[1] We all crave appreciation and wither when it is denied us.

The Apostle Paul was no different. At enormous personal cost, Paul had brought the Corinthians to Christ. With no thought of reward, he had ministered to their every need. And now they questioned his authority. Worse yet, they had turned to false apostles, to "peddlers of God's

---

[1] From Ashley Brilliant, *I Have Abandoned My Search for Truth and Am Now Looking for a Good Fantasy* (Santa Barbara, CA: Woodbridge Press, 1983).

word." But the real problem Paul had with them was that they had learned to take but not to give. They had learned to receive forgiveness and acceptance but not how to forgive and accept. And, above all, they had not learned appreciation. Maybe they were grateful to Paul. Maybe they were appreciative of one another. If they were, they kept it to themselves.

Starved for Affection

I remember hearing about Ole and Olga, who lived on a farm in Iowa.

> Olga was living on a starvation diet of affection. Ole never gave her any signs of love, and Olga's need to be appreciated went unfulfilled. At her wit's end, Olga blurted out, "Ole, why don't you ever tell me that you love me?" Ole stoically responded, "Olga, when we were married I told you that I loved you, and if I ever change my mind, I'll let you know."[2]

The Corinthians loved Paul. They were just too busy to spend much time telling him. They were like the tourists on a rush tour of Europe, whose car screeched to a stop in front of Chartres Cathedral. The husband jumped out and called to his wife, "You take the inside; I'll do the outside. Meet you here in five minutes."[3]

Paul was an incredibly gifted human being—so gifted that he easily could have spent all his time admiring his talents and feeling superior to everyone else. However, God does not allow any of us to succumb to that temptation for long. Life is simply too painful, too hard, too humiliating.

What Was Paul's Thorn?

"To keep me from becoming conceited," says Paul, "there was given me a thorn in my flesh." "A thorn in my flesh"? What was Paul's thorn in the flesh? Sexual temptation? An unhappy marriage? A painful eye condition? Epilepsy?

Or simply an overdeveloped sense of lack of appreciation? Maybe Paul felt that no matter what he did for the Corinthians, it was never enough—for them. Like all of us, he needed an occasional word of encouragement, an "'attaboy," a "way to go!"

It is so much easier to criticize, scandalize, gossip . . . to bring greatness down to our level . . . to find feet of clay. As Dale Carnegie says, "Any fool can criticize, condemn and complain—and most do."

Mutual Misery and Gossip

When I was a graduate student, most of my friendships were based on mutual misery. My fellow students and I would denigrate our professors and somehow feel that the human failings of "great men" made them no better than us neophytes.

Our currency, our medium of exchange, was gossip. Gossiping is like trading baseball cards. I will tell you some secret about so and so whom you respect, that is, whom you fear and resent, and you will give me some juicy morsel in return.

And behind it all—the failure to appreciate others is our lack of respect for ourselves. We do not know or appreciate who we are in ourselves, in relationship to others, and in Christ.

---

[2] *Pastor's Story File*, February 1985, p. 4.

[3] James Hewett in *Parables, Etc.*, July 1990.

I seldom meet anyone with exaggerated self-esteem or a superiority complex. To say that a person has low self-esteem is like saying that he is alive.

Ian Chapman, a Baptist minister, tells of his daughter, who

> was looking for a particular phonograph record and was calling several record shops trying to locate it. She called what she thought was a record shop, but instead a local plumber answered.
>
> Not realizing her mistake she asked, "Do you have 'Ten Little Toes and Fingers in Arkansas'?" The plumber paused for a moment not really knowing how to respond—and then said, "No, but I have a wife and ten children in Mississippi." My daughter asked, "Is that a record?" The plumber responded, "No, I don't think so, but I'm sure it's above average."[4]

Well, maybe none of us is setting records, but I'm sure, like the children of Lake Woebegone, we're all above average!

Unfortunately, we believe anyone who says we are sick and no one who says we are whole.

We believe anyone who says that another is sick and no one who says another is whole.

We believe anyone who says that a great person is sick and no one who says that a great person is whole.

We are content with the lowest common denominator because that excuses our being average or less than average.

Maybe Paul's thorn in the flesh was that he had transcended the gossip game. He knew he was "Paul the Apostle," the messenger and agent of God. He knew he was the one sent and empowered to bring others to Christ. He knew he was elite and elect. He knew he was non-interchangeable. He knew he was, in no way, average.

Do you know that you are Peter the Apostle, Edith the Apostle, Jim the Apostle, Diane the Apostle, Bob the Apostle, Betty the Apostle? [Insert the actual first names of several members of the congregation.]

Paul could have considered the alternatives and played it safe. He could have been like everyone else, sitting around mending tents in Damascus while he gossiped about the other apostles.

It is so tiresome to hear people's excuses for not being who they could be, for not doing what they know they ought to be doing. It is so depressing to hear constant complaints, lamentations about how everybody else is no good. It is so uplifting to be with people who spontaneously and unapologetically do whatever they do from a sense of who they are. It is so ennobling to be with people who know what their eliteness in Christ is—even if their eliteness is being chosen to a quiet, normal, ordinary existence.

It is so exhilarating to be among people who appreciate one another.

What it all boils down to is that appreciation is a form of praise and thanksgiving to God. If I had to summarize how to live a spiritual life in four words, they would be, "Be thankful" and "Show appreciation."

Show appreciation—now, while you have the chance. J. Kenneth Morris tells of a Southern mountain woman, who, in rough and uneven letters, chiseled on her husband's tombstone this epitaph: "He always appreciated."[5] Let that be your epitaph.

A few years ago, the following letter appeared in the Chicago Tribune.

---

[4] *Parables, Etc.*, May 1985, 5.3.

[5] *Premarital Counseling* (Englewood Cliffs, NJ: Prentice Hall, 1960), p. 53.

> I am not a writer but I am taking some space in the newspaper to write something special about Kathy. We weren't so special. . . . I'm just a little insurance man, but when someone makes your life so good, you just hate to let her leave the world without some kind of memorial to let people know she was alive. I want to tell people to look over at their husbands and wives and say to themselves, "My God, look what I have here." People take so much for granted. It's as if they think everyone is going to live forever and they can put off their love and appreciation until they have time.
>
> Here I am saying these things about Kathy today and it seems like I never said them to her when she was alive. She'd have come to me now with kisses. I am sitting home alone at night and I see her in the hallways. I see the furniture we bought, and I see her sitting beside me on the couch. If I could go back . . . , I would do everything different. I would let her know how much she meant to me, but I can't do that, and it seems like the only thing I can do is try to make other people know it. Look at your husband. Look at your wife. If you think you have things pretty nice, say it out loud. Don't assume that they are going to be there forever. Some day they are going to walk out the door and never come back. . . . I didn't think of that until Kathy was dead. It's too late for me, but it's not too late for you.

Show appreciation. It may teach you to appreciate yourself, for each of us is unique. I have heard about a wise teacher, who

> was speaking to a group of eager young students. He gave them the assignment to go out and find a small, unnoticed flower somewhere. He asked them to study the flower for a long time. "Get a magnifying glass and study the delicate veins in the leaves, and notice the nuances and shades of color. Turn the leaves slowly and observe their symmetry. And remember that this flower might have gone unnoticed and unappreciated if you had not found and admired it."
>
> After the class returned the teacher observed, "People are like that. Each one is different, carefully crafted, uniquely endowed. But you have to spend time with them to know this. So many people go unnoticed and unappreciated because no one has ever taken time with them and admired their uniqueness."[6]

Show appreciation. It makes a difference. There was a factory in which management conducted an experiment.

> They thought that improved lighting would boost production. To reduce the financial risk they decided to install the new lighting in only one-half of the factory first, and see what happened.
>
> To their surprise, productivity went up throughout the factory, not just in the part with improved lighting. So, bewildered and curious, they moved the lighting to the other half of the factory. Again, productivity increased among . . . the workers.
>
> Still befuddled, they tried removing the new lighting completely. Again, productivity shot up. By this time the management was totally confused, and as a last resort (of course) they asked the workers why productivity had increased each time, regardless of who had the new lighting.

---

[6] From John Powell, *The Christian Vision,* cited in *Pastor's Story File,* October 1985, p. 12.

Workers responded, "We saw all of you out here looking around, checking on us and our working conditions. For the first time, we felt like you cared what was going on out here."[7]

Show appreciation. It may pay off. In Lee Iacocca Talking Straight, the CEO of Chrysler Motors shares several stories about raising funds for the renovation of the Statue of Liberty. My favorite is about Mary Miller. Iacocca remarks:

> She was just a little old lady from New Jersey who wanted to help, and so she sent $1,000. Naturally, we sent her a nice thank-you note. I guess she must have appreciated the note, because she then sent another check—this one for $50,000.
>
> After that, I called her to say thanks again, and she said, "You guys are really nice." She was so pleased that she said she was sending along a "little envelope." When it came, it had three checks in it—one for $25,000, one for $50,000, and one for $75,000.
>
> So much money was pouring in from her that I used to kid about it. I'd say, "I never even met Mary Miller. All I did was thank her and she sent me $201,000. Imagine if I'd sent her flowers!"
>
> I was so grateful to her that I wanted to bring her over to visit Liberty Island with me. On two occasions when I was in New York I called her, but she was always too busy. She was eighty-seven, and yet her schedule seemed to be tighter than mine. The last time she turned me down for our date, she told me it was out of the question for her to get away that day. She was doing her spring housecleaning![8]

Appreciation counts. It blesses both the giver and the recipient. It makes a difference. And it pays dividends.

So show your appreciation.
Thank and praise God.
Everything else in life is a bonus!
Being appreciated is wonderful. Not being appreciated is the pits. It's as simple as that.

Amen.

—LDS

[2068 words]
[21 minutes]

❦ *Sermon 60*

❦ *Date:* Sunday Between October 9 and October 15 inclusive Pentecost, Year A

Texts:
Exodus 32:1-14
Psalm 106:1–6, 19-23
Philippians 4:1–9
Matthew 22:1–14

---

[7] *Pastor's Story File*, February 1988.

[8] Iacocca, Lee, *Talking Straight*, (New York: Bantam Books, 1986), pp. 8-9.

Theme: Those who know the peace of God cannot but rejoice, cannot help treading lightly, cannot see things any other way but from a perspective where worry just does not fit, and find that their hearts start praying even before their minds realize it.
Subject: Grace, thanks, joy

Title: Does My Spirit Need a Tune Up? Paul's Personal Checklist

There are many reasons why I go to church. But one of the most powerful is because I like to. In the words of Walt Whitman,

> I have perceived that to be with those I like is enough,
> To stop in company with the rest at evening is enough,
> To be surrounded by beautiful curious breathing laughing flesh is enough. . . .
> I do not ask any more delight . . . I swim in it as in a sea.

The kingdom of God is not a funeral. It is a celebration. If I fail to rejoice, there is something wrong—something about which I had better do something. Perhaps my inner self needs a tune-up.

The Christian life flows naturally and freely from a sense of God's unconditional love. The Christian life is more a spontaneous response than it is an attainment. It is more a receiving than a striving. At the same time, the Christian life is a journey with mileposts, a pilgrimage with a checklist that charts our progress. In the fourth chapter of his letter to the Philippians, Paul offers a simple inventory of basic spiritual equipment. Now and then, it is worth considering Paul's checklist to see if our spirits require a tune-up. So get out your clipboard and let's look under the hood.

To restate Paul's requirements in simplest terms, he recommends five basic rules:

1. Rejoice.
2. Forebear.
3. Worry not.
4. Pray.
5. Think good thoughts.

Paul's advice seems so unremarkable, so ordinary. Is there more to this than meets the eye? Let's take a closer look.

Rule 1. Rejoice

The early Christians believed that the second coming of Christ was just around the corner. Therefore, they lived expectantly. As time went by, their apocalyptical excitement waned, but their sense of the nearness of God did not. Perhaps the end of the age was farther away than they had imagined, but God was not. Their eschatology became realized. They learned directly and indubitably that the Lord had come—in their individual lives and in their life together as a family of the faithful. The same Jesus who had walked among the people of Palestine, healing, caring, and serving, was present among them, healing, caring, and serving as before.

Without a sense of the nearness of God, Paul's advice becomes meaningless prattle. Without the intimate healing, caring, and serving presence of Jesus the Christ in our midst, Paul's checklist becomes a string of tiresome platitudes. But if Christ lives in us and among us, Paul's words are not so much recommendations as an accurate report of what, by the grace of God, is happening daily in our midst. Paul does not have to direct us to rejoice, to forebear, stop worrying, pray, or think good thoughts any more than he has to command prisms to refract light.

Rejoice in the Lord always; again I say, rejoice.

I'll never forget what Fred Craddock said in this spirit at Faith Works, the United Church of Christ Experience I attended in Bloomington, Indiana. Preaching on Jesus' teaching, "Seek first the kingdom of God and his righteousness, and all these things shall be added to you" (Matthew 6:33), Craddock observed:

> you know in the New Testament the same word that is translated "thanks" is sometimes translated "grace." . . . It's the same word—charis. "Thanks be to God"—charis—for God's grace—charis. The same word. . . .
>
> In fact, some people at mealtime "express thanks." Other people "say grace." What did you call it at your house? Did you "express thanks" for the meal or did you "say grace."[1]

Craddock continues:

> Would you regard it as too simplistic, would you regard it as too naive, for me to say that according to the teaching of Jesus, the Christian life is to live all day according to the prayer you had at the breakfast table? . . . This is really very, very simple but I want you to think about it just a moment. The Christian life is to live all day by the prayer that you said at the breakfast table before you went to work.
>
> What was the first one you learned?
> God is great.
> God is good.
> Let us thank him for our food. Amen.
> Is that it?
> For health and strength and daily food,
> we give you thanks, O Lord.
> That's a good one. You can sing that one.
> Morning has come.
> The board is spread.
> Thank you, Lord,
> For giving us bread.
> And to live that all day.
> For this and all thy bounty
> Make us grateful, O Lord. Amen.
> All day!
> Bless this food to our bodies' use
> and us to thy service. Amen.
> All day!
> Blessed art thou, O Lord,
> who gives bread to the hungry
> and satisfies our hearts with good things. Amen.
> All day!

[1] Craddock, Fred, "God Reconciling," a sermon preached at Faith Works, UCC (United Church of Christ) Experience 1990, Bloomington, Indiana, June 25, 1990.

> The Christian life is to live all day what you said at the table at breakfast when you said grace.[2]

God's grace and our thanks are inseparable. Rejoice, be thankful, means: "Stop complaining." That may be the beginning for most of us. We have developed the bad habit of seeing the glass as half empty and suspecting that the half that is full is polluted. We cannot see the gifts right before our eyes because we are attuned only to the potential hazards.

Faith is never too proud to say "Thank you." If you set out each day to be thankful, you will find God's grace everywhere. If you set out each day to complain, you will find evil everywhere. Thankfulness produces good and complaining produces evil—it is as simple as that! If you expect that God's grace will fill your life, God's grace will fill your life. If you make of your heart a complaint-trap, you will accumulate pain, hurt, confusion and cause pain, hurt, and confusion in whatever you do.

At the beginning of his letter to the Philippians, Paul rhapsodizes: "Grace and peace to you from God our Father and the Lord Jesus Christ. I thank my God every time I remember you." (1:2–3) Grace and thanks are joined together. God's gifts and our joyful appreciation of life are inseparable.

Rule 2. Forebear: Be Easy on Others

"Let all men know your forbearance," the Revised Standard Version renders Paul's words. "Let your gentleness be known to everyone," says the New Revised Standard Version. "Let your gentleness be evident to all," echoes the New International Version. "Forbearance" suggests restraint, self-control, avoidance. "Gentleness" brings us in touch with touch with the third beatitude: "Blessed are the meek, for they shall inherit the earth."

The words "gentle" and "meek" suggest a person who is so gladdened and overcome by God's greatness that he counts his life as nothing, but gladly gives it for love's sake. Meekness combines goodwill toward humankind and reverent obedience toward God. Gentleness has sinew, activity. It is not sad resignation. Others claim their rights, but the gentle are concerned about their duties. Others demand notice, but the meek walk in quiet godliness.

The Jews asserted their pride of race, the Roman their pride of power, and the Greeks their pride of knowledge. The meek assert their pride in a job well done, in promises kept, in taking time to help others, in making a difference.

Rule 3. Worry Not: Be Easy on Yourself

Don't be anxious, says Paul. Stop worrying. His words echo the emphatic teaching of Jesus found in the Sermon on the Mount: "I tell you do not be anxious about your life. Your heavenly Father knows what you need. Seek first God's kingdom and his justice, and all these things shall be yours as well. (See Matthew 6:25–34.) The closer we are to our own needs, concerns, and hurts, the farther we are from God's purposes for our lives or for his world. The closer we are to God's purposes for our lives and for his world, the more things fall into place.

How can I stop worrying? Stop creating evil. Stop complaining. Stop giving other people the power to make you happy or to make you miserable. Stop playing life's victim.

---

[2] Ibid.

Start rejoicing. Start thanking God for his gifts. Live expectantly—expect God to be present in your life, expect life to be an opportunity, a challenge. Live gratefully.

Rule 4. Pray

Paul's advice to the Philippians wisely joins together prayer and lessening anxiety. Develop the instinct of prayer and fruitless worrying will diminish. Begin each day with prayer and the likelihood that your requests will give form and substance to your day will increase and your anxiety will decrease. Start with the Lord's Prayer, or a simple grace before meals, or whatever else springs from your heart. Repeat the substance of that morning prayer throughout the day. Allow it to surface in your life for a few seconds now and then. Finally, as you drift off to sleep at night, reflect on that prayer, offering to God thanks for the way in which it has been answered throughout your day.

Follow this simple advice and you will receive of God's grace without limitation or pause.Your heart will overflow with thankfulness. And you will be unable to tell where God's grace ends and your thanks begins.

Rule 5. Think Good Thoughts

Degunk your thinking, says Paul. The images we entertain, the thoughts we think, the news we see and hear, the representations of reality we take into our lives change us.

Whatever you think, thinks you. The human body responds to powerful images, thoughts, imaginings, and fantasies much the same way it responds to actual experiences. Think about biting into a lemon and your mouth will pucker. Fantasize about being honored and respected by your colleagues, and you will feel worthy of honor and respect. Your parents may have told you, "Be careful what you ask for. You may get it." Our deepest wishes, fantasies, and daydreams have a way of transforming themselves into realities. Perhaps not exactly as we might expect, but into realities nonetheless.

So mind what you think. Paul approaches the matter positively. He does not tell us what to avoid thinking, but what to think about. Whatever is true, whatever is honorable, whatever is just, whatever is pure, whatever is lovable, whatever is well spoken of, whatever is virtuous, whatever is praiseworthy—consider these things. The Jesus whom Paul and the Philippians worshiped filled the bill. The Christ-nature of each Christian today, the part of us which we nurture and which nurtures us, conforms to the requirements. The life of a community of Christians, who rise above pettiness and rancor, who labor side by side in the gospel, who run the race together that all may win the prize—they are worth considering.

Years ago, when I was a member of a Rotary Club, I was asked to observe "The Four Way Test of the Things We Think, Say, or Do." In my dealings with my fellow human beings, I was urged to ask myself

1. Is it the TRUTH?
2. Is it FAIR to all concerned?
3. Will it build GOODWILL and BETTER FRIENDSHIPS?
4. Will it be BENEFICIAL to all concerned?

I learned a similar four-way test in Sunday School as a teenager. Before saying anything about another person, this test insists, ask yourself:

1. Is it true?
2. Is it necessary?
3. Is it loving?
4. Will it build up the church?

Unless what you plan to say meets all four criteria, don't say it. Whatever does not pass the four-way test is gossip, and like all complaining it produces evil in the life of the one who speaks, the one who hears, and the one spoken about. If you want your life to be blessed, start blessing.

What Paul says cannot be broken into separate components. He is not saying if you want peace of mind either rejoice or forebear or rejoice or pray or think good thoughts. He is not prescribing as much as he is describing. Those who know the peace of God, which passes all understanding, are those who cannot but rejoice, cannot help treading lightly, cannot see things any other way but from a perspective where worry just does not fit, and find that their hearts start praying even before their minds realize it. And, above all, such persons are intolerant of junk—idle chatter and gossip. They are drawn to excellence as iron filings are to a magnet. They see the hand of God at work in their lives. They are aware of his grace. They are thankful. Their lives generate goodwill and friendship. They build up the church. For they are cradled, tenderly and lovingly, by the God of peace. Their souls are fine tuned and ready to run. VAROOM!

Amen.

—LDS

[2100 words]
[21 minutes]

❦ *Sermon 61*

❦ *Date:* Whenever appropriate

Text:
Luke 13:10–17

Theme: Jesus heals. Praise be to God.
Subject: Healing, praise

Title: Freed by Jesus. Praise Be to God!

I'm taking my stole off so that I may become, for a few minutes, not your pastor, but rather a poor, crippled woman named Rebekkah. My robe is no longer the fine linen of priesthood, but the simple, dirty, scratchy wool of poverty. As the woman Rebekkah, I can no longer stand erect and strong before you, no longer can I look you straight in the eye. For I am now the woman of the gospel story, bent over, for eighteen years bent over with paralysis of my lower back. We are in a synagogue in Israel, the people are gathered on this Sabbath day for worship, and this new, powerful teacher, Jesus of Nazareth, is here with us.

I stand this way because the bones of my lower back have fused together, and I stand this way because of the pain, which is excruciating like this, but it's less than if I tried to stand up straight; it hurts less to stand this way. I can't move my head either, for my whole spine is affected by my disease. I can only walk in small steps, and slowly, and I can only see you by peering up.

There's a lot I can't see, I don't see. It's harder to breathe this way, but I've learned over the past eighteen years to breathe slowly and carefully.

I came into the synagogue as you all did, through that door back there, to worship and to hear this new teacher Jesus, the young man from Nazareth. But I usually stay back there in the women's section, out of sight. Something about how I look makes people mad—they tell me to go away, call me sinner. And something about how I look makes people scared, they look away, pretend I don't exist. That's why I stay in the back, and usually I just keep my eyes down. I know the words of the service and I don't want to see the eyes of the worshipers, their hate and fear of me.

But today I looked up to see this teacher, and he looked back at me, he saw me, really saw me. And then, he called me to come forward next to him. I was terrified. All the people murmured in hate as I walked through them. It was bad enough that I was there at all. If I were a man and wanted to be a priest, I couldn't have, because of my disfigured body. But there I was, a woman, and disfigured going to the front of the synagogue, where only men are supposed to go.

Jesus ignored their hateful murmurings. He looked right at me, spoke right to me. All he said was, "Woman, you are free from your infirmity." He put his hands on my back, his touch was gentle yet stirring. And I could stand up. The pain was gone. I could move back and forth. I could see, I could breathe. I shouted out, "Praise be to God!"

The people in the synagogue were mad. Their leader stood up and spoke angrily at Jesus and me: "There are six days for working. Come on those to be healed, and not on the Sabbath." I was used to hearing words of hatred like this, but I hadn't been able to look people in the face for so long that I was shocked by the looks of hatred in their faces. Here God had acted in their midst, here was the crooked made straight, and they hated me, and they hated Jesus.

I just wanted to leave, and I was sure that I could now move pretty quickly. But Jesus put his hand on me again, this time to stop me from going and to comfort me. Then he turned to the people, as angry as they, but controlled in his words. "You hypocrites! Don't you each untie your animals on the Sabbath and lead them to water? Should not this daughter of Abraham, whom Satan has bound for eighteen years be loosed from her bond on this day?"

It was then that I remembered what he had said to me moments before, that he had "freed" me, "Woman you are free of your infirmity," not that he had healed me, but freed me. It's the same word we use in our language for release, to release people from prison, the same word he said to the people about being untied from bonds, loosed from restraints.

And that's how I felt, freed. I had heard Jesus in another synagogue say he had come to free the captives, but I thought he meant people in jail. No, he meant all of us who are tied to habits or hatred, all of us who are prisoners of fear, of frustration. Now, through him, we are free from habits or hatred, from fear of frustration. The door is open, we can stand tall and look people straight in the face. We are free.

There was silence after Jesus' words. And then the people felt what I had just felt. They stood up a little taller too. They looked at each other not in fear or envy, but right at each other, with looks of love and compassion. They understood that this being freed is what worship, what the Sabbath is all about, not an escape from everyday life, but a celebration of God's transforming love, a celebration of how God makes the crooked straight, turns the fearful into the strong, the captive into the free.

Suddenly they echoed my words, "Praise be to God!" And we all turned to worship our Lord. Praise be to God!

Amen.

—Deborah Streeter

[1,000 words]
[10 minutes]

Sermon 62

Date: Thanksgiving Day, any year

Texts:
Deuteronomy 8:7–18
Psalm 65
1 Corinthians 9:6–15
Luke 17:11–19

or Fourth Sunday After Epiphany, Year C

Text:
Jeremiah 1:4–10

Theme: When God calls us to do something, God provides the resources with which to do it.
Subject: Abundance, calling

Title: An Economy of Scarcity and a God of Abundance

When the Prophet Jeremiah was called by the Lord to warn the inhabitants of Judah of impending doom, he complained, "I'm the wrong man for this job. I'm not very good with words." (Jeremiah 1:4–10) But God insisted.

When the Lord called Moses to lead the children of Israel from bondage in Egypt, Moses said, "O Lord, I've never been much of a public speaker. Besides, I'm a nobody. Why should the Egyptians pay attention to me? Why should the Israelites accept my leadership?" (Exodus 3) But God insisted.

When Simon Peter first met Jesus, Peter's self-confidence fled like a startled deer and the boastful fisherman cried out, "Please go away, Lord; I'm a sinful man." But Jesus said, "Until today you have been catching fish for yourself. From now on, you will catch men for me." (Luke 5:8–10) Once again, God insisted.

Despite his shyness, Jeremiah found the courage to speak. Despite his self-abasing humility, Moses gained the charisma of irresistible leadership. Despite his impetuous and volatile nature, Peter became the rock upon which God built the Christian church.

Jeremiah, Moses, and Peter were so much like you and me. They knew their own shortcomings and they were content to remain within the narrow confines of their limitations. Until God beckoned. Until God said, "I am not interested in what you lack. I am not a God of scarcity. I am a God of abundance."

Understanding the Problem

It is my privilege to serve as a member of the Board of Directors of the northern California Conference of the United Church of Christ. The Board meets quarterly—our last meeting was just a few days ago. For nearly 6 hours, the 30 plus of us—Board members, Conference staff, and other interested parties—struggled earnestly with the problems of the conference. Often we sounded like Jeremiah, Moses, and Peter on their very worst days. You see, being a member of the Board is rather like being a trustee in a church with twenty-four thousand members, meeting at 130 locations from Monterey to Reno, from the Central Valley to Eureka.

As an entity serving its member congregations, the Conference is going through a difficult and challenging time. Financial support in 1991 fell short of the most conservative expectations by about 8 percent. That's a serious figure in a budget of nearly seven hundred thousand dollars. Current estimates for 1992 project an additional deficit of some seventy thousand dollars.

The current recession is the major culprit, but hardly the only one. Other factors in recent years include the ripple effects of a major earthquake, a disastrous crop freeze, and the Berkeley-Oakland fire. Rare indeed is a congregation in our Conference that is not suffering a cutback of 5 percent or more. And there is always the problem of unhappy customers—churches that withhold financial support because they are alienated by the Conference's social activism or its theological liberalism or the fact that it ordains gay clergy, or because Mr. W and Mrs. X at the First Congregational Church of Y just don't like Rev. Z, a member of the Conference staff.

In addition to money problems, the Conference is in the throes of major structural and staffing changes. Add to all this confusion about what services the Conference should provide in the future and how to best provide them, and a strange sense of panic mixed with exhilaration seizes the heart. In words Kipling chose not to write: "If you can keep your head while all around you are losing theirs, you probably don't understand the problem?"

Where We Are

Shortly after the beginning of the Board meeting, we divided into small "buzz" groups. The assignment of each group was to utter one to three words expressive of where the conference is and where we, its Board of Directors, are. I wrote down the responses of my group. Let me read them to you exactly as they were presented.

potential

transition

exciting

abundance

opportunity for the right use

confused; needing focus

multi-talented

too money-focused

visibility needed

Now let me bring these descriptions into focus. What my group was saying was that we are passing through an exciting and trying time. On the one hand, we know that our potential is unlimited, that we have been called by God, and that the economy of God is an economy of abundance. What does that mean"? It means that when God calls us to do something, God provides the resources with which to do it.

My group also observed that our greatest resources are the multi-talented Christians who fill our churches. The apparent scarcity of financial resources should not blind us to the abundance of human resources. The real challenge is finding the opportunities to use our resources of people and dollars wisely.

An amazing thing happens when dollars are tight. We become aware that if we had an additional million dollars a year, we could spend it without batting an eye. If we did, we would be no closer to serving the real needs of our constituency or properly utilizing our people resources.

Like most Americans, we have become too money focused. If something appears to be a problem, we want to solve it by throwing money at it. Suddenly, reality has put the Conference and many of its churches on a dollar diet. And we are forced to realize that our real focus should be on our real focus. We should be asking "why?" before asking "how much?"

The question facing the Conference shifts from "What are all the wonderful things that we could do if we had the money to do them?" to "What do we do well now and how can we do those things even better with the resources and people available?"

The Conference will simply not have the money and staff tomorrow that it had yesterday. So rather than trying to live in yesterday, it will have to create a vital and significant tomorrow.

"I am Not the Church"

Michael Kortright is the pastor of the Loomis Basin Congregational United Church of Christ—a church similar to ours in many respects. Michael and I were talking the other day and he told me of a conversation he had with one of his senior members after Sunday worship a few years ago. Michael is an ardent anti-war activist. Something he said in his sermon offended this particular member, who was not the least bit reticent to let him know. She said something like this: "I thoroughly disagree with what you just said. But I know that you are not the church. And I am not the church either. In a few years, you will probably move on. And in a few years, I will probably be dead. But the church will remain. For the church is the congregation, the community that follows Christ and lives the Gospel. And this church will survive, will continue to be the church, as long as we can be honest and loving with one another."

Churches that Grow

The church will survive. The church will continue. But will the church grow? Kelly Boyte Peters, a United Church of Christ minister, notes: "Churches that grow are churches that embody the good news in what they do and who they are. They are living the joy of the gospel even as they do the work of Christ."[1]

Note | the following anecdote is based on the history of Ladera Community Church, Portola Valley, California. Substitute the story of your congregation. Relate the events of the beginning of your church as though they had just occurred.

Let me tell you about a startup congregation in the Conference. In the beginning, there was a group of neighbors all living in the same suburban community. They were a diverse group. Many of them were young couples with children. Some were not so young. They decided to start a church but they wanted a church to be bound together by more than just the common experiences of friends

---

[1] *United Church News* (United Church of Christ), April 1991, p. 8.

and neighbors. The more they talked and prayed together, the more they realized that what they believed and valued reached beyond their local community. They felt that if they shared what they believed and valued with people in nearby communities, others would be attracted.

They said to each other, we have a mission to the larger community. So they went door to door calling on strangers. They felt a little awkward. Jehovah's Witnesses go door to door, but do mainline, middle-class Protestants?

Pretty soon, they wanted to build a structure to serve their needs. There wasn't a great deal of money. The Conference advised them to build a social hall, a multipurpose building that could be used for dinners, classes, and worship. You know the kind of structure—basketball hoops at one end, an altar at the other, folding chairs in stacks on either side. But the members of the new church had other ideas. They decided to start with a sanctuary. They wanted to say to the surrounding communities that this was first and foremost a church, a place to worship God. So they asked an architect to consider their limited resources and to design their church very, very carefully. And while he was doing that, they drew upon the fabulous wealth of people resources they had in abundance.

They built their simple yet beautiful sanctuary and people came. They called a minister, a man every bit as special as their sanctuary. And more people came. Not everyone liked this minister, or the next one, or the next. But they knew what the octogenarian at the Loomis church knew: "You are not the church. And I am not the church either. The church is the congregation, the community that follows Christ and lives the Gospel. And this church will survive, will continue to be the church, as long as we can be honest and loving with one another."

I am sure that you know the name of this church.

Doing it Well

Now I would like to direct our attention back to the list of 1 to 3 words expressive of where the Conference is and where we, its Board of Directors, are. I deliberately ignored the last item on the list. The word is "visibility." There are visible churches and invisible churches. Visible churches attract people. Invisible churches retain the people they already have. Visible churches stand out against the background of the communities in which they are found because they serve the needs of the community. Invisible churches are mostly made up of friends and neighbors bound together by their common experiences, good and bad. Visible churches live in the present and are poised to leap into the future. Invisible churches are anchored to the past.

What makes a church visible? The short answer is figuring out what it does well and doing it.

Note

> Again, the following comments pertain to Ladera Church. Replace with similar remarks about your congregation, expressed in the form of direct quotations from members of your church or in your own words.

What do we do well?

A member of our church recently sent me a letter detailing her "wish list." She has given me permission to share it with you. She has asked not to be identified. She writes:

I pray for
a place that honors the heart as well as the head

a place that welcomes the seeker and the wounded
a place with an atmosphere of acceptance, inclusion, and warmth
a place where Christian theology is translated into contemporary terms—
where knowledge gained in the last two centuries is utilized
and contemporary issues are frequently addressed
a place to serve the needs of others
a place to reflect and to pray
a place where judgment is left to God
a place to speak one's truth and to receive another's
a place that fosters the spiritual development of each member
a place of healing
a place of community

She concludes:

> I hope this is the year that we develop a collective vision for Ladera and we begin to learn from each other new steps in our collective dance.

Her letter moves me deeply, expressing not only what we can do and ought to do, but, in fact, what we already do. The challenge is to do it better.

I have made reference to a list of characteristics of the Northern California Conference expressed at the recent Board of Directors meeting. Let me repeat them:

potential

transition

exciting

abundance

opportunity for the right use

confused; needing focus

multi-talented

too money-focused

visibility needed

And like the Conference, Ladera Community Church is passing through an exciting and challenging time. It is a time of opportunity, a time to use our talents, a time to focus our energies, a time to decide what we do best, a time to do what we do best, and, finally, a time to become visible.

Our moderator, Charles Coale, has given us his vision of Ladera Church: a place "of living and dying, joy and sorrow, arguing and reconciling, hugging, consoling, affirming, . . . praying, searching, questioning, worshipping, thanking, and loving and sharing." He adds: "This church has given us something to belong to, something to share together, something to challenge us, something to provide an outlet for our talents, something to preserve, something to pass on to others, something to share in passing on to others."

When the prophet Jeremiah was called by the Lord, he protested, "I don't know how to speak." But God insisted, "You must go to everyone I send you to and say whatever I command.

. . . Do not be afraid . . ., for I am with you." The founding members of this church were not afraid. Does their spirit still live in our midst? Shall we console ourselves with excuses? Shall we let self-doubt and fear limit our vision? Or shall we trust in the God of abundance?

Amen.

—LDS

[2248 words]
[22 minutes]

❦ *CHAPTER SIX*

DEATH AND RESURRECTION

None of us is immune to discouragement. We know, for example, that death is not good and never can be. We are upset and confused by the tragedy of AIDS.

God makes us compassionate and draws us together in the midst of suffering. If one of us suffers, we all suffer. Christ is in the midst of our struggles, giving us peace and joy. In the darkest depths of despair, Jesus is our light. What he is to us, we are empowered to be to others. And as Christians we are sustained by our faith in the life to come.

Death is not only our ultimate fate, it can be the state of our daily existence. Jesus is our resurrection and life not just after death, but here and now. Wherever joy and peace come together in our lives, there is beauty. Wherever there is beauty, there is God.

Frustration and pain are real, but they do not have the last word. By the power of Christ's resurrection, we have courage to stop being a part of life's problems and start being a part of the solution. By the grace of God, we are called to change the way things are into the way they ought to be.

Sermon 63

Date: Sixth Sunday in Lent, Year C
or Palm Sunday, Any Year

Text:
Luke 19:37–42

Theme: Dealing with discouragement requires that we see the big picture.
Subject: Discouragement

Note

> This sermon makes use of an outrageous device, a delayed-reaction-time-bomb joke. It is also a deeply moving, confessional sermon. Combining these elements is risky!

Title: Dealing with Discouragement

As you review the great names and personalities of the Scriptures, you become aware very quickly of the fact that almost all of them knew, at one time or another, great discouragement. Job is described as the noblest man living in his time, but after the troubles that were his, he cried out, "My days are swifter than a weaver's shuttle and are spent without hope." Moses is described as the meekest (that is, the most disciplined) and the greatest of all of the Old Testament personalities. And Moses, as he leads the children of Israel out of Egypt finds in them truculence and frustration. They want to return to the sweet cucumbers of the slavery they've known before, and this becomes so discouraging to Moses that at last he cries out, "O Lord, why have you afflicted me? I am not able to bear these people. They are too heavy for me."

We find similar expressions of discouragement in Ezekiel and Daniel and Nehemiah and Jeremiah and Elijah, and yes, even in our Lord himself, for at the conclusion of his incarnate ministry, when he came to Jerusalem, the city he loved most on the face of the earth, and looked out upon it, he was filled with profound discouragement. Weeping, he said, "O Jerusalem, would that even today you knew the things that make for peace. But now they are hid from your eyes."

The company of the discouraged is a very noble company. Not too long ago, the Hayden Planetarium in New York City issued an invitation to all those who were interested in applying to be a part of the crew on the first journey to another planet. Eighteen thousand people applied. They gave the applications to a panel of psychologists, who examined them thoroughly and came to the conclusion that in the vast majority of incidents, those who applied did so because they were discouraged with their lives here and hoped they could find a new life somewhere else.

All of our lips have spoken the words of discouragement. All of our hearts have felt it. Every one of us has known at one time or another the slap of setback. So to be discouraged is to be in good company, is not to be a part of an exclusive group, but it is a costly fellowship. What I would like to share with you in our brief time this morning are four steps you can use in dealing with discouragement.

The first step is to take a short look at the problem. Notice I say a short look. That is, you recognize that you are discouraged, but you don't focus upon that. The birds of discouragement may crow and fly about you, but you don't let them build nests in your hair, if you have any.

You perhaps have heard of the sales managers' device of holding up a large piece of paper with a small orange spot down in one corner. He sales to his salesmen, "What do you see?" They all report that they see that orange spot, and he says, "That's your weakness as a salesman. You see the spot and don't see all of the open opportunity before you."

We don't want to focus on our discouragements, because as one thinks in one's heart, so one is. To major in discouragement soon makes all of life discouraging. Yet we must at least take a short look at it for two reasons. First, to acknowledge that it's true. There are some individuals who think somehow it's sub-Christian to be discouraged. They need to acknowledge it and to recognize that our Lord Jesus himself knew how discouragement feels. So we need to admit that for our souls' sake.

But we need also in that quick look at discouragement to discover whether or not we're the ones who have caused the situation to be discouraging. Many times we are not the cause of our own discouragement. If that is the case, in a moment of discouragement it's important that we know that so we don't add to the weight of the discouragement the burden of blame.

You remember how they came to Jesus and said, "Those Galileans who died—was it because of their sin?" Jesus said no.

"Those on whom the tower fell in Siloam, was it because of their sin?" Jesus said no.

They brought a blind man to him. "Is he blind because of his sin or the sin of his parents?" And Jesus said no.

Many times we are not the cause of our own discouragement, and a quick look will ascertain that.

I have in my notes that I am supposed to tell a joke at this point, and my secretary says this joke is no good. But I'm going to try it anyway.

There was a farmer who had a barn, and it burned down. And so he built a new barn, and it blew down. So he decided he would build a third barn better than the other two, and the third barn he built entirely of brick—brick floor, brick walls, brick roof, thousands and tens of thousands of bricks. When he was finished, he had one brick left over. He stood there contemplating that one brick. What do you think he did with that one brick? He just threw it over his shoulder and walked away. [No response.]

My secretary was right. I'll take that out next time.

The point is, you just take a short look at those kinds of things. You don't have to focus on them. When Jesus came to Jerusalem, he wept over it but he didn't sit there all day sobbing. He got up and went down into the city, and that brings us to the second step.

You take a narrow look at yourself, that is, you remind yourself of your capacities and assets—the things that are going for you. Edison said that the body exists to carry the mind around. That's not altogether true and not altogether wise, but there is a great deal to be said for the fact that we remember in the discouraging moment the things that we still have going for us. There's an interesting story in 1 Samuel where David, because of a military blunder, leaves some cities unprotected. They are attacked by the Philistines, and some of the relatives of David's soldiers are slain. David, it says, is discouraged. But in 1 Samuel 30, it goes on to say that David went off and "encouraged himself in the Lord his God." He encouraged himself by reminding himself of all of those things that were still his.

Just because you miss one train doesn't mean you have to cancel the whole vacation.

Here's a man sitting on his porch in Kentucky. He's only recently retired from the post office, and he's sitting there when his first Social Security check is delivered. He's very, very discouraged. He thinks to himself, Is this what life is going to be from now on—sitting on the porch waiting for my check to arrive? He decided he wouldn't settle for that, and so he made a list of all of the things he had going for him, all the blessings and the capacities, the unique things that were in him. The list was long because he listed everything he could think of, and in the list was the fact that he was the only person on earth who knew his mother's recipe for fried chicken. It used eleven different herbs and spices.

So he went to a nearby restaurant and asked if he could cook the chicken, and they said yes. It soon because the most popular item on the menu. So he opened his own restaurant, and then others, and a string of restaurants. Eventually, Harland Sanders sold the Kentucky Fried Chicken franchise across all of America. He finally retired a second time (all this happened, you remember, after he had retired from the postal service), and he continued in the service of the company as a public relations representative for a quarter of a million dollars a year till his death. Now here was a man who did not allow himself to be defeated by discouragement. He took a look at it, recognized it was there, but then went on to look at what he had with which to deal with it and used that.

Jesus wept over the city, but he knew there were certain things to be done in that city that only he could do. There was a temple to be cleansed. There were teachings to be offered. There was a Last Supper to be known. And there was a cross to be climbed. Only he could do these things, and so he set about the doing of them.

The third step is to take a long look at God, to remember that we are loved of God. My dear friend Benjamin Weir was held captive by terrorists in Lebanon for eighteen months. Fifteen of those months he was in solitary confinement. In talking with him about those days, I was thrilled to discover how he endured the face of it.

They took him into a room, a small room, and in the room there was a mattress on the floor and a radiator beside it. That was the mattress on which he slept and on which he sat, because one arm was always handcuffed to the radiator. The window had Venetian blinds. There was no other furniture. Interestingly enough, there was an old stuffed bird sitting over in one corner, a poor example of the taxidermy art. There were some cracks in the walls, and where there had been a chandelier in the ceiling, it had been taken away and there were three loose wires sticking down. This was all there was in the room.

Ben said, "I began to use what was there to remind myself of the love of God. Those three wires coming down—well, they reminded me of the way God's hand comes down and touches the hand of Adam in Michelangelo's Sistine Chapel ceiling. You remember how the gift of life is given in such a way? This meant God's gift of life." He counted the various slats in the Venetian blinds, and he used the Venetian blind to remind himself that he was surrounded by a cloud of witnesses. The bird, though it was very old and dirty, he used to represent the Holy Spirit, sometimes symbolized in Scripture, as you know, by the dove.

The cracks in the walls, the places in the plaster that were marred—each and every one of them he identified with some promise in Scripture. He would repeat to himself every day passages which he had long ago hidden in his heart: "May the peace of God which transcends all understanding guide your heart and your mind into Christ Jesus;" "Call upon me and I will do great and wondrous things that you know not of."

He remembered all of those things, and out of this he kept hold of himself for fifteen months alone—a long look, a remembering, a focusing upon the love of God.

Notice that when Jesus went down into that city for that week, he went in the power of his Father's love. John, writing about the foot-washing scene says, "And Jesus, knowing wither he came and wither he was going, girded himself with a towel." Or Jesus says, "He who has seen me has seen the Father." Or there is that magnificent word at the end of the experience on the cross when Jesus says, "Father, into thy hands I commit my spirit." Remembering the love of God.

The fourth step is to take a wide look at the possibilities. There was a woman riding on a train, and she had a dog she liked very much. She had purchased a seat right beside her for the dog to ride in. The man in front was smoking a very foul-smelling cigar, and the smoke was drifting back into the face of the dog. So she tapped him on the shoulder and said, "Would you mind extinguishing your cigar?"

He said, "Madame, there are nonsmoking cars on this train and there are smoking cars. This is a smoking car. If you didn't want me to smoke, you should have been seated in another car. I will continue to enjoy my cigar."

By this time the little dog was coughing and panting, so she tapped him on the shoulder again and said, "You can see it's really troubling my dog. Won't you please put it out?"

And he said, "Madame, I consider my pleasure to be of much more importance than the happiness of your animal. I will not put it out."

By this time the little dog was down on his side. He was white when he got on the train, but he was turning blue. So she reached over and opened the window, and then reached around, yanked the cigar out of the man's mouth, and threw it out the window. He got up, grabbed the dog, and threw it out of the window. And she went into hysterics and began to scream, pounding on the man's back.

At this point, the train is slowing down as it comes into the city, and the conductor is running, of course. He hears all this screaming. The man starts down the steps and she's walking behind him. When they get to the foot of the steps on the platform, here comes the little dog running up. And guess what he had in his mouth? He had that brick the farmer threw over his shoulder!

Now the reason you didn't laugh at that the first time is because you hadn't heard all of it, and that's what you need to do with discouragement. You need to see the whole thing.

There was a story in the paper in Chicago this last weekend about a man who was being pursued by his wife. To escape her he jumped over a five-foot wall. He never knew he could do that before. That's what you call the stimulation of unrecognized resources. As he looked back on that discouraging moment, he suddenly leaned something he hadn't known before.

See the possibilities. Here's a fellow who sold insurance, and he went after a particularly difficult customer, a man whom no one had been able to sell. Eventually he sold him a fifty-thousand-dollar policy. Back in 1883 when this occurred, that was a very large policy. He took out his pen and handed it to the man to sign the contract. When the man tried to write, the pen wouldn't write. He tried several times without success and finally handed the pen back with the contract and said, "I'd better think this over a little while longer." The man lost the sale.

He went home disappointed and discouraged because he had lost the sale, and he determined right then and there that he would never lose another sale because of a fountain pen that didn't work. So he sat down and invented his own fountain pen. His name was Louis Waterman, and the Waterman Fountain Pen became the premier writing instrument of America for the next fifty years. Out of discouragement, great possibility.

Here's a man working in St. Mary's hospital in London. He's growing some cultures, and a careless laboratory assistant leaves a window open and some material blows in, settles in the cultures, and ruins them. The doctor is very discouraged. His name is Fleming. As he decides which of the cultures to throw out and which he might be able to save for some other use, he begins to notice mold growing there. Out of that Fleming developed penicillin. A possibility out of discouragement.

The Franciscans were the first ones to grow grapes systematically in California. They grew the muscat grapes to make muscatel wine. One year they had a terrible drought, and the grapes withered on the vine. The growers thought they were going to lose them all, but they took those grapes down into the towns and sold them as what they called "Peruvian delicacies." That was the beginning of the Sun Maid Raisins Company.

Out of what was discouraging came—well, Jesus, when he went down into that town in the midst of discouragement, brought out of it Easter.

I know that in talking about discouragement this morning I've told some jokes and perhaps some of you think I've been too simplistic or too flippant. I know what discouragement is. I know of the discouragement of fighting my excess weight for fifty years. I know the discouragement of open-heart surgery that was not successful, though every bit as painful, as it was supposed to be. I've stood beside my father's casket, knowing the discouragement of saying goodbye for awhile to the man I loved most on the face of the earth. I've known the discouragement of being betrayed by a very close friend. I've known the discouragement of having a congregation, to which I gave everything I had, turn against me and reject my ministry. I've learned the discouragement, and know it still, of loneliness, for I am a bachelor. I have no wife, I have no children.

Believe me, I know what discouragement is. But I've discovered in my own experience that if you'll take a short look at the problem, admit it exists, and discover where the blame lies; take a narrow look at yourself, that is, be prejudiced in behalf of the things God has given to you; take a long look at God, remembering his love, hiding Scripture in your heart that testifies to it; and if you take a wide look at the possibilities, the dividends that you can find in discouragement—if you do those things, you can be like that little old lady I was sitting beside flying to Europe. She was very nervous. I said, "Is this your first flight?"

She said, "No, I'm always nervous when I fly. But it won't be bad this trip."

I said, "Why?"

She said, "We're flying toward the morning. We're flying toward the dawn."

That's the thing to hold onto, sisters and brothers. As the disciples of Jesus Christ, we're flying into the sun, always and forever into the sun.[1]

Amen.

—Bruce Thielemann

[3083 words]
[31 minutes]

Sermon 64

Date: Any Appropriate Occasion

Texts:
Luke 2:22–40

Theme: Death is not good and never can be. Hospices attempt to mitigate the horror of death. Hospices provide the opportunity for the dying to die well.
Subject: Hospice, death and dying, loss, grief

Title: "Lettest thy servant depart in peace"

A year ago this week I was in Sun City, Arizona, visiting my parents and celebrating my mother's birthday. It was difficult to do this because my dad was dying of cancer. It was hard for him to go out because of the pain he was suffering and the morphine he was taking.

We went to a local restaurant, and when the waiter came to take our orders my father said, "I want you to bring my friend here a Beefeater's martini on the rocks with lots of olives." Shortly the waiter returned with our drinks and my dad looked at me and said, "Say, could you spare your olives?" That moment summed up what was happening to us as a family, and particularly what

---

[1] Copyright 1987, *Preaching Today* (*Preaching Today* is a series of audiotape cassettes published by *Christianity Today* and *Leadership*, 465 Gundersen Drive, Carol Stream, IL 60188). Used with permission.

was happening between my dad and me who have been the very best friends for my forty-seven years.

When I was a youngster, the family ritual was that I would get to have the olives out of Dad's martini, which he had on special celebrations. As I grew older, Dad and I would always celebrate the ritual of having a martini together at these special family events. It was the one way that we bonded to each other.

Dad could no longer have martinis or any other alcoholic drink to celebrate with because he was taking a lot of morphine and other medications. In a vicarious way, and in a way of reversing our roles, Dad could get that little bit of a taste of the martini in the olive, and we could celebrate who we were and what our life together had meant.

In a few months, my dad would die. I had the wonderful opportunity of being with him constantly for the last six weeks of his life. We talked about good things and bad things, wonderful memories and disappointments. I had the chance to enter into his world and help him and hold him, clean him, feed him.

Dad, like Simeon in the Temple, was not only looking back over the benchmarks of his life, but also, like Simeon, he was looking forward, he was looking into me and into the future of life that would go on after he left, life that he created and life that would be lived out for him and the values that he believed in.

It was the babe Jesus the Jew who was brought to the temple in Jerusalem to be presented to the Lord as Jewish law required.

Waiting at the temple, for the presentation of this Jewish infant, was Simeon. This elderly perhaps terminally ill man, who had been waiting for the "consolation of Israel," was promised that he would not see death before he had seen the Christ. When he saw Mary and Joseph, and most of all when he saw their child, he said, "Lord, now lettest thou thy servant depart in peace according to thy word" (Luke 2:29). Simeon saw in this babe new life, life into the future, in very human terms as well as the redeemed spiritual life of humankind. He said, "I've waited as long as I could. I'm old. I am ill and infirm. I should have died, but I have waited for this and now I've seen him. Not only do I look back with joy, but I look forward with joy and I see the future. I have reached the watershed. I am willing to go on. Now I have what I need to complete the journey."

Simeon is such a good example of what hospice is to those of us who participate in it. In one way or another as we help a patient and family, as a volunteer or as a professional, there is the opportunity to assist someone to look back at the benchmarks of their life and find meaning, and to look forward into the future as it will be lived out in their loved ones and the values that they lived in.

I can think of many examples of people waiting to die. They are waiting for something important to them, such as the birth of a child or grandchild or something they need to accomplish, so that they can say good-bye, and they can say, "a good job well done." Like Simeon they will take with them into the cocoon the vision not only of the past but of the future.

My grandmother, Minnie, a Methodist minister's wife, and so proud to have been that for many years, lived beyond the death of my grandfather, John Bury, by ten years. She was eighty-six and failing. When given permission to die by my father, she said to him, "Walt, give me a couple more weeks. I want to die on our anniversary, because that is who I was, I am, and I will be, as I am lived out by you and the grandchildren and the great-grandchildren.

She looked very well that anniversary Sunday morning when the nurse got her up to make her bed. Grandma sat in the rocking chair and when the nurse completed the making of the bed she turned around and Grandma was dead.

As a professor, I remember years ago working with a colleague, our dean, who was dying of cancer. He had been such a strong, capable, and directed person. However, things seemed to be falling apart all around him and he was greatly agitated and depressed.

In talking with him, I finally found out what the problem was. There were so many things that he needed to complete that he could not let himself deal with his dying and allow himself to die. We sat down together and made a list. We did it by prioritizing those things that he had to get done before he could die. These were important things. These were issues about professors waiting on tenure, or waiting on salary increase, or waiting on promotion. There were budgetary concerns that he had been responsible for. He knew that if he did not get these items completed, colleagues could be left stranded. We made the list of twenty tasks he wanted to do.

You know the end of the story. After he finished number twenty, he died. Like Simeon, he died in peace. Not only did he look back at these important benchmarks, but these benchmarks spoke to him about people whom he cared for deeply, whom he felt responsible for. He, too, could say as Simeon has said, "Lord, now lettest thou thy servant depart in peace."

That is what hospice is about—to help people die with as much peace as possible, whether we have in-depth philosophical discussions with them, or help prioritize the major issues of their life, or just sit with them so that their spouse can get some time away at the barber shop, or for a round of golf.

Some people erroneously talk about hospice helping provide a "good death." To presume that there is anything good about death for any person is a travesty. Death, particularly the death we know in hospice, which is usually a death from cancer or AIDS or occasionally respiratory or cardiac disease, is not good. However, I have no doubt, as a Christian, that it is good after death.

In hospice we try to mitigate the horror of death. We want to be able to alleviate it not only for the patient but also for the survivors, so that they can truly let the dead bury the dead and to pick up and go on with their lives as survivors in the process of healing.

I have worked as a chaplain in two hospitals, and I find the more that I serve, the less I know and the fewer answers I have for people who are dying and for their loved ones. I find that there are no elaborate "for certain" answers. There are some things that help me, and I try to share these with patients. I know that God is with us in the living person of Jesus. God has experienced the worst type of pain and death imaginable, that of crucifixion. Rarely will any of us experience death from any disease that could equate to this. Yet God experienced that pain. Therefore we need to count on the fact that God understands the pain that we are going through. We can say that God has walked in our moccasins. God has faced everything that we have to face, the experience of loss. God knows our death, God is aware of our death.

In hospice we name death. We do not use euphemisms. We do not talk about passing away or just sleep. We use the words dead, die, death, and we use these words as much as we can. We try to get the threat and fear out of them. Dying is a step in our biological process, in our eventual and expected biological breakdown.

If hospice does nothing else, it is important because it attempts to bring death out of the closet and sit it at the dining room table so that we can talk about it in concrete, realistic, and effective ways. We need to get death out of the slumber room at the mortuary, and we need to talk about its real presence with us, with real words and real feelings, so that it will not have the power of naming, owning, and haunting us for the rest of our lives.

When I talk to people about hospice I reflect on the first chapter of Ruth, where she says, so eloquently, "Entreat me not to leave you or to return from following you; for where you go I will go, and where you lodge I will lodge; your people shall be my people, and your God my God" (1:16). Ruth is what presence is all about—as Our Lord Jesus has always promised to be present for us and to be constant and enduring. Ruth promised, and hospice promises, to follow the terminally ill patient into the burning bush. Hospice is willing, through its volunteers and its professionals, to say to a dying person and his or her family that "we will be constant and true with you until you have died and until those of you who are survivors have begun to manage your grief."

Our primary response is presence, and more often than not the highest level of presence is silence. We come to be with, and we come to listen to, and, oh yes, we come to do the windows if somebody asks, or run somebody out and about for an errand. When a family calls the hospice office and talks to the volunteer coordinator, she implements a response of constancy and of presence that people who are dying and their families can depend on. Not so they can have "good death" but so they can try to do it as well as possible.

I would like to challenge you by saying that death is not good and never can be. But, in dying and in helping someone die, we can do as Plato has said, "when you do something, do it well." We can provide the opportunity to do this in the best way possible, and if we mitigate, even just a bit of pain, inconvenience, or fear, we will have done that.

I paraphrase from a great book, Aristotle's Nicomachean Ethics, specifically rule no. 1109a:

> Anyone can die. That is easy. But to do this in the right place, at the right time, with the right motive, and the right way, that is not for everyone, nor is it easy; wherefore, goodness is both rare and laudable and noble.

When it comes to dying, death, and bereavement, it is our responsibility to help learn, not only about death, but also about life and about doing both well.

I knew my dad would die Friday night because it was 118°F in Sun City and the air conditioner broke down. As Dad always said, crises never come one at a time. I was thinking as I stood outside at midnight, holding the flashlight for the repairman that "this is it." Dad died that morning at 6:00. I found no difficulty being with him and looking at him and feeling the tremendous presence of his goodness and spirit rise up. His body looked peaceful and, as I left the hospital, I looked up at the sky and the clouds in the sky were etched in bright colors. I had never seen a sky in the morning with the richness of a sunset like I saw then.

Amen.

—John Bury

[2111 words]
[21 minutes]

❦ *Sermon 65*

❦ *Date:* Third Sunday After Epiphany, Year C

Texts:
Nehemiah 8:1–3, 5–6, 8–10
Psalm 19
1 Corinthians 12:12–31a
Luke 4:14–21

Theme: True peace comes in knowing "the wrath of love."
Subject: AIDS

❦ *Title:* The Wrath of Love

In today's gospel we see the difference between John the Baptist and Jesus. John preaches repentance or doom—a message of woe to "broods of vipers." Jesus brings good news—in the words of Isaiah which he reads in the synagogue. He talks of Good News for the poor, of release of those who are captive, of sight to the blind, of liberty to those oppressed. Like John the Baptist,

Jesus knew the wrath of God, but in the words of William Barclay, it was always "the wrath of love." It was always the wrath of love.

What could Barclay mean by "the wrath of love?" This morning I would like to venture an opinion. In light of today's gospel and epistle I invite you to think about three words: compassion, evil, and integrity. For when these three elements come together, we are confronted with the wrath of love.

Compassion

Compassion—according to Webster's, is a sympathetic consciousness of others' distress, together with a desire to alleviate it. A synonym is sympathy—to be with someone passionately. It is not a sweet word—it's a word which points to real life—life's blood.

It's a concept which is unavoidable when hearing today's epistle. St. Paul compares the Kingdom of God to a human body—all members drinking of one spirit. Paul says, "God has so composed the body, giving greater honor to the inferior part, that there may be no discord in the body, but that the members may have the same care for one another. If one member suffers, all suffer together. If one member is honored, all rejoice together."

It is the spirit of compassion that Jesus preached. God's spirit bringing people together, bringing individuals to be free of all that captivates or blinds them to the truth of God's will. In the spirit of God human beings work together to be of one holy compassionate purpose.

Evil

On the other hand, it is the presence of evil which separates. The word "diabolical" means to split apart, to bring chaos. In the words of John Sanford, "Evil may be described as the power which works for dissociation; it exerts specifically wherever a part seeks to take over the whole."[1] Sanford uses the example of a cancer, seeking to take over a total organism, or a psychosis, which destroys the unity of a personality. As you know, the traditional story of Satan is about an angel who breaks away from the community in the name of his own desires. His desires separate him from God's ways, and the ways of God's community.

So evil, that which separates us from God, also serves to separate ourselves from others, and so evil is the opposite of the compassion of today's readings.

Integrity

If we are to take these readings for what they are—descriptions of the Christian call to any and all disciples (and you!)—then we need to talk about integrity.

Integrity is the (1) quality or state of being complete, whole, unbroken. It speaks to us about (2) soundness and (3) sound moral principles, or uprightness. It's the movement from the chaos of evil to the unity of compassion. Have you ever had a moment when you finally accomplished something, or learned something, glimpsed the truth about something, and felt complete—that was a moment of integrity. It is a moment far from the chaos of evil, a moment very close to the unifying movement of compassion. I would say it was a moment close to God.

As Christians we can look at human history as the drama of integrity. Was it present or not? Here are some illustrations.

---

[1] Sanford, John, *The Kingdom Within: A Study of the Inner Meaning of Jesus' Sayings* (New York: Paulist Press), 1970.

A historical example of a people's struggle to move from separation to wholeness is the civil rights movement of "integration" itself—removing social or legal barriers which separate one group of people from another. When racial barriers are destroyed the world is closer to God.

An example of the loss of integrity, the separating of one person from another in diabolical greed and power was the Nazi's persecution of the Jews—a moment in real-life history that we find difficult to face up to because of the blatant absence of compassion in the face of the blatant presence of evil.

The AIDS Crisis

Today, in this moment of history, there is something as challenging as integration, and as challenging as the evil of the holocaust. That something is AIDS, and the moral crisis surrounding a disease that separates one person from another, one surgeon from another, one politician from another, one Christian from another, and one sibling from another. As Christians we cannot avoid the challenge of AIDS.

It is difficult, as you know, to talk about AIDS without talking about sexuality and homosexuality. It is difficult to say much about either in a short sermon, but I want to say something about both because I think that homosexuality and AIDS have every thing to do with evil, compassion, and integrity. One reason it is difficult is because it's risky. Controversy surrounds the issues. Yet Christians, in following Christ, are called to confront controversy. To have integrity is to try to be open to God's voice in different moral situations. Please allow me to take a personal risk.

Homosexuality itself is a reality that I try to understand. It is frightening because it is outside of what many call "normal"—yet I have gay friends who inspire me with their faith in God and Christ, friends who are examples to me of what it means to be a Christian. So homosexuality is a personal issue for me, as is AIDS. This is all the more so because I have a brother who is homosexual and who recently tested positive for HIV, the virus which causes AIDS.

My Brother and Me

I want to tell a story from my childhood about that brother. It's an emotional story for me and difficult to share so I may shed some tears. I'm saying this simply so that you don't become uncomfortable. But I believe it's a story which has shaped my sense of evil, compassion, and integrity.

My brothers and I were playing in a back bedroom. We were fairly young. I remember taking a red crayon and writing the name of my brother, Dennis (two years younger), on the white baseboard. No one saw me write it. I then walked into the kitchen and told my parents that Dennis had written his name on the wall. My father came back and asked us to leave the room. I stood out in the hallway. My father, trying to be fair, told Dennis, "All you have to do is tell the truth and you won't be punished." He asked, "Did you write your name on the wall?" Dennis told the truth. He said, "no." My father spanked him. And I heard Dennis scream and I was horrified. My father, again, and again, and again, asked him to tell the truth. Each time Dennis did so. And each time he was hit and screamed. Out in the hallway I was frozen, unable to move—horrified at what I had done.

Now this story is about a lot of things—it's about a kind of evil, it's about a surprised guilt, but mostly it's about a surprised compassion—about my horrified realization that the brother I had judged to be deserving of punishment—for whatever childish reason, deserved not punishment and pain, but my brotherly love. It's about my father's attempt at integrity but his failure to judge correctly. I couldn't formulate those thoughts but I thought, what have I done and what did Dennis do to deserve this?

And it's a story about my failure—which is understandable as a child—to act with integrity and walk into the room to stop my father from punishing Dennis for something he didn't do and confess to my father that it was I who wrote the name of my brother on the wall. A child is not expected to act with integrity because he is yet learning how to be a whole person. I couldn't muster up the strength to overcome my traumatic fear.

But as St. Paul once wrote, "I am no longer a child." I am an adult who has glimpsed the truth in my life, and I am not willing, God give me the strength, to stand still fearful in the hallway anymore. Unlike my response as a child, as a Christian adult I know I am called to act and not stand idly by when others are suffering.

My brother's life has been nothing but hell—struggling to live with the reality of his sexual identity—he came to hate himself and turned to drugs and alcohol and then to promiscuity. But Dennis does not deserve punishment from me or anyone else. I've already learned the hard lesson of judging others. Only God can judge the way Dennis has lived his life. My response to my brother and other people HIV positive, or people with AIDS, is conditioned by two simple questions: (1) What would Jesus do if he were with us today—about the disease of AIDS? and (2) What do we do as his followers?

Given what we know, I say that Jesus would remain true to his belief in the wrath of love, a compassion which does not separate but brings people together in the powerful name of God's mercy—especially those who are suffering. Especially those who are outcast. Jesus would be in the midst of them.

I give thanks to God that Dennis found the strength—and he found it in God—to cleanse himself of his addictions. Even when he tested positive for HIV he said, "I'm still happier than I've ever, ever been."

I honestly believe that it was the continued love and compassion of his parents and family—the desire to bring him home rather than separate from him—to stand with him in compassion rather than to distance themselves from his pain and suffering—that helped Dennis to bring himself closer to a life of integrity. He is still, and will always be, a gay man. And he is now a man who believes in and responds to God's compassion.

When I die and meet my maker I do not believe his first communication with me will be a question about how well I was able to judge others in terms of their righteousness. The first question will be: "How did you care about people who longed for compassion? How did you spread my love in the world so that righteousness would spring from inside people themselves?"

The words of St. Paul echo in my mind: "If one member suffers, all suffer together. If one member is honored, all rejoice together." I rejoice in my brother's spiritual health, and I feel overwhelmed at the thought of all who suffer in the world. We can only do so much, but it is my prayer that all of us may find ways to struggle together—because we all need help—to struggle together to discern God's will for compassion. We need to recognize evil when we see it—in the world or in ourselves. We need to offer our compassionate help to those who struggle to overcome evil. We need to join our efforts together with theirs as we strive for integrity. And, above all, we need to recognize that Christ is there in the midst of those struggles to light the way, to lift burdens, to open doors, to keep us from leaving the hallways, and to give us true peace and joy in knowing the wrath of love.

Amen.

—Matthew McDermott

[1900 words]
[19 minutes]

Sermon 66

Date: Any Appropriate Sunday

Text:
Matthew 7:21–29

Theme: God welcomes us to Heaven. But where or what is it?
Subject: Heaven

Title: Looking for Heaven

Professor Himmel is my name, Himmel, that's German for heaven, and that is the subject of my guest lecture with you today, heaven that celestial place, or that state of being we dream of, and hope for, heaven. I am grateful to your pastor for inviting me here to speak with you on a subject dear to my heart, Himmel, my own name, heaven.

I have studied this topic in depth, in college, graduate school seminary, and post–doctoral research. I have written several articles and books on heaven, the best known is my volume, *Heaven; Up, Down and All Around.* Or perhaps you have heard of my article in the periodical, *Heaven Studies,* "Pearly Gates and Angel Choirs: Is Heaven Sweet and Fluffy, or Does Christ Have Something Else in Mind for Us?" I know your pastor quotes these works to you weekly.

Because, you see, to understand heaven, one must study it. To understand heaven one must read these long entries on heaven in theological dictionaries, one must know Greek and Latin and Hebrew, one must read Paul and Augustine and Aquinas. Oh, and Jesus, Jesus too, yes. But mostly the scholars. Actually, that is my idea of heaven, a group of scholars, Augustine and Aquinas and Paul, perhaps even me, Professor Himmel, sitting around discussing heaven. Ah, that would be heaven.

Actually, that's how I used to feel about heaven, that only scholars, only those past greats, could understand heaven. The others, simple folk, all they thought about were pearly gates and angel choirs. I knew better. Or so I thought. Something dramatic and painful happened in my life that challenged all years of study and writing on heaven. A small event, insignificant (to the world at least). My son was born. He grew. He loved life. He seemed blessed with all God's gifts, especially (I think he got it from me) the gift of curiosity. "What is heaven, Mommy, where do we go after we die?" I quoted to him many authorities on heaven (so I thought.) "You'll never get to heaven if you want to go alone" or "You can't go to heaven if you haven't sent your heart there first," or from Shaw: "To be in hell is to drift, to be in heaven is to steer." My son seemed satisfied and stayed curious. But then, this is what did it, one day, he died, my son, my Theo, I had named him Theodore, literally, a gift of God, me heaven and him a gift of God, and he died, too young, age fifteen. Is he in heaven? I hope and pray so. But no longer did all my theories comfort me.

But let me tell you first about those theories, those ideas, for they are sound, I believe, as far as they go. First, heaven is where God lives. All throughout the Bible God says, I am in the heavens, all throughout the Bible, people pray to God in heaven, Our Father, who art in heaven. Certainly God lives other places too, the temple, mountaintops, and visits here and there. But heaven's God's main domicile.

Second, heaven is where we go after we die—if we are good. Actually, that idea about heaven as a reward is completely absent from the Old Testament. The Hebrew people believed that after we die we are reunited with God, but nothing about heaven and hell, just reunited with God. It was Jesus, no, actually, it was the early church, and oh that medieval church that became obsessed really, with heaven, hell, and purgatory. The whole scale of judging who was good and bad. Sort of like our own Kris Kringle, what do you call him, Santa Claus, God makes a list, checks it twice, finds out who's naughty and nice. There was a list in heaven, of all places, the idea went, of the, what do you call them, good guys. Everyone else was assigned to purgatory—or worse. Now Jesus did plant the seeds of these ideas, the final judgment, sheep and goats, the coming of God's Kingdom. But it was those medieval clerics who set up the whole system of who got into heaven. As if God wasn't loving, forgiving. As if the priests and not God were in charge.

Thankfully the Reformation came along, Martin Luther and the gang. No, heaven was the reward for faith, not works, for faith. And another twist, heaven was not just in the future, but here too, the Kingdom of God is within, Jesus said. The reformers reminded us that heaven was not just something to look forward to, to hope for, heaven could be here, now. This was radical. Most people ignored this idea. Be good, parents said, be good, ministers said, or you won't go to heaven. Threat and bribe, good old religion, threat and bribe.

One more point I made in that first book, "Heaven, Up, Down and All Around": those old Hebrews, Jesus, Paul, and their heirs, Augustine and Aquinas—they thought the earth was flat, heaven up, earth here, hell down there. Scientists and explorers said the earth was round, not flat, that it went around the sun; they scorned them, killed them even. Even in our own century, people thought the astronauts would go up and see God and the pearly gates, and were disappointed when they didn't.

You know, I used to be very critical of these old Hebrew, simple flat world ideas of heaven. So old fashioned. The hymns, for heaven's sake (for heaven's sake!), God come down, descend upon my heart, God high in heaven. For goodness sake, the earth isn't flat, heaven isn't up there, heaven is all around, up, down, all around. God, too.

Oh, I thought I knew it all. I had great confidence that my volumes on heaven would earn me quick entrance into the very place of my study. Then my son died, Theo died. All of a sudden I knew why authors spend so much more time talking about hell than heaven, why so many books have in their index citation after citation on hell, nothing on heaven. It's the pain, the loss, the loneliness, the anger, the grief. That's hell. How could God do this to me, to my little boy. Where is he now?

My books were of no help. They seemed dry, sterile. I was lost, I cried, I wandered. One day, I wandered into our church (that's how I came to know your pastor). A lovely spot here, quiet, peaceful, cool, and open always, open your church is, open, never locked—it seemed like heaven, this place. I sat, just sat. I read from the Bible, Lord thou has searched me and known me, even in heaven, thou art there. God took Elijah up into heaven, promised through Jesus eternal life, heaven if we love our neighbor.

I prayed. To God, to Theo, to all spirits of the dead. Tell me what happens after we die, reassure me, comfort me, tell me what I had so confidently written of—what is heaven?

The answers came slowly. Heaven is peace. Both now and in the future. Peace. Peace and freedom. Freedom from pain, anger, violence. Once, here, in prayer, I so clearly saw Theo I thought I could touch him. And he was at peace, he was free, free from pain, the violence of our world and of his death, free and at peace. That I know for Theo, that I could hope for me and for everyone.

I never had a vision of hell in the future, of a place of punishment. I have known hell on earth, but I don't think a loving, forgiving God spends one moment stoking the fires of hell, figuring out punishments. No, God is hard at work trying to save us, to give us peace, freedom. We need to get out from our own fears, our own needs, our own concerns, and let God in, let God give us peace and freedom. Let God welcome us to heaven.

Then we will know heaven. I've come to know heaven as both now and in the future. If I spend all my time waiting, hoping for heaven, I may miss it all around me. And it is a sure hope, a promise, with no threat, that God will grant me after I die, some kind of peace and freedom. Of what exact nature, who knows? Is it spirit and body, or just spirit? What kind of consciousness—

who knows? I do think I will be with Theo in some sense, that loved ones are reunited as spirits at least. I still hope to have a spirit contact with Aquinas and Augustine. But mostly with Theo. I don't think it's going to be pearly gates and angel choirs. But it will be sweet. So sweet.

And the whole business of the flat earth, my scorn for this simple mythology. No more. Sure, I know if God is up, God is also down and all around. But there is something special about the sky, the precious rain that comes from above, the healing warmth of sunlight. I know why they said Jesus went up after he died, rather than down into the earth. Heaven is out there, up there, bringing us the bounty of warm rain and illuminating sun and healing warmth. I hope for heaven, I know it daily in small moments of peace and freedom. And I believe in the resurrection, and the life of the world to come.

Thank you for leaving your sanctuary open all day and all night so I could have a bit of heaven here. And thank God for heaven. Thank heaven for God.

Amen.

—Deborah Streeter

[1600 words]
[16 minutes]

Sermon 67

Date: Fourth Sunday in Lent, Year A

Texts:
1 Samuel 16:1–13
Psalm 23
Ephesians 5:8–14
John 9:1–41

or Sunday Between October 23 and October 29 inclusive Pentecost, Year B

Texts: (NCL)
Mark 10:46–52

Theme: Jesus the Christ brings light, that in the darkest depths of despair he is the light, and that what he is we may be also.
Subject: Suffering, handicaps

Title: "Wake up, sleepy head"

We are all handicapped. We are all limited. We are all impaired, disabled, challenged.

We are all born blind. I felt this when I was a teenager and wrote a poem, "My Son Born Blind," to express the conviction:

My Son Born Blind

His eyes are blue
as airless space

Where dust bands breathe
their gloomy sigh.

And yet how can
such joy be told
by one who has
not seen the sky?

How can his never
seeing eyes
reflect the
morning light

when all that they
will ever know
is emptiness
and night?

This poem has been published a number of times over the years. Once it was recorded as the introduction to the rock song, "Snow Blind." And inevitably I have been asked if my son were really sightless. The poem, written when I was about thirteen, is, of course, about neither physical blindness nor a biological child. It is about spiritual blindness and the child of its title is the poet himself.

In the story of Jesus' healing of the man born blind, blindness is a metaphor. Yet, like all metaphors, it is based on something real, something that we experience every day of our lives—pain and suffering.

It would take a very naive human being to insist that there is a direct means-end, causal connection between sin and suffering. If life teaches us anything, it teaches us that suffering is not meted out as punishment for sin. Life is unfair.

Two Views of Suffering

There are two biblical views of suffering: Deuteronomic and Jobian. The Deuteronomic view says that obedience to God's will produces health, wealth, and long life, while sin produces illness, poverty, and early death. We read in the Book of Deuteronomy that shortly before his death, Moses exhorted the Hebrews as follows:

> *See, I set before you today life and prosperity, death and destruction. For I command you today to love the LORD your God, to walk in his ways, and to keep his commands, decrees and laws; then you will live and increase, and the LORD your God will bless you in the land you are entering to possess. But if your heart turns away and you are not obedient, and if you are drawn away to bow down to other gods and worship them, I declare to you this day that you will certainly be destroyed. You will not live long in the land you are crossing the Jordan to enter and possess. (Deuteronomy 30:15–18)*

The Deuteronomic theory seems to work best when it is applied to social realities. Nations that forget their roots, heritage, values, and traditions can lose their reason for existing, and soon decay, and die. The same thing can happen to the building block of society—the family. When society no longer fosters and nurtures the family, the family no longer fosters and nurtures society.

The second view, which may be called realistic or even pessimistic, is found in such biblical books as Job and Ecclesiastes. It describes life from a highly individualistic point of view. When life is considered person by person, it is grossly unfair. Faith, the realists of the Bible tell us, is no talisman to ward off tragedy. Good men can fail and evil men prosper. Listen to the eloquent but despairing words attributed to King Solomon:

> *"Meaningless! Meaningless!" says the Teacher. "Utterly meaningless! Everything is meaningless." What does man gain from all his labor at which he toils under the sun? Generations come and generations go, but the earth remains forever. . . . All things are wearisome, more than one can say. The eye never has enough of seeing, nor the ear its fill of hearing. What has been will be again, what has been done will be done again; there is nothing new under the sun. (Ecclesiastes 1:2–9)*

Or as Job demands of his comforters,

> *Why do the wicked live on, growing old and increasing in power? They spend their years in prosperity and go down to the grave in peace. Yet they say to God, 'Leave us alone! We have no desire to know your ways.' One man dies in full vigor, completely secure and at ease, his body well nourished, his bones rich with marrow. Another man dies in bitterness of soul, never having enjoyed anything good. Side by side they lie in the dust, and worms cover them both. . . . the evil man is spared from the day of calamity, . . . he is delivered from the day of wrath. Who denounces his conduct to his face? Who repays him for what he has done? (Job 21:7, 8, 13, 14, 23–26, 30, 31)*

Jesus subscribed to both theories. He exhorted the nation Israel to return to its calling. Israel, he taught, is God's fig tree. If it fails to produce, God will tear it up by its root. And Jesus recognized that the world in which we live as individuals is not what it ought to be. He was bold enough to acknowledge that God is not in control of the present world. If he were, why would Jesus have taught us to ask our heavenly Father: "Thy kingdom come. Thy will be done. . . "? The prayer makes it clear that it is not so already.

A few years ago, I wrote of a friend of mine, who was dying. I remarked:

> The therapy which is extending [Joe's] remaining months is painful and exhausting. He is in his forties and has a wife and three children. He is a minister of the gospel. And his parishioners, attempting to comfort him, are always telling him to accept his lot as the will of God. He becomes angry and tells them that he cannot worship a God who would allow him to suffer and would leave his family without a husband and father. Joe tells them: "Disease and death are not the will of God. They are the consequences of a world out of control, a world which shunned the will of God in the beginning and which continues to shun it at every moment. And as it drifts its meaningless way like some great machine run amok, it is killing me, afflicting me with pain, and denying me a future with my loved ones."

Joe decided that the pain with which he paid for each day's continuation of his life was not worth it. He discontinued his treatment and died.

The Reality of Evil

Evil is real. Life is unfair. Sometimes nice guys finish last. Hard work is not always rewarded. And we all make mistakes. We all cause harm and grief even when we try to make things better for our friends and loved ones.

If God is loving and all-powerful, why does he tolerate evil? If suffering is punishment for sin, why is it that the righteous are afflicted while the unrighteous prosper? Why does he let us make mistakes? Why do Christians suffer when they are doing the best they can? Why do so many of our decisions turn out to be disasters? Why do we still feel that we could have done better even after we have made a decision?

The only basis for affirming the meaningfulness of life in the face of the insurmountable evils of human existence is the recognition that our tribulations are also the sufferings of God, that our struggle to realize good despite all that opposes us is at the same time God's ongoing creation of order out of primal chaos. Unless God himself participates in the heartache and sorrows of our earthly state, then all striving is in vain.

Why do Ethiopian children starve while our children flourish? Because God does not intrude to take away our freedom even when we mismanage his creation. If he intervened every time we were about to act selfishly, violently, or heedlessly, we would have no real freedom and no responsibility. Why is life unfair? Because it is, because it expresses our basic alienation from nature, from one another, and from our true selves. God did not create it this way. He does not want it to be this way. And according to the Christian gospel, he gave what was dearest to himself to do something about it.

Partnership with God is costly. To worship God as God means that one must be open to respond without ever knowing if one is doing the absolutely right thing. To live is to be guilty of inflicting pain and committing injustice. We cannot even breathe or eat without destroying life. We make mistakes and will continue to make mistakes.

We live in a confusing and evil world—confusing because we project our own confusion on it—and evil because it is not yet redeemed, because it is not yet created. The creative spirit which works in each of us enables us to become instruments of peace for ourselves, for our neighbors, and for our world. But the process of creation is filled with pain, contradiction, confusion, and suffering. In this suffering we are not alone, for what we experience mirrors the struggle of the divine with us and with our world.

Every Life an Opportunity

It is through crucifixion and death that God in Christ reconciles the world to himself. And it is through our courage, our affirmation of life, our turning of chaos into meaning, our suffering and pain that we are instruments of the divine purpose. For, as the story of the man born blind informs us, every life is an opportunity for God to be glorified.

Consider Helen Keller—blind and deaf, a major force in the struggle for human rights.

Think of Christy Brown, almost totally paralyzed, whose contributions to the arts and literature are the subject of the recent Irish film, *My Left Foot.*

Regard Franz Rosenzweig—Jewish theologian, who wrote his major work, The Star of Redemption, while his entire body was immobilized with the exception of the muscles in his eyelids. By blinking in code, he "dictated" his book to his wife, one letter at a time.

We are rediscovering the humanity of the handicapped, the worth of the physically and mentally challenged, the value of those who are not normal according to our conception of normality.

Even if the man born blind had not been healed, his life could have glorified God. For it was his recovery from spiritual blindness that really counted. In contrast were the religious authorities who rejected Jesus because he did not conform to their stereotype. What blinded them? The same things that blind us: prejudice and self-righteousness.

Jesus Brings Light to Our Despair

The real message of the story is that Jesus the Christ brings light, that in the darkest depths of despair he is the light, and that what he is we may be also.

As Paul says in Ephesians, "For you were once darkness, but now you are light in the Lord." Not "you are influenced by the light" or "you are full of light" or "you are bearers of the light" or "you are enlightened," but "you were once darkness, but now you are light in the Lord." We are all born blind and crippled and limited and handicapped. And we are born with the smallest spark of the divine in us, a spark that may be fanned into a conflagration. We are born to glorify God and to enjoy him forever.

When I was a child, my father would wake me on Sunday mornings so that we could have breakfast together, listen to the radio, and read the Sunday funnies. "Wake up, sleepy head. Open your eyes," he would urge in his gentle voice.

"Wake up, sleepy head," says our heavenly Father. "Open your eyes."

Amen.

—LDS

[2000 words]
[20 minutes]

❦ *Sermon 68*

❦ *Date:* Fifth Sunday in Lent, Year A

Texts:
Ezekiel 37:1–14
Psalm 130
Romans 8:6–11
John 11:1–45

Theme: There is no reward in being dead and being alive is much more fun!
Subject: Death, abundant life

❦ *Title:* When Dead Bones Live Again

Crucifixion

The rugged fall
In God's presence.
Drop the lakes of blood incessant?
We bewildered,
Arms uplifted,
Celebrate a mass once more.
Man on man
Against his brother.
Sea of mothers' tears
Rain on
Till the last drop
Or the One Mind;

Till the heart of love asunder
Flows with water and with blood.

—LDS

Last week, the gospel reading reminded us that we are all handicapped—that we are born blind and that not only is Jesus the light of our world but that what he is we are also.

This week's gospel reading, the account of the raising of Lazarus, informs us of something even more radical: We are all dead and Jesus is our resurrection and life.

Physical Death as Separation

Lazarus was dead. Physical death is separation. Physical death is the separation of consciousness, memory, and feeling from the physical shell in which we live. We die. We are gone. Only the memory of our influence for good and for evil persists.

Lazarus was dead. Death is frustration. It is the ultimate limit, the end, the point of no return. With death, all the bright hopes for a particular life are over.

Lazarus was dead. Death is destiny. The only prediction that a soothsayer can make with 100 percent certainty is that all will perish. The exact moment when I shall die is shrouded in mystery, but the certainty is unavoidable.

Jesus loved Lazarus. He loved those who shared his love for Lazarus. Their sorrow and grief touched his heart, leaving him confused and troubled. "Jesus wept," we are told. And these two words, the shortest verse in the Bible, speak volumes of the compassion of the God whom Jesus images.

"Jesus wept." Remember these words the next time you are angry with a friend, or hurt by a loved one, or confused by a stranger's way of life, or troubled by circumstances over which you have no control.

Lazarus was dead and Jesus wept for him. And then Jesus did something about his sorrow. He looked death right in the eye; announced his defiance of separation, frustration, and destiny; and overcame them.

Even in the midst of life, we are all dead. Death is separation. We are all victims of the little murders, the small suicides, that deprive us of life. There is so much pain in each of us—the pain of not having been loved enough, the pain of being afraid to ask for what we want, the pain of realizing that we have harmed those we love.

We deny the pain. We choke it back. We make everyone around us wrong. We wallow in being right. And, in the process, we cut ourselves off from our neighbors, our friends, our spouses, and our children. We pay the price of always being right, and the price is separation.

Death as Frustration

Even in the midst of life, we are all dead. Death is frustration. We begin life as pure potential. At each milestone in our early lives, we are told that we are the future of the world. We are raised on mother's cooking, on father's moral exhortations, and on our media-spawned dreams of romance and success. But life does not turn out the way that we are led to expect. We make mistakes. We lose courage. The fires of romantic love cool. We compromise for the sake of security or because we have responsibilities. We find out that we are as flawed and limited as those imperfect adults who reared us, those imperfect men and women we promised we would never be like!

So we do exactly what our parents did—we transfer our expectations to our children. We expect them to climb higher up the ladder of success than we did, to be better educated, to make better choices, to have more, to do more, to be more. And then we walk the floors at night, just as our parents did, frustrated and disappointed. We worry ourselves sick because our children waste their potential and defeat themselves in ways that we could scarcely have imagined in our own youth.

Death as Destiny

Even in the midst of life, we are all dead. Death is destiny. The movie is over. The hero has kissed the heroine. The villain has been vanquished. The words, "The End," have flashed on the screen. The credits are rolling and only a handful of people remain in their seats.

Everything has an end, a limit, a culmination.

What is is and what isn't isn't, and the sooner we realize it the more we will stop worrying about adding years to our life and start adding life to our years. Which of you by worrying, Jesus asked, can add a foot to his height or an hour to her life? (Matthew 6:25, Luke 12:25)

"To be or not to be—that is the question," Hamlet mused. It remains the question for us. Separation, frustration, and destiny did us in. We have been dead in many ways, for many years. And then this upstart, Jesus, comes and stands just beyond our reach, and shouts at us in a voice that blasts our eardrums like a cannon shot. "Lazarus, come out! Come out of your separation. Give up your frustration. Transcend your destiny."

I think of those remarkable words of Jesus when he was challenged by those who did not believe in the resurrection of the dead:

> *in the account of the bush, even Moses showed that the dead rise, for he calls the Lord "the God of Abraham, and the God of Isaac, and the God of Jacob." He is not the God of the dead, but of the living, for to him all are alive. (Luke 20:37–38)*

God is the God of the living—not of the dead. In Jesus the Christ, God annuls the power of separation, frustration, and destiny. He gives us the authority to live.

Living in the Face of Death

How can you and I appropriate that authority for ourselves? How can we respond to the God who calls us by name and tells us to get out of our caves of isolation?

First, we must accept the truth of God's verdict. We are all dead. As Paul tells us in his letter to the Romans: "All have sinned and come short of the glory of God. . . . [and] the wages of sin is death . . ."(3:23 and 6:23). We are separated from God, from one another, from nature, from our own true identities. As the bumper sticker aptly says, "Death is nature's way of telling us to slow down." And the recognition of the little murders and the small suicides we have committed and continue to commit day by day is the beginning of breaking the power of death in our lives.

Get out of your grave, says the One who is the Resurrection and the Life. Stop blaming. Stop whining. Stop feeling sorry for yourself. Reach out. Forgive. Reconcile. Restore. Rebuild. Dare to let the other guy be right and yourself be wrong. Accept responsibility for your own hurt feelings.

Reexamine your expectations—for your own life and for the lives of those you love. Are you allowing yourself to live or using your disappointment as an excuse for staying in the cave? In your most cherished relationships, are you a life-giver or a life-denier? Are you a grave-dweller or a death-defier? Are you a life-avoider or a life-affirmer? Are you a source of love and comfort or the voice of frustration and disappointment? Are you the home to which children may come regardless of their successes or failures or the place of confinement from which they must seek escape all the days of their lives?

Accept what is. Accept yourself as you are—warts and all. When God commanded us to love our neighbors as ourselves, he clearly expected that we would be able to love ourselves. When Jesus called this the second greatest commandment, he indicated that he shared that expectation. Unless you can admit your failings to yourself, forgive yourself, and begin to honor and respect your own life as the gift from God, which it is, you will never be able to overcome the deadness that robs you of life.

And unless you can learn to knock off the judgmental attitude, the tendency to exclude from your acceptance all those whose lives differ from your own, you will remain mired in the grave of separation, frustration, and destiny. God accepts us just because we are. When we were still sinners, Christ died for us. (Romans 5:8) Not when we were perfect or lived up to God's expectations—when we were yet sinners. This does not mean that God approves of everything we think or do, let alone of all that we fail to do or think. God is a just and righteous God who hates sin, who detests the harm we daily do to ourselves, our neighbors, and our world. The brokenness of our lives breaks God's heart. That is why Jesus wept.

And yet God calls us to life. He speaks his word and we are reborn. He calls us to repentance and restores us to himself. He forgives us and revitalizes us. He invades our lives and we are born from above. He cannot tolerate our deadness. After all, he is the God of the living.

There is no reward in being dead and no need. And being alive is so much more fun! Lazarus, get those dead bones out here. It is time to live!

Amen.

—LDS

[1600 words]
[16 minutes]

❦ Sermon 69

❦ *Date:* Easter, Year A, B, or C, Sunrise Service

Theme: As Dostoevski said: "In the end beauty will save the world." Wherever joy and peace meet, there is beauty.
Subject: Beauty, resurrection

❦ *Title:* Easter Morning Reflections

Dostoevski once said, "In the end beauty will save the world." What a surprising statement. We view beauty as such a fragile thing, like the flowers of spring that fade all too quickly, or the autumn trees that shed their radiant plumes of russet and gold in one furious storm.

What's more, in our frantic search for the almighty dollar we seem to give little thought to beauty today. We relegate it to coastal drives, or expensive art. Rollo May writes: "We have lost touch with the real power of beauty which is its power to keep us in touch with the eternal. The experience of beauty is the experience of joy and peace. Many things can make us joyful from a wedding to a football game. Other things can give us a sense of serenity. A beautiful thing gives us both at once."[1]

---

[1] May, Rollo, *My Quest for Beauty* (Dallas, TX: Saybrook Publishing Company, 1985), p. 20.

When we see something beautiful we tend to be silent, and out of this silence comes a feeling of ecstasy and of eternity, of something that lasts forever. Why else do we gather ourselves up, most of us only this one time of the year, and come out in the cool of the morning and whisper to each other and wait for the sun to rise. Sunrise at Easter is a symbol that affects more than our mind, it seeps within us, and rests deep down in our core. This is beautiful. This is an experience of the power of beauty. It is an experience which can have a profound effect upon our lives if we so allow it.

Hilltops are often thought of as beautiful places. I have been to a hill this past week that is anything but beautiful. I have been to hell and I have come to tell you that Christ is risen.

At least I have been to what I imagine hell to be like. Last week our youth group visited the "Colonia Pan America," a community of some 500 people who live at the site of the old dump outside of Tijuana. These people are the poorest of the poor. As little as three years ago, the dump was still being used. Fires, caused by spontaneous combustion, would break out so smoke would hover over the hillside. The fires provided some heat for families unable to afford fuel, but they also threatened children and pets with asphyxiation.

The picture of hell, that Jesus referred to as Gehenna, is that of a dump where fires burned and the souls of the lost were tossed aside and left to rot. The hill upon which Jesus was crucified was probably near the dump outside of Jerusalem, where the rotten bodies of the crucified could be tossed after they had served the purpose of demonstrating to the community the powerlessness of rebellion. Hell is the antithesis of beauty. There is no joy and there is no peace.

On our tour of hell, however, we became witnesses of something remarkable. A community has literally risen from the ashes. Local leaders of the colonia decided something had to be done. They had dreams of building a life out of the rubble. The church became involved. An evangelical group started services. A Lutheran mission board got involved. Heifer project (which we have supported) provided forty-two piglets to start a pig farm. (One of the fires sprouted just below the pig enclosure and the smoke killed thirteen of the pigs, a near disaster for the venture.) Houses made out of cardboard and flattened barrels, were constructed by another church group. Soon Habitat for Humanity will be organizing a housing program which will employ residents as builders of their own homes. A development fund was put together. It only amounts to about fifteen hundred dollars, but a business can be started for as little as three hundred dollars.

Suddenly in the midst of hell a real-life community is emerging. We ate at the local restaurant, not a four-star eating establishment, not even a one star. The building was a shack, 15 feet by 20 feet. It had no door. The flies hovered in the ceiling, but stayed off the food. This was also the church and the heartbeat of the colonia.

I don't know if our young people realized it, but they were witnesses to the resurrection. Christ was in that place calling people together. Christ, who was crucified on a dump like this, was here reclaiming his own people. We may not have recognized him because of all the dirt, disease, the mangy dogs, and hostile children, who wanted money and threw rocks at us as we left. But he was there. We didn't see him because we were too shocked.

Like Mary who didn't see Jesus standing next to her that Easter morning. She thought he was a gardener, and probably wanted him to go away so she could mourn in private. But, he was there calling to her. And when she looked up it was beautiful.

"Beauty," says Solzhenitsyn, "grips the soul." It takes us deeper than so-called rational consciousness is able. It takes us outside our present worries and fears and expands us. We see that on a morning like this when we are filled with the spirit, and full of hope, and look at the neat and ordered affairs of our life—it seems beautiful. It fills us up. It expands us so we can take it all in.

Beauty affects us on so many levels. It affects our hearts and our minds. It is the power of beauty to connect us with one another and with the timelessness of the human spirit that is perhaps the greatest sign of the resurrection in our midst. Where joy and peace meet, there is beauty. But even before joy and peace are possible, there is God, calling us out of hell.

On this morning when I stand on this beautiful hill, I wonder what it is like outside Tijuana, at the dump. I know they will be worshiping today in the little church. I wonder if they will see the beauty of their day. I do know they have hopes, and they have dreams, and what is more, they have the risen Christ with them. "I have witnessed the resurrection and it is beautiful."

Amen.

—W. Matthew Broadbent

[1000 words]
[10 minutes]

❦ *Sermon 70*

❦ *Date:* Good Friday or Easter, Year A, B, or C

Texts:
Good Friday, Year A, B, or C
Isaiah 52:13–53:12
Psalm 22
Hebrews 4:14–16; 5:7–9
John 18:1–19:42 or John 19:17–30

Easter Sunday, Year A
Acts 10:34–43 or Jeremiah 31:1–6
Psalm 118:1-2, 14–24
Colossians 3:1–4 or Acts 10:34–43
John 20:1–18 or Matthew 28:1–10

Year B
Acts 10:34–43 or Isaiah 25:6–9
Psalm 118:1-2, 14–24
1 Corinthians 15:1–11 or Acts 10:34–43
John 20:1–18 or Mark 16:1–8

Year C
Acts 10:34–43 or Isaiah 65:17–25
Psalm 118:1-2, 14–24
1 Corinthians 15:19–26 or Acts 10:34–43
John 20:1–18 or Luke 24:1–12

Theme: Frustration is real, but it does not have the last word.
Subject: Easter

❦ *Title:* "It's Friday, but sunday's acomin'"

We may think it is Easter Sunday, but it is still Good Friday. Evil still seems to have the upper hand. But Sunday is just around the corner. An elderly, experienced black pastor in West Philadelphia says it like this:

> It was Friday, it was Friday and my Jesus is dead on the tree, but that's Friday, Sunday is acomin'.
>
> Friday, Friday, Mary is crying her eyes out, the disciples are running in every direction like sheep without a shepherd. But it's Friday, Friday. Sunday is acomin'.
>
> Friday, Friday, those are looking at the world and saying as things have been so they shall be, you can't change nothing in this world. You can't change nothing in this world. But they didn't know it was only Friday. Sunday is acomin'.
>
> Let's try one more time here, Friday, Friday, them forces that oppressed the poor and keep people down, them forces that destroy people, them forces is in control and they are going to rule, but they don't know it's only Friday. Friday, Friday, Sunday is acomin'.
>
> Friday, Friday, people are saying darkness is going to rule the world, sadness is going to be everywhere, but they don't know it's only Friday, Sunday is acomin'.[1]

And here in our lives and in our community, [even on Easter Sunday] it seems like it's always, Friday . . .

the rich are getting richer,
while the poor and working fathers and mothers are paying the bill.

But Sunday is coming. . . .
by the grace of God you and I will change the way things are to the way they ought to be,
the rich will pay their fair share,
and the needs of the poor and working fathers and mothers will be met by a society that cares, that has compassion, that knows there is no future for any of us unless there is a future for all of us.

It is Friday. . . .
we are killing our children with dope, booze, speed, and AIDS,
our children are killing themselves,
junk and bunk are polluting their minds,
and there is nothing worth living for.

But Sunday is coming. . . .
when getting high on the gospel of Jesus Christ is the greatest thrill in the world,
that living for others makes life worthwhile,
and the truth shall set us free,
and the young shall see visions and dream dreams,
and know that to live is Christ.

---

[1] Cited by Anthony Campolo in "It's Friday, But Sunday's Comin'," audiotape presentation, (Waco, TX: Word, Inc., 1982).

It is Friday. . . .
and the unloved and wretched of the earth have no way of dealing with their hurt other than hurting others.

But Sunday is coming. . . .
but here and now and the lion shall lie down with the lamb,
and loving and caring and listening shall never be in short supply,
And no one will have to harm his brother or sister ever again.

It is Friday. . . .
and all that we have tried, all that we have lived our lives for, seems doomed to futility;
our husbands and wives no longer love us and we can't talk to our children anymore.

But Sunday is coming. . . .
God makes all things new,
we stumble, we fall, but he picks us up again,
we confess our shortcomings and ask our loved ones to allow us to love them and they love us in return.

It is Friday. . . .
the environment is battered and bruised and bleeding.
Mother Earth is dying and no one seems to care,
we are spending our substance for things of no value, and using up in one generation the endowment of centuries.

But Sunday is coming. . . .
we are learning our lessons and, one by one, beginning to do something about it.
Earth shall endure and we shall be reborn, regenerated with her.

It is Friday. . . .
and life is not fair
and depression clings to us like a heavy, wet coat.
we see nothing at the end of the tunnel but more tunnel
and no one gives a damn.

But Sunday is coming. . . .
but he shall fill our souls with gladness, our hearts with laughter. He shall turn our sorrow into dancing,
darkness shall fade and the light of God's presence break through—not in the "sweet by and by," but now,
and here in his church God shall give us brothers and sisters who love us with a faithful and constant love, with His own love.

It is Friday. . . .
there are unpaid bills and peeling paint and leaks everywhere—leaky faucets, leaky roofs, leaky bank accounts,
and always a surplus of what we don't want and a shortage of what we desperately need.

But Sunday is coming. . . .
when God shall carry us in his bosom as a shepherd carries his lambs,
when God shall stroke our foreheads and hug us and walk with us and talk with us and tell us we are his own,
where the Word of God is preached and heard, God shall fill our hearts and minds and

stomach with good things, with sweet and tender things that nourish us forever,
and we shall never hunger nor thirst again.

It is Friday. . . .
and we are one step closer to the grave, to the end, to futility, to nothingness,
and terror clings to us like a mean and ugly pit bull.

But Sunday is coming. . . .
and we are one step closer to the house of our Father, the house where Jesus has prepared a place for us,
and we are filled with the wonder and awe that God shares his own life with us and that this life can never be extinguished. For God is among us, filling us with hope.

It is Friday. . . .
and the politicians are crooked and the cops take graft and the IRS is out to get us.

But Sunday is coming. . . .
the kingdom of God is at hand,
the first shall be last and the last, first,
and all the crooks and thugs will answer to God,
and, starting today, we will be part of a world that works for everyone.

It is Friday. . . .
and we don't know who we are or what we are supposed to do with our lives.

But Sunday is coming. . . .
we shall know even as we are known by God,
and our lives will have purpose, meaning, and fulfillment.

It is Friday. . . .
and our poems don't rhyme,
we can't find the right words to express ourselves or the right notes for the melody,
the colors and shapes and proportions of our paintings are all wrong,
and our architecture collapses.
When we try to ask for help, the words stick in our throats.

But Sunday is coming. . . .
God shall be all and all,
the crooked shall be made straight,
the desert shall bloom,
we shall be unstuck and released and redeemed and creative,
and our expressiveness shall know no limitation.
We shall make a difference.

It is Friday. . . .
and the elderly are tucked away in foul-smelling nursing homes,
and the mentally ill sleep in parking lots,
and women make half as much as men but have twice the responsibility.

But Sunday is coming. . . .
when the wisdom of the old shall save the young from folly,
and the sick shall be made whole,
and our demons shall be cast out together with their demons,
and all shall receive what they need and give what they can.

And there shall be honor and respect for caregivers,
and all shall carry the burden of work and family together.

It is Friday. . . .
and looks count and stature means height,
and who you know counts for more than what you know.

But Sunday is coming. . . .
when the only beauty is inner beauty,
and the only one worth knowing is one's own true self.

It is Friday. . . .
and the horror of war revolts us,
and the bloated stomachs of starving children offends our sensibilities,
and we do nothing about it.

But Sunday is coming. . . .
we shall beat our swords into plowshares,
and turn our munitions into foodstuffs,
and everyone of us shall accept responsibility for doing something to ending war now
and wiping out hunger today.

It is Friday. . . .
and men drink cheap wine and Sterno and sleep in alleys,
and families sleep in their cars,
and the night in the shelters belongs to the rats and the roaches,
and the comfortable and content wag their fingers and cluck their tongues and close out the outside world with their garage door openers and shut off their TVs with their remote controls and seal themselves off from the homeless in their midst.

But Sunday is coming. . . .
and Jesus shall say, "I was homeless and you let me die in the streets." And we shall say, "When, Lord?"
And we shall get the point and realize that nothing will change unless we change it and change ourselves in the bargain,
And there shall be jobs and dignity and homes to go around.

It is Friday. . . .
and we lock men up in cages like animals,
and abuse women for being women,
and kill one another in hot blood, in cold blood, because we want to, and because we are too heedless to know we are killing.

But Sunday is coming. . . .
love shall annul fear and set the prisoners free,
women shall be called blessed once again,
and human beings shall live at peace with one another and with all other living beings,
And God shall reign, forever and ever!

Sociologist/preacher Anthony Campolo says it well:

People, that's good news. When we take the gospel seriously this is what will happen. Our psychological needs will begin to be met. Our capacity to love will be developed. Our appreciation of the miraculous will cause us to expect great things from God. And

> the Spirit of God that possesses us will motivate us to give ourselves to those who are suffering in a way that we have failed to do up to this day. And when all of that happens, this is the good news, this is the very good news, that even though this world is rotten as it is right now we know it's only Friday.[2]

It may be Friday, but wherever the Good News is proclaimed and lived, wherever men and women have the courage to stop being part of the problem and start being part of the solution, Sunday is coming!

It may be Friday. . . .
But Sunday is coming!

Amen.

—LDS

[1700 words]
[17 minutes]

---

[2] Ibid.

❦ *CHAPTER SEVEN*

HOPE, ADVENT, AND CHRISTMAS

Advent is not the season that proclaims the coming of Christmas—but the coming of Christ. Advent is a season of darkness and a season of light. As the days grow shorter, we face the darkness within—our frustrations and disappointments. Yet in the midst of darkness, we find illumination. We find hope beyond all reasonable expectations.

Advent is the season for the preparation of the coming of God in our lives. It is a time of repentance and expectancy. We wait for renewal. Advent offers us the validity of God's promises of a new world, a new set of relationships, and fresh possibilities.

On Christmas we celebrate the Good News: God is for us, with us, in us, and among us. And we are thankful. As God chose humble peasants and shepherds to reveal his purposes, so does he select us today so that his power may be made perfect in our weakness.

Sermon 71

Date: First Sunday of Advent, A 1992

Texts:
Isaiah 2:1–5
Psalm 122
Romans 13:11–14
Matthew 24:36–44

Theme: Our eyes behold God's glory. Can we await the coming of Christmas without losing sight of the coming of the Christ?
Subject: Christian life

Title: Trying on the Armor of Light

Tip

> Make use of the most familiar material you know such as the lyrics to the "Battle Hymn of the Republic" to grab your listeners attention and make them feel that they already own what you have to say.

Advent begins today. Advent is not the season that proclaims the coming of Christmas. Advent is the season that proclaims the coming of the Christ. In the words of Fred Craddock, "Advent is not a period of Christmas preliminaries but a season in itself, with its own integrity and its own announcement."[1]

The Glory of God's Coming

> Mine eyes have seen the glory of the coming of the Lord,
> He is trampling out his vintage where the grapes of wrath are stored.

Abolitionist Julia Ward Howe gave us these words. For Howe, the Civil War was the apocalypse, the coming of God. Hers was the awful realization that God had called the nation to judgment for tolerating the enslavement and dehumanization of millions of blacks. "As he died to make men holy, let us die to make men free! While God is marching on." In her vision, the death of the Christ and the sacrifices of the war dead fused together.

She saw the end of slavery as truly a new beginning, the end of an age of degradation and despair and the start of an era of equality and hope. When the conflict ended, Mrs. Howe was so moved by the plight of war widows that she became a major figure in the women's suffrage movement.

---

[1] *Preaching the New Common Lectionary, Advent, Christmas, Epiphany, Year A* (Nashville, TN: Abingdon Press, 1986), p. 19.

The point is that Julia Ward Howe looked for the coming of God not in the hereafter but in the crises and opportunities of the present moment. She knew what Christians of all ages have realized—that the kingdom of God is just as truly here and now as it is yet to come.

Mrs. Howe completely agreed with the Apostle Paul, who taught that the kingdom of God is at hand. In his words,

> *The night is nearly over; the day is almost here. So let us put aside the deeds of darkness and put on the armor of light. (Romans 13:12)*

God's Coming Here and Now

What do we need armor for? Not as fireproofing against the day of judgment, but for now. Protect yourself against yourself. With the sense of urgent expectancy characteristic of the church in the first decades of its history, Paul declares "The Lord is coming." But the fact that the church has a history, that the end was not as close as Paul surmised, teaches us the lesson that the struggle that we face is not apocalyptic—not at the end of the world or the end of the present evil age, but right before our eyes. It is a battle between two life-styles, two ways of living in the present. Those who do the deeds of darkness experience the wrath of God not as a far-off torment but as an anguish, an emptiness, a falling apart, a coming to naught of everything even in the midst of the greatest apparent success. As the author of the Fourth Gospel proclaims, "The one who has the Son has life—here and now, and the one who does not have the Son does not have life but God's wrath rests upon him—here and now." (John 3:35)

> *The night is nearly over; the day is almost here. So let us put aside the deeds of darkness and put on the armor of light. (Romans 13:12)*

Paul could have chosen any number of vices in his description of the children of darkness. He settled for orgies, drunkenness, sexual immorality, debauchery, dissension, and jealousy. And he never watched a soap opera! Some of the vices listed by Paul were no doubt the sins of "those people," individuals outside the church, outside the calling to be God's people. But lest Christians pat themselves on the back for being better than anyone, Paul includes the all too human failings all too common among God's elect—dissension and jealousy.

From this passage, one could come to the fallacious assumption that virtue is the avoidance of vice. That being a good person is the same thing as not being a bad person. To set the matter straight, one should read chapter 6 of Paul's letter to Ephesians. Once again the motif of armor is central, the metaphor here elaborately developed. Says Paul,

> *Finally, be strong in the Lord and in his mighty power. Put on the full armor of God so that you can take your stand against the devil's schemes. . . . Stand firm then, with the belt of truth buckled around your waist, with the breastplate of righteousness in place, and with your feet fitted with the readiness that comes from the gospel of peace. In addition to all this, take up the shield of faith, with which you can extinguish all the flaming arrows of the evil one. Take the helmet of salvation and the sword of the Spirit, which is the word of God. And pray in the Spirit on all occasions with all kinds of prayers and requests. (Ephesians 6: 10–18)*

Equipped for God's Coming

The children of light are not perfect, not sinless, not beyond reproach. What sets them apart from the children of darkness is their superior equipment: their willingess to tell the truth and have the truth told to them, their commitment to a just world, their readiness to respond where love requires, their faith, their openness to the saving work of God in their lives and in their midst, the intensity with which they listen to the word of God and for the word of God, and their willingness to accept a God who accepts them.

Being a child of light means telling the truth—keeping one's word. Being a child of light means preparing oneself body, mind, and spirit for the task of being an instrument of justice, of God's righteousness. Being a child of light means cleaning up one's own act and being a model to others.

Wearing the armor of light, living a Christian life, is a matter of discipline, training, and conditioning. One can no more become a championship caliber Christian than he or she can be a world-class swimmer or tennis player or golfer by merely entertaining sincere feelings and being inoffensive.

Ray Stedman, the pastor of Peninsula Bible Church in Palo Alto, California, once asked a nine-year-old boy what he wanted to be when he grew up. The boy answered, "A returned missionary." As Ken points out,

> the boy looked ahead not to the years of graduate study, not to the years of separation from home and loved ones, not to the months and years in steaming jungles or parched deserts—but to the final state of recognition and acclaim. It's hard to skip the preliminaries and still reach a final goal. The musician's finger exercises, the Olympic athlete's daily push-ups, and the Christian's daily stint in the prayer closet can't be bypassed.[2]

The Christian life requires that time and effort be directed to discerning the word of God as it is spoken to each of us in the Bible, in our personal lives of prayer, and through our participation in the life and sacraments of a local Christian community.

> *The night is nearly over; the day is almost here. So let us put aside the deeds of darkness and put on the armor of light. (Romans 13:12)*

Our eyes have seen the glory of the coming of the Lord! Because we have prepared ourselves to respond, we do respond. In those moments when you and I have no choice but to decide, no choice but to do with our whole being what is right, what is human, what is humane, what is just, what love requires—in those moments the Christ meets us face to face. Our eyes behold his glory. He has come.

Amen.

—LDS

[1270 words]
[13 minutes]

---

[2] *Parables, Etc.*, August 1981.

Sermon 72

Date: First Sunday of Advent, Year B

Texts:
Isaiah 64:1-9
Psalm 80:1–7, 17-19
1 Corinthians 1:3–9
Mark 13:24–37

Theme: Advent is a season of darkness and a season of light.
Subject: Darkness, Advent

Title: A Season of Darkness, A Season of Light

1994

[choir]

O Come, Thou Dayspring, come and cheer
Our spirits by Thine advent here;
O drive away the shades of night
And pierce the clouds and bring us light.

Rejoice! Rejoice! Emmanuel
Shall come to thee, O Israel.

Advent is a season of darkness and a season of light.

The days are growing shorter and shorter. There is a chill in the air that cuts right through us. And sometimes the darkness takes hold of our spirits like an intruder grabbing us by the throat. We can bundle up against the cold. We can set bright blazes in our fireplaces. We can festoon our homes with multicolored lights, jolly Santa Clauses, and festive decorations of all sorts. But the darkness is always there, waiting like a hungry beast of prey, threatening to devour us.

For the thousandth time, we can watch *It's a Wonderful Life* and *A Christmas Carol*, attend performances of Handel's Messiah and The Nutcracker Suite, and still not escape the lurking beast.

O Come, O Come, Emmanuel. Come, God, be with us. Come, God, take away our depression, our frustration, our disappointment. Take away the bittersweet nostalgia—the memories of holidays past, Yuletides that we have romanticized and recreated in our memories. Take away the expectations that torment and pain us now.

"'Tis the season to be jolly. . . ." Why is it such hard work? And what does our joviality cover over? It is so easy to project our inner needs on others—and it is not a bad thing to do. If we give our last dollar and spend ourselves into debt for the sake of others, maybe the darkness will lift. Maybe we can sing "Joy to the World!" and feel it ourselves.

A Season of Self-Examination

Advent is so much like Lent. Its call to self-examination is as unavoidable. The diversions, frills, commercializings, folk customs are so similar. The temptation is the same—to try to avoid the darkness of the season and the darkness of our spirits by turning life into one endless round of wassailing and Mardi Gras-ing, a perpetual Miller Time.

But the beast of reality has us in his jaws. And we quickly learn that before we can enter into life, we must first pass through death. Before the light of the eternal flame may blaze in our souls, we must pass through the death of illusion and false hope.

Advent is a season of darkness and a season of light. Advent confirms our worst fears. Look around. This is a dying world. The plucky evergreens cannot disguise the facts. The world is dying morally, spiritually, and physically. All we acquire, achieve, earn, borrow, or steal is like so much sand slipping through our fingers. The more tenaciously we hold on to it, the sooner it is gone. Ashes to ashes, dust to dust.

Advent is a season of darkness and a season of light. A new world is coming. The light is coming into our lives and nothing we do can extinguish it. The king is almost here. We fret and worry and feel frustrated. And our frustration is appropriate. It is exactly where we should be, what we should feel on the eve of his coming. He is not coming to make us secure in business as usual. He is not coming to set his seal of approval on how we have managed our world. He is coming not only to comfort the afflicted but to afflict the comfortable.

He is coming to disrupt our lives and our world. He is coming to demand that we change. He is coming to demand that we lay aside our egos and our hurt feelings and our "why don't you live up to my expectations?"

We anticipate that God's coming is bad news to "bad people," to those who exploit, harm, and abuse others. Aren't we the "good guys" as individuals and as a nation? But the one who comes is not going to pat us on the head. He is coming to insist that we unflinchingly reexamine our values, standards, and attitudes. He is coming to ask us what we have done with his creation. He is coming to ask us what we have done with our responsibilities as parents and guides of the young. He is coming to ask us what we have done with the intellects, dreams, and aspirations with which he has gifted us. He is coming to ask us what we have done for the poor, the needy, and the newcomer in our midst. He is coming to ask us why we have tolerated injustice, why we have not stood with the powerless.

Advent is a season of darkness and light. The tunnel of our everyday lives is long and dark, but there is light at the end of the tunnel. Focus on the light and the darkness gives way. God is with you in this tunnel. God is at the end of your way. Jesus is about to be born in our midst and in our lives.

The Hope that Banishes Darkness

The hope that banishes darkness is not sold in the malls. It is not advertised in the newspapers or on TV. It cannot be found in family gatherings or in garishly wrapped presents under our Christmas trees. The hope that banishes darkness is so close to us that if it were a living being we would feel its breath.

For Christians, Christmas is the most dangerous time of year. Let that Christ child be born in you and you and your world will never be the same. Let God's rule of justice and compassion reign in your heart and it may cost you more than you would ever contemplate paying. Let the light come into your life and you may discard the lies and excuses of today as you once gave up the toys of childhood. Then you would be fully alive and fully responsible.

Zechariah, the father of John the Baptist, looked forward to the birth of his son and the coming of the one to whom his son would point with these words: "the rising sun will come to us from heaven to shine on those living in darkness and in the shadow of death, to guide our feet into the path of peace." (Luke 1:78–79) The path begins when we stop denying the darkness, when we stop trying to fill up the emptiness. The path begins with the shattering of all we treasure—including our misconceptions, our prejudices, and our expectations.

Darkness, it turns out, is not our enemy but our guide and our deliverer. For the darkness blots out "the restrictive forms," "the shapes of oppression and paralysis that beset us and keep us from living half of what we would."[1] Advent is an odd time, a time that we both welcome and dread.[2]

Come, O Come, Emmanuel. Walk with us through the darkness and the darkness shall be our light.

[choir]

O Come, Thou Dayspring, come and cheer
Our spirits by Thine advent here;
O drive away the shades of night
And pierce the clouds and bring us light.

Rejoice! Rejoice! Emmanuel
Shall come to thee, O Israel.

Amen.

—LDS

[1100 words]
[11 minutes]

Sermon 73

Date: Third Sunday of Advent, Year C

Texts:
Zephaniah 3:14–20
Isaiah 12:2–6
Philippians 4:4–7
Luke 3:7–18 1994

Theme: Outrageous hope is one of the core convictions of Advent; outrageous hope—beyond all reasonable expectations.
Subject: Hope

Title: Outrageous Hope, Unseemly Preparation

The Prophet Zephaniah assures his people: There is a mighty one coming! Your suffering will not be in vain. Your deliverance will be a cause for rejoicing. "Sing, O daughter of Zion; shout, O Israel! Rejoice and exult with all your heart, O daughter of Jerusalem!" This sounds like religious cheerleading, and would mean nothing more than positive reinforcement if it wasn't for the context of the prophecy. Zephaniah is speaking from the Babylonian captivity, to a people who watched their temple destroyed, their religious structures dismantled, their cultic practices desecrated, and their people deported to a foreign land. They were a people of no future, and this was an outrageous prophecy of hope.

---

[1] *Proclamation 3: Aids for Interpreting the Lessons of the Church Year, Advent-Christmas* (Philadelphia: Fortress Press, 1984), p. 14.

[2] Ibid.

Outrageous Hope

Outrageous hope is one of the core convictions of Advent; outrageous hope—beyond all reasonable expectations.

I went looking for a really outrageous story for an illustration, and I was having a hard time until I went shopping this week and there it was right in front of me at the end of the checkout counter. There sat a tabloid with one outrageous story after another. Notice that the more reasonable stories start out in small print, the more incredulous the premise the larger the print. Here are some examples: "Doc Weds Girl He Delivered 21 Years Ago"—that's understandable. "Healer Cures Impotence by Telephone"—possible. "How the Duke's Ghost Helps U.S. Presidents to Govern America"—so that's the problem. Slightly bigger print reads "Mom Puts Roast in Crib—Baby in Microwave." I read the story, the child is OK, but I'm not sure about its future. Second largest headline is a little more gruesome: "Woman Eats 24 Large Pizzas in 10 Hours—And Explodes"—disgusting. But the headline that caught my eye was "Explorers Find Adam and Eve: Biblical Pair Still in Garden of Eden." Outrageous, all of it.

The outrageousness of the tabloid comes from lies, or, at best, the clever stretching of truth. "Adam and Eve," it turns out, are a primitive tribe in the, until now, unexplored regions of deepest Africa. Of course, there are no pictures, no corroborating evidence from the band of Australian explorers, but facts are not important here.

Joy Through Faith

The outrageous joy of the Scriptures, however, comes from facing hard reality, and yet discovering that the joy is just waiting to be received. It comes as a surprise completely unexpected, and can only be assumed by faith. During World War II a Jewish girl escaped from Warsaw and hid in a cave. She died there just before the war ended. The following inscription was found on the wall: "I believe in the sun, even when it is not shining. I believe in love, even when not feeling it. I believe in God, even when he is silent."

Dutch theologian Johannes Halkendijk shares another story from that war. During the Nazi occupation, a Dutch resistance group was formed. Almost immediately, the Nazis planned to deport Jewish children to concentration camps. One arm of the resistance decided to do what they could to save these children.

A group of three hundred people, children and resistance members, was assembled and went into hiding. What they didn't realize was that someone in their own group had betrayed them to the Nazis. They were found and taken to a detention center, from which they heard they were not going to a concentration camp but to a crematorium.

When the day of deportation came, both Christian resistance fighters and Jewish children boarded the cattle cars together to face the same fate. Halkendijk did not say how long the trip lasted. But one morning, just after sunrise, word was passed among the three hundred that they were to get out of the now stopped train.

But instead of finding themselves surrounded by guards, they were standing in the middle of a pasture. They were not in Germany, but in Switzerland. The train, in the very act of taking them to their death, had been liberated in the night. These three hundred people were not the recipients of death, but were surprised by a new life.

Against the Rules

Even with examples such as these, this conviction of outrageous hope violates our reason and our modernism. We have imagined our world closed and all the pieces are already in place. To speak of God coming as a completely new event is theologically primitive and intellectually embarrassing. Things don't happen like that in our world.

In Zephaniah we have a staggering poem of promise. It is God's own self who comes. Twice he says, "the Lord is in your midst." It is God's own self who comes in power, and the coming of God is entirely good news. The message is that while you have become victims of political caprice, God, who is faithful, will "restore our fortunes" (v. 20). God will take situations of disaster and displacement (v. 19) and transform them into a reality of liberation, health, and homecoming.

Good News in Tragedy

A few years ago in Armenia, a disaster of incredible proportion occurred. Whole villages crumbled, families were burned, tens of thousands of people were dead. This was a national disaster, but it has the dimensions of biblical myth. We are caught in the moment of decision. Nations which have been poised with weapons of obliteration are drawing together to assist the human needs of the disaster victims. Enemies are feeling compassion—and this is at least a twinge of hope. This is a hint of the good news under the hard reality of life.

How can I say "good news" in the face of such tragedy? Good news is not the same as happy news. The news—hoped for, witnessed, remembered—is that the power of God has come mightily into situations of wretchedness and made things new. The news is about the newness wrought by the power of God. Notice that Zephanaiah's poem does not explain or tell how newness happens. It invites us to reckon with the inscrutable, inexplicable power of God that cannot be harnessed or resisted by us.

The good news is that no matter what your situation "God is in your midst." Or as Paul says, "The Lord is at hand . . . [so that] in any and all circumstances I have learned the secret of facing plenty and hunger, abundance and want. I can do all things through him who strengthens me."

This good news is an outrageous claim because it doesn't sound like good news, that is, happy news, and it comes with unseemly preparation. An earthquake in Armenia is not happy news, but if out of the wretchedness, the human family is able to learn some new ways to model working together in compassion for one another, it will be profoundly good news, especially if it can help break the cycle of hatred between peoples.

The coming of God's new consciousness may be a terrible threat or a wondrous gift. It depends on whether one is ready. This is the lesson of John the Baptist. His "good news" doesn't sound like good news at all—more like judgment. Here are all these people from the cities suddenly getting religion and coming to be baptized and what does he say: "You brood of vipers! Who told you to flee before the wrath to come."

This is bad news, but it gets our attention. Clarence Jordan, in his Cotton Patch version of Luke makes this passage very clear as he translates it into the southern vernacular.[1] "Here's what [John] was saying to the crowds who were coming out to get dipped by him: "You sons of snakes, who put the heat on you to run from the fury about to break over your heads?" You must give some proof that you have had a change of heart. And don't start patting one another on the back with that "we-goodwhite-people" stuff, because I'm telling you that if God wants to, he can make white people out of this pile of rocks. Already the axe is lying at the taproot of the trees, and every tree that doesn't perform some worthwhile function is chopped down and burned up."

Our passage ends: "So, with many other exhortations, he preached good news to the people." This is good news? It is serious good news. The lesson concerns getting ready for the coming of God in Christ who will change the order of what is important.

---

[1] Jordan, Clarence, *The Cottonpatch Version of Luke and Acts* (New York: Association Press, 1962), p. 22.

What are we to do then? John is asked this question three times by three different groups of people about their specific situation. "What shall we do?" To the multitude he answers, share. Some obviously have more than enough clothes or food while others have none. Life goods must be redistributed. To the tax collectors, John answers, stop exploiting. Tax collectors, who worked on commission, were notorious for exploitive economic practices. We may take this instruction as a mandate not only for our private economics, but for the ways we participate in oppressive policies that work for some to the disadvantage of others. To the soldiers, who were mercenaries of a foreign occupation force, John answers, end the brutality, the violence, intimidation, and deception.

If you are preparing yourself to receive Christ in your heart, then do something about sharing, stopping exploitation, and ending brutality. If Christ makes a difference it must show in the fruits of your behavior. Pay attention to the Good News. For whatever gets your attention gets you!

Giving Our Attention

Saint Paul urges us to focus on the good things of God, even as John urges us to choose the good ways of God. We will be pulled by those good things into the focus of Christ. Thus we will be drawn into Christ-likeness. Advent says Christ is out ahead of us drawing us by attraction into the future, and when we are finally at a place where we can see with Christ as our lens, we will see things clearly. (1 Corinthians 13:12)

What is the source of our joy, then? How can we receive the peace of God? What gives us the serenity to accept life as it is presented to us, whether we "are abused, or abound . . . in plenty and hunger, abundance, and want."

It's all a question of what gets our attention. Give your attention to Christ and joy, peace and contentment come. This is the Good News.

Amen.

—W. Matthew Broadbent

[1858 words]
[19 minutes]

❦ *Sermon 74*

❦ *Date:* Second Sunday of Advent, Year C 1994

Texts:
Malachi 3:1–4
Psalm 126
Philippians 1:3–11
Luke 3:1–6

Theme: Christmas is a time for nostalgia. Advent is the season of preparedness, encouraging us to do the work of repentance, of turning to the God of our future, in hope, faith—trust.
Subject: Repentance

❦ *Title:* A Deep Yearning

Nostalgia

Christmas is a time for nostalgia. It is a time to remember when feelings were pure and being a child was the standard of goodness. Christmas, the season of giving and surprising, and loving and cherishing, may be the one time when the greatest number of people feel the greatest degree of acceptance for just being themselves. The rest of the year we compete with each other for our place in the scheme of things. We are judged and found wanting.

Christmas is a time to remember back to when we were not judged, just loved, not found wanting, but given toys, and socks, and scarfs, and useless gifts that wouldn't work past the Christmas vacation, just for the pleasure of it. No wonder we yearn to return to the attitude of a child at this time of the year. We become nostalgic for what was.

I have a special memory at Christmastime. You remember the poem, "'Twas the night before Christmas and all through the house . . ." I grew up in that house. It wasn't the actual house of Clement Clark Moore, but it was like all of the illustrations I have ever seen for that poem: nestled in the southern Connecticut countryside, snow on the roof, a fire in the fireplace, and the Christmas tree set up in the front bay window. Christmas breads baked in the old oven that stood on tall cast iron legs in the kitchen, and underneath Dinah suckled her kittens in a box my brother and I had prepared.

On Christmas Eve, we would sneak down the stairs and peak through the banister, just like they do in a Disney film, and we would watch Mom and Dad finish decorating the tree until they caught us and chased us back to bed. It was the longest and most exquisite night of the year. It still is.

I only lived in that house for the first four years of my life, but it still sits within me like a jewel, an ideal I wish to return to.

I wonder if the past has that kind of hold on you as well. It is as if the special memory is a reference point for our lives. There is this ideal home, which we left long ago and to which we have a deep yearning to return, back to the days when it just felt right, and safe and good.

This is the purpose of tradition, to help us fix in practice those things that recall the past. This is particularly true at Christmas. Sing the carols, light the lights, do it exactly as you did it last year, because we don't want to change a thing. We want to recapture that feeling we once had, even though we may have outgrown it; we want to recapture the memory of "home."

Changing the Rules

Change anything and we may be in trouble of ruining the whole mood. A couple of years ago my wife and I were busy and stressed on Christmas Eve. We got the presents all wrapped and under the tree early, so we could come home from the late-night service, relax, and get some sleep. We decided the children were old enough that we didn't have to play that old game of hiding presents and then putting them under the tree after they were asleep. In the morning they woke up to exactly the same number of presents as they saw when they went to bed.

We have never heard the end of that terrible mistake. We ruined Christmas that year. At first I thought, "What selfish kids, not to be satisfied with what they received," until they explained it had nothing to do with the number of gifts, but with the magic of being surprised in the morning. Santa Claus didn't come that year, Bah-humbug.

Tradition keeps us from losing touch with that first, purest, and best feeling. It locks the memory in place, so we can play it over and over again.

The terrible truth is—there is no real returning to that home of the past, because the past no longer exists. I went back to that house of my childhood and was dismayed to see what people had done with it over the years. It was so small, as if all those who had lived there had eaten it from the inside out and the outer skin had shrunk to fit what was left. It wasn't the home I imagined.

Advent is a season of returning. Many people return to church, to check things out, see if it is the same, because of a yearning to reclaim what was given up in their youth—a sense of values. The popular political atmosphere has capitalized on this idea of returning to "traditional American values." We have a cultural yearning to return to, if not the way it was, then the way it should have been.

In his day, John the Baptist was appealing to the same yearning for the way it was. Luke places John in the middle of the power brokers of the age, both political (Caesar, Pilate, Herod, and his brother Phillip) and religious (Annas, Caiaphas). As Brueggemann points out, "This is real-life dangerous stuff." It was in this milieu that "the Word of God came to John . . . in the wilderness; and he went into all the region about the Jordan, preaching a baptism of repentance for the forgiveness of sins."

We are told that John headed a popular movement. People streamed to him from the big cities of Jerusalem and Jericho. They had a feeling that if they could just get their religious values straightened out, if they could get back to the roots of their faith, they would free themselves of the oppression of the Romans. God would reestablish the Davidic kingdom, and Israel could reclaim its independence and identity.

This may have been the same thought, this deep yearning for the way it was, in the minds of the exiles in Babylon to whom Malachi was speaking. He prophesied a homecoming led by the messiah, "behold, he is coming . . . the messenger of the covenant in whom you delight . . ." "We are going to return to the way is was," they might have thought . "Repent, turn back to your old faith in God." "Give me that old time religion, if it was good enough for Ma and Pa Levi, it'll be good enough for me."

Redeeming the Past

Unfortunately, what is true of our memories of Christmas is true of our spiritual life, and is true of our historical reality. You can't go back, because it doesn't exist anymore. The past is past. It is gone. You can't reclaim it, and there is only one way to redeem it.

You can't even reclaim it in your memory because memory is always a present interpretation of what you thought was in the past, and some of us are very creative interpreters.

There is only one way to redeem the past, and that is to commit yourself to the future. And this can be very frightening and dangerous, because you don't know what to expect. This is the warning of Malachi: "But who can endure the day of his coming, and who can stand when he appears? For he is like a refiner's fire, and like fuller's soap; he will sit as a refiner and purifier of silver, and he will purify the Sons of Levi, and refine them like gold and silver." The old ore will become the new gold; it will be like that of the days of old, but it will be a new thing.

When John quotes Isaiah, he is saying something similar, for Isaiah, too, is speaking to the returning exiles: "Prepare the way of the Lord, make his paths straight." You are returning to the old land, but a new thing is happening.

And this is the redemptive message of Advent. You are hearing an old story and you are interpreting it through your childhood memories, but you are facing a new situation. Repent! Turn from your sinfulness, that is, anything that separates you from God, and turn to a new direction.

Now, repentance means to "turn away from" that which is wrong and sinful, and necessarily refers to something that was done in the past. Repentance would seem to imply that we return to the past and correct our error, and commit ourselves never to do that again. But if we do this we will always be frustrated because the past is not real. It is gone. You can't replay it again.

There is only one way to turn—the future, and it is the most difficult turning because we can't know what is out there. We can only live in faith, in the trust that God is there already waiting to welcome us home.

Advent is the season of preparedness, encouraging us to do the work of repentance, of turning to the God of our future, in hope, faith—trust. It is a season to recognize our deep yearning for that pure life of the spirit we have glimpsed in the past. It is a reminder of the hard work of turning our attention from the comfortable memory of the past to the risk and danger and the opportunity of the future. It is a season to ponder who this one is for whom we wait. It is a season to become pregnant with expectation as we prepare to give birth to Christ, and thus experience the joy that is waiting for us. Then we shall sing like the psalmist:

"When the Lord restored the fortunes of Zion, we were like those who dream.

Then our mouths were filled with laughter, and our tongue with shouts of joy; The Lord has done great things for us; we are glad." (Psalm 126)

Repent! Rejoice! God is our future. Believe it! This is real.

Amen.

—W. Matthew Broadbent

[1660 words]
[17 minutes]

Sermon 75

Date: Third Sunday of Advent, Year B

Texts:
Isaiah 61:1–4, 8–11
Luke 1:46b–55
1 Thessalonians 5:16–24
John 1:6–8, 19–28

Theme: Don't wait for life to begin. Wait only for God's coming.
Subject: Waiting

Title: Dr. God's Waiting Room

Advent is a time of waiting and a time of hope.

Mother Earth waits for the coming of longer days, the return of the sun, the emergence of new life.

Humankind waits for the coming of justice, the passing away of tyranny and oppression. The hungry wait for food, the homeless for shelter, the unemployed for jobs. Prisoners wait for release, orphans and victims of circumstances wait for the embrace of a loving family. Victims of prejudice and hate wait for a fair chance, an opportunity. The weak and the poor wait for humane treatment.

You and I wait for the lifting of lonesomeness and sadness from our hearts. "I know what family Christmas gatherings are all about," a young woman said to me years ago. "It's when all the lonely people get together so that instead of being lonely apart they can be lonely together."

Each of us in his or her own life is waiting. That's what life is all about—waiting. When does life begin? A priest, a rabbi, and an Episcopal minister discussed this question at a Rotary luncheon.

"We believe that life begins at conception," said the priest.

"I would argue that life begins at birth," added the rabbi.

The Episcopalian said nothing until he was pressed by the others. "Well," he said, "for me life begins when the children go to college, my mother-in-law moves to Florida, and the dog dies!"

And like the Episcopal clergyman we are always waiting to live. We wait as though life cannot begin for us until we graduate from high school or college, until our first child is born, until we get that big promotion, until the children are married, until the house is paid for, until retirement. . .

I know about waiting. I have lived much of my life as though I were a patient in Dr. God's waiting room.

I don't always know what I can do about injustice, crime, stupidity, and greed. I don't always know what I can do about world hunger, global pollution, and the thousand natural shocks that flesh is heir to. But I know what I can do about my own waiting. I can wait hopefully, realizing "I know not what the future holds, but I know who holds the future."

And I can live expectantly and fully as a member of a community of faith. I can wait with those with whom I enjoy waiting. And as I wait, I can comfort those who also wait. I can comfort them with a dollar here and a kind word there, with a joke here and a hug there, with a protest here and a vote there.

Don't wait to live. You can start that right now, this very moment. If you must wait, wait for God. Expect him in this season and at all times. And he will come.

Amen.

—LDS

[478 words]
[5 minutes]

Sermon 76

Date: First Sunday of Advent, Year C

Texts:
Jeremiah 33:14–16
Psalm 25:1–10
1 Thessalonians 3:9–13
Luke 21:25–36

Theme: Advent is a time for reflection and self-assessment. The gift of Advent is the gift of hope
Subject: Advent, self-assessment, hope

Title: Jeopardizing the Present: Seizing the Future

We are in love with technology, overly impressed with our achievements, imagining that our ability to create new things, and manage our lives, are somehow signs of our well-being. We are tempted to conclude, "It doesn't get any better than this."

Even when we imagine what the future might hold we are enchanted with the idea of technological improvement. Last week Star Wars played on network television. Here is a film about the future, but has anything changed? There are new and amazing spaceships and lasers, and cosmic communications, that's true, but, as far as humanity is concerned, or what poses as humanoid life, it appears that life has regressed. Gone are the democracies of the world, and back are princes and empires, and soldier–statesmen called "Jedi" who are nothing more than medieval knights with a nuclear power pack, or samurai warriors with their own brutal code of ethics. The technology has changed, but the spiritual life has been reduced to the knowledge of a special cult.

Science fiction doesn't so much show the future as it describes our present attitudes. We are in love with technology, think of it as savior, and thus desperately hold to the way things are. We resist change. Einstein said: "The unleased power of the atom has changed everything save our modes of thinking . . ." We have the technology of the nuclear age and the morality of the stone age.

We resist change in the way we think, concentrating on the things we make, rather than on who we are. Fourteenth-century mystic, Eckhart said: "One must not always think so much about what one should do, but rather what one should be. Our works do not ennoble us; but we ennoble our works."

Even in this brave new age of rapidly escalating technological knowledge, we resist change when it counts. We begrudge the intrusion of what is new, and we assume a posture of defensiveness to guard our way of life.

Seeing Things as They Are

Advent is an invitation to see the world differently. Advent invites us not to be so enmeshed with the present, not to be so overly impressed with things as they are, not to be so committed to and defensive of all the current arrangements. Advent is an assertion that all our present stands under judgment. The present will end—and we cannot stop it from ending. It will be displaced by another arrangement of life that God will give. Advent is an invitation to live precisely at the juncture where the present is jeopardized and God's new future starts to emerge.

Tolstoy wrote The Kingdom of God Is Within You: "A Christian cannot promise to do or not do a given thing at a given moment, for he cannot know what the law of love, which is the rule of his life, may require of him at that moment." A friend of mine put it this way, "You can't write the end of the story before you experience it." It is an uncomfortable place to be, but it is precisely where we are asked to stand, between the judgment of the present and the promise of God's future.

In Jeremiah we hear that God promises a new reality, shaped as righteousness and justice. This theme of righteousness and justice is central to the biblical witness. Righteousness and justice are the two legs upon which the law stands. It is a vision of new relations between God and the world, between neighbor and neighbor, between human creatures and all of creation. In other words, it is a change of the heart. This new way of relating is one in which there is no threat or fear or hurt or exploitation. God will overcome the power of evil, destructiveness, and death. All will "dwell secure" (v. 16) with no one afraid of any other. And this new age will be called "The Lord is our righteousness."

The teaching of Jesus speaks clearly about this promise of a new day. The newness of Jeremiah—which sounds so wonderful—will not come easily because it is drastic. It will not be welcomed, because it is a threat to all our present arrangements. We won't even give up what we know is proven, destructive behavior. It is safer to live with our known misery, than to risk potential joy.

The parable of the fig tree is a way of speaking of the nearness of judgment and the time for change. Jesus and the early church believed that the kingdom of God, the new power arrangement, the establishment of God's new right relations is very near and will happen soon. I'd push that thought a little further. Jesus says in Luke 17:21: "The Kingdom of God is in the midst of you." It is already present, growing like a tree in the yard. When you become conscious of it, you can pick of its fruit and be nourished and have life. If you remain unconscious you will die for want of the food that is of greatest importance.

Getting Ready for the New

Advent is about an emerging consciousness, in which we ponder the newness that is near, a newness that threatens us and for which we must be ready.

Advent is about readiness. "Take heed to yourselves lest your hearts be weighed down with self-indulgence (dissipation and drunkenness) and with the cares of this life (v. 34)." This is not an inappropriate warning this time of the year. We may consider such self-indulgence as consumerism that reduces all life and all persons to commodities. We may consider the "cares of this life" to refer, among other things, to economic anxiety, our mad pursuit of profit, security, affluence, and control.

Advent is a time for reflection and self-assessment. It is a time for taking stock of how enmeshed we are in modes of self-indulgence and how overly impressed we are with our ability to take care of ourselves. In 1987 when President Reagan threw the switch for the national Christmas tree, he said: "For every unemployed there are nine of us who do have jobs." Had he left it there it would have been a cold and callous remark, but with typical charm the President went on to say, "How about those of us who are employed making sure that those who are not will nevertheless have a Merry Christmas?" The least this season can cause us to do is reflect and be sensitive to those who are not included in the blessings of the season.

What becomes discouraging in our reflection, however, is that a rising economic condition does not necessarily mean rising levels of compassion. In an article in the *San Jose Mercury News*, it was pointed out the "Per capita giving (in the Silicon Valley) is much lower than other parts of the country—and this is one of the richest." Wealth is not a good benchmark of benevolence. Families making $10,000 or less give almost twice the percentage of income of families making $50,000 to $75,000.

We are invited to "take heed" (v. 24). We are invited to "watch and pray" (v. 36), to wake up and become conscious of the signs of God's reign, and submit to its newness.

Jeremiah focuses on a new king (the branch of David's line). Jesus focuses on the coming "son of man." The church sees both motifs fulfilled in the recognition of Jesus as Christ child. Jesus is "the sign of embodiment of God's new age of righteousness and justice," writes Brueggemann, "The gift of right relations, right distribution of power, right attitudes and actions of caring. The rule of Jesus makes new behavior possible."

Advent asks us to consider the validity of God's promises. If we accept them on faith, which means we trust in God, we could receive a new world, a new set of relations, a fresh possibility. We could start again. But that means being willing to face the judgment of the present systems, disengage from old habits of defensiveness, and join in new practices of compassion.

It's a dream, I know. But it is God's dream, and we are part of that dream. If we watch and wait and pray we may become conscious of the small signs of God's life in our midst. We may see the tree and eat of the fruit of God's love.

This is the gift of Advent: the gift of hope.

Amen.

—W. Matthew Broadbent

[1435 words]
[14 minutes]

Sermon 77

Date: Third Sunday of Advent, Any Year
or Christmas Eve, Any Year

Texts:
Christmas Eve
Isaiah 9:2–7
Psalm 96
Titus 2:11–14
Luke 2:1–20

Theme: The Good News is true: God is for us. God is with us. God is in us. God is among us. And we are thankful.
Subject: Christmas

Title: Until Christmas

Tip

> Conclude your sermons with three or four short sentences. This makes it easy for the congregation to remember your main point and carry it away with them.

Christmas is almost upon me. There are only a few days left for me to think about how best to regather our scattered family, to worry about giving and getting, to sort out any accumulated holiday hurts, and to deal with my well-earned weariness. I am looking forward to the Christmas Eve Eucharist at our small church, to those few quiet minutes for contemplating the mystery of our faith. I believe that this observance of the Eucharist only minutes before the day that celebrates the birth of King Jesus is at once the most sublime and paradoxical act that can ever be performed. For by our sharing of the Lord's Supper, we are uniting our joy and gratitude for the coming of the true king with our sorrow and repentance that for each of us he must suffer and die.

With God, all things are possible, for God is the almighty, everlasting, perfect, holy, and divine ruler of the universe. His power and knowledge are limitless. Until the coming of the Christ. Until the birth of his son. Until the sovereign Lord of Creation surrenders himself to the state and fate of humankind. From the very moment that the Christ child is born, God lays aside his omnipotence and places the fulfillment of his purposes in our hands. The initiative remains his. But by our response we may accomplish or frustrate the divine plan for our lives, our loved ones, our society, or our world.

Many years ago when I was a teenager, some friends and I were in the observation tower of the then tallest structure in Chicago, the Prudential Building. As we peered down at the automobiles shrunken by the distance to the size of toys and the pedestrians to the dimensions of scurrying ants, the most religious of my companions remarked: "This must be how we look to God." His innocent words expressed a sense of childlike awe and wonder. But they also ignored the message of Christmas. God is no emperor of an intergalactic federation who monitors us with refined instruments of scientific scrutiny. He is with us now and for all time—closer to each of us than we are to ourselves. He is present in the life of each Christian—striving to perfect you and me in love, luring us into the discovery of what we can be, seducing us, tricking us into sharing, caring, loving, and being loved.

Most of the time, we do not respond to one another as human beings but as categories. I put you into some hard and fast category and respond not to you but to my own mental construct about you. And you may do the same to me. When I am introduced to a stranger, he asks me, "What is it that you do?" And whatever I reply becomes the basis for 90 percent of all the thoughts or feelings he will ever entertain toward me. If I say, "I am a minister," he will be careful not to tell off-color jokes in my presence, apologize for having missed church last Sunday, and be sure that I am not invited to his next cocktail party. If I were to say that I were retired, he would want to know "retired from what?" so that he would be able to pigeonhole who I was and what I was like as a person. If he could not comfortably work me into a preestablished category, he would always feel unsettled in my presence.

The Chinese have a saying which they use to explain prejudice and hatred toward others: "Call a dog a bad name and shoot it." Once you have categorized someone, you are no longer responsible to treat him as a human being. We characterize our enemies as insects, animals, or things and then feel justified to exploit them or take their lives. When someone disagrees with us or acts in a manner of which we do not approve, we declare that person "sick" or "crazy" or "brainwashed." From that point on we can react to the label and pay no attention to the reality of the person. But the ministry and example of the Christ challenges every assumption as to who is good and who is evil, who is worthy of our caring and who is not. Jesus enjoyed the company of the most despised of his countrymen. That does not mean that he spurned such conventionally upright individuals as Nicodemus and Joseph of Arimethea. He knew men and women of every class and condition, knew them inside and out, and was impressed not by their titles, stations, and positions, but only by who they were.

The lesson to be learned is that when I respond to you and you respond to me without prejudice and preconception, we are both changed. We know and are united with one another. We know and are restored to ourselves. Where any life touches another life deeply, each person is able to be who he or she is and be responded to as who he or she is. When to you I become a real flesh-and-blood person and not just the categories in which you place me, you will find out who you are and reveal it. And when I respond fully to you, I will find out who I am and reveal it. As we noted earlier, through such openness and only through such openness can the healing, teaching, reforming, and redeeming of persons be accomplished. To paraphrase the Apostle John, don't tell me that you love God, show me by loving me. (1 John 4:19–21)

If you and I want to hear the voice of God, it is time for us to start listening to one another. We must forget everything we think we know about one another and allow ourselves to feel the loneliness, the pain, the fullness, the joy of our brothers and sisters. Only if we ignore the categories, the shallow psychologizing about one another, can we discern the willingness to share, to serve, to love (as well as the hunger for sharing, service, and being loved) which fills us like a cloud of incense whenever two or three of us are gathered together.

The test of a religion is not the degree of its theological development or the beauty of its worship or the intensity of its devotional life, but the sensitivity of its adherents to the needs of their fellow human beings—to the needs of the stranger next door, the friend in the next pew or at the next shop bench, the lonely, the confused, the hungry, the sick. And how does one acquire this sensitivity? By the simple and yet profound act of accepting the gift now and always offered—the living God who stands ready to plunge himself into our lives, to bless and enhance the highest highs and the deepest lows or our existence so that in, through, and despite us, the miracle of Christmas, the sacrifice of Good Friday, and the promise of Easter may daily be renewed.

For, to paraphrase Meister Eckhart, if the Christ is born in Bethlehem a million times, and trudges the dusty roads of Palestine, preaching for a million years, but is not born in your heart and life—and in my heart and life—then what difference does his Gospel make? But if you and I are crucified with the Christ and yet we live because he lives in us, then the good news is true: God is for us. God is with us. God is in us. God is among us. And we are thankful.

Amen.

—LDS

[1315 words]
[13 minutes]

Sermon 78

Date: Christmas Season

Text:
Luke 2:1–20

Theme: God chose some shepherds to be the first to hear about Jesus' birth, because He loves to choose the weak to get powerful things done.
Subject: Weakness, humility

Title: The Unlikely Shepherds

God Chose the Shepherds

Isn't it interesting that when God sent His Son Jesus to this earth that first Christmas, He didn't advertise a la Madison Avenue, He didn't spread the word to the power brokers of the day.

It was the greatest event to hit our planet—and yet He announced it to a few shepherds in the field.

If you were buying a puppy from a litter of newborns, you wouldn't choose the runt, the one that's small and sickly, would you? You'd choose a strong, healthy one. Or if you were choosing up sides for a ball game you wouldn't deliberately pick a bad player.

But out of all the people God could have revealed the birth of His Son to, He chose shepherds. They were definitely an unlikely group for this big honor. Shepherds weren't known for their goodness, in fact they were considered such liars, shepherds weren't allowed to testify in court! So you'd think they wouldn't get much attention when they told people about the Messiah they have seen.

But God sent His angels to declare the Christmas announcement to lowly shepherds. Imagine it! God chooses inconsequential people for Himself. He deliberately picks weak ones.

Out of all the nations in the world God picked Israel to be His own. No super-power. Just a small nation of shepherds and farmers. And when the disciples thought Jesus shouldn't waste His time on children (after all, there were important people around) Jesus said,

> *"Let the little children come to me . . . for the kingdom of heaven belongs to such as these."*

God chooses children for His kingdom, and shepherds to be His ambassadors. It doesn't make any worldly sense, but it's God's perfect way.

1 Corinthians 1:26 and 27 says,

Brothers, think of what you were when you were called. Not many of you were wise by human standards; not many were influential; not many were of noble birth. But God chose the foolish things of the world to shame the wise; God chose the weak things of the world to shame the strong."

God Chose You

My friend, if you're a believer, God chose you. You may not think you're much, but God wanted you for Himself; He considers you precious. Isn't that Good News?

God chose some shepherds to be the first to hear about Jesus' birth, because He loves to choose the weak to get powerful things done. We can accept that the Lord would let Shepherds, "unacceptable" people, into the family, but at least keep them in the background. His upfront people ought to be sharp and impressive. Right? Wrong. That's not His way.

The Lord uses the weak. He makes unlikely people his representatives. As Paul says in 1 Corinthians 2,

When I came to you, brothers, I did not come with eloquence or superior wisdom . . . I came to you in weakness and fear, and with much trembling. My message and my preaching were not with wise persuasive words, but with a demonstration of the Spirit's power, so that your faith might not rest on men's wisdom, but on God's power. (vss. 1–4)

God Blesses the Weak

Surely the reason God uses weakness is so there'll be no question that the power is His, not ours. Don't put your hopes in human abilities and cleverness! Offer God everything you are, but it may well be your weaknesses, not your strengths, that He uses. And even when you say, "Lord, I have nothing to offer you, but I'm yours," then God does something wonderful through your nothing.

The key is, "but I'm yours." If you wait to be strong before offering yourself to the Lord, you'll never get there. Offer yourself to the Lord just as you are, my friend, and He will use you.

That Jesus' birth was revealed to poor shepherds tells us (1) God chooses the weak, (2) God uses the weak and (3) blesses the weak.

The appearance of the angels was scary, but it was also wonderful. It was a unique gift to these shepherds from God. Angels had visited a very few other people before (not many), but this was different. When angels visited the parents of Abraham and then later of Samson, they came in human form. It wasn't until afterward that Abraham and Manoah realized they had been talking to angels. But when these mighty beings showed themselves to the shepherds, Luke 2 says,

An angel of the Lord appeared to them and the glory of the Lord shone around them.

And then,

Suddenly a great company of the heavenly host appeared with the angel, praising God . . .

And it's true today, that it's the poor and the weak who get blessed by God. Jesus taught,

Blessed are the poor in spirit

Not "Blessed are those who assert themselves and try to get ahead in this world," but

Blessed are the poor in spirit, for theirs is the kingdom of heaven.

Happiness isn't looking out for number one; it's admitting what we really are, and receiving God's blessing.

The qualities of those whom God blessed are given in the Beatitudes, and they're deep and amazing, not at all what the world would describe as "blessed." But God says mourning, meekness, mercy, purity, peacemaking, and hunger for righteousness—these things will make you usable and powerful in His hands. He blesses the weak!

Queen Victoria once visited a business and saw men sorting old filthy rags that had been reclaimed from trash. She asked what in the world those rags could be good for and was told that they're made into paper. Afterward the owner of the business sent the queen some delicate white stationary with her picture embossed on it. He said that it had been made from the very dirty rags that she had seen.

That's a picture of what God does for you. He reclaims you from your dirty, useless state; He makes you clean and beautiful and useful; and then He even stamps His own personal image on you!

You see, first God chooses the weak; second, He uses the weak; third, he blesses the weak; and then last, God changes the weak. You become strong in His hand.

Jesus is your example of this. He came into this world as a totally helpless baby. Babies can't even get across a room without being carried. And Jesus lived His life in vulnerability—that's weakness. And He allowed His enemies to kill Him. That's the great mystery of all the ages, that in Jesus Christ God Himself became weak! He even called Himself a shepherd! So it was appropriate that His birth was announced to simple shepherds.

Of course, that lowly birth and life, and that humiliating death, wasn't at all the end for Jesus. The end was followed by the beginning—in His resurrection and ascension! And He's coming again in great glory! So when in the book of Revelation angels sing about a slain lamb, and they bow down singing, "Worthy is the Lamb who was slain"—that's the marvelous contradiction of God. Christ's very triumph came out of His weakness.

God will take your weakness, my friend, and change it into strength. He did that for Paul. God told him.

"My power is made perfect in weakness."

After learning this Paul could say,

I delight in weakness . . . For when I am weak, then I am strong.

The way to "up" is "down." God wants your weakness. He wants you to admit it humbly and yield to Him. Then He can change you.

God opposes the proud but gives grace to the humble. (James 4:6)

God can't use who you pretend to be. He can't use who you intend to be, when you get your act together. But He will use who you are, as you humbly admit it and offer the "real you" to Him.

Let's pray.

—Ray Ortlund[1]

[1300 words]
[13 minutes]

---

[1] "Haven of Rest," radio broadcast, December 20, 1990. Used with permission.

CHAPTER EIGHT

BIRTH, BAPTISM, AND FAMILY

Every Christian belongs to two families—the family into which he or she was born and the church, the family of God. Entrance into the first family is by birth, into the second by baptism.

Baptism is a promise made either by the one receiving the sacrament or by parents and sponsors on a child's behalf. But unless the individual is committed to hearing and obeying God's word, baptism is an empty act.

The demands of modern life tear us apart, bit by bit. Again and again, we leave a part of ourselves behind, we are dismembered. Through baptism we remember and are remembered. We reassert the promises of the past, and we are reattached to the Christian community.

Physical birth is a metaphor for our re-creation in God's image. Pregnancy and birth are compelling symbols of our spiritual journey, our struggles to be a people of God.

Mother's Day and Father's Day give Christians opportunities to celebrate the calling of parenthood. Motherhood is a calling to the will of God on behalf of others. Fatherhood is a calling to support children by being there, being aware, and being real. Through the nurture of their parents, children hear the voice of God.

Never has it been more difficult to be parents. Parenting isn't easy. Parenting takes courage. But it is the job most of us wanted all along.

Child abuse is one of contemporary society's greatest problems. The concluding sermon in this chapter deals with the causes and prevention of the cycle of family horror. In the words of a survivor of child abuse, "There's more than anger, more than sadness, more than terror. There's hope."

Sermon 79

Date: First Sunday After Epiphany, Year B

Texts:
Genesis 1:1–15
Psalm 29
Acts 19:1–7
Mark 1:4–11

Theme: Unless we daily hear and obey the word of God, our baptism is an empty act.
Subject: Baptism

Title: "Stop, Children! What's That Sound?"

Prophet with the Magic Cure

The good guys were uncomfortable. Life seemed awkward, out of joint, confusing. The bad guys were in power. And the good guys, were paying for it in every way. They were being ground down, humiliated, exploited, ignored, neglected, and taxed to the hilt.

Not that the guys with the upper hand were having such a great time. Like all oppressors, they were chained to those they enslaved, terrified of what would happen when the rage of the oppressed found expression. When a nation becomes a prison, no one is free.

Word spread in the city that help was only a few miles and a few hours away. Something was going down—in the middle of nowhere. Something electric was in the air. The city people could feel it in their bones. They could almost taste it. It wasn't clear what it was, but it had to be better than chaos and confusion. It had to be better than waiting for the volcano to erupt. Anything would be better.

So the people from the city flocked to the wilderness to see the wild holy man. Some came looking for easy answers, quick fixes, momentary highs. Some came to ridicule him and to entertain themselves. Others came in desperation, knowing nothing else had worked. Maybe this strange prophet had the magic cure.

The New Age at Hand

It is a road we travel, swarming to Woodstock, to the March on Washington, to Altamont Pass, to Chicago, to Tiananmen Square. We want to know "what's happening." We want to be "where it's at." Sometimes we go in person; sometimes we let the electronic eyes and ears go in our stead. But one way or another, we are there. As Buffalo Springfield sang, "You've got to stop children. What's that sound? Everybody look. What's going round?"[1]

---

[1] Buffalo Springfield, "For What It's Worth," words and music by Stephen Stills, Cotillion Music, Inc., 1967.

If only something wonderful and exciting would happen so we could label life "new and improved." If only the chaos—my chaos, my family's chaos, my society's chaos—would give way to meaning and the confusion to certainty.

They came to John and he told them to repent and be baptized. So they wrung out of themselves every last tear of sorrow and regret, wallowed in pity until they were exhausted, and soaked themselves in the water of the River Jordan until all the color was washed out of their clothes and themselves.

And there they were, in the middle of nowhere, wet and despondent, mired in the old age with old ways, old habits, old hurts, and old blind alleys.

They needed something new—a new year, a new age, a new way. And John offered them only repentance and baptism, emotion and religion. They were more confused than ever. The chaos worsened. Most of them packed up and headed back to the city.

And even as they did, the new year was at hand, the new age was breaking, the new way was staring them in the face. As they left the wilderness, they may have passed it on the road. But how could they know? For amid the tumult of the public events, something private and personal, something taking precedence over all the mass lamenting and religiosity, was happening. And amid the tumult of our busy lives, something powerful is here, within reach.

And So It Begins

Mark tells us:

> *At that time Jesus came from Nazareth in Galilee and was baptized by John in the Jordan. As Jesus was coming up out of the water, he saw heaven being torn open and the Spirit descending on him like a dove. And a voice came from heaven: "You are my Son, whom I love; with you I am well pleased."*

According to Mark, nobody saw the heavens open or witnessed the descent of the Spirit or heard the divine utterance except for the thirty-year-old Galilean carpenter. According to this report, the earliest account of the baptism of Jesus, not even John knew what was happening. This epiphany was not for the crowd. This shining forth of the divine light was not for the crowd. This overwhelming coming of God's presence was not for the harbinger of God's coming, but for Jesus only.

In an instant, in the blinking of an eye, Jesus knew who he was and to what he was called. It all came down to two words: son and servant. He received the message: "You are my son, my beloved, in whom I am well pleased." As the words echoed in his mind, he thought of the Old Testament song of coronation, the second Psalm: "I will proclaim the decree of the LORD: He said to me, "'You are my Son, today I have become your Father'" (v. 7). And he recalled the Prophet Isaiah's ode to God's suffering servant: "Here is my servant, whom I uphold, my chosen one in whom I delight; I will put my Spirit on him and he will bring justice to the nations" (42:1). Son and servant, king and victim, bearer of the Spirit and bringer of justice—the thoughts blend together in the words from heaven.

And so it begins—his ministry, his career, his vocation. The Spirit leads him out into the desert to wrestle with his own doubts and confusion, to give up the last vestige of his prebaptism assumptions and desires. But the Spirit does not leave him there, to meditate and ponder forever. The words heard at his baptism provide the form and shape of what he is to be. The forty days of solitude add content and direction. He is God's Son and our servant. He is the one with authority to heal our sicknesses, cast out our demons, divide our good from our evil. He tells us who we are.

He calls us not only to find meaning but to create it. He calls us not only to overcome our confusion but to dispel confusion in the lives of others. And so begin our ministries, our careers, our vocations.

Take your baptism for granted and it is an empty gesture. Take your baptism seriously and it will empower you, fill your life with significance, hour after hour, day after day, and forever.

Starting Over

In the beginning there is always chaos. There is always waiting for the creative, lifegiving word of God. It was so at the creation of the cosmos. It is so when we are called forth from the waters of our mothers' wombs. It is so when we are overcome by the flood tides of circumstances and suffering and gasp for comfort like beached whales gasping for air.

It is so when we declare ourselves for Christ and his gospel. It is so when we start our lives all over again where he started his career—through the act of baptism. It is so when we take seriously for ourselves the vows made on our behalf by our parents and their church. It is so when we declare that their faith is our faith, that what they believed and valued is now what we believe and value.

Whether we were baptized as infants or stepped forward on our own as believers, the act is hollow unless it is followed by commitment, by openness to God's word, by obedience to God's will. Until baptism becomes for each of us an outward and visible sign of an inward grace, chaos and confusion will prevail. Until we respond to the God who calls, who speaks, who transforms, we remain in the empty and uncomfortable wilderness.

When Jesus knew who he was, the Spirit led him. When we acknowledge who we are as baptized Christians, the Spirit leads us. When Jesus chose silence amid the confusion of the scene, the message and the messenger became one. No happy ending, no special effects. The beloved son did not ascend into heaven or accept David's throne while trumpets sounded, choirs sang, and laser beams flashed. The son became the servant and went out to be tested, to heal, to cast out demons, to offer his life to us and for us.

The light and the darkness were separated. The choice was made clear. The Spirit had descended, hovering, brooding, molding, penetrating to the very core of our being. The Spirit is here in our midst. Look for the signs. Look for endings to chaos and confusion—not a big, dramatic once-for-all end, but many, many endings to chaos and confusion.

The baptism of Jesus is a moment of destiny and decision. God calls and his child responds. Grace and power are given without limit to him and through him. The career of Jesus begins as he hears and obeys the word of God. For each of us, today is the day of destiny. Now is the hour of decision. May we hear the call of God above the tumult of life. May we be ready to serve as we are called. May we thoughtfully and deliberately renew the promises of our own baptism.

Amen.

—LDS

[1500 words
15 minutes]

Sermon 80

Date: Fourth Sunday in Advent, Year A

Texts:
Isaiah 7:10–16
Psalm 80:1-7, 17-19
Romans 1:1–7
Matthew 1:18–25

or Sunday Between August 7 and August 13 inclusive Pentecost, Year C

Texts:
Hebrews 11:1–3, 8–16
Luke 12:32–40

Theme: We play an active part in the creation of God's realm, and at the same time we can only trust and hope in the new creation that God is birthing through us.
Subject: Birth

Title: The Gift of Birth: An Advent Sermon

I was four months pregnant with my son Owen. I was sitting on the stage of a huge auditorium at Eastern Washington University, near Spokane. Thousands of students and faculty and journalists filled the auditorium to help the university celebrate its hundredth anniversary. I was on the stage representing my family, for a century earlier my great-great-grandfather had helped the university get started. And I was there to present an award, in my great-great-grandfather's name, to former President Gerald Ford, who was the keynote speaker for the event.

I was the only woman among the dignitaries, and the academic cap and gown did little to hide my growing belly. I was flushed with all the attention, and the bright lights of the TV cameras. I was trying hard to look attentive to President Ford's speech. In this unusual, and highly unlikely place, the most miraculous thing happened.

I felt it move. I felt the fetus that was to become my son move inside me. For the first time, I felt the flutter of life, the stirring and stretching of a person to be, I felt it growing and groaning. Ford talked on and on about politics and education and peace through strength, and I sat there, looking out at a sea of faces, thinking, "It's moving, it's alive."

Most mothers have some such story. You may not have been sitting on a podium with President Ford, but most mothers know this miraculous feeling: the hiddenness of the first stirrings of life, while the outside world goes on about its usual business. Now, whenever I read the definition of faith, of which you need a lot during those nine months, offered by the author of Hebrews, faith is the assurance of things hoped for, the conviction of things not seen (11:1), I think of faith as that moment, the conviction of things not seen.

The Gift of Birth

Both our Old and New Testament readings for today speak of the conception and birth of a savior, a child called Emmanuel, Hebrew for "God with us." God with us in the form of a baby. And so we celebrate the fourth gift of Advent, the gift of birth itself.

The gift of birth. The origins of this sermon are extremely personal, because for me being pregnant and giving birth were perhaps the most profound religious experiences of my life. Since then, the Bible accounts of Jesus' birth have had new meaning for me, and the metaphor of pregnancy and birth has become for me a central symbol of what it means to be a person of faith. We are all filled with God's spirit. We all struggle and labor to bring forth new life. We nurture and gently care for our faith and the faith of others. We each, men and women, parents and nonparents, as people of faith, are pregnant, and waiting and creating and laboring and nurturing. We are each a Mary and a Joseph, on the road to Bethlehem.

There are very few stories in the Scripture about pregnancy. There's an awful lot of begetting, and lists and lists of names of children as they are born. But not much in between the begetting and the naming, not much about the nine months of waiting, the wondering, the fearing, the delighting, the quickening. We read little about labor and labor pains, about nurturing and caring for the young child. This is not surprising, since the Bible is in general written more from a male than a female perspective and was for the most part written by men.

But for this very reason the few accounts there are of pregnancy and birth stand out. Only in Luke do we read the lovely story of Mary's friendship with her cousin Elizabeth, and their mutual surprise and delight at their respective pregnancies, Elizabeth in her extreme old age and Mary in her extreme youth. I remember from my own pregnancy this bond with other pregnant women.

The one account in scripture that does describe the first feeling of movement in the womb is in this story. Elizabeth sees her cousin Mary coming up to her house, and she says, "My baby leapt for joy in my womb." As I was that day in Washington, so Elizabeth was delighted and surprised by this first movement, by what some people call quickening, the first feeling of life. This story shows a remarkable sensitivity to birth from a woman's perspective. Luke in general includes many more stories than do the other gospel writers about women. It is Luke who gives us the wonderful description of Mary after the birth, "Mary heard all these things and pondered them in her heart." I know that feeling, of just sitting and pondering it all.

Pregnancy, and then birth. You know, the gospels of Mark and John say absolutely nothing about Jesus' birth; they begin with Jesus as a grown man, His birth is not important to them. They may very well have heard the stories, but they chose not to include them. But Matthew and Luke do, and we must ask, why? What were they trying to tell us about Jesus, by beginning with the stories of him as a baby?

I think they used the birth stories to say two things. They wanted to say that Jesus was born of human parents, that he was flesh, just like other babies. And they wanted to say at the same time that he was special, different from other babies. I don't want to go into all the controversy about the virgin birth. The point is not the so-called facts, was she or wasn't she? The point is, I think, that Luke and Matthew wanted to say, this man was born in a different way from other babies, he was a child of human parents, but he was also a child of God.

He had angels and kings as some of his first visitors. That's unusual.

But I think we have to read these accounts also by saying that Jesus' birth was not so unusual.

Actually you could say that the controversy about Mary's virginity has to do with Jesus' conception, not his birth. The virgin conception, not the virgin birth. As far as we can tell, his birth was perfectly normal. Even being born on the road, away from home, in a barn, was not that unusual for a people whose life-style was nomadic and rural.

Just like all other babies, Jesus came into the world naked and vulnerable and hungry. His mother cried out in pain. She nursed him. His father held him and walked with him through the hours of crying and teething. The stories of Jesus' birth are an Advent gift themselves, a marvelous gift to us, for they tell us how special Jesus is, that angels sing at his birth, that kings fall on their knees at his birth. And they tell us how much he is our brother, our friend, who knows what human life is all about because he lived it himself.

What else is there in the Bible about pregnancy and birth? Well, if you look in a biblical concordance under labor or delivery or nursing, or babies, what little you find, much of it appears in the book of Isaiah. Our Old Testament readings this Advent have all been from Isaiah, and we have heard over and over how he looks with hope to a time when a child shall lead them, when a son will be born whose name is "Wonderful Counselor, Mighty God, Everlasting Father, Prince of Peace" (Isaiah 9:6). But listen to these other passages from Isaiah, which were the basis of our call to worship this morning. I will cry out like a woman in labor. Can a woman forget her sucking child? Will she have no compassion on the son of her womb? Yes, even she may forget, but I will not forget you. I have made and I will bear. I will carry and I will deliver. Behold I will extend peace to you like a river, like a flowing stream. Then ye shall suck, ye shall be borne upon her sides and be dangled on her knee. As one whom his mother comforts, so will I comfort you. (See Isaiah 13:8, 21:3, 26:17, 49:15, 44:4, and 57:18)

As one whom his mother comforts, so will I comfort you. It is God who is speaking these words. It is God who is the pregnant mother, crying out in the pain of creation. Isaiah sees God as a nursing mother, feeding and carrying and caring for her children. God is the young mother never forgetting the child of her womb. God is the playful mother, dangling her child on her knee.

I know these passages are surprising. As much as we think of Mary as a virgin, so much more do we think of God as male, and as a confirmed bachelor, and an old one at that. For me, this is another gift of birth, at this time of Advent time of year, this time of arrival, of the coming of the new. We are given the image of a God who cares about us as deeply as a mother cares about the child of her womb, who has given as much to us as a mother gives to her child, who sacrifices body and blood, who risks death to give life to another. Such is our God, the one who has given us life, the one who has given us birth. I have made and I will bear. I will carry and I will deliver.

Birth and the Journey of Faith

I offer you one more reflection on the religious aspects of pregnancy and birth, one more way I think God has given us a gift in birth. I've referred to it already. Pregnancy and birth are powerful symbols for our own journeys of faith, our own struggles to be a people of God.

We are all like Mary and Joseph, pregnant with new life inside us, traveling toward Bethlehem, toward birth. Like them, we are actively walking, making choices, decisions. We have decided to take this road, to join a church, to have a baby. We have freedom in our choices. We are partners with God in creation, co-creators.

And at the same time, "it is he that hath made us and not we ourselves." We are partners in grace, captive to a power beyond our control. God has chosen us, God has announced to us what is being borne by us and in us. For all the power in pregnancy we also know its powerlessness, that feeling of a life beyond our human control, a faith moving and stretching within us. Pregnancy is the ultimate experience of grace. Grace is being filled with a spirit that is new life.

On our journey of faith, our trip to Bethlehem, we have at times to wait, to be patient, in scriptural language to wait until the hour is come, to wait for the fullness of time, to wait until our days are accomplished. Like a seed, our faith germinates in the dark and the warmth of a womb.

And then comes the labor of birth, the crisis of faith, the movement into new life, the birth and rebirth of ourselves as children of God. This birth can be hard, it can be painful. We can seem all alone, we want to give up. We cry out like a woman in travail, in labor.

We are a pregnant people. We play an active part in the creation of God's realm, and at the same time we can only trust and hope in the new creation that God is birthing through us. Like Paul, we can say, ". . . I no longer live, but Christ lives in me." (Galatians 2:20)

Amen.

—Deborah Streeter[1]

[1,900 words]
[19 minutes]

❦ *Sermon 81*

❦ *Date:* First Sunday After Epiphany, Year A

Texts:
Isaiah 42:1–9
Psalm 29
Acts 10:34–43
Matthew 3:13–17

Theme: The meaning of Jesus' baptism is that we should honor the vows made at ours.
Subject: Vows, baptism

❦ *Title:* New Things I Now Declare

[Music: This sermon might be preceded by a quartet of little children singing "This Little Light of Mine, I'm Going to Make It Shine."]

As Jesus instructed his followers in the Sermon on the Mount,

> *You are the light of the world. A city on a hill cannot be hidden. Neither do people light a lamp and put it under a bowl. Instead they put it on its stand, and it gives light to everyone in the house. In the same way, let your light shine before men, that they may see your good deeds and praise your Father in heaven. (Matthew 5:14–16)*

As the Apostle Paul taught,

> *For God, who said,"Let light shine out of darkness," made his light shine in our hearts to give us the light of the knowledge of the glory of God in the face of Christ. (2 Corinthians 4:6)*

---

1 This sermon was preached at First Congregational Church of Sonoma, Sonoma, California, on December 18, 1983, as the fourth in a series on "The Gifts of Advent." I am greatly indebted to Elizabeth Hambrick-Stowe's book *Expecting: A Christian Exploration of Pregnancy and Childbirth* (Valley Forge, PA: Judson Press, 1979). —DS

The Meaning of Epiphany

Today is the First Sunday after Epiphany. The word Epiphany comes from the Greek *epiphaneia,* which means "shining upon" or "showing forth," a commemoration of the revealing of the Christ child to the Three Wise Men and, subsequently, to the whole world, beginning with our Lord's baptism. It seems appropriate that during these short days of winter when the sun has disappeared before we return home at the end of the workday, we should feel in our souls the need to be reilluminated by the Light of the World. Likewise, it seems proper that, as we are once again energized by the Light within, we should show forth that light, shining it on the darkness of the world around us.

Epiphany or Twelfth Night, which is observed on January 6, is one of the most ancient celebrations of the Christian Church, probably a century older than Christmas. Epiphany originally focused on the baptism of Jesus rather than on the visit of the Magi. Frederick Houk Borsch, the Episcopal Bishop of Los Angeles, observes:

> Since the third century the Orthodox churches of the East have used the story of Jesus' baptism as the Gospel reading for the Epiphany. For them it is the first of Jesus' epiphanies or manifestations of who he is for all humanity.[1]

The Baptism of Jesus

Matthew's telling of the story of the baptism of Jesus presents us with a riddle. Why should the Son of God, the one who "knew no sin," be baptized by John? What sense does it make for John, the messenger of repentance, the harbinger of the Messiah, to apply the cleansing waters to the one whose shoestrings he was not worthy to tie?

The key to the riddle is the recognition that Jesus came voluntarily to his cousin as he had come freely to our world. This central concept of Christian theology can be stated in a thousand different ways, but however it is expressed, it always means the same thing: In the person and work of Jesus of Nazareth, God has surrendered himself to the limitations of human nature. Therefore, the Christ begins his career by submitting himself to the same ritual that his church will later offer to all humankind.

In our rather informal church, it is easy to overlook the significance of baptism—either our own or our Lord's. Therefore, I will spend a few minutes stressing the meaning and importance of Christian baptism and the baptism of the Christ.

It all comes down to a single phrase from Isaiah: "See, the former things have taken place, and new things I declare; before they spring into being I announce them to you." What Matthew was saying was that by his baptism, Jesus "shines forth" as the Son called out of Egypt; that is, he is the chosen servant, the one through whom and in whom God is bringing not just Israel but all the nations of the world to himself. When Matthew describes the Son of God as stepping into the water of baptism and out of those waters to begin his ministry, Matthew is saying in his way what the author of the Fourth Gospel says in very different words:

> *In him was life, and that life was the light of men.*
> *The light shines in the darkness, but the darkness has not understood it.*
> *There came a man who was sent from God; his name was John.*

---

[1] *Proclamation 4: Aids for Interpreting the Lessons of the Church Year, Series A: Epiphany* (Minneapolis: Augsburg Press, 1989), p. 15.

He came as a witness to testify concerning that light, so that through him all men might believe.
He himself was not the light; he came only as a witness to the light.
The true light that gives light to every man was coming into the world. (John 1:4–9)

For Matthew, the baptism of Jesus was the fulfillment of the Exodus. As the nation Israel, God's servant-people, had been called into existence by passing through the waters of the Red Sea, so now was God presenting to the world the chosen Servant, the one whom he loves, the Son in whom he is well pleased. As the waters of the Red Sea dealt death to those who rejected God's word but life to those who obeyed him, so now the waters of the Christ's baptism would mean death and darkness to the Son who would lay down his life for us and life and light for us who were called to follow him.

There were other motives behind Matthew's telling of this story. The early church had its problems with disciples of John the Baptist who refused to accept Jesus as the Messiah. That tension is still felt in the brief argument between John and our Lord. "If Jesus is really the Christ, the one anointed by God to establish his kingdom," the followers of John must have argued, "Why did he ask John to baptize him?" Their logic seems impeccable. Isn't the one who cleanses superior to the one who is cleansed?

Matthew's reply is obvious in his telling of the story. The Son of God has come to fulfill not to destroy. With the baptism of Jesus, a line has been crossed—once and for all. Jesus brings justice. That had been the responsibility of the Hebrew kings. But they had failed miserably. Jesus proclaims God's reign. That had been the job of the Old Testament prophets. He would now complete what they had started, establishing through his death and resurrection a new covenant. Jesus would make clear what God requires of each human being. That had been the task of the priests of the Old Covenant. But their system of rituals and sacrifices was about to pass away forever.

Jesus had come to the waters of baptism because God had told him to come. It was as simple as that. The former things had come to pass, the message of the Old Testament had been fulfilled. No longer would the will of God be revealed through prophet, priest, or king. The Spirit of God, which had brooded over the face of the waters when God created the world, had hovered over the waters of the River Jordan and had descended. From this moment on, God is with us, God is in our midst, God is for us.

The Meaning of Our Baptism

And what of our baptism? Have we forgotten what the Apostle Paul teaches, that "if anyone is in Christ, he is a new creation; the old has gone, the new has come" (2 Corinthians 5:17)?

In our personal lives, our baptism means that we are dead to selfishness, to selfcentered existence, to never-to-be-satisfied demands of ego and pride. Our friends at the social transformation organization, Creative Initiative, used to advise us to "think globally and act locally." I think the meaning of Christian baptism is much more simple: in the Christ, "I, me, my, mine" gives way to "we, us, our, ours." John N. Gladstone, the senior minister at Yorkminster Baptist Church in Toronto, remarks:

> At Mount Rushmore, South Dakota, are the carved figures of four United States presidents—Washington, Jefferson, Lincoln, and Theodore Roosevelt. The sculptor was Gutzon Borglum. Asked how he did it, he replied whimsically: "Well, those figures were there for forty million years. All I had to do was dynamite 400,000 tons

of granite to bring them into view." Isn't this what Christ is seeking to do: to bring into view the real person he knows us to be?[2]

That is how each of us fulfills his or her baptismal vows—by allowing God to blast away the tons of debris—the laziness, carelessness, apathy, fear, misconception, and stubbornness that stand between us and our true spiritual selves.

At this church, there is a sense of excitement and expectancy. Old things are passing away, and new things are coming. This church has undergone its own baptism. It has suffered, it has died a little, and it is awaiting rebirth. The light may have flickered a bit, but it has never failed. But I have a secret for you, the new things will not be brought to this community by a hero on a white horse anymore than they were brought to Israel by Conan the Barbarian. Jesus was not what we today would call a strong leader. Power, manipulation, and control of others was not what he was about. He had a powerful sense of mission, followed it wherever it carried him, invited those whom he encountered to join him. He took no polls to discover whether or not he was popular. He withstood criticism, abuse, and misunderstanding and still pursued his calling.

In the words of Isaiah 42, God's servant does not break a bruised reed or snuff out a smoldering wick. Yet "in faithfulness he will bring forth justice; he will not falter nor be discouraged till he establishes justice on earth." You and I have been called to the same mission. We are God's servant church, caring for one another and reaching beyond our fellowship to those in need of the message and comfort of God's Good News.

Epiphany is the season of "showing forth" or "projecting" our light out into the darkness, of letting our friends and neighbors know what we are made of. Epiphany is a season of rededication to our mission as individual Christians and as a church. It is a season for pursuing the light of God's word, following it with deliberation and intensity. Epiphany is a time for honoring the vows made when we were baptized—whether we made those promises ourselves or they were made on our behalf by our parents or sponsors.

Epiphany is a time to honor the promise of our baptism, to show forth the light of God in our lives and in our community.

Amen.

—LDS

[1732 words]
[17 minutes]

❦ *Sermon 82*

❦ *Date:* Mother's Day

Texts:
Proverbs 31:10–31
Luke 11:27–28

Theme: Motherhood is a calling.
Subject: Motherhood

❦ *Title:* Motherhood is a Calling

[2] "What's in a Nickname?" *Best Sermons 1* (San Francisco: Harper & Row, 1988), p. 80.

Mother's Day! Letter carriers have their bags fuller than usual this week. Greeting card companies have made a significant percentage of their yearly sales during the past week, and the same is true of florists. And long-distance phone companies are certainly not hurting for business today.

Though not a holy day, still it is a time many churches pause to think about mothers, parenthood, and families. The term "Festival of the Christian Home" has replaced "Mother's Day" on most church planning calendars.

As special as this day is for most moms, Mother's Day can be one of the worst days of the year for some people. We think about

A woman recently divorced, whose husband got custody of the children

A mother whose only child died, and who wonders if she is still a mother

A woman who has tried to become a mother, but was never able to conceive

A woman who consciously decided not to become a biological or adoptive mother, for very private and personal reasons, yet finds herself unsettled by the emphasis on motherhood in the marketplace, the broadcast media, and even church

Men and women who have had traumatic conflict with their own mothers, resulting in developmental wounds as yet unhealed

It may sound subversive, but I want to suggest today that we refrain from doing three things: let's not (1) sentimentalize, (2) idealize, or (3) idolize mothers and motherhood.

Sentimentalizing Motherhood

My wife Roberta and I made our annual pilgrimage to the greeting card store last week, seeking appropriate cards for Ella and Helen, our mothers. Amid all the flowery, gushy mush, I was able to find a simple card with a nice note of humor. But I could wish for a better selection, without having to wend my way through all the trivial schlock.

To me, *sentimentalizing* mothers and family relationships serves only to trivialize what is by nature profound and indeed a gift of God.

Idealizing Motherhood

We have *idealized* motherhood. Just listen to some of these images of mothers:

> The best friend that God ever gives us.
> —Christian Nestell Boree

> A mother is . . . the holiest thing alive.
> —Samuel Taylor Coleridge

> God could not be everywhere, so He made mothers.
> —Jewish Proverb

In contrast, I am reminded of that hilarious portrayal by Erma Bombeck of the ideal woman who manages a household, takes care of her kids and most of the neighborhood, carries a bucket of soapy water to clean wherever she goes in the house, volunteers for a dozen good causes, managing all the while to be a cheerful and erotic wife for her husband.

But listen to this prison made of words:

> Maids must be wives and mothers, to fulfill the entire and holiest end of woman's being.
> —Frances Anne Kemble

Idealizing can be so oppressive! So I'm appealing to all of us today not to idealize mothers, motherhood, or family relationships.

Idolizing Motherhood

And of course we could *idolize* mothers, which is roughly the equivalent of making gods of them. I have known of families where the world revolves around mother, living or dead. Mothers are not all-powerful or all-knowing or all-righteous. In our childhood imagination we might have thought they were or felt compelled to say they were.

Mothers and everybody else are served best when no human being is idolized.

Celebrating Motherhood

So what shall we do today, if we don't sentimentalize, idealize, or idolize mothers and motherhood?

I would hope today we could do this:

Encourage mothers and all women.

Liberate mothers and all women, as well as all the rest of us regarding appropriate and inappropriate roles of mothers, women, and all the rest of us.

First, I would invite us all to celebrate the fact that it's a new world! The 1980s and beginning of the 1990s have seen amazing cultural changes. And I'm glad. Women increasingly assert themselves as self-directed persons. The quest for liberation is being felt everywhere. All of us can find reason to be glad for that.

Yet some people are apparently frightened by competent women. There are those who want women in positions subservient to men. Is it the only way they can feel adequate as a man? Or is it because of misguided literalistic reading of selected verses of St. Paul's writings? Just as today's woman is not locked into stereotypes of yesterday, neither is she a conformist to any particular movement.

I had to appreciate Barbara Bush when she responded to things said by some of the women of Wellesley College not long ago. You may recall the incident. Some did not want her to be a speaker on campus because she did not fit their image of the modern, liberated woman. The first lady's response was that while she appreciated their position, they also needed to realize she made a conscious decision about how she was going to live her life. She made that decision from among alternatives. It had been fulfilling for her.

Seems to me that liberation has to include personal choices, whether or not it conforms to somebody else's notion.

Remembering Our Mothers

Any consideration of Mother's Day compels us to consider *our own experiences with our mother*, whether birth mother, adoptive mother, or nobody in particular serving as mother for us.

My mother always worked when I was growing up. As an adolescent I learned to cook and clean house. I learned child care by taking care of my little brother. That was part of the price to be paid for Gus and Ella to be able to buy their first and only house. It required two incomes. That meant I had to provide the child care in the afternoons and do some of the housework.

At the time, I must confess, I felt deprived. I was quite sure most of the other kids, whose moms didn't work outside the home, had warm cookies and milk waiting for them when they got home from school. And they didn't have to take care of their little brother either, of that I was certain!

(Correction: I said most of the other kids' mothers didn't work. Fact is, most of the other white kids' moms didn't work. Roland's mom worked. Roland was black. His mom took care of white kids, while her older kids took care of her younger children after they got home from school.)

Today I'm glad I learned those skills, necessitated by the two pay-check marriage. Mom worked outside the home. She was a hard worker who took great pride in her particular skill. She was also an excellent money manager. She taught me some things about that too, for which I am grateful. And though she wasn't a perfect mother, she was pretty good, probably good enough. I know she did the best she could at the time. Isn't that all we can rightly expect of anybody? I am grateful for her, and I try to let her know that often.

Men and Motherhood

We have talked a lot about women as mothers and wives. *But what about men? This is not just Mother's Day, but Festival of the Christian Home.*

"Motherhood" has been thought of in our culture as a nurturing role, thus a job for women. Men taking care of children has been seen as a kind of humorous aberration, as in "Mr. Mom," as though the man is only filling in awkwardly for a brief time, until the woman can get back on the job and do what is, after all, "women's work!"

I suggest that when a man takes care of his children, he is not being "Mr. Mom." He is being a father! A father does not "baby sit." He takes care of his children!

And where is it written that a woman can't be the principal wage earner for the family? Where is it declared, except among some who don't like change, that a man can't be the person who is the principal homemaker and child nurturer?

And who says women must be married, bear children, or care for children, in order to fulfill what God created them for? Some indeed say it. But it doesn't have to be so.

I think a person would really be straining the point to find that kind of view in the Bible.

The Calling of Motherhood

I want to suggest that motherhood is a calling. Motherhood is a holy calling. But being a mother does not mean being perfect. Nobody should expect mothers to be perfect. Mothers shouldn't expect it of themselves.

Like all callings, a person has a choice. I believe that some women are called to be mothers, and they fulfill that calling admirably. God bless them! Thank God for mothers! I believe that some women want to be mothers, but probably shouldn't be. I believe that not every woman is called to motherhood. And that's got to be OK.

I wish that in the cultural revolution of which some of us have been a part, we could achieve yet another milestone, namely, that all women could realize they are not lesser beings if they aren't mothers.

Some women are wonderful nurturers of other people. And some are not.

Some, like my niece Julia who is hearing impaired, are brilliant at mathematics, computer science, writing, engineering, and mechanical things. Some day Julia may become a mother. But today I am grateful we live in a world where Julia does not have to be seen as an aberration, either for her hearing impairment or for not being married and a mother.

Everybody has a mother. Let's honor our mothers today, remembering not to sentimentalize, idealize or idolize them. Mothers are neither holier nor less holy than anybody else, greeting cards notwithstanding.

Today on Mother's Day, let's remember all the people who nurtured us and helped us to grow this far in life.

Today I think of Ella, my mother. I'm also remembering Aunt Mattie and Aunt Mary fondly. They were both caregivers for me when I was a small child.

Let's think of those nurturing people in the church who help keep the church alive and well.

Let's remember Jesus' mother Mary, who nurtured the Son of God. We remember that Jesus honored her and the way he honored her—by being who he was called to be. Jesus followed his calling though it led him to Calvary. And on the cross he demonstrated his unfailing concern for her by committing her to the care of his beloved disciple. While he honored and respected his mother, he established his identity apart from her and pursued his career of service. And so should we.

Thanks be to God for mothers!

Amen.

—Harold L. Rucker

[1800 words]
[18 minutes]

❦ *Sermon 83*

❦ *Date:* Mother's Day

Texts:
Matthew 12:46–50 or
Mark 3:31–35 or
Luke 8:19–21

Theme: A mother is a woman who really does the will of God on behalf of another.
Subject: Motherhood

❦ *Title:* Who is My Mother?

Barbara searches. She gets down on her hands and knees and looks at frogs with her children. She reads Shakespeare late into the night. She finds easily young people who need a surrogate aunt, an older friend, and makes them part of her life. She writes them, and all of us, long, funny letters. Barbara searches. She is a mother, and God loves her.

Teresa touches. She touches all manner of people whom no one else will touch. She touches especially the dying. She gives them a safe and loving place to die (although she has never given birth from her own body). Teresa has the title mother. Mother Teresa. These days she touches especially those who have AIDS, young men and women and children. Teresa touches. She is a mother, and God loves her.

Sarah says yes. Sarah was pregnant once, only once, and miscarried, and almost died herself. Now she is a foster mother of hard-to-place teenagers. She feels in her body their loneliness and fear and to them she says yes. Often her yes is in the form of a loving no to these teenagers, but these kids adore her. Sarah says yes. She is a mother and God loves her.

Mothers come in all shapes and sizes, all ages and colors. Some might even say all sexes, that men too can be nurturers and teachers and leaders (that's at least what mothers are—nurturers, people who care and teachers who teach and leaders who lead). Sure men do that too and do it well. But their day comes in June and I get to preach then too. That will be Chapter Two.

Chapter One is about mothers. All women, that is. All women have mothers, we all share that gift. And in my book all women are mothers, for we all, regardless of what we have chosen to do or been able to do with our own bodies, women care for those who need care, teach those who need to learn, lead those who are seeking direction. Mothers.

Toni works. Every mother is of course a working mother, and so is Toni. She has her own grown children and she takes care of four young ones whose own mothers and fathers both work. Her house is their second home, during the day, and she holds and wipes, changes and feeds, rocks and loves. They too will grow up and leave, and she is sad to see them go. Toni works. She is a mother, and God loves her.

Rosalie survives. She had her baby when she was still a teenager and unmarried. Not as she had planned, not as she had dreamed as a little girl of Prince Charming and then the baby. Rosalie had some hard choices to make when she found herself pregnant, had to keep working, find child care, endure stares and scorn. Later she was lucky to find a man who loved not just her but her daughter as well; most single mothers don't. Rosalie survives. Rosalie is a mother, and God loves her.

Elizabeth mourns. Her grown son Ben, Ben Linder, an American engineer working for the Nicaraguan people, was killed this past week by the Contra forces as he worked bringing electricity to a remote village. Elizabeth and her husband and their other children flew to Nicaragua for Ben's funeral, and Elizabeth, knowing Spanish, translated her husband's words at Ben's funeral. Like many Nicaraguan women on both sides of the civil war, Elizabeth mourns for a dead child. Mother's Day is hard for these women. Their children are dead; they are mothers, and God loves them.

Elizabeth Linder is a member of Mothers for Peace, and so she must know the origins of this day, Mother's Day. It has nothing to do with Hallmark Cards or FTD Florists. It was started by Julia Ward Howe in 1872. Howe was a prominent leader in the struggle for freedom for women. She also wrote the words of the "Battle Hymn of the Republic." And she called for that first Mother's Day in 1872. She made an appeal to mothers throughout the world to combine their voices in unified opposition to the bloody Franco-Prussian war. She later wrote, "I was visited by a sudden feeling of the cruel and unnecessary character of the war. It seemed to me a return to barbarism, the issue having been one which might easily have been settled without bloodshed. The question forced itself upon me; why do not the mothers of mankind interfere in these matters to prevent the waste of human life in which they alone bear and know the cost? The august dignity of motherhood and its terrible responsibilities now appeared to me in a new aspect, and I could think of no better way of expressing my sense of these than of sending forth an appeal to womanhood throughout the world, which I then and there composed."[1] That same year, 1872, Mother's Peace Day was celebrated in the United States, London and Geneva, Constantinople and all around the world. I wish we would remember the origins of Mother's Day and struggle with Julia and Elizabeth and all mothers for peace.

---

[1] Howe, Julia Ward, as cited in *Resources for Worship,* edited by Diane Dulin, The Northern California Conference, United Church of Christ, April 1, 1987.

Ruth dotes. She is proud to be a mother and a grandmother. Sometimes she doesn't understand her children or even approve of what they do, but in the long run her love for her family is strong and prevails. She is proud of her offspring and loves them. Ruth is a mother, and God loves her.

Erica creates. She writes books, articles, essays. She writes compulsively and with passion. She has a wide circle of friends, but ultimately she is alone. She has never married. When she's writing she goes into seclusion. Her friends say then that she is "with book." Each creation is a new birth. Erica creates. She is a mother, and God loves her.

Jean copes. She's got the same bumper sticker on her car as Anseth has: "I can handle anything, I've got children." Her work is never done and she loves it. In the words of Proverbs, "Strength and dignity are her clothing, and she laughs at the time to come. She opens her mouth with wisdom, and the teaching of kindness is on her tongue. She looks well to the ways of her household and does not eat the bread of idleness. Her children rise up and call her blessed; her husband also, and he praises her; 'Many women have done excellently, but you surpass them all.'" Jean copes. She is a mother, and God loves her.

Who is my mother? Jesus asks rhetorically. Whoever does the will of God is my mother, he answers. Barbara searches. Teresa touches. Sarah says yes. Toni works. Rosalie survives. Elizabeth mourns. Ruth dotes. Erica creates. Jean copes. These are mothers, and God loves them.

Amen.

—Deborah Streeter

[1100 words]
[11 minutes]

Sermon 84

Date: Mother's Day

Texts:
Isaiah 46:3–4; 49:14–16a; 66:10–13
1 Kings 3:16–28
Matthew 12:46–50

Theme: Who is a mother today?
Subject: Motherhood

Title: Fastlane Frenzy and Mother's Daze

Today is Mother's Day, but today what exactly is a mother?

Let me tell a story about three generations of mothers.

Ellie became a mother in 1940. She got married in 1939 because that's what women did. She really wanted to go to college and become a lawyer, but her parents had four boys to educate, and, after all, she was only a girl.

So she married William, a struggling, young attorney, a sole practitioner. He worked long hours, six days a week and many evenings, leaving her alone with their children. By 1945 there were four of them.

By eleven each morning, Ellie had completed the housework, washing, ironing, and marketing. She would recline on the sofa the rest of the day, reading women's magazines. There were many of them in the 1940s and the articles were long.

Ellie was often depressed. She became angry with everyone and frequently took it out on her children.

When her last child entered school, Ellie decided to get a job. But her lack of education and skills restricted her options. For fifteen years she worked as a filing clerk. Then she took over the management of her husband's law office.

Ellie's daughter Nancy is a college professor in the East. She teaches psychology and also maintains a private practice. She speaks at conferences throughout the United States. She has three children. Her husband Tom teaches geography at the same university. When the children were young, he was the family's househusband. He handled the shopping, cooking, cleaning, and chauffeuring duties with élan. He was affectionate and supportive to his children.

In 1971 Nancy and her husband separated. Nancy felt that marriage restricted her. In 1973, Nancy and Tom were divorced. The children by their own choice and Nancy's remained with Tom. They are adults now. They keep in touch with Nancy by phone and visit her once or twice a year. Nancy keeps in touch with Ellie by phone and visits her about once every other year.

Nancy's daughter Maya works at a health food store in Palo Alto. In the evenings, she is a crystal healer, Tarot card reader, and massage therapist. Maya is divorced. She has one daughter, Willa. Maya and her daughter live with Julia, who is also a divorced mother. Julia has a son and daughter. The two women intend to live together at least until their children are grown. Currently Julia works full time and Maya part time so that Maya can be home in the mornings and late afternoons to care for the children.

Ellie, Nancy, and Maya—mothers all, but as unlike one another as sugar, salt, and vinegar. Ellie was brought up in a chocolate or vanilla world. There were few choices. Nancy could choose from seven or eight flavors. Maya lives in a Baskin-Robbins universe—thirty-one flavors. When Willa is an adult, she will be able to choose a hundred flavors plus sugar-free plus low-fat plus no-fat plus frozen yogurt. Of course, her health-conscious mother would be happy if she avoided ice cream all together.

The Divided Mother

Solomon offered to divide the one child between the two mothers. Today's world tries to divide the one mother into many demanding and sometimes incompatible roles. The result is "mother's daze"—the malaise of our time. Ellie was a wife and mother. Nancy was a wife, a mother, and a professional. Maya is a worker, a mother, a social activist, an environmentalist, a counselor for three telephone hotlines, and a leader of a local women's consciousness-raising group.

On Mother's Day, we glorify the traditional family. We sentimentalize and even trivialize motherhood. We act as though it were still 1940 and we forget what a mixed blessing motherhood was for the Ellies of yesterday.

About thirty years ago, in 1959 Phyllis McGinley wrote that women's bodies

> are shaped to bear children, and our lives are a working-out of the processes of creation. All our ambitions and intelligence are beside that great elemental point.[1]

---

[1] Phyllis McGinley, "The Honor of Being a Woman," *The Province of the Heart* (1959); cited in *The International Thesaurus of Quotations*, compiled by Rhoda Thomas Tripp (New York: Perennial Library, Harper & Row, Publishers, 1970), p. 663, number 34.

The Perfect Mom

We used to celebrate the perfect mom of fact, song, and fiction. She was sacrosanct, an icon. "God could not be everywhere, so he made mothers," says the Jewish proverb. "Mother is the name of God in the lips and hearts of little children," said the novelist Thackeray. Silent film maker Mack Sennett recalled:

> We never make sport of religion, politics, race, or mothers. A mother never gets hit with a custard pie. Mothers-in-law—yes. But mothers—never.[2]

We loved her. We feared her. She nurtured and protected us. We thanked her and respected her. When we were children, we were afraid she would abandon us. We depended on her totally and unconditionally, and, of course, we came to resent her. That's what happens in all dependent relationships. When we became adults, we, in one way or another, abandoned her. Sometimes we made her the butt of our jokes, for example, the Jewish mother, the Italian mother. Consider the following apocryphal sayings attributed to mothers of the famous:

> Alexander the Great's mother: "How many times do I have to tell you—you can't have everything you want in this world."
>
> Franz Schubert's mother: "Take my advice, son. Never start anything you can't finish."
>
> Achilles' mother: "Stop imagining things. There's nothing wrong with your heel."
>
> Sigmund Freud's mother: "Stop pestering me! I've told you a hundred times the stork brought you!"

But even as we glorified and teased Mom, we were coming to the realization, as Milton R. Sapirstein had noted in 1955, "The ideal mother, like the ideal marriage, is a fiction."[3]

Economic necessity, women's lib, divorce reform, and changing social expectations tore her from home and hearth. Mom lost her place on the pedestal and was blamed for all manner of societal ills, ranging from teenage drug addiction to illegitimate pregnancy.

In recent decades we seem to have lost faith in her together with many of the other longtime pillars of society. With considerable exaggeration, a "Bloom County" cartoon of a few years ago expresses our cynicism: Opus, the penguin, is suffering a crisis of faith. While standing in front of the television set, he says, "I believe in our government," only to have the TV announcer say, "Today the President admitted sending a personally inscribed copy of Leo Buscaglia's Living, Loving and Hugging to Khadafy." Opus walks into the next room and says, "I have faith in the forces of Capitalism." Just then Milo reads from the newspaper, "Today on Wall Street everybody but the hot dog vendors were busted." Continuing into another room, Opus says, "There's always religion." And Steve Dallas reads from a magazine, "Oral Roberts strangled Jimmy Swaggart and ran off with Tammy Bakker's drug counselor." Stepping outside onto the back porch, Opus queries, "What can a fellow believe in anymore? Are there no more bastions of purity?" Just then he spots a pregnant woman and rushes to embrace her and exclaims, "Motherhood." She responds, "Surrogate!"

---

[2] *The New York Times*, November 6, 1960.

[3] *Paradoxes of Everyday Life* (1955), p. 3.

The Commercialized Mother

As hard as it may be to believe, Mother's Day did not start as a celebration of home and family. It began as a day of social protest. A hundred twenty years ago, we called this special occasion "Mother's Peace Day." Julia Ward Howe, poet, abolitionist, and suffragette was the guiding spirit. Having pleaded the cause of the widows of the American Civil War, she was sickened by suffering caused by the Franco-Prussian conflict. Mrs. Howe called on mothers throughout the world to combine their voices in united opposition to violence. She wrote:

> I was visited by a sudden feeling of the cruel and unnecessary character of the war. It seemed to me a return to barbarism, the issue having been one which might easily have been settled without bloodshed. The question forced itself upon me: Why do not the mothers of mankind interfere in these matters to prevent the waste of human life in which they alone bear and know the cost? The august dignity of motherhood and its terrible responsibilities now appeared to me in a new aspect, and I could think of no better way of expressing my sense of these than of sending forth an appeal to womanhood throughout the world, which I then and there composed.[4]

In 1872 Mother's Peace Day was celebrated in many major American cities, in London and Geneva, and as far away as Constantinople. Such celebrations continued well into the early twentieth century. But little by little, the emphasis shifted. The greeting card companies and the florists came to the fore. One observer notes:

> By World War I the process of commercialization leading to the present form of Mother's Day was well under way. And in 1914 President Wilson declared this day one of reverence for mothers.
>
> What an ironic twist! A movement of mothers into the public arena of international politics has become a day to honor their role in the private arena of home and family![5]

Mothers, to be sure, are still desperately needed in the private arena—perhaps more today than ever. But they have other vital contributions to make—contributions on the local, national, and international scenes.

Let their unified voice be heard as they demand a world of peace and justice, a social order that protects and comforts all. Let us join with them and enable them to do the important job of childrearing—the job without which no civilization can survive. Let us empower them to dream their dreams of contributing to society and to their own aspirations. Let us together remove from them the burdens of irrational limitations and false expectations. Let us, their friends, lovers, children, and fellow citizens, be for them and with them. Together let us nurture and be nurtured.

Stay-at-home moms like Ellie, working moms like Nancy, childrearing single moms like Maya and Julia—"Just who is a mother?" Jesus posed a similar question. In the Gospel according to Matthew we read that Jesus asked, "Who is my mother?" His reply: the one who does the will of my Father in Heaven (Matthew 12:46–50).

---

[4] Howe, Julia Ward, as cited in *Resources for Worship,* edited by Diane Dulin, the Northern California Conference, United Church of Christ, April 1, 1987.

[5] Adapted from *Resources for Worship,* edited by Diane Dulin, the Northern California Conference, United Church of Christ, April 1, 1987.

The Mother We Honor

In the eyes of God, who is a mother? The one who does what God wants. The one who cares for another, the one who puts the needs of another first, the one who teaches another, the one who guides another, the one who listens before speaking, the one who comforts with a touch, the one who toils to support another, the one who works for peace, the one who laughs at what cannot be changed, the one who mourns for the hurt that others do to themselves. In the eyes of God, these are mothers. And on this special day we honor them.

Amen.

—LDS

[1800 words]
[18 minutes]

❦ Sermon 85

❦ *Date:* Father's Day

Text:
1 Samuel 3:2–9

Theme: Thank God for fathers who help children and young people hear the voice of God.
Subject: Father's Day

❦ *Title:* Faith of a Father

Ironically, Eli was a rotten father. The first two shots he took at raising boys were an abysmal failure, and he gave the world two monsters. So God must be a gracious God, because he gave Eli a third chance. When Hannah and Elkanah presented their precious young son for service at the temple, this time Eli performed.

Eli, what is your job description in the raising of Samuel?

Answer: My mission is to raise this young man that when the voice of God is heard, he will know how to decode the noise and respond obediently to it. There could be no higher call for the man who was privileged to be called father.

Any healthy male past the age of puberty can become a father, but it takes a man who understands this mission to be a father. The mission of the man called father is to raise children in such a way that, like Samuel, they may be able to decode the voice of God and make a proper choice as to whether or not they shall respond. This encounter happened in the tabernacle at Shiloh, for God called people to himself in special places.

In Lexington, Massachusetts, where Gail and I and our children, Mark and Kristi, lived for thirteen years, we lived on Grant Street in a small, ranch-type house with six or seven rooms and one bathroom. I now shake my head in consternation to realize I raised a family with one john. One year ago, my wife and I said goodbye to Grant Street. As we got into the car, I said, "Why don't we go back into the house one more time. Let's tour each room and see if we can form one final memory of something that happened so we can carry it with us." And so we went from room to room and decided the most memorable experience that had happened in the vocation of mothering and fathering during those thirteen years.

The first room is the breezeway, sometimes the family room. It was a marvelous place to eat and have a lot of fun in as a family. I remember coming home one day when our children were probably around the ages of nine and six. As I entered the breezeway, the two of them were standing nose-to-nose, ripping each other apart. I was amazed at the words and the anger. I was grieved, as a father would be watching his children rip each other apart. Then I put my hands on their shoulders so they maintained this limited distance, and I said, "Listen carefully. This place is called home. It is unlike any other place. When you enter into a home, people do things differently. In a home, they build each other. Did you hear that word? They build each other. Say it for me, very slowly." And both children said, "Build each other." Say it again louder, so I can hear you better." "Build each other." "Yes, that's what you do in a home. You build each other. Outside that door, people carve each other up. They compete with each other. And sometimes you have to look over your shoulder to see who may be coming up behind you. You should never have to do that in a home. I anticipate from this moment forward that the content of your conversation will always be in the mode of building, because here we are growing human beings to the glory of God." That's a definition of a home, a place where people are built. The rest of the world is a place where people are discriminated against, are denied their rights, are made to feel something less than they are. But in a home, the number one task of parents is to build people, to create an environment in which people can grow.

I stood one day at the edge of a newly planted lawn. I loved the cleverness of the planter who had put a sign there that said, "Please do not walk on this ground; seeds are at work." A sign like that could go on the front of every home. Seeds are at work. Children are being grown. People are being built.

Our cliché becomes build. It came home to roost one day when I said an idle word to my wife and one of our children said to me, "Now Dad, was that a building statement? Why don't you say it again to Mom and see if the second time you can do it right."

I believe one day men entrusted with wives and children will stand before God and among the first questions God might ask would be, "Did your child and spouse grow to be all that I designed them to be in the environment you created?" In the breezeway, the great memory was the admonition to build.

You go from the breezeway to the kitchen. At one end had been a lovely old table we had refinished, and around that table we ate our meals. When it was time to eat, the phone came off the hook because for the hour we were at that table, the family was the ultimate priority. That did not happen by accident, for as our children began to enter the preteen years, Gail and I discovered that our family schedule was falling into the hands of everybody outside the house. The children were victimized in a positive sense by the wonderful things to do in the school. The church had its own programs. The community had its programs. If we did not have control of our family calendar, before long we would be going in four different directions, having almost no useful time together.

One day my wife made an announcement with my support. She said, "From this day forward, every evening at supper time, we are going to eat together. It is an inviolable part of the daily schedule. I don't care what time we eat, as long as you tell me when you all can be here." My contribution was to suggest that supper time is more than eating. It is a relational event in which people talk. That, I believe, is the second mark of a home in which people grow; people learn to talk with each other. No one will learn to talk if the time is not taken and if interruptions are not minimized. As we stood in the kitchen of the empty house, we began to think of all the great conversations that happened around that old table: The evenings when one of the children came home defeated in an event at school and the opportunities to give vent to feelings and frustrations; the moments when the interesting questions merged into long conversations about sex, about marriage, or how you hear the voice of God.

If your children are anything like mine, they don't like to talk. "How was your day?" "Good." "Is that all, good?" "Yeah." "But, that's the way it was yesterday, and the day before that." So fathers have to be creative, like, "If you don't tell me what was the most interesting part of your day, it will cost you a quarter." Sometimes it takes a father who admits to his children that he also had struggles that day or that he has failed. But sooner or later, because the time is taken, families learn to talk.

When you leave the kitchen, you come to the living room. Our living room had a large, plate glass window, and my memory as I entered that room was of our daughter, Kristi, who often sat on the love seat looking out the window. I often saw her there at 5:30 in the morning, when, for an hour with her Bible and journal, she would spend time ordering her world and bringing it into reconciliation with God.

She often did her homework out there. And it was not unusual to walk into the living room and see eight or ten young people sitting around the fireplace as she and the others talked about the Scriptures or a summer mission trip. The living room was a lovely place, and Kristi liked it very much. But one Saturday afternoon, Kristi sat in front of that window, and I knew the thoughts this time were difficult thoughts. Gail had alerted me that Kristi was struggling, and maybe it was time for her father to enter the act. The issue was simple. She had to make a big decision as to where she was going to attend high school. One group of friends thought she ought to go to the public school, and the other group thought she ought to go to the Christian school. She knew that to make a decision would hurt one group. Here was a fourteenyear-old child, more girl than woman, wrestling with a massive decision.

As I listened to her talk, I finally heard myself saying, "Kristi, all men and women, be they teenagers or adults, have moments when they are like an oak tree or a tulip. The trick is to know which you are. Oak trees grow and stand tall. They take a long time, but when they get to full growth, no one messes with them. You walk around them, because oak trees stand by themselves. They are strong and beautiful and tall. And, Kristi, I have seen you when you are an oak tree. On the other hand, tulips grow to fullness and beauty also, but even at their greatest height and beauty, they need to be protected. You need to build a fence around a tulip, but you don't have to worry about an oak tree at all. So, it's important for fathers to ask their daughters, 'Are you today an oak tree or a tulip?' because if you are an oak tree, Kris, I'll leave you alone. But if you are a tulip, I'll build a fence around you today.

She pondered the alternatives, and then came the tears and finally the quiet voice, "Daddy, today I'm a tulip." With those code words, father knows it's time to protect. Thank God, there are moments when fathers have that opportunity to build a fence. And thank God for the moment when he gives us the spirit of discernment to know when our children need the fence because they are tulips and when we need to stand aside because they are becoming oak trees.

If you walk down the hall, there's a bedroom where our son, Mark, lived. I remember that bedroom vividly. And now a memory quickly came to me. Mark was a sixth grader when the event happened. He had rushed in the door of our home after school and said, "The kids have asked me to go with them to Cape Cod this weekend There are fourteen of us going, seven boys and seven girls. It's going to be fantastic!" Sixth grade. For seventy-two hours. I took one look at him and with all my good interventive techniques, said, "No way!" Sixth grade is generally the year when boys and girls form peer groups, when popularity becomes an issue, when being in the in-group is the most important thing in the world. To be invited to go to the Cape for a weekend is a special privilege, and to hear from your parents that there's "no way" is devastating.

Mark quickly disappeared, and for a half hour I didn't hear anything from him. I began to search the house, but I couldn't find him. Then suddenly my mind turned back to the bedroom, and I realized there was something unusual about that bedroom; the closet door had been shut. So I went back into the bedroom and opened the closet door. There, back in the corner, was my son, sitting with his knees wrapped up to his chest, quietly weeping. I'd never seen him do that before.

There are no textbooks that tell a father how to perform in a moment like that, but instinct told me I ought to join him. I found myself closing the closet door behind me and getting down on the floor in that darkened closet. I sat in the darkness for ten minutes and listened to my boy weep. Finally, when there were no more tears, I began to rethink the decision I had made and whether I had been too arbitrary. "Son," I said, "let's talk. It's obviously very important to you. Tell me about the ground rules. Tell me what's going to happen." And with that, the story came out, the story I had been too gruff to listen to. When he finished, I said, "Bud, I'll back off. You go. But I want you to promise you will watch everything that happens this weekend. Watch the way the adults act and the way they treat their son. Watch the way the young people interface with each other. Promise that the minute you get back, the two of us will sit down and have a long talk about everything you saw and how you felt about it."

He said, "Dad, I promise." He went, and thank God, he had a thoroughly miserable time. "It was crazy, Dad. Those parents didn't care what their kids did. The kids were left on their own, hour after hour. Something wrong could have gone on. You and Mom would never have acted that way. I'm really pleased that you let me experience that, because I saw how different families treat each other." From that weekend, because I made a choice to flex as a father, my son and I have a different relationship, which lasts until this day. He learned and I learned that part of good fathering is to have principles and convictions but also to learn how to negotiate and flex and allow one's son or daughter to take a few chances for the possibility of learning valuable lessons on their own.

Down the hall is the bedroom where Gail and I lived. When we reached that room, we laughed a bit as we remembered that it was to that room late in the hours of the night that the children often came with all sorts of wonderful and troubling stories. There was the night at 12:30 when a soft knock came on the door and a rather quiet male voice said, "Dad, can I come in for a moment?" The door opened and our son walked in at the age of seventeen. He was breathing hard. He said, "Dad, I don't know how you are going to take this, but I got a speeding ticket tonight. You warned me, and I've gotten it and I'm very, very sorry." And he sat on the edge of the bed and he talked about how he made the mistake. You said to yourself, "Thank God we have achieved a point where the boy can admit he's wrong." We talked about what we were going to do about it. We gave each other an embrace, and he went to his bed.

Or there was the night when the same kind of knock came on the door, and this time it's a feminine voice: "Daddy? Mom? Can I come in?" And a little girl now turned seventeen sits on the edge of the bed and tells you about a handsome guy she has met, and how he has feelings for her, and she has feelings for him. You look mesmerized as the little girl unfolds the fact that now she has become a women, her heart has been captured. Just two weeks ago I walked her down the aisle to commit her to that young man, but there in that bedroom, we first heard the story of a budding romance.

Gail and I looked at each other in that empty bedroom and remembered moments like that when there was the admission of pain and the first seeds of joy, and we said to ourselves, "Thank God, our children know this was a room to which they could come no matter what the hour talk about what was in their hearts."

The garage brought us to the memory of a red pickup truck that was housed in it for many years. When our son turned sixteen, the learner's permit was hardly dry or in his billfold when he came to me and said, "Dad, next Friday I have a date; I'd like to take her in the truck." I said, "Well, Bud, you can't do that. You only have a learner's permit, and you can't go out at night without someone who has a license." "Dad, she has a license." But the licensee has to be eighteen." "Dad, she's eighteen and a half." "Where is the date?" "Boston." "What time does it start?" "Five-thirty." "Have you ever driven in Boston at 5:30 on Friday afternoon?"

I wanted to say, "No way!" but I had learned my lesson. I said, "Bud, give me two hours to think about it." "I called the father of the girl and said, "Don, you know your daughter and my son have a date next Friday, don't you?" He said, "Yes, I do." "How would you feel if you knew that Mark was going to drive on that date with just a learner's permit because your daughter has a driver's license?" He said, "Gordon, I trust Mark's judgment. If you feel he should do that, it's fine with me." The two hours were almost gone, and I said, "Mark, my answer is yes under one condition. On the night before your date, you and I will drive the route to the date at the same time of day, and you will permit me to create any kind of circumstance and you will have to react to it." He said, "Sure, Dad." So the next Thursday at 5:30, we started out in rush hour traffic, bumper to bumper. I suddenly said to him, "Son, I'm sorry, but your right front tire just blew out." "What do you want me to do?" "What do you do with tires that have just blown out?" "You change them."

"Then get over there and change it!" So we pull over into the breakdown lane with me praying that a cop wouldn't stop and make me explain all this. Mark climbed under the truck to get the jack, and he was under there for ten minutes. When he appeared, there was no jack. Jacks in most pickup trucks are under the hood. Mark found out that afternoon. He also discovered what to do when an alternator burns out. He discovered what you have to do when you plan to go down an exit ramp and the freeway is blocked because of construction, and you have to take an alternate route. He also learned what happens if the truck completely breaks down and you have to make a decision late at night whether to call the girl's father or not. When we got home that night, I think Mark knew every contingency about driving a pickup truck to Boston on a Friday afternoon. I smiled about that as I stood in the empty garage in the home on Grant Street. But that's the act of fathering. It's releasing the child to face the possibilities and to grow through experience once you have taught him everything that's possible to give him.

The last room we walked through was the dining room, and the memory I have of the dining room is not as happy as all the others. It came the night of a birthday party for me. Gail had cooked my favorite food. She put together a beautiful cake. The presents were all wrapped. The lights were now low, and the family gathered for the supper. But it was clear from the onset that the children were not in sync with the evening's activities. They were caught up too much in their own thoughts. Soon they got to complaining about a vegetable they didn't like (which I did), and they started bickering with each other. Then they sprang up from the table and announced they were going to watch a favorite television show and they'd appreciate it if we'd wait for them. We sat at the table for thirty minutes, me saddened that the kids had forgotten it was my birthday, that they were spending too much time thinking about things that were important to them. We were tempted to ask the question parents ask on occasion. Where did we go wrong?"

Finally after an hour they came up and one said, "Where's the cake? When are we going to open the presents?" I said, "I'm sorry, the party has been canceled." "It can't be canceled. This is your birthday." I said, "I know it's on the calendar, but a party is a party only when the people determine its supposed to be a party and act in a party mood. Two of the four of us decided today to party by themselves. So maybe we'll have the party in another few nights. But not tonight. The party's over."

It was not a pleasant scene as our children walked away with tears. Later that night, sitting at the edge of the bed with my son and listening to him apologize to God and to his father because of his selfishness, I realized there are moments in the raising of a family when fathers have to make difficult decisions and say and do painful things. In my journal that night, I wrote these words: "It would be so easy, God, to make simple decisions dictated by convenience and the desire to be liked. But just as I withdrew the hand that offers pain to my children, you remind me, God, that one never learns and grows and blooms when the climate is easy. Teach me, therefore, God, like a father to thank with eyes and ears, to brood with a heart just like yours, which sees in the scope of eternity's process what makes people, even my children, become like your Son, Christ. The ecstasy of this one moment when simple decisions might bring temporary tranquility is not to be compared with the maturity of all the tomorrows through which my children must live."

For the final time, we locked the door on the house on Grant Street. It's not quite the same place with the furniture gone and the curtains down and the pictures off the wall and the shouts and the joys and even the tears of the children no longer there. It's just an empty-fourwalled structure that a new family will fill with its artifacts in another day or two. A house is not made of dry wall, studding, and plate glass windows. No, a house is a place that becomes a home when there is a decision on the part of a father and a mother to make the people inside it grow. And there comes a day when, having grown, the children leave and become what their choices are making them become. As we drive up Grant Street, leaving behind us the empty house, we are able to pray, thanking God that he gave us a home where children grew.

For some of you, that is a dream yet to happen. For others, it's a dream in progress. For many of you, like me, it is a past memory. But thank God for fathers who help children and young people hear the voice of God. It is one of the greatest privileges in the world.

Amen.[1]

—Gordon MacDonald

[3963 words]
[40 minutes]

Sermon 86

Date: Father's Day

Text:
Luke 15:11-31

Theme: Great fathering requires three things: being there, being aware, and being real. Everything else is dessert.
Subject: Fathering

Title: "Help Wanted, Dad. Ask for Calvin and Hobbes."

What Do Daddies Do?

Six-year-old Calvin is talking to his stuffed tiger, Hobbes:

Calvin: Here's a box of crayons. I need some illustrations for a story I'm writing. You can draw something besides tigers, can't you?

Hobbes: Sure, leopards, pumas, ocelots . . . you name it.

[Time passes and we find Calvin in bed with his stuffed tiger, ready to be tucked in by his father.]

Calvin: Here Dad, read this story tonight. I wrote it and Hobbes illustrated it.

Dad: . . . Um. OK. [He reads aloud.] "The Dad Who Lived to Regret Being Mean to His Kid."

---

[1] Copyright, 1987, *Preaching Today*. Used with permission.

Calvin: What are you pausing for. Keep reading.

Dad: Barney's dad was really bad. So Barney hatched a plan. When his dad said, "Eat your peas!" Barney shouted, "NO!" and ran.

Barney tricked his mean ol' dad and locked him in the cellar. His mom never found out where he'd gone, 'cause Barney didn't tell her.

There his dad spent his life, eating mice and gruel. With every bite for fifty years he was sorry he'd been cruel. THE END.

Calvin: You know how a lot of stories have morals to them . . .?

Dad: [With great annoyance] I get it. I get it![1]

What are the primary tasks of being a father? And how should we perform them?

Fathers protect. Fathers teach. Fathers model. Fathers instill values. Fathers empower (or disempower), and Fathers are a child's point of contact with the wider world. In particular, a father is essential for the development of his children's sense of values. In simplest terms: No dad, no conscience.

Dads provide leadership by example and encouragement; the key words—to repeat—are example and encouragement. A child sees as possible what Dad says is possible and what the child sees as possible in Dad's life. Soon enough, the same child will realize that Dad's word is not the only word or necessarily the final word. That comes later.

Taming the Barbarians: Dad and Discipline

[Dad is sitting at a desk in the living room, balancing his checkbook. Calvin enters carrying a clipboard.]

Calvin: Dad, your polls took a big dive this week. Your "Overall Dad performance" rating was especially low. [He hands the clipboard to Dad.] See? Right about yesterday your popularity went down the tubes.

[Dad protests vehemently]

Dad: CALVIN, YOU DIDN'T GET DESSERT YESTERDAY BECAUSE YOU FLOODED THE HOUSE!!

[Calvin walks away as he replies.]

Calvin: I'd suggest a new line of work, "DAD" . . .[2]

Dads not only empower; they set limits. And when the limits are transgressed, it is Dad's job to discipline the wayward. In the words of Dr. Alberta Siegel, a professor of psychology at Stanford University:

---

[1] Watterson, Bill, *The Calvin and Hobbes Lazy Sunday Book* (Kansas City: Andrews and McMeel, 1989), p. 45.

[2] "Calvin and Hobbes," by Bill Watterson, June 11, 1991.

> When it comes to rearing children, every society is only 20 years away from barbarism. Twenty years is all we have to accomplish the task of civilizing the infants who are born into our midst each year. These savages know nothing of our language, our culture, our religion, our values, our customs or our interpersonal relations. The infant is totally ignorant about communism, fascism, democracy, civil liberties, the rights of the minority as contrasted with the prerogatives of the majority, respect, decency, honesty, customs, conventions, and manners. The barbarian must be tamed if civilization is to survive.[3]

That is not to say that discipline is only Dad's job or that it is Dad's sole job. But just as fathers represent the possibilities of the outside world to their children, so also do they react as agents of that world.

Leaving Dad Behind

Calvin: I wanna horsey ride!

Dad: [stirring paint] I'm busy Calvin.

Calvin: You know, Dad, it won't be long before I'm all grown up. One day you'll wake up and wonder how all the years slipped by. You'll look back and say, "Where has the time gone? Calvin's so big. It's hard to remember when he was small enough that I could give him horsey rides . . . But those day will be lost forever.

[Calvin is on Dad's back as they gallop toward a fence.]

Dad: I think I've worked through my potential guilt now.

Calvin: No, no! Jump the fence![4]

In one of my memories of my childhood, I am about ten years old. My playmates have bicycles, and I want one, too. My father discovers that the Chicago Herald-American is selling Schwinn bicycles to its carriers for nineteen dollars. He convinces the local newspaper distributor to sell one to him. It is delivered, unassembled in a cardboard carton.

For most of a weekend, we work together in the basement of our apartment building assembling the red, one-speed, balloon-tired bicycle. It proves a formidable task, which I assist by passing him tools and asking impatiently when he will be finished.

Finally, it is done. Dad rides the bike around the block, tinkers with the chain some more, and rides it again.

Then he has me mount it. He walks alongside, steadying the bike. At first, he grips the handle bars. Then he holds the saddle as I practice steering and pedaling. He walks faster and faster. Soon he is running. As the bike picks up speed, he lets go, and I lose my balance and fall in the street. We repeat the sequence again and again. Balance still eludes me. He demonstrates, explains as best he can, and we try again. It is after dark when we quit.

A few days later we try again. He rides the bike for several minutes and has me try. He steadies the bicycle again. I manage a few yards on my own, become frightened, and stop. Then we try again. I add a few more yards to my range. We try again. Finally, to his surprise and mine,

---

3 *Stanford Observer,* October 1973, p. 4.

4 "Calvin and Hobbes," June 25, 1987.

I am riding alone. I am frightened and excited. I glance back over my shoulder. Dad is waving at me, smiling, and shouting encouragement as he recedes into the distance. I am on my own!

I am still unsure and wobbly. In the next few days there are spills and scrapes. Trying to stop, I scratch the paint on a car door about three blocks from home. I explore new neighborhoods, meet new boys my own age. About a mile from home, a bully stops me, tries to goad me into a fight, and tells me to stay out of his neighborhood. From month to month, my self-confidence and range increase. Some days, I bicycle from morning to night. I am on my own!

Psychiatrist Martin Greenberg states:

> As fathers, we struggle to get our children on the "cycle" of life. We race alongside of them, panting—exhausted sometimes—and, finally, they're able to ride off on their own, and we are saddened because we feel we've been left behind. But indelible memories can keep you running alongside that bike.[5]

Permanently etched in our very being, influencing our sense of self, are what we as sons and daughters remember about our father's teaching us. For Dad was there from Day One instructing us how to pee other than in our pants or ride a bike or shave or flirt or gut a fish or entertain guests at a pretend tea party or start a lawn mower or shag flies, in sum, to "be a man" or "act like a lady." These memories color not only our relationships with our father, but with all other human beings as well. The memories of a son, in particular, surface again and again in the way he acts as a father with his own children. In his book, The Birth of a Father, Greenberg states that he often thought of his father and his own first bicycle-riding lesson just after his own son was born. He comments:

> The images captured the closeness that I have with my father and yet the reality that I was leaving him behind, that I was moving on to a new phase of my life. My recollection of my father running beside me filled me with a need to be near my own child, to be a part of his life, recognizing nevertheless that at one point he would also leave me behind.[6]

Dad is our teacher and our model. He recedes into the distance—yet is always there. For a lifetime, we idealize him, fight him, blame him, and resist him. But when we become fathers ourselves, we catch ourselves repeatedly using his very words and duplicating his very reactions. We keep telling ourselves that we are smarter than he was, that we will never make the same mistakes with our children that he did with us. Consciously and unconsciously, we keep asserting: "Look, Dad, I'm on my own now!" But we never are.

[Calvin's Dad is in his chair, drinking coffee and reading the newspaper.]

Calvin: How come you're still home? Why aren't you at work?

Dad: I took the day off. [Calvin looks horrified.]

Calvin: Say, Dad. Can I have a look at the classified section?

Dad: As soon as I'm through with it.

---

[5] "Father's Day Can Be a Celebration of All Kinds of Ties," by Al Morch, *San Francisco Examiner*, June 21, 1987, p. E-4. See also Martin Greenberg, *The Birth of a Father* (New York: Avon Books, 1985), pp. 71–72.

[6] Ibid., p. 72.

Calvin: Gosh, Dad. I'd sure like to borrow that section right this minute. Why don't you read the editorials?

Dad: [Looking astounded, reads aloud,] "New Dad wanted. Frequent traveler preferred. Liberal views on discipline a must. Ask for Calvin during normal work hours."[7]

Fathering Made Easy (?)

[It is a quiet Sunday afternoon. Calvin's dad is sitting on the patio reading. Calvin walks by, covered with mud.]

Dad: Wow! How did you ever get so muddy?!

Calvin: Well, I was just standing there, minding my own business, when all of a sudden, a horde of dirty cannibals comes . . .

Dad: Forget it.

[Calvin wanders off. Dad throws back his arms and takes a deep breath.]

Dad: Boy, what a delightful afternoon. Sometimes I feel like I work all the time to afford this place, and never get to sit back with a good book and enjoy it. Well, at least I have the weekends to . . . [Dad's reverie is interrupted by his wife's scream.]

Mom: CALVIN! YOU GOT MUD ALL OVER THE HOUSE! LOOK AT YOU! AIEE—THE COUCH! WHAT'D YOU DO?! DID YOU WALK ACROSS THE COUCH?!

Calvin: I didn't do it! Someone else must have! I saw a muddy guy go running from . . .

Mom: OUT! OUT OF THE HOUSE! NOW!

Calvin: OK, OK! I'm going! You don't need to push! I can tell when I'm not wanted! Hey! Leggo! Ow! All right, goodbye!

[Dad sits with his book in hand, staring into space. Calvin reappears.]

Calvin: Hey, Dad, catch the water balloon. [Dad and his book are drenched.] Great reflexes, Dad. By the way, don't go in the house like that. Mom's in one of her moods again.

Dad [talking to himself]: I'll bet I could get a lot of work done at the office on weekends . . .[8]

So here we are on this weekend—on Father's Day no less, trying to brush up on our fathering skills. When we took on this job, no one gave us a guidebook, but there are a few obvious rules.

First, as a father realize that your only responsibility is to do the best that you can do, to be aware of the impact you have on your children, and to respond as fully as you can to their needs.

---

[7] "Calvin and Hobbes," August 25, 1987.

[8] Watterson, *The Calvin and Hobbes Lazy Sunday Book*, p. 75.

Second, do the best you can do under the circumstances just as your father did the best he could do.

Third, do whatever you do for your children because it gives you pleasure to do it—not because you have to or because it's good for them—and expect nothing in return.

Fourth, accept responsibility for your own happiness and stop expecting your spouse or your kids to do it for you.

Fifth, start now to make positive contributions to your children's memories of their childhood. You cannot guarantee that their memories will not accentuate the negative while ignoring the positive, but you can create a basis today for being remembered as a great father tomorrow. It is all in the execution. Time and focus are all that separate a good father from a rotten father. There is no such thing as a few minutes of "quality time." Quality means attention, dedication, commitment, talent, and, above all, ample time.

Great fathering requires three things: being there, being aware, and being real. Everything else is dessert.

Being there, wanting to be there, committing oneself to being there, being proud of being there, putting up with the messes and the disappointments and one's own shortcomings, and still choosing to be there for this child—that is what fathering is all about.

And don't worry too much about not having all the answers. That's what children are for!

Calvin: Dad, can you get my ball out of the gutter again?

Dad: This is the third time this afternoon! I thought I told you to play out back!

Calvin: Relax, Dad. It's just a ball in the gutter. It's not as if I've been embezzling money or killing people, right? Aren't you glad I'm not stealing and murdering?

[Dad walks away. Calvin turns toward the reader.]

Calvin: I always have to help Dad establish the proper context.[9]

Amen.

—LDS

[2100 words]
[21 minutes]

Sermon 87

Date: Father's Day

Texts:
Jeremiah 31:7–9
Psalm 103:8–13; Psalm 136
Ephesians 6:1–4
John 13:1–17

Theme: The secret of fatherhood is controlling one's ego and strength, directing one's energies to serving one's sons and daughters, laying aside power and prerogative in order to share one's life with one's children.

---

[9] "Calvin and Hobbes," August 21, 1987.

Subject: Fathers

❦ *Title:* The King Who Cried

God Is No Bully

I love good fathers, those who are committed to their families and not afraid to admit their mistakes and clean up their own messes. What bothers me are cruel and unreasonable fathers who use the Bible as their excuse, citing a few passages from Proverbs and the Apostle Paul. If God were the kind of father to the human race that such petty despots would have us imitate, we would have all perished long ago. But such a God never has made an appearance in the Bible as I understand it. To be sure, the God of the Old Testament is wrathful, punitive, and demanding, but he is also long-suffering, caring, forgiving, and restoring. Fundamentally, his love is as unconditional as it is capricious. He loves whom he loves, when and where he chooses to love. "Jacob have I loved and Esau have I hated." His gifts and promises are unearned and undeserved. But there are limits to his patience and favor. For he is a moral as well as a loving God.

Hence, he initiates the Covenant of Sinai. His message to the children of Israel is "You will be my people and I will be your God." And the sign of this adoption is obedience to the Torah, the Law which binds every man, woman, child, beast, and possession to him. The strict observance of the Law sets this people apart from all other nations as chosen and holy. But to break the Law—by worshiping other gods, by living like every other people, by ignoring the demand for justice, and by oppressing the poor and the weak—is to abrogate the Covenant and unleash the wrath of a jealous deity.

And when his chosen nation breaks the rules and defies God, it is scattered among the Gentiles, its institutions, sacred places, and leadership destroyed. But even then, God chastises but does not reject. In his mercy, he offers his chosen people a way back. He sends his prophets to the exiles to teach them the lessons which their fathers had ignored: "He has showed you, O man, what is good; and what does the LORD require of you but to do justice, and to love kindness, and to walk humbly with your God." (Micah 6:8) In his punishment, there is restoration and redemption. He swears a new and unalterable covenant with his people that shall culminate in a reign of peace for the whole world. And he calls his chastened and reeducated people back to the land of promise: "With weeping they shall come, and with consolations I will lead them back, I will make them walk by brooks of water, in a straight path in which they shall not stumble; for I am a father to Israel . . ." (Jeremiah 31:9)

The God of the old covenant is no tyrant, crushing the spirit of his wayward offspring. His wrath is balanced by a tenderness which we, in our own day, would probably (and foolishly) describe as maternal. His heart aches for his children even as he corrects them. In the words of Psalm 103,

> The LORD is merciful and gracious,
>   slow to anger and abounding in steadfast love.
> He will not always chide,
>   nor will he keep his anger for ever.
> He does not deal with us according to our sins,
>   nor requite us according to our iniquities.
> For as high as the heavens are high above the earth,
>   so great is his steadfast love toward
>   those who fear him;
> as far as the east is from the west,

so far does he remove our transgressions from us.
As a father pities his children,
so the LORD pities those who fear him. (vss. 8–13)

And throughout the Old Testament, we find images of a nurturing, protective, empathetic, responsive, and involved father, whose "love is eternal." (Psalm 136) In no way is he a model to the autocratic father.

Nor does the patriarchal bully find much comfort in the New Testament. "Father" is a key word, appearing more than four hundred times. However, the authoritarian paradigm, that is, that to disobey Dad is to rebel against God, is scarcely a normative doctrine. The example of Jesus of Nazareth makes short shrift of images of fatherhood based on domination. The child Jesus not only ignored the guilt-tripping of his earthly parents so that he could be about his heavenly father's business, but, as an adult, he encouraged his followers to put first things first even if that meant placing family obligations last. He knew that even as primal and powerful a relationship as the father–child bond would eventually have to dissolve as the child became a free and responsible agent.

Moreover, Jesus' teachings are an offense to the autocratic father. The Parable of the Prodigal Son is sufficient to demolish patriarchal pretensions. The wastrel's father welcomes and restores his son. A self-righteous tyrant would have beaten him, thrown him out, and written him out of the will. But more decisively, our Lord's description of his relationship to his father speaks the language of intimacy and unity rather than of power and domination. The son, to be sure, is submissive—"obedient unto death, even death on a cross." (Philippians 2:8) For it is in submission and service that he reveals his true greatness, his oneness with the Father. The message is that whatever such love is, God is. The implication for fathers is that the one who serves and influences is greater than the one who commands and dominates.

John the Baptist had preached that the kingdom of God was at hand. He probably envisioned it as a rigid *theocratic monarchy*. But Jesus offered it to his disciples as a *cooperative kinship*, a new family in which rank and recognition depend on service to others. The model lord of the household is neither a taskmaster nor a benevolent despot. He is a servant.

To share in the life of the new family by serving others is to participate in the unity of Father and Son. In the fellowship of believers, in daily lives open to the presence of God and responsive to the needs of others, we experience a God who is available, intimate, compassionate, self-giving, and constant.

The King Who Wore a Towel

Every father is a king. But for Christians the model is the King of Kings, who took the form of a servant, who girded himself with a towel and washed the feet of his apostles, who was touched with our infirmities and was not ashamed to weep for our sorrows.

The greatest manifestation of the Christ's power was neither in his miracles nor his resurrection but in his restraining that power, using it only on behalf of others, and surrendering himself totally to our state and fate. *Here is the secret of fatherhood—controlling one's ego and strength, directing one's energies to serving one's sons and daughters, laying aside power and prerogative in order to share one's life with one's children.*

Dads are needed to put on the towel of the servant-king. Dads are needed to follow the example of the King of Kings, who humbled himself, became one of us, and on the night of his betrayal girded himself in a towel to wash the feet of his disciples. Dads are desperately needed to be there, to be aware, and to respond. They are needed as hands-on fathers. For a man, no relationship is more fulfilling, lasting or magic than that which he sustains with his own children.

Hobbies come and go, careers end, marriages are dissolved, but I will always be my father's son and I will always be my children's father. What they are to me and I to them cannot be sundered by circumstances, misunderstandings, or death. It is not a bed of roses. In the indissoluble bond of being a father, there is pain, there is frustration, there is disappointment. But, this side of heaven, only in fathering can a man find permanence, a sense of at-homeness and belonging, and the experience of immortality. But the quality of our relatedness as father and child (or as grandfather and grandchild, or stepfather and stepchild) does not come by accident. Such rapport must be tended, fed, and cherished.

In sum, Dad is needed to be free, creative, dedicated, caring, wise, and empowering. He is needed in his children's lives as a bearer of a love like God's which makes strong demands but which never lets go of the beloved. *Being there, wanting to be there, committing oneself to being there, being proud of being there, putting up with the messes and the disappointments and one's own shortcomings, and still choosing to be there for this child—that is what fathering is all about.* And the more Dad is there—alert, aware, and responsive—the more Dad is himself fulfilled. Fathering, stepfathering, grandfathering, and godfathering are creative relationships that begin when someone big and powerful takes someone little and powerless into his arms, smiles, and receives a smile back. Like marriage and friendship, like loving God with all your heart and your neighbor as yourself, being a father is what you make it.

Amen.

—LDS

[1500 words]
[15 minutes]

❦ *Sermon 88*

❦ *Occasion:* Talk for a Parents' Group or PTA

Theme: Parents influence their children by example.
Subject: Parenting

❦ *Title:* Parents—The Bravest People in the World

You are the bravest people in the world. Never in my lifetime has it been more difficult to be a parent. And never has it been more difficult to be a child [teenager].

Today's young people face greater opportunities, temptations, challenges, and threats than any generation in American history. With virtually no adequate information, they face decisions about sex, drugs, career preparation, and so on at ever-younger ages. Their peers cannot help them—they are no better prepared. The schools do the best they can, but their best is not good enough.

That leaves the burden exactly where it belongs—in Mom and Dad's hands. Being a parent is a dirty job, but somebody's got to do it. And let's face it—it is the job you really wanted all along.

The Tools of Parenting

Being a parent requires time, attention, and concentration. It requires more than an intensely focused moment of "quality time" every now and then. Unless we are committed to rearing our children; are there for them when they need us, are willing to try, make mistakes, and try again, we will more likely than not fail at this job.

Parents have the greatest lifelong influence on their children. They can do the most good or the greatest harm. If parents create an atmosphere in which their children feel accepted, free to communicate, and respected, their children will be open and receptive to their advice—at least, some of the time. The very closeness of the family both intensifies and limits the effectiveness of parents as advice-givers. What they do—the example they set, the self-control they maintain, the honesty of their dealings with their family members and with others—is the most powerful educational force in the world.

What parents *say* is another matter. Although children are influenced by their parents' words as long as the parents live and long thereafter, the influence can be positive, negative, or mixed. Ambivalent persons appreciate advice even when they outwardly resist it. And there is the natural defensiveness of children when it comes to parental urgings. As children struggle to become their individual selves and achieve independence, they may be poor receivers for parental advice. This does not mean that parents should ignore the problems of their offspring. It simply means that they will have to learn when to offer help and when to back off and allow their children to make their own mistakes.

Parents must recognize that even the best of families must ultimately disintegrate in a natural way. The goal of parenting is the final freedom for our children from all that limits our children—including their relationship with us. The test of a loving family is its ability to respect the decisions made by its members—even if these decisions are painful, confusing, and alien to that family. As a parent, I must grant those whom I love the same freedom I demand for myself.

Is it possible to disasterproof our children? to guarantee that they will never use drugs or join a cult or hook up with a loser as a potential life's mate? The best defense against the problems of the young adult years is the creation during childhood days of an atmosphere of free and open communication. Most of the young adults I counsel feel that they were never able to discuss their deepest feelings with anyone—family, friends, or professionals. They report a wall of reticence, busyness, and impatience which stood between them and their parents during their adolescent and college years. The willingness of the instant family provided by the cult or sect or their drug-using peers or their girlfriend or boyfriend to listen sympathetically is for many clients their first experience of unconditional emotional support. Or so it seems.

Protecting a child against tomorrow's follies requires a deepening of interpersonal intimacy, the willingness to listen, and more. Good college teachers are often praised for encouraging their students "to think for themselves." For whom have these young adults been thinking during the previous twenty years? Being autonomous is an art which requires constant practice and much support. Keeping the next generation of children out of trouble requires that we carefully and cleverly explain to them how everyday decisions are influenced by peers, advertising, parental expectations, and one's own insecurities. We need to praise independence and responsibility in decision-making. The real villain is gullibility—the inability to examine our actions critically and the unwillingness to say no.

Cults, drugs, and antisocial life-styles have little fascination or power of attraction for those who know who they are, what they believe, how to think for themselves, and where their lives are going. Parents can do a great deal to encourage the development of a sense of identity, to foster a positive self-image, and to provide an island of unconditional acceptance in the midst of a lonely and threatening world. Parents can and should articulate ethical values and religious beliefs. None of these actions can guarantee that one's offspring will be happy, successful, or trouble free. But not doing them is a prescription for disaster.

Parents as Models

Remember—*attitudes are caught not taught.* Children imitate the only role models they have—their parents. Children have no innate knowledge about religion, money, sex, interpersonal relationships, or anything else.

The child of parents with clear commitments has something against which to react, attitudes to reject or refine, and a haven to which he or she may return if all else fails. "Live and let live" provides no sense of direction. No one can find a fixed point of reference in a stress-filled world by reacting to such an attitude as that reflected in the often-heard parental cop-out: "I don't believe in forcing my children to do anything they don't want to. I think they should have the right to think for themselves, to decide on their own values and beliefs. I think that when they are adults they can choose their own religion, morality, and politics." If parents who feel this way would only realize that they are telling their children: "I really don't care what you believe or how you choose to behave as long as you don't hurt yourself or embarrass me. I just make out the best I can from day to day. I don't know what I believe; so how can I encourage you to follow in my steps?" How much better it would be if we admitted our own lack of faith to our children instead of patting ourselves on the back for our superiority to those who compel their children to conform to parental standards of faith and practice!

I think a much sounder approach is strengthening self-image, enhancing the ability to communicate feelings and needs, and emphasizing the importance of accepting responsibility for one's own decisions. And I also think that careful consideration of a child's moral and religious education cannot be neglected. From all outward appearances, we are one of the most religious societies in the history of the world. The vast majority of us believe in God, consider ourselves Christians, regard Jesus as divine and the Bible as God inspired, and belong to a church. But most of us provide our children with less guidance on religious matters than we do on how to mow the lawn properly.

The fundamental role of parents is setting an example. Equally important is reinforcing positive behavior with praise and affection. The family can avail itself of an opportunity which no other institution can equal for instilling values, creating an atmosphere for the safe expression of needs, and molding character.

Parents and Children

Even as parents have responsibilities to their children, so too do children toward their parents. In childhood, sons and daughters should honor and obey their parents. A family is not a democracy. It is more like a constitutional monarchy. Someone has to accept the responsibility for providing food, shelter, education, and guidance. With such awesome responsibility should come respect. For a child to withhold respect from a parent is as serious as a parent withholding love and sustenance from a child.

If parents for just a moment would pretend that they were their children's counselors rather than Mom and Dad, if they would do what all good counselors do—they would be eager to listen, to listen again, to hear their child's implicit complaint, "you don't love me enough to trust me," and would be willing to negotiate a resolution. And if children would imitate this example, they would listen until they have heard their parent's implied plea to them: "Love me as much as I have loved you."

Parents influence their children by example. Children influence their parents by following that example and by being appreciative. There is a folk tale about a mother bird who is able to rescue only one of her three fledglings from a rising tide. She asks each of her offspring in turn why she should save him. The first says, "Save me, and I will take care of you in your old age." The second says, "Save me, and I will sing so beautifully that all the creatures of the forest shall be made glad." The third says, "Save me, and I will care for my children as dutifully as you have cared for me." The mother rescues the last child.

The little bird had learned well. Mother bird's attitude toward parenting had been caught, whether or not it had been taught. Perhaps if we start doing the job we accepted when we became parents, our own fledglings will not have to be rescued.

Being a parent is not an easy job—but neither is being a child. Since we have no choice, let's do the best that we can—together. The test of successful parenting is simple. If you want to be a great parent, live today in such a way that tomorrow or twenty years from now or forty years from now, you will be able to say: "I gave it my best shot. I was there when I was needed. I juggled a career and a family, but I was there. I made mistakes, but I was there. And I am still here."

Amen.

—LDS

[1700 words]
[17 minutes]

Sermon 89

Date: Third Sunday After Epiphany, Year A

Text:
Psalm 27 (read responsively before sermon)

Theme: There are explanations for child abuse, but no excuses.
Subject: Child abuse

Title: Victims of the Victims of the Victims

The Cross and the Open Tomb

It is a shame, in a way, that the cross has become the central symbol of our faith. For the use of the cross suggests victimization and hints at masochism. But the gospel of Jesus Christ is the good news that God has transformed suffering into life, pain into personal growth, sorrow into justice. The essence of Christianity is found as much in the open tomb as in the cross.

The two symbols—cross and open tomb—need to be held together. The cross says that your suffering and my suffering are the suffering of God. God is with us in our pain, sorrow, and anger. But suffering is not the last word. The open tomb proclaims the power of God—a power that enables us to change, to start over, to transcend the past, to break the chain.

We are survivors, not pawns. We are victors, not victims. God cares for us. God enfolds us in a boundless love. God strengthens us to triumph over all adversity.

David, the author of today's psalm, was a man of deep religious faith. Yet there were times when not all the king's horses and all the king's men could put his emotional health together again. His greatness of his faith in God was equaled only by the depth of his self-doubts. In today's psalm, he sounds like a quivering bowl of insecurities as he tries to reassure himself with the statement: "Though my father and mother forsake me, the LORD will receive me."

I have chosen to say a few words this morning on behalf of those millions of children who have truly been forsaken—children who are neglected or abused by adults. "The basic relationship between children and their elders," asserts Roger Rosenblatt, "is that adults do things to children, and children are done to."[1] The things that adults do to children affect them for the rest of their lives.

The Case of Wally

Consider the case of Walter Patrick Bissell. His family knew him as "Wally," the public as Patrick Bissell. At age 20, he broke upon the New York ballet scene as the partner of some of the most famous ballerinas in the world. His mother, Patricia Bissell, recalls:

> Exceptionally strong at six-foot-two, [he] could effortlessly spin the ballerinas. His charming robust personality carried over into his dance, and he was known for helping his partners look good and perform well. Critics raved about him . . . he enjoyed extraordinary success. At the peak of his career, he was earning $250,000 a year.[2]

On December 29, 1987, a few days after his thirtieth birthday, Patrick Bissell's fiancee found his body in his Hoboken, New Jersey, apartment. An autopsy revealed that "his system was crammed with every imaginable drug." Only a few months earlier, he had been released from a cocaine-addiction treatment program.

His mother reports: "When the terrible news reached us, I was sick with remorse. It was agonizingly clear to me that I had led my child to this tragic end." "I had led my child to this tragic end"? Patricia Bissell blamed herself. She saw her son as her victim, just as she viewed herself as a victim of others. Patricia Bissell was a victim of child abuse—and, at Patricia's own hands, so was her son.

Walter Patrick Bissell or "Wally" as he was known in his family was the unwanted child of a troubled mother. He and his fraternal twin were the fourth and fifth children born to a depressed and distressed twenty-nine-year-old mother. She remembers:

> [Wally] was a wonderful child—effervescent, confident, smart and adventuresome. . . . But no matter what he tried to do for his mother—and he never ceased trying—I refused to grant him even the smallest hint that he pleased me. . . . I never hugged him or kissed him. Not once did I cradle or comfort him.

Patricia attended church regularly. She sang in the choir and taught Sunday School. "But," she says, "emotional and physical violence flowed from me. . . . Almost from the beginning, I battered my children—screaming at the younger ones and beating the older ones with a leather belt. . . . The tiniest transgression would set me off. I battered the children's self-esteem as much as I battered their bodies—and in some ways those wounds probably were worse."

Wally, the bright spot in a terrifying environment, became her chief target. She relates:

> For a normal person, it's nearly impossible to understand how a mother can beat her child. But little Wally learned early about me. He knew when he'd done something to provoke my rage, I'd launch into a screaming tantrum over something like a messy room. Soon guilt over my irrational anger would fuel my physical violence. As I would

---

[1] "From the Children in the Shadows," *U.S. News & World Report*, October 31, 1988.

[2] Excerpted with permission from "A Mother's Plea" by Patricia Bissell, *Reader's Digest* October 1988. Copyright © 1988 by the Reader's Digest Association, Inc.

> furiously flail Wally's legs and back, I'd hold one of his arms to keep him from running. He would stare directly into my eyes with a steady, composed look. . . . So I would swing the belt harder, bringing more guilt, and more frenzied rage. It would end in a crescendo of humiliation when I finally conquered that look, and his eyes clouded with pain and fear.

Once, when Wally was about seven, she stopped beating him for a moment, jerked him out side, marched him down the street, and shoved him into the darkness. "Why don't you just run away!" she screamed. "I don't want to be your mother anymore!"

When Patricia looks at family photos, she can chronicle the destruction of her son's spirit. She states:

> Early pictures show a smiling face with warm, lively eyes. But in successive images, as he grew older, his face radiates sadness, then fear and wariness. Finally, at the age of 15, his eyes seem set in dull defiance. He had at last found the comfort and solace I had so thoroughly denied him. He was firmly into drugs—a deadly companion that would be with him the rest of his life.

Half of Wally's all-too-short life would be dominated by drugs and alcohol. He did not use them as a crutch to prepare himself for the stage. As his mother explains: "He actually sought refuge in drugs and alcohol after his successes." He once told an interviewer:

> I do good performances, and then I punish myself with drugs. I try to destroy myself. It's a weird kind of cycle. You don't know why the brain does the things that it does.

But Patricia thinks she knows why Wally's brain did the things it did. She explains:

> No matter how well he performed—or how wildly appreciative audiences and critics were—he still felt he didn't measure up. This sense of failure was the terrible legacy I gave my son. I don't think he ever had a chance.

Victim of a Victim

According to Patricia, Wally was her victim just as she was her father's and grandmother's. Patricia's constant assault on the person and psyche of Wally is inexcusable, but it is not incomprehensible. The pain and suffering Patricia inflicted on her son was her twisted revenge for the pain and suffering inflicted on her as a child. She relates:

> I was born in 1928 to an affluent family plagued by demons that must have lurked in dark crooks of the family tree for generations. By any measure, my childhood was a relentless horror. Before I was two years old, my mother died . . . [my father] detested me . . .
>
> We went to live with my father's mother, a stern and self-righteous woman who was viewed as a community and church leader. Every memory I have of my early childhood is gripped by overwhelming fear of my father. He beat me practically every day with his leather razor strop—a practice my grandmother endorsed. Other times he locked me in a closet.

She adds:

> The only photograph I have of my father and me shows us standing in front of the house. He is smiling, holding me in his arms. Terror is etched across my small face. I am clearly pushing away from him with all my strength.

By age six, sexual abuse was added to physical abuse.

Years later, Patricia married a shy and gentle man, "completely confident," she comments, "that our love could overcome the shame of my childhood." She was eager to have children of her own, she says, "for I assumed they would love me and I would be able to love them."

During the ensuing years, she relocated sixteen times to thirteen different cities, as her husband moved up the corporate ladder. Her husband was usually away on business. Frightened by her own uncontrollable rage, she went to doctors, ministers, and counselors, admitting that she was "too hard" on her children. She twice attempted suicide. Still no one took her confessions of child abuse seriously. The doctors merely tranquilized her. In her words, "they simply maintained the maternal monster I had become."

Breaking the Pattern

When Wally died, she came forward with her story in order to break the pattern. She came forward so that her surviving children could be equipped to triumph over the legacy she had given them. Hear her moving words:

> I do not believe that any mortal alone has the strength to break this powerful cycle of horror. But all around you, caring people are ready to come to the rescue.

Referring to the National Child Abuse hotline,[3] she states: "A lifeline is as close as your telephone." And she adds her personal hope that "never again will anyone, alone and helpless, have to face the kind of searing anguish of my life and the life I gave to my son."

Patricia Bissell recognized that her son was a victim of a victim. There is a lesson here for all of us: We are all the victims of the victims of the victims. Her statement, "I was born in 1928 to an affluent family plagued by demons that must have lurked in dark crooks of the family tree for generations," may make it sound as though she has little in common with us "normal people." But that is not so.

Perhaps we were not physically or sexually abused by those entrusted with our upbringing—perhaps we were. Perhaps we were encouraged, bolstered, and sustained by our parents—maybe not. Enough shameful things have been done to each of us to justify all manner of shameful behavior on our part. Most of us have experienced disappointment and harm sufficient to give us an excuse to disappoint and harm others for decades to come. Rage and abuse can always find a justification. Addictions can always be understood. Ending them is another matter.

Patricia Bissell abused her children. Her father and grandmother abused Patricia Bissell. There is no necessary causal link between these sentences. When, as an adult, she was overwhelmed by personal stress, she reverted to the pattern she had learned from her elders. But no necessity made it so.

---

[3] Childhelp USA's National Child Abuse hotline: 1-800-4-A-CHILD. For information, write to National Committee for the Prevention of Child Abuse, P.O. Box 2866, Chicago, IL 60690. For reprints of Patricia Bissell's article, write Reprint Editor, *Reader's Digest,* Box 406, Pleasantville, NY 10570. The price is $5 for ten copies.

Likewise her son's self-esteem was damaged by his childhood experiences. He found solace from his pain and humiliation in substance abuse. I can understand that. But I also know that self-destruction was not his only choice.

When I hear a story like Patricia's I feel compassion and sadness. It may sound trite, but I think "There but for the grace of God go I." I agree with Patricia. No mortal alone has the strength to break this powerful cycle of horror. But the invisible circle of caring rescuers is not the solution.

If we were or are someone's victims, there is only one way to break the chain and that is by breaking the chain. If we are hurting someone else through abusive behavior—whether that abuse is physical, psychological, or verbal, there is only one way to break the chain and that is by breaking the chain.

The only way out: First, admitting that there is a problem. Second, accepting responsibility for doing something about it. Third, making a plan to break the cycle of being victimized or of victimizing others. Fourth, getting help. Fifth, finding a community that will support you as you recreate your life, free of the abusive patterns of the past. Sixth, turning in humble faith to the God who will never forsake you no matter what you have done or what others have done to you.

Only God can break the cycle of horror. Only the grace of God can enable us to stop being victims and making victims of others. Only a community of God's people can help the individual break the chains of abuse and violence.

Together we are survivors, not pawns. We are victors, not victims. God cares for us. God identifies with our deepest need, our most profound hurts. God enfolds us in a boundless love and strengthens us to triumph over all adversity. In the words of Edith Horning, a forty-six-year-old survivor of child sexual abuse, "There's more than anger, more than sadness, more than terror. There's hope."[4]

Amen.

—LDS

[2170 words]
[22 minutes]

❦ *Sermon 90*

❦ *Occasion:* Infant baptism

Theme: Remarks at an Infant Baptism
Subject: Baptism

❦ *Title:* Remembering and Being Remembered

The lives we live and the society in which we live them are characterized by separation, estrangement, and alienation. It is as though we begin life as whole creatures and are gradually, steadily dismembered by reality. We leave the homes and families of our childhoods to find our own way in the wider world. We end up hundreds or thousands of miles from the neighborhood that nurtured us and from the family members, friends, and neighbors who shaped our attitudes and values.

---

[4] Cited in Ellen Bass and Laura Davis, *The Courage to Heal* (New York: Harper & Row, 1988), p. 7.

We pursue careers, marry, raise families, make friends, and begin again. We put down roots only to tear them up repeatedly. We change jobs, we move, friendships fade, children go their own way, sometimes marriages fail. We begin again and again. But each time, it is as though we left a part of ourselves behind. We are being dismembered.

Only our commitments keep us in one piece. Only the promises we make and keep allow us to endure. In, through, and despite each change in our lives, only God is constant. Our ideas, beliefs, doubts, and fears change as we change, but God does not.

The church is a place for remembering—for getting in touch with what really matters, counts the most, cannot be forgotten. The church is a place for being remembered, for being reattached.

The birth of a child is a time for remembering—in both senses of the word—for reasserting the promises of the past ("I remember and declare to this community who I am") and for being reaccepted, readmitted, reconnected, remembered.

God has given this life to these parents. He has given them as a family to one another and to us as a church. Our first reaction is joy and thankfulness. Our second is an awesome sense of responsibility. Parents, sponsors, and this entire congregation are joining hands, are being remembered. We are making solemn promises that will change our lives forever.

Sonnet Faith Ludwig and Jacqueline Kay Emery [Note: Use actual names of those being baptized], you are now bone of our bone and flesh of our flesh. You belong to us and we to you. We are members one of another. As your pastor, I am giving you an additional middle name. In my heart, I shall know you as Sonnet Faith Ladera Ludwig and Jacqueline Kay Ladera Emery [use actual name of your church].

Amen.

—LDS

[400 words]
[4 minutes]

❦ CHAPTER NINE

BUILDING THE CHRISTIAN COMMUNITY

"Let this mind be in you," wrote the Apostle Paul to the church at Philippi, "which was also in Christ Jesus." As Jesus surrendered to our state and fate, so also should we give up our self-centered individualism for the sake of a community of persons who care about one another.

Building the Christian community requires that we remove the major obstacles—vicious anger and destructive criticism. Jesus taught if you are angry with someone, do something about it. Get it settled. Reconciliation is powerful.

Criticism is of value only when the critic is committed to the community and to solving its problems. Otherwise, criticism is just squawking!

Building the Christian community requires stewardship. We give because the church needs and deserves our gifts and because it is good for us to give. How we invest our money is an important indication of how we invest our lives.

In the end, we recognize that it is God's Spirit who woos us and empowers us to be a community. But just what are the characteristics of a Spirit-filled church? Are we ready for the answer?

A selection of brief materials for special times within the life of a community (dedication of a new facility, a memorial service, a retirement observance, and a birthday celebration) is offered.

Sermon 91

Date: Sunday Between September 25 and October 1 inclusive, Year A

Texts:
Exodus 17:1-7
Psalm 78:1-4, 12-16
Philippians 2:1–13
Matthew 21:32

or Palm/Passion Sunday, Year A

Texts:
Isaiah 50:4–9a
Philippians 2:5–11
Matthew 21:1–11

Theme: Within a community of persons who care about one another, individualism loses its cancerous power.
Subject: Responsible individualism

Title: Glimpsing the Face of Christ

"Let this mind be in you, which was also in Christ Jesus: Who, being in the form of God, thought it not robbery to be equal with God. . . . And being found in fashion as a man, he humbled himself. . . ." (Philippians 2:5–8 KJV). More has been written about these few verses in Paul's letter to the Philippians than about any other part of the Bible with the exception of the Sermon on the Mount. For these words from an early Christian hymn express the central mystery of the Christian faith, the surrender of Jesus to our state and fate and his exaltation as our Lord.

If you want to know what the early Christians believed, you will have to wrestle with these words. But don't expect to find a simple formula that exhausts all efforts to explain the relationship of Jesus and God. After having studied these verses for many years, I am still not sure I know what they mean. But I know why Paul used them. He was concerned about the divisive individualism that threatened the unity of the church. Each Philippian felt entitled to his or her own opinion. They formed little cliques and factions based on these differences. The principal players were two strong-willed women, Euodia and Syntyche. They and their respective followers were at one another's throats when Paul founded the church at Philippi. Nine or ten years later when he wrote to them, they were still at it. And sad to relate, the Philippians were bickering a generation later, when the Church Father Polycarp visited them.

Like many of our churches today, the church at Philippi had a personality, a distinction character that persisted long after its original members had passed away. They never seemed to get the message that unrestrained individualism is deadlier than cyanide.

The Bonds of Love

None of us is an island. None of us exists apart from our relationships to other human beings. Yet each of us is an individual, and as individuals we may enter into bonds of love and compassion, or we may operate in a constant state of war against others. Individualism can be creative or destructive. It can stimulate healthy growth, or it can inhibit it. What Paul was saying to the Philippians was that within a community of persons who care about one another, individualism loses its cancerous power.[1]

Let me repeat that thought: within a community of persons who care about one another, individualism loses its cancerous power. We are a nation of free individuals. Yet what we most cherish—our marriages, our families, our communities, our churches—depends on our willingness to balance our wants and needs with the wants and needs of others. The freedom of the individual is the foundation of the greatness of our way of life. But unrestricted and unbalanced by a commitment to others, individualism destroys all that makes life worthwhile. Freedom without responsibility is the most contemptible and ruinous of all human fates.

According to Paul, the only cure for malignant individualism is sharing the mind of Christ. "Let each of you look not to your own interests, but to the interests of others. Let the same mind be in you that you have in Christ Jesus," says Paul (2:4–5 NRSV, alternate reading). Verses 5 to 11 may be part of an ancient baptism liturgy. As such they would have conveyed that by dying with Christ through baptism, we also rise to new life in Christ after baptism. As Jesus emptied himself, surrendering whatever claims he had to be one with God, humbled himself by being our servant, humiliated himself by dying the meanest of deaths, so also has he been exalted and given the rank, title, and honor accorded only to God. As he has been lifted up by God, so does he share with us the power of his glorification.

The whole faith of the early church is here in the words: "God has given him the name that is above all names, that at the name of Jesus every knee should bow and every tongue confess that Jesus Christ is Lord to the glory of God the Father." "Jesus Christ is Lord." If these words speak to your heart and condition then the message of Paul to you is that the same Jesus empowers you to humble yourself, to put the interests of others ahead of your own, to experience the exaltation of being like Christ because Christ lives in you.

If you are troubled by the claims made by Paul and the early church, let these words say to you that Jesus of Nazareth is a model of what true humanity is all about, that whatever you may believe or not believe about him, he is an example worth imitating.

Disabled by "Can't"

Paul like Jesus before him had a profound understanding of the human condition. The way we view people, the expectations we project on them even before we have a chance to know them, the manner with which we value them or devalue them can greatly affect them. Over the years, I have met several celebrated and successful individuals, who confided in me that they were afraid of only one thing: singing in public. In each case, the story was the same. It went something like this:

> When I was in grade school, my teacher singled me out and told me before my classmates, "Some of us can carry a tune, and some can't. And I'm afraid that you are one of those who can't. But if you stand in the back row and move your lips when the class sings during the next assembly, no one will notice."

---

[1] Miller, Patrick D., Jr., *Proclamation 3, Series A, Pentecost 2* (Philadelphia: Fortress Press, 1987), p. 61.

If I told you who some of these self-confident, outgoing men and women were, you would be surprised that they still carried with them the sense of shame and inhibitions of experience of forty to fifty years ago.

The words "you can't" have disabled more young people than infantile paralysis. And the words "you can" have given more assurance and self-assurance than all the psychiatrists, psychologists, and social workers who have ever lived.

Affected by Attitudes

When you value the other fellow as highly as you value yourself, you will think for a second before uttering words that empower or words that disable. When you value the other fellow as highly as you value yourself, you will resist the impulse to gossip, attribute negative motives to others, or denigrate his or her accomplishments. No one ever became an inch taller by reducing the stature of someone else.

But there are much more positive consequences of valuing the other fellow as highly as you value yourself. The way we view others affects their response. If we are hostile to others, the chances are that they will be defensive and closed to us. If we are open and approachable, others will be joyful and open with us. Consider Mother Teresa. As Charles Rice, the editor of Word & Witness, notes,

> Mother Teresa is an obvious example of [how] one's attitude can affect the response of the other person. She sees the face of Christ in every dying person, every beggar, everyone sick of body or sick in heart. In her presence everyone feels precious and worthwhile.[2]

Appreciation and Self-Esteem

Without a doubt, the greatest reward in valuing the other person as highly as you value yourself is that the more highly you value and thus enhance the life of another person, the more highly you come to esteem yourself. If you see the world as filled with jerks, you will soon see a jerk in the mirror. If you see the world as filled with ordinary human beings, most of whom are doing the best they can, you will see an ordinary human being in the mirror, who is doing the best that he or she can. And if you habitually see the world as filled with potential saints, the image in your mirror may turn out to be more Christlike than you would ever have suspected.

There once was a monastic community.[3] Over the course of many centuries, the fellowship had slowly shriveled up and was ready to die. Only seven monks and their abbot remained, and they were in their seventies, discouraged, and exhausted.

One day the abbot was talking to a local rabbi who often visited the monastery to enjoy the seclusion it offered. He and the abbot swapped stories of how difficult it was to share their faith with the modern, materialistic, me-first generation. "What keeps you going?" the abbot asked of the rabbi.

---

[2] Rice, Charles, World & Witness, September 30, 1990, p. 3.

[3] Like M. Scott Peck, who cites this story to open his book, *The Different Drum: Community Making and Peace* (New York: Simon & Schuster, 1987), I cannot remember where I first heard this tale.

"It is simple," the rabbi replied. "I tell my congregation that the messiah might be one of us, and I believe it."

That night at dinner, the abbot told the monk about his conversation with the rabbi. He repeated the words: "The messiah might be one of us." Each of the monks thought to himself: "The messiah, the Christ, could be one of us." And something profound happened as a result. Each of the monks began treating his fellow as though he were the Christ. Soon they became more caring, compassionate, and open with one another.

As their mutual respect for one another grew, so also did each monk's self-respect. "If any of us could be the Christ, then I could be the Christ," each of them thought. And each of them began acting as though he might be the Christ.

The monks began to make their huge but largely unused estate available to the local populace for picnics and special occasions. Their beautiful spirits touched all who visited. Soon the visitors began to show interest in what made these monks the men they were. The monks sought to convert no one, but when asked they spoke honestly about their faith and the history of their community.

Within a few months, men and women who found themselves alone, unloved, and without anyone to care for sought the monks' advice on starting a spiritual community. The monks aided them. Then by two and threes, men from the neighboring town and men from far away began knocking at the doors of the abbey, seeking acceptance as brothers. Women came from far and near to learn to pray and to lead disciplined Christian lives. Several of them joined similar communities for women in the region. Others returned regularly to the monastery for special retreats and Bible study groups.

You have probably caught on by now. I am not telling you about a monastery in some foreign land. I am offering a parable about our own church. I am presenting a vision of things to come, a prediction of what can be, what will be if we take the advice of the Apostle Paul: "Let each of you look not to your own interests, but to the interests of others. Let the same mind be in you that you have in Christ Jesus."

Amen.

—LDS

[1800 words]
[18 minutes]

❦ *Sermon 92*

❦ *Date:* Sunday Between September 4 and September 10 inclusive, Year A

Texts:
Romans 13:8-14
Matthew 18:15–20

or Sunday Between September 11 and September 17 inclusive, Year A
Fifteenth Sunday After Pentecost, A

Texts:
Romans 14:1–12
Matthew 18:21–35

or Sunday Between August 28 and September 3 inclusive, B
Fifteenth Sunday After Pentecost, Year B

Texts:
James 1:17-27
Mark 7:1–8, 14–15, 21–23

or Sunday Between September 18 and September 24 inclusive, C

Texts:
Amos 8:4–7
1 Timothy 2:1–7
Luke 16:1–13

Theme: Jesus taught us that if you are angry with someone, do something about it. His teachings on this subject are among the most neglected in the Bible.
Subject: Anger and forgiveness

Title: Getting Angry and Doing Something About It

Jesus taught: If you are angry with someone, do something about it. Get it settled and behind you. His teachings on this subject are among the most neglected in the Bible. We speak as though other people and circumstances make us angry. The truth is that we are angry to begin with. Anger is the natural overflow of a person's essential irritability. Each of us has his or her own boiling point. Annoyances do not so much anger us as provide us with an opportunity to express our underlying aggravation.

Consider a group of aggrieved drivers in heavy traffic. What is it that keeps the chain reaction of offended drivers from erupting into an explosion of violence and homicide? Only the phenomena of divergent boiling points and dissimilar expressiveness. No two of us erupt at exactly the same level of provocation, and our responses are as varied as our temperaments and backgrounds.

The New Testament message is that a human being cannot control the fact that he is angry, but he can choose the form of expression. The automatic form of expression is a learned behavior. Inappropriate responses can be unlearned and replaced with productive ones. In the words of the Apostle Paul: "Be angry but do not sin; do not let the sun go down on your anger . . . . Let all bitterness and wrath and anger and clamor and slander be put away from you, with all malice, and be kind to one another, tenderhearted, forgiving one another, as God in Christ forgave you." (Ephcsians 4:26; 31–32)

Jesus could become highly irritated and could express that anger with words and actions. His critics, enemies, and followers felt the sting of his denunciations, reprimands, and rebukes. The cleansing of the Temple was scarcely an act of nonviolent civil disobedience. For Jesus, anger was an opportunity. His anger energized him to confront issues, demand change, comfort the afflicted, and afflict the comfortable.

Anger is a power, an elemental force. And like all energy it may be used for good or evil. Unleashed and out of control, anger becomes destructive. Channeled and directed, it has the potential for deepening relationships, harmonizing incompatible egos, and building community.

In all real relationships between real human beings, anger is inevitable. The repressed rage—the accumulated resentments, hurts, and misunderstandings—lurks in each of us like a starving predator waiting for an opportunity to pounce. Sometimes the reaction is "justified" by the lack of consideration, insensitivity, and rudeness shown to us by the object of our anger. Indeed, there are broken promises and neglected commitments enough to excuse every angry word that any of us will ever utter or every vindictive deed which we will ever perform. The question is not: Do we have the right to get angry? The question is: Do the "justifications" make our anger appropriate? or do we act out our anger because we are fundamentally angry to begin with? And even if our anger is completely justified, is it productive? Does it get us what we want, or is it "full of sound and fury, signifying nothing"?

Jesus taught: If you are angry with your brother, do something about it. Go directly to your brother with your grievance, and talk it out. Don't gossip. Don't hold it all inside. Don't kick the family dog—or your spouse and children. Take your aggravation to the source. For when you confront the other person, you have entered into dialogue and created an opportunity for the Spirit of God to lure you into partnership. For while we may address God in the solitude of our devotional life, it is in the confrontation of human being with human being that God addresses us.

When confrontation doesn't work, try mediation. Jesus prescribes seeking the help of two or three members of the church. If that fails, he instructs, try laying your grievance before the church governing council or the entire congregation. The Apostle Paul gives similar advice, chastising the Corinthians for taking their squabbles into the secular courts and urging them to appoint a member of the church as a mediator when disputes arise. These directives on mediation are probably the most ignored verses in the Bible!

Jesus regards the presence of unreconciled disputants within a community as destructive to the spiritual and social well-being not only of the foes but of the community as well. Making peace with one's fellow Christian is considered more important than is fulfilling one's religious obligations. Insulting a brother or harboring resentment toward him is a violation of the spirit of the commandment "Thou shalt not kill." Jesus realized that unvented anger is more explosive than dynamite, and just as lethal.

The remedy which Jesus recommends is forgiveness. To paraphrase his teaching, get your head out of the past with its hurts and resentments. Put yourself into living relationship—here and now. Don't get even; get together. To withhold forgiveness is to condemn oneself to life's rubbish heap. Each party of a dispute is right—and each is wrong. And no matter what the other person did or said, rage wells up from personal reservoirs of spite which existed long before the argument at hand.

We are really angry because we have not been loved as we perceive we ought to have been loved. Is this perception true? It is and it isn't. We are all the victims of the victims of the victims. At birth, we were placed in the hands of imperfect human beings. No matter how conscientious they may have been, they could never give us the sense of self-acceptance for which we yearned because no one ever gave it to them. On the other hand, our demands for acceptance and approval are boundless. For the first few years of our lives, each of us believes that he or she is the center of the universe, that his or her will is all powerful, and that just wishing for comfort, affection, and pleasure can bring immediate gratification. When we are thwarted by reality, we pout, wail, and throw tantrums. Not getting our way is the first cause of anger. Not being loved enough is our first excuse.

Our own basic anger causes us to exaggerate what has happened, to see the other person through a filter of self-justification and prejudice, and to color our recollections to suit our needs. To emphasize the point that holding on to our grievances lessens our humanity, Jesus adopts the radical stance that our forgiveness by God depends on our willingness to forgive others. (The apostles appealed instead to the example of God: As we have been forgiven, so ought we to forgive others.)

Being able to forgive is a matter of gaining perspective—of realizing that anger invents or exacerbates its own causes. Forgiving is a matter of accepting oneself as flawed and imperfect and as the cause of one's own deepest hurts and disappointments. Forgiveness for others begins with an internalized awareness that God in Christ has reconciled us to himself, that he loves us despite our unworthiness. God's acceptance of us bestows worth and lovability on us. When we accept God's forgiveness, we forgive ourselves. And when we accept ourselves, it is a small task to impute acceptability to others.

Forgiveness also grows out of appreciation and thankfulness, out of the perception that those who love us today and those who have loved us since birth are gifts of God. The grateful heart returns generosity for generosity, kindness for kindness. And in the process of loving, forgiveness is spontaneous. If a man who owes me a hundred dollars gives me a gift of a thousand, will I harbor a grudge about his debt to me?

Forgiveness does not remove responsibility. The forgiven person is still responsible for his actions, still accountable. When I forgive a friend, I ignore his excuses. I do exactly what God has done in Christ, I accept my friend's guilty plea and release him with time served, accepting him in God's general amnesty. I hold him accountable only for his words and deeds—not for my projections upon his words and deeds. To forgive is to avoid exaggerating or plugging today's annoyances into yesterday's store of grievances. Forgiveness means recognizing the reservoir of resentment within oneself and knowing that what our friend has done has nothing to do with it. And, finally, I realize that when I confront the obdurate, insensitive resistance in others (or in myself) that there is no need for me to act as an instrument of retribution. There is a cosmic justice that sees to it that in the case of deliberate, harmful behavior the punishment always fits the crime. And that punishment is that we are who we are, and we cannot escape from ourselves.

It is no more possible to avoid ever being angry than it is to avoid ever being hungry. But just as I can choose from a dozen options for satisfying my hunger—from stuffing myself with junk food to dining at a gourmet restaurant—so also can I choose how I will respond to my own anger. I can let anger control me and destroy my relationships with others. Or I can view my anger as an opportunity to build, to create, and to grow together with those I love.

Jesus taught: If you are angry with someone, do something about it. Get it settled and behind you. His teachings on this subject are among the most neglected in the Bible. May they never be neglected in our lives.

Amen.

—LDS

[1558 words]
[16 minutes]

❦ *Sermon 93*

❦ *Date:* Fourteenth Sunday After Pentecost, Year A

Texts:
Exodus 12:1-14
Psalm 149
Romans 13:1–10 or 8-14
Matthew 18:15–20

Theme: Reconciliation is powerful.
Subject: Reconciliation, community

❦ *Title:* "How Can I Row with Only One Oar?"

"For where two or three are gathered in my name, there am I in the midst of them." (Matthew 18:20 KJV) Surely, these are among the most beautiful and encouraging words in the Bible. How many churches have emblazoned them on the exterior of the sanctuary or the interior of the Sunday School facility or over the archway to the fellowship hall? How many business meetings, prayer sessions, and worship services have been called to order by the recitation of this promise?

These words remind us of the most basic truths of the Christian faith: (1) that Christianity is not a one-person game; (2) that it is God who gathers us; (3) that the church to which he calls us is made up of imperfect human beings like ourselves; and (4) that despite our mutual differences and misunderstandings, reconciliation is powerful.

I. *Christianity Is Not a One-Man or a One-Woman Game.* Although God calls us to his church one by one, the church to which he calls us is a community, a gathering together of those called by God to fellowship with one another.

You are not alone, these words remind us. Being a Christian is like sitting in a rowboat and discovering that there is only one set of oars and that they are eight feet apart. It takes more than one to get anywhere.

II. *It Is God Who Gathers Us.* ". . . where two or three are gathered. . .." As always, the initiative is God's. It is God who lures us, leads us, draws us, impels us to himself. It is God who has created us with an inborn hunger that can only be satisfied in him. The New Testament Greek word for church is *ekklesia* (from which we get the word "ecclesiastical"). It literally means "those who have been called out." Imagine yourself at a professional baseball or football game. The score is tied. The excitement in the stands is unbearable. You are sitting on the edge of your seat. No. You are on your feet, pushing aside the shoulders of the fans standing in front of you, straining to see the action. Then suddenly you hear your name being called on the public address system. Your presence is urgently requested in the stadium office. You think you have made a mistake. It only sounded like your name. Then a written message forms on the electronic score board. There is no mistake this time. There in sixteen-foot-tall letters is your name, likeness, and social security number. You don't know why, but you have been called out.

Those who are gathered in the name of Jesus are called out—out of lives of compromise and despair, out of personal chaos and confusion, out of drifting and selfishness, out of isolation and fear. We are called out by name, as individuals, with all our pains and hurts and mistakes. We are called out of lives that work and lives that don't work, successful lives and lives of failure.

III. *We Are Called to a Local Congregation That Is Not Perfect—That Can Never Be Perfect for It Is Made Up of Imperfect Human Beings Just Like Ourselves.* We are called to a place where the Word of God is preached and the sacraments are observed. The church is not a social club or a special interest group, not a civic center or a theater, not a school or a museum. It is a special place where God is at home and invites us in to be with him.

Isn't God at home everywhere? Isn't it just as possible to worship God in the mountains or at the seashore as in a cathedral? And isn't it easier to worship God when one is not distracted by all those hypocrites who clutter up Christian churches?

I am present, says Jesus, where two or three are gathered in my name. We fool ourselves into thinking that the appreciation of nature and the freedom from interpersonal tension are the same thing as worshiping God, that mindlessness is the same thing as devotion. Worship without a church is like marriage without a spouse. It may sound wonderful in the abstract but it is essentially nonexistent. Unless a committed, covenanted life of mutual concern is at the core of one's spiritual existence, religion degenerates into sentimentality, clichés, and pretensions. Without the focus, discipline, shared history, and give-and-take of community, there is simply no there there!

A selection from Martin Buber's classic work, *Between Man and Man,* comes to mind. Says Buber:

> The word of him who wishes to speak with men without speaking with God is not fulfilled; but the word of him who wishes to speak with God without speaking with men goes astray.
>
> There is a tale that a man inspired by God once went out from the creaturely realms into the vast waste. There he wandered till he came to the gates of the mystery. He knocked. From within came the cry: "What do you want here?" He said, "I have proclaimed your praise in the ears of mortals, but they were deaf to me. So I come to you that you yourself may hear me and reply." "Turn back," came the cry from within. "Here is no ear for you. I have sunk my hearing in the deafness of mortals."[1]

Buber concludes:

> True address from God directs man into the place of lived speech, where the voices of the creatures grope past one another, and in their very missing of one another succeed in reaching the eternal partner.[2]

Buber's words are such an apt description of the local congregation of Christians. Is not this church "the place of lived speech, where the voices of the creatures grope past one another, and in their very missing of one another succeed in reaching the eternal partner"?

IV. *Despite Our Mutual Differences and Misunderstandings, Reconciliation Is Powerful.* A moment ago, I said: Without the focus, discipline, shared history, and give-and-take of community, there is simply no there there! Notice how the word "discipline" crept into that sentence. We Christians seldom pay attention to the context in which the words about our Lord's presence were uttered. They are the coda that brings to a close a thorny speech on discipline in the church. No congregation can survive as an anarchic mob of individualists. There must be some principles of order, some process for settling grievances.

Just because Jesus is in the midst of us does not mean that there will not be misunderstandings and disagreements among us. It is because he is a party to every attempt to resolve our disputes that they can be resolved at all. Jesus was not talking about prayer meetings or Sunday socials when he promises his presence in our midst. He was talking about what we seldom talk about, what we resist talking about, what we are too nice to talk about.

It boils down to this: I don't know you and you don't know me. The less I know you the more likely I am to project some unflattering picture of who I think you are on you and the more likely you are to do the same to me. Pretty soon I not only don't know you but I don't like you, and you don't like me. Before long I add an ally or two to my dislike of my mentally constructed image of you and you add an ally or two to your dislike of me.

Jesus had an incredibly clear teaching about defusing such a potentially explosive situation, and—as we Christians are prone to do with all his clear teachings—we ignore it. "If your brother [or sister] sins against you, go and tell him [or her]. . . ." It sounds so simple and yet so complicated. We psych ourselves out. "John won't pay any attention to me. He'll just make fun of me or patronize me. You just can't be honest and open with some people. Besides who needs him?" It's hard to go to someone with a grievance when you already have your mind made up as to how that person will respond and what the eventual outcome will be.

But the odds are you are wrong. A friend of mine, whom I will call "Ron," tells the following story:

---

[1] Buber, Martin, *Between Man and Man* (New York: Macmillan, 1965), p. 15.

[2] Ibid.

> For longer than I care to remember, I was angry with two of my college professors. I felt they had been unsympathetic and unsupportive during my student days. I felt they had undermined my self-confidence. And I often told my wife and friends about my unhappiness.
>
> One day my wife said, "You've been complaining about these two guys for twenty years, and, frankly, I'm sick of hearing about them. If you have a problem with them, why don't you make an appointment with each of them and work it out face to face?"
>
> "They won't pay any attention to me. They'll just deny that they ever intended to harm me. Or they'll say that it was all in my head," I protested.
>
> "Do it!" she replied.
>
> So I did just what she recommended. First, I went to Dr. X's office, but before I could utter a word, he took my hand in his frail arthritic grip and began crying. His daughter was in serious trouble and he begged me to help her.
>
> All the anger I had felt for all those years disappeared. I guess it was replaced with pity.
>
> Then I went to Dr. Y. Before I could say anything to him, he said, "I'm so glad you came to see me. I'm so proud of you. You've taken what you learned here and have put it to practical use. I'm still teaching the same courses from the same yellowing notes and I'm bored to death!"
>
> Once more the anger melted away.

So without uttering a word of accusation Ron had confirmed for himself just what Jesus had taught.

Reconciliation is powerful. Look at the words of Jesus with which we began, but this time give them their proper setting. Jesus says: Thrash out your differences. Get together as brother with brother or sister with sister or brother with sister, and then, in the context of your reconciliation, "if two of you agree about anything they ask, it will be done for them by my Father in heaven. For where two or three are gathered in my name, there am I in the midst of them."

Now the key word is "agreement." Shooting from the hip, telling the other person "the truth" without listening, is not reconciliation. Ventilating without getting the facts, without sympathetically seeing, hearing, and feeling the other person's point of view leads nowhere. If "jumping to conclusions" were an Olympic event, many of us would be gold medal winners. "Being honest," "sharing your feelings" is not enough. Unless both parties speak and are heard there is no agreement.

If Ron had gone to his old professors and said, "You know what's wrong with you," he would not have been heard. If he had not listened, he would not have been reconciled. He would not have been freed from the anger that had formerly ruled him. In his heart and life, the professors would have continued to have the power to make him miserable, the power that Ron had given them for twenty years.

If his professors had left their respective meetings with Ron feeling dumped on, Ron would have added a sense of guilt to his earlier sense of outrage and his professors would have had no opportunity to disclose and examine their own lives.

I know what I am talking about. I am Ron.

Amen.

—LDS

[1900 words]
[19 minutes]

Sermon 94

Date: Seventh Sunday After Epiphany, Year A

Text:
Matthew 5:43–48 or Matthew 7:1–6

or Seventh or Eighth Sunday After Epiphany, Year C

Text:
Luke 6:37–49

Theme: Criticism is valuable when the critic is committed to the flock and to solving its problems.
Subject: Criticism

Title: Lessons of the Honking Geese

Tip

> The following parable sermon was used as a communion meditation. Horns and ratchet noisemakers were distributed to the congregation at the start of the service. When the word "Honk" was read, I gave a "thumbs up" sign and the horns were blown. When "Squawk" was read, I gave "thumbs down" and the noisemakers were employed.

I saw a flock of Canada geese flying in formation high overhead a few months ago. Geese are one of my favorite sights. So I strained by eyes and ears to find out what was going on.

The lead goose was breaking the air resistance for the others in the flock. This made it easier for them. They appreciated what he was doing and HONKed in encouragement. Since I studied classical Goose in graduate school I could translate their HONKs. "Attaboy, brother! Way to go! Kccp up thc good work!"

The lead goose did not take time to HONK a response. He was too busy plowing through the air. When he got tired, he let the current carry him to the back of the formation. Then he HONKed his encouragement of the new lead goose.

Pretty soon the number three goose and the number sixteen goose decided that they did not like the speed or direction of the flight. They called for a meeting in the pond ahead. So the flock landed to give three and sixteen an opportunity to express their opinions. The geese listened patiently as three and sixteen SQUAWKed and rustled their feathers.

Three was a young goose. He felt that the flock was moving too slowly. "Let's pick up the pace. I want to get to Canada while their is still enough food for all of us."

Sixteen was a wise old goose. He had been with the flock for many migrations. He thought that the flock was flying too fast. It was hard for the old geese and some of the fledgling flyers to keep up.

The geese took a vote and decided to keep flying at the same speed but to set down a half hour earlier each day. Three was very unhappy with the decision but decided to stay with the flock. He even volunteered to be the lead goose when they took to the air again.

Sixteen shrugged his feathers and said that he too would be glad to lead the formation. And off they went to Canada.

I was really glad classical Goose had been a required subject where I went to college. And I was glad for the lesson I learned. Criticism is valuable when the critic is committed to the flock and to solving its problems. As a member of God's formation, I restrain my natural tendency to criticize my fellow flyers except when I am willing to join them in solving the problem at hand. Every one is entitled to his or her opinion. I am just as entitled as anybody else. But unless I am willing to be part of the solution, I should probably keep my SQUAWKing to myself.

I once belonged to a flock that was mostly SQUAWKing and little flying. Each goose insisted on getting his or her own way and flying in his or her own direction. When we did get into the air together, we offered no encouragement to the lead goose. Instead of HONKing, we whispered to each other, "You call that lead flying. My gosling sister could do better than that in her sleep." The lead goose got very discouraged and took to hopping a few feet at a time. Needless to say, we never got anywhere.

We also had a nasty habit of SQUAWKing about one another all the time. You know how it is—Goose three doesn't like the way that Goose twelve combs his tail feathers and directs his complaint not to Goose twelve but to every other goose in the formation. Of course, since it is a small formation, Goose twelve hears every SQUAWK anyway. And when he does, ice forms on his wings and his flight becomes erratic. Oddly enough, the same thing happens to every goose in the formation. Squawking to anyone but the direct object of your SQUAWK will do that every time. And as the ice forms, the geese in the formation start flying every which way until there is no formation at all. So if you've got a SQUAWK, don't spread it around. Direct it to the goose whose tail feathers bother you. If you do, your feathers and his will actually get lighter and your flying will be truer and speedier than ever. Not only that but the flock will have a better chance of getting where it is supposed to be getting.

It is so wonderful being a member of a first-rate flying formation. There is a member of my formation who is a frequent flyer goose with more than twenty migrations to his credit. He has been through more squalls, storms, jet plane wakes, sunrises, sunsets, and gentle breezes than I. Now and then he SQUAWKs at me. "Say, brother goose, don't you know there is an easier flight path? I'll bet you don't know about the great pasture near Medford, Oregon." And whether or not I agree with him, I always pay attention. And he always pays attention to me. That doesn't mean that we have not been known to SQUAWK up a storm at each other every now and then.

The point is that we keep flying—together—in the formation and for the sake of the formation.

And sometimes, when he is lead goose, I SQUAWK at him: "Hey, brother goose, I'm getting tired. . . . I'm getting hungry. . . . I'm getting cold. . . . I don't like some of the geese in this formation and some of them don't like me." And the next time we set down, he always says the same thing to me: "Brother goose, don't SQUAWK your problems at me; HONK your solutions."

Who can argue with him? Whether you are on the flight path to Canada or to the heavenly goose city, if you are not part of the solution, you are part of the problem.

Amen, or as we say in classical Goose, HONK!

—LDS

[982 words]
[10 minutes]

Sermon 95

Date: Any Sunday During a Stewardship Campaign

Texts:
Matthew 6:24–34 and 7:7–12
Acts 20:32–35

Theme: It is more blessed to give than receive.
Subject: Stewardship

Title: Why I Pledge

It is the season of harvests, time to reap what has been sown, to gather, and to give thanks to God. If we were still a land of farmers, we would be garnering the fruits of the land and storing them up for the winter months. Instead, throughout the past months, we have been sowing loving deeds in the lives of our children. We now gather together with them for a harvest of mutual commitment and concern. In a few short weeks, it will be Thanksgiving, our national day for gratitude.

It is also a time to be aware of the needs of others and to share with them the bounty with which we have been blessed. It is a time to remember the strangers, the orphans, and the widows in our midst. It is a time to reach out with compassion to the sick, the handicapped, the lonely, and those whose lives have been shattered by circumstances.

It is also the time for our annual Stewardship Campaign. During these few weeks, we ask members of our church family to renew their commitment, to plant with us that we may all share in the harvest of spiritual and community blessing that lies ahead.

As your pastor, I follow the tradition of this church and leave the important work of fund raising to our Stewardship Committee, trusting in them to do their usually fine job. After all, it seems self-serving for ministers to beat the drums for pledges and donations.

Out of respect for such feelings, I will not urge you to give. Rather I will tell you why I do. For when it comes to stewardship, I am just as accountable to God as any church member for how I use my time, talent, and money.

I pledge to the support of the church because I believe in its work and importance. I not only conduct worship services here, I *worship* here. I have been called not only to a position of leadership, but to be a *member* here. I not only preach, I open my ears to *hear* the word of God for me in this place. As a Christian, I know that I cannot survive and flourish as a spiritual Lone Ranger. I need my brothers and sisters and this place of worship and service. I have the sense that together we can do exciting and significant things—greater things than any of us can do individually. And I know that those responsible for the financial affairs of our congregation need to know what to expect. They need to know just how committed we are to having our beautiful house of God.

I give to the church because the church needs and deserves my gifts. I give because it is good for me to give. I discovered some time ago that the more generous I am, the more open I become to the blessings of God in my life. The more freely I give, the more sensitive, the more receptive I become. The more I love others by giving, the more I am able to respect myself. If I have learned anything it is that two things make life worth living—generosity and the appreciation of generosity. And so with an awareness that by the grace of God I have harvested abundantly, I open my heart and my wallet. Jesus was right: it is more blessed to give than to receive!

Amen.
—LDS

[578 words]
[6 minutes]

Sermon 96

Date: Any Sunday

Texts:
Daniel 7:9–14
Psalm 145:8–13
Hebrews 10:11–18
Mark 13:24–32

Theme: What can we ever give in return in proportion to what we have received? Nothing!
Subject: Stewardship

Title: Giving Back a Portion

A Tale of Two Brothers

There is an old rabbinic story about how God decided where to build the Temple. Two brothers were partners in a grinding mill in Jerusalem. At the end of each day, they took the grain they had milled and divided it equally into two separate sacks. One night the bachelor brother thought, "This is not right. I am alone and don't need much, but my brother has a wife and a family. He deserves the larger share." So, sneaking back to the mill each night he took part of his share and poured it into his brother's sack.

The married brother also thought one night, "This is not right. When I am old, I will have children to support me, but my brother will be all alone. He deserves the larger share." So, sneaking back to the mill each night, he took part of his share and poured it into his brother's sack. They thought it a miracle to find their sacks refilled each morning.

One night, however, the brothers left home at the same time to sneak back to the mill, and by coincidence, met on the streets with their sacks in hand. Instantly, they knew what was happening and fell into each other's arms weeping.

God looked down upon the scene, according to the story, and said, "Here is where love meets. Here I will build my Temple."

Giving as Christ Gave

During the seasons of stewardship campaigns, we are being asked to give back a portion of what we have received so that the "temple" will continue to be built that all will be able to recognize that this is a place where love meets.

A portion, in proportion to what we have, is all we are asked to give. It is not a pound of flesh—though it may feel like a pound of flesh, and budgets may sound like begging—it is not, it is but a portion of what we have.

Sometimes we are made to feel that we must give as Christ gave. A noble thought, but none of us in this room is prepared to do that, because Christ gave more than we have proven ourselves capable. ". . . Christ . . . offered for all time a single sacrifice for sins . . .," says the writer of Hebrews. We might say it this way: "It was a singularly unique sacrifice of self that bridged the gap that separates us from God."

That was the point of the much discussed film *The Last Temptation of Christ*. It was not that Jesus experienced temptation, or even succumbed in his fantasies. The point was that in the end he didn't. In the end he remained faithful to God and was a shining example of God's faithfulness to us.

The writer of Hebrews goes on: "For by a single offering he has made whole for all time those who are sanctified. . . . This is the covenant I will make with them after those days says the Lord: 'I will put my laws on their hearts, and write them on their minds . . . . I will remember their sins no more.'" (Hebrews 10:15–17)

How can we give anything in proportion to what we have received? Not only have we been given life by the Creator, made to be, as the psalmist says "little less than God," but we have also been freed by forgiveness from our arrogance when we pretend to play God. What have we to give in return?

We live by God's grace. Can grace be portioned out? M. Scott Peck writes: "Grace is the gift unearned, the wonderful unanticipated present, the blessing undeserved. It is sunshine in a place where only the darkness can be explained. It is the bursting presence of love at a time when we have the right only to expect condemnation, emptiness, and aloneness."[1]

Giving in Response to Grace

When I came to California, Barbara and I were separated. Papers had been filed in Vermont, and an automatic legal separation was granted. We were just waiting out the six months. I had resigned from the church I served in Vermont, I was burned out and hurting. I wasn't sure I wanted to continue in the ministry. It had been a painful journey so far. I was living through the feelings of condemnation, emptiness, and aloneness.

I ended up in a little church no one wanted, in a town about as far removed from my experience as I could imagine, but it was there that I found a loving, healing group of people. When Barbara and I decided the separation was a grand mistake, we started up our life together in this little town in the foothills of the Sierra. The day I picked up Barbara and the children we returned to the parsonage next door to the church only to find that the Women's Fellowship was meeting. Barbara looked at me as if to say, "I can't believe that after all we have been through, the first day I see you I have to deal with the Women's Fellowship."

I shrugged my shoulders, "I'm sorry," I said. "We have to go say 'hello.' We can't avoid them." We climbed out of the borrowed van and walked into the Social Hall. The group of women were sitting in a circle having tea and coffee. When we stepped into the room they stopped their conversation, stood up, and immediately greeted us with hugs and kisses and an outpouring of affection. It was for us a moment of grace—unearned, unanticipated, undeserved. It was a moment of healing for this broken family.

What can we ever give in return in proportion to what we have received? Nothing!

What should a proper response be to such love? The answer is obvious: gratitude. And gratitude is more than being thankful; it means an attitude that sees the world filled with grace upon grace upon grace, in a graceful dance of harmony. Even the evil in our lives is swept to the side in this swirl of wonder. You have given me so much, dear Lord, what can I give back in return?

What God wants back is our love. Remember the first of Christ's two commandments: "Love the Lord your God, with all your heart and soul and mind." God wants the true adoration of the total person. Christina Rossetti wrote a Christmas poem that later became a lovely carol. The third verse begins: "What can I give him Poor as I am? If I were a shepherd, I would bring a lamb."

---

[1] Peck, M. Scott, *What Return Can I Make?* (New York: Simon & Schuster, 1985), p. 36.

Later Emerson wrote: "The only gift is a portion of thyself. A poet brings his poems; the farmer his corn; the miner his gem." What God wants is ourselves.

But how is such love to be manifest. Is it only a feeling? Once again Scott Peck notes that genuine love is not a feeling. "Genuine love is always manifested in loving behavior. It is not a matter of empty words; it is a matter of deeds." Thus the second great commandment asks us to love our neighbors as ourselves. What would such love be like?

God has given us life. To love God and cherish life is to love and cherish the gift, even the gift we are to each other. It means to love every expression of existence, to have what Albert Schweitzer called a "reverence for life." To nurture life and each other is our obligation. We cannot love God without assuming it. We are called to nurture ourselves. We are called to nurture our children and our grandchildren. We are called to nurture, in love, and respect, our elders. And we are called to nurture the Russians, the Sudanese, the South Africans, the Nicaraguans; the wolves and the whales, the beaches and the forests; the whole rich gift of God's creation.

In other words we are responsible for each other. Jesus commanded his disciples, "Love one another as I have loved you." To love one another means that we care for one another enough that we will do for one another. To love is to care, to care is to do.

And what can we do? We can give a portion of what we have for the ministry of our church so that we can nurture one another in love, and so that we can reach out in love to those who don't expect it, but who need it. If we give a portion of what we have in response to the love we have received we will experience the miracle of the two brothers at the mill; our essential needs will be filled each morning because we have taken care of each other.

Consider carefully your pledge of support to our mutual ministry. Where you invest your money is an important indication of where you invest your lives. Jesus said: "I was hungry and you fed me. I was naked and you clothed me. I was sick and in prison and you visited me. I was a stranger and you received me." Let all we do be done in love.

Amen.

—W. Matthew Broadbent

[1500 words]
[15 minutes]

❦ *Sermon 97*

❦ *Date:* Pentecost Sunday, Any Year

Texts:
Year A
Acts 2:1–21
1 Corinthians 12:3b–13
John 20:19-23 or 7:37-39
Year B
Acts 2:1–21
Psalm 104:24–34, 35b
Romans 8:22–27
John 15:26–27, 16:4b–15
Year C
Acts 2:1–21
Romans 8:14–17
John 14:8–17, 25–27 or **25–31**

Theme: We wait for God's Spirit to make us what we have been called to be.
Subject: Holy Spirit

Title: "Come, Holy Spirit!" Can Progressive Protestants Put Up with Pentecost?

[This sermon uses the Mission Statement of a particular church. Substitute your congregation's statement or covenant.]

[Solo: "Where the Spirit of the Lord Is"]

On Sunday mornings as they began class, the fifth graders would line up and each would recite one phrase of the *Apostles' Creed.* This went on for about four months, until one Sunday. The class began the usual way. The first girl recited her line flawlessly, "I believe in God the Father Almighty, maker of heaven and earth." The second, a boy, stood up and added his sentence, "I believe in Jesus Christ, his only son, our Lord." But then silence descended over the class. Finally, one girl, who felt she knew what was wrong stood up and announced, "I'm sorry, sir, but the boy who believes in the Holy Ghost is absent today!"[1]

And that's the way it is in most Christian churches: the Holy Spirit is strangely absent. Yet were it not for the giving of the Spirit, there would be no Christian Church. We celebrate Pentecost not only as the birthday of the Church, but because there is something about the strange, ecstatic events of that day long ago that is available Sunday after Sunday in this church and in every church.

They were there:
Peter, John, and James, and the other apostles.
They were there:
the women and Mary the mother of Jesus
and his brothers.
They were there
and they joined together constantly in prayer
and they sought the guidance of the Scriptures.

They were there "all together in one place" when the wind and the flame of God's presence came. They spoke a language that all humanity could comprehend. They spoke a language that reversed the confusion of Babel. They spoke a language that ended the separation of races, nations, and cultures. They spoke a language that lifted women from their second-class status as men's property and child-bearing machines—for when the Spirit fell upon them, it made no distinction between male and female.

They were there also:
those who did not yet believe, did not yet belong.
They were there
for the Feast of Harvest, the Day of the First Fruits,
assembled from many nations, cultures, and climes.
They were there
and they reported,
"We hear the wonders of God in our own tongues."

We read that Peter preached boldly, quoting from the Hebrew Scriptures, that thousands were converted, that they "devoted themselves to the apostles teaching and to the fellowship, to

---

[1] *Parables, Etc.*, March 1984, 4.1.

the breaking of bread and to prayer." We read that everyone was filled with awe and wonder, that miracles were daily occurrences. We read of a unity of spirit that touched not only their hearts but their wallets: "All the believers were together and had everything in common. Selling their possessions and goods, they gave to anyone as he [or she] had need." We read that they met together daily, "praising God and enjoying the favor of all the people." We read that "the Lord added to their number daily."

They were there when the Spirit descended. And today we are here, waiting as they waited for the gift of God's Spirit.

We wait for God's Spirit to heal us, to take away the wounds of the past, to take away our sense of having been shamed and betrayed by those who were supposed to love us. We wait for God's Spirit to heal our bodies of illness and weakness. We wait for God's Spirit to heal our minds of doubt and fear and loneliness. We wait for God's Spirit to heal us of self-centeredness, of self-pity, of self-loathing.

We wait for God's Spirit to renew us, to give us visions and dreams so powerful that the very utterance of them pulls us toward their fulfillment.

We wait for God's Spirit to release our creativity, to call forth our gifts and talents.

We wait for God's Spirit to recreate us as the Church, just as the Holy Spirit melded and empowered the ragtag band of which we read in Luke's account of Pentecost. And if God's Spirit fills and indwells and excites and validates and commissions us, what will be the result? What can we expect as we together approach a new century?

As I prepared this sermon, I returned again and again to the "Mission Statement" of this church. This morning I want to lift it up so that each of us may own it as his or her own. Let me read it to you:

> The mission of the Ladera Community Church is to provide a sanctuary where the congregation can worship God according to the teachings and spirit of Jesus Christ; to nurture the spiritual, moral, and intellectual growth of each person in our congregation; to serve God with our talents, our time, our energy, and our money, accepting full stewardship for our community—the World; to encourage others to join us in our ministries.

Now that, ladies and gentlemen, is a reason for being. That, sisters and brothers, is a call worth responding to.

Our Mission Statement is a vision of Ladera Community Church as it moves toward the year 2001. It is a vision of the emergence of a Spirit-filled church. And what exactly is a Spirit-filled church? Let me mention a few characteristics. Some I will emphasize; others I will only list.[2]

1. A Spirit-filled church is a Christ-centered church

What is this church's greatest asset or any church's greatest asset? its buildings? its programs? its worship services? its music? its finances? its wonderful people? Truly, it is none of these. For these are only the temporal building blocks. The eternal foundation of this church or of any church is the will of God revealed in the person of Jesus, the teachings of Scripture, and the ongoing work of the Holy Spirit.

---

[2] The list of characteristics of a Spirit-filled church was suggested by a talk, "The Pastor as Evangelist," given by Henry Simmons (pastor of St. Alban's United Church of Christ, Queens, New York) during the Annual Meeting of the Northern California Conference, United Church of Christ at Asilomar, California, May 18, 1991.

Understand Jesus in any way that suits you. Regard him as a prophet, a sage, a seer, a holy man, God's most perfect image, God incarnate, the coming king, the heavenly judge.

Consider him an historic being shrouded in mystery and ambiguity, as a shaman or holy man. Know him as the divine spark within each of us, the true Self at the core of each person. Know him as Jesus the man or as the cosmic Christ, as the teacher of moral maxims or as the eternal Word through whom all things were made.

Know him in any way, shape, or form you can, but know him.

2. A Spirit-filled church is a worshiping church

A church is a sanctuary, a place of refuge, a place to celebrate, to rejoice, to praise God. Worship is the central act of the believing community. It is the single act that constitutes and maintains the community as a community. Coming to church is coming to a sacred place at a sacred time to bind ourselves deliberately to God and to one another. Let anything take the place of the worship of God in our lives and the church degenerates into a mailing list.

Worship is the intentional, God-directed, Christ-centered, Spirit-charged act of the total personality within the fellowship of believers. Accept no substitutes.

3. A Spirit-filled church is a biblically literate church

The story is told of the time when Leopold Stokowski was conducting a dress rehearsal of Bach's *St. Matthew's Passion:*

> Stokowski went through the work once with the several hundred singers and orchestra, tapped for silence, and said, "Well, I guess you know the notes well enough. But the spirit is lacking. I want each of you to sit down tonight with your Bible and read St. Matthew's account of the life of Christ. Try to grasp it all. Who knows—perhaps that message is just what our listeners need in a time of doubt and despair. Then let's come back to our performance and try to convey to our audience the meaning and inspiration of these sacred words." The singers were startled to hear this advice from the worldly, debonair Stokowski. But they did as they were told. At the performance the next night they sang their hearts out.[3]

The secrets of life and death are there—in the sacred text. The message that each of us needs in a time of doubt and despair is there. But we resist and we ignore that message. We fear most what we understand least.

4. A Spirit-filled church is a tithing church

Worship is our way of telling God that we love him; stewardship is our way of showing him. All that we have comes from God. He is the source of our lives and the landlord of the universe. Tithing is merely paying the rent due to our Creator. The tithe or 10 percent of one's income has been the standard for giving since Old Testament times.

Nothing more obviously reveals commitment to a church than one's personal giving pattern. Show me a person's check stubs and I will show you what he or she really believes.

Nothing creates greater excitement and forward movement in a church than increased financial support. And nothing better enables a church to do the work to which it is called. If I had to choose between belonging to a small church of tithers or a large church of moderate givers, I

---

[3] *Parables, Etc.*, October 1987.

would instinctively choose the tithers. For financial commitment breeds enthusiasm and outreach as surely as soil, seed, water, and light produce crops.

Moreover, people who are generous with their money are generous in their appreciation of one another. They see life as a gift and live it with gratitude and zest. Nothing cures depression and low self-esteem like generosity.

5. A Spirit-filled church is a love-centered and caring-through-sharing church

6. A Spirit-filled church is a praying church

Prayer is the stretching out of the divine within each of us to the God who made us in his own image. As Henri Nouwen writes,

> It is eternity in the midst of mortality, it is life among death, hope in the midst of despair, true promise surrounded by lies. Prayer brings love alive among us.[4]

Prayer lies at the heart of all personal godliness. Prayer throws us onto the frontier of the spiritual life. As Richard Foster states,

> Of all the Spiritual Disciplines prayer is the most central. . . . it is the discipline of prayer that brings us into the deepest and highest work of the human spirit. Real prayer is life-creating and life-changing.[5]

I am convinced that every activity of a Christian church and every day of every individual Christian's life should begin and end with prayer.

7. A Spirit-filled church is a culturally aware and socially active church

8. A Spirit-filled church is a progressive church

Phillips Brooks has written:

> We never become truly spiritual by sitting down and wishing to become so. You must undertake something so great that you cannot accomplish it unaided.[6]

And I would add, the place for greatness is here. The time for greatness is now.

9. A Spirit-filled church is an evangelism-intensive and evangelism-affirming church

A Christ-centered, worshiping, biblically literate, and generous church cannot help but attract members. A caring, praying, aware, and progressive church will always draw like-minded and like-spirited people as surely as a magnet draws iron filings. A Spirit-filled church is a secret that cannot be kept. A Spirit-filled church cannot keep itself from reaching out to others.

And even as we reach out, those who are who are hungry for the Spirit of God will be find us, and those who are being fed will stay.

---

[4] Nouwen, Henri, *Gracias* (San Francisco: Harper & Row, 1983), p. 12.

[5] Foster, Richard, *Celebration of Discipline* (cited in *Pastor's Story File*, May 1989), 33.

[6] Brooks, Phillips, *Parables,Etc.*, March 1985, 5.1.

They were there and they reported, "We hear the wonders of God in our own tongues."

We are here this morning, ready for the wind and the flame of God's Spirit, ready to be part of the wonders of God here and now. And our hearts cry out, "Come, Holy Spirit, come!"

Amen.

[Round: "Father, I Adore You"]

—LDS

[1976 words]
[20 minutes]

❦ *Occasion:* Dedication of a New Facility

We meet today to dedicate the new [name of purpose] building. We are grateful to God for the memory of our brother [sister] [full name]. As his [her] faithfulness was an example to all of us, so we pray, shall this building be an instrument of God's will in our midst.

We are grateful for our memories of [first name], for the gift that his [her] presence was in our lives. As we open this new building and dedicate it to its purpose, we dedicate ourselves to follow in [name's] footsteps for the sake of God's kingdom.

Amen.

[90 words]
[1 minute]

❦ *Occasion:* Memorial Service or Funeral

Theme: Thankfulness for the Life of the Deceased
Subject: Eulogies, memorial services, remarks and prayers of thanksgiving

As well as I knew [first name], there are many of you who knew him [her] longer and better. I was his [her] pastor. You were his [her] family member, coworkers, and friends. Instead of attempting to eulogize him [her], I am asking you to help me. I would like to invite each of you who feels so moved to express your thanks for the gift that [first name] was to you. In just a sentence or two, tell us what [first name] meant to you. When you have done so, let us all respond by saying: "*We thank you, O Lord, for the gift of your servant [first name].*" Let me begin.

[First name] always showed more interest in me and my work that I could ever show in him [her]. I will never forget his [her] earnest caring and warm sense of humor.

Response: "*We thank you, O Lord, for the gift of your servant [first name].*"

Remarks

There is so much and yet so little to say. I could take hours to rehearse all the acts of kindness and caring that were so characteristic of [first name]. We have all been changed forever and for the better by the life of [full name].

The poet Emily Dickinson has said, "Parting is all we know of heaven and all we need of hell." Because [first name] is no longer with him [her], our hearts and minds are full of his [her] kindness and caring. We remember and cherish our moments together, the jokes we shared, the smiles and hugs, the quiet sense of humor. They glow incandescent in our memories. And we realize that we have been forever changed because [first name] was part of lives. We think of [first name] and we cannot help but smile. Our hearts rejoice and we call out. "*We thank you, O Lord, for the gift of your servant [first name].*"

And then we realize how much we have lost. We are aware of an influence in our lives that can never be replaced, and that we shall miss [first name] for the rest of our lives. We were not prepared for the pain, the loneliness. Something that we took for granted is gone from our lives. All that we have earned together through our mutual caring and work seems to have slipped through our fingers.

But as Christians we know that death has not spoken the final word. We have lost [first name] only for little while. As Jesus our Lord before him, [first name] has gone to prepare a place for us that we may be together forever.

But even here and now, we know that we are not alone, that the goodness and kindness of [first name's] life has not disappeared. For he [she] is with us. what was fleeting and temporary has become eternal in our lives. And we are blessed and enhanced because [full name] was, and continues to be, part of our lives.

Amen.

—LDS

[471 words]
[5 minutes]

❦ *Occasion:* Retirement or Departure of a Fellow Employee

Theme: Our friend has been God's gift to us.
Subject: Goodbye

[First name] is leaving us. It does not seem possible, but it is so.

To say that he will be missed is true but as far as expressing what we are feeling, it is the tip of the iceberg. To say that there is no one else like him [her], that we can find someone else to fill his [her] job, but that no one can ever take his [her] place is also true, but equally inadequate.

The daily banter, the handshakes, the shared smiles, the mutual frustrations, our coffee hours together— all that we have taken for granted as though they would go on forever; these are over. The memories, the lessons we have learned together, the moments of regret for feeling left unsaid—these all lie ahead.

[First name], you have been God's gift to us in this place. In all of our lives, people come and go, but few truly make a difference. You are one of the few. And so we honor you and thank God for you and wish you and your loved one's all the best.

—LDS

[185 words]
[2 minutes]

❦ *Occasion:* Birthday

❦ *Title:* Birthday Blessings

We have come together to honor our very special friend, [full name]. His [her] life has touched us and changed us forever, and we are grateful.

[First name], we wish you a happy birthday—for a richly deserved happiness. We wish you a hundred more birthdays so that your life may continue to bring happiness to ours.

No present that we could give you on this day can equal the gift that you are to us. May God bless you and keep you. May he make his face to shine upon you and be gracious to you on this birthday and on many to come.

Amen.

—LDS

[100 words]
[1 minutes]

❦ CHAPTER TEN

COMMITMENT AND CARING

The commitments we make and honor determine who and what we are. It is up to each of us to ask ourselves, What do I stand for? What do I believe? To what and to whom am I committed?

The plea "I am too busy" is always a lie. It is an excuse for not caring, for not fostering the relationships that really count. Jesus transforms our lives, sparking our concern for our fellow human beings, especially for the hungry, the homeless, and the oppressed. Our apathy is inexcusable; it is inhuman.

From beginning to end, the Bible speaks of God's concern for orphans, widows, and newcomers. The test of our faithfulness as Christians is our commitment to the lonely, the depressed, and the abandoned. Kindness is the glue binding us to one another and uniting us with God.

Commitment and caring constitute our reason for living. Every day we are reminded that our actions have consequences.

❦ *Sermon 98*

❦ *Date:* Sunday Between November 6 and November 12 inclusive, Year A

Texts:
Amos 5:18–24
Psalm 78:1-7 or 70
1 Thessalonians 4:13–18
Matthew 25:1–13

Theme: You are the commitments you make and honor minus the commitments you break. Everything important you ever achieve is as the result of commitments made and honored.
Subject: Commitment, keeping one's word, stewardship

❦ *Title:* Ready, Willing, and Able: How 'bout One Out of Three?

> Recommendation: Use this sermon on the Sunday before Pledge or Stewardship Sunday.

The Meaning of Commitment

The minister says: "Do you take this woman to be your lawfully wedded wife?" or "Do you take this man to be your lawfully wedded husband?" You say, "I do," and nothing is ever the same again. Before God and your fellows you have made a commitment.

A child is born. It is your child. You hold him or her close to you and feel an undeniable oneness. "This child is mine," you say in your heart. "This is my son (or daughter)," you say to everyone else. Nothing is ever the same again. You have made a commitment.

You make friends—many friends over the years. But one of them you hold onto no matter whatever happens. You go through happy times and sad times together. You remember one another—each of you becomes a living record of the other's life. You talk together, cry together, laugh together. You share your innermost secrets—secrets you would not even tell your spouse. You both grow older and busier, yet you refuse to allow the tides of circumstances to separate you. You have made a commitment and you honor it.

You embrace a calling, a vocation, a profession. You adhere to its standards and discipline. You do your best because you have promised to, because you want to, because you like the way you feel when you do. You do your best because you do your best—not because you are afraid of the consequences if you don't or because you earn a lot of money if you do or because you are recognized for what you do. You give your word and you keep it. As a result, you make a difference.

You fall out of love. You don't even like one another anymore. Your paths diverge. There is sorrow and pain. You go your separate ways. Now and then you recall the good times. A commitment is broken and a price is paid.

You are the commitments you make and honor minus the commitments you break. Everything important you ever achieve is as the result of commitments made and honored. You give your word and you keep it. As a result, you make a difference. Or you give your word and you break it. And you make a very different kind of difference.

When you can't or won't keep your word, you feel diminished and guilty. So you own up to it. You make no excuses. You admit your failings and you accept the consequences. And you expect the same from others that they will keep their word to you. When they don't, you hold them accountable.

So far, so good? Or does it sound too idealistic, too unreal? If so, is that because it is too idealistic, too unreal or because you have made a choice to tolerate a world in which no one keeps his or her word, in which there are not commitments but only empty words?

Things change. The promises uttered today do not cover the situation tomorrow. Does that absolve you of the need to maintain your commitments? Or does it mean that you have to refocus, sharpen up, renew your commitments?

Commitment and Community

A community is a network of overlapping commitments. We are here because we choose to be here, because we are willing to do what is required to stay here. Our responsibilities toward one another are not always clear, but we do not deny that there are responsibilities. And as they become clear to us, we respond.

The church is a covenant community. It consists of individuals, each of whom has sworn solemn promises before God. You have said, "I do" to life as it is shared and enhanced in this place. You have held this fellowship of brothers and sisters to your heart and have allowed them to embrace you in return.

You have befriended us and been befriended by us. You have responded to the call of God and bound yourself to answer it here.

Our gospel reading for this day is a story told by Jesus, which is known as the Parable of the Foolish Virgins or the Parable of the Improvident Bridesmaids.

In this parable as in all the parables of Jesus, there is a single general concept. As Paul Scott Wilson observes: "It is the idea of the Realm (Kingdom) of God: this Realm is in contrast to the ways of the conventional world."[1] The realm of God is not heaven—not a place "up there" where disembodied souls go after death. It is "any location or event in which God's justice, mercy, and love are breaking in."[2]

We are fond of the parables about mercy and love. The Parable of the Prodigal Son and the Parable of the Good Samaritan are everybody's favorites. Yet we tend to forget that judgment and mercy are balanced in the teachings of Jesus, that for every verse that speaks of the unconditional welcome extended by God there is a parable that warns us of being unprepared for that welcome. For example, in the Parable of the Great Supper in Matthew 22, a king sends his messengers to scour the countryside to find guests for a magnificent banquet and then the king throws out a poor wretch who arrives without proper attire. How that story must have sent shivers up and down the spines of its hearers! God's grace is a gift, but if we accept it we must be prepared to be changed, to be held accountable.

Ready or not—God's justice, mercy, and love are breaking in. God is coming to your life; he is coming soon—the parables say. Is he coming as a judge or friend? as a consuming fire or as a comforting balm? God is a destabilizing influence. So be prepared.

One writer notes that today's parable

---

[1] Wilson, Paul Scott, *Imagination of the Heart: New Understandings in Preaching* (Nashville, TN: Abingdon Press, 1988), p. 209.

[2] Ibid.

> speaks, not to those who have made no preparation for the Lord's coming, but to those who have made insufficient preparation. The foolish young women are those who have taken some oil along, but not enough for the journey. They may have made a good start on the Christian way, but they are now faltering. They have neglected to refuel the inner resources necessary to sustain a Christian commitment.[3]

"to sustain a Christian commitment . . . "—what a challenge! I'm a good person; isn't that enough? I give a few dollars now and then to the church and my favorite charities; isn't that sufficient? I was baptized, confirmed, and exposed to years of religious education when I was a child; aren't I finished, aren't I done?

The improvident maidens of our story had bought new dresses, traveled all the way from who knows where, and waited hour after hour for the errant groom. Why pick on them? Why pick on Christians who fail to sustain a Christian commitment?

Because they were willing but neither ready nor able. And one out of three isn't good enough. Because they didn't stay the course, because they didn't grow in grace, because they failed to make of their spiritual lives a lifelong learning experience, because they were no more generous after decades of enjoying God's gifts than they were at the beginning.

Sustaining Commitments

Saying "I do" and feeling romantic does not guarantee a successful marriage. Being proud of a newborn child and feeling sentimental about childhood does not prepare that child to cope with the demands of daily life. Exchanging Christmas cards and feeling goodwill does not maintain and foster a true friendship.

Commitments are sustained by giving and keeping one's word. Commitments are sustained by deeds and not just words. Commitments are sustained through gifts of self and gifts of cash. Show me a man or woman's check stubs and I will show you his or her true character.

In the end, all that any of us has is time. We can squander it, use it, abuse it, turn it into paychecks and bonuses, invest it in causes or fads, numb ourselves with alcohol or diversions so that it slips away unnoticed, try in vain to save it. Or we can allow eternity to break in, to redeem the hours and us with them. How do we do that? By making and honoring a commitment to God—a commitment to love, to serve, to be human. And by honoring that commitment with everything we are, everything we have, everything we do.

There's a place for us—and it's here!

There's a time for us—and it's now!

Amen.

—LDS

[1400 words]
[14 minutes]

---

[3] *Prayers for Worship*, November 11, 1990.

Sermon 99

Date: First Sunday After Christmas, Any Year

Texts:
Isaiah 45:18–22
Romans 11:33 to 12:2
Luke 2:41–52

Theme: Each of us belongs to God.
Subject: Commitment

Title: After Christmas

Tip

> The opening portion of this sermon was inspired by a then hit TV series, "Mork and Mindy." Adapt the theme of a current top television program, movie, or best-seller to involve your audience.

Observing the Week After Christmas

Imagine the report of an alien who had been assigned to spy on us from December 1 to 31:

Of all the earth months which I have observed, the month known as December is clearly the most curious, stimulating, and interesting. The observer is struck by great flurries of activity, high emotional excitement, much rushing about characterized by many breakdowns in transportation and communications facilities, and a dramatic increase in the size and frequency of commercial/mercantile transactions.

We note also a great attenuation of emotions—gaiety, filial devotion, compassion tinged with nostalgia, regret, loneliness, depression. These moods are probably influenced by meteorological phenomena, that is, the relative absence of sunlight, the need for massive amounts of artificial lighting, and the effects of contrasting darkness and illumination on the nervous systems of the subject species.

During the latter part of the period, a midweek day of rest was observed, rather like their weekly Sabbath. On this day, the birth of one Jesus Christ, a religious figure from their tribal past, is celebrated. Religious services are observed by some, and clan gatherings are held for the purpose of exchanging tokens of affection and regard. In addition, the attempt is made in these clan gatherings to exhaust provisions of foodstuffs which have been meticulously selected and prepared during the above-mentioned period of commercial/mercantile transactions. It is apparently the conviction of the subject specimens that all items which have been earned, received, or otherwise obtained during one solar year must be destroyed before the inception of the next to prevent the contamination of the new solar year by the old.

The following few days, there occurs a remarkable charade as the inhabitants of the subject land pretend to return to mundane practical concerns. In fact, their thoughts and energies are devoted to a special ordeal. On the one hand, they are obligated to meditate upon their personal failures, shortcomings, and excesses so that they may properly resolve to mend their ways during the next solar cycle or year. On the other hand, they are expected to engage in public displays of debauchery, drunkenness, and sonar dissonance, and the witnessing of organized gladiatorial spectacles in which armored young men collide headlong with one another for three hours at a time while a leather covered egg of some huge avian species is flung, kicked, and avidly clung to. Since the auditoria are ovaloid and at least two of them are monitored by huge ovaloid flying machines which bear the wish, "Good Year," it is to be supposed that the inhabitants are worshipers of a cosmic egg from which the next solar cycle or year is believed to emerge.

How this period of joint repentance and irresponsibility through which the cosmic egg is worshiped is related to the celebration of the birth of the so-called savior, Jesus Christ, which we witnessed scant days ago is not immediately apparent to this observer. Nor, according to the interviews which I have conducted, is it apparent to any of the subject specimen. Further research is indicated and this observer's application for additional funding as well as his expense vouchers are enclosed. Finally, in the words of the subject specimens, "Merry Christmas and Happy New Year," whatever that means!

Three Journeys to Jerusalem

Turning away from our fantasy, let me add that as odd as the transition from Christmas to New Year's Day may be for us at the end of 1992, I note a similar strange transition in the Gospel According to Luke. At one instant, we are in Bethlehem with Mary, her infant son, and shepherds as angels proclaim, "Glory to God in the highest, and on earth peace, good will to men." A verse later, we are in the Temple at Jerusalem for the ritual of circumcision, as the eight-day-old baby Yeshua or Joshua or "God is Salvation" or, as we know him, Jesus, is dedicated by his family through an ancient ritual to belong to the covenant which God had made with the descendants of Abraham, Isaac, and Jacob, the covenant later crystallized for all time in the Law of Moses. A few verses later, with no mention by Luke of the sojourn in Egypt, we are again in Jerusalem for the Feast of Passover, the great reminder to the covenant people of the God who had chosen them and led them out of Egypt with a strong hand. Now Jesus is a young man, an adolescent discoursing with experts about the Law, a pre-teenager who had not bothered to tell his parents of his whereabouts, who in the first assertion of his role as giver of the new covenant begins to go his separate way, to pursue his heavenly father's business, to be in his father's house, begins to cause his parents the pain and anxiety of leaving them to be what he had been born to do. As we know, there would be yet another journey to Jerusalem. This final journey, recorded by Luke, began with joyful praises, "Blessed is the King who is coming in the name of the Lord!" An irate Jesus drove out the peddlers and provoked his own death at the hands of the guardians of the establishment.

Three journeys to Jerusalem. Circumcision. This child belongs to this people and its ways. The Passover visit. This child is almost an adult, responsible for his own actions, ready to take his place freely as one of us and yet ready to be what only he can be. The triumphant entry. He condemns us for our failings, questions the very foundation of our institutions. We kill him. Yet instead of destroying the threat, we enable him to fulfill his mission, to annul one contract or covenant, and through his death and resurrection to establish for all nations and peoples the very meaning of his name, "God is salvation!"

In our own way, each of us must make these journeys to Jerusalem. We are each a child of the covenant. Mother and father hope. As long as we live, we are theirs. We belong to them. And we will struggle with this identity, their expectations, and their values long after they have passed from this earthly stage. Each of us is the product of a host of relatives who loved us, comforted us, were there for us, and as human beings failed us now and then. Nurture that child. Live every day with thanks for those who cared. And learn through those failures before you are doomed to make them yourself. To each of us as children, much was given and of us little was expected. And in so many ways, nothing has changed for any of us. God gives freely and we are loved—when we but let ourselves be loved.

Each of us is responsible. Each of us must listen for himself or herself to the voice of God. And when we respond to the calling of God, to the unique vocation which sets each of us apart, We must risk losing our secure place as someone's child or disciple or pupil or employee or spouse. "To stand for something, we must take a chance of being misunderstood by our peers and loved ones." It is not easy to be about our Father's business nor is it easy to let go of our children so that they may respond to what calls them.

None of us is called to make the final trip to Jerusalem. Christian theology tells us that Jesus did that for us once and for all. And yet he walks that road in and through us today. He calls us to die to self and be reborn as instruments of God's peace and justice. Jesus would not accept business as usual. He would not accept the excuses of those who compromised principle because it was easier that way. He warned of the judgment that was about to befall his nation. In forty years, the Temple would be gone, the people dispersed. And in forty, fifty, sixty, seventy years, all of us will likewise be gone. And if our lives are to count for anything, we must reexamine and reassert our covenants, our personal trips to Jerusalem. Each of us must ask: To whom do I belong? Whose child am I? Whose love and caring made me the person I am today? What mistakes did they make? How can I avoid those same mistakes?

What do I stand for? What do I believe? What kind of world do I want for myself and my children?

What is my calling? What is my mission? Am I willing to nurture that sense of my truest, my highest self? Whose business am I about? In whose house do I reside?

Can I serve even if there is no triumphant hosannas and thank yous? Can I humbly and gratefully accept the love which God showers on me through those who love me for myself when I but let them?

Amen.

—LDS

[1500 words]
[15 minutes]

❦ *Sermon 100*

❦ *Date:* Sunday Between July 17 and July 23 inclusive Pentecost, Year C

Texts:
Colossians 1:15–28
Luke 10:38–42

Theme: Being too busy is always a choice.
Subject: Busyness, commitment

❦ *Title:* Too Busy?

We have all bought into a lie. We have convinced ourselves that not being busy is a sin, is a sign of failure. We have persuaded ourselves that being too busy guarantees success or, at the very least, is as likely to produce prosperity and ward off calamity as anything that anyone can do.

"Too busy" is always a lie. We use being too busy as an excuse for not caring, not investing ourselves in what really matters—family, friends, our neighbors, our own development spiritual human beings. We mean by "too busy" that we have no control over our time, our lives, or what happens to us. We rarely admit to ourselves that "too busy" is a choice, a decision to allow ourselves to be overwhelmed by things and worries and make work and anything else that shields us from intimate contact with other human beings or with the divine lover of our souls.

"Too busy" is poison. It kills marriages, families, and friendships. It kills personal happiness, and intellectual growth. It kills spiritual life, moral reflection, and civic responsibility. "Too busy" denies us recreation in the true sense of being re-created and refreshed. "Too busy" brings everything to naught. Life is yearned for but never lived. We become something less than persons. We become random patterns of addiction. Addiction to anxiety, depression, and busyness. We run because we run because we run because we run.

God is there in the midst of our busyness. The still, small voice whispers to us despite the noise to which we willingly subject ourselves. "I know you," says the voice. "I know you better than you know yourself. Your excuses and rationalizations for not living fully neither astound nor confound me. Before you were born, I had read the book of your life and knew every line of dialogue, every character who would play a part, every twist and turn, every surprise ending . . . ."

The volume of our busyness swells like the finale of the *1812 Overture*. We defend ourselves against our inner discomfort, saying in our hearts: "I don't want to hear you, Lord. I don't want to listen. You disrupt my rhythm, make it impossible for me to get everything done, make me ask myself why I am on this treadmill. I want to be too busy. I'm afraid to stop—afraid of what I will find out if I allow the silence to rush in. 'Not good enough' is what the silence will say. 'Not worthy of being loved.' 'Not able to love.' The silence knows that I am a failure. God knows."

And yet each of us yearns to be known, to be accepted, to be able to relax in the embrace of joy, to think those idealistic "big thoughts" that once excited us, to believe that one person can make a difference, to believe that I could be so important in the life of another that the other would be changed for the better, and that another could be so important to me that the caring and sharing would. But we interrupt our musings, saying to ourselves, "Enough of such foolish, romantic dreams! There is work to be done and I'm really too busy to think about such foolishness." And so each of us drifts off into unconsciousness, exhausted by his or her own busyness. "Yet," says the psalmist, "when I awake, I am still with you!"

The mystery of God, hidden for ages and generations, is now known, says the apostle. The mystery is made known, I would add, only to those who refuse to be too busy, who have the time to see, hear, taste, smell, and touch it. "Mystery" is one of those loaded words in the New Testament. A mystery is something revealed to a muse or mystic. A mystery is a ceremony restricted to the initiated in the cults of the Hellenistic gods. A mystery is participation in an energy so powerful, overwhelming, and penetrating that it is as much to be avoided as sought. Remember what happened to the fellow who stretched out his hand to steady the Ark of the Covenant. The divine energy struck him dead!

This gospel of Jesus Christ is nothing to fool with. It can turn us inside out, revealing the emptiness of our excuses, and the insignificance of your busyness.

We understand Martha. Somebody has got to take care of business. But what really counts? What is really needed? Sitting still as much as raging about, listening as much as speaking. I would be willing to bet that the people who have loved you in a way you never deserved to be loved were not the most educated, most accomplished, successful men and women you have known. I'll bet that the loved ones for whom you mourn, whose passing left you bereft and bewildered, amassed little. What made them special?

The living Christ was there—in them, loving, caring, reconciling, supporting, taking time, being there, being aware, responding.

There is so much more that I, your preacher, could say. The Scriptures for today are so pregnant with meaning. But I have to stop. I am too busy to say any more and you are too busy to listen. And so I say "adieu" for now so that I can get back to all those things that I must do.

As Paul said, "To this end I labor, struggling with all God's energy, which so powerfully works in me." And God keeps me very, very busy!

Amen.

—LDS

[1000 words]
[10 minutes]

Sermon 101

Date: Last Sunday After Pentecost, Year A
or Sunday before Memorial Day, Any Year

Texts:
Ezekiel 34:11–16, 20–24
Psalm 100 or 95:1-7a
Ephesians 1:15-23
Matthew 25:31–46

Theme: Jesus, the transformer of human lives, sparks our concern for our fellow human beings and expects our hearts to burst aflame with compassion. Jesus, the liberator of the downtrodden, identifies with the hungry, the thirsty, the newcomer, the unclothed, the sick, the prisoner.
Subject: Compassion, transformation

Title: The Five Dollar Song and the God of the Unseen

Note

> This sermon may be used for either the coming of the Advent season or for Memorial Day. Special material for each occasion is indicated in marked brackets.

The Battle Hymn of the Republic

She was married to a renowned humanitarian, a physician whose dedication to those in need was known far and wide. He had risked his life in a foreign war of liberation, serving as a soldier and a surgeon for six years. Back in his native Boston, he founded programs for the blind and championed the cause of retarded children. His dedication to duty and to his country had brought them from their home to Washington, D.C.

She was a sensitive and compassionate woman in her early forties, the devoted mother of four. She hated oppression and she loathed conflict. Her heart filled with distress as the nation drifted toward war. And when war came, she watched the troops go by and heard them singing the strains of a raucous marching song.

One day as she watched a parade of soldiers with a visiting friend, her former pastor from Boston, the minister turned to her and said: "Why don't you write some decent words for that tune?" She promised that she would.

The next morning, she recalled:

> I awoke in the grey of the morning, and as I lay waiting for dawn, the long lines of the desired poem began to entwine themselves in my mind, and I said to myself, "I must get up and write these verses, lest I fall asleep and forget them!" So I sprang out of bed and in the dimness found an old stump of a pen. . . . I scrawled the verses almost without looking at the paper.[1]

She sold her poem to The Atlantic Monthly for five dollars. Sung to the tune of an old camp song, it quickly became one of the most popular songs ever written, finding its way into every hymnal and every collection of patriotic songs.

At the height of the terrible war, it was performed by a soloist at a large patriotic rally attended by the president. When the singer finished, the audience erupted in applause. With tears in his eyes, the president cried out, "Sing it again," and it was sung again.

Her song gave courage to a dispirited America. It brought renewed conviction and purpose to the men on the battlefield. And when the war ended, the mother of four dedicated her time, energy, and considerable talents to a series of noble causes. She led a crusade to provide for the widows of the long war—widows on her side of the battle line and on the enemy's. Five years after the war, she organized women throughout the world in an effort to end war for all time. She campaigned tirelessly for equal educational, professional, and business opportunities for women. She wrote travel books, biography, drama, verse, and songs for children. When she was ninety-one, just twelve days before her death, she was awarded an honorary Doctor of Laws degree by Smith College.

Her name is Julia Ward Howe, and her song is known as "The Battle Hymn of the Republic." For me, it is a beautiful and passionately moving hymn, which far transcends the American Civil War.

[Pre-Advent text: And it is so appropriate on this Sunday, the last Sunday in our church year and the Sunday before the season of Advent. Memorial Day text: And it is so appropriate on this Sunday, the day before our nation observes a special day to remember the dead of the Civil War and all our other conflicts.]

The God of the Oppressed

The Scripture readings for today warn us of God's impending judgment on nations that neglect the needs of the helpless and oppressed.

---

[1] Cited by Kenneth W. Osbeck, *101 Hymn Stories* (Grand Rapids, MI: Kregel Publications, 1982), p. 35.

[Pre-Advent text: Next Sunday, Advent begins with its message of God's coming to our world in the person of the infant of Bethlehem. "The Battle Hymn of the Republic" is virtually a commentary on our gospel readings for today and next week. Memorial Day: "The Battle Hymn of the Republic" is virtually a commentary on our gospel readings for today and next week.]

Jesus taught that powerful nations would rise and fall not on the basis of their gross national product or their military might, but on the basis of their concern for the helpless and oppressed. In like manner, Mrs. Howe's song reminds us of a just God who "is sifting out the hearts of men before his judgment seat." She knew that wherever there is enslavement, wherever there is denial of human rights, wherever there is abuse or neglect of one class of human beings by another, there are to be found God's marching orders.

And Julia Ward Howe also knew that the justice of God is inseparable from the mercy of God.

[Pre-Advent text: Just as our Scripture readings move us from warnings of divine retribution to preparation for the coming of the Christ child, so also does Mrs. Howe turn from the theme of judgment to the scene of a manger. Memorial Day text: Note how Mrs. Howe turns from the theme of judgment to the scene of a manger.]

In the beauty of the lilies
Christ was born across the sea,
With a glory in His bosom
that transfigures you and me. . . .

Julia Ward Howe believed in Christ the transformer of human lives, Jesus the liberator of the downtrodden. She was no evangelist. Her theology was as liberal as that of our most ardent radicals of today. She was an active member of the Unitarian Church, a frequent guest preacher in Unitarian pulpits. She tenaciously maintained: "Nothing of what I have heard or read has shaken my faith in the leadership of Christ in a religion which makes each man the brother of all, and God the beneficent Father of each and all."

We read this morning of the coming king who will sift the hearts of men and women at the throne of judgment. We read of the transformer of human lives who sparks our concern for our fellow human beings and expects our hearts to burst aflame with compassion. We read of the liberator of the downtrodden who identifies with the hungry, the thirsty, the newcomer, the unclothed, the sick, the prisoner.

Liberation and transformation—that is the call. It is easy to turn the challenging words of Jesus into a demand for contributions to charity. It is easy to respond with our gifts for the poor and needy, to feed a few families for a few days and return to business as usual [Pre-Advent add: until the next holiday season appeal]. Don't misunderstand me. I thank God for every dollar given, every night of shelter provided, every meal offered [Pre-Advent add: at this time of year]. But let us recognize that Jesus was demanding something much more extreme.

The Unresolvable Dilemma

Jesus was plunging us into an unresolvable dilemma. How do we empower the needy? How do we help them without making them dependent on our help? How do we show respect for who they are and not expect them to become "good people" just like us, with our virtues, values, and vices? How do we offer the Good News that God's just reign is here and now for them without treating them like second-class citizens? How do we honor what makes them different and yet give them the opportunity to participate fully in the "good life"? As Norman Gottwald muses,

> how do we give the basics of life to people today with love and respect for them and with an efficacy that will change their inner and outer conditions in a lasting way? Will it be more charity or a step toward liberation, or both, and how do we figure out the difference?[2]

God is sifting out our hearts before his judgment seat. God is on the side of the downtrodden, the oppressed, the exploited, the neglected, the abused. The invisible God is the God of all invisible people—the people without whom we could not exist but whose existence we ignore.

Invisible Populations

As you know, most prime-time television shows are produced right here in California, a state with an enormous and growing Third World population. Yet, according to a recent study, "Almost all minority characters on TV are black. There are as many extraterrestrials on TV as Hispanic and Asian characters."[3] What has happened to our Third World population? We have rendered it invisible.

The same study notes: "Women on prime-time television shows usually are young and often scantily clad. . . . Women tend to be supporters and sidekicks. . . . Women help, but rarely overshadow men." Older women are grandmas and moms, while older men have authority and power. "In the real world," the report says, "women don't disappear at age 40, they don't wear bikinis when they answer the door and they rarely need to be rescued." And real women in the real world have economic power and social influence. In other words, TV has rendered real women invisible.

How many other populations have we turned invisible? AIDS patients, cancer sufferers, the mentally ill, the retarded, drug abusers, children at risk? Isn't it ironic that while we have turned our most basic natural resources, the air we breathe and the water we drink, toxically visible, we have rendered more and more of our neighbors invisible?

Abruptly our friend, the meek and mild Jesus, Jesus lover of our souls, stands before us as our king. And Christmas morn turns into Judgment Day!

We come to church on Sunday mornings as though it were a spiritual filling station.[4] We call this hour a "service," don't we? We drive up and expect to be serviced. But the king demands that we serve him. "But, Lord, when have we ever failed to serve you?" we bleat like terrified sheep. And suddenly all those invisible people whom we have ignored take visible form standing

---

[2] Gottwald, Norman K., *Proclamation 4: Aids for Interpreting the Lessons of the Church Year, Series A: Pentecost 3* (Minneapolis: Fortress Press, 1989), p. 64.

[3] "TV Heroines Lost in a Bimbo Limbo," *San Jose Mercury News*, November 15, 1990, p. 6D.

[4] Ortlund, Ray, "You Were Made to Worship God," *Haven of Rest*, radio broadcast, November 14, 1990, written by Sherry Ortlund Harrah.

there beside our Lord. He points to them—the hungry, the thirsty, the newcomer, the poorly clothed, the sick, the prisoner, the exhausted working mother, the cast-aside elderly, the homeless, the war ravaged, the victims of human mistakes and the victims of natural calamities.

As they become visible, do they make us ashamed? Do they make us feel guilty? Or do they ignite our inner fire? Do they fan the flames of compassion? Do they inspire us to create a world that works for everyone? For Julia Ward Howe was right. As surely as God is calling us to judgment, he is inviting us to partake of the glory that transfigures you and me.

[Pre-Advent: Our church year ends today. Next Sunday, the Season of Advent returns to remind us that Christ child is coming soon. But before we get lost in the warmth and glow of Yuletide, let us remember that the same Christ is coming in this season and in all seasons as our king and judge. As our eyes open to behold God visible in human form, so may they see those in need of our compassion, who stand at his side.]

[Memorial Day: The season of spring ends soon. Summer begins with its sunny days and recreation. But before we get lost in the busyness of our travel plans, let us remember that in the coming season as in all seasons, Christ is our king and judge. As our eyes open to behold the wonders of God's creation in our summer travels, so may they see those in need of our compassion, who stand at his side.]

Amen.

—LDS

[1732 words]
[17 minutes]

❦ *Sermon 102*

❦ *Date:* Sunday Between July 10 and July 16 inclusive (if after Trinity Sunday) Pentecost, Year C

Texts:
Colossians 1:1–14
Luke 10:25–37

Theme: Apathy is inhuman; caring counts.
Subject: Apathy, caring

❦ *Title:* A Thorn in My Paw, second in a series (See also sermons 21 and 59.) [or Who Cares?]

The Fallen Comrade

I was standing at the elevator when he collapsed. I was stunned. A colleague lay at my feet, limp and motionless.

Seven or eight of his fellow professionals were within four feet. Another twenty were within thirty yards.

Two of us bent over him to see if he was breathing. "Yes, he's still alive," we reported to a few anxious viewers. By now, those on the periphery of the scene had disappeared.

He came around—was conscious again—confused, disoriented, but conscious. "I'll be all right," he said. All but three of us took his words as a cue to depart. As he was struggling to his feet, an elevator door opened and a new actor arrived. "I'm a nurse," she said. "Don't let him move," she chided the few of us who still stood watch.

"I just want to get to my room," he protested, his embarrassment obvious. Another male staffer and I followed him into the elevator. On the way to the third floor, he fainted again. We caught him and held his body upright between us. He revived in two or three seconds. "I can't understand what's wrong," he stammered. "I'll be all right if I can just lie down." We accompanied him to his room.

"I'll be OK," he insisted.

"Are you sure?" I asked. He nodded his assent and closed the door.

I ran to the information booth and reported the incident to the office staff of the National Mental Health Association—the group whose conference I was attending. A secretary, in turn, directed me to a member of the professional staff.

Our colleague recovered within an hour and returned to the conference activities.

The Bleeding Hand

My stream of consciousness carries me to another incident—personal, trivial, petty, to be sure. I was at an outdoor cocktail party at Staff Council in Brainerd, Minnesota, shortly after I joined the Mental Health Association family. Somehow I had gotten an ugly and painful thorn in my right hand. The more I tried to remove it, the more it embedded itself. After ten fruitless minutes, I wandered from staffer to staffer asking for help. "Do you have a pair of tweezers?" I asked. "Not here. In my cabin," an occasional women staffer would answer. Then she would turn her back and return to the conversation I had interrupted.

The same scene repeated itself a dozen times as I disrupted conversations by displaying my, by now, bleeding hand. The body language of my hearer always conveyed "Go away." The actual words were, "What a shame. Wish I could help, but I'm busy at the moment. Perhaps the Lodge has a doctor or a nurse. . . ." (We professionals call that rendering "information and referral"!)

I felt as though I had phoned the suicide prevention hotline and had been greeted by an answering machine. I felt rejected, depressed, disillusioned. These were overreactions to be sure, but real feelings, nonetheless. I went to my cabin, poured after-shave lotion over the thorn, cut it loose with a razor blade, grabbed the thorn between my teeth and spit it out. With a styptic pencil borrowed from my absent roommate's shaving kit, I stopped the bleeding.

After my return to the festivities, one of those whom I had asked for help inquired, "Did you want something? I didn't quite understand what you were asking."

"That's OK. It wasn't important," I replied.

I was executive director of the Mental Health Association in Delaware when these incidents occurred. I remember thinking: "We are citizens who make a difference—that was our motto. We professional staffers *care* for a living. Yet most of us would walk away if one of our number needed our attention. Apathy rather than caring would be our first response. Why?"

Sometimes we refuse to care because we are afraid of the inconvenience

Allow me to illustrate with an apocryphal story. I was in line at the Menlo Park post office when the man ahead of me purchased a postcard. He turned to me and asked, "Would you mind addressing this card for me?"

Thinking the poor fellow could not write, I gladly helped him out. When I handed the card back, the man needed another favor. "I hate to bother you again," he continued, "but would you mind writing a short message on the card for me?"

I agreed to this second request and wrote out the message as the man dictated it. I gave the completed card to the man who looked at it for a moment and then asked one more favor. "I know this is an imposition, but would you mind doing one more thing for me? At the end of the message, would you apologize for the horrible handwriting?"

Sometimes we refuse to care because we are sure that our caring is neither wanted nor needed

Allow me to illustrate with a true story. In 1972 I was in Boston on a promotion tour for my book, *The Jesus Trip.*[1] I had arrived an hour and a half early for a television interview. So I decamped at a Howard Johnson restaurant next to the studio and spent ninety boring minutes picking away at a hamburger and French fries.

I looked up and noticed a familiar looking, bald-headed man, sitting alone across the room. I recognized him as Otto Preminger, the film actor and director. I was tempted to go over and introduce myself and ask if he would like some company. How I would have like to talk to him about Laura and Exodus. But I convinced myself that he could not possibly be interested in anything I had to say.

When I got to the studio, I was introduced to the guest host of the local talk show on which I was to appear. The guest host? Otto Preminger.

The interview went well. Preminger and I lingered in the studio when it was all over. He had many questions for me about contemporary religion in general and my religion in particular. He told me of his early career as an actor in Vienna, his interest in Hinduism, and his personal spiritual search. He asked me: "Why didn't you come over and join me for lunch? I was nearly bored to death having to wait there for an hour and a half?" If only I had acted on my original impulse. If only I had realized that everyone I meet in life, no matter how secure he or she may seem, has need of me. If only others would realize as they meet me that no matter how secure I seem, I have need of them.

Sometimes we refuse to care because we are angry and hurt because no one has cared for us

We have trapped ourselves in a vicious cycle. We have become cynical. We are like Lucy in her relationship with Schroeder. In a "Peanuts" cartoon strip, Lucy says, "Guess what? . . . If

---

[1] Streiker, Lowell D., *The Jesus Trip: Advent of the Jesus Freaks* (Nashville, TN: Abingdon Press, 1972).

you don't tell me that you love me, you know what I'm going to do? I'm going to hold my breath until I pass out!"

Looking up from his piano, Schroeder informs her, "Breath-holding children is an interesting phenomenon. . . . It could indicate a metabolic disorder. . . . A forty milligram dose of vitamin B_6 twice a day might be helpful. . . . I think that's probably it. . . . You need vitamin B_6 . . . you might also consider eating more bananas, avocados and beef liver. . . ."

As he goes back to his piano, Lucy sighs, "I ask for love, and all I get is beef liver!"

Sometimes we refuse to care even though caring is in our best interest

A few years ago a traveling minister stopped at a gas station. It was a rainy day, yet the station workers were industriously taking care of the customers. He was impressed by the diligent service and fully understood the reason when he read a sign on the front door of the station:

Why Customers Quit

1 percent die

3 percent move away

5 percent form new friendships

9 percent find lower prices elsewhere

14 percent become dissatisfied with the product

But 68 percent quit because of an attitude of indifference toward them by some employee![2]

Sometimes we refuse to care because apathy is safe but caring costs

Donald L. Anderson tells of a visit to the Hillhaven Hospice:

When I interviewed the Chaplain on a Tuesday morning, he told me that 8 of their 30 patients had died over the last weekend.

Knowing how close-knit a family (care-takers and care-receivers) they were, I asked him about the effect of so many deaths on the staff. He replied that it was tough—but then recited for me the most moving story I have ever heard.

It was the story of one patient—one death. He told me that on Saturday one of their patients who had been there a couple of months had a visit from her teenaged son. The staff said that it must have been a great visit because there were laughs and jovial conversation. At noon the boy said, "I'm to have lunch with some friends, I'll be back later, Mom." After he left, the patient called her favorite nurse and said, "I think this may be it. I may be dying." The nurse checked her vital signs and replied honestly, "It's possible that you are." The patient then said to her nurse friend, "Will you hold me? I think if you hold me I can do this well." The nurse got into the bed and cradled that emaciated little body in her arms—and held her into eternity.

---

[2] *The Bible Illustrator*, November 11, 1988, p. 6, adapted.

Anderson comments:

> What a story! All I knew to ask the chaplain was, "What about the nurse? What did it do to her?" He replied that she had taken four days
>
> off to go to the mountains to think and feel and decide whether to come back to work again. I asked whether, in his judgment, she would return to the job.
>
> "She'll be back," he said. "You learn in a place like this that caring hurts—*but when you really care you offer something special—and become special yourself.*"[3]

". . . when you really care you offer something special—and become special yourself."

Sometimes we refuse to care because we have forgotten how to.
Sometimes we refuse to care because the way we live numbs
us to our responsibility, because often our lifestyle is based on apathy

As a boy, I spent my summers away from the tenements of Chicago in the small town of Maywood, a few miles west of the city. My grandfather was a beverage distributor. It seemed that everyone knew him personally and recognized me instantly as his grandson. My successes and failures were magnified a thousandfold by their awareness of my existence. Our responses to one another were open and spontaneous.

Now I am an adult who lives in a medium-sized city, the suburb of a larger city. My relationships with all but a handful of people are mechanized and superficial. Our goal seems to be the avoidance of disrupting one another's routine. When we want to express our feelings, we hire specialists to ritualize the process. We seem to be crying, "Teach me the rules so I can feel now."

When I spent those spring and summer vacations in Maywood, I helped my grandfather cultivate his half-acre vegetable garden, accompanied him as he delivered cases of Orange Crush and Old Colony Ginger Ale, puttered in the kitchen with my grandmother as she made Challah (egg bread) and chicken soup. I played with neighbor children, conversed with adults. Here was reality, connection, immediacy, and *responsibility.*

Much of the alleged freedom we Americans so cherish is borne of anonymity. There is a freedom in being unknown, uncared about, beyond the grasp of personal responsibility. I can afford to be rude to a stranger in a supermarket. As my grandparents' grandson, I never would have dared to insult a neighbor at the corner grocery store. As a stranger, I can pass by an injured or distressed fellow stranger. In Maywood, I would have felt it necessary to respond to the lost house pet of an acquaintance who lived half a mile away.

Many of us have freed ourselves of old taboos, inhibitions, and values—just as we have sundered the old person-to-person responsiveness of the neighborhoods of our youth. At times, our rootlessness is positively invigorating. It is wonderful to be free to be one's true self for the sake of oneself alone. But as liberated as we may want to be, a somber truth remains: No one can endure alone, without belonging, without caring, without being cared for. We think we have transcended the limitations of the past, but what we have left behind are the personal, nurturing, relationships that enable us to be human at all.

A thorn in my hand is nothing. A fainting staffer means little. There is no going home to the village life of an earlier time. But apathy is reversible.

---

[3] Anderson, Donald L., "Caring Really Counts—And Costs," Opening Convocation, Fall 1987, *Princeton Seminary Bulletin*, (Vol. 8, No. 1), emphasis added.

Apathy is giving up, acting as if no single individual counts. Apathy is believing that abstract forces, an ill-defined they, rule our destiny. Apathy is letting the other guys do it all, letting George think, feel, decide, act and react. Apathy is copping out.

Caring counts. Responding to another makes a difference—a difference to the one for whom we care—and, just as important, a pronounced difference to the one who cares. When I think of the people I revere, I discover not the famous nor the accomplished nor the brilliant nor the powerful men and women I have known. Instead, I think of the generous of heart, who love, who comfort, who care.

Because of them, I can be human. I can share. I can love. I can accept love.

Who cares? Because of them, I do.

And caring counts.

Amen.

—LDS

[2274 words]
[22 minutes]

❦ *Sermon 103*

❦ Date: Sunday Between October 16 and October 22 inclusive, Year A

Texts: (NCL)
Ruth 1:1–19
Psalm 146
1 Thessalonians 1:1–10
Matthew 22:15–22

Theme: Ruth's gift of herself silences her bitter mother-in-law. Ruth commits herself to Naomi; Naomi accepts. It is a sacred moment.
Subject: Faithfulness, commitment, widowhood

❦ *Title:* Women in the World: Wistful Widows on the Way to Where?

[First in a series of three sermons: "More Than Is Required"—The Book of Ruth and Women of Today. It is suggested that this sermon be followed by sermons 104 and 53. Each sermon may be used independently.]

Three wistful widows set out on the road to where? One will turn back. Two will press on, leaving the graves of loved ones behind, trusting in what lies ahead, never looking back.

On Being a Widow

What is it like to be a widow? Let me tell you what I have learned from the many widows I have known and especially from my friend Barbara Ellis Long. Barbara is a psychologist and a widow.

First, there is the panic of abandonment. There is the feeling of being totally, hopelessly alone. There is the sense of emptiness and the isolation.

Then, there is the anger. The widow is mad at her husband for leaving her, angry at the doctor who did not save him, hostile toward whatever contributed, toward whatever could have been different, furious with the cold, cruel world for not caring. Those near at hand are often the targets for this anger—although they scarcely deserve it.

Such anger may turn inward. Many a widow becomes angry with herself for not having achieved her potential, for having accepted an auxiliary and subservient role as a good wife and perfect mother. Having thought of herself for forty to fifty years as part of a couple, she is confused and bewildered by her newfound status.

I was preaching once on the need for Christians to put others first. A widow in the congregation told me that putting another first had been the story of her life until her husband's death. Now for the first time in her adult existence she was discovering what it meant to live for herself. She let me know that I had left her out of my sermon. And she was right.

Often, there is depression, the helpless and hopeless feeling that sucks all the energy out of one's life, that clings like a leaden overcoat.

And there is the gut sense that the world is no longer a safe place. There is the fear of outliving one's resources, no matter how much one actually has. Many widows become misers, holding on to whatever they have rather than starting a new life.

Naomi and Ruth

Let me tell you about the widows "on the way to where?"

"Hey, you kids, stay away from those people across the way," the townsfolk warned. "You young follows, don't have anything to do with those wild girls," the solid citizens of Bethlehem admonished. The people of Moab were the neighbors and the relatives of the Israelites. The Israelite men lusted after and hated their women, accusing the women of being temptresses and seductresses. Those who abuse women always accuse them. Things haven't changed much.

In stories told around campfires for hundreds of years before they found their way into the Scriptures, the children of Israel recounted the shameful origins of the Moabites. While God was calling Abraham to be the father of a great people and blessing him at every turn, Abraham's nephew Lot was lucky to escape from Sodom with his life and his two daughters. Lot's wife, we recall, did not share their good fortune. While the three hid in a cave, Lot became drunk and impregnated both daughters. "The firstborn bore a son," comments the writer of Genesis, "and named him Moab; he is the ancestor of the Moabites to this day." (19:37)

It was the women of Moab, we read in Numbers 25, who had tempted the children of Israel even before the Israelites had entered the promised land. These foreign women had lured men of Israel into taking part in ritual prostitution, in the worship of fertility gods. The women of Moab had seduced the Israelites both physically and spiritually.

Like a jilted lover, Yahweh, the God of the Israelites, was infuriated. He sent a plague upon the Israelites. Phineas the priest was also infuriated. When he found the Israelite Zimri making love to his pagan wife Cozbi, he killed them with a spear. Only then did the plague abate. Twenty-four thousand lives were lost.

Around the campfires and in the market place, the whispers continued: "Don't have anything to do with the Moabites. They are a plague. They are accursed. They will be our undoing. And, above all, stay away from their women—their alluring, bewitching, attractive women."

Elimelech, his wife Naomi, and their sons were not frightened by such stories. They were not afraid of divine wrath. After all, it had already come their way. They were poor barley farmers and the crops had failed. So they trekked from the insignificant village of Bethlehem up into the more fertile farmlands of the Moabites and settled there unmolested.

Naomi missed her family and friends, but she made what she could of her husband's decision to resettle in this strange place among these strange people. She was not happy when her boys selected local girls as wives. But what mother is ever thrilled by the girl that her son chooses? And, as it turned out, they were fine, hardworking, loving girls. So what's not to like? Indeed, she came to love them as though they were her own.

"So perhaps Yahweh isn't really interested in us," she thought. "Perhaps he has enough to do, looking after my people at home in Bethlehem." She heard from travelers that things were better there. The crops and the flocks were the best they had been in years. But travelers also brought her bad news: one after another, almost all of her relatives and her husband's relatives had died. Most of her childhood friends were gone as well. The thread that bound her to Bethlehem and to the God she had worshiped in Bethlehem was becoming thinner and thinner.

Ten uneventful years passed. And then the disaster that had dogged their relatives in Bethlehem tracked down Naomi's family in Moab. Naomi's husband Elimelech died of some mysterious malady that was going around. Her son Mahlon became weak and sick. Within months, he died. Her remaining son Chilion, who had never gotten used to the climate of Moab, started coughing up blood and soon he too perished.

Naomi found herself alone in the world with her two daughters-in-law. Her situation was desperate. She had little more than the clothes on her back. She sold her personal possessions to buy food for her sons' widows and herself, but that would soon be gone. And then she remembered the small piece of land she had inherited from her father's estate. It was not much, but if she could sell it to a generous relative and find some cheap housing and a job working as a maid, perhaps it would all work out.

Naomi was afraid to think of the future. Without a man to provide for her, to protect her.... And she was so lonely. Her daughters-in-law were pleasant companions. Their chatter was entertaining. They helped the hours go by. But as she lay awake at night, worrying about what lay ahead, they were no substitute for her Elimelech, Mahlon, and Chilion.

"If only we had stayed in Bethlehem.... If only we had been rich and could have hired the best healers.... If only I had been a better wife and mother.... " Wide awake in the darkness, Naomi tormented herself. "Why has God done this to me? Why am I being punished?"

She became bitter and hostile toward her neighbors, even toward the daughters-in-law she so loved. She was sorry for the way she felt, for the way she was acting. In her heart, she knew it was time to go home—to go to whatever home there might be for her in Bethlehem.

And so three wistful widows set out. Naomi tried to send them back to their own people, to the houses of their fathers. She thought: "I can scarcely provide for myself on this journey. How can I take care of them? It will be hard enough for me to find acceptance from the few relatives who might remember me. How will they react to my Moabite daughters-in-law? I am no threat to any woman—not the way that affliction has robbed me of the beauty of my youth. But Orpah and Ruth are young and attractive. My relatives will have nothing to do with me if I bring them along. I don't want them ending up selling their bodies to survive or to support me."

So she told the girls: "You have done everything for me that anyone could expect of you. You are on your own now. Go home to your people and to your god and I will go home to mine." Mahlon's widow, Orpah, stopped arguing. She knew the older woman was right. Her eyes filled with tears, she turned back.

But Ruth would have none of it. She paid no attention to Naomi's reasons, complaints, or insults. When Naomi tried pushing her away, Ruth restrained her with and an embrace and said simply: "Don't urge me to leave you or to turn back from you. Where you go I will go, and where you stay I will stay. Your people will be my people and your God my God. Where you die I will die, and there I will be buried. May the LORD deal with me, be it ever so severely, if anything but death separates you and me." (1:16–17)

And, finally, Naomi had the good sense to shut up.

Enabling a Widow to Return to Life

What helps a widow to turn the corner, to get on with life?

Widows (and widowers) can help themselves by realizing that life is a matter of choices and consequences. What is is. What is not is not. What will be depends on decisions made today.

Without denying the pain, the anger, the loneliness, or the vulnerability of widowhood, widows can accept what cannot be changed. The years ahead are not a curse, they are an opportunity. They are years of freedom as well as limits. More than one widow has blossomed after the death of a life's mate, has found her true self as though finding a long lost friend.

Relatives, friends, and fellow church members can help by refusing to allow the grieving ones to cocoon themselves up in their fear, anger, and misery. Don't argue with a hurting person—at first. Listen carefully. Help guide her or him through the despondency, the sense of abandonment, the loneliness, the depression. Be there and be with. And gently, persistently, lovingly draw your loved one back into the land of the living. Never allow anyone you love to wall herself or himself up in the living death of perpetual mourning.

Angry with God

Naomi was mad at God. That was a perfectly all right response. When the pain of a spouse's death causes us to lash out with rage, we can do real damage. We can hurt our friends, our children, our neighbors, but there is no way that we can hurt God. God has a thick skin. The sooner the anger is vented, the sooner the energy needed to start over returns.

When Naomi has exhausted her rage against God, when she has given voice to her sadness at the loss of what was and what might have been, Ruth speaks. Ruth speaks with such love, commitment, and force that her words reassure Naomi and empower her for what lies ahead. Ruth offers the gift of herself—her love, her loyalty, and her courage. Ruth has the strength of character that enables her to give and Naomi has the sense to accept.

A Sacred Moment

Ruth refuses to leave and Naomi is speechless. It is a sacred moment—a sacred moment for Ruth and Naomi and a sacred moment for each of us and those to whom we commit ourselves. Ruth gave more than was required. She gave more than Naomi or anyone else could expect. She gave more than custom or tradition obliged her to give. She gave herself—her word, her deeds, her life. And Naomi stopped protesting and without as much as a "thank you," she accepted and gave herself to Ruth in return.

Although they never suspected it, Ruth and Naomi were on the road to the will of God. Even before they left on their journey, they had already arrived. God is scarcely mentioned in this story. God seems to take no initiative, to perform no miracles. God sends neither messengers nor messages. God seems to be on the margins of this tale, but he is not. Through the unremarkable lives of barley farmers, their widows, and their kin, his purposes are the very heart of the story. And his purposes are the very heart of your story and mine!

A young widow commits her life to an elderly widow. The older woman responds in kind. It is enough. It is a sacred moment. In a poem echoing the eloquence of Ruth's words, Susanne Vander Lugt says:

> Sacred time and sacred space
> It is ours alone

Where we meet our God
Tender, passionate, strong,
Loving us with Abandon and
Connecting us to all of creation,
To all parts of ourselves,
Our past, our present, our future.

Sacred time and sacred space
It is ours alone
Where the cosmic lover of our souls
Lifts us up and
Wipes away the tears from our eyes.
The place of intimacy.

Sacred time and sacred space
It is ours alone
To take as we journey on[.]
Our own sacredness,
Our own giftedness,
To live out [of] and love out of.

Sacred time and sacred space
It is each one of us,
A gift from God.[1]

Amen.

—LDS

[2300 words]
[23 minutes]

Sermon 104

Date: Sunday Between October 23 and October 29 inclusive, Year A

Texts: (NCL)
Ruth 2:1–13
Psalm 128
1 Thessalonians 2:1–8
Matthew 22:34–46

Theme: Kindness and magnanimity are the glue binding human beings to one another and uniting human beings with God.
Subject: Kindness, magnanimity

Title: Women in Harm's Way: Perils and Protectors

[1] Vander Lugt, Susanne, *Word & Witness*, October 21, 1990, p. 4.

[Second in a series of three sermons: "More Than Is Required"—The Book of Ruth and Women of Today. Each sermon may be used independently. See also sermons 103 and 53.]

When you are harvesting in your field and you overlook a sheaf, do not go back to get it. Leave it for the alien, the fatherless and the widow, so that the LORD your God may bless you in all the work of your hands. When you beat the olives from your trees, do not go over the branches a second time. Leave what remains for the alien, the fatherless and the widow. When you harvest the grapes in your vineyard, do not go over the vines again. Leave what remains for the alien, the fatherless and the widow. (Deuteronomy 24:19–21)

Do not pick your fields clean. Do not strip your vineyards bare. Why not? Because I am the sovereign God, who adopted you when you were orphaned among the nations, when you were strangers in the land of Egypt, when you were as vulnerable as any widow. (Leviticus 19:9–10)

From beginning to end, the Hebrew Scriptures speak of God's concern for orphans, widows, and newcomers. They speak of the way that the children of Israel treat the helpless as an indicator of the status of the nation. For when orphans, widows, and aliens are cared for, the nation prospers. And when they are exploited or neglected, the nation falters.

Do not strip your fields bare. Leave the gleanings for the poor, the newcomer, the orphan, and the widow. Ruth was poor. She was a newcomer. She was an orphan. She was a widow. She qualified on every count.

A Woman in a Man's World

And she was a woman in a man's world. Like all widows in ancient Israelite society, her existence was precarious. A widow could not inherit property from her husband's estate—whatever he owned passed to his male relatives. If he had no male relatives, his property passed to his daughter if the daughter married into her father's clan. If the widow's late husband had male relatives, a marriage could be arranged to keep the widow and her potential offspring in the family, but this was not always possible. If the widow had neither children nor parents willing and able to care for her, her prospects were dim. The only career available to an unmarried woman was unsavory. Hence, for a good woman like Ruth the choices were limited: she could rely on public charity or she could glean.

Women of Ruth's day had no direct access to power or decision-making. They had few rights. They relied totally on men for their protection and sustenance. As the stories of Sarah, Rebecca, and Rachel, the matriarchs of the Israelites, demonstrate, women in this period made cause their mark either by directly influencing their husbands or by trickery.[1]

Modern women may be troubled by Ruth's subservience and obsequiousness. She is humble to the point of groveling. No one today would throw himself or herself at the feet of a benefactor as she did. Yet there is something about her that is profoundly charming and ingratiating. And it is not her servility that captivates Boaz. It is her strength of character. Even before their chance meeting, her reputation has preceded her. Their conversation is as mannered as a Japanese tea ceremony, but there is a spark of mutual admiration and respect. Ruth is profoundly grateful to Boaz and Boaz is profoundly impressed not by her gratitude to him but by who she is.

---

[1] *Harper's Bible Dictionary* (San Francisco: Harper & Row, Publishers, 1985), p. 1138.

Women and men no longer live in the patriarchal world of earlier times. The problem is they do not comfortably live in an alternative world either. Women have struggled for equality of opportunity and have made some hard-won gains. Yet, again and again, biology upsets their plans.

Women's Liberation has freed women to have what they never wanted—unachievable expectations. For women cannot be perfect wives, perfect mothers, and perfect careerists, all at the same time, without an extraordinary amount of skill, luck, and the support of their husbands, their families, and their bosses. Women have been set free to make terrible choices. No one can tell them which choice is correct, but everyone can and will tell them when their choice is wrong. Working mothers are blamed for social ills ranging from juvenile delinquency to teenage sexual promiscuity, from low grades to poor nutrition.

Women are supposed to want it all: husband, home, family, and career. If they are caught by their peers not wanting it all, they are treated as lepers. If they catch themselves not wanting it all, they wonder what's wrong with themselves. If they want it all, but don't get it all, they are miserable. If they want it all, and get it all, they are too exhausted to enjoy it. What's wrong with this picture?

And one thing is clear—whatever progress may have been made by women in the economic arena during the past few decades, women are more at risk than they have ever been. Even as women take their places in houses of legislature, on the highest courts, in the cabinet, as corporate CEOs, as network news personalities, as talk show hosts, an ugly, merciless countertrend rears its ugly head. Women are being abused, molested, and murdered by men at a rate that seems to increase exponentially from year to year.

And because of modern techniques for determining the sex of the fetus in utero, girl fetuses are being aborted, being denied the opportunity of living, because they are less valued by mothers and fathers alike. In the next fifty years, we may pass from a society with a surplus population of women to a society with a serious shortage.

It is a dangerous and a difficult time to be a woman—and it was then, three thousand years ago when in a barley field outside of Bethlehem Ruth met Boaz.

Kindness

The Book of Ruth is about kindness. It is not about what human beings owe one another, but what they can give to one another. It is not about what is demanded of us, but what we are capable of when we do more than could ever be expected. And, this beautiful short story makes clear, whenever individuals commit themselves to one another, whenever life touches life deeply, God is at the center of the action.

Kindness is contagious. A single act of kindness can create a debt in the recipient that colors and shapes his or her whole life. A stranger bought me a cold drink when I was a child. More than forty years later, I am obliged to every small child in need whom I encounter. A supervisor at work, an elderly woman, offered to lend me money if I would return to college when I was twenty. I would not borrow a cent from her. But her encouragement helped propel me through ten years of university study. Because of her, I am obliged to be kind and supportive—for the rest of my life!

Ruth was entitled to glean in any field she chose. The Law of Moses entitled her to as much. Yet she asked Boaz for permission. She didn't take her rights for granted. She entered into relationship with the guarantor of those rights.

Women today are entitled to equal pay, equal treatment, and equal respect. The law says so. But the law cannot guarantee what is most needed—basic, human kindness between men and women. For kindness requires the establishment of rapport.

Showing kindness is more than being inoffensive and nice. Showing kindness is more than contributing to charity. Kindness imitates the divine initiative, the unmerited favor of God, which comes without being deserved.[2] Kindness is evoked by a "plus factor" because of which we do more than is required of us.

Magnanimity

What is this plus factor that predisposes one human being to act with kindness toward another? Let us call it "magnanimity." How long has it been since we have termed anyone "magnanimous"? It sounds like such an old-fashioned word. Consider the synonyms for magnanimous: generous, benevolent, big, chivalrous, considerate, grandiose, lofty, noble. Boaz is the very exemplification of every word. He appreciates the extraordinary caring and kindness that Ruth demonstrates toward her mother-inlaw Naomi and is moved to extraordinary caring and kindness of his own.

This tender tale adds a dimension to the central concept of the Hebrew Scriptures: covenant. We tend to think of covenant as a contract made between God and his people: you will make me happy and I will reciprocate. It is as though the favor of God had to be earned. If you really love me, you will do what I want you to do, and if you do what I want you to do, I will love you back. But the message of the Book of Ruth makes evident that such an understanding of God's covenant with the children of Israel or later with the remainder of the human race is governed by a loftier law—the rule of magnanimity. God loves his people because God loves his people—freely and unconditionally. Human righteous acts do not gain God's favor; they are evoked by God's favor.

God is in the kindness business. Wherever there is true kindness between human beings, God is the giver and sustainer of that kindness. God does not reward us for being kind. He is present in our kindness—giving, luring, testing, enhancing, opening up our hearts, re-creating us in his image. Kindness is its own reward and that reward is God himself.

The Book of Ruth is about persons acting as God to one another—acting benevolently, magnanimously, generously, appreciatively. Yes, Boaz is powerful and Ruth is weak. Yes, the way that God acts in this touching drama is by having a strong, chivalrous male take a poor but humble woman under his wing. It is scarcely a tale of two equals attaining parity.

Holding the Door

Let me tell you something undramatic and unremarkable that transpired a few days ago. I went to the local branch of my bank. As I was about to enter, I looked over my shoulder and saw a small Asian woman approaching, encumbered by a husky baby. Without thinking, I paused for a moment so that I could open the door for her. She thanked me and rewarded me with a smile. After I had made a deposit and was about to leave, I noticed a young woman, probably about twenty, a few feet behind me. I stopped at the door and held it open for her, too. She thanked me and we exchanged a few pleasant sentences of conversation.

Years ago, as Women's Liberation was breaking on the scene, I attended a "sensitivity training" weekend in New Jersey. The trainer explained at length how humiliating it is to women to treat them as frail, weak, and in need of male assistance. The words made sense, but they hardly moved me.

I was as empathetic as I could be. But I still hold doors open for women, help women out of motor vehicles, help them on and off with their wraps, and so on. Perhaps someday when I am old and frail and in need of assistance and protection, some young woman will hold a door for me, help me out of my car, help me on with my coat. . . . That will be all right. It will be wonderful!

---

[2] Campbell, Edward F., Jr., *Ruth, The Anchor Bible* (New York: Doubleday, 1973), p. 81.

I'm glad that Ruth and Boaz did not argue about who owed what to whom, that they could be kind and appreciate kindness when they saw it. Maybe kindness cannot erase centuries of injustice or make it possible for women to be all things to all persons or get men to shoulder a fair share of the burden of rearing and supporting their families. Maybe a magnanimous spirit here and there will not put an end to the virtual war of women now being waged on our streets, in our homes, and in the workplace. But it is a start—and it can't hurt.

It delights me to read that poor, hard-working Ruth showed kindness to Naomi. She didn't have to. Her kindness revealed who she really was. It heartens me to read that rich, strong Boaz helped and protected a young woman at risk in a man's world. His magnanimity demonstrated who he really was.

May our simple acts of kindness tell the world who we really are as well.

Amen.

—LDS

[2075 words]
[21 minutes]

❦ *Sermon 105*

❦ *Date:* Any Sunday

Texts:
Genesis 4:1–16
Luke 10:25–37
Joshua 24:14–15

Theme: Actions have consequences.
Subject: Responsibility

❦ *Title:* Truth and Consequences: The Meaning of Responsibility

We were thirteen years old, sitting around a campfire at Boy Scout Camp. It was a rare moment of semiseriousness, and I can still remember the passion with which we debated the question that had been put to us. The leader had described a hypothetical situation and had asked us what we would do. Here's the way it went.

You and a friend have gone mountain climbing in the Rockies in wintertime. Because conditions are icy, you are roped together by a 30-foot-long rope. Things go well at first, and then you come to an icy ledge, with a sheer drop-off on either side. The two of you are edging your way up when your friend loses his footing and goes over the side. He dangles helplessly from the rope. You had managed to hold on during the first shock, but you haven't the strength to pull him up. In fact, you are growing weaker and are slowly being pulled toward the edge yourself. You can do nothing. In a moment, it will be over the side, and the two of you will be gone.

But you have an ice ax, and one swing of the ax, and the rope would be cut. Though your friend would die, at least you would be saved. Inch by inch the edge draws closer, the question is: Would you cut the rope?

In the intervening years, I have heard that same question discussed in dormitory bull sessions and in church youth groups, and half a dozen other settings. The questions and opinions of the thirteen-year-old philosophers at Scout Camp were essentially the same raised in every other group through the years. Would you cut the rope?

The word for today is responsibility, and it is easier to say than it is to define fully. What are the dimensions of responsibility for us? Where does my responsibility begin and end in this world? In our complex society, I am roped to so many people who, from time to time, need help—a spouse, some children, friends, business associates, a community. Someone has observed that he feels like a corporation that has gone public, and everyone owns a controlling piece of him.

So the question—where does our responsibility focus? Where does it end? Back up on the mountain ridge, can we cut the rope?

Don't Cut That Rope!

I. No, you can't cut the rope, many would say. Especially in the Christian tradition, there is something abhorrent about the thought of saving one's life by cutting the rope. Yes, your friend is doomed anyway. No, you're not going to save his life by going down with him. Yes, you have a family, little children to think about. But even with all this, why is it that most groups, arguing the issue in theory, abstractly, why is it that the majority in most groups say they wouldn't cut the rope?

From the dawn of time, there has been an instinct within us that binds us to others. In one of the Bible's oldest stories, Cain kills his brother Abel and cries out to God, "Am I my brother's keeper?" Strongly implied in the question is the answer—yes, yes, you are. When the Pharisees asked Jesus, "Who is my neighbor?" Jesus proceeded to tell a story about a Good Samaritan who did not abandon a wounded traveler in need. And did not Jesus say, "Greater love has no man than this, that he lay down his life for his friends?" (John 15:13)

We don't live on little isolated mountain peaks—we are bound to one another. A black civil rights leader said to a white person, "Your ancestors came over on the *Mayflower,* and mine came over on a slave ship, but we're all in the same boat now." And we are, tied together in our communities. One of the obstacles we face in solving our community problems is the quickness, almost the eagerness of some of us to cut the ropes that bind us to others in the community. If they're going to drown, we don't have to go with them—and the rope is cut, and where are we?

The cartoon showed two fellows talking religion. One says to the other, "Sometimes I'd like to ask God why he allows poverty, famine, and injustice when he could do something about it." "What's stopping you?" asks the second. And the first replies, "I'm afraid God might ask me the same question."

What about it? Have you in your own mind cut the rope already to the large parts of the community? Jesus said emphatically, "everyone to whom much is given, of him will much be required." (Luke 12:48) Do we assume here that he didn't mean us? Would you cut the rope? A strong Christian instinct says "No!"

Don't Take Me with You!

II. But there's another way of looking at the story. Yes, you not only can cut the rope, but sooner or later you should. To be responsible does not mean to be foolish. I am tied to others, yes, but not when their careless or foolish actions send them down to the inevitable results. I cannot keep them from stumbling stupidly down many a precipice, but I can keep myself from going too. That is my first responsibility.

You hear this argument? It is powerful, and has enough truth in it to demand attention. Talk all you will about being tied together to others in the community and around the world, but face it! If you rope yourself to much of modern society, you're in trouble.

And that is basically what Joshua decided in our text for today. "Now therefore, fear the Lord," he said, "and serve him in sincerity and in faithfulness. . . . And if you are unwilling to serve the Lord, choose you this day whom you will serve, whether the gods your father served in the region beyond the river, or the God of the Amonites in whose land you dwell." (And here we hear Joshua raising the ice ax to cut the rope.) "But as for me and my house, we will serve the Lord" (Joshua 24:14–15).

Joshua wanted others in his community to be faithful. He urged this upon them. But if they weren't, he wasn't going down with them. His first responsibility was to himself and his family. We live in a society of some very dangerous liaisons, and what do you do when the community is dragging you down with it? Whether that has to do with the prevailing use of drugs, or the abuse of sex, or diluted integrity, or whatever—if the community or someone in it is bound for hell, you don't have to go with them.

And sometimes when you deliberately cut the rope and do what is right, everybody else profits. Someone has told of an office worker in a university back east. Every day he parked his car and walked through a twenty-foot swath of lawn to get to work. The lawn was littered with every form of debris imaginable. It bothered him, and he thought of writing a letter to the editor about it or organizing a clean-up program. "Then one day he got an idea; he would take ownership of the plot. He didn't tell anyone—it was probably against some regulation or other. But he made himself responsible for this twenty-foot swath of lawn. Every day, going to and from his car, he picked up the litter. He made a game of it, limiting himself to ten items each way. At first he carried it home, but then a curious thing happened. Large trash barrels appeared at each end of the lawn. Finally, he reached the point where he was picking up litter faster than others were depositing it. His twenty-foot lawn was beautifully green and free of trash. The rest of the campus was as littered as ever—but that was someone else's problem. He was taking care of his own."[1]

Whether it is littered lawns or minds or souls, you and I have a plot we are responsible for, and it is our first responsibility. "As for me and my house, we will serve the lord," and any tie that prevents me from doing that should be cut as quickly as possible. Would you cut the rope? Absolutely.

Actions Have Consequences

III. But back to the mountain top. Would you cut the rope? If we take responsibility seriously, we don't let ourselves get into predicaments like this, when every option is bad. That is the difficulty with this conundrum—either option is bad! Common sense says that it is foolish to remain tied to that doomed friend and die needlessly. But while we might save our lives by cutting the rope, forever after we would remember an icy ledge and a deserted friend. Both options are bad.

That's where the real solution starts, in staying out of those predicaments where there isn't any good choice anymore. We are there because we have already made a bad choice, a mistake in judgment. If a poor choice had not already been made, someone would not be debating now the subject of abortion and its alternatives, if a wrong choice had not been made, we would not face the dilemma of capital punishment. If we really want to discuss responsibility, we start long before we are standing on some mountaintop with ax in hand. Responsibility means that we stay out of these situations in which every option brings pain to someone.

Down in Dallas over the past six months, a remarkable and tragic real-life drama has been played out. A year ago, a football team of Carter High School was winning every game. It was a tremendous team, playing before huge crowds of admiring fans. They proceeded to win every

---

[1] *Pulpit Digest,* March 1989, p. 29.

game, and became champions of the Class 5A schools in Texas. Many of the seniors won college scholarships.

Then in April, a stunning story broke, shocking the community. Ten stars of that team were arrested for a series of armed robberies. Was it true? The boys confessed—it was true. Sons of hard-working, professional, religious families, the boys had, in twos and threes, committed twenty-five armed robberies of stores in Dallas. Found guilty after recent trials, ten of the twelve were sentenced to prison terms of up to twenty-five years. Right now, instead of being nineteen-year-olds enjoying the excitement of freshmen years at college, they are in the state prison beginning their sentences.

The article in the *Dallas Times Herald* that told of the sentencing began this way: "It is a statement of fact so simple, so self-evident, that most people take its truth for granted. Yet when the words were uttered Friday by State District Court Judge Joe Kendall, their meaning stunned a packed courtroom, changed forever the lives of twelve teenagers, and brought anguish to the hearts of parents and friends. In pronouncing their prison sentence, Judge Kendall looked at the boys and said simply, "Young men, actions have consequences."[2]

Isn't that the best argument for responsibility? Actions have consequences, and because we are inextricably tied to others, when we hurt ourselves, so many others are hurt too.

And so you are fifteen hundred miles from home on a business trip, and the choice is suddenly put to you—do you do this, or not? No need to wait for some rope-cutting moment in the future. Now is the critical moment. Actions have consequences, and if you do it, who may have to pay the bill you are running up?

A business decision comes up, a border-line decision, and maybe you can get by with this, but maybe you can't. Actions have consequences, and who will pay this bill?

You're a young person, and stand considering the matter. Should you try it or not? Will anyone know? Actions have consequences, and to whom will this bill be sent?

So may people think they are cutting some ropes, but when it's all out in the open, when the bill comes in, it's likely to be some precious little children who pay it, or some hurt parents who pay it, or a devastated spouse who pays it, and it's not much fun left alone on the ledge with those ropes dangling. Actions have consequences.

The word is responsibility, and Joshua said it for us. "If you be unwilling to serve the Lord, choose you this day whom you will serve. . . . But as for me and my house, we will serve the Lord."

Amen.

—Eugene Brice

[2100 words]
[21 minutes]

---

[2] *Dallas Times Herald,* September 24, 1989, p.1.

❦ CHAPTER ELEVEN

FREEDOM AND RESPONSIBILITY

More than two hundred years ago, we declared our national independence. But the questions remain: What are we free from? and What are we free for? Freedom without responsibility is the worst form of slavery.

There is a cost to freedom, a price that each of us must pay. We live in a country worthy of our commitment. The time has come for us to rededicate ourselves to this nation and the purposes for which it was founded. In our lives, the dream of the Pilgrims, Washington, Lincoln, and King continues.

However, before we as a nation can achieve that dream, we must deal openly and effectively with such major problems as drug addiction, environmental pollution, international conflict, and civic apathy. Jesus is at war with our tolerance of "business as usual." Until we respond to these problems, there can be no ceasefire.

Sermon 106

Date: Independence Sunday (Sunday Before the Fourth of July)

Text:
Romans 13:1–8

Theme: We have devised our own personal religious constitutions, whether it is written or not, consciously identified or not, by which we declare what we are free *from* and what we are free *for.*
Subject: Freedom and responsibility

Title: Do You Have a Constitution?

Do you remember July 4, 1976? It seems but an instant ago for some of us. It was our nation's bicentennial, and it fell on Sunday. Two hundred years earlier, the Declaration of Independence had been signed, and we were a free nation. Remember the celebrations? The great ships in the New York harbor, the exploding fireworks, the oratory? Our Declaration of Independence was two hundred years old.

Ten years after the Declaration of Independence, another event occurred of equal, or perhaps greater, importance. On September 17, 1796, after years of struggle and debate, the Constitution of the United States was signed and forwarded to the states for ratification. Two events of monumental significance, but which, in your estimation, was more important: the Declaration of Independence, or the Constitution?

I remember Labor Day weekend, 1948. My own personal Declaration of Independence was issued, if not signed. At age seventeen, after years of devoted service to the king and queen at my house, the yolk of servitude became oppressive, and I declared independence. I was off for college, finding there a freedom that was exhilarating and full. No checking when I came in at night, no reminder of homework, no tips about table manners or dress codes. That first week of complete freedom was a dizzying experience. Then reality set in, and I discovered that either I found some sort of discipline, or else I would be returned rather quickly to the dependence of home.

It is one thing to be independent, to be free, but some sort of order has to be imposed from without or from within, or that freedom becomes destructive anarchy.

So with our nation in 1776, freedom was grand, but it would be lost if some sort of order could not be voluntarily devised and accepted for the nation. So, in that critical decade from 1776 to 1786, the free and independent nation sought a constitution.

Why did it take so long? Anyone who has sat on a committee trying to decide what color to paint a classroom ought to know. Fierce differences of opinion existed about almost every conceivable issue raised, and negotiations and compromise were necessary at every turn. Those decisions made more than two hundred years ago have given our nation its cast and character of today.

How should the states be represented in Congress: according to their population, or equally? A compromise was reached: the Senate could be apportioned with equal representation, the House according to population.

How should slaves be counted in the population? Illustrating the fact these decision makers were far from perfect, they decided that each slave should be counted as four-fifths of a free person.

How should taxes be levied? Who should decide on disputes between states? Where did states' rights end and federal authority prevail? How strong an executive should there be? What role should legislative, executive, and judicial branches play in the enactment and enforcement of laws?

Again, freedom was heady and exhilarating, but unless the states could accept a constitution that voluntarily limited freedom, the new nation could not be born. And there were those who fiercely resisted the new Constitution, and opposed any federal restrictions of freedom.

Remember Patrick Henry? It was Patrick Henry's fiery words that had led to the Declaration of Independence. Who can ever forget those words spoken in May 1776? "Is life so dear or peace so sweet as to be purchased at the price of chains, or slavery? Forbid it, Almighty God. I know not what course others may take, but as for me, give me liberty or give me death!"

Patrick Henry was great at rebellion or revolution, but after the war was over and the United States were struggling for order, for a constitution, Patrick Henry kept right on rebelling. He refused to attend most of the Constitutional Conventions, and when the Virginia legislators considered ratification of the Constitution in 1788, Patrick Henry's fiery oratory rang out against it to the bitter end. He objected, for example, to the way it began, "We the people of the United States," because the people never got to vote on it, only the state legislatures. So his suggestion was that the preamble should begin with "We the States," not "We the people."

Finally, after long and intense struggle in the legislatures of each of the thirteen states, the Constitution was formally ratified in July 1788. What an incredible creative and significant document the Constitution was and is. For the first time in world history, a harness had been devised for democracy that made it workable. It was not perfect, of course, but it included devices for careful and ordered change.

No political system, no form of government, can ever substitute for the integrity of its citizens. But the Constitution, now over two centuries old, gave us a way to make democracy stable and workable. That is what we also celebrate and thank God for, this weekend.

Again, it should be stated clearly, freedom is magnificent, but order and discipline have to be imposed from within or, without it, the sparkling freedom turns sour and produces nothing. This principle applies to each of us in our own personal lives. Many a person who has, in a moment of courage, declared independence from some tyranny and gained freedom has never devised a constitution by which to order his or her life, and that freedom has gone bad.

Young single persons experience this struggle more than most others. Once school is over, a job received, obligations minimized, debts paid, a pretty good salary coming in, we experience a period of freedom we haven't ever known before and probably won't ever know again. There is no warden closing the gates and ringing the bell. We don't have to keep declaring our independence in this period; it is there, for all to see.

But many find that a glut of freedom doesn't bring the rewards they thought it would, and the order that some impose on themselves, the obligations they freely accept—the chains, if you will, that they wear—seem to bring them more joy than does boundless independence. Only when their declarations of independence give way to some voluntarily accepted constitution or order does meaning come.

Often we emphasize our freedom in matters of religion more than our responsibilities and obligations. We declare independence in religion, but we stop short of devising a religious constitution for ourselves, setting forth what we want to be free for.

It is easier to devise declarations of independence of religion than constitutions. Consider the old evangelical question, "Brother, sister, are you saved?" The emphasis is usually on what we are saved from—we are saved from guilt, from sin, from death, from eternal damnation. Get saved, and you are free from all these things. But saved for what?

At home we sometimes say, "Are we going to save this or that article? Yes? Then put it in the attic if we want to save it." Some would see the church as a sort of religious attic into which saved persons are put. But this is obviously incomplete. Saved for what? What do we intend to do with our freedom from guilt and sin? To be born again means to be born to a life of integrity and responsibility and righteousness, and most persons need some sort of personally ratified constitution which guides them in turning religious freedom into responsible living.

Each one of us has devised some sort of religious constitution, whether it is written or not, consciously identified or not.

Does my unwritten religious constitution say anything about how often I worship God?

Does my constitution count people of other races as four-fifth of a person or as whole people?

Does my constitution ever direct me to the aching needs of hungry and hurting people around the world, or does it keep me focused only on my own needs?

Does my constitution point me in any way to people in this world whose struggle for freedom continues, or does it direct my gaze to what I have attained?

Does my constitution say anything about gossip and slander and fault finding? Does it cover how much of my income I give away? Does it deal with clean language or honesty or decency?

You see why many a person who declares independence in religion never creates a constitution. No wonder that religion remains unsatisfying to many. They never give it order and structure, so it can have no strength. In this sense, then, constitutions are more important than declarations of independence, and unless you have one for your life and until you get one, this freedom you enjoy will be lacking something.

John Killinger writes about a lovely young woman who came to his office with a baby in her arms and a slightly older child pulling at her dress and acting up. Killinger says: "She had only a few minutes to talk because she was picking up her third child from the preschool when she left. She apologized for her hair which she had not had time to comb properly for that morning, and for her dress which had been clean when she left home but now showed traces of milk and juice and a shade or two of baby food. We had already discussed what she came to see me about and she was readjusting one child on her hip, pacifying the other, picking up scattered toys from the floor. "Wow!" she said. "When I think that five years ago I was dying to get married and move out of my parents' house in order to be free, it almost blows my mind!"[1] And yet it was in her gladly accepted chains that she found freedom's meaning, fulfillment, and joy.

Back, then, to our nation. The Constitution is, in a sense, the Dr. Spock for raising justice and freedom. But justice and freedom are messy babies. They spit up on us and they cry all night. But they are worth raising!

Thank God, then, for freedom and for those patriots who brought it to us. But thank God even more for our kind of constitution, national or personal, that takes freedom and puts it to work in responsibility.

Amen.

—Eugene Brice

[1700 words]
[17 minutes]

---

[1] *Pulpit Digest*, July 1987, p. 299.

Sermon 107

Date: Independence Sunday (Sunday Before the Fourth of July)

Texts:
2 Chronicles 7:11–16
Matthew 22:16–22
John 8:31–36

Theme: There is a cost to freedom and each of us must pay the bill.
Subject: Freedom

Title: Free Indeed! But Who Pays the Bill?

Interwoven in this sermon are five authentic songs from the early years of our national history:
"Chester," by William Billings of Boston, America's first professional musician. Music composed in 1770, lyrics in 1778.
"War and Washington," to the tune of *The British Grenadier,* these lyrics about Continental soldiers were written about 1776.
"The Battle of the Kegs," a sarcastic ditty by Francis Hopkinson, written in 1778. Hopkinson represented New Jersey in the Continental Congress, painted portraits, and designed the Stars and Stripes.
"The World Turned Upside Down," played when Cornwallis surrendered at Yorktown.
"Ode to the Fourth of July," sung on July 4, 1789, the first Fourth since Washington's inauguration. Written by Daniel George and Horatio Garnett.
The music and lyrics are included in Samuel Eliot Morison's *The Oxford History of the American People* (New York: Oxford University Press, 1965).

The Declaration of Independence boldly begins:

> When in the Course of human events, it becomes necessary for one people to dissolve the political bands which have connected them with another, and to assume among the Powers of the earth, the separate and equal stations to which the Laws of Nature and of Nature's God entitle them, a decent respect to the opinions of mankind requires that they should declare the causes which impel them to the separation.

They never should have done it. They never should have declared independence from England, from their mother country. That's what many Americans thought.

They really didn't want to, at first.

Song: Chester

It begins in Massachusetts on April 18, 1775. Major John Pitcairn leads eight hundred troops to destroy patriot munitions stored in Concord. At Lexington, a grim band of seventy Minutemen block Pitcairn's line of march. Pitcairn orders them to disperse. A shot is fired, "a shot heard round the world." No one knows who fired first. Both sides reply. The Minutemen retreat, leaving eight dead and ten wounded on the green.

The British march to Concord where they ransack the town and set ablaze the blacksmith shop and the courthouse. The smoke attracts patriot militias from several nearby communities. At Concord's North Bridge the Americans are fired on by the British and fire back.

The American Revolution. The War for Independence. It has begun.

❦ Song: War and Washington

Word of Lexington and Concord had barely reached the scattered colonies when the Second Continental Congress met at Philadelphia on May 10, 1775. No more distinguished company would ever assemble in this country.

> Twenty-four were lawyers and jurists. Eleven were merchants, nine were farmers and large plantation owners, men of means, well educated.[1]

Benjamin Franklin was there. And John and Samuel Adams and Thomas Jefferson. And Benjamin Rush and John Witherspoon. And John Hancock.

The leaders of the patriot cause did not rush to divorce themselves from Great Britain. Fourteen months would pass between the opening of hostilities and the Declaration of Independence.

Emotionally, they were torn apart. After all, they belonged to the greatest empire in history. Everything that made them the people they were was English.

What would become of the colonies if they departed from English rule? Who would govern them? If the answer was not a person but a democratic form of government, what model would they follow?

The thought of a Republic terrified them. "In the past, republics had been turbulent and of short duration. . . ."[2] When England proclaimed itself a republic in 1649, it had swiftly become a military dictatorship. No European colony had ever thrown off dependence on a mother country, or even wanted to.

If separated from England, the diverse colonies would probably clash continually among themselves. Is it possible, they asked themselves, "to bring together under a common and enduring government mariners of Maine with tobacco planters of Maryland, South Carolina aristocrats with Pennsylvania German farmers, Yankees with Dutch New Yorkers, proud Anglican gentlemen of Virginia with equally proud Rhode Island Baptist traders?"[3]

The Americans also realized they could not win or maintain their independence without the armed intervention of France or Spain. How could they be sure that once they expelled the British, they would not end up as colonies of the French or the Spanish?

❦ Song: The Battle of the Kegs

Even after Washington assumed command of fifteen thousand undisciplined troops and began molding them into a united army, even after Continental soldiers had blundered into Canada in a vain attempt to bring it into the rebel fold, the Continental Congress pressed for reconciliation.

---

[1] *Illustrations Unlimited,* edited by James Hewett (Wheaton, IL: Tyndale House, 1988), pp. 398–399.

[2] Ibid.

[3] Alden, John R., *A History of the American Revolution* (New York: Alfred A. Knopf, 1969), p. 234.

In the Olive Branch Petition of July 1775, Congress implored the king to repeal the Coercive Acts that had led to war and to bring about "a happy and permanent reconciliation."

The British government refused to forward the petition to the king. On August 23, 1775, George III proclaimed the American patriots rebels and ordered that "utmost endeavors should be made" to suppress the rebellion and bring the traitors to justice. Britain sent German mercenaries, instigated terrorism through appeals to Indian tribes and Negro slaves, and banned all trade with the colonies.

As the delegates to the Congress hesitated, waited for instructions from their home legislatures, and debated, a remarkable pamphlet by an otherwise unimpressive Quaker corset maker began to circulate. The pamphlet was called "Common Sense" and its author was Thomas Paine. Paine saw government, at best, as "a necessary evil," "a badge of lost innocence." Of all the forms of government, he contended, none is worse than monarchy. A king is a kind of neighborhood bully, who extorts submission from others. Moreover, Paine argued, the notion that any person can inherit the right to rule over others is ridiculous.

As for America's debt to England, we had long since paid it in full. Whatever we had received, England had taken from us tenfold in economic profit. Paine eloquently exclaimed:

> Every thing that is right or reasonable pleads for separation. The blood of the slain, the weeping voice of nature cries, "'TIS TIME TO PART.'"

Paine suggested that the colonists replace British rule with self-rule by forming a federation of commonwealths. The time for tyranny was over. The time for a new nation to come forth as a haven and an example of liberty for all humanity was at hand.

Historian John R. Alden notes: "Sophisticated and less informed Patriots alike more and more reached the conclusion that they could most effectively defend their rights, their property, and even their lives by leaving the empire."[4] Practical Americans realized that independence would mean free trade, free navigation, and the freedom to manufacture what they pleased as they pleased.

Finally, the logic of violence took its toll. Alden comments:

> Wounding words and economic blows do aggrieve, but killing, maiming, and plundering create deep and enduring rancor. The American militiaman who killed a redcoat at Bunker Hill and fled to safety before royal troops wielding bayonets found it difficult to continue to look upon the British as affectionate cousins.[5]

The Declaration of Independence continues:

> We hold these truths to be self-evident, that all men are created equal, that they are endowed by their Creator with certain unalienable Rights, that among these are Life, Liberty, and the pursuit of Happiness.—That to secure these rights, Governments are instituted among Men, deriving their just powers from the consent of the governed,—That whenever any Form of Government becomes destructive to these ends, it is the Right of the People to alter or to abolish it, and to institute new Government, laying its foundation on such principles and organizing its powers in such form, as to them shall seem most likely to effect their Safety and Happiness.

The tide turned. In May, the Virginia legislators heard with outrage that the king was sending twelve thousand German mercenaries. On June 29, they adopted a constitution for an independent

---

[4] Ibid., p. 233.

[5] Ibid., p. 229.

Commonwealth of Virginia. Georgia authorized its delegates in Philadelphia to vote for independence. South Carolina and North Carolina empowered their delegates to follow suit.

On June 7, Richard Henry Lee presented a resolution to the Continental Congress, stating:

> That these United Colonies are, and of right ought to be, Independent States . . .

Although the job of preparing the Declaration of Independence was assigned to a committee, its principal author was Thomas Jefferson. The elegantly written document turns on two fundamental assumptions: (1) natural rights and (2) government as a political contract. According to the Declaration, people adopt governments to protect their basic, unalienable rights—life, liberty, and the pursuit of happiness. Government is a contract between rulers and those whom they govern. If a government fails to protect the rights of the governed, if it usurps of the prerogatives of the people, then it is the right—no, the duty—of the governed to rebel, to annul the contract.

The Declaration of Independence concludes:

> We, therefore the Representatives of the United States of America, in General Congress, Assembled, appealing to the Supreme Judge of the world for the rectitude of our intentions, do, in the Name, and by Authority of the good People of these Colonies, solemnly publish and declare, That these United Colonies are, and of Right ought to be Free and Independent States. . . . And for the support of this Declaration, with a firm reliance on the Protection of Divine Providence, we mutually pledge to each other our Lives, our Fortunes, and our sacred Honor.

And the cost of their commitment would be great!

Song: The World Turned Upside Down

John Adams and Thomas Jefferson would both later serve as presidents of the United States. The accomplishments of Franklin and Rush are too numerous to recount. Witherspoon, the only clergyman among them, was the president of the college now known as Princeton University. But what of the others who signed the Declaration of Independence? When they placed their names on the Declaration they knew full well that the penalty would be death if they were captured. One writer tells us:

> Five signers were captured by the British as traitors, and tortured before they died. Twelve had their homes ransacked and burned. Two lost their sons in the Revolutionary Army, another had two sons captured. Nine of the 56 fought and died from wounds or the hardships of the Revolutionary War.
>
> . . .
>
> Carter Braxton of Virginia, a wealthy planter and trader, saw his ships swept from the seas by the British navy. He sold his home and properties to pay his debts and died in rags.
>
> Thomas McKean was so hounded by the British that he was forced to move his family almost constantly. He served in the Congress without pay, and his family was kept in hiding. His possessions were taken from him, and poverty was his reward.
>
> Vandals or soldiers or both, looted the properties of Ellery, Clymer, Hall, Walton, Gwinnett, Heyward, Ruttledge, and Middleton.[6]

---

[6] *Illustrations Unlimited*, loc. cit.

At the Battle of Yorktown, Thomas Nelson, Jr., saw that the enemy General Cornwallis was using the Nelson home as the British headquarters.

> The owner quietly urged General George Washington to open fire, which was done. The home was destroyed, and Nelson died bankrupt.
>
> Francis Lewis had his home and properties destroyed. The enemy jailed his wife and she died within a few months.
>
> John Hart was driven from his wife's bedside as she was dying. Their 13 children fled for their lives. His fields and grist mill were laid waste. For more than a year he lived in forests and caves, returning home after the war to find his wife dead, his children vanished. A few weeks later he died from exhaustion and a broken heart.
>
> Norris and Livingston suffered similar fates.
>
> Such were the stories and sacrifices of the American Revolution. These were not wild-eyed, rabble-rousing ruffians. These were soft-spoken men of means and education. They had security, but they valued liberty more. . . .
>
> They gave us an independent America.
>
> —author unknown[7]

Historian Samuel Eliot Morison declares:

> If the American Revolution had produced nothing but the Declaration of Independence, it would have been worthwhile. . . . the beauty and cogency of [these words] . . . have lifted the hearts of millions of men and will continue to do so. . . .[8]

For these words are more revolutionary than anything written by Robespierre, Marx, or Lenin. They are more explosive than the atom. They remain a continual challenge to us and an inspiration to the oppressed of all the world.

Today we extol those who pledged their lives, fortunes, and honor. We thank them for fulfilling their promises. Today we look back on two centuries of history. We look back on golden days when the hopes of those patriots were fulfilled. We look back on black days when as a nation we lost our way. We look at a world longing to be freed from hunger, disease, and violence. We look at a world threatened by massive armaments, unstable leaders, and pollution of the environment.

We look at men, women, and children demeaned by discrimination. We look at those in bondage to the false gods of pleasure, materialism, and greed. We look at lives enslaved by loneliness and despair. We look at a society in need of the dedication, commitment, and labor of all its citizens.

Day by day, God sheds his grace on this country. But the cost is our willingess to involve ourselves in the responsibilities of citizenship. Two hundred thousand Americans risked their lives—thousands gave their lives—in the War for Independence. They paid the cost and so must we. Day by day, God sheds his grace on each of us—setting us free from the past, from loneliness,

---

[7] Ibid.

[8] Ibid., p. 223.

from despair. The power of God in our lives is a free gift. But it cost God his only Son. And accepting this gift obligates us to respond to others with everything we have and are.

Our founding fathers were right. The time for tyranny is over. The time for this nation to come forth as a haven and an example of liberty for all humanity is at hand. The time for each of us to join the battle is now.

God bless America!

❦ Song: Ode to the Fourth of July

—LDS

[2100 words]
[21 minutes]

❦ *Sermon 108*

❦ *Date:* Sunday Before Presidents' Day

Text:
2 Chronicles 7:11–22

Theme: Lincoln has shown us the way to rededicate ourselves and our nation.
Subject: Rededication, patriotism

❦ *Title:* Lincoln's Lessons for a Nation at War[1]

Note

> This sermon was written during the 1991 strife in the Persian Gulf. References to that war can readily be replaced with mention of current conflicts or tensions involving our country.
> The words of Lincoln indicated by italics can be read aloud by a second person from a location other than the pulpit. Quiet musical accompaniment ("The Battle Hymn of the Republic," "When Johnny Comes Marching Home Again," "The Cruel War") may be used at appropriate points during the sermon.

Abraham Lincoln came to Gettysburg to dedicate a cemetery and to rededicate a nation.

Fourscore and seven years ago our fathers brought forth on this continent a new nation, conceived in liberty, and dedicated to the proposition that all men are created equal.

Abraham Lincoln had a dream—a vision of America as a great nation. His vision drove him to save the Union, not for its own sake, but because the nation embodied the ideal of self-government. This ideal was not just for Americans but for men and women of all nations. For Lincoln, America was the light of hope to all who were crushed by tyranny and oppression.

---

[1] For an excellent general introduction to Lincoln, see Richard N. Current, *Encyclopaedia Britannica* (Chicago: Encyclopaedia Britannica, 1974), Vol. 10, pp. 985–991. Current's article provides the factual basis for this sermon.

Lincoln did not invent this vision. He learned it from the founding fathers who had gone before him those "fourscore and seven years." Writing for Newsweek on the occasion of our nation's bicentennial, historian Barbara Tuchman reminded us of their vision. She said:

> The United States is a nation consciously conceived, not one that evolved slowly out of an ancient past. It was a planned idea of democracy, of liberty of conscience and pursuit of happiness. It was the promise of equality of opportunity and individual freedom within a just social order. . . . It was a new life for the oppressed, it was enlightenment, it was optimism.[2]

We honor Lincoln for his vision and for freeing the slaves. Although he detested the institution of slavery, he loved the Union more. Lincoln loathed slavery—of that there is no question. In 1854 he said of Stephen Douglas' attitude of indifference toward the spread of slavery into new territories:

> *I hate it because of the monstrous injustice of slavery itself. I hate it because it deprives our republican example of its just influence in the world; enables the enemies of free institutions with plausibility to taunt us as hypocrites. . . .*

In 1855, he wrote to his friend Joshua Speed about a steamboat trip that the two men had taken on the Ohio River years earlier:

> *You may remember, as I well do that from Louisville to the mouth of the Ohio there were on board ten or a dozen slaves, shackled together with irons. That sight was a continual torment to me; and I see something like it every time I touch the Ohio, or any other slave-border.*

In his debates with Douglas, three years before the outset of hostilities between the States, he accurately predicted:

> *A house divided against itself cannot stand. I believe the government cannot endure permanently half slave and half free.*

At the beginning of the Civil War, he would gladly have accepted the continuation of slavery in the South if the Union could be saved. In 1862 he wrote to Horace Greeley:

> *My paramount object in this struggle is to save the Union, and is not either to save or to destroy slavery. If I could save the Union without freeing any slave I would do it; and if could save it by freeing all the slaves I would do it; and if I could save it by freeing some and leaving others alone, I would also do that.*

The Emancipation Proclamation of January 1, 1863 had little direct effect on the institution of slavery. It declared the freeing of slaves only in the areas then controlled by the Confederacy. The Proclamation pertained neither to those regions loyal to the Union nor to those under federal military control. In substance, Lincoln freed the slaves over whom the Union exerted no effective control. As historian Richard N. Current observes,

> Directly or indirectly the proclamation brought freedom during the war to fewer than 200,000 [out of four million] slaves. Yet it had great significance as a symbol. It

---

[2] Tuchman, Barbara, "On Our Birthday/America as Idea," *Newsweek*, July 12, 1976, p. 9.

> indicated that the Lincoln government had added freedom to reunion as a war aim, and it attracted liberal opinion in England and Europe to increased support of the Union cause.[3]

Lincoln did not depend on the Proclamation to achieve his aims. After his reelection but before the new Congress convened, Lincoln skillfully shepherded the Thirteenth Amendment forever abolishing slavery through the lame duck Congress.

According to Professor Current,

> He rejoiced as the amendment went out to the states for ratification, and he rejoiced again and again as his own Illinois led off and other states followed one by one in acting favorably upon it.[4]

Whatever honor we have bestowed on Lincoln as the Great Emancipator is an honor well deserved.

Lincoln knew that the road to civil rights for freed slaves would not be an easy one. He realized that more than Union ascendancy and Constitutional amendments would be required to incorporate millions of African Americans into a predominantly white nation. Although he treated the black Americans who visited the White House with courtesy and respect, he never envisioned the multiracial society that was to come.

I wonder what he would think if he were alive today. How would he advise us to rid ourselves of the stain of racism? How would he react to our acceptance of tyranny and oppression in many parts of the world? How would he respond to the modern forms of enslavement—the disparity between rich and poor within nations and between nations? How would he meet the challenge of our enslaved environment—exploited, humbled, and humiliated by the same unreasoning greed that once enslaved human beings?

Abraham Lincoln came to Gettysburg to dedicate a cemetery and to rededicate a nation.

> *Now we are engaged in a great civil war, testing whether that nation, or any nation so conceived and so dedicated, can long endure. We are met on a great battlefield of that war. We have come to dedicate a portion of that field as a final resting place for those who here gave their lives that that nation might live. It is altogether fitting and proper that we should do this.*

Today this nation is again at war—to free the enslaved of Kuwait, to resist a merciless dictator, to fulfill our sense of calling as mankind's Marshall Dillon, to guarantee that the economies of major industrialized nations will not starve for lack of oil, and for many other diverse and murky reasons. Wars are like that—confused and confusing, idealistic crusades for the rights of others, on the one hand, and the exercise of brute force for the sake of brute force, on the other. Lincoln's war was no different.

Lincoln saw his war as a terrible necessity. And, rightly or wrongly, Lincoln interpreted necessity as the hand of God. Here was a man of such gentle sensitivities that he regularly pardoned convicted deserters and granted hardship discharges to men whose families had previously lost fathers and sons. Yet as commander-in-chief Lincoln vigorously prosecuted what, bloody battle by bloody battle, would prove to be, in terms of human life, America's costliest war.

---

[3] Current, *Encyclopaedia Brittanica*, pp. 985–991.

[4] Ibid.

Total casualties, killed and wounded, amounted to ten percent of the nation's entire population. Imagine if you can a modern war in which America were to sustain thirty million casualties and you will have an idea of the enormity of the Civil War.

Although Lincoln saw the war as the hand of God, he claimed neither for his cause nor for himself any special place in the divine order. It is reported that

> Early during the Civil War Abraham Lincoln was chatting with a clergyman who said, "Let us have faith, Mr. President, that the Lord is on our side in this great struggle." To this, Lincoln is reputed to have said, *"I am not at all concerned about that, for I know that the Lord is always on the side of the right; but it is my constant anxiety and prayer, that I and this nation may be on the Lord's side."* [5]

Abraham Lincoln came to Gettysburg to dedicate a cemetery and to rededicate a nation.

> *But, in a larger sense, we cannot dedicate—we cannot consecrate—we cannot hallow—this ground. The brave men, living and dead, who struggled here, have consecrated it, far above our poor power to add or detract. The world will little note nor long remember, what we say here, but it can never forget what they did here. It is for us the living, rather, to be dedicated here to the unfinished work which they who fought here have thus far so nobly advanced. It is rather for us to be here dedicated to the great task before us—that from these honored dead we take increased devotion to that cause for which they gave their last full measure of devotion—that we here highly resolve that these dead shall not have died in vain—that this nation, under God, shall have a new birth of freedom—and that government of the people, by the people, for the people, shall not perish from the earth.*

The promise of new life for the oppressed, equality of opportunity within a just social order, was our founding fathers' dream. It was Abraham Lincoln's dream. This vision dominated the first century of our national existence. And then we became successful, wealthy, and powerful. In the process, we lost our bearings. As Barbara Tuchman observes,

> Our sins of the twentieth century—greed, violence, inhumanity—have been profound, with the result that the pride and self-confidence of the nineteenth century have turned to dismay and self-disgust.[6]

From top to bottom, she fears, our society is pervaded with a contempt for standards of decency, honesty, and justice. Says Tuchman, "The average citizen, trying to hold a footing in standards of morality and conduct he once believed in, is daily knocked over by incoming waves of venality, vulgarity, irresponsibility, ugliness, and trash in all senses of the word."

During my lifetime, we have stood for and stood by few who could remotely be called the friends of humanity and liberty. In the name of the one who gave his life to set us free, I call us to repentance as individuals and as a nation. Through the power of the Gospel, I declare that we are summoned to a renewed sense of dedication to the promise of America. The promise of equality of opportunity and individual freedom within a just social order is not dead. Like the message of Jesus and the vision of Abraham Lincoln, its truth is marching on!

But today our vision must transcend the boundaries that separate nation from nation. Joseph Campbell has said:

---

[5] *2500 Anecdotes for All Occasions*, edited by Edmund Fuller (New York: Avenal, 1942).

[6] Tuchman, *Newsweek*.

> When you see the earth from the moon, you don't see any divisions there of nations or states. This might be the symbol for the new mythology to come. That is the country that we are going to be celebrating. And those are the people that we are one with.[7]

> And Campbell adds:

> We need myths that will identify the individual not with the local group but with the planet. A model for that is the United States. Here were thirteen different little colony nations that decided to act in the mutual interest, without disregarding the individual interests of any one of them.[8]

In the midst of the cruelty and insanity of war, can we catch a glimpse of the light? Can the nations of the world start acting "in mutual interest, without disregarding the individual interests of any of them"? Can we?

The story is told of a mother and her small daughter, who, in recent years, were walking past the house in Springfield, Illinois, where Abraham Lincoln once lived.

> The lights were burning inside, making the home seem warm and inviting. They paused for a few minutes as the mother told the girl what a great president Mr. Lincoln had been and how the whole nation mourned when he died. The youngster listened with rapt attention. Then, noticing the glow coming from the windows, she said, "Look, Momma. When Mr. Lincoln went away, he left the lights on."[9]

Lincoln has left the light on. The time has come for each of us to turn the light on as well.

When the Civil War was drawing to a close, Lincoln delivered his Second Inaugural Address, on March 5, 1865. His words are as appropriate today as they were then:

> *With malice toward none; with charity for all; with firmness in the right as God gives us to see the right, let us strive on to finish the work we are in; to bind up the nation's wounds; to care for him who shall have borne the battle and for his widow and orphan—to do all which may achieve and cherish a just and lasting peace among ourselves, and with all nations.*

Let us strive on to finish the work to which God has called us. Let us bind up this nation's wounds and the wounds afflicted by humankind on this planet. Let us bind up the wounds of Arab and Israeli, of Kuwaiti and Iraqi, of friend and foe. Let us strive together for a world where mothers and their infants can sleep safely through the night. Let us resolve to rain down on our brothers and sisters neither bombs nor missiles but rather spiritual and material blessings.

Abraham Lincoln came to Gettysburg to dedicate a cemetery and to rededicate a nation. As we pass through these painful days, may we rededicate ourselves as well.

Amen.

—LDS

[2233 words]
[22 minutes]

---

[7] Campbell, Joseph, *The Power of Myth* with Bill Moyers; Betty Sue Flowers, editor (New York: Doubleday, 1984), p. 32.

[8] Ibid., p. 24.

[9] *Pastor's Story File*, January 1985, 3.

Sermon 109

Date: Sunday Before Martin Luther King, Jr.'s Birthday

Occasion: Martin Luther King, Jr.'s Birthday

Theme: The dream of Martin Luther King, Jr., continues
Subject: Brotherhood

Title: Martin and Me: The Dream Continues

Tip

> This sermon is a running commentary on Martin Luther King, Jr.'s classic speech, "I Have a Dream." King's words may be read by the preacher or by a member of the congregation.

> I still have a dream. It is a dream deeply rooted in the American dream. I have a dream that one day this nation will rise up and live out the true meaning of its creed: "We hold these truths to be self-evident—that all men are created equal." . . . I have a dream that my four little children will one day live in a nation where they will not be judged by the color of their skin but by the content of their character.

I was there thirty years ago in Washington, D.C., on that warm August afternoon when Martin Luther King, Jr., spoke these words. I was there in a wool suit and a black clerical shirt with a stiff celluloid collar. I had been sitting on the grass by the reflecting pool. Suddenly I felt overcome—by the sun, the heat, the crowd, the emotion. As King's words rang out over the public address system, I drifted to the bus. I heard most of King's speech on a small transistor radio belonging to the bus driver.

We were there—a quarter of a million of us—because we wanted to do something about racism and injustice. A few months earlier, President John Kennedy had gone on television to address the nation. That very day, George Wallace got out of a school doorway so that black students could register at the University of Alabama. As Arthur M. Schlesinger, Jr. recalls, Kennedy's speech

> was a response not alone to Birmingham and Tuscaloosa but to an entire springtime of gathering outrage and atrocity—the white postman from Baltimore murdered on a "freedom walk" in Alabama; black demonstrators in Mississippi slugged, stomped on and then arrested for disturbing the peace; protests, riots; hardening resolve, hardening resistance. The President, deeply disturbed, decided the time had come to assert leadership and appeal to the nation.[1]

The president declared:

---

[1] Schlesinger, Arthur M. Jr., *Robert Kennedy and His Times* (Boston: Houghton Mifflin, 1978), p. 343.

> We are confronted primarily with a moral issue . . . as old as the scriptures and . . . clear as the American Constitution.
>
> . . . Who among us would be content to have the color of his skin changed and stand in [the Negro's] place? Who among us would be content with the counsels of patience and delay?
>
> The time has come, for this Nation to fulfill its promise of freedom.

That very night, a white gunman shot down Medgar Evers in front of his house in Mississippi. A few weeks later, fifteen sticks of dynamite blasted the Sixteenth Street Baptist Church in Birmingham, Alabama. Four small girls, who were in the basement, changing into their choir robes were killed.

The time had come to do something. The time had come to make equal access to places of public accommodation a matter of law, to guarantee the voting rights of all citizens, to take a stand for equal opportunity in employment. If Congress failed to act, the debate would turn to the streets. Already young revolutionaries were challenging Martin Luther King's leadership of the civil rights movement. King believed in the American system of government—believed that it could be cajoled, persuaded, and convinced to do the right thing. His faith was not shared by more militant black leaders.

Bayard Rustin proposed a march on Washington in support of the proposed civil rights bill. A march was the last thing John and Robert Kennedy wanted. The President warned that a march on Washington would create an atmosphere of intimidation—which would give some members of Congress just the out they sought.

King agreed that the march might be "ill-timed." But, he insisted, "I have never engaged in any direct action movement which did not seem ill-timed." Blacks were already in the streets. Better for them to be there under nonviolent leadership.

"If the march could not be headed off, the Kennedys decided that it would have to be made a success."[2] It would be a masterpiece of planning and execution. So on August 28, 1963, we came to Washington, a quarter of a million strong.

> I have a dream today.
>
> I have a dream that one day the state of Alabama . . . will be transformed into a situation where little black boys and black girls will be able to join hands with little white boys and white girls and walk together as sisters and brothers.

I had only known a few blacks. When I was a toddler, I had played with the children of the black family who lived next door to my grandparents in Maywood, Illinois. There were fourteen children in the converted storefront that housed them.

My mahogany skinned playmates were a marvel to me. Why were the palms of their hands and the soles of their feet so white? I had wondered. And why was I not allowed to play in their house nor they to play in my grandparents'? Why could they not go with me to the bright and shiny playground a block to the west? And why could I not go with them to the small, rundown playground two blocks to the east?

Why did I have to stop playing with my black friends when I started school?

---

[2] Ibid., p. 350.

Why did my grandparents talk about their black neighbors behind their backs and sneeringly refer to them as *Schwartzahs*. The word only meant "black" in Yiddish, but the tone connoted something else.

> I have a dream today. . . . that we will be free one day.

> This will be the day when all of God's children will be able to sing with new meaning "My country 'tis of thee, sweet land of liberty, of thee I sing. Land where my fathers died, land of the pilgrim's pride, from every mountainside let freedom ring." And if America is to be a great nation this must become true. So let freedom ring from the prodigious hilltops of New Hampshire. Let freedom ring from the mighty mountains of New York. Let freedom ring from the heightening Alleghenies of Pennsylvania. . . . But not only that; let freedom ring from Stone Mountain of Georgia. Let freedom ring from every hill and mole hill of Mississippi. From every mountaintop, let freedom ring.

In the neighborhood where my family lived in Chicago there were no blacks at all. There were no blacks on the streets, in the classrooms, at the movies, at the YMCA, at the Boys' Club, in the stores.

When I went to high school, there was one black student among my four thousand classmates. His name was Abe Woodson. He was the star of our football team. His family did not live in our school district. He had been allowed to transfer from the black high school district.

When I met Ted, a black student from Marshall High School, who was a leader in Jr. Red Cross, I stared at him as though he were an exotic animal at the zoo. I admired him. I enjoyed his company. But I never asked what his father did for a living or told him what mine did. I never asked him where he wanted to attend college or what career he wanted to pursue. I never invited him to my home. He never invited me to his. We lived two blocks from one another, but some invisible barrier separated us. I let it.

During my undergraduate years, I lived in Germantown, an integrated neighborhood in Philadelphia. I was astounded to find blacks at the supermarkets, the drugstores, the department stores, the movie theaters, the public schools.

In 1969, some white picketers asked me not to shop at the local dime store because blacks were barred from Woolworth's lunch counters in the South. I failed to see the connection between my purchasing a ballpoint pen in Philadelphia and the segregation in Alabama. So I brushed past the demonstrators.

In my early twenties, I was pastor of a Congregational Church in an all-white, economically depressed neighborhood in Philadelphia. A riot erupted when a family tried moving into a row house down the street from the church. The rumor was that the husband was part Indian or part Negro. I tried to convince my congregation that we should welcome blacks, Puerto Ricans, and other dark-skinned peoples when and if they arrived in our community or came to worship with us. I was told by some of my members about other inner-city churches in other inner-city neighborhoods that had been "ruined" by such newcomers. Angry, frightened members declared: "Let them stay where they belong. We don't want them here. Besides they will be more comfortable with their own kind."

During my first year in graduate school, I joined the Princeton Association for Human Rights, an organization made up in equal parts of whites and blacks. The whites were faculty, professional people, and graduate students. The blacks were residents of the local ghetto. Our major concern as a group was fighting discrimination in housing. The black members had a hard time restraining their impatience with the way things were in America in general and Princeton in particular. Sometimes that impatience would be vented at us good mannered, polite, grammatically superior, socially concerned liberals. I was beginning to get angry at people who were angry at me all the time. Another invisible boundary.

When word came of the March on Washington, the Association rented a bus and arranged to join the caravan. I arrived at our departure point in comfortable clothes. One of my religious friends insisted that I go home and change into clerical garb "as a witness" to the support of the churches. En route to Washington we sang "freedom songs" and received instructions on how to handle ourselves if we were attacked by racist goons.

> When we let freedom ring, when we let it ring from every village and every hamlet, from every state and every city, we will be able to speed up that day when all of God's children, black men and white men, Jews and Gentiles, Protestants and Catholics, will be able to join hands and sing in the words of the old Negro spiritual, "Free at last! Free at last! Thank God almighty, we are free at last!"

I had become uncomfortable not only with my clothes but with myself. The March was all too big, too star studded, too controlled. I couldn't make myself go with the flow. I couldn't fit in or see how I could make a difference. I couldn't make contact with anyone but the white friend with whom I had come. After the March, I never felt comfortable in the Princeton Association for Human Rights. Something no longer was right.

I had still not invited a black person to my home or been invited by a black person to his. I was waiting for it to happen. That was the problem. I was waiting for "them" to come to me. I was allowing myself to be totally passive. I wasn't listening. I wasn't discovering what they wanted or needed. I wasn't reaching out.

As King orated, some in the crowd joined hands, swayed back and forth, and chanted ecstatically, "Dream some more." But one black man shouted furiously: "To hell with that dream, Martin. Now, damit, NOW!"[3] That made me angry and gave me an excuse to leave the civil rights battlefield to others.

It would take me five years to come out of my shell, to want to commit myself to making a difference, to feel open to those who still struggled for racial justice. I was set to work for Robert Kennedy's presidential campaign. But 1968 was a bad year to make such a choice. It was the year in which both Bobby and Martin were murdered. When Kennedy was killed, Don Hesse's editorial cartoon for the day portrayed a field of clouds. In the background, almost out of our sight, John Kennedy places his arm around his brother's shoulder as Robert says: "Things haven't changed much, Jack."[4] The artist could have included Martin in that picture.

Racism remains entrenched in American society. Poverty is worse than it was in the 1960s. Millions of blacks remain herded together like cattle, with little to eat and nothing to do. In the words of Thomas Merton, prejudice "hems them in with its four insurmountable walls. . . . thousand upon thousand of souls are destroyed by vice and misery and degradation, wiped out, washed from the register of the living, dehumanized."[5]

I want to be part of a community that actively welcomes men, women, and children of all races and national origins. I want to be part of a community that stands against racism, agism, sexism, and all the other destructive isms. I want to be part of a community that makes a difference, that enhances, that sustains, that nurtures, that cares.

I still have a dream.

---

[3] Adapted from ibid., p. 351.

[4] *The St. Louis Globe-Democrat,* June 7, 1968.

[5] Merton, Thomas, *The Seven Storey Mountain* (New York: Harcourt, Brace, 1948), p. 338.

Amen.

—LDS

[2130 words]
[21 minutes]

❦ *Sermon 110*

❦ *Date:* Any Sunday

Text:
Hosea 11:1-11

Theme: We are a people held hostage to drugs and alcohol. How as Christians should we respond to this crisis?
Subject: Drugs, alcohol

❦ *Title:* Burnt Offerings to Idols: Christians and the Drug Crisis

The Tragedy of Adam Dorris

When Adam Dorris was born, his mother was drunk. She came into the delivery room drunk. She had been drunk most of her pregnancy. The delivery room reeked of Ripple, the nurses said. And when Adam Dorris was born, he was drunk too. He had spent nine months in the uterus feeding through the umbilical cord between him and his mother on the occasional healthy meal, and mostly on booze. When the doctor cut the cord, Adam got the shakes, the DTs, in the first moments of his life he was forced to go cold turkey.

The story of Adam Dorris, a victim of fetal alcohol syndrome, is told most movingly by his adoptive father, Michael Dorris, in this new book, The Broken Cord. It's a story of the father's growing realization that this little baby he had adopted was not normal, would never be normal, was severely learning disabled, regularly had seizures, had an IQ of 70, and had ahead of him a life of helplessness, pain, and sorrow. All because his mother was addicted, addicted to the drug alcohol. Within three years of his birth she was dead of that addiction. The broken cord; Adam and his mother both had the cord of love between them and their God, broken, severed, never to be reunited.

The cord of love, the cord broken in Adam Dorris's life, that cord of love is what God speaks of in a Hosea passage, I used it as the introductory quote on the order of worship, "I led them with cords of compassion, with the bands of love." It is this cord of compassion that connects us to God, as the umbilical cord connects us, provides us with a lifeline, with our mother. Severed, we are on our own. God says to Hosea, I cannot let you go, I can never forget you, even though I am angry, enraged at your faithlessness, at your worship of idols, offering burnt offerings to false gods. Still, I have with your bonds of love, ties of compassion.

Worshiping False Gods

Surely God's anger at us persists today. When we abuse drugs or alcohol, we too are worshiping idols, false gods of the quick fix, the easy numbness, the lonely despair. And drugs is not a problem out there suffered by other people, other families, other kids. We're all tempted to worship that false god, to be hooked by a society addicted, lured, drugged into looking for other gods of numbness and escape. And even if drugs and alcohol abuse do not touch us directly (and if you aren't practicing good old denial, drugs probably are touching your life in some way) at least it touches you in that the body of Christ, the whole of creation, is addicted. I mean if one member suffers, we all suffer. We are addicted, we suffer.

And the ones who suffer most are the children. Children like Adam and others suffering fetal alcohol syndrome. Children like the crack babies you have read about and seen on television. Babies born addicted, babies born drunk, toddlers abandoned in crack houses, children coming into school now with severe learning disabilities, with no real home to go home to. And then of course there are the high schools, colleges, work places. But think of the children.

I spent a lot of time the last couple of weeks at a local hospital, visiting the sick, and each time I was there I would pass a most moving art exhibit in the corridor of the first floor. They usually have some community art show there, and these days it is drawings by children, ages four through twelve, kids in the alcohol rehab program for children of alcoholics. Simple, incredibly moving pictures: my father drunk, my father sober; a broken heart and tears, a rainbow of hope; a detailed picture of different drugs and booze, captioned hugs, please not drugs; a lonely child crying out, daddy, please pick me up. These kids know, they hurt, their cord of love is broken.

I want to point out that I'm including alcohol in this sermon for a reason. Alcohol is a drug. Now we drink it here every Sunday, as part of communion, and lots of us drink it every day. I enjoy drinking myself. But it is a drug. Just as caffeine, nicotine, diet pills, tranquilizers are all drugs. We can use them and we can abuse them. Our society suffers from the desperate fallout of drug and alcohol abuse.

One Crisis—Many Forms

Now the drug crisis takes many forms. It is a physical crisis—people's bodies are destroyed, babies are born drunk. It is a sociological crisis—families are torn apart, elementary education, high school, college, all are strained. It is a political crisis—now we have a drug czar (why he's called a czar I don't know) and a huge budget item; it even impacts our foreign policy—what exactly was the nature of our relationship with Noriega? How corrupt is the Colombian government? Where did the Contras get their money? And it is an economic crisis: whole nation's economies depend on the drug trade. Surely, I believe, that if we had economically, real job opportunity and full employment in this country, if, I even dare to propose, we decriminalized some aspects of drug use, we could remove the financial incentive of drug dealing and the desperate use of drugs by people with empty lives. Not to mention the middleman who make a yearly salary we can all envy. That's the only connection I can make with our scheduled gospel reading; those old middlemen, like the steward, screwing his masters' customers by charging a huge commission as all middlemen do. Jesus seems to approve of such machinations if they make money. But then he reminds us that we can't serve two gods, God and money. The drug crisis is an economic crisis because so many people choose money rather than God.

For you see, I am convinced that ultimately the drug and alcohol crisis is a spiritual crisis. Drugs and alcohol are golden calves, our false idols. If we were a people centered on God, connected to God by cords of love, we would not want or need to abuse drugs and alcohol. Put simply, in the theology of bumper stickers, we should be able to get high on life, not drugs. Loving God is getting high on life. Taking drugs is worshiping the false idols of the quick fix, the easy numb, the tremendous profit, succumbing to the hollow deposit or violent rage of a lonely and meaningless life. We need to do a lot more than "just say no" to drugs. Much more. We need to say yes to life, yes to God, yes to that cord of love.

What then should a Christian response be to drug and alcohol crisis? Well, I've said some things already. We shouldn't point the finger—oh, that's their problem, that family, that community, that nation. It's our problem, as the body of Christ; we are addicted, our cord of love is severed, we all suffer.

And so we should be truth tellers, honest, we should trust that the truth really will set us free. I found this very good and highly recommended book in the library, Not My Kid, A Parent's Guide to Kids and Drugs. There's a great chapter on parent denial, "Not my kid, oh, just late coming home, eyes just red from the swim team"—all forms of denial.

Talk with your kids, it says, honestly, openly; Christ called us again and again to tell the truth—which means to keep communication open. Jesus comforted and loved the outcasts of his day, those with whom no one else would talk. Learn simple, caring communication. Not judging, rejecting, scorning. I've read that we say "no" to our children 25 times for every time we say "yes." Open, honest communication does not mean just saying "no" all the time. Now, of course, we must all learn to say "no" to drug and alcohol abuse. Clearly Adam Dorris's real mother needed to learn to say "no" to drugs, to booze, and she never could. But she needed a lot more in her life than the simple slogan, "Just say no." I have to say I'm not too impressed with the whole theme, "Just say no." You can't simply "Just say no" to a crisis that is physical, sociological, political, economic, and spiritual and expect it to go away. No, there's got to be some yeses too, yeses to life, hugs not drugs, get high on life.

For you see, I don't think Christians used to be afraid of getting high. Yes, I think God wants us to get high all the time. Does this contradict all I have said so far? No, I'm still convinced drug and alcohol abuse are a severed cord of love, choking out connection with God. If we get high only to escape, to keep separate from God, that is of course unfaithful.

Getting High on God

But getting high on life, getting high on each other, on the world, getting high on God, that is a worshipful celebration of beauty, a loving engagement with the world. We need to do more than "Just say no" or to teach our children to "Just say no." We need to give them something else to fill that void, something else to say a big "Yes" to. We all need to learn to get high on life, on God.

I am, of course, saying these things to get a conversation going afterwards, to shake us up, but I really am concerned about what I see as a new prohibitionism, a new era like the attempts earlier in this century to outlaw liquor, a style of dealing with problems that's founded on repression, denial, loss of personal freedom, punishing the victims, and which simply won't work. The whole metaphor of the war on drugs smacks of that same attitude, the drug czar, all the money for the military and police and not much for education, social services, employment, counseling, drug rehab, all the money for the no, and not much to help people learn to get high on something else. I even heard a well-meaning drug rehab counselor use the war metaphor, referring to new money available for drug rehab programs, he said, now we have more ammunition, more bullets to shoot into the community. It's not the victims of the drug crisis we need to kill in a war on drugs. We don't need to kill anything. We need to promote life, not death. Our world does not need another war. We need to promote human peace.

Any drug testing, too, becomes a part of the new prohibition. Sure, I think some people should be tested, especially airplane pilots and captains of oil tankers. The citizens of Alaska would agree. But when our former president ordered drug testing of all federal employees, when the NCAA requires testing of all college athletes, I think we are succumbing to a paranoia and an ethic of fear. How can we teach people to be responsible and trustworthy when we give them no tools to be responsible or trustworthy. How can we expect people to love life when all we say to them is "no"?

No, as Christians we need to speak the truth to acknowledge our own forms of addiction and learn which God we really worship, the God of life or the idol of death. And we need to try each day to get high on life, on God, on that blessed tie that binds. And we need to reach out to those whose cord of compassion is strained or severed, and reconnect them, retie them, one to another, to our God.

Amen.

—Deborah Streeter

[1979 words]
[20 minutes]

Sermon 111

Date: Earth Day or United Nations Environmental Sabbath

Texts:
Genesis 1:1–2:3
Psalm 19:2–5
Isaiah 24
Romans 8:18–28

Theme: Something about Earth Day is terribly wrong.
Subject: Ecology, the environment

Title: What's Wrong with Earth Day?

Note | Originally an editorial and later a brief sermon, What's Wrong with Earth Day? was prepared for Earth Day 1990, but may be adapted to any year.

Something about Earth Day 1990 is terribly wrong.

It goes beyond the way the media are covering it, and I know something about that. Our metropolitan newspapers and local television stations are employing the calculated overkill that comes from having an editor in charge of Earth Day coverage, someone whose performance—and career prospects—are judged by whether all possible stories are written.

The result is too many words and too little thinking.

These phenomena in the press are matched by fundamental problems with how corporate America is responding to Earth Day. Most companies give the job to their marketing departments. It is seen as a marketing opportunity rather than as a time for fundamental reexamination of how a business, primarily in the way it produces and distributes its products, affects the earth's environment.

Earth Day 1990 is too corporate, at least to those of us who recall the original version.

Twenty years ago, the original Earth Day grew out of political and intellectual ferment on college campuses. It had enormous impact, creating a political force that has become mainstream—if not dominant—in local, state and national affairs.

Before Earth Day 1970, we had conservationists who wanted to save wilderness, but Earth Day created environmentalists.

It helped begin the process of making complex connections between urban and industrial issues and the quality of our air and water. It forced us to look at how many resources we in the developed world consume as compared to the poor nations of the planet where the bulk of the world's population lives.

Nothing so profound has emerged from the mishmash of Earth Day 1990.

Today our environmental issues involve trade-offs, generally between economic opportunities and environmental conservation but also between individual choice and the broader social or global good.

What, for example, is the biggest environmental problem in the Bay Area?

Air pollution caused by our overreliance on the automobile.

Will the environmental movement have the guts to take on our car-craving culture?

Today, being for the environment is comfortable and politically safe. Telling Californians they must get out of their cars is not politically safe, but it is politically necessary.

The grass-roots elements of Earth Day 1990, as distinct from the corporate hangers-on, hope to create a mass movement demanding a cleaner, healthier environment. Having a big polluter or a profits-before-environmental corporation for an enemy can help environmentalists prevail—on the right issues.

It's a lot tougher when we are the enemy, when our love for the automobile causes our worst pollution.

Another question.

What is the world's most serious environmental problem?

Overconsumption by those of us in the richest nations. It's been too long since I read the precise figures, but citizens of the developed world consume an enormous share of the planet's limited natural resources: oil, minerals, steel, and timber.

It will be hard to build a political movement that captures the mainstream if it preaches the unpopular message that Americans consume too much, or drive too much.

Nor is the business community—or at least the corporate marketers who have hijacked Earth Day—likely to rally to the cause of lower consumption.

How do we, as responsible world citizens and, in this setting, as Christians, respond to Earth Day 1990?

We recycle.

We recall the backpackers' credo about the wilderness: Take nothing but pictures, leave nothing but footprints. And we figure out how to take a similar attitude in how we affect our planet's fragile environment.

We listen when our nature loving friends tell us the natural habitats of birds, wildlife and flowers are shrinking. Daily. And we learn why it matters.

And maybe, just maybe, we carpool to church.

Amen.

—Tim Clark

[600 words]
[6 minutes]

Sermon 112

Date: Third Sunday in Lent, Year B

Texts:
Exodus 20:1–17
Psalm 19
1 Corinthians 1:18–25
John 2:13–22 [or 13:25]

Theme: "Business as usual" is no excuse.
Subject: Righteous indignation

Title: Throw the Rascals Out!

His eyes were ablaze that day. His friends thought he had gone mad. Jesus was angry—angrier than they had ever seen him or would ever see him. He was getting ready to throw the rascals out.

John, unlike the Synoptic tradition, places this incident right at the beginning of Jesus' ministry. Matthew, Mark, and Luke place the cleansing of the Temple in the final week of Jesus' career. They describe it as the act that precipitated the death of Jesus.

We can sympathize with the Jesus of their accounts. After months of rejection in city after city, a very frustrated prophet comes to Jerusalem for one last attempt to reform the religion of his people. Here at the heart of his nation, the population swollen to four times its normal size by pilgrims from every corner of the earth, Jesus tries one more time—knowing full well that he will not be heard. So he loses it! And it gets him killed.

But John does not see it that way. His Jesus is no frustrated street agitator. The cleansing of the Temple is not the tactic of a desperate messianic claimant who lets his emotions get the best of him. He is no martyr. No one takes his life from him. He is in control of circumstances; circumstances do not control him.

Everything is going well when Jesus comes to Jerusalem for his first visit and first Passover. He has performed the first of his miraculous signs at Cana, changing water into wine. He is attracting attention and followers. So why is he so furious?

Business as Usual

After all, the money changers were only performing a necessary service. As William Willimon explains,

> Roman coins, the only kind used in Jerusalem, could not be used to pay the temple tax. One needed shekels. So . . . if you wanted to offer your money, you had to deal with money changers. And if you wanted to offer God an unspotted ox or sheep or pigeon, as scripture required, then you had to buy one from a temple merchant.[1]

What's the big deal? What's the point? If you and I had been there, we could have given Jesus some good advice. "Chill out, Jesus. Don't be so uptight. So the Temple officials and money

---

[1] *Biblical Preaching Journal*, Winter 1991.

changers have their little racket. Everybody's got to make a living. So what if the pilgrims get rooked? If the money changers and the animal brokers don't get their money, those out-of-towners will only spend it someplace else. Maybe at home or on the road somewhere. It's better to have that cash in the local economy, isn't it? That way it trickles down to all of us."

But Jesus doesn't look amused. He keeps right on braiding those cords into a scourge. Don't try "business as usual" or "It's OK—everybody's doing it" on him. He isn't buying.

"Come on, Jesus, don't embarrass us. Not here in God's house. Not now on this sacred occasion." But he goes on plaiting that whip. And there is fire in his eyes. And we shudder.

And he tells us something we cannot understand—not yet. Sacred places and sacred ceremonies and duded-up worshipers mean absolutely nothing. What counts is knowing the secret of God's real temple. "What is a temple anyway?" his irate looks seem to ask. We try to answer: "A place where God is known. A place where his presence is felt. A place that reveals him to others, to the whole world."

"These stone buildings are not God's temple—I am," says Jesus. "Destroy it and God will raise it up. I am God's temple—the house of his presence, the mirror of his light, the magnet drawing others to him. I am God's temple—and so are you. And when you don't get that it ticks me off."

"Now, just a minute, Jesus," we want to protest. "Just be calm. You're supposed to be 'meek and mild'—right? All this anger isn't good for you. You'll give yourself an ulcer. Now just put down that ugly thing for a moment and listen to some good advice. Remember what that lovely nun, St. Catherine of Siena, had to say? 'There is no sin nor wrong that gives a man such a foretaste of Hell in this life as anger and impatience.' Or think of Ben Franklin's words: 'Anger is never without a reason, but seldom a good one.' And you'll get a chuckle out of Will Rogers, who said: 'People who fly into a rage always make a bad landing.'"

But Jesus just stares at us with those blazing brown eyes of his. And we begin to get it and to think of other words such as those of Jean Baptist de la Salle: "There is a holy anger, excited by zeal, which moves us to reprove with warmth those whom our mildness failed to correct." Or the words of Thomas Fuller, "Anger is one of the sinews of the soul. He who lacks it hath a maimed mind."

"OK," we admit, "Those guys have a point, too. You've got a point. But didn't Thomas Secker say it so well? 'He who would be angry and sin not must not be angry with anything but sin.'"

And suddenly Jesus puts down the whip and gives us each a hug. So that's it! "Be angry with sin: Never tolerate excuses from anyone including yourself for missing the mark, for not caring, for doing a sloppy job, for taking rather than serving. Never rationalize away somebody else's right to live and to prosper. Don't get so cozy with "business as usual" in yourself or in your world."

Remember when "business as usual" killed a hundred thousand men, women, and children in the Persian Gulf. And they are a drop in the bucket. Greed, self-interest, and apathy kill that many every day, sometimes every hour of every day.

Remember that poem you learned as a child, the one by John McCrae, the young Canadian physician who was killed during the waning days of "the Great War"?

In Flanders Fields

In Flanders fields the poppies blow
Between the crosses, row on row,
That mark our place; and in the sky
The Larks, still bravely singing, fly
Scarce amid the guns below.

We are the Dead. Short days ago
We lived, felt dawn, saw sunset glow,
Loved and were loved, and now we lie
In Flanders fields.

Take up our quarrel with the foe:
To you from failing hands we throw
The torch; be yours to hold it high.
If ye break faith with us who die
We shall not sleep though poppies grow
In Flanders fields.

And I reply, "John, I have met the enemy and I am he. And it angers me. I hate oppression. I hate killing and torturing for land or minerals or money. I hate the hurt and the harm I do heedlessly, unconsciously, day by day in order to live my life, to maintain my life-style. I hate the apathy that ignores the sufferings of others.

I hate the "business as usual" attitude that feels no pangs of conscience in making a buck selling the implements of mass destruction to the least stable nations in the least stable parts of the world.

I hate the real politik that makes ruthless dictators our friends one minute and our enemies the next.

The Eternal Conflict

So I take up your quarrel with the foe, the real foe, the enemy within and without. And I pray that the Sovereign Lord may bless us with a just and lasting peace. When I heard of the cease-fire in the Persian Gulf, I thought of Churchill's immortal words, "Now this is not the end. It is not even the beginning of the end. But it is, perhaps, the end of the beginning." It is, perhaps, the end of the beginning of talking instead of shooting, of sharing instead of grabbing, of bringing justice rather than power politics to our Arab brothers.

In my own poem, "Armistice," I write:

The field is peaceful now.
No more the cannon's glare.
Determined by a vow,
Yet death is everywhere.

We victors now rejoice.
Success is ours today.
But yet I hear one voice,
Its sound is of dismay.

"Today why should you cry?"
I ask, so soft, so clear.
"Those tears you must now dry
For victory is here."

"You ask, sir, why I weep,"
She says in sad reply.
"My love forever sleeps
For country he did die."

The field is peaceful now.
No more the cannon's glare.
Determined by a vow,
Yet death is everywhere.

The mothers, sisters, wives, and lovers of a hundred thousand young men are weeping. And I am weeping with them. Americans, Kuwaitis, Iraqis, Israelis, Britons, and others are weeping. How angry Jesus would have been with all of us. For we allowed "business as usual" to drown out the open dialogue of human being with human being.

There can be no peace between Jesus and "business as usual." British mystery writer Dorothy Sayers tells us:

> The people who hanged Christ never accused Him of being a bore—on the contrary; they thought Him too dynamic to be safe. It has been left for later generations to muffle up that shattering personality and surround Him with the atmosphere of tedium. We have very efficiently pared the claws of the Lion of Judah, . . . and recommended Him as a fitting household pet. . . . But He had a "daily beauty in his life that made us ugly," and officialdom felt that the established order of things would be more secure without Him. So they did away with [him] in the name of peace and quietness.[2]

But in his war against "business as usual," he observes no armistice. In his war against our blindness to the presence of God in our own lives and in those of our brothers and sisters, he offers no cease-fire.

He is on our case. His eyes are ablaze.

Amen.

—LDS

[1686 words]
[17 minutes]

---

[2] Sayers, Dorothy, *The Greatest Drama Ever Staged*, as cited in *Parables, Etc.*, August 1983, 3.6.

❦ *CHAPTER TWELVE*

TRANSFORMATION AND CHANGE

Jesus had little patience with self-centered people. His message was: You have to change. Change is painful and difficult. But it is also unavoidable. Things change and, like it or not, so do we.

Don't be a conformist; be a transformist. The pattern of the world is isolation. The message of the Gospel is community and mutual concern. Here's what Christian life is all about: finding the gap between the way things are and the way they ought to be and throwing ourselves across the gap. The world, to paraphrase Shaw, sees things as they are and says, "Why?" but Christians dream things as they never were, and say, "Why not?"

By the amazing grace of God, our lives have meaning, purpose, and direction. We are neither helpless nor hopeless. Despite difficulties and setbacks, we are joyfully confident.

Sermon 113

Date: Sixth Sunday in Lent, Year A
Passion Sunday

Text:
Matthew 26:14-27:66

Theme: Ride the tides of opportunity while they are yours.
Subject: Opportunity

Title: Tide Riding

The Power of the Tide

During the troubled years of World War II, the Italian forces were driven out of Eritrea in North Africa. In an effort to make the harbor unusable to the Allies, the Italians took great barges, filled them with concrete, and caused them to be sunk across the entrance to the harbor. When the Allies entered, their problem was to remove those barges in order that the harbor might become usable.

They did so in a very ingenious way. They took great gas tanks—not the kinds of tanks we have on our cars or in our homes, but those huge tanks which are used to hold hundreds of thousands of gallons of fuel in great oil refineries. They sealed those tanks so they would float, and they caused them to be floated over the place where the barges were below. When the tide was out, they chained the tanks to the barges. When the tide came in, the barges were lifted by the tanks floating with the tide. The barges were pulled from the sucking sand at the bottom of the bay. It was then a relatively easy matter to remove them and make the harbor usable again.

Think of the power in that! The barges were chained to the tanks. The tanks were dependent upon the tides. The tides were pulled by the gravitational attraction of the moon, and the moon was moving in accord with the whole cosmos, the great sidereal system. Tremendous, unimaginable, dynamic power belongs to the tides.

It's this idea which Shakespeare emphasizes in the fourth act of Julius Caesar, when he puts these words upon the lips of Brutus trying to enlist Cassius in his aid. (Note how Shakespeare speaks of the power of the tides and then adds another serious consideration concerning them.) He writes:

> There is a tide in the affairs of men
> Which, taken at the flood, leads on to fortune;
> Omitted, all the voyages of their life
> Is bound in shallows and in miseries.
> On such a full sea are we now afloat
> And we must take the current when it serves
> Or lose our ventures.

What Shakespeare is saying is not only that the tides have great power, but that they also are irretrievable, unstoppable, unrecallable. Their lifting strength comes for but a few hours and then is gone. And if you miss the flood, you will be left in shallows and in miseries, having lost your ventures.

The Garden of Gethsemane

Now I ask you to come with me to a place that's not at sea, but rather is thirty-five miles inland from the sea. It is a garden called Gethsemane. Jesus has come there for prayer—on the same night in which he was betrayed. Judas has already gone to betray him. Jesus leaves eight of the disciples at the gate of the garden, and three, those closest to him, Peter, James, and John, join him in a kind of inner glade. And Jesus urges them to pray with him.

Then he goes apart and throws himself out flat upon the earth and prays that the cup of the world's sin might not be forced upon him. He is in a tremendous agony of spirit. All the hideous hurt of the whole world's history is flowing through the single channel of his great heart.

Having so prayed, he goes back to the disciples for some word of encouragement and finds them asleep. "Would you not watch," he asks, "even for an hour? Watch and pray, lest you yourselves enter into temptation. Your spirit is willing but your flesh is weak. Therefore, watch and pray."

Again he goes apart to pray, and this time the Scriptures say his prayer was so intense that his sweat came, as it were, like great drops of blood falling in a kind of crystalline rosary at his feet. Once again he goes back to the disciples, seeking some word of support and help. And once again he finds them asleep. This time he permits them to remain asleep (that's a very significant detail in the story) and goes back to pray alone.

A few minutes later he sees torches flickering through the branches of the olive trees. Soldiers of the high priest have come. He goes back to his disciples and says, "Arise. My betrayer is at hand." He is led off to the house of Caiaphas, the high priest, and the disciples are left hiding among Gethsemane's bushes. They are left in the shallows and they are left in miseries, because they have missed the tides.

The Opportunity to Grow in Character

First, they missed the tide of opportunity to grow in character.

Every one of us is in need of growth in character. Not long ago I was talking to some young men who are part of the Word of God Community in Ann Arbor, Michigan. One of these young men asked me why it was that there is so little thought about character in our time. And what I said to him, I share with you this morning.

In a day when behavioral psychology is the dominant psychology of the time (a psychology which teaches us character is nothing more than the influence of our environment), and in a time when moral relativism has settled across the land, as some think, like stinking fog so that there are no absolutes recognized as being right or wrong, and in a time when the pseudosophisticated laugh at the very notion of character, it should not surprise us that there is so little serious talk of character, let alone focus on growth in character. But we all need to grow in character, and we need to recognize such growth cannot occur at every moment and under every circumstance. There are tides in the development of character. Catch them, and growth is yours. Miss them, and you are left in shallows and in miseries.

My first pastorate was in McKeesport, Pennsylvania, which was famous at that time for having the world's largest steel-tube rolling mills. The mills created a seamless tube that was unparalleled. Many was the time I stood in one of those great machines (the command module was called the pulpit, incidentally) with the man operating the machine. I'd see a great serpent of molten metal come slithering down into the machine, and it would be chopped off. Then the machine would grab it by its end and begin to spin. By centrifugal force, that bar of molten metal would open from the inside out, forming a perfect tube of steel without seam and without blemish.

Many times I asked the men directing those machines, "What's the most important ingredient in the process?"

The answer was always the same: "It's the temperature of the metal. If it is too hot, it will fly apart; if it is too cold, it will not open as it ought. Unless you catch the molten moment, you cannot make the perfect tube."

Unless we catch those molten moments when character can develop, we miss our opportunity just as the disciples did. They missed such an opportunity there in Gethsemane. They had the opportunity to see how Jesus handled suffering and hurt. They had the chance to see him face ugliness straight on—not run away from it, not attempt to deny it, but confront it, and so defeat it. In observing him they could have learned about courage, and patience, and hope, and endurance, and pity, and mercy, and fortitude. All of these precious lessons could have been theirs. But they slept, and so missed the tide.

I do not know what would constitute a molten moment for you. Perhaps it might be your own suffering. Maybe it is the death of someone you love very much. Perhaps it is some inner urge you cannot explain—the voice of conscience. Maybe it's the example of someone you admire; a bit of Scripture; a piece of lace you find, which once belonged to your mother; a letter from an old friend; the words of a sermon; the words of this preacher in this sermon. Whatever it is, it suddenly causes within you the feeling that you wish to expand and develop your character beyond that which you have known before.

Claim that moment. Don't sleep through it. Jesus says to the disciples, "Could you not watch? Watch and pray lest you, yourselves, enter into temptation."

The Opportunity to Grow as God's Children

The disciples of Gethsemane also missed the opportunity to grow as the children of God. Any one of us can strike a match. Any one of us can light a candle. Any one of us can ignite a bonfire. But no one of us and no group of us and not even all of us together can enkindle the flaming power of the Holy Spirit of God. Jesus says that the Holy Spirit comes and goes like the wind, utterly outside any direction or control from us. There in Gethsemane that night, the Holy Spirit was moving. His hot breath filled that place. And the disciples slept through it.

Notice that while Jesus wakened the disciples the first time, he did not waken them the second time. In verse 44, we are told that when he found them sleeping again, he went away. In other words, one cannot depend on the Holy Spirit of God to interrupt in such dramatic fashion each and every time. If we turn away from the enkindling power of the Spirit, we may never know that power again.

I often think of it in terms of our great space shot. Do you remember a few years ago when we sent that sophisticated space vehicle out to take pictures of the planet Jupiter? For a period of more than two years, that space vehicle was moving toward Jupiter. And then there came a time of closest approximation. In those moments, the cameras on board that vehicle took and sent back to us remarkable pictures of Jupiter. But then, having completed its task, the vehicle continued out into space, and it continues so until this very minute. Never again will it come close to Jupiter.

Just so, there are times when we come very close to God, and the hot breath of his Holy Spirit is all about us. In that time of closest approximation, let us claim what it is to be a child of God. For if we miss that moment, it may never come for us again.

David Brainerd, the great missionary to the American Indians, was on one occasion witnessing to a chief, who was very close to deciding for Christ. But he held back; there was some pause or hesitation. Brainerd got up, took a stick, drew a circle in the soft earth about the chief, and said, "Decide before you cross that line." Why this passion and urgency? Because Brainerd recognized that at that moment that chief was close to God. If he missed that moment, he might never be so close again.

It is said that Satan once called to him the emissaries of hell and said he wanted to send one of them to earth to aid women and men in the ruination of their souls. He asked which one would want to go. One creature came forward and said, "I will go."

And Satan said, "If I send you, what will you tell the children of men?

He said, "I will tell the children of men that there is no heaven."

And Satan said, "They will not believe you, for there is a bit of heaven in every human heart. In the end everyone knows that right and good must have the victory. You may not go."

Then one last creature came forward, this one from the darkest place of all. And Satan said to him, "And if I send you, what will you say to women and men to aid them in the destruction of their souls?"

And he said, "I will tell them there is no hurry."

And Satan said, "Go!"

That spirit is still abroad on the face of the earth. "There is a tide in the affairs of men which taken at the flood leads on to fortune." Missed, and we are left in shallows and in miseries. "The spirit is willing, but the flesh is weak." Awake, because the tides may be running for you at this very moment. Don't miss riding those tides.

The Opportunity of Jesus' Friendship

One last thought: Those disciples in Gethsemane also missed the opportunity to grow in friendship with Jesus. It is a wonderful thing to have friends, and that, of course, is particularly so in the time of trouble. When we're battered by the hammer of hardship, that's when we need our loved ones close. That's the reason Jesus, who in the Scriptures is recorded most often as going off to pray alone, on this occasion took his disciples with him. He knew the deep agony of spirit which was going to be his, and he wanted their comfort close. He wanted to feel their shoulders beside his own. But they slept.

When he came back the first time from his prayer, his robe was dirty. He had thrown himself upon the ground, but there was no one there to brush him off or to give him words of love. When he came back the second time, his sweat was like great drops of blood. But there was no one awake to wipe away that perspiration or to give him words of encouragement and support. To all his other burdens was added the burden of loneliness.

It's a tragic irony that this Christ who was so filled with compassion—this one who looked upon the multitudes and saw them as sheep without a shepherd, this one who took the separated and united them, who healed the sick, who uplifted the broken, who gave himself in the service of others—in the moment when he needed service, found none.

Peter went on to become the prince of apostles. James went on to become leader of the church in Jerusalem. John went on to write that great vision which is the book of Revelation which was our Scriptures close. But no one of these men has ever been able to say that at the moment when Jesus needed them the most, they were there. And they never had such an opportunity again.

Don't miss the tide which gives you the opportunity to serve the Jesus in others. You know as well as I that before this same date roles around next year, some we know will no longer be with us. They will have either gone from this earth or moved far beyond where we can reach them. Perhaps there is on your mind right now someone to whom you ought to speak: a word of encouragement you should bring, a word of reproof, a word of witness, a word of apology. Don't miss the opportunity when it is yours. Don't forsake the tide which might be flowing in your heart of hearts at this very moment. Claim this day, for in very truth, there will never be another one like it.

Two summers ago I received a telephone call from my physician, who also happened to be the physician of my most beloved seminary professor. He called to tell me that my old prof, who had been retired for many years—he was in his eighty-sixth year at that time—had been taken to the hospital and that he would not be coming home from the hospital. I said to the doctor, "Is Prof's death imminent? Will it be today or tomorrow?"

"Oh," he said, "I doubt it. But it won't be too long. And he won't be coming home."

I had a commitment for that night which I had scheduled almost two years in advance, but I broke that commitment in order to go to the hospital. When I walked into the hospital room, I found my old professor with another of his former students whom I knew well sitting beside him. As I came to the door, he looked at me and said, "Thielemann, old chap, you've come to help me die."

I said, "No, Prof, I'm sure you can do that by yourself."

We began to talk and to share, and he decided he would like to confess his sins. He said things like, "I taught you boys too much theology. I should have taught you more about Jesus. I'm taking my final examinations, and I find I wouldn't even be able to write my name on the paper were it not for my Savior." And he talked about his love for his wife.

As he talked he moved a bit on the bed, and I went over at one point to move him back to his pillows again. I remember I was astonished at how little he weighed. There was so little of the body left, and yet that great spirit was still sparkling. At last he said, "Boys, I think I'm going to go to sleep now. And I don't think you should wait, because it may be a very, very long sleep."

As he said that, he reached out and took the nurse's hand. And I said to him, "Prof, I don't think you ought to hold that nurse's hand."

"Why?"

"Because if you're going to go now, I have a feeling you're going to go like Elijah in a fiery chariot, and I don't want her to be singed!"

He said, "If I'm going to go that way, then I'm going to take her with me!" He fell asleep holding her hand, and the tides came and took him away.

But I was there, and no one will ever be able to take that from me. I was there.

The greatest message any minister can bring to a pulpit is the message that addresses the human soul. I have spoken to you of growth in character, a growth as a child of God, and of growth in the service of Jesus. All of these are matters of the soul. I have held Jesus before you as example, as opportunity, and as need.

Please don't say anything to me about *tomorrow. Tomorrow* is the word the Bible does not know. If you can find me any place in the Scriptures where the Holy Spirit of God says tomorrow, I will step down from this pulpit and never step into it or any other pulpit for as long as I live.

The Holy Spirit's word is the word today. "Now is the accepted time; now is the day of salvation." "Today, if you will harden not your heart and hear my voice. . . ."

Don't say tomorrow. "Tomorrow and tomorrow and tomorrow creeps in this petty pace from day to day . . . and lights fools the way to dusty death."

The word is *today.* Come to Christ today. Grow in Christ today. Serve in the name and in the spirit of Christ today. Ride the tides while they are yours.

Amen.

—Bruce Thielemann

[3179 words]
[32 minutes]

Sermon 114

Date: Sixth Sunday of Easter, Year C

Texts: (NCL)
Acts 15:1–2, 22–29
Psalm 67
Revelation 21:10, 22–27
John 14:23–29

Theme: Jesus gives us peace, enabling us to endure and to make a difference.
Subject: Peace

Title: The Real Peace

Jesus is preparing to say good-bye to the disciples. What he says seems so simple and yet it is difficult to comprehend his actual meaning.

Jesus says those powerful words:

Peace I leave with you; my peace I give to you not as the world gives do I give to you. Let not your hearts be troubled, neither let them be afraid.

The Peace of God

The core of John's Gospel for this lectionary reading is that Jesus gives to the apostles, and to us, a gift. The gift is peace, not the type of peace that the world knows of, but the peace of the Father. Not a peace that means "the absence of trouble." The peace of the world is a peace of escape, an avoidance of trouble, a peace that comes from refusing to face things.

In this sanctuary today, all of our lives are defined by pain more than anything else. The life of Jesus on this earth, God's very own son among us, does not strike me as a life of peace. The more we commit ourselves to following in the moccasins of our brother Jesus, the more we commit ourselves in being Christians, the more pain we are going to see because we are more sensitive to those around us who are in pain.

What Jesus is giving to us is a peace of confrontation, a peace of different values, a peace that may even involve death on the cross. His vision of peace might call us to advocate for the nameless and strangers in our midst. He said that no experience of life can ever take this kind of peace from us. No sorrow, no danger, no suffering. It is independent of outward circumstances. It has an existence of its own.

The Jerusalem Council, reported in Acts 15, was an historical event that showed us how the Church was getting bogged down with its own internal issues. At the time of the council the church was only fourteen years old. Fortunately, it was also an experience of individuals who knew Jesus' type of peace. Paul, Barnabas, James, and Peter were all at this council and all stood up for what they believed. They were willing to confront others with their understanding of what the Body of Christ meant. Theirs was a peace from knowing who they were and having the courage to stand up for who they were. This was the peace that Jesus was giving us.

A contemporary example of this type of peace comes to mind. The Catholic Saint Archbishop Oscar Romero of El Salvador is a contemporary martyr whom many people say has been the closest to that of a modern-day Jesus of any person.

A Man of Peace

Oscar Romero was born in 1917 in a very poor family of eight children. At the age of ten he was an apprentice to a local carpenter. He was very devoted to pious traditional dogmatic Catholicism, and at age thirteen he went off to seminary and priesthood.

At first he was a very unassuming, retiring priest, without much hope for a future in the church hierarchy, and he was assigned to a backwoods, hole-in-the-wall town. But he was reassigned to the capital city by the bishop. And there he rose to importance, because he was such a noted traditionalist. He felt Vatican II was too worldly for his theology, and he was against it. He was never controversial; he was always pious and spiritual. He was primarily a ceremonial person dealing only with the rich and having little to do with the poor. He said, and I quote, "If you cultivate the friendship of the rich, eventually you'll be able to help the poor." The old trickle-down theory. In 1970, already six years after Vatican II, he took over the archdiocese's newspaper, to promote his anti-Vatican II values. He went after Protestants, substance abusers, and pornographers. I'm not sure in what order.

In 1977, Oscar Romero was made archbishop of San Salvador. Needless to say, this greatly dismayed the progressives. He persecuted those priests who supported Vatican II. He was a persecutor of the church just like St. Paul.

Only nine weeks after he was made Archbishop, a large demonstration took place in San Salvador against the death squads, led by one of the archbishop's priests, Father Luna. More than one hundred people were killed by the military. For the first time, Oscar Romero began to wonder about what was happening. Two weeks later, Father Grande, a young inspired priest and a close friend of Romero, was tortured and killed by soldiers who placed his beaten body on the altar. The bishop saw in this priest the (transtigmata), the Body of Jesus. He picked up the body of his friend and cradled it in his arms and walked across the town square. In front of all who were gathered, he promised God that he would from then on pattern his ministry after Father Grande.

He closed all churches and schools for the funeral so that everybody could come. Fifty thousand people attended, and his homily was broadcast by the Catholic radio station. During this sermon, Romero excommunicated the killers.

From then on, the archbishop changed the whole style of the mass and had it broadcast each Sunday by the Catholic radio station. People from labor, the universities, and the women's movement participated in the services. His sermons became the center of attention for the news media, since there were no opposition newspapers. His voice was the only significant voice of any importance that contradicted what the repressive military was doing.

This put the archbishop's life on the line, and he and everyone knew it. A friend and professor of mine, Jorge Lara-Braud, traveled from New York City as a representative for the National Council of Churches to talk with the archbishop to see if assistance could be provided. He discovered that things were becoming very violent. One day in November of 1979 the death squads gunned down twenty-five civilians. Romero felt that he had to lead the demonstration against these killers. He said in regards to the danger he was being exposed to, and I quote him, "a shepherd does not seek the protection that the sheep do not have. I shall rise again in the Salvadoran people."

Jorge also discovered that the archbishop was everything that the peace of the living Jesus and the risen Christ was and is all about, as we know from John 14. He knew what he believed in. He knew the righteousness of his cause. He knew that he had to commit himself without qualification to his people as their shepherd. My friend commented a number of times how the archbishop was so completely at peace with himself—not worried, not anxious, and knowing that he would be resurrected, as we all will be.

By 1980, three years after he was installed as archbishop, everything was unraveling. During the next three years, it is said that the lights went out in El Salvador. Over thirty thousand nonmilitary, noncombatant civilians died violently at the hands of institutionalized killers.

On March 23, 1980, in his radio broadcast, Oscar Romero said to the military, "Do not obey your orders . . . to kill your brothers and sisters. In the name of God, stop!" With this, the archbishop signed his death warrant.

The next day he was conducting a funeral for the mother of a friend. In his sermon, Archbishop Oscar Romero said: "God's reign is already present in our earth in mystery. When the Lord comes, it will be brought to perfection. That is the hope that inspires Christians. We know that every effort to better society, especially injustice and sin are so ingrained, is an effort that God blesses, and God wants, that God demands of us." He was preaching from John 12 about the grain of wheat. He said, and I quote again, "We give ourselves in service out of love for Christ. We will live like the grain."

He was holding the chalice up as he said, "The Blood of Christ, the New Covenant." At that moment a bullet tore through his body and he fell dead upon the altar. The nun who was with him said, "his body broken, and his body drained."

But Oscar Romero lives on. Today, in the fields of El Salvador, when the rolls are called, they call out in reply, "Oscar Romero is here, Oscar Romero presente."

The Peace of Courage

The peace that Jesus left us, the peace that he gives us now, in the body of this Christ, is not a peace that this world knows. This is not a peace where one runs away from responsibility and hides in the closet of one's job or the womb of business and accumulated belongings or, perhaps, the womb of being too spiritual. The peace of Christ is the peace of Oscar Romero, the peace of courage, of willingness to see and act on the truth. The path Christ calls us to is worth the risk. This peace is the reality to embrace hope and resurrection, and know it is a risk worth taking.

One of the incredible things that finally hit me about this passage in John, when Jesus says, "My Peace I give to you and my Peace I leave with you," is that I kept trying to hear this in a way that would make me feel good, protected and secure. However, when I was reading the commentary of William Barclay, he said that Jesus was leaving a peace that could only be arrived at through giving up security for commitment and confrontation. As I thought this through, I said, "Yes." Jesus certainly didn't live a peaceful and secure life on this earth. But he had peace inside of himself, because he was about his Father's business. That is the highest and finest level of peace there is.

Christ's peace is our willingness to see the reality of this world, and to yet have the strength and the commitment to see ourselves within this reality.

More than anything else Christ's peace is that Christian word "hope." We have Christ's peace when we have the hope of who the living Jesus was and the risen Christ is now in our lives. The word "hope" from its Greek origin, means to endure, and that's what we do with the strength of Christ's peace in our life, we endure as the terminally ill patient endures, and through the endurance see the presence of Christ.

"Peace I leave with you: my Peace I give to you, not as the world gives do I give to you."

Oscar Romero Presente.

Amen.

—John Bury

[1745 words]
[17 minutes]

Sermon 115

Date: Any Sunday

Text:
Luke 5:27–39

Theme: Change is unavoidable. How change is dealt with makes all the difference in the world.
Subject: Change, renewal

Title: No Whine Before Its Time

Tip

In next to final paragraph, use a local illustration, for example, a restaurant or other well-known business of many years' standing that has recently closed its doors.

"You have to change," Jesus said. "You have arrived at your turning point." Nobody liked it much when he said that. But he said it again and again. He often used the word "repentance" (metanoia) to get his idea across.

"The time has come," he said. "The kingdom of God is near. Repent and believe the good news!" (Mark 1:15) ". . . unless you repent, you . . . will all perish." (Luke 13:3) He made it as simple as simple could be: change or else. Don't just think about changing. Don't just feel sorry for the way you are. Don't just sit there content with yourself. Turn your life around—now.

Jesus had little patience with self-satisfied people. He didn't like to hear "We've never done it that way before" or "We've always done it this way." He taught, "I have not come to call the righteous, but sinners to repentance." (Luke 5:32) When he found people who were ready, willing, and able to change, it delighted his heart. He said, "I tell you . . . there will be more rejoicing in heaven over one sinner who repents than over ninety-nine righteous persons who do not need to repent." (Luke 15:7)

When he left us, he gave us the job of changing and encouraging others to do the same. "Your responsibility," he said to the early church, "is to preach repentance in my name to all nations, beginning at Jerusalem." (Luke 24:47 paraphrased) "Change!" those early Christians proclaimed. "Stop loving yourselves and start loving God and your fellow human beings." They preached about a God who insisted, "Don't just tell me you love me. Show me." As the Apostle Paul explained his mission to King Agrippa: "First to those in Damascus, then to those in Jerusalem and in all Judea, and to the Gentiles also, I preached that they should repent and turn to God and prove their repentance *by their deeds*." (Acts 26:20)

The Turning Point of the Merchant of Death

I stumbled across a story of one person who came to a turning point and decided to change:

> A number of years ago a man picked up the morning paper, and, to his horror, read his own obituary. The newspaper had reported the death of the wrong man. The caption read: "Dynamite king dies." The story identified him as a "merchant of death." He

> was the inventor of dynamite and he had amassed a great fortune from the manufacture of weapons of destruction. Moved by this disturbing experience, he radically changed his commitment to life. A healing power greater than the destructive force of dynamite came over him. It was his hour of Pentecost. Thereafter, he devoted his full energy and money to works of peace and human betterment. Today he is best remembered as the founder of the Nobel Peace Prize—Alfred Nobel.[1]

Churches come to turning points, too. They go through cycles of change. They are born in response to challenges. They grow, mature, decline, and sometimes die. They can dissipate their resources, or like Alfred Nobel, they can devote their full energy and money to works of peace and human betterment.

At heart, we are all like Charlie Brown's sister. One day little Sally is frantic. She complains to her brother, "I'm doomed! I have to write a report on rivers and it's due next week, and I just know I'll get a failing grade!" Charlie Brown says, "Well, why don't you work real hard and turn in the best report that you can possibly write?" She looks at him in amazement and says, "You know, that never even occurred to me!" Whether change is thrust upon us or we initiate it ourselves, change is hard work. It requires our deliberate intentions and our best efforts.

Change for the better requires imagination and vision. One of my favorite "Peanuts" cartoon strips shows Linus and Charlie Brown sitting and talking about what they will do when they grow up. Linus says, "When I get big I'm going to be a humble little country doctor. I'll live in the city see, and every morning I'll get up, climb into my sports car and zoom into the country! Then I'll start healing people. I'll heal everybody for miles around!" and he concludes this speech with "I'll be a world famous humble little country doctor."

That's how I'd like the church to which I belong to be known—as the world-famous humble little suburban healing community.

Everything Changes

Life happens. Yesterday fades away and today takes its place. Old friends move away. Children grow up and start families of their own—sometimes around the corner but often hundreds of miles away. Our spouses change. Our relationships change.

Things change—not necessarily for the better or for the worse. They just change.

And how we whine and resist. Our point of view is so narrow, so self-centered. At a college reunion, thirty years after graduation, one man said to another, "See that fellow over there? Well—he's gotten so bald and so fat he didn't even recognize me!"[2]

We take it so personally. The network cancels our favorite television series. The morning news team replaces the weather reporter. The physician who has looked after us for twenty years decides to do something else with his life. We ask, "How can they do this to me?" We feel unsettled, threatened, anxious, maybe even a little depressed.

And just as we get used to the new TV series, the new weather caster, the new physician, things change some more. The boss retires and we don't like the new one nearly as much. Or we retire and don't quite know what to do with ourselves. Or our spouse retires and hovers over us, getting in the way. Or the child who grew up and got married gets divorced and comes back to live with us.

---

[1] Colaianni, James F., *Sunday Sermons Treasury of Illustrations,* Vol. 2 (Pleasantville, NJ: Voicings, 1983), p.430.

[2] *Parables, Etc.,* August 1982, 2.6.

Why can't things stay the same? Why can't they be the way they used to be? And we paint rosy pictures of past glories that never were. We long for the simple, peaceful days of old, conveniently forgetting the tensions and uncertainties of earlier times.

The Face of Change

And then we look in the mirror. We look in the face of the change we fear the most—our own. "You move sixteen tons and what do you get? Another day older and deeper in debt." It's written right there, in the mirror.

I like being older. I just don't like growing older. Let me admit it. I'm just as uncomfortable as the next one when familiar things disappear, when the neighborhood changes, when friends leave my life, when I'm forced to adjust. I'm just as prone as anyone to try to defend my unwillingness to grow and mature by resorting to those tired, canned responses: "We've never done it that way before" or "We've always done it this way." So I try to catch myself and have a good laugh at my own expense.

A young girl watched her mother prepare a ham and notice that her mother cut off the end of the ham before placing it in the baking pan. "Why do you do that?" the child asked. The mother could only say, "That's the way your grandmother always did it." So the little girl asked her grandmother, who responded, "That's the way my mother always did it." Visiting Great-grandmother, the girl asked her the same question. The old woman replied, "All I had was a small pan, so I had to cut off the ends to make it fit."

"We've always done it this way," we insist as though the way we do things was dictated by God. Whenever we catch ourselves saying "We've always done it this way," we should think of the little girl and the truncated ham, and stop for a moment and have a good laugh. It helps.

Our Narrow Confines

Methodist minister Mark Trotter offers an illuminating illustration:

> Years ago the Denver Zoo had a difficult decision to make. They were offered the gift of a beautiful, large polar bear, but the problem was that there was no existing room for the bear. At the time of the gift the Board of Directors was in the middle of a fund-raising campaign to renovate the zoo. They changed the strategy to include a magnificent habitat for the polar bear in their renovation plans.
>
> In the meantime the bear was put in a small, temporary cage. The space was so small that it could only take three steps, turn around and walk three steps back.
>
> Because of unforeseen delays the construction took three years, but its new home was indeed grand: waterfalls, spaciousness, caves. The bear entered its new home, looked around, took three steps, turned around, and took three steps back, turned around.
>
> Trotter observes:
>
> It is a parable of human life. The promise to all of us is that life has infinite possibilities, a vast environment to explore. Yet most of us settle for a routine that narrows our life to the dimensions of a prison.[3]

---

[3] "Minister's Musings," *Outlook,* First United Methodist Church of San Diego, cited in *Parables, Etc.*, June 1987, p. 7.4.

Changes in the Church

Changes, changes. At least, God never changes. We can always count on God. But what are we going to do with the church? Every time we turn around, there is something new to contend with. There are those constant changes to the church service. What's happened to the "thees" and "thous"? Why are we reading that ugly new translation instead of the majestic King James Version? What's become of the beloved old hymns? What's this business about inclusive language? Why can't we refer to God as father?

I heard about a woman who had been a member of her church for twenty-five years. As she walked toward the pastor, who stood waiting at the sanctuary door after the service, it was obvious that she had something on her mind. She exclaimed, "Reverend, if God were alive today He would be shocked at the changes in this church!"[4]

Now we all want the church to grow. We want more young families with more young children. We want more help and more money. We just don't want anything to change. Because fundamentally you and I don't want to change. Change is difficult. Change is painful. Change is confusing. Change is demanding.

Alas, change is inevitable and will happen whether we want it or not. If we resist it, it will sneak up on us like a thief in the night and rob us of everything we have. But if we open our hearts and minds to the new—to new ideas, new people, new opportunities, new leadership, new challenges—change can be invigorating, transforming, and exciting. If we let it, change will come into our hearts and into our church like the reappearance of the long-lost love of our youth.

Whining, gnashing our teeth, fastening on to the present, glorifying the past may soothe our qualms for a moment. But no amount of grumbling can stop the clock. The life and ministry of Jesus was something new and threatening to his peers. The rule of God had broken out in their midst like a measles epidemic but they tried to ignore it or control it. When life or God demands that we change, we can celebrate the possibilities or we can complain.

I know this is a difficult subject. So let's forget about change for a moment. Let's indulge ourselves in clinging to things as they are. Let's get together Friday night and watch "Dallas." What's that, you say? We can't? It's not on any more?

As someone once remarked: "Just when you think you see the whole picture of life clearly; the channel changes."[5] And whether we like it or not, so do we.

Amen.

—LDS

[1947 words]
[20 minutes]

❦ *Sermon 116*

❦ *Date:* Thirteenth Sunday After Pentecost, Year A
Labor Sunday (the day before Labor Day)

Texts:
Exodus 19:1–9
Psalm 114

---

[4] *Christian Leadership Letter* (World Vision), February 1982.

[5] Sheppard, Arnot L., Jr., source unknown.

Romans 12:1–13
Matthew 16:21–28

Theme: Don't be a conformist; be a transformist!
Subject: Conformity, transformation

❦ *Title:* Always Transforming; Never Conforming

"Do not conform any longer to the pattern of this world, but be transformed by the renewing of your mind. Then you will be able to test and approve what God's will is—his good, pleasing and perfect will." (Romans 12:1)

Do not be conformed but rather be transformed—how these words from Paul's letter to the Romans have pursued me throughout my Christian life. When I was a teenager, their meaning was simple. Don't smoke, drink, dance, attend movies, or watch television, and you will be the kind of Christian God wants you to be.

In other words, if you avoid vice, you will be virtuous. In practice, this meant cutting oneself off from good as well as bad—from art as well as from obscenity, from entertainment as well as from pornography, from innocent pleasure as well as from depravity. I once worked for a Christian publication that would not print photographs because pictures of human beings might tempt young people to become models and movie actors.

If you avoid vice, you will be virtuous. Something seemed to be missing from the equation. Couldn't Christians preach the gospel through the arts and the media of communications? Wasn't it possible to sing, dance, paint, write plays, or produce motion pictures to the glory of God? Weren't there many prophetic messages in the arts—condemnations of racism and injustice. Weren't many representations of the human condition the expression of a search for something real, fulfilling, and transcendent? If they were, why should we ignore them? Weren't they preparing the hearts of humankind for the coming of Christ?

The Pattern of the World

I did not want to be conformed to the pattern of the world, but I sensed that unless I entered into dialogue with that pattern, neither I nor it would ever truly be transformed. Alas, the pattern of the world turned out to be more resistant to transformation than I suspected.

Television

Take television for example. As Peter G. Horsfield observes,

> Far from being a neutral communication medium, television in America has become an integrated symbolic world filling the socially functional role demanded of it by its viewers and its advertisers.[1]

---

[1] Horsfield, Peter G., *Religious Television: The American Experience* (New York: Longman, 1984), pp. 47–48.

Television has taken on the role of promulgating the central, dominant myths of our society. According to William Fore, the assistant secretary for communication in the National Council of Churches, these myths include

> The fittest survive.
>
> Happiness consists of limitless material acquisition.
>
> Consumption is inherently good.
>
> Property, wealth, and power are more important than people.
>
> Progress is an inherent good.[2]

Fore maintains, "the whole weight of Christian history, thought and teaching stands diametrically opposed to the media world and its values."

If Fore is right, I am forced back to making a choice: either television or Christ. Or perhaps I am confronted with a more responsible option. I may choose to articulate to others and commit myself to a responsible, humane, human, and, thus, Christian response. Consider, for instance, television's version of responsible sex: he has a condom. The gospel's version of responsible sex: he and she have committed themselves to one another in a relationship of love and trust of which the sexual act is an expression.

Do not be conformed to the pattern of the world. But do more than resist the pattern. Understand it. Respond to it. With appropriate humility, offer an alternative. And be willing to live by it. That is the ministry of every Christian. As biblical scholar Walter Brueggemann insists, our task is "to nurture, nourish, and evoke a consciousness and perception alternative to the consciousness and perception of the dominant culture around us."[3]

The Rich and the Poor

The pattern of the world is ever-increasing disparity between rich and poor. According to a recent report issued by the Washington-based Center on Budget and Policy Priorities,

> The gap between rich and poor widened so much in the 1980s that the richest 1 percent now receive nearly as much of Americans' total income after taxes as the bottom 40 percent.

Ten years ago, the top 1 percent received only half as much. The report says, "the most affluent Americans received large income gains during the '80s, while middle income people gained little and the poor fell behind." "Shifting tax burdens, fueled by tax changes of the 1980s, are also a factor in the changes. . . ." The rich pay a smaller percentage of their income in taxes today than they did ten years ago. Lower-income households pay a larger proportion.[4]

Good-paying jobs in production-industries are disappearing, while poor-paying jobs in retail trade, business, and health service are increasing. "The average real income for families headed by parents under 30 has dropped by 26 percent since 1973," says Assemblyman Tom Bates,

---

[2] Fore, William F., "Mass Media's Mythic World: At Odds with Christian Values," *Christian Century*, January 19, 1977, pp. 34–35.

[3] Brueggemann, Walter, T*he Prophetic Imagination* (Philadelphia: Fortress Press, 1978), p. 13.

[4] "Gap Widens in '80s Between Rich, Poor," *San Jose Mercury News*, July 24, 1990, p. 3F.

co-chair of the California Legislature's Task Force on the Changing Family. Likewise, the Children's Defense Fund notes that "earnings for young families with children" are "at sharply reduced levels. . . . Families with children headed by persons under age 30 virtually have been severed from the national economy. Nearly 36 out of every 100 children living in young families lived in poverty in 1987, nearly a 50% increase since 1979."[5] "At the same time," comments The Washington Spectator, the publication of The Public Concern Foundation, "the young poor are shown dazzling pictures of affluence on television and know that they can never reach it. They are easy marks for crack."[6]

The response of the gospel is the call for responsible stewardship. The response of the gospel is the call for equal economic opportunity, for a sharing of wealth that expresses compassion. The response of the gospel is the call for a moral revolution, the declaration that people are more important than possessions, that unless our society works in the most basic dollar-and-cents terms for everyone, it works for no one. As the King of Id complains in a recent cartoon strip: "There is only one drawback in keeping the peasants so poor. . . . It puts the castle in the middle of a ghetto."[7] In practical terms, the gospel would have us attack homelessness by sharing our homes, by empowering the poor to build and buy homes of their own, perhaps even by showing our willingness to pay a more equitable share of the costs of our society through a more equitable tax structure.

Isolation

The pattern of the world is isolation. Hour by hour, we shut others out of our lives. We become too busy. We move away. We divorce ourselves from them. We buy and rely on the gadgets of alienation. We transact our banking with ATMs instead of bank tellers. We allow our telephone answering machines to converse on our behalf. We "network" through our personal computers rather than face to face. Our garage door openers enable us to disappear into our homes without ever seeing or being seen by our neighbors.

The pattern of the world is isolation. The message of the gospel is community and mutual concern. The church is more than a spiritual filling station where the lonely and harassed find momentary comfort so they may return to their loneliness and harassment. In opposition to all isolation, it is a community.

The Death of the Family

The pattern of the world is the destruction of the family. Notes journalist Joanne Jacobs, "There are more working mothers, more single-parent families, more yours-mine-and-ours families, more poor children, more elderly and very elderly households, and a lot more stress."[8] She adds:

> it's pretty obvious that we're not going back to what's called the Ozzie and Harriet family. We don't know how to make young people marry before they have children,

---

[5] Cited in *The Washington Spectator*, November 15, 1989, p. 3.

[6] *The Washington Spectator*, p. 3.

[7] Hart, Johnny, "The Wizard of Id," August 10, 1990.

[8] Jacobs, Joanne, "Design Laws to Catch Up with Families of the '90s," *San Jose Mercury News*, August 17, 1989, p. 7B.

> or to stay together. I don't think we can raise the incomes of young men high enough to make it feasible for most women to be full-time homemakers and mothers.
>
> We can adapt some of our laws, regulations, business practices, health and retirement benefits, communities and traditions to deal with the varied families of the '90s instead of the hallowed myth of the '50s.
>
> June Cleaver doesn't live here anymore.

The problem is that when government—local, state, or federal—becomes aware of family problems it tends to respond with programs that serve only to weaken the family further. We are all familiar with the self-perpetuating nature of welfare. Just how far are we willing to entrust the future of the family to government? As Jacobs cautions: "There is a delicate balance between supporting families' ability to do their job, and taking over their job."

The pattern of the world is ignore, replace, or destroy the family. The message of the gospel is enhance, support, and sustain the family. The message of the gospel is: critically examine all assumptions about the shape of the family in the 1990s. Look for the real needs and find out how to step in and respond to them. If working mothers are the weak link, then the mainline Protestant churches with their graying population should step in as adoptive grandparents, surrogate parents, assistant parents, and caregivers. A senior citizen committed to the life of an overwhelmed working mother and her children can effect more good and prevent more harm than a legion of government programs.[9]

Too Busy

The pattern of the world is "so much to do and so little time to do it." In the words of writer Anna Kolson:

> In the last several months, the media have proclaimed a severe "time famine." They have called workaholism the disease of the '80s and have declared time the precious commodity of the '90s (surpassing money).
>
> It feels as if we're busier than ever. We think we're busier than ever. But are we?[10]

A Harris poll finds that between 1973 and 1984 the amount of leisure time for Americans shrank by 32 percent to eighteen hours a week. Harris claims that during the same period the average workweek increased from just over forty hours to nearly forty-seven hours. Since Harris polls are based on questionnaires, we could say this is what Americans think or claim.

When social scientists examine the actual time records kept by Americans, a different picture arises. By studying time diaries, sociologist John F. Robinson came to the conclusion that spare time is actually on the rise. Men report that they have exactly the same amount of leisure time today—forty hours a week—as they reported in 1965. Women report that they now have thirty hours of free time a week, five more than they did in 1965.

---

[9] Ibid.

[10] Kolson, Anna, "People Feel Busier, But Experts Say We Have More Time," *San Jose Mercury News*, October 31, 1989, p. 2E.

Whether or not the number of free hours has increased or decreased, the common perception is that the pace of life has increased substantially. For today's two-income families, life has become a scheduling nightmare. Many experience the lack of time as a greater privation than lack of money.

Our lives are screaming: "I'm running as fast as I can. I'm running faster than I ever have. Yet I can't keep up." Kolson comments:

> Fax machines, overnight mail, computers, car phones, microwave ovens make life faster, faster, faster. The idea of instant gratification is almost a reality. But much of the frenzy, the pressure, may be self-imposed.

Having enough time, not being too busy, seems positively unAmerican.

We work so we may have time for leisure. But leisure has become highly suspect. Vacations become marathon races against the clock. Retirement is experienced as more grueling than one's preretirement career. Notes Kolson, "Americans like to boast of not having enough time. Even retired people think they have less free time. They told Harris pollsters they had only about one more hour daily of leisure than working people." But no matter how much time they have, it is not enough. Their leisure is not very leisurely; it is undetaken the same way they pursued their work: with a vengeance.

Arranging one's life so there is never enough time has become a major addiction of the 1990s. And while it is not nearly as deadly as substance abuse, its effects on our lives are every bit as catastrophic. For busyness addiction causes us to swap what is really of value in life—aesthetic enjoyment, creative achievement, the comfort of longterm personal and family relationships, and peace of mind—for the moment by moment need to be doing something.

The message of the gospel is busyness addiction is bunk. To be or not to be—that is the question. To be too busy or not too busy—that is your decision—and mine.

In the newspaper comic strip, "For Better or For Worse" by Lynn Johnson, Ellie, the central character, a middle-aged, suburban, wife and mother is shown sitting on the living room sofa in her bathrobe, a mug of coffee in her hand, Farley, the family dog nestled in her lap. She asks the dog: "Why aren't people content with what they have, Farl? Why do we always want more? Why, when we have everything we need, do we still want the biggest, the best, the loudest, the fastest, the most exciting. . . .? Why do people throw away something perfectly good—for the sake of something new?" She concludes: "If money isn't the root of all evil . . . maybe insecurity is."[11]

Ellie has discovered the pattern of the world. While Farley snoozes in her lap, she is on her way to deciding for herself whether or not she will be conformed to it.

The real-life Ellie, cartoonist Lynn Johnson, is a divorced, single parent. The fictional Ellie is committed to her dentist-husband and family. Her struggles as woman, wife, and parent encourage millions of readers. This person has been transformed. And through her, so are we.

Here's what the Christian life is all about: finding the gap between the way things are and the way they ought to be and throwing oneself across the gap; discerning the pattern of the world, and altering it—never conforming, always transforming.

And so it goes.

Amen.

—LDS

[2200 words]
[22 minutes]

---

[11] Johnson, Lynn, "For Better or For Worse," January 24, 1990.

Sermon 117

Date: Sunday Between November 13 and November 19 inclusive, Year A

Texts:
Zephaniah 1:7,12–18
Psalm 76
1 Thessalonians 5:1–11
Matthew 25:14–30

Theme: Jesus had a radical notion: the present depends on the future. The quality of our life today depends on our vision of the future.
Subject: Dream, vision

Title: Savers Weepers, Losers Keepers

The kingdom of God is like the demanding, self-made CEO who was about to go to Hong Kong to build a new factory. Before leaving he called in his three top VPs and asked them to manage eight million dollars from the company retirement plan.

To the VP in charge of product development, whose division was having a wonderful year, he gave five million dollars.

To the VP in charge of marketing, whose division was having a good year, he gave two million dollars.

To the VP in charge of budget management, whose division was having a safe and sane normal year, he gave one million dollars.

And then the CEO hopped on the corporate jet and was gone.

The first VP bought several small companies with promising, innovative technologies. A few of them yielded nothing profitable, but two were real winners. Within a year, their products netted ten million dollars.

The second VP increased the company's advertising and promotion budget by two million dollars. Sales increased by ten million dollars. The company netted four million.

The third VP worried a lot and tried to cover his backside. He thought about investing his million in the stock market, but was afraid of the risks of a volatile market. He thought about buying real estate, but felt that the timing was wrong. He considered gold and silver, but who could predict what they might be worth in the future?

He talked to a number of investment experts and got contradictory recommendations. He consulted astrologers, numerologists, and phrenologists, but he found their advice ambiguous. He thought of putting the money in CDs, but the banks and S&Ls were so shaky. He came to the conclusion that the best course was no course. So he carefully documented all his research in a three-hundred-page memorandum. Meanwhile the boss's cashier's check for a million sat safe and secure in the company vault.

By the time the CEO got back, there was a recession. Things weren't going so well for the company. The new products people were spending more than they were earning. Sales were flat. There were layoffs and lawsuits. The third VP heaved a sigh of relief. No risks had meant no losses.

Then the boss sent for him.

The third VP knew there was something wrong the minute he walked into the boss's office. The boss's breathing was heavy. His face was red. His eyebrows arched ominously. The first and second VPs sat quietly on chairs in front of the boss's desk. An empty chair waited for the third VP.

The prudent VP extended the cashier's check to the boss, expecting that it would change the CEO's mood. Surely the boss was mad at the risk-takers who had lost his seven million dollars.

"What's this?" asked the boss gruffly.

"It's your million dollars," the VP replied.

"If I had wanted to keep a million idle dollars safe and secure, I could have kept the check in my wallet!" he scoffed.

"But I took no chances," the VP said in his own defense.

The boss took the check and gave it to the first VP, saying, "I know that things will turn around soon. They always do. Keep up the good work. I didn't build up this company by avoiding risks."

The third VP is now a part-time tax preparer for H&R Block.

Thankful for Investors

There are two kinds of evil: the evil of the wrong decision and the evil of indecision. Doing the wrong thing is never as bad as doing nothing at all. When it comes to what to do with one's life, investing is always better than saving.

We are thankful this morning for our brothers and sisters who have chosen to invest rather than save. They have invested their time, talents, and treasure in this church. We are thankful for those who have made commitments of hours and dollars and have honored those commitments, year after year. We are thankful for those who do the work of this church, quietly and steadfastly, unheralded and often unacknowledged.

We are thankful for an abundance of talents in our midst. For singers and painters and planners and cooks and teachers and conveners and chairpersons and caregivers and newsletter editors and flower arrangers and neateners and fixers and menders and leaf rakers and weed pullers and blossom planters and balancers of checkbooks and tenders of budgets. We are thankful for those who pray and teach us to pray, those who stimulate our minds, those who prod our consciences, and those who set an example of faithfulness and piety.

We are thankful for those who weep with us when we mourn and rejoice with us when we are joyful.

But most of all, we are thankful for those who have a vision of the future and will risk themselves—their time, their abilities, their financial support here and now.

The Need for a Hopeful Future

The third VP believed that if he took care of the present the future would take care of itself. He believed that the future depends on the present.

But Jesus had a radical notion. The present, he taught, depends on the future. The quality of our life today depends on our vision of the future. Whether we experience life as frightening or exciting, whether we worry or rejoice, whether we feel purposeful or bored, depends on our image of the future. A depressed person is one who lacks a hopeful vision of the future. An anxious persons is one without faith in tomorrow. A selfish person is one who cannot see beyond his or her here and now.

Churches are like people. If they attempt to save their lives by keeping things exactly as they have always been, they will lose them. As it is written in the Book of Proverbs: "Where there is no vision, the people perish." (Proverbs 29:18 KJV) Speaking of the death of a friend and fellow prisoner in a Nazi concentration camp, Viktor Frankl recalls:

> The prisoner who lost faith in the future—his future—was doomed. With his loss of belief in the future, he also lost his spiritual hold; he let himself decline and became subject to mental and physical decay. . . . Those who know how close the connection is between the state of a man—his courage and hope, or lack of them—and the state of immunity of his body will understand that the sudden loss of hope and courage can have a deadly effect.[1]

Frankl's friend had believed he would be liberated from the death camp by March 30, 1945—a dream had told him so. When March 30 came and went, his vision of the future was thwarted. His body was found the next morning. Frankl's friend had lost hold on the future and with it he had lost his life. Frankl comments: "The ultimate cause of my friends's death was . . . [that] he was severely disappointed."

Some visions of the future are so powerful that their very declaration transforms the present. Martin Luther King, Jr., had such a vision. He declared:

> I have a dream that one day this nation will rise up and live out the true meaning of its creed: "We hold these truths to be self-evident—that all men are created equal." I have a dream that one day on the red hills of Georgia the sons of former slaves and the sons of former slaveowners will be able to sit down together at the table of brotherhood. . . . I have a dream that my four little children will one day live in a nation where they will not be judged by the color of their skin but by the content of their character.

And we are still being transformed by his vision.

Do we have a transforming dream? Can we see a future that is so overwhelmingly beautiful, compelling, and irresistible that it forcefully lures us to itself? Can we declare the future with such conviction that our dream will transform itself into reality? Can we allow ourselves the courage to be overcome by our vision? In the words of George Bernard Shaw,

> You see things [as they are]; and you say, "Why?" But I dream things that never were; and I say, "Why not?"[2]

Amen.

—LDS

[1300 words]
[13 minutes]

---

[1] Frankl, Viktor, *Man's Search for Meaning: An Introduction to Logotherapy* (Boston: Beacon Press, 1959), pp. 74–75.

[2] Shaw, George Bernard, *Back to Methuselah* (1921), pt. 1, act I.

❦ *Sermon 118*

❦ *Date:* First Sunday in Lent, Year A

Texts:
Genesis 2:4b–9, 15–17, 25:3–7
Psalm 130
Romans 5:12–19
Matthew 4:1–11

or Second Sunday After Pentecost, Year A

Texts:
Genesis 28:10–17
Psalm 91:1–10
Romans 5:12–19
Matthew 10:24–33

or Fourth Sunday in Lent, Year B

Texts:
2 Chronicles 36:14–23
Psalm 137:1–6
Ephesians 2:4–10
John 3:14–21

Theme: God's amazing grace bestows life, meaning, purpose, and direction.
Subject: Grace

❦ *Title:* Amazing Grace—But No Free Lunch

In the parish cemetery in Olney, England, a granite tombstone reads: "John Newton, clerk, once an infidel and Libertine, a servant of slavers in Africa, was, by the rich mercy of our Lord and Savior Jesus Christ, preserved, restored, pardoned, and appointed to preach the Faith he had long labored to destroy."

Beginning at age eleven, John Newton sailed on many ships. In addition, he captured slaves on the West African coast for sale to traders. Eventually he became captain of his own slave ship, providing slaves to the plantations of the West Indies and America.

On March 10, 1748, while returning to England from Africa, Newton's vessel was beset by recurrent storms that threatened to sink ship and crew. In the midst of waves and gales, Newton began reading Thomas a Kempis's devotional classic, The Imitation of Christ. The peace he found on the tempest-tossed sea would eventually lead him away from the slave trade and to the ministry of the Church of England. In fact, he would become one of the major voices of antislave agitation in the British Empire.

Newton was a popular minister who held public services in any structure which could be obtained for the purpose—an innovative approach for an Anglican priest. When the available supply of hymns proved inadequate for his purposes, he and his friend, William Cowper, produced Olney Hymns, which contained 272 lyrics by Newton and 67 by Cowper.

The song that we know as "Amazing Grace" was originally named "Faith's Review and Expectation." Newton's lyrics were inspired by 1 Chronicles 17:16–17: "Then King David went in and sat before the LORD, and he said: 'Who am I, O LORD God, and what is my family, that you have brought me this far? And as if this were not enough in your sight, O God, you have spoken about the future of the house of your servant. You have looked on me as though I were the most exalted of men, O LORD God.'" The tune is an early American folk song, a plantation melody.

What is the "amazing grace" which the song exalts? Can we find in our own lives in 199__ what the "infidel and libertine," John Newton experienced in 1748? Or turning to our Scripture passages for today, are the same resources available to us in our daily lives as those which enabled Jesus to resist temptation and triumph over evil? As mainstream Protestants, can we retrieve for ourselves a heritage that seems to have gone by default to the pietists and fundamentalists?

The texts for today oppress us with their remarkable unity. They speak to us of Adam and Jesus, of fallen humanity and redeemed humanity, of death and life, of unfaithfulness and obedience. The lessons for this day harass us with "the 's' word"—SIN—a word with which we middle-of-the-road Protestants are not quite comfortable. At one moment, we are in the Garden of Eden, awash in the myth of the fall of humankind. In the next moment, we are in the wilderness, sharing with Jesus in the experience of testing. Finally, we are with Paul the theologian as he writes to the Corinthians of the cosmic drama—the juxtaposition of man's rebellion against his own true nature with God's intervention. In the words of Robert Hughes, "At the start of the Lenten journey, from the peak of temptation, we see back to the garden and ahead to the cross."

Four themes stand out in these familiar texts: (1) the abuse of freedom, (2) the abdication of responsibility, (3) the attribution of blame, and (4) the acceptance of God's gift.

The Abuse of Freedom

What does the Garden of Eden mean to us? We look at the familiar pattern: freedom, restriction, transgression, and consequences. We know all too well that here is the pattern we repeat every day of our lives.

We read that "the LORD God formed the man from the dust of the ground and breathed into his nostrils the breath of life, and the man became a living being." The breath of God gives us life, gives us meaning, gives us purpose, gives us direction. But we, like Adam, the earth creature, and his mate want more—more knowledge, more power, more pleasure, more control—more, more, more. We want to be as God. We want to get what we want when we want it "without cost or obligation." We not only want a free lunch—we want free breakfast, free dinner, free dessert (several times a day), free between-meal snacks—all with no regrets and no consequences. And life tells us again and again that the lunch is not free and that it may even be harmful to our health! But we pay no attention. And therein lies the abuse of freedom.

The Abdication of Responsibility

The breath of God led Jesus into the wilderness to be tested, to face temptation. And the breath of God howls across the wilderness of our existence—unsettling, reproving, thundering, accusing. "What have you done to my Garden?" God demands. What have you done to the world over which I gave you dominion? What have you done to the comforts of family and home? What have you done with the mate I gave you to shelter you from loneliness?

We dodge responsibility. We insist on defining life in our own terms. We act as though the rules apply to everyone but us. We make excuses. But life keeps presenting us with a bill for the damages. Finally each of us is forced to admit, "I messed up, OK?" We offer excuses. We make ourselves too busy to deal with the problems we have caused. We deny that there are any problems. We hire professionals to be human beings in our stead. In sum, we offer excuses instead of repentance. We abdicate our responsibility instead of cleaning up our messes.

The Attribution of Blame

"But it's not my fault!" each of us insists. Adam, the earth creature, our progenitor, first copped that plea: "The Woman you gave me, she made me break the rules. It's not my fault!"

So we blame others. After all, we rationalize, there is always a snake in the grass—the serpent in Eden, the devil in the wilderness. "It's not my fault that my life, my world, my family are in such a mess. I'm only human."

"The woman is to blame," said the first man. "The devil made me do it!" added the first woman. The story is told of an unloving and unloved man who died after willing his farm to the devil. The next of kin sued to have the will voided on the ground that this was a case in which the will of the deceased could not be carried out. After much legal research and judicial pondering, the court decision read as follows: "It is decided that every effort should be made to carry out the deceased's wish. And the best way to carry out the wish of the deceased is to allow the farm to grow weeds, and the soil to erode, and the well to run dry, and the house and barn and fences to rot. In the opinion of the court, the best way to leave something to the devil is to do nothing."

The breath of God whispers to us in a still, small voice—reminding us that we have done those things we ought not to have done and have left undone those things we ought to have done. Our own guilty conscience echoes in agreement. So we find some one (our parents, our spouse) or something (our job, our allergies, our horoscope) to blame.

The Acceptance of God's Gift

I said before that the pattern is freedom, restriction, transgression, and consequences. I left off "the rest of the story." The pattern is freedom, restriction, transgression, consequences, and *grace*.

The breath of God departs from a body on the cross. God has surrendered himself to our state and fate. God does not desert us. When we triumph, God is with us. When we fail, he is there. When we are tempted, convince ourselves that we are above the rules, and learn to our sorrow that we reap what we have sown, he is still with us, offering us forgiveness and a new beginning.

The breath of God's presence is breathed on us as we are given the Holy Spirit by the risen one. God is in us. God is with us.

The breath of God blows as a "mighty wind" on Pentecost, gathering men and women of all nations, gathering all of us today, into the church, and showering us with gifts.

The content of the faith we profess, that in *which* we believe—no matter how tentative and provisional it may be—is a gift. The faith that possesses us, the faith *with which* we believe is a gift. The care and concern of those who love us are gifts. The talents that serve us and hold us together are gifts. Each day we live, each breath we take, each mouthful of food we eat, each sip of water we swallow, each roof that shelters us, each dollar in our pocket—each is a gift.

Even temptation is a gift, offering us the chance to exercise our freedom, to think for ourselves, to choose. This is the most dreadful gift of all! It would be so much easier if God made the decisions for us, if God removed all the risk from our lives. Instead he gives us the opportunity to fall flat on our faces! And the chance to be his partner in the ongoing redemption of the world.

Our freedom has its limits. We try to live as though we hold all the aces, call all the shots, make up the rules as we go along. We try to live as gods in our own worlds, until we bang our noses on the stubborn, unyielding, unforgiving real world. Reality can be harsh. There is no free lunch. Every choice has its consequences and its cost.

God so loved the world, says the Fourth Gospel, that he gave his only son so that we would not have to pick up the tab. John Newton called that "amazing grace." Here then is the meaning of the Lenten season: God's grace is his free gift to us, but, oh, what it cost him!

"Amazing grace—how sweet the sound—That *saved* a wretch like me!" How often I have wanted to argue with Newton, to tell him I am convinced that he got his verb tense wrong. He should have said, "saves" not "saved." Salvation is not something that occurs once for all in a moment of religious ecstasy. God's free gift is at hand, to be received, to save me, to save us , here and now, every minute of every day. But, of course, Newton knew that too. "'Tis grace," he said, "hath brought me safe thus far, And grace will lead me home."

When Jesus was preaching at Capernaum, a centurion came to him, begging for help. "Lord," he said, "my servant lies at home paralyzed and in terrible suffering." Jesus said to him, "I will go and heal him." The centurion replied, "Lord, I do not deserve to have you come under my roof. But just say the word, and my servant will be healed." (Matthew 8:4–8) And each of us says today, "Lord, I do not deserve to have you come under my roof. Just say the word, just breathe on me and I will be healed." And once again, if we but receive, the breath of God bestows life, bestows meaning, bestows purpose, bestows direction. What amazing grace!

Amen.

—LDS

[1900 words]
[19 minutes]

Suggestion: Include "Amazing Grace" as a hymn just after the sermon. John Newton originally wrote six stanzas, at least two of which are usually omitted from modern hymnals. I have included all the verses with which I am familiar. The fourth stanza was written by John P. Rees.

Amazing Grace

Amazing grace—how sweet the sound
That saved a wretch like me!
I once was lost but now am found,
Was blind but now I see.

'Twas grace that taught my heart to fear,
And grace my fears relieved;
How precious did that grace appear
The hour I first believed!

Thru many dangers, toils and snares
I have already come;

'Tis grace hath brought me safe thus far,
And grace will lead me home.

When we've been there ten thousand years,
Bright shining as the sun,
We've no less days to sing God's praise
Than when we'd first begun.

The Lord has promised good to me,
His Word my hope secures,
He will my shield and portion be
as long as life endures.

Yes, when this heart and flesh shall fail,
and mortal life shall cease,
I shall possess within the veil,
a life of joy and peace.

The earth shall soon dissolve like snow,
the sun forbear to shine;
But God, who called me here below,
will be forever mine.

❦ *Sermon 119*

❦ *Date:* Twenty-third Sunday after Pentecost, Year B

Texts:
Jeremiah 31:7–9
Psalm 126
Hebrews 5:1–6
Mark 10:46–52

Theme: There are two kinds of people in the world: Those who are helpless and hopeless—and those who are joyfully hopeful.
Subject: Hope, healing, addiction

❦ *Title:* The Helpless and the Hopeful

"There are two kinds of people in the world: Those who are helpless and hopeless—and those who are joyfully hopeful." Would you agree with that? No? It's too simplistic you say? I agree.

It would be better to say, "There are two kinds of behavior: Behavior which is hopeless and behavior which is hopeful." The truth is that for most of us we move back and forth between these two extremes.

I want to address this morning the tension between helplessness and hopefulness. We can begin with the premise that we have free will—a gift of God which reflects God's own being, God's own unlimited freedom. In our freedom we must inevitably, if we are honest with ourselves, come to recognize two things: (1) We are in one sense helpless—ultimately we do not control our lives. (2) Even though ultimate control is beyond us we must struggle as Christians to take control of our lives and act with Christian moral responsibility.

Today's gospel illustrates for us the tension between helplessness and hopefulness. Jesus and his disciples are heading triumphantly to Jerusalem. The beggar Bartimaeus, who cannot see, hears that Jesus is near and so cries out, "Jesus, Son of David, have mercy on me!" Here is someone who appears helpless—a poor, blind person in the street. Yet even the disciples who rebuke him for some reason can't keep him from his hope of finding healing through Jesus. The helpless has hope, and this faith led to Jesus restoring the beggar's sight. He then becomes a disciple. What a person of hope he must have become! What an admirable role model he is for us today. We have much to learn from this blind beggar, and this gospel if we but open our eyes.

For like the beggar we too—if we are honest with ourselves, must first accept the fact that we are in need of help, that we can't always see what may actually be true, and second, we must overcome the reality of our limitations, and act, behave, move with hopefulness, even if people try to stop us, even if forces or events are in the way, even if one of these forces is part of our very selves.

So Bartimaeus represents for us part of our journey toward God—the realization of our own needs—Bartimaeus knew he was blind—we too have a blindness which keeps us from God's truth. That's why we have a confession as part of this Eucharist. Once we acknowledge our limitations, our real humility, we then move closer to communion with God and a new hopefulness in the presence of Christ, re-presented to us in the Sacrament. It's a paradox of truth. That's why we have a confession as part of this Eucharist. Once we acknowledge our limitation, our real humility, we then move closer to communion with God and a new hopefulness in the presence of Christ, re-presented to us in the Sacrament. It's a paradox of truth. In the tradition of Jesus Christ we die to ourselves so that we may be made new, for God is the great healer.

I want to share with you some stories of God's healing which illuminates both our need to acknowledge our helplessness and our call to allow that realization to free us up and move us towards hopefulness. Three stories from a recent trip:

Two weeks ago I was in my home state of Ohio to be with my family because my brother, Dennis, had begun a thirty-day alcohol and drug treatment program. For fifteen years his way of dealing with life was to do drugs and drink alcohol, and he became addicted to both. After struggling with my family on how best to help him, I went home in celebration of his decision to change and to support him. The time with him and my family were precious moments of healing, for if you know about alcoholism and addiction, you know that it is a disease which affects the whole family in deeply basic ways. Both my grandfathers were seriously sick alcoholics and abusive to my parents, and sitting in a room with my parents and four of my siblings we all realized just how much we all live with the legacy of this disease, even if we aren't abusers ourselves. We all realized, too, that we were both victims of the disease and yet champions of change. My parents had made great progress over the years in changing their own behavior, which had been learned in the presence of such abusive parents. They had been both helpless and hopeful. I was so proud of my family that day—because we were facing unpleasant truth, but we did it in a way which said, "I still love you." The healing of those real wounds—Dennis's and the whole family's, could not have happened if weeks before Dennis had not reached the point of saying, "OK, I'm not in control of my life. I'm helpless." And once in treatment he realized, rationally, that he had a disease, he inherited a disease, and he had learned how to become an addict. This realization was the freeing moment.

As I sat in a room and listened to the residents in treatment for their addictions I heard them say, "I have a disease. I've ruined my life because once I take that first wrong step, that first drink, that first drug, my body won't stop. I'm helpless. Therefore, I must do everything I can not to take that first wrong step. That is my only hope." They are victims, yet they can be champions of change. They are helpless, yet they can be hopeful.

As I sat in that room I realized that I'm no different from them. I'm not an alcoholic. I'm not addicted to drugs. But I don't have ultimate control of my life either. And I have to overcome weakness, and struggle to be hopeful and behave hopefully. I realized that everyone in that room—residents and family and friends—were all in the same boat. We were all helpless to a degree. We need support from others in a community of faith to remain hopeful. And if we think we do not need help from others or God to be hopeful we are fooling ourselves—like an alcoholic who doesn't want to admit his or her addiction even when deep down they know it's true. We all have addictions—it's not a matter of degree—yes, and it may be chocolate—it may be work—it may be peanut butter and jelly sandwiches—but the truth is that to become healthy we must admit who we are. It's no wonder Alcoholics Anonymous is such a spiritual program. For the alcoholic is in one sense a metaphor for all Christian pilgrims. There is a higher power who brings us to power in recognizing our weakness. For us it is Jesus Christ and the Holy Spirit of God.

While I was in Ohio I went to see my former high school English teacher. We were discussing our work with young people, specifically the pressures, when he told me about one of his favorite students—a gifted student and athlete—who went to Annapolis this fall, and eventually jumped out of the window of a fifth story building, killing himself. You may have read about it. Why didn't that teenager know it was OK to feel helpless? Why couldn't he feel any hope?

As I flew home from Ohio I was sitting in my seat and I thought about my time at home, my own life, and decided to write down some notes for this sermon. I know I wanted to talk about the feeling of helplessness. I eventually struck up a conversation with the man next to me—who turned out to be a lieutenant colonel in the Marines, who was also a lawyer who worked in the parole system for the Marines and the Navy. We talked about young people, and alcoholism, and parole, and rehabilitation. When I told him I was an Episcopal priest he said he was Episcopal also; in fact his brother was a priest. He himself was married by Shunji Nishi, a former professor at CDSP, while he was at Bolt Law School in 1966. We eventually came to this talk about healing, and I shared my new sense of the need for true recognition for our helplessness. He proceeded to tell me about coming down with cancer. Melanoma cancer that had spread to his lungs. He lay in bed overnight and couldn't sleep—so he told his wife he was going out running—at 2:00 in the morning. That was his "addiction," he joked. In the course of that run he just stopped and said, "God, it's out of my hands—I'm just gonna give it up to you. I don't know what else to do." He surrendered. I said, "That must have been hard—surrendering as a Marine—that's not something that was in your training was it?" He said, "No it wasn't." But within a week he went back to the doctor and had another X-ray and there was nothing there. No disease. He still has both X-rays. Before and after.

Now even as a minister, when people start talking about physical healing I get a little uncomfortable. My rational mind says, "Slow down." But I believe this man spoke truth. How rational can you get—a lieutenant colonel in the Marines, a lawyer, an Episcopalian—now come on? I imagined meeting St. Peter at the pearly gates and him saying, "Matt, what do we have to do? Come on!"

God is alive and well. I met a Bartimaeus on an airplane. The Holy Spirit empowers us. But we must remember, with Christ as our example, we are empowered through our weakness—a weakness which leads us to compassion. Our compassion for our own helplessness, and for the helplessness of others leads us to hope. Let's let go of all the other addictions and hold on to that compassion.

Amen.

—Matthew McDermott

[1700 words]
[17 minutes]

Sermon 120

Date: First Sunday After Christmas (New Year's Sunday), Any Year

Text:
Psalm 111

Theme: Having a happy New Year depends on our understanding of "happy" and "new."
Subject: New Year

Title: A Seriously Frivolous Happy New Year!

I love Christmas. Well, let's say, I can handle Christmas. Why some years I even have a knack for Christmas.

Maybe I don't always get what I want. Sometimes I get things I don't want. And now and then I have the feeling that Christmas takes advantage of me—I give to it more than I get from it. But on the average I come out way ahead. All my Christmases may not be white, but they certainly are warm.

Now New Year's is another matter. By the time Christmas has come all my enthusiasm (like all my cash) has gone. The week between Christmas and the first of the year is a parenthesis, an afterthought, a vacation for the mind and the heart. Those ghosts of Christmas may have cured Scrooge of his Yuletide bah-humbugs, but an army of New Year's elves cannot make me eager for a second celebration. Couldn't we postpone the New Year until March or April, until I have rested up and all the Christmas bills have been paid?

I don't drink—never have, really. Being religious has nothing to do with it. Some people drink too much. Some drink too little, I guess. And being a minister, I don't get invited to many New Year's Eve parties. There's a prejudice we ministers face. We're all thought of as party poopers.

I was half-invited to a New Year's Eve party once. A friend said he'd like me to meet his fiancee. All of a sudden he slapped his forehead and remarked: "That's right. You don't drink. Well, I suppose I can find you a little holy water." Then he started apologizing to me because he and his group would be having a good time and obviously I wouldn't fit in.

Serious people can actually have a good time—a seriously good time. Sometimes we can even have a frivolously good time. And, wonder of wonders, we have even been known to have a seriously frivolous good time.

It all depends on how one combines the two basic elements of a happy New Year: happy and new.

Americans have a great capacity for being entertained as though happiness were something that you could pay other people to do to you or for you. Americans are tolerant. We say to our children, "You do whatever you want to, dear, just as long as it makes you happy. If it makes you happy, it makes me happy, too." We *say* such things all the time. Maybe we don't *mean* them, but we do say them.

Americans pursue happiness with a vengeance. After all, life, liberty, and the pursuit of happiness are the foundations of the American way of life. It says so in the Declaration of Independence.

But there's the rub. Happiness and *independence* are at best kissing cousins. They are really not as closely related as are happiness and *interdependence.*

There is a simple formula for happiness: "You should do something every day to make other people happy, even if it's only to leave them alone."[1] What we really should be saying to our children is: "Do whatever you want to, as long as it makes others happy—including me." I know it feels strange, but it would be infinitely more honest and definitely truer.

And there is something else we can do. We can take the advice of Abraham Lincoln, who once said, "I have found that most people are about as happy as they make up their minds to be."[2] Here is a revolutionary thought. Other people, things, and circumstance do not make anyone happy or miserable. We do that for ourselves. Were you ever happy when you were poor and struggling? Some of the time or most of the time? Are you happier now that poverty and suffering are behind you? Some of the time or most of the time?

Reginald Thomas, a great Welsh Presbyterian preacher I knew many years ago, became frustrated with a women parishioner who continually faulted his sermons. During one conversation, she lamented, "Dr. Thomas, I just don't get a blessing from your preaching." Losing his patience, Thomas blurted out: "It's a shame you expect your blessings from sermons and not from God!" I might have put it differently, but I know how Reg felt. No minister, not even the greatest, can make anyone happy. That's between each of us and God.

Happiness, you see, isn't a product. It's a by-product. The more you try to find happiness, to acquire happiness, to make yourself happy, the more misery you accumulate. Happiness, I have found, is the natural state of a human being doing what he or she is called to do. As Joseph Campbell advises: "Follow your bliss!" Do what you are best at, what thrills and excites you, what challenges and stretches you, what expands your mind and imagination, and you will never lack happiness.

Need more of a blueprint for happiness? Read the Beatitudes in Matthew 5. If you want to be truly happy, says Jesus, you have to acknowledge the poverty of your spirit and be willing to let God make up for it with his inexhaustible riches. If you want to be truly happy, you have to let yourself be touched by the pain and hurts of others. If you want to be truly happy, you have to insist on justice and be willing to pay the price to make a world that works for everyone. If you want to be truly happy, start being compassionate and merciful. If you want to be truly happy, clean up your own act, take the rafter out of your own eye before you demand that your brother take the speck out of his. If you want to be truly happy, stop insisting on being right and start bringing peace and harmony to others. If you want to be truly happy, decide what counts and commit yourself to it—no matter what it costs.

Well, that should give us all the happiness we can handle in the coming year. Now if we can just get ready for the newness of the new year. We all have a tendency to resist the new, but opposing the new is an exercise in futility. Things change—whether you are ready for them or not. G.K. Chesterton remarked:

> It would seem that if you leave things alone, you leave them as they are. But you do not. If you leave a thing alone, you leave it to a torrent of change. If you leave a white post alone, it will soon be a black post. If you particularly want it to be white, you must be always painting it again. Briefly, if you want the old white post, you must have a new white post. But this which is true even of inanimate things is in a quite special and terrible sense true of human beings. If we want the good old church, we need to risk the good new church; the good old days need to risk the good new days.[3]

---

[1] *Pastor's Story File*, January 1987.

[2] Ibid.

[3] Ibid., January 1989.

As a friend reminds me, "Progress always involves risks. You can't steal second and keep your foot on first."

Making a big deal out of the passing of one year and the arrival of the next is kind of silly, isn't it? I mean, do we really have a choice? One calendar year ending and another beginning is like aging. I would avoid it entirely if it weren't for the alternative.

I like the old year. I'm comfortable with it. I know my name and address in the old year—who I am and where I belong. The new year is a scary business. The old year is a story from which I can learn and, for the most part, of which I can be proud. The new year is unwritten. It's a school assignment that never can be handed in. The what, who, why, where, when, and how of it is so—unknown—yes, that's the word.

It's also so exciting—not merry-warms-the-cockles-of-your-heart-tear-the-wrappingpaper-off-the-gifts-exciting like Christmas but sometimes-up-and-down-and-around-at-the-speed-of-light-like-a-roller-coaster-ride-designed-by-Alfred-Hitchcock-exciting. Exciting like something you can't control and yet which you are co-writing and co-producing and co-directing even while it takes you for a ride.

Couldn't we just leave well enough alone and allow the New Year to sneak in without balls descending in Times Square? Couldn't the new year just happen without all those bowl games and parades?

So what am I opting for? New Year dignity! Holding the lessons of the old year very close to our hearts and waiting expectantly for new challenge, threats, and opportunities. Expecting the year to be both happy and new and committing ourselves to making it so. We can do it! We are hardy souls. We have survived Christmas. We ought to be able to make it through New Year's Day!

Amen.

—LDS

[1530 words]
[15 minutes]

❦ *Sermon 121*

❦ *Date:* New Year's Sunday, Any Year

Text:
Matthew 7:24–27

Theme: Take the new year under construction and build something lasting and worthy from it.
Subject: Opportunity

❦ *Title:* Danger: New Year Under Construction

Every person here was given exactly 8,760 of them. You were given that many, and so was the person sitting beside you. The President was given that many, and so were Madonna and Joe Montana. 8,760! Are you wealthy? No difference there, you got no more than the poorest among us. The Equal Rights Amendment may not have been ratified but it is in effect here: Male and female, all got the same—8,760. And all of us here have already used up exactly 83½ of them.

Hours! Eight thousand, seven hundred sixty hours this year. Time makes up the building blocks of this new year now under construction, and we have been given: 8,760 hours, to do with as we will. The only difference is that, given exactly the same set of circumstances, we can respond in a wide variety of ways.

The story from a generation or two ago tells of two fellows who were sent out into a remote part of the Ozarks to sell shoes. Almost immediately, one of the salesmen sent a telegram back to the home office, "Am returning at once," he wired. "Can't sell shoes here. Everyone goes barefoot." No word came from the other salesman for a few days, until a letter arrived at the home office. It came in a bulky, bulging envelope. The letter said: "Fifty orders enclosed. Prospects unlimited. Nobody here has shoes."

Same situation, different interpretation! Same amount of time each of us is given, same world we live in, same people we work with, but what different results emerge from us. The annual coming of a new and fresh year highlights our assignment for us: to take this unused year now under construction and build something lasting and worthy from it. That is God's assignment to you and to me, put most simply. Opportunities beyond number, needs to be filled, growth to be reached for, and 8,760 hours to do it in, this building of a new year.

But recognize that there are dangers involved in such an effort. Hard hats are required around the construction site, for falling debris is frequent and mistakes are easy. Here on this first Sunday of the year, consider how these dangers affect you as you build your own new year.

Danger number one is our excessive determination to hold on to the past and let it have too much voice in building this brand new year. By its very nature, building is a future-tense assignment. In his parable of the builder (Matthew 7:24ff.), Jesus' main point is the good builder's awareness of what the future might bring, and the foolish builder's disinterest in this. In the original greed of this passage, the language conveys the understanding that the foolish man not only built his house on the sand but that he kept on building it there, a stubbornly continuing action. To supply too many details is to overwork Jesus' story, but the implication is there that the foolish builder was tied to that sandy site by the past and, despite its bad record as a place to build, was never willing to move away and try another place.

It's one of the dangers encountered in building a new year, that ghostly hand that reaches out from the past and knocks down anything that we try to build. It may represent loved ones whom we have lost, places we've lived that we like better than the present one, jobs we've had that have been taken away, children who have gone with the wind. Myriad things reach into our lives from the past and grasp the reins of our life. One and all, they represent a past that will always be there in memory. But that past makes a most uncertain foundation upon which to build a future.

One of the most dramatic moments in the history of this hemisphere came in 1519 when Hernán Cortés landed his six hundred fifty men on the east coast of Mexico. Once they were ashore and all the supplies had been unloaded, Cortés ordered the ships burned. When hardships would develop on the expedition at hand, he did not want men whose attention was centered on easy trips back to Spain. That little company of men stood and watched those ships burn, knowing that any return to Spain would have to depend on new ships being built or new expeditions sent out.

In a symbolic way, every December 31 is a time when old ships are burned and new expeditions are embarked upon. But there are so many people today who still try to sail away in ships burned by time, who stand looking across an ocean of years or miles to times and places that won't be again—unaware that even as they stand looking back they are standing on the shore of a continent of time and opportunity grand beyond description, if only they will claim it.

But, it requires future-tense thought to do it. The past is a treacherous foundation on which to build our house. It is tomorrow that we are going to be living in and living up, and if we want tomorrow to be any better than today, we have to plan for it. It will be just as miserable and as hopeless as we choose to make it, or it will be as joyful and exciting as we choose to make it. We choose the building site, and one danger we face is that we cannot turn loose of the past as we move on.

Dathane Stanley writes about her daughter who "came down the stairs one evening and said, 'Have you ever pushed and pushed on a door, and then discovered it was a wall?'" She had turned off the light in her bedroom and then in the darkness tried to force open what she had mistakenly thought was a door."[1]

Doesn't that little story cause just a quick spark of recognition in all of us? Pushing on walls! Standing there, stubbornly, trying to make life something it isn't and can never be! Playing games with ourselves about the realities of life! We are game-playing people, aren't we? The sign that was seen in the window of a loan company said, "Now you can borrow enough to get completely out of debt!" Pushing on walls, indeed!

To put it clearly, "The past is a wall, not a door. The door is the future, and if we can realize this, we will have successfully dodged one real danger as we go on constructing this new year.

Danger number two is that we will be satisfied with too little as we build this new year. The provocative detail that Jesus leaves out of his parable of the builders is this: Why was the foolish builder content to build his house on such a questionable foundation? Why did he settle for so little? Did the past tie him to that one site, as we suggested a moment ago? Was it an expensive place, one that cost him nothing? Why did he settle for it? Jesus leaves this to our own imagination, and wisely so, for one reason would do for the builder, as no one reason will do for us.

Why do we settle for so little? Given these 8,760 hours, given these opportunities, given the fact that we are going to be living in this house we build, why do we settle for so little? The ironic point in the parable of the builders is that it takes just as much hard work to build a house on a poor foundation as it does on a good one. The work involved is basically the same. But the results are so vastly different. Clearly, one danger encountered in this new year under construction is our strange willingness to settle for so much less we might in what we make of our lives.

While visiting the zoo one day, a certain man paused before the lion's cage, watched for a few moments, and was puzzled at what he saw. The lion's cage had recently been enlarged greatly and remodeled in order to give the animal more open, natural space. But strangely, the lion still paced back and forth within the small, now unseen, boundaries of his old cage as it was before enlarging. Back and forth he went, turning in the same place each time, where the wall once had been, ignoring all the extra space beyond. The animal's keeper wandered by and the visitor asked for an explanation. "Why does the lion pace back and forth in this narrow space, instead of exploring his new area?" The keeper answered quickly: "It's the same old story. The lion is busy making a cage of his own."

Busy making a cage of his own! Doesn't that capture some of us completely? Who says we have to build our house on sand? We do the choosing! Who says life has to be so constructed and narrow? When you awaken tomorrow morning, in that instant before you get up, who determines what kind of day it will be for you? Your boss, you say quickly? Not completely. Circumstances may choose the frame of the day, but you paint the picture that goes in it. If you choose nothing but blacks and grays, that's the picture you'll paint. But you do the choosing! And so many people, even as this new year begins, are already busy pacing up and down in little unwalled prisons of their own making, settling for so little.

It's a point that runs like a thread through all the teachings of Jesus. You are in charge of your life. You are not a helpless victim of circumstances, you are in charge. The prodigal son decided on his own to leave home, and then decided on his own to come back again. The good Samaritan decided to stop alongside that road between Jerusalem and Jericho. The wise builder decided to build his house on a rock. Each person is in charge of his or her own life.

Why is this such a hard fact for us to understand and accept? It must be hard for us to grasp, because so many of us are standing waiting for life to happen to us. We are waiting for something

---

[1] "The Secret Place," February 6, 1961.

to happen to make us happy. We are waiting for that perfect set of circumstances to come along, people and places and things, and then life will be complete and full. Don't you believe it! Life is going to be just what you decide to make of it.

I challenge you at this moment to put this truth to work. You've taken the trouble to get here today, and you've listened well, so don't let this sermon go floating out into thin air. Right now, let there be some resolution within you, some specific goals set. One year from now, you'll be looking back on this year, used up and discarded. What do you want to see there as you look back? What goals and accomplishments do you want to have achieved? Set those goals high, and then aim at them, work for them. Good things seldom happen accidentally. They happen because someone thought about them and worked for them.

One point I often share with young couples sitting in my office talking about getting married is this: "Ten years from now, what do you want to have happened in your married life together? What do you want your life to be like? If we could visit in your home a decade from now, what would you want us to see there? That is your goal, your destination you want to have arrived at ten years hence, and there is a road that leads inevitably to that destination, if you want to take it. Then don't just sit there waiting for a good marriage to happen to you! Work on it, plan for it, and aim high.

That truth applies to all of us, for we stand equal here. There are 8,760 hours in the new year, hours that will be filled up with all sorts of building material, jobs and assignments, friends and families, opportunities for learning and for growth. The one indisputable fact is that we are going to build something with all this, and one year from now, we will be living in that which we build.

So let the new year be abuilding, but be alert to the hazards. don't let the past bind you down as you build. And don't let too limited a vision blind you. Perhaps Robert Sharpe's words sum it up:

Isn't it strange
That princes and kings,
And clowns that caper
In sawdust rings,
And common people
Like you and me
Are builders for eternity?

Each is given a bag of tools.
A shapeless mass,
A book of rules;
And each must make
Ere life is flown.
A stumbling-block
Or a stepping stone.[2]

Which will it be for you in this new year?

Amen.

—Eugene Brice

[2175 words]
[22 minutes]

---

[2] Sharpe, R. L., "A Bag of Tools" in *The Best Loved Poems of the American People,* selected by Hazel Felleman (New York: Doubleday, 1936), p. 99.

RESOURCES FOR PREACHING

The editor strongly recommends the following materials. Items marked with an asterisk are commended as having particular merit.

As is the case with all materials based on the New Common Lectionary, look for new versions based on the just published Revised Common Lectionary (1992). The Common Lectionary is officially endorsed by the following traditions: Methodist, Presbyterian, Reformed, and United Church of Christ as well as the Anglican Church of Canada, the United Church in Canada, and the Evangelical Lutheran Church in Canada. It is also used by many congregations within the Episcopal, Lutheran, and Roman Catholic Churches.

Books

Brown, Burch. *Transfiguration: Poetic Metaphor and the Language of Religious Belief* (Chapel Hill: The University of North Carolina Press, 1983). A serious consideration of the language of preaching.

Brown, Robert McAfee. *Unexpected News: Reading the Bible with Third World Eyes* (Philadelphia: The Westminster Press, 1984). Liberation theology comes to the local church.

Brueggemann, Walter. *The Prophetic Imagination*, (Philadelphia: Fortress Press, 1978). The author exemplifies his own title.

*Craddock, Fred B., *Preaching* (Nashville, TN: Abingdon, 1985). The standard against which all guides to homiletics are judged.

*Craddock, Fred B., John H. Hayes, Carl R. Holladay, and Gene M. Tucker. *Preaching the Common Lectionary* (Nashville, TN: Abingdon Press, 1985, 1986, 1987). Each liturgical year (A, B, and C) is covered in three volumes. This series is the finest commentary available on the Common Lectionary, skillfully blending biblical scholarship and preaching suggestions.

Handbook for the Common Lectionary, edited by Peter C. Bower (Philadelphia: The Geneva Press, 1987). Developed by The Office of Worship of the Presbyterian Church (U.S.A.). A well-produced guidebook offering a one-page "map" of each Sunday of all three liturgical years as well as other days of the liturgical calendar (Christmas Day, Maundy Thursday, Good Friday, etc.). Included are summaries of the message of each lectionary passage, suggested music for each psalm, hymns for the day, and anthems for each day. This inexpensive, vinyl-bound volume includes suggested resources, an exhaustive bibliography, and indexes of all scriptures. Thus, if you already have written a sermon on Psalm 91:9-16, you can discover that it would fit into the Common Lectionary schedule on the First Sunday in Lent, Year C (1992 or 1995).

*Hewett, James S. *Illustrations Unlimited* (Wheaton, IL: Tyndale House Publishers, Inc., 1988). A compilation of more than 1,700 anecdotes, quotations, and stories from *Parables, Etc.* and *Pastor's Story File*, selected by the founder of the two publications. The best one-volume collection of illustrative material. Lacks documentation of origianl sources.

Keck, Leander, *The Bible in the Pulpit* (Nashville, TN: Abingdon, 1978). Biblical preaching is an art and a skill.

New Common Lectionary for the United Methodist Church, Revised Standard Version (Wichita, Kansas: St. Paul's Publishing Company, St. Paul's United Methodist Church, 1356 N. Broadway, 67214. The complete text of the lectionary readings for each Sunday of years A, B, and C, conveniently arranged in a small spiral-bound, vinyl-covered book. Inexpensive. Lacks indexes.

Proclamation 1 (1973-76), 2 (1979-82), 3 (1984-87), and 4 (1989). Similar to *Preaching the New Common Lectionary*. Each year's readings are covered in a set of eight thin volumes. Quality ranges from adequate to excellent.

Soards, Marion, Thomas Dozeman, and Kedall McCabe. *Preaching the Revised Common Lectionary* (Nashville, TN: Abingdon Press, 1992). A 12-volume series combining commentary with suggestions for preaching, worship, and music.

Troeger, Thomas H., *Imagining a Sermon* (Nashville, TN: Abingdon Press, 1990). The author invites the reader to watch as he creates fascinating, imaginative sermons. The question remains: can it be done week after week?

Wagley, Laurence A., *Preaching with the Small Congregation* (Nashville, TN: Abingdon Press, 1989). What if preaching arose out of dialogue with the congregation on Sunday Morning?

Willimon, William H. and Robert L. Wilson, *Preaching and Worship in the Small Church* (Nashville, Tennessee: Abingdon Press, 1980). The small church is different; and it requires appropriate preaching.

Other Publications

**Biblical Preaching Journal*. Exegeses and Sermons based on the New Common Lectionary. Of high quality. Write to Biblical Preaching Institute, 321 Fourth Court East, Carmel, IN 46032.

Celebration—A Creative Worship Service. A monthly packet of resource materials based on the Common Lectionary, including feature articles, cartoons, artwork, liturgy, book reviews, and homilies. For information, write P.O. Box 419493, Kansas City, MO 64141.

*Duncan, King. *Who's Afraid of a Hinged-Tail Bingbuffer* and *I Am a Promise*. Collections of object lessons/sermons for children. Available from Seven Worlds Publishing.

**Dynamic Preaching* and *The Positive Pastoral Preaching Service*, Seven Worlds Publishing, P.O. Box 11565, Knoxville, TN 37939. Two of the best edited sources of model sermons, illustrations, and anecdotes. Also available on computer diskettes.

Emphasis: A Preaching Journal for the Parish Pastor. Supplies illustrations for each lectionary text and three sermon outlines for each Sunday. Write to C.S.S. of Ohio, 628 South Main Street, Lima, OH 45804.

**Homiletics*. Resources for sermon preparation including exegetical and homiletic suggestions illustrations, liturgy, and hymns. Follows the Common Lectionary. Annual subscription $31.95. Address: Communications Resources, Inc., 1425 West Maple Street, P.O. Box 2625, North Canton, OH 44720.

Homily Service: An Ecumenical Resource for Sharing the Word. Exegetical and homiletical notes on each lectionary reading. Follows the Roman Catholic lectionary with cross references to the Common Lectionary. Available from Liturgical Conference, 810 Rhode Island Avenue, N.E., Washington, D.C. 20018.

King's Treasury of Dynamic Humor. Seven Worlds Publishing, P.O. Box 11565, Knoxville, TN 37939. Also available on computer diskette.

Lessons from Ladera. Sermons by Lowell D. Streiker from Ladera Community Church. Issued about 40 times a year. Annual subscription $40. Write to Ladera Community Church, 3300 Alpine Road, Portola Valley, CA 94028.

**Parables, Etc. and Pastor's Story File.* These two monthly newsletters are a gold mine of sermon illustrations, anecdotes, and usable quotations, published by Saratoga Press, Box 8, Platteville, CO 80651. The editor, Michael Hodgin, is extremely generous with his advice to preachers via correspondence or telephone. His bookstore offers many fine resources for sermon preparation. Both publications are available on computer diskette.

Preacher's Illustration Service. Stories and illustrations. Write to Voicings, Post Office Box 3102, Margate, NJ 08402-9900. Also from the same source: **Sunday Sermons, The Illustration Finder* (software). and **Sermon Ware* (a collection of 328 sermons on disk). These excellent products flow from the creative mind of James F. Colaianni, a master of the use of humor in preaching.

Word and Witness. Bimonthly publication. Four pages of commentary, worship suggestions, illustrations and quotations, and a sample sermon for each Sunday. Published by Liturgical Publications Inc., 2875 South James Drive, New Berlin, WI 53151

Computer Resources (IBM PC or compatibles)

For writing and editing sermons, *WordStar, WordPerfect*, Microsoft *Word*, or *PC-Write*. For checking grammar and style, *Right Writer* from Que Software.

There are several Bible study programs of excellent quality. I rely on **Word Search Computer Bible* from NavPress Software, P.O. Box 6000, Colorado Springs, CO 80934. It has excellent concordance search capabilities; will write selected text directly into your favorite word processor; and may be obtained in such popular translations as the King James Version, the New International Version, and the New Revised Standard Version. A Greek and Hebrew "lookup" module based on Strong's Concordance is available. The program is fast and easy to learn. An add-on program called **The Bridge* allows the user to access all features of the program directly from a word processor. Hence, texts can be imported directly into a sermon without leaving the document. I have also found very useful *MegaWord* from Paraclete Software (1000 14th Street, Suite 425, Plano, TX 75074).

After *Wordsearch* my favorite software is the **Infosearch Hymnal,* also from NavPress. This program is one of the most useful tools I have yet discovered. Indexed to twelve major hymnals, it searches out and displays lyrics to hundreds of songs. Simply enter a topic, a biblical text, or a few words of the song, and, in seconds, you have a listing of appropriate selections. If you are not familiar with a given song, type a single letter ("u"), and the program plays the melody! If you want to include the lyrics in your sermon or Sunday bulletin, press a few more keys and the words are copied to a text file.

If you want to include the lyrics in your sermon or Sunday bulletin, press a few more keys and the words are copied to a text file.

Gofer from Microlytics, Inc., features string-search software for locating text and inserting it into your sermon. Not as elegant as NavPress' *Bridge*, but extremely valuable. Truly indispensable when used with the computer diskette versions of Saratoga Press and Seven Worlds publications.

Excellent, inexpensive software for Bible study and sermon illustration is available from Parsons Technology, 375 Collins Road N.E., P.O. Box 3120, Cedar Rapids, IA 52406-3120.

For authoritative reviews of all church-related software, see *Church Bytes: The Church Computing Magazine*. For subscription information, write to Church Bytes, Inc., 562 Brightlead Square #9, 905 West Main Street, Durham, NC 27701.

Many of the mentioned programs are available for Apple MacIntosh computers.

Contributors

Rev. Eugene Brice is Senior Pastor of the University Christian Church in Fort Worth, Texas. His latest book is *Illusions of Excellence* (Christian Board of Publication). His address is 2720 S. University Drive, Fort Worth, TX 76109.

Rev. W. Matthew Broadbent is Pastor of the First Congregational United Church of Christ, 900 High Street, Santa Cruz, CA 95060.

Rev. R. Geoffrey Brown, Ph.D., has been a pastor in the Presbyterian Church (U.S.A.) since 1974. He holds a doctorate in Christian Ethics.

Rev. John Bury is Pastor of the First Congregational United Church of Christ in Newark Valley, New York (P.O. Box 605, Newark Valley, NY 13811).

Rev. James S. Hewett is Pastor of the Walnut Creek Presbyterian Church, P.O. Box 5606, 1720 Oakland Blvd., Walnut Creek, CA 94596. He is the founder of *Parables, Etc.* and *Pastor's Story File* (Saratoga Press). He is the editor of *Illustrations Unlimited* (Tyndale House Publishers) and the author of *How to Live Confidently in a Hostile World* (Word Publishing).

Mr. Tim Clark is the editor of the *San Francisco Business Times* (325 Fifth Street, San Francisco, CA 94107).

Rev. Elizabeth Chandler Felts is pastor of Danville Congregational Church (United Church of Christ). Her address is 3450 Granada Ave. #70, Santa Clara, CA 95051.

Rev. Donald E. Lewis, a methodist minister, was a U.S. Army Chaplin during World War II and the Korean conflict.

Rev. Matthew McDermott is Assistant to the Rector and a Minister to Youth at Holy Trinity Episcopal Church, 350 Ravenswood Road, Menlo Park, CA 94025.

Gordon MacDonald is an author and pastor. His address is 30 River Rd., Apt. 12-L; New York, NY 10044.

Ray Ortlund is President and Speaker for the Haven of Rest radio broadcast, which is heard daily on stations throughout the United States and Canada. His latest book is *Confident in Christ* (Word Publishing). Dr. Ortlund's address is 2410 Hyperion Blvd., Los Angeles, CA 90027.

Rev. Harold Rucker is Pastor of the Island United Church in Foster City, California. Island is affiliated with the United Methodist Church, the Presbyterian Church in the U.S.A., and the United Church of Christ. His address is 659 Cygnes Lane, Foster City, CA 94404.

Rev. Eugene A. Schneider is Marketing/Education Coordinator for the Office of Communications, United Church of Christ, 700 Prospect Avenue, Cleveland, OH 44115-1100. He leads spiritual renewal events and has produced four videotapes on the subject.

R.C. Sproul is chairman of Ligonier Ministries. He is professor of Systematic Theology and Apologetics at Reformed Theological Seminary in Orlando, Florida. His address is Ligonier Ministries, 598 S. North Lake Blvd., Altamonte Springs, FL 32701.

Rev. Deborah Streeter is Pastor of the Woodside Village United Church of Christ, 3154 Woodside Road, Woodside, CA 94062.

Rev. Lowell D. Streiker, Ph.D., is Pastor of the Ladera Community Church in Portola Valley, California. He has written, co-authored, edited, and contributed to 16 books. His most recent books are *Fathering: Old Game, New Rules* and *New Age Comes to Main Street,* both published by Abingdon Press. His address is Ladera Community Church, 3300 Alpine Road, Portola Valley, CA 94028.

Rev. Barbara Taylor is an Episcopal priest in the Diocese of Atlanta. She is the author of two volumes of sermons, *Mixed Blessings and The Seeds of Heaven.* Her address is All Saints Episcopal Church, 634 West Peachtree N.W., Atlanta, GA 30308.

After serving prominent Presbyterian pulpits on both coasts of the United States, Dr. Bruce Thieleman is retired and living in Pittsburgh, Pennsylvania. He carries on a wide ranging teaching and preaching ministry in this country and abroad. He may be contacted in care of First Presbyterian Church, 320 Sixth Avenue, Pittsburgh, PA 15222.

INDEXES

Numbers refer to specific sermons. For page numbers, see Table of Contents.

TOPICAL INDEX

INDEX OF DATES, HOLIDAYS, AND SPECIAL OCCASIONS

SCRIPTURE TEXT INDEX